BROADWAY MUSICALS

Sandra Church and Ethel Merman in the final moment of perhaps the greatest Broadway musical of all time, *Gypsy*.

BROADWAY MUSICALS

THE
101 GREATEST SHOWS
OF ALL TIME

KEN BLOOM & FRANK VLASTNIK

FOREWORD BY JERRY ORBACH

Black Dog
& Leventhal
Publishers
NEW YORK

Ziegfeld Follies is recreated in *Funny Girl*: Barbra Streisand declares that John Lankston's love makes her beautiful. Even in her third trimester.

Copyright © 2004 by Ken Bloom and Frank Vlastnik

Permission to reproduce photographs is outlined on page 336, which constitutes an extension of this copyright page. All rights reserved. No part of this book may be reproduced in any form or by any electronic or mechanical means, including information storage and retrieval systems, without written permission from the publisher.

ISBN 1-57912-390-2

Library of Congress Cataloging-in-Publication Data
Bloom, Ken, 1949-
 Broadway musicals : the 101 greatest shows of all time / Ken Bloom and Frank Vlastnik.
   p. cm.
 Includes index.
 ISBN 1-57912-390-2
 1. Musicals—New York (N.Y.)—Encyclopedias. I. Vlastnik, Frank. II. Title.

 ML102.M88B56 2004
 782.14´097471--dc22
        2004015066

Book design: Scott Citron

Manufactured in China

Published by
Black Dog & Leventhal Publishers, Inc.
151 West 19th Street
New York, New York 10011

Distributed by
Workman Publishing Company
708 Broadway
New York, New York 10003

g f e d c b a

ACKNOWLEDGMENTS

A BOOK OF THIS SIZE AND scope requires the cooperation and friendship of many people. We'd like to thank the following for their assistance and support: Jerry Orbach for kindly providing a wonderful Foreword; Deborah Brody, a good friend who brought us together with Black Dog; and speaking of Black Dog, to our publisher J. P. Leventhal, a particular fan of *Flahooley* (#102), our thanks for his vision and support. Our editor, Laura Ross, ably navigated us through the perils of this huge undertaking. Her enthusiasm, insights, knowledge of the theatre, and sense of humor were greatly appreciated. Our designer, Scott Citron, created a marvelous template and spent hundreds of hours in front of the computer with two rabid authors breathing down his neck—and he did so gracefully! Kenneth Kantor helped us with encouragement, ideas, and proofreading—his contributions were a major part of this enterprise. Others who shared their encyclopedic knowledge of the musical theatre, offering suggestions and proofreading the final draft, are Laurent Dubrovine, Peter Filichia, Barry Kleinbort, and David Schmittou. Believe us when we say we couldn't have done this book without their help.

The photographs in this book are much more than the usual sparse illustrations. We wanted them to provide the reader with a vivid sense of how the shows and stars looked. The majority of the photos came from two sources: Photofest and the Billy Rose Theatre Collection of the New York Public Library at Lincoln Center. Photofest's Howard Mandelbaum and Ron Mandelbaum are themselves experts in the musical theatre, and their enthusiasm and generosity is greatly appreciated. At the Billy Rose Theatre Collection, Jeremy Megraw and Louise Martzinek are always wonderfully patient, good humored, and unfailingly helpful. We would also like to thank Robert Taylor, Curator of the Theatre Collection and his colleagues Karen Nickeson, Susan Chute, Christopher Frith, Christine Karatnytsky, Annette Marotta, Daniel Patri, Louis Paul, Olive Wong, and Roderick Bladel. Our research meant many trips into the stacks for Patricia Darby and her staff: Brenta Agard, Caleb Cadet, Veneshia Gordon, Andrene Hunter, Karen Opokua, Gregory Rodriguez, Sean Velez, and Afisha Williams. Thanks also to photographers Martha Swope, Paul Kolnik, Joan Marcus, and Carol Rosegg, as well as Caitlin Thorne and Erin Baiano. Will Rhys of the Goodspeed Opera House Library also generously supplied historic photos from their impressive collection.

Thanks also to Adrian Bryan-Brown of Boneau/Bryan-Brown, Peter Barros and Tim Bennell, Michael Borowski of the Publicity Office, Manoah Bowman, Michael Cassara, Barry Day, Brian Drutman of Decca Broadway, Michael Feinstein for the Ira Gershwin photo and so much more, Andrew Glant-Linden, Mark Trent Goldberg—Executive Director of the Ira and Leonore Gershwin Trusts—for the color photos of George Gershwin and Ira Gershwin; Joe Harris, Jerry Herman, Geoffrey Johnson, Robert Kimball, Lynn Lane, Jeff Lunden, Nick Markovich of the Yip Harburg Foundation, Larry Moore, Richard Norton, Anthony J. Petrillose and Gary Van Dis of Condé Nast, Frank Pisco, Cory Plowman, Pat Plowman, Richard Traubner, Joseph Weiss, Tom Wilson, and Wayne Wolf.

A stein-wielding Patricia Morison hates men in *Kiss Me, Kate*. But we toast everyone.

Bebe Neuwirth, Ann Reinking, and Allison Williams, airborne in the 1986 revival of *Sweet Charity*.

CONTENTS

FOREWORD
BY JERRY ORBACH

TURNING THE PAGES OF THIS BOOK brings back a lot of memories of my forty-five years in musical theatre. It seems I had just arrived in New York when I found myself, at age twenty, on stage at the Theatre DeLys in Greenwich Village, acting in the historic revival of Kurt Weill and Bertolt Brecht's *The Threepenny Opera*. I remember my costars—Bea Arthur, Ed Asner, Charlotte Rae, and John Astin—but most of all I still remember how much in awe I was of Lotte Lenya, not only Kurt Weill's widow, but one of the greatest actresses of all time. I celebrated my twenty-first birthday while in that show, singing "Mack the Knife." My next show turned out to be the longest running musical in theatre history, *The Fantasticks*, in which I introduced my first standard, "Try to Remember."

My Broadway debut was in David Merrick's production of *Carnival!*, directed by the genius Gower Champion, alongside Anna Maria Alberghetti and Kaye Ballard. I played Charlie Davenport with the legendary Ethel Merman in the historic revival of *Annie Get Your Gun*. I guess I was naive, but for a while I thought that every show that came my way would be a hit—then I made my straight play debut in *The Natural Look*, and our opening night was also our closing night. More memories come flooding back: *Promises, Promises*, with its brand new sound by Burt Bacharach and Hal David, its great book by Neil Simon, and its wonderful director, Robert Moore; *Chicago*, starring two of the great ladies of musical theatre, Gwen Verdon and Chita Rivera; and my most recent Broadway show, the remarkable *42nd Street*, my third show for David Merrick.

Believe me, I know I was a very fortunate man. Just how fortunate is illustrated on the pages of this book, for all of my original musicals (save *42nd Street*) are represented in this celebration of the greatest shows of all time. It's a thrill for me to relive those terrific experiences and see all of the magnificent people with whom I was privileged to work.

Please enjoy this rich volume, every page covered with photographs (most of them never-before published and many of them so rare that I'd never even seen some of the ones of me!); expert commentary by two authors whose breadth of knowledge is downright scary, and information not found in any other place that I know of. Reading it makes me proud to be in a line that stretches over an entire century and into the next. And when you're done, put down the book and go to the theatre! Broadway history is being made eight times a week—and we can only guess what the 101 greatest musicals of the 21st century will be.

ABOVE: Jerry Orbach bides his time in *Promises, Promises* while his bosses entertain "friends" in his apartment.

LEFT: Got Milk? Gwen Verdon is Jerry Orbach's Charlie McCarthy in "We Both Reached for the Gun" from *Chicago*.

INTRODUCTION

WELCOME TO THE WORLD OF the American musical theatre—well, our look at that world, anyway. Our primary goal in writing this book was to examine the 100-year-plus history of the Broadway musical in all its glorious variety. We had no intention of creating a definitive history, though many of the great shows (more than just the 101 featured ones) and hundreds of significant artists are covered one way or another through-out these pages. We like to think of this book as a celebration of the countless wonderful performers, directors, songwriters, librettists, designers, and producers who have enriched the true American art form.

Before we go any further we'd like to point out that our book's subtitle includes the word "Greatest" rather than "Best." Not all of the musicals in this book would appear on our "best" list, but each show has been selected because it was extremely popular and/or groundbreaking in some way, and has had an undeni-able influence on the form. Admittedly, it is subjective list (as all lists are), and we understand that your list would certainly differ from ours. The only real ground rule we set for ourselves in selecting the shows was that we wouldn't include any musical whose score was originally composed for another project (a film, for example), thereby eliminating such worthy shows as *The Lion King*, *Crazy for You*, and *Ain't Misbehavin'*. As it turned out, we have included a roughly equal number of shows from each decade—and we made a concerted effort to include every sub-genre of musical theatre, from the operetta to the big book musical to the revue.

Chita Rivera dances for joy in Gower Champion's *Bye Bye Birdie*.

In addition to the 101 featured shows, we've included some special chapters on subjects that deserve attention and are not fully covered elsewhere, such as Original Cast Albums, Guilty Pleasures, Off Broadway Shows, Posters, and Broadway Theatres. We've also included at least one sidebar per show that spotlights a particular artist, producer, or even theatre. We didn't have room for all of the features and sidebars we would have liked to include, but we tried hard to cover the important people, places, and institutions of the American musical theatre.

We made a concerted effort to avoid using photos that have been published over and over again, and are very proud that the vast majority of photos in this book are being seen here for the first time anywhere. We hope that the hundreds of marvelous archival photographs provide a real sense of how Broadway has looked over its rich history. We can't go back in time to see the opening night of *Show Boat* or *South Pacific*—but these photos should help evoke the experience.

You'll notice that in writing the text, particularly in the Backstage items and photo captions, we've kept our tongues firmly in our cheeks. Although we're serious about our love of musical theatre, there's no point in being *too* serious. We also want to rejoice in the sometimes ridiculous, over-the-top side of the musical theatre—which is, after all, a form of popular entertainment.

Any book of this size and detail is bound to have a mistake or two, though we've tried hard to avoid them. We welcome all comments—pro or con—and corrections (care of our publisher, whose address is listed on the copyright page), and promise to fix any errors we are made aware of in future editions.

We truly hope you enjoy revisiting your favorite shows, becoming acquainted with new ones, and recalling the great songs, stories, and stars of the Broadway musical.

Ken Bloom and Frank Vlastnik

ANNIE

OPENED APRIL 21, 1977; ALVIN THEATRE; 2,377 PERFORMANCES

Finally finding a happy home and a beautician who can give a really great perm, Annie (Andrea McArdle) celebrates with her new daddy (Reid Shelton).

Synopsis

Orphan Annie brings joy to her fellow orphanage mates, though they are all kept virtually hostage by the mean and spiteful Miss Hannigan. Annie, meanwhile, meets the millionaire Daddy Warbucks, bringing joy into his life as well. Miss Hannigan plots evil things but is thwarted. Annie continues to bring joy to everyone, including the mutt Sandy.

Cast

Grace Farrell	Sandy Faison
Rooster Hannigan	Robert Fitch
Miss Hannigan	Dorothy Loudon
Annie	Andrea McArdle
Oliver "Daddy" Warbucks	Reid Shelton
A Star to Be	Laurie Beechman
Molly	Danielle Brisebois
Kate	Shelley Bruce
Lily St. Regis	Barbara Erwin
F.D.R.	Raymond Thorne
Drake	Edwin Bordo
Bert Healy	Donald Craig
Sandy	Sandy

"Ughhh, I hate it."

—Thomas Meehan when Martin Charnin proposed a musical version of Little Orphan Annie

"OLIVER IN DRAG" was what naysayers dubbed it, but the Charles Strouse/Martin Charnin musicalization of the *Little Orphan Annie* comic strip struck a chord with millions of prepubescent girls, and its anthem, "Tomorrow," was their rallying cry. There was, of course, a proud tradition of comic strips adapted into Broadway musicals. The litany goes back to at least 1906 and *Foxy Grandpa*, and there was a very successful series of Mutt and Jeff musicals that toured the country, though they never came into New York. The importance of the funny papers in American life shouldn't be underestimated, with Irving Berlin's topical revue *As Thousands Cheer* boasting a song titled

"Easy Street" with Barbara Erwin, Robert Fitch, and Dorothy Loudon—outrageously talented and shameless muggers all—gave a much-needed burlesque lift to the adult visitors to *Annie*.

"The Funnies." During a newspaper strike (in a scene reenacted in the musical *Fiorello!*), New York City mayor Fiorello LaGuardia read the comics, including *Little Orphan Annie*, over the radio so kids—and their parents—wouldn't miss an installment of their favorite strip. In more recent times, there have been Broadway musicals suggested by the strips *Superman*, *Li'l Abner*, and even *Doonesbury*; but by far, the most successful comic-strip musical of all time is *Annie*.

The project started out inauspiciously at the Goodspeed Opera House in East Haddam, Connecticut. The reviews were not at all kind, but producer Lewis Allen believed he had the germ of a gem of a show that could be developed further. He called in his friend Mike Nichols, who agreed to coproduce and become an uncredited artistic advisor. The results on Broadway were astounding given the poor reception at Goodspeed, receiving mostly rave reviews and going on to a long, long run and many tours. A lot of the credit goes to the music of Strouse and the book by Thomas Meehan, not to mention the original cast, which included Andrea McArdle as the title character, a petite Merman with pipes of steel, and Broadway veteran Dorothy Loudon as Miss Hannigan, the piece's comic villain. Most importantly, Loudon

provided a heart and humor behind the bluster, and audience members (especially the more cynical ones) deeply empathized with her lament, "Little Girls."

The show was so successful that Charnin and Strouse attempted to make lightning strike again with two sequels—*Annie 2*, which closed out of town, and *Annie Warbucks*, which played Off-Broadway to little acclaim. But the original *Annie* remains one of the most produced musicals of all time, with thousands of little girls belting to the best of their abilities its uplifiting score.✻

THE SONGS

ACT I "Maybe" · "It's the Hard-Knock Life" · "Tomorrow" "We'd Like to Thank You (Herbert Hoover)" · "Little Girls" "I Think I'm Gonna Like It Here" · "N.Y.C." · "Easy Street" "You Won't Be an Orphan for Long"
ACT II "You're Never Fully Dressed Without a Smile" "Something Was Missing" · "I Don't Need Anything But You" · "Annie" · "A New Deal for Christmas"

RIGHT: Forced to scrub floors in the middle of the night, Annie thoroughly depresses the other orphans by reminding them that her parents are still looking for her.

Dorothy Loudon

Dorothy Loudon, a singer/comedienne whose reactions were often three-act plays in themselves, had a vibrant throb of a voice, a compulsion to please audiences, and the ability to turn her comic gifts on a dime into deeply affecting pathos. She became the comeback kid for the ages with her star-making turn as Miss Hannigan in *Annie*, after surviving the flops *Nowhere to Go But Up*, *The Fig Leaves Are Falling*, the out-of-town casualty *Lolita, My Love*, and others. After *Annie*, she returned to the world of shows whose ledgers ended on the debit side, albeit this time in a classy failure with her performance as widow Bea Asher in Michael Bennett's *Ballroom*. After replacing Angela Lansbury with a wildly different yet entirely valid Mrs. Lovett in *Sweeney Todd* and a brilliant turn in the backstage, nonmusical farce *Noises Off*, she returned to the world of the flop with the revue *Jerry's Girls* and yet another out-of-town fiasco, the sequel *Annie 2: Miss Hannigan's Revenge*. Critics and audiences lamented her string of bad luck in shows that were unworthy of her great talent. Still, her comic creation of Miss Hannigan has never been equaled, and her performance of "Fifty Percent" in *Ballroom* ranks with Dorothy Collins's "Losing My Mind" and Helen Morgan's "Bill" as one of the greatest torch song moments on the Broadway stage.

ABOVE: Dorothy Loudon always gave 110 percent onstage, but only needed "Fifty Percent" in her eleven o'clock stunner from *Ballroom*.

Backstage

The music to "Something Was Missing" was previously used by Strouse as "You Rat You" from the film *The Night They Raided Minsky's*.

Bill Berloni found the original Sandy in a dog pound, saving his life and making him a Broadway star. Each succeeding Sandy was also rescued from the pound to live a life upon the wicked stage.

LEFT: In *Jerry's Girls*, Loudon and Chita Rivera did a maniacal spoof of Shirley Temple singing "Tap Your Troubles Away." They are soon to be joined onstage by Leslie Uggams (as Shirley Temple Black?).

In *Bells Are Ringing*, Peter Gennaro stopped the show by teaching Judy Holliday the cha-cha in one easy, touchy-feely lesson.

Peter Gennaro

Peter Gennaro started out as a dancer in the chorus of *Guys and Dolls* and *The Pajama Game*. After an early choreography gig creating the spectacular "White and Gold Ballet" for Chita Rivera in the 1955 flop *Seventh Heaven*, he returned to performing with a supporting role in *Bells Are Ringing*. His enthusiasm gave the show's choreographer Bob Fosse the confidence to let Gennaro stage part of his show-stopping "Mu-Cha-Cha" dance with Judy Holliday. His talent and flair grabbed the attention of *Bells'* director Jerome Robbins, who tapped Gennaro to be co-choreographer of *West Side Story*. Gennaro once again lent his knowledge of Latin styles to "Dance at the Gym," and the fiery steps in "America" are largely his. *West Side*'s success led to a busy career creating athletic, super-high-energy dances for shows such as *Fiorello!*, *The Unsinkable Molly Brown*, and *Bajour*, reuniting him with old friend Chita Rivera. In *Annie*, his clever use of the ensemble in "N.Y.C.," his high-kicking, bucket-wielding orphans, and the down-and-dirty bump and grind in "Easy Street" were vastly underappreciated, though they greatly helped the seamless flow of that show.

LEFT: Peter Gennaro's stylish use of the treadmill and quick costume changes made the twelve-person ensemble of *Annie* seem like a cast of thousands in "N.Y.C."

ANNIE GET YOUR GUN

OPENED MAY 16, 1946; IMPERIAL THEATRE; 1,147 PERFORMANCES

An unusually subdued Ethel Merman and Harry Bellaver, as Annie Oakley and Chief Sitting Bull.

ANNIE GET YOUR GUN

Produced by Richard Rodgers and
Oscar Hammerstein II

Music and Lyrics by Irving Berlin
Book by Herbert Fields and Dorothy Fields
Musical Director: Jay Blackton
Music orchestrated by Philip J. Lang,
Robert Russell Bennett, and Ted Royal
Vocal Arrangements by Joe Moon
Piano Arrangements by Helmy Kresa

Directed by Joshua Logan
Choreographed by Helen Tamiris

Scenic Design by Jo Mielziner
Lighting Design by Jo Mielziner
Costume Design by Lucinda Ballard

Synopsis

Annie Oakley, an uneducated hillbilly, proves her sharp-shooting mettle when Buffalo Bill's Wild West Show comes to her hometown. She's soon hired for the show, but comes up against the ego of the star attraction, Frank Butler. Annie and Frank love each other, but their competitive natures keep them apart. It's only when Annie remembers singing "You Can't Get a Man with a Gun" in the first act that she purposely loses a shooting match with Frank, thereby winning his heart.

Cast

Annie Oakley .... *Ethel Merman*
Frank Butler .... *Ray Middleton*
Chief Sitting Bull .... *Harry Bellaver*
Tommy Keeler .... *Kenny Bowers*
Mary .... *Ellen Hanley*
Little Jake........................... *Bobby Hookey*
Charlie Davenport .... *Marty May*
Winnie Tate........................ *Betty Anne Nyman*
Col. Wm. F. Cody .... *William O'Neal*
Dolly Tate .... *Lea Penman*

"You may think I'm playing the part, but inside I'm saying, 'Screw you! You jerks! If you were as good as I am, you'd be up here!'"

—*Ethel Merman on unresponsive audiences*

THE ROAD TO BROADWAY is fraught with dangers, and the fact that, despite the death of its original composer, *Annie Get Your Gun* became a smash hit is an amazing testament to the tenacity of its producers, Richard Rodgers and Oscar Hammerstein II.

By 1944, the songwriting team was established as a musical theatre powerhouse based upon their previous collaborations, as well as the remarkable achievement of *Oklahoma!* the previous year. Rodgers and Hammerstein decided to become producers not only of their own works but of the works of others, and their second offering in this capacity was to be a musical based on the life of Wild West legend Annie Oakley. The idea was originally librettist/lyricist Dorothy Fields's, who brought the project to Rodgers and Hammerstein, along with her brother Herbert as co-librettist. The plan was for Dorothy to write the lyrics and Jerome Kern to write the music. All fell into place, and Kern arrived in New York from Hollywood to begin work on the new show.

Tragically, while walking in Manhattan, Kern suffered a fatal stroke. Despite their grief, Rodgers and Hammerstein approached Irving Berlin to write this most-American musical. Berlin was reluctant to take over from Kern, even though the great master had not written any songs for the show. But after going away for a few days to think it over, Berlin returned with five songs. For the lead role of Annie Oakley, Ethel Merman was summoned, and she gave one of her most indelible performances, exceptionally well served by Berlin, who provided no fewer than six smash-hit songs. On the flip side were the totally subpar songs "Who Do You Love, I Hope?" and "I'll Share It All with You," written for the clichéd secondary romantic couple in the newly minted Rodgers and Hammerstein musical theatre formula.

Surprisingly, *Annie Get Your Gun* wasn't revived on Broadway until 1966, when Richard Rodgers himself produced it for the Music Theatre of Lincoln Center starring (who else?) Ethel Merman. Though she was twenty years older than her "Frank Butler"—Bruce Yarnell was young enough to be her, well, nephew—as soon as she opened her mouth to belt out "Doin' What Comes Naturally," the audience forgot their quibbles about an October/April romance and became enthralled again with the power of La Merm.

A second revival showed up on Broadway in 2001, starring Bernadette Peters, who seemed to make a little career detour playing roles originated by Merman (her next Broadway appearance was in a revival of *Gypsy*). For this revival, Peter Stone decided to make the show "politically correct," an unnecessary exercise in disembowelment that hurt the show greatly, as did his decision to add the ultimate plot cliché—a story within a story—and begin the proceedings with "There's No Business Like Show Business." A succession of replacements followed Peters with varying degrees of success, including soap opera star Susan Lucci, Charlie's Angel Cheryl Ladd, and country singer Reba McEntire. McEntire earned raves from critics and audiences for her stage debut. ❋

Howard Lindsay, Russel Crouse, and Irving Berlin share a rare happy moment during rehearsals of their 1962 *Mr. President*.

Irving Berlin

Irving Berlin, composer of the most enduring popular songs of the twentieth century, including "White Christmas" and "God Bless America," also wrote the scores to many Broadway shows, from *Watch Your Step* (1914) to *Mr. President* (1962). He wrote for the *Ziegfeld Follies* and his own *Music Box Revues*, contributing hit song after hit song. After *As Thousands Cheer* in 1933, he spent most of the decade in Hollywood writing scores for Alice Faye and the team of Fred Astaire and Ginger Rogers. He returned to New York with *Louisiana Purchase* in 1940, and composed and starred in the World War II revue *This Is the Army*, stopping the show with his rendition of "Oh, How I Hate to Get Up in the Morning" (from his World War I revue, *Yip, Yip Yaphank*). Subsequently, he wrote his all-time greatest hit, *Annie Get Your Gun*, spinning off more standards than any other Broadway show: "They Say It's Wonderful," "The Girl That I Marry," "I Got Lost in His Arms," "Anything You Can Do," "Doin' What Comes Naturally," "You Can't Get a Man with a Gun," and the unofficial showbiz anthem, "There's No Business Like Show Business" (originally written by Berlin as a throwaway to cover a scene change). Revitalized by *Annie*'s success, he continued with *Miss Liberty* and *Call Me Madam* (again for Merman) before taking a twelve-year hiatus. The last song he wrote (at the age of seventy-eight!) that was performed on a Broadway stage was "An Old-Fashioned Wedding" for the twentieth-anniversary revival of *Annie Get Your Gun*, starring a fifty-seven-year-old Ethel Merman. Amazingly, he lived another twenty-three years, still composing but rarely being seen in public.

The production team of *Annie Get Your Gun*, indeed a lineup of most of the biggest names in musical theatre history: Joshua Logan, Irving Berlin, Richard Rodgers, Oscar Hammerstein II, Dorothy Fields, and Herbert Fields standing behind Ray Middleton and Ethel Merman.

SONGS

ACT I "Colonel Buffalo Bill" · "I'm a Bad, Bad Man" "Doin' What Comes Naturally" · "The Girl That I Marry" "You Can't Get a Man with a Gun" · "There's No Business Like Show Business" · "They Say It's Wonderful" "Moonshine Lullaby" · "I'll Share It All with You" · "My Defenses Are Down" · "I'm an Indian Too"
ACT II "I Got Lost in His Arms" · "Who Do You Love, I Hope?" · "I Got the Sun in the Morning" · "Anything You Can Do"

Herbert Fields

Lew Fields, famed comedian of the team Joe Weber and Lew Fields, and noted Broadway producer, was the father of three children, all of whom would distinguish themselves as writers for the musical theatre. His daughter, Dorothy Fields, was Broadway's most successful female lyricist and librettist, while her brother Joseph wrote both musicals and plays. The third offspring, Herbert, occupied his time as an eminent Broadway librettist. He began his career as a choreographer for the original *Garrick Gaieties*. During the production of that historic revue, he met Rodgers and Lorenz Hart, and together they wrote seven Broadway musicals, including their first, *Dearest Enemy*, and *A Connecticut Yankee*. From Rodgers and Hart, he moved on to a long, fruitful collaboration with Cole Porter, resulting in another seven shows. Their musicals together were timely, hilarious fare that included the Merman vehicles *DuBarry Was a Lady*, *Panama Hattie,* and *Something for the Boys*. In 1941, with the production of *Let's Face It!*, Herbert began collaborating with his sister, Dorothy, and the high point of their eight shows together was *Annie Get Your Gun*. They also turned out witty, character-driven libretti for *Up in Central Park* and *Redhead* (the first murder mystery musical).

ABOVE: Herbert Fields with many admirers.

ABIVE LEFT: Ethel Merman sings a "Moonshine Lullaby" to her brothers and sisters in the Pullman parlor of a train bound for the Big Time.

LEFT: Country singer Reba McEntire (here with Peter Marx, Brent Barrett, and Conrad John Schuck) made an astonishingly confident Broadway debut in the 2000 revival.

Backstage

During *Love Life*, the Alan Jay Lerner/Kurt Weill musical, Ray Middleton would brace himself against costar Nanette Fabray and squeeze when he had to reach a particularly high note. The bruised Fabray asked Middleton what he was doing, and he responded that he used the technique with Ethel Merman during their run in *Annie Get Your Gun*. Fabray allowed that she was not built like the rock-solid Merman and didn't appreciate having her ribs broken.

Irving Berlin based several of his song titles on those originally suggested by Dorothy Fields to Jerome Kern. After Kern's death the song titles remained in Fields's script, and Berlin appropriated them to write some of the greatest songs of his career.

ANYTHING GOES

OPENED NOVEMBER 21, 1934; ALVIN THEATRE; 420 PERFORMANCES

ANYTHING GOES

Produced by Vinton Freedley
Music by Cole Porter   Lyrics by Cole Porter
Book by Guy Bolton and P. G. Wodehouse
Book revised by Howard Lindsay
and Russel Crouse
Music arranged by Russell Bennett
and Hans Spialek
Choral Arrangements by Ray Johnson
Staged by Howard Lindsay
Dances and Ensembles by Robert Alton
Scenic Design by Donald Oenslager
Gowns by Jenkins

Synopsis

Nightclub singer Reno Sweeney sets sail on an ocean liner along with heiress Hope Harcourt, Moonface Martin (Public Enemy #13, who yearns to inch his way up the scale to #1), Billy Crocker (who stows away to be close to Hope), Lord Evelyn Oakleigh (who is engaged to Hope), Elisha J. Whitney (Crocker's boss, who doesn't know his employee is on the ship), and some Feds looking for Martin. Hilarity and romance ensue.

Cast

Billy Crocker	William Gaxton
Reno Sweeney	Ethel Merman
Moonface Martin	Victor Moore
Hope Harcourt	Bettina Hall
Bonnie Letour	Vera Dunn
Lord Evelyn Oakleigh	Leslie Barrie
Elisha J. Whitney	Paul Everton
Captain	John C. King
Mrs. Wadsworth T. Harcourt	Helen Raymond
Babe	Vivian Vance

Three people looking for nothin' but trouble: William Gaxton, Ethel Merman, and Victor Moore.

Anything Goes IS YET ANOTHER exemplary show that survived great odds to reach the stage. In this case it was problems with P. G. Wodehouse and Guy Bolton's original script, concerning the merry adventures of passengers on a transatlantic crossing and the ship's subsequent sinking. Wodehouse and Bolton titled their show *Hard to Get*, and it went into production when, on September 8, 1934, the liner *Morro Castle* caught fire and sank, more than a hundred people losing their lives. Suddenly, the idea of a jolly shipwreck musical didn't seem quite so distingué.

At a loss, producer Vinton Freedley created a new team of writers, Howard Lindsay and Russel Crouse, to fashion a new script. The team, which would go on to become one of the most successful in theatre history, kept the ocean liner sailing but sank the sinking. A merry musical farce, *Anything Goes's* libretto was mainly an excuse to bridge the spaces between Cole Porter's outstanding songs.

It was Porter's score and Ethel Merman's history-making performance that propelled the show. *Anything Goes* contained a number of future standards,

"Beethoven, Bach, Wagner, Brahms, Mendelssohn, Debussy, Chopin, Verdi, Offenbach, Strauss, Haydn, and Francis Scott Key could have marched into the room and I wouldn't have looked up."

—Russel Crouse upon first hearing the score of Anything Goes including "You're the Top," "I Get a Kick Out of You," "Blow, Gabriel, Blow," "All Through the Night," and the title song. Porter's work achieved great renown, with *Time* magazine stating, "So popular are composer Porter's lyrics that it is now considered the smart thing to know them all by heart, to rattle them off loudly."

Merman repeated her stage success on the screen in the first film version of the show, released in 1936; unfortunately, Paramount omitted many of Porter's secondary numbers and interpolated lesser songs by lesser writers. Merman's costar in the film, Bing Crosby, repeated the role in the second film version twenty years later. In this even more disappointing version, Mitzi Gaynor, Jeanmaire, and Donald O'Connor joined Crosby. This time around, the Porter score received even less respect, with some third-rate Sammy Cahn and Jimmy Van Heusen songs added to drag down the proceedings.

Critics and audiences embraced an Off-Broadway revival in 1962, which resulted in an original cast recording on the Epic label. In 1987, Lincoln Center Theatre produced a revival starring Patti LuPone, who had the pipes to match Merman in volume but lacked the necessary diction, turning the witty lyrics into mush. The revival also featured a pointless libretto revision that hurried the proceedings along but didn't add much in the way of charm. ✲

Cole at the keys, with Hildegarde (K)Neff and Don Ameche during rehearsals for his last Broadway show, *Silk Stockings*.

Cole Porter

Cole Porter, the urbane, worldly composer/ lyricist who hailed from the exotic locale of Peru, Indiana, was the epitome of soigné wit in the 1930s, transporting the downtrodden victims of the Great Depression with the glamour and fantasy of his songs. The plots of his shows were often silly, and his songs achieved a markedly higher level of sophistication than the books. In shows like *Anything Goes*, *Jubilee*, *Red Hot and Blue!* (whose story revolved around a buttock burn from a waffle iron—don't ask), *Leave It to Me!*, *DuBarry Was a Lady* (a washroom attendant dreams he is the King of France), *Panama Hattie*, *Let's Face It!*, and *Something for the Boys* (where Merman receives radio messages through her fillings), the songs were unmistakably Porter, from his sinuous ballads ("Night and Day," "Begin the Beguine," and "Love for Sale") to delightful list songs full of up-to-date references and sometimes incredibly shocking double entendres that blissfully sailed over the heads of all but the most inside audience members ("Let's Do It," "You're the Top," the title song to *Can-Can*). During this run of hits, Porter suffered an accident that changed the course of his life. After a horse fell on him, crushing both his legs, the story goes, he worked on the lyrics for "At Long Last Love" ("Is it an earthquake or simply a shock") while waiting for help. After the failure of *Around the World in Eighty Days* (directed by Orson Welles—the sets wouldn't even fit in the theatre) the public decided Porter's career was over, but he returned after a two-year absence from Broadway with his greatest work, *Kiss Me, Kate*. After the revitalization of his career, he continued with two more excellent scores, *Out of This World*, and his second-biggest hit, *Can-Can*. His last Broadway score was for *Silk Stockings* in 1955. A virtual cripple, he endured constant pain and more than thirty operations, finally undergoing an amputation in 1957.

Ethel Merman and her sixteen Angels in 1934; due to budgetary constraints, in subsequent productions, there were fewer.

ABOVE: Ethel Merman proclaims "Anything Goes" accompanied by The Foursome.

BELOW: Bettina Hall and the Girls sing of "The Gypsy in Me."

SONGS

ACT I · "I Get a Kick Out of You" · "Bon Voyage" (There's No Cure Like Travel) · "All Through the Night" · "Sailor's Chanty" (There'll Always Be a Lady Fair) · "Where Are the Men?" · "You're the Top" · "Anything Goes"

ACT II · "Public Enemy Number One" · "Blow, Gabriel, Blow" · "Be Like the Bluebird" · "Buddie Beware" · "The Gypsy in Me"

Backstage

Ethel Merman's under-study was Vivian Vance, later Ethel Mertz on *I Love Lucy.*

Reno Sweeney was based in part on the evangelist Aimee Semple McPherson (hence the "Blow, Gabriel, Blow" number).

Robert Russell Bennett

Robert Russell Bennett, the premier orchestrator of Broadway's golden age, worked on an estimated three hundred Broadway shows, from *Daffydill* in 1922 to *The Grass Harp* in 1971. His choice of instruments to be used in a particular show, the voicing of instruments (i.e., who would play the melody or counter-melody), and even the composition of underscoring was unparalleled in his era. He orchestrated the songs of the greatest composers of the twentieth century: Jerome Kern; George Gershwin; Cole Porter; Frederick Loewe; Burton Lane; and Arthur Schwartz. Best known was his work with Richard Rodgers and Oscar Hammerstein II, where he made invaluable contributions to the musical atmosphere of *Oklahoma!*, *Allegro*, *Flower Drum Song,* and *The Sound of Music.* To think of the first notes of *The King and I*, *Show Boat,* or *Camelot*, one realizes that Bennett's arrangements are absolutely crucial in transporting the theatregoer to nineteenth-century Siam, a levee on the Mississippi, or the mythical realm of King Arthur. Composer Burton Lane remembered visiting Robert Russell Bennett in his office. There Bennett sat, with a girl on one knee, the radio blaring, while he blithely orchestrated one of Lane's scores.

GREAT SCORES FROM SO-SO SHOWS, PART I

WE'VE ALL BEEN FOOLED IN the past; you buy a CD (or an LP, for the truly ancient), give a listen, and think, How could this show have failed? It's happened time and time again; in fact, producers are often bamboozled into investing in shows, thinking that just because a score is great, the show must be, too. Wrong, wrong, wrong, for all too often, a wonderful score is surrounded by a less-than-wonderful show.

The greatest example of a great score from a flop show is *Candide*, which, despite its recent successes, definitely did not set the world ablaze in its original production. Harold Arlen hit the great score/so-so show trifecta with *House of Flowers*, *Jamaica* (it ran, but only because of Lena Horne), and *St. Louis Woman*. Almost matching Arlen's record for great songs from okay shows is Jerry Herman. He followed the smash hit *Mame* with *Dear World*, featuring the same star and much the same team—and another wonderful, if different-flavored score. Herman hit a home run with Gower Champion on *Hello, Dolly!*, but he and Champion struck out with *Mack and Mabel*. The excellence of Herman's score is breathtaking and also heart-rending, considering how poorly the show was initially received. Stephen Sondheim's score for *Merrily We Roll Along* was thrilling, augmented by Jonathan Tunick's incredible, brassy orchestrations; but the show, as seen at the Alvin, no. Arthur Siegel, a wonderful composer (he wrote the music to "Love Is a Simple Thing" from *New Faces of 1952*), a sweet man, and the person who knew more about show music that anyone, always insisted that Jerome Kern and Otto Harbach's *Roberta*, with a stunning set of songs, was a big, crashing bore in performance.

Ultimately, we are damn lucky that the beautiful songs are what survive from these less-than-stellar creations. Great shows . . . or so we tell ourselves.

CLOCKWISE FROM TOP LEFT: Pearl Bailey stops the show in Harold Arlen and Johnny Mercer's *St. Louis Woman* with "It's a Woman's Prerogative." Jim Walton, Ann Morrison, and Lonny Price, "Old Friends" in Stephen Sondheim's *Merrily We Roll Along*. Robert Rounseville (wearing the heaviest makeup this side of Grizabella, the Glamour Cat) and Barbara Cook sing Leonard Bernstein's demanding score for *Candide*. Bernadette Peters (with Robert Fitch) back when movies were movies, in Jerry Herman's *Mack and Mabel*.

AS THOUSANDS CHEER

OPENED SEPTEMBER 30, 1933; MUSIC BOX THEATRE; 390 PERFORMANCES

Ethel Waters traveled the gamut of emotions in *As Thousands Cheer*, from sexy, Caribbean sass in "Heat Wave" (pictured here), to the tragic grief of "Supper Time."

AS THOUSANDS CHEER

Produced by Sam H. Harris

Music by Irving Berlin
Lyrics by Irving Berlin
Book by Moss Hart
Musical Director: Frank Tours
Music orchestrated by Adolph Deutsch, Frank Tours, Ed Powell, Russell Wooding, and Helmy Kresa

Staged by Hassard Short
Choreographed by Charles Weidman

Scenic Design by Albert R. Johnson
Lighting Design by Hassard Short
Costume Design by Varady and Irene Sharaff

Synopsis

In this living newspaper revue (to borrow an idea from the WPA) headlines are illustrated through songs and sketches. The sections include the financial page, roto-gravure ("Easter Parade"), Broadway gossip, the weather ("Heat Wave"), advice to the lovelorn, the funnies ("The Funnies"), society, and headlines ("Supper Time" and "Not for All the Rice in China").

Cast

Helen Broderick, Marilyn Miller, Clifton Webb, Ethel Waters, Jerome Cowan, Hal Forde

Clifton Webb as Mahatma Gandhi and Helen Broderick as Aimee Semple MacPherson doing the hunger strike hokey-pokey in a Moss Hart sketch.

I RVING BERLIN WAS IN MANY ways a contradictory talent. Of course, his career spanned nearly sixty years, so it's difficult to pigeonhole such an immense body of work. One show that stands apart from his others in tone and form is the revue *As Thousands Cheer*. We all know Berlin the patriot, composer of "God Bless America" and "This Is the Army." There is Berlin the romantic, exemplified by such songs as "Always" and "What'll I Do?" And although *As Thousands Cheer* contains such typical Berlin songs as "Easter Parade" and "Heat Wave," there are surprises, too, with a more incisive and critical thrust from the composer/lyricist.

The show was conceived as a topical revue, with each scene linked to a backdrop of a newspaper headline designed and lit under the auspices of director Hassard Short, one of the unsung geniuses of the American theatre. Berlin and Moss Hart skewered such contemporary news makers as evangelist and self-promoter Aimee Semple McPherson (also satirized in Cole Porter's *Anything Goes* with Merman's "Blow, Gabriel, Blow"), John D. Rockefeller, Barbara Hutton, Douglas Fairbanks Jr., Joan Crawford, and even Gandhi.

But the number that caused all the commotion took place following a headline reading, "Unknown Negro Lynched by Frenzied Mob." The song was "Supper Time," and it personalized individuals and a segment of society largely ignored by Broadway sophisticates. Hart and Berlin were worried about the song's reception. But, as Ethel Waters recounted in her autobiography, *My Eye Is on the Sparrow,* "When I was through and that big, heavy curtain came down, I was called back again and again. I had stopped the show with a type of song never heard before in a revue, and a number that until then had been a question mark." ❋

RIGHT: Looks like an angel, swears like a sailor: ultimate charm star Marilyn Miller takes a trip on the Toonerville Trolley in the song "The Funnies."

SONGS

ACT I "How's Chances?" · "Heat Wave" · "Majestic Sails at Midnight" · "Lonely Heart" · "The Funnies" · "To Be or Not to Be" · "Easter Parade"

ACT II "Supper Time" · "Our Wedding Day" · "I've Got Harlem on My Mind" · "Through a Keyhole" · "Not for All the Rice in China"

Beloved star Marilyn Miller made her last Broadway appearance in *As Thousands Cheer* (here stepping out with future movie star Clifton Webb).

Ethel Waters

The first black star to have her name above the title of a Broadway show (when such a thing was earned rather than contractual), Ethel Waters was also the first black performer to star on Broadway in a racially mixed book show. (Bert Williams, while a great black star, appeared only in the *Ziegfeld Follies* and never with his name above the title.) Waters began her stage career in 1917, touring the black vaudeville circuits and singing blues and double-entendre ballads. She graduated to Broadway in the early black musicals *Americana, Blackbirds,* and *Rhapsody in Black.* Following her star-making performance singing "Heat Wave" and the bold, wrenching "Supper Time" in *As Thousands Cheer,* she went on to appear in *At Home Abroad* and *Cabin in the Sky;* then it was on to Hollywood, nightclubs, concerts, and plays, most notably *A Member of the Wedding.* In addition to her two Berlin showstoppers, Waters also introduced to Broadway audiences "I'm Coming, Virginia," "Till the Real Thing Comes Along," "Cabin in the Sky," and "Taking a Chance on Love." As she got older, she got religion and turned her back on her early, wild years, still retaining the chip-on-the-shoulder attitude that was nurtured in the rough-and-tumble racist atmosphere of her youth.

In a sketch spoofing Noël Coward's return to England after great success in the States, Waters, Miller, and Broderick wait on Webb (as Coward) hand and foot.

Backstage

Webb and Miller resented Waters's success and didn't want to share the curtain call with her.

BABES IN ARMS

OPENED APRIL 14, 1937; SHUBERT THEATRE; 289 PERFORMANCES

Babe Mitzi Green in the arms of Ray Heatherton, as LeRoy James looks on.

BABES IN ARMS
Produced by Dwight Deere Wiman
Book by Richard Rodgers and Lorenz Hart
Music by Richard Rodgers
Lyrics by Lorenz Hart
Music orchestrated by Hans Spialek
Musical Director: Gene Salzer
Staged by Robert B. Sinclair
Choreographed by George Balanchine
Production supervised by Dwight Deere Wiman
Scenic Design by Raymond Sovey
Costume Design by Helene Pons
Pianists: Edgar Fairchild and Adam Carroll

Synopsis

Times are tough, and the threat of a trip to the work farm inspires a bunch of theatrical offspring. How to avoid tireless drudgery? Get a barn and put on a show!

Cast

A Gang Member	Dan Dailey
Marshall Blackstone	Alfred Drake
Billie Smith	Mitzi Green
Val LaMar	Ray Heatherton
Mazie LaMar	Ethel Intropidi
Lincoln Vanderpool	LeRoy James
Nat Blackstone	George E. MacKay
Dolores Reynolds	Grace McDonald
Sam Reynolds	Ray McDonald
Baby Rose	Wynn Murray
Irving DeQuincy	Fayard Nicholas
Ivor DeQuincy	Harold Nicholas
Emma Blackstone	Aileen Poe

"We had particular fun with the scene in the kids' show in which Wynn Murray sang 'Johnny One Note.' For some reason that I can't recall, it was performed in an Egyptian setting, but instead of going in for exotic scenery and costumes, we emphasized the do-it-yourself nature of the show by having the cast come out wearing such household appliances as towels, bath mats, coat hooks, and scrub mops."

— *Richard Rodgers*

"LET'S PUT ON A SHOW!" It's a cliché now, but it began as the plot of one of the freshest entertainments ever to be seen on Broadway, Richard Rodgers and Lorenz Hart's *Babes in Arms*. By 1937, the musical theatre had been rolling along for almost a half century, with the previous decades marked by a maturation of the form; although standards were still high, a certain sameness had set in, and the musical was due for a shake-up. Ira and George Gershwin and DuBose Heyward had expanded the musical theatre with *Porgy and Bess* two years earlier, but it was definitely that rare show that was truly ahead of its time. Rodgers and Hart had been having their way for decades with their mix

of romance, sophistication, and lyricism. Their shows, like the surrealistic *Peggy-Ann* and, later in their career, the cynical *Pal Joey*, hadn't set out to be different for different's sake; it was just the team trusting their instincts and not letting the norms dictate where their ideas and talents should take them.

Babes in Arms was certainly not a sophisticated show, nor did it espouse a great ideal; it was rousing good fun in typical musical theatre style. Where it was different was in its celebration of a younger generation of performers who, it turned out, would enliven the boards for decades to come. Because of its youthful joie de vivre, *Babes in Arms* was heralded as one of the most delightful shows in Broadway history. As critic Robert Coleman opined, the conventions of musical comedy were "thrust aside in favor of novelty, surprise, and freshness."

Among its adolescent newcomers were future stars Wynn Murray, Mitzi Green, Robert Rounseville, Alfred Drake, Dan Dailey, the Nicholas Brothers, and Ray Heatherton. The bright score included many future standards, including "Where or When," "The Lady Is a Tramp," "My Funny Valentine," and "I Wish I Were in Love Again," the last with its famous lyric describing love as having "the faint aroma of performing seals."

The show was transformed by Hollywood in 1939 with its major assets intact and a cast headed by Judy Garland and Mickey Rooney. And thus a cliché was born. ❈

ABOVE: Wearing costumes made from towels and other bathroom accoutrements, the kids put on a pretty darn fancy Egyptian ballet, choreographed by George Balanchine.

Lorenz Hart

Lorenz Hart, or "Larry" as he preferred to be called, was an enigmatic genius, personally tortured and professionally brilliant. His career began at age twenty-five when he was introduced to the seventeen-year-old Richard Rodgers. They were dissimilar in most ways—Rodgers punctual with a strong work ethic, Hart not—but they blended perfectly when it came to writing songs. Their shared obeisance to excellence resulted in hundreds of classic songs, all of which, save one ("Blue Moon"), were written for stage or film projects. Although Hart did yeomanlike work for the Shubert brothers on several unproduced operettas, the entire remainder of his career was spent writing with and frustrating Richard Rodgers. Hart's unhappiness with his looks and problems in accepting his homosexuality were not helped by Rodgers's stoicism. Hart began drinking more and more, forcing Rodgers to complete the lyric assignments on several later shows. When Hart turned down the opportunity to musicalize *Green Grow the Lilacs* with Rodgers, the composer turned to Oscar Hammerstein II. Hart attended *Oklahoma!* and loved the show, making his insecurity even more acute. Rodgers's attempt to help his partner consisted of involving him in another production, a revival of their hit *A Connecticut Yankee*. Hart's condition did not improve with the assignment, and for two days following the show's opening he went missing. Found suffering from an acute case of pneumonia, Larry Hart never recovered.

Lorenz "Larry" Hart (right) and his *Jumbo* star, the one-and-only Jimmy Durante, enjoy a stogie during a rehearsal.

SONGS

ACT I "Where or When" · "Babes in Arms" · "I Wish I Were in Love Again" · "All Dark People" · "Way Out West" · "My Funny Valentine" · "Johnny One-Note"
ACT II "Imagine" · "All at Once" · "Peter's Journey" (Ballet) · "The Lady Is a Tramp" · "You Are So Fair"

Backstage

The Nicholas Brothers appeared in their first book musical singing the Rodgers and Hart song "All Dark People (Are Light on Their Feet)." The song has inexplicably been deleted from the film version and subsequent stagings of the show.

Few people realize that, when Mitzi Green's character Billie Smith sings "My Funny Valentine," she's singing to Ray Heatherton's character, whose name is Valentine.

BABES IN TOYLAND

OPENED OCTOBER 13, 1903; MAJESTIC THEATRE; 192 PERFORMANCES

BABES IN TOYLAND

Produced by Fred R. Hamlin and Julian Mitchell

Music by Victor Herbert
Libretto and Lyrics by Glen MacDonough

Directed by Julian Mitchell

Scenic Design by John H. Young and
Homer Emens
Costumes by Caroline Seidle
Orchestra under the Direction of Max Hirschfeld

Synopsis

Mean Uncle Barnaby wants to get rid of his nephew, Alan, and his niece, Jane, in order to obtain their inheritance. He arranges a shipwreck but the children survive and find themselves in a strange country. They meet many of the Mother Goose characters, including Bo-Peep, Tom the Piper's Son, Little Red Riding Hood, and Mother Hubbard. The poor mother's shoe is threatened with foreclosure by Barnaby. He then arranges for Alan and Jane to be abandoned in the Forest of No Return. Luckily, the Gypsies save them and take them to Toyland. The evil Toymaker turns his toy soldiers into real live people, only to have them turn on him and kill him. But Alan is accused of the crime and found guilty, condemned to the gallows. Finally, evidence is found to acquit the boy, and the children decide to leave the magic country. But Barnaby has one more plot up his sleeve. He decides to kill the children himself. He accidentally takes the poison and dies. The children, presumably, live happily ever after.

Cast

Jane	*Mabel Barrison*
The Master Toymaker	*Dore Davidson*
Widow Piper	*Hattie Delaro*
Uncle Barnaby	*George W. Denham*
Grumio	*Charles Guyer*
Alan	*William Norris*
Inspector Marmaduke	*Gus Pixley*
Contrary Mary	*Amy Ricard*
Bo-Peep	*Nella Webb*
Tom Tom	*Bessie Wynn*

BY THE TURN OF THE century, musical theatre and operetta (pretty much one and the same at that point) were already settling into a kind of stasis. Operettas were marked by their settings, inevitably faraway locales in exotic climes. There were the Ruritanian romances, exemplified by *The Student Prince*, and the more homegrown locales of *The Girl of the Golden West* and *Naughty Marietta*. One subgenre of offbeat locales was the fairy-tale musical. The English began the trips to Mother Goose Land in the form of holiday pantomimes (or pantos), children's entertainments that were more music hall than musical comedy. Soon these shows developed into more-or-less full-blown musicals, becoming some of the most noteworthy in the field: *The Sleeping Beauty and the Beast* (two fairy tales in one show!) and the most famous of its time, *The Wizard of Oz*, starring the beloved comedy team of David Montgomery and Fred Stone.

SONGS

ACT I "Don't Cry, Bo-Peep" · "Floretta" · "Mary Mary" · "Barney O'Flynn" · "I Can't Do the Sum" · "Slumber Deep"
ACT II "Christmas Fair Waltz" · "The Legend of the Castle" (Our Castle in Spain) · "Rock-a-bye Baby" · "Toy Soldiers' March and Military Ball" · **"Toyland"** · "My Rag Doll Girl"
ACT III "An Old-Fashioned Rose" · "Before and After" · "Jane" · "Maybe the Moon Will Help You Out"

The great success of the latter show led its producer, Fred R. Hamlin, and director, Julian Mitchell, to search for a way to make theatrical lightning strike twice. They turned to one of the most prolific and respected librettist/lyricists, Glen MacDonough, and the most beloved composer of his time, Victor Herbert, to come up with a suitable vehicle. The team exceeded all expectations with *Babes in Toyland*, a show that instantly became an enduring classic for theatergoers of all ages. Among the best offerings of an excellent score are the "March of the Toys" and "Toyland," both still staples at Christmastime. Other delights are the sweetly simple (but not cloying) "I Can't Do the Sum" and "Go to Sleep, Slumber Deep."

In addition to its aural pleasures, the show was a visual spectacle, in the manner of today's *Phantom of the Opera*, only more lush and lavish. James Gibbons Harker, writing in the *Sun*, described its magnificence: "The songs, the dances, the processions, the fairies, the toys, the spiders, and the bears! Think of them all, set in the midst of really amazing scenery, ingenious and brilliant, surrounded with light effects which counterfeit all sorts of things from simple lightning to the spinning of a great spider's web, with costumes rich and dazzling as well as tasteful, and all accompanied with music a hundred times better than is customary in shows of this sort. What more could the spirit of mortal desire?" ✤

Backstage

The Majestic Theatre where *Babes in Toyland* opened is not the present-day Majestic. The original was on Columbus Circle, where today's Time Warner Center stands.

Victor Herbert

Victor Herbert was the most important American composer of the first two decades of the twentieth century. Born in Dublin and trained in Germany, Herbert's music evolved from the European operetta tradition into the American vernacular. He started out as a cellist with the Metropolitan Opera, and his composing career took off in 1894 with his first cello concerto and his first operetta, *Prince Ananias*. In 1898, he took over the baton of the Pittsburgh Symphony while simultaneously flourishing as composer, writing more than forty operettas in all, including *Babes in Toyland*, *Mlle. Modiste* (1905), *The Red Mill* (1906), *Naughty Marietta* (1910), *Sweethearts* (1913), and *Eileen* (1917), all still performed by companies throughout the world. In addition to Herbert's great talents as a composer and instrumentalist, he is credited with safeguarding the legal rights of composers and lyricists with his founding of the American Society of Composers, Authors and Publishers (ASCAP).

Tom Tom and Bo-Peep with chorus sing "I Can't Do the Sum."

REVUES, PART I

THERE ARE GENERALLY TWO TYPES of musical revue: the first consists of sketch and musical material written especially for the show; the second builds an evening around the already existing catalog of a famous composer or lyricist. The roots of the original-material revue go back to the first *Ziegfeld Follies* in 1907—but that art form is now dead, a victim of the television variety show. The songwriter revue is a relatively recent phenomenon, starting in 1966 with Off-Broadway's *Jacques Brel Is Alive and Well and Living in Paris*. That show was so successful that it spawned many, many imitators—too many, in fact—since most songwriter revues lack theatricality and, since the songs are taken out of context, staging ideas must be imposed on the songs. The result is like staged radio, usually populated with grinning, squeaky clean performers from the *Up with People* mold (though often one person of color is included to break up the monotony).

The best songwriter revue ever was *Ain't Misbehavin'*, exceptional in every element. The cast was made up of unique individuals of all shapes and sizes, each with a distinctive personality. The Fats Waller catalogue was given a theatrical concept; not a plot per se, but with a point of view that expanded on the lyrics of the songs. Richard Maltby Jr.'s imaginative and offbeat staging kept the energy at a high level, and the show wasn't afraid to laugh at itself. Most songwriter revues feature a preponderance of ballads, and gosh, they're fun to sing, but ballad after ballad, no matter how beautiful, gets boring. The Fats Waller catalogue that formed the basis for *Ain't Misbehavin'* certainly had its share of wonderful ballads, but they were offset by its many up tempo, humorous songs. Full of surprises and making for an exciting, delightful evening, *Ain't Misbehavin'* deservedly made stars of its indefatigable cast.

TOP LEFT: One of the reasons that *Ain't Misbehavin'* (1978) was the absolute best of all songwriter revues was that director Richard Maltby, Jr., encouraged its five wildly talented performers to cut loose with their singular quirkiness. Here, Andre De Shields and Charlaine Woodard stop the show with "How Ya Baby."

TOP RIGHT: The elegant Gregory Hines, one of the sophisticated gents of the 1981 Ellington revue *Sophisticated Ladies*.

RIGHT: Nancy Dussault, Larry Kert, and Georgia Brown, the replacement cast of the 1977 songbook revue *Side by Side by Sondheim*.

THE BAND WAGON

OPENED JUNE 3, 1931; NEW AMSTERDAM THEATRE; 262 PERFORMANCES

THE BAND WAGON
Produced by Max Gordon
Music by Arthur Schwartz
Lyrics by Howard Dietz
Book by George S. Kaufman and Howard Dietz
Staged by Hassard Short
Choreographed by Albertina Rasch
Lighting Design by Hassard Short
Scenic Design by Albert R. Johnson
Costume Design by
Kiviette and Constance Ripley

Cast

Adele Astaire, Fred Astaire, John Barker, Helen Broderick, Helen Carrington, Philip Loeb, Tillie Losch, Frank Morgan, Francis Pierlot, Roberta Robinson

"In general, Adele was more popular than Fred." — *Howard Dietz*

Frank Morgan squires Helen Broderick.

Tilly Losch and Fred Astaire perform "The Beggar Waltz."

Not only the greatest of all revues but also a landmark in design and structure, *The Band Wagon* was the ultimate in theatrical sophistication in its score, sketches, and performances.

Musical revues up to this time had been dominated by four legendary series: the *Ziegfeld Follies*, the *Earl Carroll Vanities*, *George White's Scandals*, and the Shubert brothers' *Passing Shows*. Lavishness, great stars, and beautiful girls marked Ziegfeld's offerings. The *Vanities* neglected top-drawer material and skimped on costume costs. White's shows also boasted curvaceous, if barely covered chorines but were animated by wonderful scores. And the *Passing Shows*, with an eye toward the tired businessman, emphasized not spectacle nor stars nor songs and sketches, they just sent out the girls. Another revue series, the more intimate *Music Box Revues*, boasted excellent scores by Irving Berlin and good, clean, if undistinguished fun.

The Band Wagon blew them all away. It boasted great stars; classic songs; hilarious, slightly suggestive sketches; ultramodern design; and a chorus of fully clad men and women. Among its most notable inventions was its utilization of stage revolves. They had, of course, been used for decades but always out of sight and only to facilitate scene changes. Staging director and designer

Hassard Short (Howard Dietz directed the sketches) included two revolves in his design and utilized them as scenic elements in full view. The finale of the first act, a carousel upon which Fred Astaire and the cast sang "I Love Louisa," spun round to the delight of the audience. For the great hit of the show, "Dancing in the Dark," Tilly Losch and company danced while colored lights were reflected in mirrors placed in the stage floor.

The films *Dancing in the Dark* (20th Century Fox, 1949) and *The Band Wagon* (MGM, 1953) utilized some numbers from the original production (the latter even starred Fred Astaire), but otherwise bear no relation to this most theatrical of all revues. ❄

Backstage

Adele Astaire made her last theatrical appearance in *The Band Wagon*. She retired from show business during the post-Broadway tour of the show to marry Lord Charles Cavendish. Fred Astaire was left without a partner and embarked on a solo career. (He was never heard from again.)

SONGS

ACT I "It Better Be Good" · "Sweet Music" · "High and Low" · "The Flag" (Dance) · "A Nice Place to Visit" "Hoops" · "Confession" · "New Sun in the Sky" · "(What's the Use of Being) Miserable with You" · "I Love Louisa"
ACT II · "Dancing in the Dark" · "Nanette" · "Where Can He Be?" · "The Beggar Waltz" (Dance) · "White Heat"

RIGHT: Adele Astaire plays "Hoops."

Left to right: Tilly Losch, Fred Astaire, Adele Astaire, Frank Morgan, and Helen Broderick take a ride on the carousel to the tune of "I Love Louisa."

LEFT: Singing one of Dietz and Schwartz's most romantic scores, Walter Chiari, Barbara Cook, and Jules Munshin celebrate *The Gay Life*. The sumptuous turn-of-the-century costumes were designed by Lucinda Ballard, wife of Howard Dietz.

Howard Dietz and Arthur Schwartz

The songwriting team Howard Dietz and Arthur Schwartz were the masters of the revue format. Schwartz, a self-taught pianist, planned to be a lawyer and earned a doctorate in jurisprudence from Columbia University. But Schwartz wasn't happy in his law practice, and, even before his graduation in 1924, he began writing songs (his first, "Baltimore, M.D., You're the Only Doctor for Me" was published to shockingly scant acclaim in 1923). Schwartz approached Dietz with the idea of collaborating but was turned down. Five years later, having gained experience, he again approached Dietz, and a new team was born that would span thirty-four years. As they wrote, Dietz also pursued a career in public relations, eventually becoming a vice president of publicity for MGM. Throughout their partnership, they both worked with a variety of other collaborators, Schwartz teaming with Dorothy Fields (*Stars in Your Eyes*, *A Tree Grows in Brooklyn*), Desmond Carter on a series of British musicals, and Ira Gershwin (*Park Avenue*). Dietz worked alongside Vernon Duke (*Jackpot* and *Sadie Thompson*) and adapted *Die Fledermaus* and *La Bohème* for the Metropolitan Opera. Had he not devoted so much of his energies to MGM and ASCAP (he served on the board of directors for almost twenty years), Dietz's career might have equaled that of George S. Kaufman. Dietz also directed productions (usually uncredited), was a noted wit and bon vivant, and imported the party game charades to the United States from France, among many other accomplishments.

ABOVE: Composer Arthur Schwartz works with the brilliant Beatrice Lillie while recording the revue *Inside U.S.A.*
RIGHT: Howard Dietz always thought his retirement funds would come from his MGM work, but it was ASCAP that allowed him and Lucinda Ballard to live in the manner to which they were accustomed.

BELLS ARE RINGING

OPENED NOVEMBER 29, 1956; SHUBERT THEATRE; 924 PERFORMANCES

BELLS ARE RINGING

Produced by The Theatre Guild
Book and Lyrics by
Betty Comden and Adolph Green
Music by Jule Styne
Musical Director: Milton Rosenstock
Music orchestrated by Robert Russell Bennett
Vocal Arrangements and Direction by
Herbert Greene and Buster Davis
Dance Arrangements and
Incidental Music by John Morris
Directed by Jerome Robbins
Choreographed by
Jerome Robbins and Bob Fosse
Scenic Design by Raoul Pène Du Bois
Costume Design by Raoul Pène Du Bois
Lighting Design by Peggy Clark

Synopsis

A shy switchboard operator for Susanswerphone named Ella Peterson meddles in her clients' lives, disguising her voice as different characters. She falls in love with one of her subscribers, Jeff Moss, a playwright with writer's block. Among others whose lives she anonymously fixes are a songwriting dentist and Blake Barton, a Brandoesque actor. Simultaneously, the owner of Susanswerphone is being swindled by her boyfriend, who is secretly running a numbers racket out of her establishment. Hilarity ensues.

Cast

Ella Peterson	*Judy Holliday*
Jeff Moss	*Sydney Chaplin*
Sandor	*Eddie Lawrence*
Sue	*Jean Stapleton*
Larry Hastings	*George S. Irving*
Dr. Kitchell	*Bernie West*
Blake Barton	*Frank Aletter*
Inspector Barnes	*Dort Clark*
Carl	*Peter Gennaro*
Ella Peterson Standby	*Phyllis Newman*
Jeff Moss Understudy	*Hal Linden*

ABOVE: Switchboard operator Ella Peterson (Judy Holliday) wonders what "Plaza-oh-double-four-double-three" looks like, in a textbook example of a star "charm" number, "It's a Perfect Relationship."

RIGHT: Sydney Chaplin as swingin' bachelor Jeff Moss declares "I Met a Girl."

THE ORIGINAL LIBRETTO IS A rarity on Broadway. The original libretto for a successful Broadway musical is practically nonexistent. But *Bells Are Ringing* is a most felicitous exception, existing as a star vehicle for Judy Holliday and written by three masters of tailoring a show for their star: Jule Styne (music), and Betty Comden and Adolph Green (libretto and lyrics).

One reason that the show fit the talents of Holliday so well was her history with the team of Comden and Green. The three of them, along with John Frank and Alvin Hammer, made up a nightclub troupe titled "The Revuers." They played Greenwich Village boîtes such as the Village Vanguard with a blend of screwy comedy and off-kilter songs. So, when it came to fashioning a musical theatre debut for Judy Holliday, what better team to write it than her old partners, Comden and Green?

Holliday was permitted to show off her versatility as Ella Peterson, an operator with a telephone answering service who interacts with a variety of characters. Comden, Green, and Styne brilliantly accentuated Holliday's brashness and underlying insecurity. The songs "The Party's Over" and "Just in Time" became standards. The score's comedy numbers, "Drop That Name" and "It's a Simple Little System," were nimble and witty. Even the throwaway numbers for the songwriting dentist (!), though short, displayed Comden and Green's playfulness and zingy satire. ❋

If not for Judy Holliday's early death, the half-baked *Hot Spot* would have been merely a footnote in a long, brilliant career, instead of her second and last Broadway musical. She's seen here with Arny Freeman.

Judy Holliday

Judy Holliday appeared in only two Broadway musicals, but her unique personality made her an unforgettable presence. With a natural vulnerability that other comediennes could only manufacture, a much-underrated singing voice, and a zany streak that perfectly complemented her beauty and femininity, Holliday caused everyone she encountered to fall a little bit in love with her. Despite reprising her smash success as Ella Peterson in the film version of *Bells Are Ringing*, she was able to create only one more role on the musical stage, that of Peace Corps volunteer Sally Hopwinder in the 1963 misfire *Hot Spot*. Her talents made even the most mediocre of Mary Rodgers/Martin Charnin's songs shine, and she knocked the one gem, "Don't Laugh" (written with an uncredited Stephen Sondheim assist), clear out of the park. Holliday was known as a fiercely intelligent woman—she whizzed through the *Times* crossword—in ink! But she was also tender and a bit insecure—a mix that served her characters well. Her tragic death at the age of forty-three robbed theatregoers of the continued pleasure of one of the most special talents ever to weave a spell on a Broadway stage.

ABOVE LEFT: Judy Holliday (here with Dort Clark, singing "Is It a Crime?") had many comic opportunities in *Bells Are Ringing*, grabbing each one like a quarterback and scoring a Broadway touchdown.

LEFT: Ella and dreamboat dream date, oh-so-slick playwright Jeff Moss (Sydney Chaplin), do an impromptu soft shoe in Central Park, and the orchestra, somewhere in the bushes, swells up "Just in Time."

Backstage

Hot Spot was such a loser it featured a photo of Holliday in the film version of *Bells Are Ringing* on its poster!

1928's *The Five O'Clock Girl* had as its protagonist a telephone operator who falls in love with a subscriber—sight unseen.

Judy Holliday's character was based on an actual answering service operator friend of Betty Comden named Betty Printz, and the dentist, Dr. Kitchell, was based on Harold Karr, composer of *Happy Hunting*, who was a real songwriting dentist.

SONGS

ACT I "Bells Are Ringing" · "It's a Perfect Relationship" "On My Own" · "You've Got to Do It" · "It's a Simple Little System" · "Is It a Crime?" · "Hello, Hello There" · " I Met a Girl" · "Long Before I Knew You" ·
ACT II "Mu-cha-cha" · "Just in Time" · "Drop That Name" "The Party's Over" · "Salzburg" · "The Midas Touch" · "I'm Goin' Back"

LEFT: At the end of *Bells*, Jeff comes to realize that the small-voiced Mom at his answering service is really the big-hearted Ella.

"I don't think I'm going on tonight."

—Judy Holliday, the afternoon of the New Haven opening

Sydney Chaplin

Sydney Chaplin, Jule Styne's favorite leading man (and son of Charlie Chaplin), had a brief but busy career in Broadway musicals. After *Bells Are Ringing*, he played Robert Baker opposite original star Rosalind Russell in the television version of *Wonderful Town*. His next Styne musical was the 1961 *Subways Are for Sleeping*, today best remembered for a publicity stunt launched by producer David Merrick. His next role, as Nick Arnstein in a third Styne musical, *Funny Girl*, became his swan song to the musical stage. His carefree vocals on the songs "I'm Just Taking My Time" from *Subways* and "I Want to Be Seen with You Tonight" from *Funny Girl* were a refreshing new approach to a romantic leading man. Never to be mistaken for a John Raitt or an Alfred Drake, his strength was his strange blend of utter confidence and lack of technique, combined with his dark good looks and fine acting, which made for an extremely appealing package.

Chaplin, seen here with Carol Lawrence in rehearsal for *Subways Are for Sleeping*, retired in the 1960s to California, where he opened a restaurant.

BLOOMER GIRL

OPENED OCTOBER 5, 1944; SHUBERT THEATRE; 657 PERFORMANCES

Evelina (Celeste Holm) shows off her bloomers to the shock of her father (a manufacturer of hoop skirts) and the appreciation of her lady friends.

BLOOMER GIRL

Produced by John C. Wilson
Produced in association with Nat Goldstone

Music by Harold Arlen
Lyrics by E. Y. Harburg
Book by Sig Herzig and Fred Saidy
Musical Director: Leon Leonardi
Music orchestrated by Russell Bennett

Staged by E. Y. Harburg
Book directed by William Schorr
Choreographed by Agnes de Mille

Scenic Design by Lemuel Ayers
Lighting Design by Lemuel Ayers
Costume Design by Miles White

Synopsis

Against the backdrop of the Civil War, Evelina Applegate, daughter of a hoop-skirt manufacturer, is a highly progressive woman, involved with women's rights and the underground railway. Jeff Calhoun, the object of Evelina's affections, owns Pompey, one of the slaves rescued through the railway. Aunt Dolly Bloomer encourages her niece's abolitionist beliefs and also proselytizes on behalf of the bloomer, an undergarment that will spell the death of the hoop skirt.

Cast

Evelina	Celeste Holm
Horatio	Matt Briggs
Jeff Calhoun	David Brooks
Gus	John Call
Hamilton Calhoun	Blaine Cordner
Augustus	Hubert Dilworth
Dolly	Margaret Douglass
Delia	Nancy Douglass
Sheriff Quimby	Charles Howard
Alexander	Richard Huey
Ebenezer Mimms	Joe E. Marks
Daisy	Joan McCracken
Dancer	James Mitchell
Serena	Mabel Taliaferro
Pompey	Dooley Wilson
Betty	Eleanor Winter

"I hope to God it stops the show opening night and shuts their clamoring mouths."

—Harold Arlen to Agnes de Mille, on the "Civil War Ballet" and his coworkers' dislike of it

THE MUSICAL THEATRE BEGAN AS an entertainment without a thought in its pretty little head. Corseted chorines with hourglass figures, Dutch comics with checkered coats, blackfaced entertainers singing about the South when it was the shtetls they should have been extolling. It wasn't until *Show Boat* that the entertainment portion of our program was put on hold while a message was introduced. The musical had entered a brave new world that seemed to transcend the term "musical comedy." We still haven't figured out what exactly the term should be—musical drama has a bit of the pretentious about it. And one thing a good musical always promised, to the audience's relief, was an utter lack of pretension. In fact, most early comics made their marks (or Marx, as in Brothers) skewering pretension.

The introduction of "themes" drew a dividing line between musical comedy and musical theatre (that's the name that was chosen, don't blame us). It was a true master who could successfully merge the two. Kurt Weill and Maxwell Anderson couldn't pull it off with *Knickerbocker Holiday*, nor could Weill and Alan Jay Lerner with *Love Life*. George and Ira Gershwin fared better with *Strike Up the Band*, though it took them two tries to get it slightly right. George took the next step and went all classical on us with *Porgy and Bess* (thank God for John Bubbles and Ira Gershwin). And Richard Rodgers and Oscar Hammerstein's *The Sound of Music* tried to inject some Nazis into the mix, but they never stood a chance against raindrops on roses.

In fact, the number of musicals that gave us a rousing good dose of musical comedy as well as the dreaded message is very few indeed, which brings us, albeit verbosely, to E. Y. Harburg. A card-carrying liberal with a healthy

Backstage

Celeste Holm capitalized on her rave reviews for her portrayal of Ado Annie in *Oklahoma!* with her star performance in *Bloomer Girl*. But the sudden fame and recognition might have gone to her head, literally. Holm was set to make her nightclub debut and so cut her curly locks for a more modern look. The powers that be didn't much like what they viewed as insolence, and so Nanette Fabray, who wore her hair exactly as required, replaced Holm. While some wags suggested it was just an excuse to get rid of her, others believed it was Holm's ploy to exit the show as soon as she could.

Bloomer Girl was faithfully re-created for television starring Barbara Cook and Keith Andes. Although the plot was necessarily shortened, Agnes de Mille re-created her famed "Civil War Ballet."

disdain for the ruling classes no matter who they might be. Harburg had a fondness for the human spirit in all its ups and downs, along with the ego to believe his message was worth broadcasting (or rather, staging). In 1937, Harburg tried to inject a warning about warmongering into *Hooray for What!*, but Ed Wynn and librettists Howard Lindsay and Russel Crouse dampened the ardor and pulled the show back to farce and light comedy.

But with *Bloomer Girl*, Harburg put his artistic foot down and became, as William Goldman dubs it in *The Season*, the muscle—that is, the all-powerful artistic vision of the piece. Harold Arlen, a gentle soul, was content to write magnificent music, while librettists Sig Herzig and Fred Saidy followed their master's whim. And Harburg installed himself as codirector, allowing William Schorr to share the title if not the power.

Bloomer Girl boasted two main themes—women's rights and anti-slavery, and it fooled its audience into accepting them in the most entertaining of fashions. With such magnificent songs as "Right as the Rain" and "Evalina," Harburg allowed musical comedy to hold the spotlight. But he tempered the light moments with "The Eagle and Me," a soaring cry for freedom of the body as well as the soul, and "Man for Sale," which is exactly what its title promised. Agnes de Mille, the master of intellectual, psychological dance, presented a scorching "Civil War Ballet" wherein women wait, sometimes in vain, for the return of their men from the battlefield. The ballet is the dark side of the song "When the Boys Come Home," in which the women sing of "drums and trumpets, tea and crumpets out on the village green." Harburg knew war doesn't end as "a grand reunion."

Bloomer Girl was a success not because of or in spite of its messages but because the entire evening was a fully professional, exemplary, thought-provoking entertainment executed brilliantly. ✿

ABOVE RIGHT: Joan McCracken contemplates the fine arts.

RIGHT: In Agnes de Mille's powerful "Civil War Ballet," the women wait for their men, who, more likely than not, won't return home.

Harold Arlen

Harold Arlen, who wrote blues and jazz-flavored music for many of the greatest torch songs in popular music, contributed to many Broadway revues in the 1930s before his first book show, *Hooray for What?,* in 1937. He composed wonderful songs for the shows *Bloomer Girl, St. Louis Woman, House of Flowers, Jamaica,* and *Saratoga,* including the standards "Right as the Rain," "A Sleepin' Bee," "Any Place I Hang My Hat Is Home," and "Come Rain or Come Shine." Although none of his shows were smash hits on the level of Rodgers and Hammerstein's, as long as people sing about the loss and gain of love, Harold Arlen's songs will always, always be relevant. His songs "Blues in the Night," "Stormy Weather," "I Gotta Right to Sing the Blues," and "Happiness Is a Thing Called Joe" made him, a nice Jewish boy born Hyman Arluck and the son of a cantor, quite unlikely as one of the most-sung composers by African American singers. In addition, it is fascinating that "Get Happy," "Over the Rainbow," and "The Man That Got Away," perhaps the three songs most associated with Judy Garland, were all written by Arlen, his music perfectly matching her blend of intense, mournful ache and hyperkinetic joy. Arlen was a sensitive, kind, and dapper man whose lack of ego and innate gentility ensured that he would never be a household name, despite being one of the greatest composers of the twentieth century.

RIGHT: "Yip" Harburg (left) and Harold Arlen.

E. Y. Harburg

E.Y. "Yip" Harburg, whose lyrics employed slang and fantasy more than any other Broadway lyricist, made his debut in 1932 with his lyrics for the revue *Americana,* where his song "Brother, Can You Spare a Dime?" became the unofficial anthem of the Great Depression. That song set a tone for Harburg's entire career—delivering a societal message in a most entertaining way. In addition to the delightful simplicity of his lyrics for the movie *The Wizard of Oz,* he contributed the unmistakably Harburgian words to the songs of *Bloomer Girl, Finian's Rainbow, Jamaica,* and the underrated, cult shows *Flahooley, The Happiest Girl in the World,* and *Darling of the Day.* Perhaps the word "whimsical" has never been more appropriately applied than to Harburg's lyrics, with such titles as "Something Sort of Grandish," "You're a Builder Upper," and "T'morra' T'morra'." His ability to create another world was perfectly exploited by the heightened reality of the Broadway musical. To his collaborators, Harburg could be maddeningly didactic and insensitive, yet his elfin charm, loyalty, and intellect, not to mention his great talent, made them eager to work with him.

Augustine Rios admires Ricardo Montalban's catch while Lena Horne reels in a catch of her own in *Jamaica.*

SONGS

ACT I "When the Boys Come Home" · "Evelina" · "Welcome Hinges" · "Farmer's Daughter" · "It Was Good Enough for Grandma" · "The Eagle and Me" · "Right as the Rain" "T'morra', T'morra'" · "Rakish Young Man with the Whiskers" "Pretty as a Picture" · Style Show Ballet

ACT II "Sunday in Cicero Falls" · "I Got a Song" · "Lullaby" "Simon Legree" · "Liza Crossing the Ice" · "I Was Never Born" "Man for Sale" · Civil War Ballet

THE BOYS FROM SYRACUSE

OPENED NOVEMBER 23, 1938; ALVIN THEATRE; 235 PERFORMANCES

Eddie Albert and pop-eyed comedian Jimmy Savo, as Antipholus and Dromio, want to go back to "Dear Old Syracuse."

BOYS FROM SYRACUSE

Produced by George Abbott
Music by Richard Rodgers
Lyrics by Lorenz Hart
Book by George Abbott
Based on the play *The Comedy of Errors*
by William Shakespeare
Vocal Arrangements by Hugh Martin
Music orchestrated by Hans Spialek
Directed by George Abbott
Choreographed by George Balanchine
Scenic Design by Jo Mielziner
Costume Design by Irene Sharaff
Lighting Design by Jo Mielziner
Conducted by Harry S. Levant

Synopsis

Antipholus and Dromio of Syracuse are searching for their respective twin brothers. They travel to Ephesus, where they run into Adriana and Luce, the wives of their brothers. Mistaken identities abound.

Cast

Antipholus of Syracuse	*Eddie Albert*
Adriana	*Muriel Angelus*
Duke of Ephesus	*Carroll Ashburn*
Courtesan	*Betty Bruce*
Angelo	*John Clarke*
Tailor	*Clifford Dunstan*
Seeress	*Florence Fair*
Antipholus of Ephesus	*Ronald Graham*
Dromio of Ephesus	*Teddy Hart*
Tailor's Apprentice	*Burl Ives*
Luce	*Wynn Murray*
Aegon	*John O'Shaughnessy*
Dromio of Syracuse	*Jimmy Savo*
Merchant of Syracuse	*Byron Shores*
Luciana	*Marcy Westcott*

"Larry was a demon, he was like Peck's Bad Boy. I could never get to know him, he was here one minute and around the world in forty seconds."

— *Muriel Angelus*

It seems inconceivable now, but *The Boys from Syracuse* was the first musical comedy to be based on a work of Shakespeare. And it only took seventy years from the origins of musical theatre for someone to come up with the idea! That person was Richard Rodgers, who convinced his partner Larry Hart to go along with the notion. Librettist (and director) George Abbott very freely adapted *The Comedy of Errors*, keeping only two lines from the original play: "The venom clamours of a jealous woman / Poisons more deadly than a mad dog's tooth." When those lines were spoken in the show, Teddy Hart, brother of Larry, playing Dromio of Epheseus, stuck his head out from the wings and exulted: "Shakespeare!"

Adriana (Muriel Angelus) and her handmaidens bemoan the trap of "Falling in Love (with Love)."

The songwriting team wisely eschewed setting Shakespeare's verse to music, contenting themselves to write one of their best scores in their customary romantic and droll style. "Falling in Love (with Love)" is the standout, but "This Can't Be Love" comes in a close second. It's a stunning achievement for writers who were contributing almost a show a year to Broadway (in 1938 actually premiering both *I Married an Angel* and *The Boys from Syracuse*).

Later adapters of Shakespeare into musical comedy made the mistake of confusing written verse with sung lyrics, usually to soporific results. Some made their scores an uneasy mix of Shakespeare and modern phraseology. *Your Own Thing*, a freewheeling adaptation of *Twelfth Night*, contained "Come Away, Death" and "Hunca Munca" (can you guess which is based on Shakespeare?). With *Kiss Me, Kate*, Cole Porter had the good sense to start out a song with a hint of the bard and then go his own, freewheeling way. "I've Come to Wive It Wealthily in Padua" is how the song starts from then on it's pure Porter. And while several of his other song titles have a vaguely Elizabethan air about them, in one song, "I Am Ashamed That Women Are So Simple," Shakespeare actually wins out over Porter.

Other Shakespearian adaptations were not so felicitous, though *West Side Story* comes to mind as a successful retelling of the *Romeo and Juliet* tragedy. Still, for every *West Side Story* there's a *Love and Let Love* (also based on *Twelfth Night*, it opened a little over a week before *Your Own Thing*, robbing *Your Own Thing*'s producers of some sleep). Will's plays may be too rich and dense for musicalization, for musical theatre libretti need to move along briskly, using musical numbers as their own brand of soliloquy. (Unless you're *Carousel*.)

And to think it all started with *The Boys from Syracuse*, with some critics actually stating that it improved on the original. Richard Watts Jr. of the *New York Herald Tribune* wrote, "If you have been wondering all these years what's wrong with *The Comedy of Errors*, it is now possible to tell you. It has been waiting for a score by Rodgers and Hart and direction by George Abbott." ✽

George Abbott

George Abbott, renaissance man whose list of credits would require an additional volume of this book, wore numerous hats in 122 Broadway shows from 1913 (as an actor in *The Misleading Lady*) to 1987 (as director of a revival of his hit *Broadway*, which opened on his one hundredth birthday). As director and/or author of the greatest musical comedies of the Golden Age, "Mr. Abbott," as he was called by everyone who worked with him, had an unerring eye for new talent, giving young authors such as Leonard Bernstein, Betty Comden and Adolph Green, Frank Loesser, Harold Prince, Jerome Robbins, and Jerry Bock and Sheldon Harnick their first successes, as well as tapping actors Gene Kelly, Nancy Walker, Desi Arnaz, Edie Adams, Tom Bosley, Carol Burnett, and Liza Minnelli for their star-making breaks. He believed in instinct over interpretation (no Method method for him) and clarity. Subject of more anecdotes than any Broadway personality with the possible exception of Ethel Merman, there is one that stands out as an example of the quick wit and uncluttered, no-nonsense wisdom of George Abbott. When an actor asked why he had lost a solid laugh in a long-running show while doing the stage business of making a phone call, Mr. Abbott replied it was because the actor was calling the wrong number. Abbott was the greatest practitioner of the art of theatre in the twentieth century. Oh, and he lived to be 107.

ABOVE: Mr. Abbott in an uncharacteristically goofy shot, during rehearsals for *Damn Yankees*.

RIGHT: One of the many young stars whose careers George Abbott helped launch was a talented kid from California named Carol Burnett, here with Joseph Bova in her splashy debut, *Once Upon a Mattress*.

Backstage

Teddy Hart was the brother of Larry Hart. He was always being confused with the comic Jimmy Savo. Once Rodgers and Hart had settled on adapting a Shakespeare play for musicalization, the similarity between Hart and Savo made Larry Hart immediately suggest *A Comedy of Errors* as the team's next musical.

Muriel Angelus, Wynn Murray, and Marcy Westcott decide to bring swing to ancient Greece in the showstopper "Sing for Your Supper."

Eddie Albert

Had Eddie Albert concentrated on a musical career, he could have been an all-time great. A facile comedian, a lovely singer, and a graceful dancer, he had the ability and talent to work nonstop. But after *Boys from Syracuse*, he didn't appear in a musical again for a decade, when he starred in Irving Berlin's *Miss Liberty*. A fascinating, highly complicated piece followed: *Reuben, Reuben*, a Marc Blitzstein work of near operatic proportions that closed out of town in 1955. After that, despite a replacement stint as Harold Hill in *The Music Man*, Albert took his easygoing charm where the work was, jumping between films (where he appeared as Ali Hakim in the film version of *Oklahoma!*) and television, where he achieved perhaps his widest fame—with a pitchfork, as Oliver Wendell Douglas on the sitcom *Green Acres*.

LEFT: Eddie Albert and Mary McCarty strut their stuff in Irving Berlin's *Miss Liberty*.
RIGHT: Twenty-five years before *Barnum*, Eddie Albert did Jim Dale one better in *Reuben, Reuben* by not only juggling and walking a tight rope, but also eating fire.

BRIGADOON

OPENED MARCH 13, 1947; ZIEGFELD THEATRE; 581 PERFORMANCES

David Brooks, Marion Bell, heather, and hill.

BRIGADOON

Produced by Cheryl Crawford

Music by Frederick Loewe
Lyrics by Alan Jay Lerner
Book by Alan Jay Lerner
Musical Director: Franz Allers
Music orchestrated by Ted Royal
Vocal Arrangements by Frederick Loewe

Staged by Robert Lewis
Choreographed by Agnes de Mille

Scenic Design by Oliver Smith
Costume Design by David Ffolkes
Lighting Design by Peggy Clark
Musical Assistant to Miss de Mille:
Trude Rittman

Synopsis

Two hikers from the United States stumble upon the town of Brigadoon in the Scottish highlands. Brigadoon has a secret; it appears only once every one hundred years. Tommy, the more romantic of the hikers, falls in love with Fiona, but he is unable to commit to a life of popping up every century. He and Jeff, a typical cynical New Yorker, return to the States, but Tommy can't get Fiona out of his head. He returns to Brigadoon only to find an empty meadow where the town once stood. But the force of his love brings the town back, and he and Fiona join together for eternity.

Cast

Fiona MacLaren	*Marion Bell*
Jean MacLaren	*Virginia Bosler*
Meg Brockie	*Pamela Britton*
Tommy Albright	*David Brooks*
Jane Ashton	*Frances Charles*
Andrew MacLaren	*Edward Cullen*
Sword Dancer	*George Drake*
Maggie Anderson	*Lidija Franklin*
Sword Dancer	*Roland Guerard*
Mr. Lundie	*William Hansen*
Jeff Douglas	*George Keane*
Harry Beaton	*James Mitchell*
Angus McGuffie	*Walter Scheff*
Archie Beaton	*Elliot Sullivan*
Charlie Dalrymple	*Lee Sullivan*
Sandy Dean	*Jeffrey Warren*

DON'T DECRY THE FAILURE. DON'T deride the writer whose first, second, or even third show really, really stinks. Cole Porter was so disheartened by the reception to his first show, *See America First*, in 1916, that he left showbiz and joined the French Foreign Legion! Jerry Bock and Sheldon Harnick's first collaboration was *The Body Beautiful* (do you go around humming tunes from that one?). Jule Styne teamed up with Sammy Cahn for *Glad to See Ya!* It closed out of town. Way back in 1901, George M. Cohan expanded a sketch into the musical *The Governor's Son*. It played only thirty-two performances, sending the Four Cohans back to vaudeville. Howard Dietz's first show, *Dear Sir*, was written

SONGS

with none other than the great Jerome Kern. It was one of Kern's few failures. George Gershwin's first score. for the revue *Half-Past Eight*... well. you get the point. Luckily back in a healthier era of musical theatre. writers, directors, producers, and so forth had the time and opportunity to grow into their own success.

A case in point is that of Alan Jay Lerner and Frederick Loewe. The latter's first show. *Great Lady*: premiered to dismissive notices and quickly folded. Loewe teamed up with Lerner. his dream partner, and they began their collaboration with two mediocrities. *Life of the Party* (which closed out of town) and *What's Up?*. not good enough to be a hit or bad enough to be a legendary flop. After a modest effort. *The Day Before Spring*. the team persevered and created *Brigadoon*.

Brigadoon has a richly romantic score with beautifully atmospheric ballads and warmly humorous character numbers. Lerner's script. based on a German story (in which the hero does not end up with the heroine). contrasts the soulless life in the big city with the rich. simple life of the country. Agnes de Mille's brilliant choreography included Scottish tradition (the sword dance). an athletic, tension-filled chase through the woods. and a somber funeral dance.

Brigadoon's book is romantic. too. and humorous. which is only to be expected in a Lerner script. But it is the deep. rich. heartfelt ballads that make the show a perennial favorite around the world. All the characters in the show need something. and they express their wants wholeheartedly in song. Lerner and Loewe's previous scores gave no indication of the depth of emotion. humor. or sophistication that was to come in *Brigadoon* (not to mention *Paint Your Wagon*. *My Fair Lady*. and others). If we find a way to support new artists. we will all reap the rewards in good time—maybe not with their first. second. or even third show... but the fourth just might be a *Brigadoon*. ✻

Alan Jay Lerner and Frederick Loewe

Alan Jay Lerner (lyrics) and Frederick Loewe (music) shared a certain sophistication, despite their vastly different upbringings—Lerner the Ivy Leaguer, Loewe a one-time pugilist. Their mismatched personalities and working habits (Lerner was undisciplined but sensitive, whereas Loewe was exacting about his work and cold to the point of cruelty in his personal life), along with Loewe's health problems, led to an early dissolution of their partnership. They briefly reteamed to write four additional songs for the stage adaptation of their film *Gigi* and the lovely, unappreciated score for the film *The Little Prince*. Loewe, battling a heart condition, never worked again, happy to retire on his *My Fair Lady* wealth. Lerner continued to charm countless wives and frustrate countless collaborators: Burton Lane on *On a Clear Day You Can See Forever* and *Carmelina*, Andre Previn on *Coco*, John Barry on *Lolita, My Love*, Leonard Bernstein on *1600 Pennsylvania Avenue,* and Charles Strouse on *Dance a Little Closer*. Even when the shows were failures (as all his later shows were), Lerner's lyrics remained the essence of intelligent wit.

ABOVE RIGHT: Alan Jay Lerner, Moss Hart, and Frederick Loewe confer during pre-production of the heart attack–inducing tryout of *Camelot*.

RIGHT: Julie Andrews and Richard Burton, theatre royalty, as literal royalty in *Camelot*.

Backstage

Brigadoon is one of the only American musicals that enjoyed a longer run in London (685 performances) than on Broadway.

The Doon is a river in Scotland. And the word "brig" means bridge in Scots.

"The contract that he wished us to sign negated Abraham Lincoln's Emancipation Proclamation that freed the slaves."

—*Alan Jay Lerner on* Brigadoon's *first producer, Billy Rose*

LEFT: David Brooks (top) and George Keane lost in the Highlands.
BELOW: Lidija Franklin as Maggie Anderson, dancing Agnes de Mille's "Funeral Dance."

BYE BYE BIRDIE

OPENED APRIL 14, 1960; MARTIN BECK THEATRE; 607 PERFORMANCES

Synopsis

Albert Peterson's longtime girlfriend Rosie yearns for him to be an English teacher, but contents herself as secretary to Albert's music business, as he writes pop songs and manages the Elvis-like Conrad Birdie. After Conrad is drafted, Albert and Rosie cook up a scheme for Conrad to appear on *The Ed Sullivan Show* and give one last kiss good-bye to a lucky female fan. This scheme carries them all to the heart of small-town America, where everyone learns a little something about life, love, and celebrity.

Cast

Rose Grant	*Chita Rivera*
Albert Peterson	*Dick Van Dyke*
Conrad Birdie	*Dick Gautier*
Mr. MacAfee	*Paul Lynde*
Mae Peterson	*Kay Medford*
Kim MacAfee	*Susan Watson*
Hugo Peabody	*Michael J. Pollard*
Mrs. MacAfee	*Marijane Maricle*
Randolph MacAfee	*Johnny Borden*
Ursula Merkel	*Barbara Doherty*
Gloria Rasputin	*Norma Richardson*
Rose Grant Standby	*Carmen Alvarez*
Albert Peterson Standby	*Charles Nelson Reilly*

Bye, Bye, Birdie contains one of the all-time-great opening numbers, "An English Teacher," perfectly setting up the main relationship of the show: Rose (Chita Rivera) filling the audience in on her one and only dream: for Albert (Dick Van Dyke), her eight-year boss/boyfriend, to give up the pop-music business and become "An English Teacher."

A SLEEPER IS DEFINED AS A project with modest expectations that ends up making millions for its creators while everyone else stands with mouths agape. Think of yourself as a Broadway investor. You are approached by a producer who has never produced a Broadway show before. He's got the rights to a really wonderful show by a new songwriting team that has never written a complete score anywhere, Broadway, Off, or Off-Off. It will star a rising young comic whose previous Broadway appearance gained no notice whatsoever. It will be directed and choreographed by a popular television and film dancer who has never worked in those capacities on a book show. Oh, and we almost forgot, the librettist hasn't ever written a musical either. But hey, the story is up-to-the-minute. It's about rock and roll. You know, that new music that has no relation to the legitimate theatre at all.

And now the producer pops the $64,000 (or probably back then the $500) question: "Will you invest your hard-earned money in my show?" What would your answer have been? Well, hats off to all those relatives and friends and

"Sylvia and I sat there with all our friends staring at us. I only wanted the floor to open up and swallow us both."

— *Ed Sullivan at opening night of* Bye Bye Birdie, *reacting to the "Hymn for a Sunday Evening"*

friends of friends who forked over their cash to producer Edward Padula.

As you've surmised, the result was *Bye Bye Birdie*, one of the most popular musicals of all time. It enjoyed a long Broadway run, had a hit song in "Put on a Happy Face," and boasted a successful film adaptation, with some members of the original cast reprising their roles. It has also become, reportedly, the most produced show ever on the amateur stage.

The moral of the story is, when asked to invest, go with your gut reaction. (Of course, we know a fellow who was offered a £500 stake in a new show titled *Cats*. He laughed in the producer's face.)

Despite what we stated in the chapter on *Brigadoon*, musicals will always pop up in the most unexpected ways and save Broadway, the fabulous invalid, from certain creative death. ✲

THE SONGS

ACT I "An English Teacher" · "The Telephone Hour" · "How Lovely to Be a Woman" · "We Love You, Conrad!" · "Put on a Happy Face" · "Normal American Boy" · "One Boy" "Honestly Sincere" · "Hymn for a Sunday Evening" · "How to Kill a Man" (Ballet) · "One Last Kiss"
ACT II "What Did I Ever See in Him" · "A Lot of Livin' to Do" · "Kids" · "Baby, Talk to Me" · "Shriners' Ballet" "Spanish Rose" · "Rosie"

Director/choreographer Gower Champion scored with the staging of the number "The Telephone Hour," where he cleverly (and colorfully) showed the entire teenage population of Sweet Apple, Ohio, on the telephone. Simultaneously.

Charles Strouse and Lee Adams

Charles Strouse (music) and Lee Adams (lyrics) are masters of musically tuneful, lyrically colloquial songs that have an unexpected emotional kick and a gentle good humor. They followed up their *Birdie* smash with another satirical show, *All American*, where one song, the lovely "Once Upon a Time," became a semistandard. In 1964, they wrote their first musical play, *Golden Boy*, for Sammy Davis Jr. The underappreciated *It's a Bird... It's a Plane... It's Superman* and the star-vehicle *Applause* followed. In the 1970s, Strouse and Adams went their separate ways, collaborating only twice in the next twenty-five years on the flops *A Broadway Musical* and *Bring Back Birdie*, a rare (and unfortunate) musical sequel. Like his contemporaries John Kander and Cy Coleman, Strouse brilliantly disappears into the period of his shows. His turn-of-the-century, klezmer-flavored music for "Blame It on the Summer Night" from *Rags*, the urban yearning of "Night Song" from *Golden Boy,* and the romantic title song of his *Dance a Little Closer* show a composer who won't settle for anything less than absolute dramatic truth. Though the years since *Annie* have yielded only commercial failures, his work has never been less than excellent. Lee Adams's lyrics for songs like "An English Teacher" from *Birdie* and "You've Got Possibilities" from *Superman* are deceptively simple, yet spot-on, superb pieces of musical theatre character writing. Happily, Strouse and Adams have recently reteamed, musicalizing *An American Tragedy* and the television film *Marty*.

ABOVE: Charles Strouse, left (music) and Lee Adams (lyrics) in rehearsal for *Applause*.

Movie star Lauren Bacall made a smashingly groovy musical debut in *Applause*, Strouse and Adams's 1970 musical version of the film *All About Eve*.

TOP: When Harry MacAfee (Paul Lynde, with Marijane Maricle, Susan Watson, and Johnny Borden) discovers his daughter has been chosen to kiss swivel-hipped rock star Conrad Birdie (Dick Gautier) on national television, he's positively apoplectic, until he realizes he will achieve the dream of every family in America: to appear on *The Ed Sullivan Show*.

ABOVE: In the "How to Kill a Man" ballet, Rose envisions various ways to bump off her increasingly maddening mama's boy of a boyfriend, including poison, the guillotine, and, here, a firing squad.

RIGHT: Albert's mother Mae (the wonderful Kay Medford) tries every trick in the book to break up her son and Rose, including enlisting the charms of the bodacious Gloria Rasputin (Norma Richardson), who performs a split she can't quite get out of.

Susan Watson

Susan Watson, the quintessential 1960s ingénue, played The Girl in the original one-act version of *The Fantasticks* at Barnard College, but when funding for a full Off-Broadway production came through, she was unavailable, having already been tapped to play lovesick teenager Kim MacAfee in *Bye Bye Birdie*. Thrice, she replaced an actress fired during a show's out-of-town shakedown (Jacqueline Mayro in *Ben Franklin in Paris*, Donna McKechnie during the tryout period of *A Joyful Noise*, and Carole Demas during rehearsals for the 1971 revival of *No, No, Nanette*). In *Nanette*, she helped bring tap dancing back to Broadway, more than holding her own among such seasoned performers as Ruby Keeler, Patsy Kelly, and Helen Gallagher. She still performs in musicals in California, where she moved thirty years ago, her sweet soprano and winning smile unchanged.

LEFT: Despite *A Joyful Noise*'s two-week run, Susan Watson's charm and talent landed her her only Tony nomination.

Backstage

The role of Rosie was originally offered to Eydie Gorme, but she turned it down. She also turned down the role of Fanny Brice in *Funny Girl* and Flora in *Flora, the Red Menace*. She wisely chose to make her Broadway debut in *Golden Rainbow*.

Birdie's original title was *Let's Go Steady*.

The original "kids" from *Bye Bye Birdie* still get together for reunions on a semi-regular basis.

Paul Lynde took the role of Harry MacAfee on spec since the part wasn't developed. Once he signed on, the role was expanded and written to suit his personality.

BELOW: This being a musical comedy all ends well, with Albert thrilled that he once again has his "Rosie."

CABARET

CABARET
Produced by Harold Prince
Produced in association with Ruth Mitchell

Book by Joe Masteroff
Music by John Kander
Lyrics by Fred Ebb
Musical Director: Harold Hastings
Music orchestrated by Don Walker
Dance Arrangements by David Baker

Directed by Harold Prince
Choreographed by Ronald Field

Scenic Design by Boris Aronson
Costume Design by Patricia Zipprodt
Lighting Design by Jean Rosenthal

Synopsis

Set against the tawdry nightclub life of the Weimar Republic, *Cabaret* is told through the eyes of Clifford Bradshaw, an American writer looking for inspiration. He meets Sally Bowles, a marginally talented singer who appears at the decadent Kit Kat Klub, where the emcee, a creepy, leering ghoul, presides over a world inside that is in denial of the ever-increasing chaos outside. Cliff rooms in the house of Fraulein Schneider, a German, who is in love with Herr Schultz, a Jewish greengrocer. Only Cliff sees the rising Nazi tide for what it is.

Cast

Clifford Bradshaw .... *Bert Convy*
Herr Schultz .... *Jack Gilford*
Sally Bowles .... *Jill Haworth*
Fraulein Schneider .... *Lotte Lenya*
Master of Ceremonies .... *Joel Grey*
Fraulein Kost .... *Peg Murray*
Ernst Ludwig .... *Edward Winter*

"You remind me of Kurt. You sweat."

— *Lotte Lenya to Fred Ebb*

"Wilkommen, bienvenue, welcome."

TAKE THE DARK, OMINOUS WORLD of Bertolt Brecht and Kurt Weill, mix it lightly with the sequined, showbiz celebratory world of John Kander and Fred Ebb, and add a soupçon of Christopher Isherwood's dispassionate reportage. Bake well (or half bake, according to Martin Gottfried writing in *Women's Wear Daily*) and serve to enthusiastic audiences around the world.

All the critics hailed Hal Prince's carefully constructed concept for *Cabaret*. But the unsung mission was to make such dangerous and unpalatable material suitable for Jewish theatregoers from East Meadow. Perhaps not surprisingly, critics didn't much care for the book scenes between Cliff and Sally and Fraulein Schneider and Herr Schultz. Audiences, while thrilled and amused by the licentious doings in the Kit Kat Klub, also related to the book scenes. After all, the Holocaust had been fewer than thirty years earlier, and most of the audiences were of the World War II generation. It would be a good bet that many were personally affected by the venal rise of the Third Reich.

When *Cabaret* was reconceived for film, the parts of Fraulein Schneider and Herr Schultz were whittled away, while the doings in the bedrooms became every bit as raunchy as those at the Kit Kat Klub. In the recent Broadway revival, still more revisions were made: despite the production's wild success and its many bold choices, the powers that be made one unfortunate change: by deleting Cliff's song "Why Should I Wake Up," they lost track of the theme of the show as written in 1966. That left room for the movie's songs to be interpolated—after all, far more people had seen the film version, and they expected to hear "Maybe This Time" and "Mein Herr."

Like *The Sound of Music* and *West Side Story*, *Cabaret* became even more famous once the film opened. When London's Donmar Warehouse staged a revival of *Cabaret*, directed with a shocking final coup de théâtre by Sam Mendes, it was so successful that it transferred to Broadway's Kit Kat Klub (formerly known as the Henry Miller Theatre) in 1998. With a few changes for the New York production, it was a smash success, running longer than the original. Mendes and Rob Marshall, co-director and choreographer of the New York production, took a chapter from the 1996 revival of *Chicago* (which also ran longer than the original) and sexed up the proceedings, stressing the pansexual sleaze of the Weimar Era. As originally played by Joel Grey, the emcee was ghoulish to be sure, but he was dressed in a tuxedo and quite engaging in his opening number. As the evening progressed, his face slowly morphed into a skull. In contrast, the emcee of the revival, Alan Cumming, dressed only in ragged pants and suspenders, was covered with bruises and track marks, his nipples painted with glitter. He was menacing yet seductive from the outset. The production as a whole was much more blatant in its sexuality and violence, perfect for an age that has embraced such television shows as *Oz*, *The Sopranos*, and *Sex and the City*. With rockers like Ozzy Osborne entering mainstream entertainment via a "reality" show that reveals him as a family man (albeit one who makes a living biting the heads off of chickens), the new production of *Cabaret* fits right in.

Cabaret has become a classic American musical. Each successive incarnation tweaks the central core to keep up with the tempo of the times. And like other timeless classics, *Cabaret* is able to speak across the years, each generation drawing its own message from the lives of those on and off the stage of the Kit Kat Klub. ❋

Ron Field

Ron Field started his choreographic career with a big old floperoo whose title, *Nowhere to Go But Up*, proved prophetic for both Field and leading lady Dorothy Loudon. After his fantastic work in *Cabaret* and *Zorba*, he branched out into direction as well. With the hit *Applause*, Field's shepherding of movie star Lauren Bacall (heretofore not known for her musical prowess) through the minefields of her first Broadway musical was rewarded with two more Tony Awards. After *Applause*, his track record on Broadway was poor (the revival of *On the Town*, *King of Hearts*, *Rags*, and the "You can't fire me—I quit" drama of *Merrily We Roll Along*). He did, however, become a first-class stager of nightclub acts, lending his know-how to the ultraslick, flashy acts of Chita Rivera, Bernadette Peters, and Sandy Duncan. He also became a successful television choreographer for Bette Midler, for Liza Minnelli in the television special *Baryshnikov on Broadway,* and for many, many awards shows. But his best work was for the Broadway stage, where his inventiveness and playfulness found their greatest outlet.

Cabaret choreographer Ron Field in rehearsal with Lauren Bacall, the definition of the term "movie star" and the woman whose personal triumph helped *Applause* win Field multiple Tonys.

OPPOSITE: Jill Haworth invites the audience to "come hear the music play." ABOVE: Lotte Lenya (left) made a triumphant return to Broadway with her delightful, touching performance as Fraulein Schneider in *Cabaret*.

Backstage

Out-of-town, *Cabaret* went from three acts to two, while Jill Haworth, playing Sally Bowles, changed from a blonde to a brunette.

Lyricist Fred Ebb received letters accusing him of using an actual Nazi anthem, "Tomorrow Belongs to Me." People claimed they had heard the song in Nazi Germany.

FAR LEFT: Joel Grey examines his assets in "The Money Song." BELOW: Sally Bowles as the ultimate houseguest: Cliff (Bert Convy) already knows he has his hands full.

SONGS

ACT I "Wilkommen" · "So What?" · "Don't Tell Mama" "Telephone Song" · "Perfectly Marvelous" · "Two Ladies" "It Couldn't Please Me More" · "Tomorrow Belongs to Me" · "Why Should I Wake Up?" · "The Money Song (Money)" · "Married" · "Meeskite"
ACT II "If You Could See Her" · "What Would You Do?" "Cabaret"

ABOVE: The divinely decadent Sally Bowles (Jill Haworth). Oh, and if you see her mummy, mum's the word.

Joel Grey

Joel Grey's impish twinkle and otherworldly stage presence were well served in the role of the leering, ghoulish Emcee in *Cabaret*. After lending his indefatigable energy to his first full-fledged starring vehicle as George M. Cohan in *George M!*, and winning an Oscar for his reprisal of his *Cabaret* role, his very specific persona was less well served by his later shows. In *Goodtime Charley*, his presence as the Dauphin of France threw off the dramatic balance, in a story that should have focused on Ann Reinking's character, Joan of Arc. His particular charms seemed oddly manufactured as the sensitive refugee S. S. Jacobowsky in Jerry Herman's *The Grand Tour*. He played Amos in the 1995 concert version (and subsequent Broadway transfer) of *Chicago*, stopping the show with his white-gloved rendition of "Mr. Cellophane," and returned to the Broadway musical in 2003, still impish and otherworldly, as the Wizard of Oz in the musical *Wicked*.

Grey's first starring role was his powerhouse performance as another showbiz powerhouse, *George M!* (here with Jerry Dodge, Bernadette Peters, and Betty Ann Grove as the rest of the Four Cohans).

The Emcee and the gorilla his dreams.

RIGHT: Natasha Richardson was a sensation in the 1998 revival.

STAR TURNS, PART I

I N WRITING THIS BOOK, SOME names came up again and again as actors, directors, choreographers, or composers who had a major effect on the history of the Broadway musical but, for one reason or another, didn't fit into other sections of this book. Here, then, a tribute to some of the other essential lights of the Rialto:

Noël Coward

The epitome of continental flair to an adoring American public, from Broadway to Las Vegas to Hollywood, the soignée Noël Coward was the original multitasker, as composer, lyricist, playwright, director, actor, singer, dancer, and wit. He became a star in 1924 in his play *The Vortex*, and was extremely prolific through the 1920s and '30s, both musically and dramatically. In addition to his hit plays *Private Lives* and *Blithe Spirit*, he wrote songs for the revues of Andre Charlot, where his veddy British wordplay was first exposed to New York audiences, sung by two

of the greatest interpreters of his work, lifelong friends Bea Lillie and Gertrude Lawrence. He wrote and directed the London musicals *Bitter Sweet* and *Conversation Piece*, both of which came to New York. He made a real splash in the States when he starred opposite Lawrence in *Tonight at 8:30*, his evening of nine one act plays, where Coward did everything, save hem Gertie's gowns. As his star rose around the world, his home country was the one place that never seemed to give him his proper due, for many of his shows were greater successes in New York. Other than *Pacific 1860*, a flop musical for Mary Martin in the West End, Coward had twenty-two year span between Broadway musicals,

from 1939's *Set to Music* to 1961's *Sail Away*, starring Elaine Stritch. During his absence, when he graduated from actor/composer/playwright to the greater title of celebrity, he showed he had lost none of his talent to amuse, with songs such as "Useful Phrases," "The Little Ones ABCs," and "Why Do the Wrong People Travel," all socked over by the Yankee Stritch and greatly lifting the relative creakiness of the show. His final book show as composer, *The Girl Who Came to Supper*, was an even bigger disappointment, despite a wonderful performance by Florence Henderson. His final credit on Broadway was as director of *High Spirits*, a musical version of his play *Blithe Spirit*, starring an absolutely touched Bea Lillie as the wacky medium Madame Arcati.

LEFT: Gertrude Lawrence and Noël Coward, right out of a 1936 edition of *Vogue*, in the "We Were Dancing" sequence of *Tonight at 8:30*. ABOVE: Two masters of the arched eyebrow, Elaine Stritch and Sir Noël, try to out-irony each other in a publicity shot from *Sail Away*. TOP RIGHT: Jodi Benson and Harry Groener in the show that launched Susan Stroman into the choreographic stratosphere, *Crazy For You*. RIGHT: "Stro," in her trademark black baseball cap.

Susan Stroman

When Susan Stroman started out in the chorus of the 1979 revival of *Whoopee!*, those who were "on the line" with this fiercely intelligent, talented woman knew she was destined for greatness. With a passion for all styles of dance, a wild imagination, and an encyclopedic knowledge of the musical form (with a particular love of the Astaire/Rogers movies), she began by choreographing Off Broadway and regionally. Her big break came in 1990, with the immensely entertaining Kander and Ebb revue *And the World Goes 'Round*. After chorerographing Liza Minnelli's Radio City Music Hall show, Stroman's life changed forever when she was tapped to create the dances for the smash *Crazy For You*. Her work, a love letter to her beloved 1930s movie musicals, provided Broadway with the most inventive period choreography in years. Falling in love with and marrying that show's director, Mike Ockrent, she worked with him on the spectacular *A Christmas Carol* at Madison Square Garden, as well as the disappointing *Big*, in between, winning a second Tony Award for her work in Hal Prince's epic revival of *Show Boat*. Her dance marathon partnering was far and away the high point of the misfire *Steel Pier*. In 1999, the wonderful Mike Ockrent passed away, and Stroman threw herself into her work, co-conceiving (with John Weidman), directing, and choreographing the dance play *Contact*, winning raves from the press. The year 2000 also brought plans for a stage version of the Mel Brooks classic *The Producers*. Originally to have been directed by Ockrent, Stroman picked up its reins and delivered a gargantuan success, winning every accolade possible and securing her place in Broadway history. Despite a dud in *Thou Shalt Not*, "Stro" continues to make magic. Now branching out into ballet and film, her latest stage venture is directing and choreographing *Producers* star Nathan Lane in Stephen Sondheim's *The Frogs*.

Anita Gillette

Cast often as a quirky girl-next-door type, lovely Anita Gillette made her Broadway debut in *Carnival!*, understudying the role of *Lili* (and replacing Anna Maria Alberghetti during her well publicized feud with producer David Merrick). Equally comfortable as a soprano ingenue or a belty soubrette, she was cast as a supporting lead in *The Gay Life*, only to have her character (who jumped off a bridge in the opening scene) written out of the show in Detroit. She went right into *All American*, making bunny slippers seem like high fashion in her showstopper "Nightlife," following up with a similar role in *Mr. President*, with another comic gem in "The Secret Service." She was the leading lady in perhaps the most famous flop of all time, the one-performance *Kelly*, and replaced Jill Haworth in the original production of *Cabaret*. Many found her to be one of the best Sally Bowles ever, as she finally got a chance to exhibit her dramatic talents. After the floppo *Jimmy* she took a break from singing, only reappearing to replace in *They're Playing Our Song*. She has enjoyed a long career in straight plays as well, from *Don't Drink the Water* and *Chapter Two* on Broadway, and has grown into a wonderful character actress in films such as *Moonstruck* and *Boys on the Side* (reunited after thirty-five years with *Gay Life* choreographer Herbert Ross, by then a successful movie director).

Bobby Clark

With painted-on glasses and an ever-present cigar, Bobby Clark started out as half of the comedy team Clark and McCullough. Traveling the entire landscape of show business, they played minstrel shows, the circus, and vaudeville, before the risqué raunch of burlesque gave them the ideal venue for stardom. They hit Broadway in 1922, as sketch comics in *The Music Box Revue*. After more revues, in 1930 they tried their hand at a book show (albeit a pretty loose one), the political spoof *Strike Up the Band*. When his partner, the haunted Paul McCullough, committed suicide, Clark went solo and became top banana in a series of revues, including *The Streets of Paris* (costarring Abbott and Costello and Carmen Miranda) and *Star and Garter*, with Gypsy Rose Lee and a bevy of beauties to ogle. After his biggest hit, starring with June Havoc (interestingly, he worked more than once with both Hovick sisters) in Cole Porter's *Mexican Hayride* and what seemed like an odd match on paper, a revival of the Victor Herbert operetta *Sweethearts* (it was hit, by the way), he returned to a more expected brand of humor, leading the Mike Todd "tired businessman" specialties *As the Girls Go* and *Peep Show*, his last Broadway appearance, in 1950. Unfortunately unknown to most modern audiences, Clark was one of the greatest comedians of the twentieth century, inspiring a whole generation of comics, including Phil Silvers, Milton Berle, and Jackie Gleason.

TOP LEFT: The delightful Anita Gillette declares how naughty she's going to be in "Nightlife," from the 1962 Guilty Pleasure *All American*: "I wanna smoke, drink, and eat Chinese food!"

TOP RIGHT: Paul McCullough and Bobby Clark (note the painted-on glasses), go patriotic in *Strike Up the Band*.

RIGHT: Nanette Fabray and Georges Guetary in *Arms and the Girl*, which featured the hit song, "A Cow and a Plow and a Frau."

ABOVE: First Daughter Gillette and First Lady Fabray sing "I'm Gonna Get Him" from *Mr. President*.

Nanette Fabray

With the ability to be raucous or touching on the turn of a dime, Nanette Fabray made early appearances in the revue *Meet the People*, singing that old chestnut "Hurdy Gurdy Verdi," and as the youngest member of female contingent Eve Arden, Vivian Vance, and Edith Meiser in *Let's Face It*. After several flops, Fabray achieved great attention replacing Celeste Holm soon after the opening of *Bloomer Girl*, and became a star (at the ripe old age of twenty-five) as the leading lady of *High Button Shoes*, singing the standard of the show, "Papa, Won't You Dance With Me?" Following that hit, Fabray had what can only be termed rotten luck, for her next three starring vehicles (all produced in a four-year span, a remarkable achievement considering the number of new Broadway shows that open today) were all distinct letdowns. More's the pity, because all three shows had much to admire, not the least of which was Fabray herself: *Love Life*, with a fascinating concept and a score by Weill and Lerner that still begs for a complete recording; *Arms and the Girl*, where Fabray, clowning alongside Pearl Bailey, made the most of her comic opportunities; and *Make a Wish*, where she played a young French girl alongside fellow flop-prone hoyden Helen Gallagher, and, although completely un-Gallic, wonderfully singing a delightful Hugh Martin score. After a stint in Hollywood in the movie *The Bandwagon*, and great fame on television with Sid Caesar, she gave a Broadway musical one more try. Once more into the fray, and another flop, *Mr. President*, which also sent Irving Berlin packing, and once more, Fabray was the best thing going, singing the infectious "They Love Me" as First Lady Nell Henderson. In her eighties and still doing bell kicks, Fabray represents the kind of invigorating, gutsy performer that is all too rare in our jaded world. Word is they wanted Fabray for the role of Phyllis in the original production of *Follies*, but she turned it down, not willing to leave California with her children in high school. Maybe she'd been burned one too many times; frankly, who could blame her?

CARNIVAL!

OPENED APRIL 13, 1961; IMPERIAL THEATRE; 719 PERFORMANCES

CARNIVAL

Produced by David Merrick
Music and Lyrics by Bob Merrill
Book by Michael Stewart
Based on Material by Helen Deutsch
Musical Director: Saul Schechtman
Vocal Arrangements by Saul Schechtman
Music orchestrated by Philip J. Lang
Dance Arrangements by Peter Howard

Directed and Choreographed by
Gower Champion

Scenic Design by Will Steven Armstrong
Lighting Design by Will Steven Armstrong
Costume Design by Freddy Wittop
Puppets created and supervised by
Tom Tichenor

Synopsis

Lili, a simple country girl, arrives at the circus looking for a friend of her late father. She immediately develops a crush on the handsome, dashing magician, Marco the Magnificent. She makes friends with two puppets, whose handler, Paul, can express his most tender emotions only through them. As the evening progresses, Lili becomes aware that the puppets and puppeteer are one, and Paul finds a way to open his heart to her.

Cast

Jacquot .... *Pierre Olaf*
Mr. Schlegal .... *Henry Lascoe*
Gypsy/Lili understudy .... *Anita Gillette*
Marco the Magnificent .... *James Mitchell*
The Incomparable Rosalie.... *Kaye Ballard*
Lili .... *Anna Maria Alberghetti*
Paul Berthalet..................... *Jerry Orbach*

"While you're waiting for this f***ing elevator, I can write the song I know you want."

—An exasperated Bob Merrill to Champion and Stewart, who pressed him for a hit tune

W HEN THE AUDIENCE ENTERED THE Imperial Theatre to see David Merrick's production of *Carnival!*, the curtain was already up, revealing an empty stage save for a cyclorama of a landscape and a single tree. When the house lights dimmed, the members of the Grand Imperial Cirque de Paris brought on their wagons and tents and began setting up the circus. A young performer played his concertina until the stage was set and the show began. The audience of *Carnival!* became part of the audience of the circus, while barkers, jugglers, and performers strolled up the aisles.

It was a historically innovative moment in theatre history. Other such moments include the filmic transitions of Josh Logan's direction of *South Pacific*, Arthur Penn's *Golden Boy*, and Jerome Robbins and Garson Kanin's *Funny Girl*. Joe Layton did away with the singing chorus for his *No Strings*, and he also had the cast move scenery and members of the orchestra appear on the stage accompanying the songs. *Man of La Mancha* was the first show to do away with the intermission (it was put back in for many tour dates). *Allegro*

used projections as a scenic element for the first time. In *The Band Wagon*, Howard Dietz suggested the use of the revolving stage as part of the staging, not just to change scenery while the curtain was down. *Wish You Were Here* was the first show to open directly in New York because its swimming pool couldn't be lugged around the hinterland. *Pippin* boasted the first television commercial for a Broadway show. *Gigi* was the first Broadway show to be adapted from a movie musical. The revival of *Chicago* was the first staged reading masquerading as a fully produced show.

The era of the spectacular show began with the Hippodrome show *A Yankee Circus on Mars*. The theatre itself sat 5,000 patrons, and onstage, the star, Bessie McCoy, arrived in a gold chariot driven by two white horses. A thirty-foot airship landed on the stage and disgorged a Martian who asked the Americans to bring a circus to his planet. At one point, Barlow's Magnificent Hippodrome Elephants appeared behind the steering wheels of autos. The pachyderms drove ten chorus girls (there were 280 in the show) around the huge stage. And that was all before the first intermission. Next came *The Dance of the Hours*, with 150 ballerinas. Following it was the Civil War spectacle, *Andersonville, or a Story of Wilson's Raiders*. The highlight of this act was a pitched battle with more than 480 soldiers.

Carnival! couldn't lay claim to a cast of hundreds or elephants driving cars (though it was a circus). It was an exceedingly simple, human tale told with great warmth and humor. The show contains some of the most beautiful, minimalist songs, including "Mira," "It Was Always, Always You," and the stunning "Love Makes the World Go 'Round." Director Gower Champion knew enough not to gild the lily and kept the proceedings sweet, tender, and small by maintaining the focus on the principals and using the chorus for local color without big production numbers. When the show was done, the circus was struck and the actors moved on, leaving only the lone tree and the landscape of France. The curtain never came down. ✻

Backstage

Star Anna Maria Alberghetti became strangely ill early the run, after Merrick refused to allow her to leave and do a movie. Merrick sent her wax flowers when she returned to work. Alberghetti later stole Merrick's caricature from Sardi's and hung it over her toilet.

RIGHT: The magnetic dancer/actor James Mitchell, later known to millions of housewives as "All My Children" stalwart Palmer Cortland, beguiles Anna Maria Alberghetti's waifish Lili.

Gower Champion, in a shot perfectly representing the lonely job of the director/choreographer, at a rehearsal for *Mack and Mabel*.

Gower Champion

Gower Champion, first-rank director/choreographer, started as a nightclub sensation with his wife, Marge, then branched out into staging dances, first for the revues *Small Wonder* and *Lend an Ear*, then onto his first book show, the Nanette Fabray vehicle *Make a Wish*, where his "Sales Ballet" garnered most of the reviews. After a sojourn to Hollywood, dancing at MGM with Marge, and returning briefly to the New York stage to star alongside rising star Harry Belafonte in the glorified nightclub act *Three for Tonight*, he tackled the Broadway stage in earnest. The stage effects of his four consecutive hit musicals of the 1960s were all revolutionary: *Bye Bye Birdie*'s "Telephone Hour" beehive set, showing a townful of teens on the phone; *Carnival!*, which opened on a bare stage and constructed the set before the audience's eyes; *Hello, Dolly!*, which revolved an entire set piece when someone pushed on a stuck door; and *I Do, I Do*, in which he filled up the entire 46th Street Theatre with the talent of his two great stars. Some accused Champion of relying on gimmicks, but in retrospect that seems like sour grapes, for he was, above all else, highly inventive, always furthering the art form and seamlessly bridging dialogue and song to the point where an audience wouldn't know a song had begun until it was already in progress. His stock began to drop with the failure of *The Happy Time*. As successful as the 1960s were for Champion, the 1970s were just as memorable, albeit for a different reason. With the exception of *Sugar*, a modest success, and the revival of *Irene*, which he inherited and salvaged from previous director Sir John Gielgud, Champion's shows were all flops: the out-of-town casualty *Prettybelle*, the heartbreaking disappointment of *Mack and Mabel*, and two for which the less said, the better: *Rockabye Hamlet* and *A Broadway Musical*. His last musical, *42nd Street*, was a smash hit, but it will forever be remembered for the occurrences of its opening night, when David Merrick, the producer of many of Champion's shows, announced to the stunned cast and audience that Champion had died earlier that day. His death was all too real, but it had the dramatic impact of a scene from a work of fiction.

Kaye Ballard

Kaye Ballard, comedienne and singer who never forgot her Italian roots, came up through the ranks of the New York cabaret and revue scene. As Helen, she made a splashy debut in a book musical singing the hit "Lazy Afternoon" in the cult favorite *The Golden Apple*. After an out-of-town closer, *Reuben, Reuben,* she had the juiciest role of her career as the Incomparable Rosalie in *Carnival!*, flinging out Bob Merrill's "Diiiiirect from Vienna" with abandon, showing a comically vengeful side in "Humming," only to drop all brass and become suddenly vulnerable in the lovely "It Was Always, Always You." She had numerous disappointments: developing a bio-musical of the life of her idol Fanny Brice and getting scooped by Jule Styne, et al.; asking John Kander and Fred Ebb to write a song for her act titled "Maybe This Time," only to have it become a hit by that Minnelli girl. Instead, Ballard went back to the world of the flop with *Royal Flush*, which closed in Philadelphia in 1964. Fortunately, television beckoned. Ballard costarred alongside Eve Arden on the sitcom *The Mothers-in-Law* and was featured as the landlady on *The Doris Day Show*. Her last chance to be a leading lady on Broadway disappeared with the quick failure of *Molly*, the musicalization of the beloved Gertrude Berg character. Through all her ups and downs, though, Ballard never lost her love for performing, still turning it out after fifty years in the national tours of the shows *The Full Monty* and *Nunsense*.

SONGS

ACT I "Direct from Vienna" · "A Very Nice Man" "I've Got to Find a Reason" · "Mira" (Can You Imagine That?) · "Sword, Rose and Cape" · "Humming" · "Yes, My Heart" · "Everybody Likes You" "Magic, Magic" · "Love Makes the World Go 'Round"

ACT II "Yum Ticky" (Ticky Tum Tum) · "The Rich" "Beautiful Candy" · "Her Face" · "Grand Imperial Cirque de Paris" · "I Hate Him" · "It Was Always, Always You" · "She's My Love"

UPPER LEFT: James Mitchell, as Marco the Magnificent, slices, dices, and makes julienne fries out of the Incomparable Rosalie (Kaye Ballard). UPPER RIGHT: Jerry Orbach and Anna Maria Alberghetti as the embittered Paul and the naive Lili. FAR LEFT: Kaye Ballard, as Helen, the face that launched a thousand balloons, spends a lazy afternoon with the traveling salesman, Paris (Jonathan Lucas) in *The Golden Apple*. LEFT: Four of the many moods of Ballard, here in the out-of-town closer *Reuben, Reuben*.

CAROUSEL

OPENED APRIL 19, 1945; MAJESTIC THEATRE; 890 PERFORMANCES

The three leads of *Carousel* in glorious color: Jean Darling, John Raitt, and Lassie's future owner, Jan Clayton.

CAROUSEL

Produced by The Theatre Guild

Music by Richard Rodgers
Lyrics by Oscar Hammerstein II
Book by Oscar Hammerstein II
Based on *Liliom* by Ferenc Molnár
Adapted from *Liliom* by
Benjamin F. Glazer
Musical Director: Joseph Littau
Music orchestrated by Don Walker
Dance arrangements by Trude Rittman

Directed by Rouben Mamoulian
Choreographed by Agnes de Mille

Scenic Design by Jo Mielziner
Costume Design by Miles White
Lighting Design by Jo Mielziner

Synopsis

Billy Bigelow, a boastful carnival barker, catches the eye of Julie Jordan, a young, naïve girl, and soon they get married. Julie finds herself pregnant, and Billy begins to doubt his ability to provide for his offspring, especially if it's a girl. He gets involved with a ne'er-do-well, Jigger Craigin, who involves Billy in a scheme to rob a wealthy businessman. The robbery is botched, and Billy, knowing he will be caught, kills himself. After Billy spends fifteen years in purgatory, the Starkeeper, in heaven, suggests Billy might redeem himself by doing a good deed and allows the young man one day back on earth. Billy returns to find his daughter grown up and ready to graduate high school. He tries to reach out to his insecure daughter but in frustration ends up slapping her. The slap does not sting since it is motivated by love not hate. Somehow, though unseen by her, he manages to instill in her a confidence exemplified by the song "You'll Never Walk Alone."

Cast

Carrie Pipperidge	*Jean Darling*
Julie Jordan	*Jan Clayton*
Mrs. Mullin	*Jean Castro*
Billy Bigelow	*John Raitt*
Nettie Fowler	*Christine Johnson*
June Girl	*Pearl Lang*
Enoch Snow	*Eric Mattson*
Jigger Craigin	*Murvyn Vye*
Starkeeper	*Russell Collins*
Louise	*Bambi Linn*

"Whenever I get an idea for a song, even before jotting down the notes, I can hear it in the orchestra, I can smell it in the scenery, I can see the kind of actor who will sing it, and I am aware of an audience listening to it." —*Richard Rodgers*

IF YOU WERE THE GAMBLING type, would you invest in a musical in which the title character abuses his wife, commits suicide, then has a chance to redeem himself, only to revert to his violent ways? Not your basis for a typical musical theatre libretto, but in the hands of Richard Rodgers and Oscar Hammerstein, the show became *Carousel*. In searching for a property for their second collaboration, the songwriters/producers were drawn to Ferenc Molnár's play *Liliom*, but were understandably worried about the piece's dark, brutal tone. In the original play, Liliom (Billy) and Julie are not married when she becomes pregnant, and, following his suicide, he is sent to hell. After fifteen years, Liliom returns to earth to redeem himself, stealing a star as a gift for his daughter, but when she rebuffs him, he slaps her and is returned to purgatory. A tall order to musicalize, perhaps better suited to opera than musical theatre, but if anyone was up to the challenge, it was Rodgers and Hammerstein, then riding high after the tidal wave of *Oklahoma!*

They changed the original's location from Hungary to the New England coast, but even with the Americanizing and the soft pedaling of harsher aspects of the source material (when the musical was filmed, there were further changes: gone was the suicide, Billy now accidentally falling on a knife during the robbery), the plot was decidedly heavy going for audiences. Fortunately, the innovations made in *Oklahoma!* paved the way for theatregoers to accept new approaches, and *Carousel* became a major hit, its success proving that the brilliance of the first Rodgers and Hammerstein collaboration was far from a fluke. It helped set the pace for a monumental teaming, and audiences began to expect an R&H musical every season or so, and while there would be bumps along the way (*Allegro, Me and Juliet,* and *Pipe Dream*), the great critical and popular success of their classic shows far outweighed the relative failures of the three others.

The duo's remarkable track record was due in large part to the very fact that they were a team, committed to working solely with each other in a union stronger than some marriages (and sometimes more dysfunctional). Both men sought out this level of stability, and for over forty years of his career, Richard Rodgers wrote with only two partners, Lorenz Hart and Oscar Hammerstein II, and when he went lyricist hunting after Hammerstein's death and paired up with Sheldon Harnick, Stephen Sondheim, Martin Charnin, and Raymond Jessel, the results were less than inspired. Hammerstein also preferred to work with partners throughout his thirty-nine-year career as a lyricist/librettist: eight of his first ten shows were written in collaboration with Herbert Stothart, and he also enjoyed long partnerships with Jerome Kern (six shows), Rudolf Friml (five shows), Vincent Youmans (three shows), and Sigmund Romberg (three shows).

Partnership affords more than just familiarity, however, for ideal writing partners know each other's foibles, develop a shorthand, and create seamless, integrated shows. Though there are exceptions, it's interesting that Jerry Bock and Sheldon Harnick; Alan Jay Lerner and Frederick Loewe; Jule Styne, Betty Comden, and Adolph Green; Tom Jones and Harvey Schmidt; and Charles Strouse and Lee Adams all had most of their greatest successes when collaborating. Even songwriters like Irving Berlin, Cole Porter, and Jerry Herman, who supplied both music and lyrics also worked in teams, repeatedly pairing up with the same librettists.

A testament to their artistic fertility as well as their devotion to their craft, the team of Rodgers and Hammerstein created nine indelible shows in only sixteen years, plus an original film score (*State Fair*) and an original television musical (*Cinderella*). In addition, they produced some of the finest musicals and plays by others, including *Annie Get Your Gun, I Remember Mama* (play), and *The Happy Time* (play). The solidity of their professional partnership resulted in the most beloved musicals in American theatre history, and in *Carousel*, their second collaboration, the team was already operating as one to turn out a perfect amalgam of song and story. ❋

Agnes de Mille

The most famous female choreographer ever, Agnes de Mille made her Broadway debut with the dances for the underrated *Swingin' the Dream* in 1939, before Rodgers and Hammerstein saw her legendary ballet *Rodeo* and tapped her for *Oklahoma!* four years later. Hit after hit followed: *One Touch of Venus, Bloomer Girl, Carousel,* and *Brigadoon,* until her first directorial attempt, the brave experiment *Allegro,* failed and created a rift between de Mille and Rodgers and Hammerstein that never fully healed. She continued working with other major talents, spanning the globe and history with her versatile work for such shows as *Gentlemen Prefer Blondes, Out of This World,* and *Paint Your Wagon.* With classic dances like "Laurey Makes Up Her Mind" from *Oklahoma!,* "Forty Minutes for Lunch" from *One Touch of Venus,* the Civil War Ballet from *Bloomer Girl,* "Billy Makes a Journey" from *Carousel,* and the Sword and Funeral dances from *Brigadoon,* de Mille made history with her darkly subtextual, character-driven work. Following *The Girl in Pink Tights,* she never had another hit (except a moderate success with *110 in the Shade*), spending the remainder of the 1950s and '60s overseeing the de Mille legacy. Countless productions of her big three (*Oklahoma!, Carousel,* and *Brigadoon*) were restaged all over the world. Her few new projects were not on a par with her early triumphs, but her work was always classy, often standing out as high points in the middling shows *Goldilocks, Juno,* and *Kwamina.* She made a last attempt at direction with *Come Summer.* Her groundbreaking "dream ballet" began to seem tired as the form developed: dance was being used more cinematically, deeply ingrained into the texture of the show instead of in stand-alone ballets that, while assuredly forwarding the plot, stood outside the rest of the show. Extremely intelligent and a wonderful writer, de Mille was fiercely loyal to her dancers. She rehired her favorites over and over again, making stars of Gemze de Lappe, James Mitchell, Joan McCracken, Marc Platt, Lidija Franklin, and Bambi Linn. While de Mille didn't introduce the ballet to the Broadway musical, she certainly perfected it.

ABOVE: Agnes de Mille during rehearsals of *Allegro.*

SONGS

ACT I "Carousel Waltz" · "You're a Queer One, Julie Jordan" · "When I Marry Mr. Snow" · "If I Loved You" · "June Is Bustin' Out All Over" · "When the Children Are Asleep" · "Blow High, Blow Low" · Hornpipe Dance · "Soliloquy"
ACT II "This Was a Real Nice Clambake" · "Geraniums in the Winder" · "There's Nothin' So Bad for a Woman" · "What's the Use of Wond'rin'" · "You'll Never Walk Alone" · "The Highest Judge of All" · Ballet ("Billy Makes a Journey")

The weaving of music and dialogue around the beautiful "If I Loved You" (also referred to as the "bench scene"), is perhaps the most perfectly constructed nine minutes in musical theatre history. So rich with character and subtextual shifts, as Billy and Julie go from strangers to lovers, it ranks with the greatest love scenes in any play, musical or otherwise.

Backstage

Of the big hit Rodgers and Hammerstein shows, *Carousel* ran the fewest performances.

On opening night, Richard Rodgers, having wrenched his back, saw the show strapped to a stretcher and through a morphine haze.

Jean Darling sings the "Mr. Snow" reprise in Act II of *Carousel*. With songs like "You're A Queer One, Julie Jordan," "Mr. Snow," and "When the Children Are Asleep," the character of Carrie Pipperidge is a more musically developed role than Julie Jordan. Besides, as Barbara Cook (who played both characters in numerous productions) says, Carrie's a helluva lot more fun.

LEFT: John Raitt and Bert Wheeler, backed up by the gingham brigade, in the flop *Three Wishes for Jamie*.

John Raitt

John Raitt was the ultimate specimen of the masculine, rich-voiced leading man, so much so that he became an archetype unto himself, with a booming baritone, the physique of a weightlifter, and a confident stage presence. After a debut in the national tour of *Oklahoma!*, he rocketed to the top as the original Billy Bigelow in *Carousel*, making history with his strongly sung "Soliloquy." He then hit the road as Frank Butler opposite Mary Martin in the national tour of *Annie Get Your Gun*, a role he re-created with Martin in the first television version in 1957. Returning to New York, he found it difficult to find a worthwhile vehicle, ending up in the flops *Magdalena*, *Three Wishes for Jamie*, and *Carnival in Flanders*. He finally got a chance to create a second legendary role when he played union organizer Sid Sorokin in *The Pajama Game*, introducing the standard "Hey There," and reprising his role in the film version opposite Doris Day. His final role in a book show on Broadway was the disappointing *A Joyful Noise*. He publicly voiced his frustrations with the show, openly criticizing authors Oscar Brand and Paul Nassau. Despite the national tour of *Zorba* and a brief return to Broadway in the songbook revue *A Musical Jubilee*, Raitt spent most of the next thirty-five years recording and concertizing, sometimes with his daughter, the talented singer/songwriter Bonnie Raitt. Now well into his eighties, he still sings robustly and looks as if he might arm wrestle you (and quite possibly win) at the drop of a hat.

ABOVE: In *A Tree Grows in Brooklyn*, the flawed, tragic Johnny Nolan sings the beautiful "I'll Buy You a Star." Here, Billy Bigelow (a character even more flawed and tragic) does him one better, stealing a star for his daughter.

LEFT: Karen Morrow, bracing John Raitt as she delivers the news: *A Joyful Noise*, their 1967 musical, is a big ol' turkey.

CATS

OPENED OCTOBER 7, 1982; WINTER GARDEN THEATRE; 7,485 PERFORMANCES

CATS

Produced by Cameron Mackintosh,
The Really Useful Theatre Company Ltd.,
David Geffen, and The Shubert Organization

Music by Andrew Lloyd Webber
Lyrics by T. S. Eliot
Based on
"Old Possum's Book of Practical Cats"
by T. S. Eliot
Additional Lyrics by
Trevor Nunn and Richard Stilgoe
Music orchestrated by
David Cullen and Andrew Lloyd Webber
Production Musical Director: Stanley Lebowsky
Musical Director: Rene Wiegert

Directed by Trevor Nunn
Choreographed by Gillian Lynne

Scenic and Costume Design by John Napier
Lighting Design by David Hersey

Synopsis

An assortment of felines inhabit a junkyard and exhibit their various qualities in a series of songs and dances. Just when it seems that nothing very momentous will happen, Grizabella, the faded Glamour Cat, ascends to the Heavyside Layer (on an old tire) where there are pussies galore. Jumping, hissing, and aerobics ensue.

Cast

Grizabella .... *Betty Buckley*
Old Deuteronomy .... *Ken Page*
Rum Tum Tigger .... *Terrence Mann*
Mistoffolees .... *Timothy Scott*
Rumpleteazer...................... *Christine Langner*
Munkustrap .... *Harry Groener*
Skimbleshanks .... *Reed Jones*
Bustopher Jones .... *Stephen Hanan*
Cassandra .... *Rene Ceballos*

ABOVE: At the end of the opening number, the cast of *Cats* chants, "What's a Jellicle cat?" See, even they don't know.

RIGHT: Betty Buckley as Grizabella, the Glamour Cat, singing the power ballad, "Memory."

L EGENDARY APOCRYPHAL STORY OF THE Rialto: two postmenopausal women from Lawn-Guyland standing outside the Winter Garden Theatre:

> Matinee Lady A: "Have you seen *Cats?*"
> Matinee Lady B: "No ..."
> Matinee Lady A: "Well, I'll tell you what happens. There's a bunch of cats, and one of them is real sick and tired. So the other cats put on a show to cheer her up. Then they put her on a tire and shoot her through the roof."

Broadway's first show for the tired Japanese businessman, *Cats* baffled experienced Broadwayites but struck a chord with prepubescent girls, school trips from places that didn't have their own thee-ay-ter, and a few other people—we're not sure who, but it certainly ran. And ran. And ran. It pounced past *My Fair Lady*, it skimpered past *Hello, Dolly!*, it scampered past *Grease*, and it didn't break a sweat as it surpassed the runs of *Fiddler on the Roof* and *A Chorus Line* to become the longest-running musical of its time. Still and all, amid the general miasma onstage were some excellent stagecraft, talented performers, and admirable direction. There weren't really characters (or a plot, for that matter), just set pieces based on T. S. Eliot poems and a loose framework of a story, but the broad strokes and visual spectacle resoundingly registered with the English-as-a-second- (or third-) language crowd.

The success of *Cats* in London created much anticipation on Broadway. New Yorkers were curious as to what the brouhaha was all about, and casual theatregoers wanted to be the first on their block (or farm) to get tickets for a hot seller. Audiences were sometimes bewildered, but once one had bragged about copping tickets one couldn't go back and tell the sewing circle or homeroom that it was a big bore. So people fudged the truth and encouraged others to see the show—sort of an embarrassed word-of-mouth. Alternatively, some audiences loved leaving their minds at the door and relaxing into a stupor watching a show that didn't require following a plot. Whatever the reaction, *Cats* utterly transformed the Broadway theatre.

The show was originally envisioned as an oratorio of sorts, based on the T. S. Eliot poems set to music by Andrew Lloyd Webber, but it was eventually decided that *Cats* could work as an impudently offbeat staged musical. It's to Lloyd Webber's great credit that he saw within the poems a chance to create a unique entertainment, and it certainly turned out to be exactly that. Lloyd Webber's remarkably varied career has been based on his expansion of the musical form: he's worked with rock operas based on biblical themes, two complementary one-acts, a horror-romantic nineteenth-century spectacle, a twee musicalization of P. G. Wodehouse's Jeeves, and a famous film classic based in gothic Hollywood. Here's a man who doesn't let tradition affect his vision of the possibilities of musical theatre, and he's been remarkably successful in giving the public exactly what it wants. Whereas the growth of musical theatre has been mainly evolutionary, Lloyd Webber's works have been revolutionary, each unique and remarkably true to its own concept. *Cats*, basically a plotless musical, emphasized dance as no other show had, for the entire show was choreographed. Nevertheless, while one of the show's strengths was its reliance on dance, it was also a weakness, for no matter what Gillian Lynne accomplished, she never had any conflict or subtext to fuel her choreography, and the never-ending parade of numbers utilizing jazz, tap, and strong ballet technique demanded highly skilled dancers with boundless energy—but ultimately lacked focus and dramatic intent.

The runaway success of *Cats* was also due in part to an effective television commercial that emphasized the spectacle. Ah yes, the spectacle, for *Cats* had the dubious honor of being the first musical mega-spectacle. Oversize cans of beans and sardines graced the transformed Winter Garden Theatre, and the leading lady rose to heaven on the aforementioned steel-belted radial. *Cats* begat the Cameron Mackintosh empire of spectacular productions: *Starlight Express*, *Phantom of the Opera*, *Les Misérables*, and *Miss Saigon*, and crashing chandeliers, huge barricades, and helicopters became the hallmarks of the Broadway musicals of 1980s and early '90s. Once the century turned, however, people's taste seemed to change once more, and the monoliths that ruled for so long became dinosaurs, one by one reaching extinction. Like its tagline ("Now and Forever") *Cats* lives on, well past nine lives, in countless productions in schools, community theatres, and innumerable national companies. ✻

SONGS

ACT I "Jellicle Songs for Jellicle Cats" · "The Naming of Cats" · "The Invitation to the Jellicle Ball" · "The Old Gumbie Cat" · "Rum Tum Tugger" · "Grizabella, the Glamour Cat" · "Bustopher Jones" · "Mungojerrie and Rumpleteazer" · "Old Deuteronomy" · "The Aweful Battle of the Pekes and the Pollicles" · "The Jellicle Ball"

ACT II "The Moments of Happiness" · "Gus: The Theatre Cat" · "Growltiger's Last Stand" · "Skimbleshanks" · "Macavity" · "Mr. Mistoffolees" · "Memory" · "The Journey to the Heavyside Layer" · "The Ad-Dressing of Cats"

TOP: Donna King, Bonnie Simmons, and Rene Ceballos doing an Andrews Sisters thing in "The Old Gumbie Cat."

CENTER: Betty Buckley playing the title role of Edwin Drood.

RIGHT: Betty Buckley in *Triumph of Love*, doing what she does better than anyone: standing alone in a spotlight, mesmerizing audiences with her silvery voice and her intensity.

Backstage

Dame Judi Dench was the original Grizabella in London, but she tore her Achilles tendon. Recovered, she attended a rehearsal and, when exiting the stage, tripped and went headlong into the orchestra seats. Elaine Paige replaced her.

Betty Buckley

Her still, riveting presence, excellent acting, and above all, her vibrant high belt—both world weary and full of clear, innocent optimism—have made Betty Buckley one of Broadway's most beloved performers. She made a strong impression in her first Broadway role, straight off the bus from Texas, as Martha Jefferson in *1776*. After starring in *Promises, Promises* in London, she replaced in the original production of *Pippin* and Off-Broadway productions such as *I'm Getting My Act Together and Taking It on the Road*. Sandwiched in between were film roles (in the horror movie *Carrie* and the classic *Tender Mercies*) and television (as the understanding stepmother on *Eight Is Enough*). Broadway audiences were finally reunited with Buckley in her Tony Award–winning role as Grizabella in *Cats*, where her haunting rendition of "Memory" was hailed by critics and audiences alike, helping to account for the show's early success after a sound trouncing from critics. Next came a highly underrated turn in the trouser/title role of *The Mystery of Edwin Drood*, and a replacement stint in *Song and Dance*. Buckley's exposed nerves and otherworldly quality worked well for her as the mother in the legendary *Carrie*, where she replaced a bailed-out Barbara Cook and walked off with the only good notices. She was also well suited to her next role, for many thought she was the best-ever Norma Desmond in *Sunset Boulevard*, in which she sang a harrowing "As If We Never Said Goodbye" when she took over, first in London, then in New York. The unfortunate *Triumph of Love* (1997) was her most recent Broadway appearance, and her abundant talents were such that when she sang "Serenity," she almost convinced audiences that the material was first-rank.

CHICAGO

OPENED JUNE 1, 1975; 46TH STREET THEATRE; 947 PERFORMANCES

CHICAGO

Produced by Robert Fryer and James Cresson
Produced in association with Martin Richards,
Joseph Harris, and Ira Bernstein

Book by Fred Ebb and Bob Fosse
Music by John Kander
Lyrics by Fred Ebb
Based on the play *Chicago* by
Maurine Dallas Watkins
Musical Director: Stanley Lebowsky
Music orchestrated by Ralph Burns
Dance Arrangements by Peter Howard

Directed by Bob Fosse
Choreographed by Bob Fosse

Scenic Design by Tony Walton
Costume Design by Patricia Zipprodt
Lighting Design by Jules Fisher

Synopsis

Jazz baby Roxie Hart shoots her lover stone-cold dead and is hustled off to jail. Terrified when she realizes she could be hanged for the crime, she gets her dupe of a husband, Amos, to hire the oily lawyer Billy Flynn. Also serving time in the cell block is another killer diller, Velma Kelly, the current hot item in the tabloids, awaiting her own trial for murder. When she reveals her (fictional) pregnancy, Roxie steals Velma's journalistic thunder, and they become fierce rivals for the spotlight. Through some razzle dazzling by the slick Billy Flynn, Roxie is acquitted, and soon both merry murderesses find themselves pushed off the front pages. Longing for their past infamy, there's nothing else to do but join forces and kill 'em all over again, this time in vaudeville as a double act.

Cast

Billy Flynn .... *Jerry Orbach*
Velma Kelly .... *Chita Rivera*
Roxie Hart .... *Gwen Verdon*
Amos Hart .... *Barney Martin*
Matron .... *Mary McCarty*
Mary Sunshine .... *Michael O'Haughey*

Equal parts stand-up routine and egomaniacal fantasy, the "Roxie" showstopper, with its stream-of-consciousness riff on the lure of celebrity, has never been more relevant. Though it was tailored for Verdon's unique gifts (seen here), Sandy Duncan (who replaced in the 1997 revival) is the only performer to approach Verdon's magical ability to connect with an audience during the number.

THERE ARE SOME STORIES THAT seem eternal, captivating successive generations of audiences because, although manners and mores change, human nature does not. That brings us to *Chicago*, the cynical morality tale of crime paying through the glories of publicity, that has resonated with theatregoers for almost a century.

Few musicals have managed to stay in the public's imagination over a long period of time. *Babes in Toyland* premiered in 1903, has been filmed twice and televised twice, and productions are still being mounted today. *No, No, Nanette* conquered Broadway again fifty years after its premiere. (True, the libretto was shortened and the creakier jokes were eliminated to suit popular tastes, but in general, it was the same show with a little nostalgia added into the mix.) *Show Boat* is another musical that has never gone out of style, and many early operettas were still performed regularly into the 1960s.

Chicago is another story that seems destined for longevity. The original stage play *Chicago* opened on December 30, 1926, and ran a quite respectable

Jerry Orbach as the sleazy but suave lawyer, Billy Flynn, in the "Order" phase of his career.

As Mama Morton and Velma (she sure don't look like a) Kelly, Mary McCarty (left) and Chita Rivera bemoan the lack of "Class."

173 preformances, serving as the basis for the film *Roxie Hart*. In 1975, John Kander, Fred Ebb, and Bob Fosse turned the play into a musical, starring a potent threesome of Broadway stars: Gwen Verdon, Chita Rivera, and Jerry Orbach. Although somewhat overshadowed by the juggernaut success of *A Chorus Line*, *Chicago* was a hit at the 46th Street Theatre, running over two years.

Flash forward to the late 1990s, when a revival opened at the same theatre, now named the Richard Rodgers, subsequently moving to the Shubert, then to the Ambassador. Just when it seemed to be running out of steam, the film version of *Chicago* opened and won the Academy Award for Best Picture. Surprisingly, that boosted the box office of the stage version, and the production is still going strong in 2004.

Chicago's 1996 revival was a decidedly cut-down affair, originally staged for City Center's Encores series. The orchestra was seated on the stage (as it was for the original, albeit on a raised platform). There was only a unit set for the concert version—mainly in black (for that matter, the original was damned dark, too), and costumes were reduced to selections from the Victoria's Secret line. The original vaudeville conceit was largely jettisoned (although Joel Grey did perform "Mr. Cellophane" in the style of Bert Williams), and Bob Fosse's original choreography was rethunk by the woman who Rex Reed referred to as a screeching zombie, Fosse's one-time muse and former lover, Ann Reinking. For all the scrimping, however, no one really complained: whereas the original production was a high-concept musical, this *Chicago* was selling attitude and sex—especially sex. Stylish it was, but it wasn't really a representation of the show as originally envisioned.

Through all of its various incarnations, *Chicago* has remained an indestructible property. After all, it thrived with Melanie Griffith, a triple threat in the pejorative sense; and one stock production in the 1970s starred Sue Ane Langdon and "Password" host Allen Ludden! We're willing to bet that fifty years hence, if the younger readers of this book come to Forty-sixth Street in their hovermobiles, or pay the $30 subway fare, there, at the newly renamed Andrew Lippa Theatre, will be an all-hologram production of *Chicago*. And why? Because, as evidenced by a comparison of the characters of *Chicago* and the circus atmosphere of the current judicial system, human nature just doesn't change. ❊

Mary McCarty

Mary McCarty, a marvelous singer and brash comedienne, had talents perfectly suited to the knockout energy and pace of sketch comedy, where she had great success in the Broadway revues *Small Wonder* and *Bless You All*. She had her juiciest role costarring in Irving Berlin's *Miss Liberty*, where she delighted audiences with "You Can Have Him," and "Falling Out of Love Can Be Fun." After many tours, stock appearances, and TV variety shows, where her revue training served her well, she returned to the Broadway musical after twenty years, as Stella Deems in *Follies*, leading the girls in the legendary production number "Who's That Woman?" As the tough-as-nails Mama Morton in *Chicago*, she benefited from David Rounds's unfortunate dismissal, picking up her first-act showstopper, "When You're Good to Mama," in the deal. She was definitely best served in the world of musical comedy, where her heft and volume were welcome. Outside of the theatre, she was often cast as a nurse, in movies such as *Pillow Talk* and the TV series *Trapper John, M.D.*, where she had just finished the first season when she unexpectedly died of a heart attack at the age of fifty-seven.

RIGHT: A bechapped Mary McCarty sings "Flaming Youth" in the 1948 revue *Small Wonder*.

BELOW: Flying by Eddie Foy: In the revue *Bless You All*, McCarty does a hilarious takeoff on a P.T.A. production of *Peter Pan*.

"Tell Bob Fosse that Chicago in the late 1920s is not Berlin."

— Hal Prince, in a letter to Kander and Ebb on the similarities between Chicago *and* Cabaret

"All I Care About Is Love": Jerry Orbach and the ladies in their homage to Sally Rand.

CHICAGO TRYOUT CASUALTIES ABOVE: The audience is always, always the final judge of what's funny and what ain't. While the cast and crew of *Chicago* found it absolutely hysterical to see Roxie (on sax) and Velma (on drums) jazz their way through "Loopin' the Loop" in their "sister act" finale, audiences just scratched their heads. Was it intentionally, amusingly lousy or just plain lousy? Out it went. BOTTOM LEFT: In Philadelphia, Bob Fosse envisioned "Me and My Baby" with Gwen Verdon as a clapping, white-gloved Eddie Cantor and the ensemble men in diapers and baby bonnets. By New York, it had become a high-kicking strut for Verdon. TOP LEFT: The fantastic character actor David Rounds played the agent in *Chicago*, delivering a sizzling tap dance in the song "Ten Percent." The creators became aware that so many strong characters were detracting from the focus of the storyline so his character and song were cut.

Liza Minnelli

With a genetic predisposition for both onstage heights and offstage turmoil, Liza Minnelli grew up dreaming of dancing in a Broadway musical. Her unformed yet undeniable talent first came to light in Off Broadway's *Best Foot Forward* and again in her tremendous Broadway debut in *Flora, the Red Menace* in 1965. Had the show been successful, it would have propelled her to superstardom the same way *Funny Girl* did for Barbra Streisand, for Minnelli's vocals on "All I Need (Is One Good Break)," "A Quiet Thing," and "Sing Happy" are just as singular and thrilling as Streisand's. As it was, she needed another seven years to reach her zenith, with the double whammy of the film version of *Cabaret* (a role for which she was turned down for the original Broadway production) and the TV special *Liza with a Z*. After her pinch-hit stint as Roxie in *Chicago*, she returned to Broadway in a show that was special only because of Minnelli's presence. *The Act*, once again written by her guardian angels John Kander and Fred Ebb, provided her little more than a shadow of a story around a Vegas act, while *The Rink*, reteaming her not only with Kander and Ebb but with her friend Chita Rivera, gave Minnelli a rare opportunity to play down the glamour and tackle a dramatic role. Personal demons made the pendulum swing wider and wider, and she made her biggest misstep (save her most recent marriage) when, fragile and in poor voice, she replaced an ailing Julie Andrews in *Victor/Victoria*.

Star on the rise: Liza Minnelli in *Flora, the Red Menace*, singing "The Kid Herself," yet another tryout casualty (replaced in Philly by "All I Need Is One Good Break").

BELOW: In the Leonard Bernstein flop *1600 Pennsylvania Avenue*, Patricia Routledge sang a song titled "Duet for One." Here, Verdon and Rivera (left) sing a Solo for Two, "My Own Best Friend." When Liza Minnelli (right) filled in for an ailing Gwen Verdon, the duet became a solo, recalling her mother's slightly strange solo version of "A Couple of Swells."

Backstage

In 1992, a production was mounted in Long Beach, California, directed by Rob Marshall, who would eventually direct the film version. That production starred Bebe Neuwirth, the star of the Broadway revival. Also in the Long Beach production were Juliet Prowse, Kaye Ballard, and original cast members Barney Martin and Michael O'Haughey.

In some ways, the most famous music from *Chicago* is the overture, the music of "Loopin' the Loop," a song that was cut in Philadelphia. A good deal of the credit for *Chicago*'s infectious sound should go to arrangers Peter Howard and Ralph Burns.

SONGS

ACT I "All That Jazz" · "Funny Honey" · "Cell Block Tango" "When You're Good to Mama" · "All I Care About (Is Love)" · "A Little Bit of Good" · "We Both Reached for the Gun" · "Roxie" · "I Can't Do It Alone" · "My Own Best Friend"
ACT II "I Know a Girl" · "Me and My Baby" · "Mister Cellophane" · "When Velma Takes the Stand" · "Razzle Dazzle" · "Class" · "Nowadays" · "R.S.V.P"/"Keep It Hot"

A CHORUS LINE

OPENED JULY 25, 1975; SHUBERT THEATRE; 6,137 PERFORMANCES

Clive Clerk (left) as dance captain Larry and Robert LuPone as the exacting director Zach put the auditioners through their paces.

A CHORUS LINE
Produced by Joseph Papp
A Production by the
New York Shakespeare Festival
Book by James Kirkwood and Nicholas Dante
Music by Marvin Hamlisch
Lyrics by Edward Kleban
Music orchestrated by
Bill Byers, Hershy Kay, and Jonathan Tunick
Musical Director: Donald Pippin
Vocal Arrangements by Donald Pippin

Conceived, Directed, and Choreographed by
Michael Bennett
Co-Choreographer: Bob Avian

Scenic Design by Robin Wagner
Costume Design by Theoni V. Aldredge
Lighting Design by Tharon Musser

Synopsis

A Chorus Line takes place at an audition for the ensemble of an unnamed musical. Zach, the imperious, sometimes cruel director, puts seventeen dancers through an intense, personally invasive process to cast eight roles. One by one, the applicants come forward, and in song or monologue tell a little bit about why they chose to dance for a living, how they feel about the theatrical process, and how they get through the constant highs and lows of life upon the wicked stage. Cassie, past girlfriend of Zach, wants to rejoin the chorus although she has been a featured dancer; Val, not always the stunner that she is now, is testing out her recently augmented "features"; Sheila, the sardonic wisecracker, fell in love as a young girl with the magic of the ballet. Others, like Paul, a one-time drag queen, have issues that transcend the theatrical milieu. At the end of the piece, Zach must choose his ideal chorus, and the tension builds for the performers as well as for the audience members who have made their own choices. As we are treated to one final, costumed production number, all the dancers, employed and un-, get to step into the spotlight and shine.

Cast

Sheila	*Carole Bishop*
Val	*Pamela Blair*
Mike	*Wayne Cilento*
Richie	*Ronald Dennis*
Connie	*Baayork Lee*
Diana	*Priscilla Lopez*
Zach	*Robert LuPone*
Cassie	*Donna McKechnie*
Bobby	*Thomas J. Walsh*
Paul	*Sammy Williams*

WITH MINIMAL SETS, UTILITARIAN COSTUMES (save the Theoni Aldredge sequin specialties in the finale), and no spectacle whatsoever, *A Chorus Line* is the ultimate musical for many aficionados. Lacking all the trappings of the glitzy Broadway extravaganza, all it can boast is first-rate craft, intelligence, heart, and, most important, humanity. Unlike *Cats*, this is an intensely personal, flesh-and-blood dance musical, featuring fully rounded characters. Audiences are irresistibly drawn to the lives of a group of dancers whose worth is repeatedly (literally) put on the line. Moreover, while the seventeen characters represent performers vying for a Broadway show, their experiences have a basic universality that anyone, plumber to priest, housewife to hooker, can relate to.

In a show in which the book, music, lyrics, performances, and physical production all serve the concept, razor-sharp intelligence and simple poetry of direction are its strongest attributes. Genius Michael Bennett dreamed of creating a musical that celebrated the Broadway gypsies, those immensely talented artists of the ensemble who acted as a supporting unit, submerging their individuality for the betterment of the show.

In 1974, twenty-four dancers got together to discuss their careers, lives, and the business in which they worked. Bennett drew upon the tapes of these chat-fests as he developed the show. One of the dancers, Nicholas Dante, helped Bennett edit the tapes and form it slowly into a dramatic construct, and Joseph Papp, one of the most influential producers in the history of the American theatre, offered Bennett funding and a space to workshop and explore the material. James Kirkwood, a young playwright, joined Dante in working on the libretto, while Marvin Hamlisch, once a rehearsal pianist and arranger and by then an Academy Award–winning composer, came on board to supply the music. Edward Kleban, an untested lyricist who worked for Columbia Records, joined Hamlisch to create the score.

By April of the following year, the show was ready for a paying audience.

"The show is dedicated to anyone who has ever danced in a chorus or marched in step ... anywhere."

—*The creators of* A Chorus Line

and the Public's Newman Theatre was the site of one of the most important openings in American theatrical history. Even before the critics arrived, news of the unique brilliance of *A Chorus Line* swept the industry, and after 101 performances at the Public, Broadway's Shubert Theatre became the home of *A Chorus Line* for the next fifteen years, the modern theatre's first long-running smash hit.

What few critics noticed is that while the show is plotless, the stories in *A Chorus Line* follow a rough chronology tracing the life of a dancer, giving the show an underlying, almost undetectable structure. The sophistication of the material, juxtaposed with the simplicity of the production, emphasized the emotional aspects of the script, and drew audiences into the lives of the dancers in a way that has never been equaled in the theatre.

Surprisingly, with the exception of Marvin Hamlisch, *A Chorus Line* was not only the highlight of the authors' careers but their only Broadway musical credit. Nicholas Dante and James Kirkwood never wrote another musical, and Edward Kleban's many ideas for shows never came to fruition. It wasn't until *A Class Act*, a biographical musical on Kleban's life that was produced by his estate, as set forward in his will, that any of Kleban's other works were heard by audiences.

Also, save Hamlisch, the designers, and Bob Avian—Bennett's confidante, co-choreographer, and editor—all the creators are dead. That the show has remained a milestone is a great testament, not only to the brilliance of Bennett, Dante, Kirkwood, Kleban, and Papp, but to the heart and courage of everyone who contributed their time and talent to create one of the most emotional two hours ever spent in the theatre. ✳

RIGHT: Kelly Bishop won a well-deserved Tony Award for playing the iron butterfly Sheila, propelling her career from chorus dancer to very fine dramatic actress.

LEFT: Brian d'Arcy James, John Lithgow, Bernard Dotson, and one of the authors of this book in a scene from the Marvin Hamlisch/Craig Carnelia/John Guare musical *Sweet Smell of Success.*

Marvin Hamlisch

Like George Gershwin and Harold Arlen before him, Marvin Hamlisch began his career as a rehearsal pianist. Forever a fan of the musical theatre, and never losing his great love for the stage, he was the perfect composer for the ultimate backstage (or onstage) musical. After his work as a pianist on *Funny Girl* and *Fade Out—Fade In*, he arranged dance music for the Steve and Eydie epic *Golden Rainbow*. After a few years in Hollywood (bagging Academy Awards for "The Way We Were" and *The Sting*), it was back to the boards with one of the greatest hits of all time, *A Chorus Line*, where he not only wrote dense, sophisticated musical scenes, but created one of the rare standards to come from a Broadway musical in the 1970s ("What I Did for Love"). Unlike his collaborators, Hamlisch continued writing, for hit or flop, and he has always seemed to get a real kick out of the process. He returned to Broadway, after another Hollywood hiatus, with 1979's bouncy, long-run pop hit *They're Playing Our Song*, with lyrics by Carol Bayer Sager and a slick, funny libretto by Neil Simon. He followed it with the ultra-ambitious failure, *Jean Seberg*, produced in London. His next project, 1986's beauty pageant satire, *Smile*, first boasted a wonderful score by Hamlisch and Carolyn Leigh. When Leigh died during the writing of the show, Howard Ashman stepped in to write a new score with Hamlisch. Although the show wasn't a success, both sets of songs are wonderful, among the most underrated scores of the last twenty years. Hamlisch and Simon paired up again in 1993 for the woebegone *The Goodbye Girl*, which, through no fault of the authors, suffered from bad producing, weak direction, and a truly hideous design. His latest musical, *Sweet Smell of Success* (2002), was ahead of its time, a favorite of long-time theatregoers but savaged by especially virulent reviews.

BELOW: Hamlisch and Donna McKechnie confer during rehearsals of *A Chorus Line.*

Donna McKechnie

Vulnerable, spirited, and inexhaustible, Donna McKechnie is the finest female dancer of her generation, inspiring the finest choreographer of his generation, Michael Bennett, to create a series of spectacular set pieces for Broadway. After a start in summer stock, McKechnie landed on Broadway in the chorus of *How to Succeed in Business Without Really Trying*. Following an early nondancing gig as Philia in the national tour of *A Funny Thing Happened on the Way to the Forum*, she worked with her mentor and future husband Bennett while appearing on television's *Hullabaloo*. She was inspired and freed by the brief solos her fellow dancer choreographed for her, and after a featured role in *The Education of H*Y*M*A*N K*A*P*L*A*N*, she scored a featured dance role in *Promises, Promises*, where, along with Baayork Lee and Margo Sappington, McKechnie stopped the show with the infectious, relentless "Turkey Lurkey Time." Stopping the show again with her solo dance (again by Bennett) "Tick Tock" in Stephen Sondheim's seminal musical *Company*, McKechnie graduated to a starring role in the 1971 revival of *On the Town*, playing the elusive "Miss Turnstiles," Ivy Smith. After a sojourn in Hollywood, playing the Rose in the movie musical *The Little Prince*, she returned to Broadway a full-fledged star, in a role that solidified her fame as a brilliant triple-threat talent: the heartbreaking, heartwarming Cassie in 1975's *A Chorus Line*. Aside from the best sung Charity Hope Valentine ever, in the national tour of the 1986 revival of *Sweet Charity* (where she got to revel in comedy, something she rarely got to play), her only other Broadway role

was in David Merrick's last Broadway production, the failed *State Fair*. Embracing rather than dodging the monolithic shadow of *A Chorus Line*, McKechnie has worked steadily, appearing regularly in concert and at special events. It's unfortunate for both fans and musical theatre history that in recent years, Broadway has been denied her great talent.

TOP: Donna McKechnie, in her last Broadway appearance to date, sings "You Never Had It So Good" in *State Fair*.

ABOVE: With a song written specifically for her high-belt soprano voice; a scene perfectly utilizing her wry humor and vulnerability; and a marathon solo dance tailored to her singular, mercurial jazz/ballet style, McKechnie shone in "The Music and the Mirror," making the most of her nine minutes alone onstage to do what she does better than anyone

SONGS

"I Hope I Get It" · "I Can Do That" · "And ..." "At the Ballet" · "Sing!" · "Hello Twelve, Hello Thirteen, Hello Love" · "Nothing" · "Dance: Ten; Looks: Three" · "The Music and the Mirror" · "One" · "The Tap Combination" · "What I Did for Love"

TOP: "Just a dash of silicone...": In the perfect segue to the next chapter, Pamela Blair shows off the "T" in T & A, in the showstopper delicately titled "Dance Ten: Looks Three."

ABOVE: She's a Brass Band: McKechnie made a wonderful *Sweet Charity* in the national tour of the 1986 revival; it was on its opening night in Washington, D.C., that Bob Fosse collapsed and died on the street outside the National Theatre.

T&A, PART I

The late 1960s was a time of revolution, both social and sexual. This was reflected on Broadway in the second era of stage nudity. Around the same time as *Hair*, with its notorious nude scene, literal T & A came to Broadway with the arrival of *Oh! Calcutta!* in 1969. With an opening number titled "Taking off the Robe," the revue became a mainstay on Broadway through the 1970s and '80s, becoming a favorite stop for many non-English-speaking tourists. (After all, nudity needs no translation.)

The 1970s brought the term T & A to the mainstream with *A Chorus Line*, in which Pamela Blair's character of Val (based on the life story of original workshop member Mitzi Hamilton) sang of her newly formed accoutrements in "Dance: Ten; Looks: Three," while the chorus lines of the Bob Fosse shows *Pippin*, *Chicago*, and *Dancin'* always included the most strikingly gorgeous women dancers in the business.

The splendor of the Ziegfeld era has returned of late, with the statuesque chorus girls of *Crazy For You* and *The Will Rogers Follies*, but for the most part, nudity has been toned down as society has become more conservative. Commonplace in the New York theatre of the late 1960s and early '70s, skin has become more of a rarity, what with the rise of modern morality and the Disneyfying of Broadway. What was once used to shock and titillate, is now, as in the case of *The Full Monty*, presented in a humorous, almost genteel fashion.

SEX HAS BEEN A MAINSTAY of the Broadway theatre since the very beginning. Of course, through the decades, society's idea of sexiness and sexuality has changed. When *Florodora* premiered in 1899, the *Florodora* Sextette scandalized theatregoers, even though the girls were covered from the neck on down. The many revues of the early part of the last century also "glorified the American girl," in varying levels of taste from the poised, elegant Ziegfeld girls, whose rarefied beauty was so otherworldly that they were viewed as unattainable goddesses (that is, except to the occasional millionaire), to the lower brow *Earl Carroll Vanities*, whose costumes placed them just this side of a girly show. Nudity was legal on the Broadway stage as long as no one moved. And so, Ziegfeld presented tableaus designed by Ben Ali Haggin, artfully posed topless women, often in Grecian or Roman settings. Earl Carroll's *Murder at the Vanities* contained the immortal number "Virgins Wrapped in Cellophane." The Shubert Brothers's *Passing Show* (which actually featured a runway into the audience) and *Artists and Models* series were the most risqué. The 1924 edition of *Artists and Models* invited men in the audience to "Pull Your String." When they did as requested the ladies' costumes were pulled off.

TOP LEFT: *Li'l Abner*'s stupefyin' Julie Newmar. TOP RIGHT: It's "Dress Up Day" for Gwen Verdon in *New Girl in Town*. ABOVE: Welcome to T & A Josh Logan-style, in this pyramid from the "Physical Fitness" number in All American.

CITY OF ANGELS

OPENED DECEMBER 11, 1989; VIRGINIA THEATRE; 879 PERFORMANCES

ABOVE: James Naughton (left) and Gregg Edelman, as creation and creator, in the first-act closer of *City of Angels*, "You're Nothing Without Me," which blew the roof off the Virginia eight times a week. Oh, and you haven't lived until you've heard Steve Lawrence and Eydie Gorme sing it.

RIGHT: Randy Graff, as the faithful-to-a-fault secretary, Oolie.

CITY OF ANGELS

Produced by Nick Vanoff, Roger Berlind, Jujamcyn Theaters, Suntory International Corporation, and the Shubert Organization

Book by Larry Gelbart

Music by Cy Coleman
Lyrics by David Zippel
Music orchestrated by Billy Byers
Vocal arrangements by
Cy Coleman and Yaron Gershovsky
Musical Director: Gordon Lowry Harrell

Directed by Michael Blakemore
Musical Numbers staged by Walter Painter

Scenic Design by Robin Wagner
Costume Design by Florence Klotz
Lighting Design by Paul Gallo

Synopsis

Novelist Stine (no first name) is hired to write the screen treatment of his hit novel. Along the way he encounters the typical meddlings of the Hollywood brass. Meanwhile, in his head, he sees the film unfold, and the audience meets his characters, along with the people populating Stine's life. He soon finds that the control he has over his characters doesn't translate to real life, where people have their own agendas. In a *Follies*-esque moment, Stine's central creation, the hardboiled detective Stone, confronts his creator, and two worlds begin to blur. Stone finally empowers Stine to regain control, both of his work and his life.

Cast

Stone .... *James Naughton*
Stine .... *Gregg Edelman*
Oolie/Donna .... *Randy Graff*
Alaura Kingsley/Carla Haywood ... *Dee Hoty*
Bobbi/Gabby.............................. *Kay McClelland*
Irwin S. Irving/Buddy Fidler .... *René Auberjonois*
Mallory Kingsley/Avril Raines ...... *Rachel York*
Jimmy Powers .... *Scott Waara*
Munoz/Pancho Vargas .... *Shawn Elliott*

C Y COLEMAN BROUGHT JAZZ TO Broadway in a new way with his marvelous score for *City of Angels*. He had introduced jazz rhythms in *Sweet Charity*, having previously written standard Broadway scores for *Wildcat* and *Little Me*. Coleman, an accomplished jazz pianist/composer in his own right, extended the ideas he explored in *Sweet Charity* and created a score that was swinging, hip, and sexy.

Jazz was an integral part of Broadway almost from the beginning. Early black musicals contained elements of jazz and ragtime, and notable jazz singers and instrumentalists interpreted shows like *Girl Crazy*, albeit in a popular vein. The late 1930s saw a spate of swing musicals on Broadway, and they all seemed to have "swing" in their titles, from the Eubie Blake show *Swing It* (1937) to *The Swing Mikado* and *The Hot Mikado*, which opened within a month of each other in 1939 and updated the rhythm of the original Gilbert and Sullivan score. Later that year, *Swingin' the Dream* (a jazzy rendition of Shakespeare's *A Midsummer Night's Dream*) featured jazz greats Louis Armstrong and Maxine Sullivan onstage and both the Benny Goodman Sextette and Bud Freeman's Summa Cum Laude band in the pit. The Jimmy Van Heusen and Eddie De Lange score boasted a standard, "Darn That Dream," but it was basically a pop score with jazz arrangements.

Fran Landesman and Tommy Wolf had written a jazz score for *The Nervous Set* (1959), but it made little impact except in three areas: (1) It featured Mary Martin's son, Larry Hagman; (2) The song "Ballad of the Sad Young Men" became a gay anthem; (3) A cut song, "Spring Can Really Hang You Up the Most," became a true jazz standard. *Doctor Jazz* followed *Sweet Charity* in 1975. George Wolfe scrunched the songs of Jelly Roll Morton (the self-proclaimed inventor of jazz) into the musical theatre idiom in 1992's *Jelly's Last Jam*.

Then came *City of Angels*. Cy Coleman's rhythms and melodies, as interpreted by Billy Byers's percussive orchestrations and the hot vocal arrangements by Yaron Gershovsky and Coleman, made for a unique score. The music evoked the period sound of the 1940s while keeping closely rooted in the present.

And the Cy Coleman/David Zippel score wasn't the only element of *City of Angels* to push the bounds of Broadway tradition. Audacious is a word used all too indiscriminately, but it's the perfect word to describe *City of Angels*. Here's not a show within a show, but rather a film within a show; that is, until the main character of the film steps into the real world to confront his creator and alter ego, and the two worlds collide. The Raymond Chandleresque 1940s film *noir* is presented to the theatre audience entirely in black and white, while the accompanying story of the writer's personal life is seen in glorious color, with characters in real life having counterparts in the screenplay. The razor-sharp dialogue by great wit Larry Gelbart is a spot-on riff on the noir genre, but never falls into parody.

Cy Coleman, currently the country's busiest composer, trumped even his work on *Sweet Charity*. Unfortunately, though, while the latter's songs enjoyed success away from the score, times had changed in the years between *Charity* and *Angels*, and only Tony Bennett was left of the great jazz and pop singers. Radio had, for all intents and purposes, given up on standards, so songs like "You're Nothing Without Me" and "With Every Breath I Take" had no chance for wide, popular appeal.

With the renewed popularity of the movie musical, wouldn't it be interesting if *City of Angels* were made into a movie, a show within a film? What with Turner Classic Movies on cable and the triumph of the DVD, those old film noir gumshoes may just be back in vogue. ✷

LEFT: In the screenplay half of the show, the delish Dee Hoty plays the duplicitous Alaura Kingsley, here getting full service from Doug Tompos's tennis pro. BELOW: Carolee Carmello, Lonny Price, and Randy Graff in the tuneful and touching biomusical, *A Class Act*. BOTTOM: Kay McLelland (in Technicolor real life) and Randy Graff (in black-and-white film noir) in a number showing off director Michael Blakemore and designer Robin Wagner's incredibly clever use of a cinematic effect, the split screen.

"Did I get a pile of scripts after winning the Tony? No-o-o-o." —Randy Graff

Randy Graff

Randy Graff, one of the finest singing actresses currently on Broadway, made her debut as a replacement in *Grease*, the premiere launchpad for young talent in the 1970s. After a supporting role as Tovah Feldshuh's sister (they were two of the most unlikely actresses to play Brazilians) in the Mitch Leigh flop *Sarava*, her big break came when she was tapped to play the tragic Fantine in the original Broadway company of *Les Misérables*. After a Tony for *City of Angels*, she deftly took on roles in two straight plays, *Laughter on the Twenty-third Floor* and *Moon over Buffalo*, and was one of the few bright spots in the stage adaptation of the movie musical *High Society*. Rarely out of work, she has graced musical stages of late in *A Class Act* and the revival of *Fiddler on the Roof*. Her showstopping performance of the swinging Coleman/Zippel tune "You Can Always Count on Me" in *City of Angels* bemoans the curse of dependability, and while it causes heartache for the characters she plays in the story, "dependable" is perhaps the best way to describe Graff herself, for no matter the quality of the surroundings, theatregoers can always be assured of her warmth, her wonderful singing, and her expert timing.

COMPANY

OPENED APRIL 26, 1970; ALVIN THEATRE; 690 PERFORMANCES

Dean Jones as Bobby, Bobby-Baby, Bobby-Bubi, Robby, Bob, Rob-O, etc.

COMPANY
Produced by Harold Prince
Produced in association with Ruth Mitchell

Music by Stephen Sondheim
Lyrics by Stephen Sondheim
Book by George Furth
Musical Director: Harold Hastings
Music orchestrated by Jonathan Tunick
Dance Arrangements by Wally Harper

Directed by Harold Prince
Musical Staging by Michael Bennett
Associate Choreographer: Bob Avian

Scenic Design by Boris Aronson
Costume Design by D. D. Ryan
Lighting Design by Robert Ornbo
Projection Design by Boris Aronson

Synopsis

Five couples try to convince their bachelor friend Bobby that marriage is a good thing, but he refuses to see past his married friends' petty problems, preferring a life of unemotional one-night stands. Finally, he allows himself to open up to the possibility of sharing his emotions (and life) with another person.

Cast

Sarah	*Barbara Barrie*
Larry	*Charles Braswell*
April	*Susan Browning*
David	*George Coe*
Peter	*John Cunningham*
Paul	*Steve Elmore*
Amy	*Beth Howland*
Robert	*Dean Jones*
Harry	*Charles Kimbrough*
Susan	*Merle Louise*
Kathy	*Donna McKechnie*
Marta	*Pamela Myers*
Jenny	*Teri Ralston*
Joanne	*Elaine Stritch*

"Could you remind me again what it is?"

—Beth Howard, when Sondheim pointed out that she wasn't singing the correct melody to "Getting Married Today"

EVERY DECADE SEEMS TO GIVE birth to a musical that propels the art form to a new level or at least sends it in a new direction. In the 1900s, George M. Cohan's *Little Johnny Jones* (1904) ushered in an all-American sound and soul for the musical comedy. Jerome Kern's Princess Theatre shows, with their intimate, American-based locales, marked the 1910s. The 1920s began with the *Ziegfeld Follies of 1919* and the ascendancy of Irving Berlin and ended with the groundbreaking *Show Boat*, the best attempt thus far at merging song and story. The 1930s brought *The Band Wagon*, the ultimate Broadway revue featuring a new sophistication of writing, stagecraft, and staging. The 1940s saw Rodgers and Hammerstein's *Oklahoma!* and a whole new formula for the musical comedy. In the 1950s, the musical reached its peak with *My Fair Lady*. The 1960s were ushered in with *The Fantasticks* and the birth of the Off-Broadway musical. And the 1970s had *Company*.

A shockingly modern musical when it first opened and still a remarkably insightful (if a little dyspeptic) view of late-twentieth-century relationships. *Company* explores the games, the angst, the loneliness, and the badinage in an alternatingly brittle and heartfelt manner. *Company* is really a revusical, that is, a string of nonlinear scenes around a single theme. Howard Dietz had invented the revusical with his productions of *At Home Abroad* (1935) and *Inside USA* (1948), shows that featured a theme and continuing characters but that were revues otherwise.

When it first burst upon the scene, *Company*'s take-no-prisoners attitude was revolutionary. No chorus, no leggy chorines (save Donna McKechnie's "Tick Tock"), no salve for the tired businessman. All it had was Sondheim's brilliant metropolitan score; Jonathan Tunick's incomparable, metallic orchestrations; Boris Aronson's antiseptically urban set; George Furth's cagey and revealing book; and Hal Prince's sparse, knowing staging.

Company (the first real "Sondheim" score) was the show that introduced us to the Sondheim/Prince/Aronson/Tunick collaboration that would wrenchingly change the course of musical theatre—and lead to a hundred second-rate imitations by Sondheim wannabes. ❈

Stephen Sondheim

Stephen Sondheim, the brilliant composer/lyricist who forever changed the landscape of the musical in his five collaborations with Hal Prince in the 1970s, made his Broadway debut as lyricist to Leonard Bernstein in *West Side Story*. After another smash as lyricist on *Gypsy*, Sondheim finally made his bow as a composer with the farce *A Funny Thing Happened on the Way to the Forum*. In spite of the show's success, Sondheim's score was consistently overlooked as a major contribution, failing even to be nominated for a Tony Award when every other aspect of the show was so honored.

After the disappointing *Anyone Can Whistle*, he grudgingly returned to lyric writing with *Do I Hear a Waltz?* Determined to be known for more than lyrics, he set to work and made theatrical history just as his mentor, Oscar Hammerstein II, had done forty years earlier with *Show Boat*. With the electric current of the nervy, ultramodern *Company*, he embarked with Hal Prince on a journey of shows, including *Follies*, *A Little Night Music*, *Pacific Overtures*, and *Sweeney Todd*, which, if not always financial hits, can absolutely not be dismissed as failures in any sense, as they undeniably made waves with their brave forward strides.

In some ways these five shows were a double-edged sword, for they not only raised the bar for an entire generation of imitators who could never begin to approach his genius and complexity, but Sondheim's string of artistic coups ultimately harmed the other, more traditional writers of his generation. While these other artists possessed talent to spare and great strengths of their own, they were often unfairly denigrated as lightweight, shallow, or, horror of horrors, hummable. After another wonderful score for the disappointing *Merrily We Roll Along*, Sondheim and Prince parted professional ways for two decades, and Sondheim worked with others, primarily James Lapine, on the shows *Sunday in the Park with George*, *Into the Woods*, and *Passion*. His latest, a reunion with Hal Prince, has been, at various points in its five-year gestation, titled *Wise Guys, Gold!*, and finally *Bounce*. It had its premiere at the Goodman Theatre in Chicago in 2003, traveling next to the Kennedy Center, while 2004 promises Broadway productions of his two most challenging works, the überdark *Assassins* and *Pacific Overtures*.

Though his music is often dismissed as tuneless, chilly, and esoteric, nothing could be further from the truth. Former collaborator Jule Styne, who knew about such things, was quoted as saying that the rich Sondheim melodies for *Sweeney Todd* were something he himself could never, ever begin to write. In light of his deep intellect and complicated talents, perhaps Stephen Sondheim is best summed up by a slogan used in television commercials: Often imitated, never duplicated.

LEFT: Donna McKechnie dances "Tick Tock."

RIGHT: The bewitching and irreplaceable Joanna Gleason made the Baker's Wife in Sondheim's fractured fairy tale, *Into the Woods*, alternately deeply touching and highly contemporary.

CENTER RIGHT: Sondheim hits the wall during the Boston tryout of *Follies*.

Backstage

Dean Jones opened in *Company* and appears on the original cast album. He quit the production and was replaced by Larry Kert. When the entire original cast of *Company* went to London, CBS chose simply to rerelease the original cast recording, overdubbing Jones's voice with Kert's. Still, if you listen closely with headphones, you can hear the ghost of Jones bleeding over on his fellow singers' tracks.

The vignettes that make up *Company* were originally a series of one-act plays written for Kim Stanley. Harold Prince suggested to George Furth and Stephen Sondheim that the one-acts become the basis for a musical.

Boris Aronson

Among the most eclectic stage designers, Boris Aronson came to America in the early 1920s after a youth spent in his native Russia and Germany. His first designs were for the vital Yiddish theatre. In 1926, he gained wide notice with his sets for the Maurice Schwartz production, *The Ten Commandments* at the Yiddish Art Theatre. Within a year he had an exhibition of his set models and in 1928, Waldemar George, a famous art critic, wrote a book on Aronson's work. In 1932 he began designing for Broadway and soon became a leading designer with the Group Theatre. He was among the first designers to utilize projected scenery which he used extensively in the late '30s and early 1940s. Always an experimental, challenging designer, his work fell out of favor in the '40s and '50s. In 1953, he began a long artistic relationship with playwright Arthur Miller, designing six of his plays. His constructivist roots lent his works a bigger than life style which made him perfect for the concept musicals in the 1960s. His evocative settings for *Fiddler on the Roof* (1964) led to a long collaboration with producer/director Harold Prince. *Company* (1970) was the perfect example of his constructivist style and he went on to design such Prince/Sondheim shows as *Follies* (1971), *A Little Night Music* (1973), and *Pacific Overtures* (1976).

Elaine Stritch

The dry, sardonic actress/singer with vulnerability behind every zinger first came to the attention of New York theatregoers with her comic lament "Civilization" in the 1947 revue *Angel in the Wings*. Following revivals of *On Your Toes* and *Pal Joey* (stopping the show with "Zip"), she gave stellar performances in the less-than-stellar *Goldilocks* and *Sail Away,* and their failures led producers to the mistaken conclusion that Stritch was unable to carry her own vehicle. The boozy, sarcastic Joanne in *Company* is so identified with Stritch's voice and delivery that every subsequent actress who has tackled "The Ladies Who Lunch" has sensed her peering over their shoulders, while her 2002 smash one-woman show, *At Liberty,* proved that Stritch as Stritch is as riveting as any fictional character she has ever portrayed.

TOP: When Elaine Stritch proposes a toast, she means business, still electrifying audiences with "The Ladies Who Lunch" thirty-five years after the premiere of *Company.*

ABOVE: Elaine Stritch and Russell Nype (in *Goldilocks*), whose longtime friendship dates back to their days in *Call Me Madam,* when Stritch stood by for Ethel Merman (for the hilarious details, please consult the DVD of *Elaine Stritch: At Liberty*).

LEFT: Stritch, as cruise hostess Mimi Paragon, reaped the benefits of costar Jean Fenn's dismissal in *Sail Away,* which elevated her to romantic leading lady status. Here, she stops the show in her customary fashion with her opening number, "Come to Me."

A CONNECTICUT YANKEE

OPENED NOVEMBER 3, 1927; VANDERBILT THEATRE; 421 PERFORMANCES

Constance Capenter and William Gaxton find that their love transcends the centuries.

A CONNECTICUT YANKEE

Produced by Lew M. Fields and Lyle D. Andrews

Music by Richard Rodgers
Book by Herbert Fields
Lyrics by Lorenz Hart
Musical Director: Roy Webb
Adapted from Mark Twain
Music orchestrated by Roy Webb
Vocal Arranger: Clay Warnick

Staged by Alexander Leftwich
Dances by Busby Berkeley

Scenic Design by John F. Hawkins Jr.
Costume Design by John F. Hawkins Jr.

Synopsis

Martin, our hero, is flirting with a young girl at a party. His fiancée sees red and bonks Martin on the head with a frying pan. He goes out of the frying pan and into the fire when he dreams he's back in King Arthur's Camelot. About to be burned at the stake, he remembers an upcoming eclipse and magically makes the sun disappear, to the amazement of the court. Set free, he proceeds to industrialize King Arthur's domain. When Martin awakes from his dream, he realizes he's been in love with the wrong girl all along.

Cast

Gerald Lake/
Sir Galahad..........................*Jack Thompson*
Martin/
The Yankee..........................*William Gaxton*
Fay Morgan/
Queen Morgan Le Fay ....*Nana Bryant*
Alice Carter/
Alisande La Carteloise.........*Constance Carpenter*
Arthur Pedragos/
King Arthur of Britain ....*Paul Everton*
Lawrence Lake/
Sir Launcelot of the Lake .....*William Roselle*
Merlin/Merlin.......................*William Norris*
Mistress Evelyn La Belle-Ans..*June Cochrane*

IN 1921, HERBERT FIELDS, LORENZ HART, AND RICHARD RODGERS saw a filmed version of Mark Twain's classic novel *A Connecticut Yankee in King Arthur's Court*. The trio thought the story would make an ideal musical comedy, and they tracked down Charles Tressler Lark, the lawyer for the Mark Twain estate. The agent was overjoyed at the idea of a musical, even if it were to be musicalized by a trio of unknowns, so he gave them the rights for free. Unfortunately, because they were unknowns, no producer would consider putting up the money for the show. So as not to lose out completely on a good idea, the writers wrote a show called *A Danish Yankee in King Tut's Court* in 1923. It was produced for charity at the Institute of Musical Art.

Cut to 1927, when the now-famous trio decided to revisit the material, convinced that they would have no problems getting the show on the boards. This time Lark asked for a healthy advance and royalty from the team. Luckily, Lew Fields, father of Herbert (and Dorothy), teamed with Lyle D. Andrews to produce the show, and it was set to open at the Vanderbilt Theatre (which Andrews happened to own).

"The audience reaction was so strong that it was like an actual blow."

—*Richard Rodgers, on conducting the opening night of* A Connecticut Yankee

Backstage

"To Keep My Love Alive," written for the 1943 revival, was Rodgers and Hart's last song together.

As is all too typical of shows trying out, the creators lost sight of some of their creation's qualities. When Lew Fields insisted that a Rodgers and Hart song that combined modern language and sensibility and archaic slang (much like the show did) be cut, the songwriters defended their song and "Thou Swell" became one of the big hits from the score. This is not to say that Rodgers or Hart were always protective about their output; after all, they were at the peak of their abilities, and dashing off a new number was relatively easy. As Rodgers once said, "I'm not married to my tunes. I never was. And Larry wasn't married to his words. There were plenty more where those came from. We were interested in making the show work. If a song didn't fit, or if the audience reaction told us it was wrong, out it came."

One of the other hits from the score, "My Heart Stood Still," had a much longer gestation. While in Paris, Rodgers and Hart were riding in a taxi with two lady friends when another cab nearly hit them. Their taxi screeched to a halt, and one of the women exclaimed, "Oh, my heart stood still!" Larry Hart piped up, "Say, that's a good name for a song." Rodgers, still catching his breath, wondered how Hart could think of song titles at such a time, but the composer nevertheless made a note in his little black book. Later, in London, Rodgers came across the words "my heart stood still" in his notebook. He sat at the piano and immediately wrote out a tune, and when Hart showed up, he quickly came up with a lyric. As Rodgers has pointed out, the lyric is remarkable, consisting of only six two-syllable words, the rest one syllable.

The song was put into an English revue, *One Damn Thing After Another*, but just before *A Connecticut Yankee* was to open in New York, Bea Lillie and her producer, Charles Dillingham, asked that "My Heart Stood Still" be added to their new show, also about to open. Rodgers and Hart didn't feel that Lillie would do justice to the song, so they insisted that the song was slated for the score of *Yankee*. Since they had used this excuse, they felt obliged to follow through, but Cochran owned the rights to the song as the show was still running in London. Finally, Rodgers and Hart agreed to a cut in their British royalties for the right to include the song in their new production.

Connecticut Yankee was the biggest hit of the 1920s for Rodgers, Hart, and Fields. At the end of the Rodgers and Hart collaboration, Richard Rodgers, in the mistaken belief that keeping Larry Hart busy would stop his self-destructive behavior, proposed a revival of *A Connecticut Yankee*. It was 1943. Herbert Fields updated the book, adding a World War II setting, and the songwriting team cut five numbers from the original score, writing a half dozen new numbers. Rodgers's plan worked for a time, for during the writing and out-of-town tryout, Hart was on the wagon, but as soon as his work was done, he went back to drinking heavily. On opening night, Hart showed up at the theatre and watched the show from backstage. At intermission, he went to a nearby bar without an overcoat and returned, soaked and drunk, calling out the script and lyrics in a loud voice. Dorothy Hart, Larry's sister, took him home and put him to sleep on her couch. When she awoke, Hart was missing. The composer Frederick Loewe finally found Hart sitting in a gutter in the pouring rain, in an alcoholic stupor. Suffering from pneumonia, he was taken to the hospital, where he died a few days later. ❄

TOP RIGHT: Constance Carpenter, Nana Bryant, and William Norris.

LEFT: Lady in a cage: Constance Carpenter is a prisoner of love.

SONGS

ACT I "A Ladies' Home Companion" · "My Heart Stood Still" · "Thou Swell" · "At the Round Table" · "On a Desert Isle with Thee" · "Ibbidi Bibbidi Sibbidi Sab"

ACT II "Nothing's Wrong" · "I Feel at Home with You" · "The Sandwich Men" · "Evelyn, What Do You Say?"

Lew Fields

Lew Fields, half of the team of Weber and Fields and patriarch of the Fields theatrical family, formed an act with fellow Lower East Side resident Joseph Weber. They became a huge hit in the theatre as the German-accented characters Mike and Meyer. Specializing in perfectly choreographed, gymnastic, slapstick routines, Weber and Fields incorporated burlesques of contemporary shows and politics, becoming masters of topical humor. The titles of some of their shows indicate their lighthearted tenor: *Whoop-Dee-Doo*, *Fiddle-Dee-Dee*, *Twirly-Whirly*, and *Whirl-i-gig*. Weber and Fields were so successful, they soon opened and operated a theatre. After dissolving his partnership with Weber, Fields had his own theatre, appropriately named the Lew M. Fields Theatre, and branched out into producing more refined musical comedies and operettas. He produced several shows by composer Victor Herbert, including *Old Dutch*, in which Helen Hayes made her Broadway debut at the age of nine. Lew Fields was responsible for producing the first works by the then-young team of Richard Rodgers and Lorenz Hart, many of them written in collaboration with his son, librettist Herbert. Lew Fields was also the father of the brilliant lyricist Dorothy Fields, whose first book musical, *Hello, Daddy*, he produced. Fields's third child was playwright Joseph Fields, best remembered for teaming with Jerome Chodorov on a series of plays and the librettos to *Gentlemen Prefer Blondes*, *Wonderful Town*, and *Flower Drum Song*. Weber and Fields reunited after a thirty-year hiatus to open Radio City Music Hall in 1932.

DAMN YANKEES

OPENED MAY 5, 1955; 46TH STREET THEATRE; 1,019 PERFORMANCES

ABOVE: Eddie Phillips gives Gwen Verdon a leg up in "Who's Got the Pain?" In the film version, Verdon's dance partner was Bob Fosse.

RIGHT: Ray Walston, in an eerie foreshadowing of his *My Favorite Martian* antennae, does an out-and-out vaudeville turn in "Those Were the Good Old Days."

DAMN YANKEES

Produced by Frederick Brisson, Robert E. Griffith, and Harold S. Prince

Music and Lyrics by Richard Adler and Jerry Ross
Book by George Abbott and Douglass Wallop
From the Novel
The Year the Yankees Lost the Pennant
by Douglass Wallop
Musical Director: Hal Hastings
Music orchestrated by Don Walker
Dance arrangements by Roger Adams

Directed by George Abbott
Dances and musical numbers
staged by Bob Fosse

Scenic and Costume Design by
William and Jean Eckart

Synopsis

The *Faust* legend is played out on the fields of baseball. Joe Boyd, a typical, suburban middle-aged fan, sells his soul to the devilish Mr. Applegate in order to help his beloved Washington Senators win the pennant. Transformed into the strapping Joe Hardy, he improves the Senators' record, reaching the final game of the season against those damn Yankees. Joe grows homesick for his wife, Meg, discovers an escape clause in his contract, and attempts to break the agreement, so Mr. Applegate sends the seductress Lola to convince Joe to honor his contract. In the end, Joe returns to Meg.

Cast

Lola	*Gwen Verdon*
Applegate	*Ray Walston*
Joe Hardy	*Stephen Douglass*
Joe Boyd	*Robert Shafer*
Gloria Thorpe	*Rae Allen*
Meg Boyd	*Shannon Bolin*
Van Buren	*Russ Brown*
Smokey	*Nathaniel Frey*
Sister	*Jean Stapleton*

PROVING WRONG THOSE WHO SAID baseball and theatre couldn't mix, *Damn Yankees* was the third (and last) of the Richard Adler/Jerry Ross collaborations. It turned out to be a reunion of most of the team of *The Pajama Game*: helmer George Abbott; dance man Bob Fosse; producers Brisson, Prince, and Griffith; and the music department of Don Walker and Hal Hastings. (The cast was new, of course: *The Pajama Game* had opened only a year before, and the gang down at the St. James was still going strong; even so, couldn't most of the *Pajama Game* crew have played well in *Damn Yankees*? Eddie Foy as Applegate, John Raitt as Joe, Carol Haney as Lola, Janis Paige as third base...) The creative team worked exceedingly smoothly, and out of town, only two major changes occurred. First, the response to Gwen Verdon in her first starring role was so strong, Adler and Ross quickly wrote "A Little Brains, A Little Talent" so Lola could enter the action earlier in the act. Second, there was the matter of the "Baseball Ballet." This was Fosse's major choreographic set piece, his version of Jerome Robbins's "Keystone Kop Ballet" from *High Button Shoes*, complete with a game of musical chairs, multiple entrances, exits, and an absurdist gorilla. The ballet was cut, much to Fosse's unhappiness, after he had worked and reworked it countless times.

It was a perfectly grand mid-1950s Broadway musical comedy romp, with a solid book, quick pacing, and a tuneful score. Above all, though, it was absolutely seminal as the first pairing of one of the greatest marriages, both onstage and off, in Broadway history. Although it opened as a George Abbott show, *Damn Yankees* has become known in the intervening years as a Fosse/Verdon show. In other hands, the comic seduction "Whatever Lola Wants" could have been viewed as lewd, but with Verdon's unparalleled ability to kid her sexuality, along with Fosse's witty, quirky staging, it became the showstopper that the sometimes prudish matinee blue hairs screamed for the loudest. Outside of Fosse's dances, there was much else to admire, including the performances of Abbott regulars Nat Frey, Rae Allen, and Jean Stapleton; the understated vaudevillian devil of Ray Walston (truly the unsung hero of the show, for Walston seeped in around the edges and insinuated himself to center stage); and its touching love story, really a triangle, among Shannon Bolin and the two Joes—young and old—Stephen Douglass and Robert Shafer.

Damn Yankees was also faithfully filmed, with the Broadway cast mostly intact (again, much like *Pajama Game*, with one movie star substituted for a principal. This time it was Tab Hunter as the Doris Day ringer). A bizarre 1967 television version with Lee Remick and Phil Silvers was more acid trip than Broadway musical, and the 1994 Broadway revival was dead from inception, suffering the tragic casting of Bebe Neuwirth as Lola. Neuwirth, an extremely talented triple-threat performer, lacked the one thing that any Lola must possess first and foremost: charm. As the publicity-hungry Velma Kelly or the jaded Nickie in *Sweet Charity*, she was right on the money: hard, slick, and deadpan; as Lola, Neuwirth was adrift in a platinum-blond wig.

One final thing: when the show first opened, the logo featured Gwen Verdon in a baseball uniform, coyly looking over her shoulder. It was decided to lead with their strongest suit, so the producers revamped the look (even reissuing the cast album with the new photo) to sport Verdon clad in her striptease tights against a devilish red background. It made all the difference in the world, putting the emphasis on the "Damn" instead of the "Yankees." One wonders if Bob Fosse recalled this important marketing lesson twenty years later when *Pippin* opened to extremely mixed reviews. The television ad he directed not only saved the show but opened a whole new frontier in Broadway promotion. ❋

ABOVE: Albert Linville, Nat Frey, Jimmie Komack, and Russ Brown declare that they've got "Heart."

BELOW: Bob Fosse surrounded by his *Dancin'* cast, including longtime favorites Vicki Frederick (front row, left), Christopher Chadman (back row, second from left), Wayne Cilento (front row, right), and Ann Reinking (front row, center).

Bob Fosse

Bob Fosse grew up wanting to be the next Fred Astaire. Luckily for the Broadway musical, he was too short, balding, and frankly, his reputation as a great ladies' man notwithstanding, not a highly masculine presence, which, by the time of his arrival in Hollywood, had become de rigueur in musical stars. Choreographing his first Broadway show, *The Pajama Game*, Fosse began to develop his singular vocabulary, and in his second, *Damn Yankees*, he found, in Gwen Verdon, a muse for his idiosyncratic style, with a body perfectly suited to his knock-kneed precision. With a string of successes (*Bells Are Ringing*, *New Girl in Town*, and *Redhead*, the latter two starring Verdon, by then his third wife), Fosse became heir apparent to the mantle of Jerome Robbins. When Verdon took time off to have a baby, Fosse steamed along, rechoreographing *How to Succeed . . .* and devising the hilarious dances for *Little Me*. After *Sweet Charity*, he branched out into film, and in 1972, everything he touched turned to gold: the television special *Liza with a Z* (Emmy), the movie version of *Cabaret* (Oscar), and, in a real magic act, *Pippin* (Tony), which he made into much more than its middling material exhibited on the page. His next Broadway show, *Chicago*, which nearly killed him from a heart attack, was a brilliant example of Fosse's ability to draw from all traditions, in this case his vaudeville and burlesque salad days. More a dance concert than a musical, *Dancin'* was a marathon of a show for the cream of the crop of Broadway dancers of the 1970s. Away from theatre for nearly eight years, Fosse returned with *Big Deal*, his last show and not a success. While attending to the Washington, D.C., opening of the national tour of his successful 1986 Broadway revival of *Sweet Charity*, Fosse collapsed and died, his alter ego of over thirty years, Gwen Verdon, at his side.

SONGS

ACT I "Six Months Out of Every Year" · "Goodbye, Old Girl" · "Heart" · "Shoeless Joe from Hannibal Mo" "A Man Doesn't Know" · "A Little Brains, A Little Talent" "Whatever Lola Wants" · "Not Meg" · "Who's Got the Pain"

ACT II "The Game" · "Near to You" · "Those Were the Good Old Days" · "Two Lost Souls"

Backstage

The day after the opening Prince, Griffith, and Abbott called a rehearsal. They cut one number, switched another from the second act to the first, cut twenty minutes from the script, and rewrote the ending. The changes went in that evening. Walter Kerr even came back to rereview the show.

The role of Lola was originally offered to Marilyn Monroe, Zizi Jeanmaire, and Mitzi Gaynor.

LEFT: Joe Hardy (Stephen Douglass) his resolve dissolving, gives in to the Lola of Gwen Verdon, who hasn't even resorted to taking her dress off yet.

RIGHT: Sunshine Girl Verdon was heartbreaking as the reformed prostie, Anna, in *New Girl in Town*.

BELOW: For "Essie's Vision" in *Redhead*, Fosse created a marathon dance number for Verdon, ranging from ballet to can-can to military march to this tambourine-shaking gypsy tarantella.

Gwen Verdon

Nicknamed "Boots" for the orthopedic shoes she wore to correct rickets, Gwen Verdon, Broadway's greatest dancing star ever, was raised down the street from MGM, where her father worked. After seeking work in nightclubs to support her son, she became a protégé of choreographer Jack Cole, assisting him on several Broadway shows and many movies at Twentieth Century–Fox (where she taught Marilyn Monroe to dance). As the lead dancer in *Can-Can*, she saw her role whittled down to little more than an ensemble part, primarily through the machinations of threatened star Lilo. Verdon's talent shone through, though, and she became a star when, on open-

ing night, she was dragged onstage from her dressing room, clad only in a towel, the audience chanting "We want Verdon!" Another lucky break occurred when she was cast as the sexy temptress Lola in *Damn Yankees*. Her first show with future husband Bob Fosse, she became a superstar, and her photo in strip-tease tights one of the most iconic Broadway images ever. In four more Broadway shows, all with Fosse, Verdon owned Broadway: *New Girl in Town* (where she proved herself as a very fine dramatic actress), the murder-mystery musical *Redhead* (where she won her fourth Tony Award in seven years), *Sweet Charity* (where her over-the-shoulder stance became as famous as the *Damn Yankees* Lola pose), and her swan song, as the greatest Roxie Hart ever in *Chicago*. While continuing to act in such films as *Cocoon* and *Marvin's Room*, she was just as happy behind the scenes, as dance captain of Fosse's *Dancin'* and coach to Debbie Allen for the revival of *Charity*. With a better singing voice than she was given credit for, boundless comedic gifts, and a "who, me?" quality as much satire as sex, Gwen Verdon appealed equally to men and women, gay and straight, young and old. She is truly missed.

THE DESERT SONG

OPENED NOVEMBER 30, 1926; CASINO THEATRE; 471 PERFORMANCES

ABOVE: The Red Shadow (Robert Halliday) embraces the woman he loves, Margot Bonvalet (Vivienne Segal), in a typical operetta clinch.

RIGHT: The distaff side of the French Foreign Legion.

THE DESERT SONG

Produced by
Laurence Schwab and Frank Mandel

Music by Sigmund Romberg
Lyrics by Otto Harbach and
Oscar Hammerstein II
Book by
Otto Harbach, Oscar Hammerstein II,
and Frank Mandel
Orchestra under the Direction of Oscar Bradley

Book directed by Arthur Hurley
Musical Numbers staged by Robert Connelly

Scenic Design by Woodman Thompson
Modern Costumes designed by Vyvyan Donner
Costume Design by Mark Mooring

Synopsis

The Red Shadow, the leader of a rebel band known as the Riffs, kidnaps Margo Bonvalet, a comely French woman. In a twist reminiscent of *The Scarlet Pimpernel* and *Naughty Marietta*, the true identity of the Red Shadow is Pierre, the supposedly milquetoast son of the governor of Morocco, General Birabeau. When the rebel band is tracked down, the Red Shadow finds himself in the unenviable position of having to duel his own father. Pierre backs down, much to the derision of his not-so-merry band. General Birabeau's aide, Captain Paul Fontaine, is determined to bring the Red Shadow to justice until a jealous Arab girl, Azuri, reveals the true identity of the mystery man to him. Fontaine does the only decent thing, showing the general the burnoose of the Red Shadow and declaring the interloper vanquished, thus keeping secret forever the identity of the general's offspring and making safe the presumed marriage of Margot and Pierre.

Cast

Sid El Kar	*William O'Neal*
Benjamin Kidd	*Eddie Buzzell*
Captain Paul Fontaine	*Glen Dale*
Azuri	*Pearl Regay*
Margot Bonvalet	*Vivienne Segal*
General Birabeau	*Edmund Elton*
Pierre Birabeau	*Robert Halliday*
Susan	*Nellie Breen*
Ali Ben Ali	*Lyle Evans*

RUDOLPH VALENTINO WAS MESMERIZING WOMEN in his silent turns in *The Sheik* and *Son of the Sheik*; T. E. Lawrence was sending back almost daily reports through journalist Lowell Thomas; in French Morocco, an actual band of rebels called the Riffs was making things hotter for the French. All things exotically Arabian were in vogue—so what better time to present a Saharan operetta?

The true hero of *The Desert Song* isn't the Red Shadow, however; it is composer Sigmund Romberg, whose masculine, martial melodies propelled the action forward. Even the comic songs "It" and "One Good Man Gone Wrong" have certain incessant, rhythmical underpinnings. The score's momentum and lusty vocal arrangements typify the operetta form. "The Riff Song" is in the vein of testosterone-driven marches like *Naughty Marietta*'s "Tramp, Tramp, Tramp"; *Rio Rita*'s "March of the Rangers"; and *Rose-Marie*'s "Stout-hearted Men."

In the late 1920s, operetta coexisted peacefully with more modern musical comedies: The same month when *The Desert Song* opened, the Gershwin brothers' *Oh, Kay!* received huzzahs from audiences. An English version of the French operetta *Mozart* opened at the Music Box Theatre the day before *The Desert Song*, and the original French version of *Mozart* opened at the 46th Street Theatre a little over a month later. Richard Rodgers and Lorenz Hart's *Peggy Ann*, the first psychological, surrealistic musical, opened the same day as the revival of *Mozart*. (Astoundingly, Rodgers and Hart's next show, *Betsy*, opened the next day!)

As the 1920s wound down, however, the operetta was slowly supplanted by the musical comedy. A little over a year after the debut of *The Desert Song*, *Show Boat* opened, on the surface an operetta but set in America, and the Broadway musical would never, ever be the same. Even with that groundbreaking show changing the course of the musical, the greatest operettas live on to this day, with their stirring songs and romantic (though creaky) plots still offering thrills to audiences who are willing to leave their preconceptions in the lobby. True, these shows may have stilted dialogue and lyrics by today's standards, and their plots might rely a little too much on coincidence, but the emotions are deeply felt and emphatically richer than those in today's musicals. In addition, these shows don't stay within the confines of their corny stereotypes. They are loaded with modern notions, cynicism, and even self-deprecating humor—what they don't contain is irony, a singular attribute of today's modern musicals. The world of operetta is a tribute to the past, promoting a respect for audiences and an unabashed joy in the drama of kisses, swordfights, unrequited love, good versus evil, a good cry, and a good laugh. *The Desert Song* has all these elements, and it is still performed to enthusiastic audiences almost eighty years after its premiere. ✳

SONGS

ACT I "High on a Hill" · "Ho!" · "Margot" · "Why Did We Marry Soldiers?" · "French Marching Song" · "Romance" "Then You Will Know" · "I Want a Kiss" · "It" · "The Desert Song"
ACT II "My Little Castagnette" · "Song of the Brass Key" "One Good Man Gone Wrong" · "Eastern and Western Love" · "Let Love Go" · "One Flower in Your Garden" · "One Alone" · "The Saber Song" · "Farewell" · "All Hail to the General" · "Let's Have a Love Affair"

Vivienne Segal listens as Robert Halliday proclaims her the finest actress in the land—and he was right, too.

Backstage

Sheet music of songs from the show that bear its original title, *Lady Fair*, are prized as a Holy Grail to music collectors.

In the style of the day, Oscar Hammerstein II sloppily wrote the lyrics for opening numbers, reasoning that audiences were coming in late, getting settled, and not really listening. When he heard the opening number of *The Desert Song* in London, however, and the audience was on time, attentive, and listening to every bad lyric clearly enunciated and projected, Hammerstein decided that he would never again be cavalier about an opening number.

Vivienne Segal

The beautiful and talented Vivienne Segal was one of three women who had the ability, taste, and intelligence to break out of the operetta world and cross over to even greater fame in musical theatre. While Jeanette MacDonald and Irene Dunne decamped to Hollywood, Segal made her career in New York, remaining a great star of the musical theatre. She got her start on Broadway at eighteen, singing Sigmund Romberg's "Auf Wiedersehn" in 1915's *The Blue Paradise*, and her clear, round soprano and natural beauty caught critics' and audiences' eyes and ears. After appearing in the legendary production of *Miss 1917*, Segal's natural, commanding stage presence was used in Jerome Kern's early musical comedy success *Oh, Lady! Lady!* After costarring with Vernon and Irene Castle in *Castles in the Air*, she became a superstar in two of the greatest operettas, *The Desert Song* and Rudolf Friml's *The Three Musketeers* (1928). While on the West Coast filming the early movie musical *Viennese Nights*, she befriended Richard Rodgers and Lorenz Hart, who convinced her to return to New York in *I Married an Angel*. She followed that success with her greatest role, the glamorous sophisticate Vera Simpson in the controversial and groundbreaking *Pal Joey*, introducing "Bewitched, Bothered, and Bewildered." Lorenz Hart, one of her greatest admirers, wrote his last song, "To Keep My Love Alive," for her appearance in the 1943 revival of *A Connecticut Yankee*. She retired from the stage after the immensely successful 1952 revival of *Pal Joey*.

TOP LEFT: General Birabeau (Edmund Elton) listens as Azuri (Pearl Regay) explains that operetta is here to stay.

ABOVE RIGHT: Vivienne Segal is in a Spanish mood in the flop, *Music in My Heart*.

LEFT: Comic couple Benjamin and Susan (Eddie Buzzell and Nellie Breen) take a ride on a donkey.

DESTRY RIDES AGAIN

OPENED APRIL 23, 1959; IMPERIAL THEATRE; 472 PERFORMANCES

Andy Griffith, in his first gig as a small-town sheriff, gets a howdy from the Bottleneck welcoming committee, Dolores Gray, singing "I Know Your Kind."

RIGHT: George Reeder, Swen Swenson, and Mark Breaux in the number that caused all the trouble backstage at *Destry*, Michael Kidd's "Whip Dance."

DESTRY RIDES AGAIN

Produced by David Merrick

Music and Lyrics by Harold Rome
Book by Leonard Gershe
Based on the story by Max Brand
Musical Director: Lehman Engel
Vocal Arrangements by Lehman Engel
Music orchestrated by Philip J. Lang
Dance Arrangements by Genevieve Pitot

Directed and Choreographed by Michael Kidd

Production Design by Oliver Smith
Costume Design by Alvin Colt
Lighting Design by Jean Rosenthal

Synopsis

Bottleneck is one of the most corrupt, lawless towns in the Wild West. Gambling magnate Kent controls the town, and he has the sheriff killed when a nefarious land scheme is discovered by the lawman. When the town drunk, Wash, is elected sheriff, he calls upon his friend Tom Destry, the son of a legendary keeper of the peace. Destry shows up, but he's not what the community expected. He's a slow-moving, drawling country boy who doesn't even carry a gun. Kent sets the saloon entertainer Frenchy on Destry, to woo and disarm him. Destry uncovers one after another of Kent's schemes and, when the time comes, straps on his guns and confronts Kent and his gang. Frenchy saves Destry's life, and order is introduced in Bottleneck.

Cast

Frenchy	*Dolores Gray*
Destry	*Andy Griffith*
Kent	*Scott Brady*
Clara	*Rosetta LeNoire*
Mayor Slade	*Don McHenry*
Wash	*Jack Prince*
Chloe	*Libi Staiger*
Rose Lovejoy	*Elizabeth Watts*
Gyp Watson	*Marc Breaux*
Rockwell	*George Reeder*
Bugs Watson	*Swen Swenson*

IT'S A RARITY AMONG BROADWAY musicals—the Western. *Whoopee* and *Girl Crazy* preceded *Destry Rides Again*, both featuring easterners coming west to humorous effect. but *Destry* was a traditional Western with prostitutes in the local saloon. gunfights. jailbreaks. hangings. and hoosegows. It might not have had any horses. but the movie upon which it was based also took place mainly in the saloon. Michael Kidd provided his usual athletic. stylized choreography. with a hint of Martha Graham and a soupçon of Agnes de Mille thrown in for good measure.

The highlight of the choreography was the famed whip dance. in which three rugged fellows cracked bullwhips which resounded off the walls of the theatre. Dolores Gray was promised a part in the whip dance before she signed her contract. Gray didn't want to play a clichéd saloon singer and wanted a darker cast to her character. Merrick refused to put the promise in writing. but he gave Gray his solemn oath. She knew she'd have to be ready to crack the whip (literally) when the time came. so she went out and purchased one of her own. The dance was hard work—the tip of the whip actually breaks the sound barrier when it snaps—and it exhausted the actress. But she was a professional and persevered. becoming fairly efficient with the prop. When it came time for the choreography. Michael Kidd didn't want to use her in the number at all. She begged to be included in some way. She would throw the whips to the dancers. She would just crack the whip once. But it was no dice.

Relations between Gray and Kidd grew more and more tense. Their mutual loathing peaked after a performance and they blew up at each other. Kidd called Gray a slut, and she slapped the choreographer. He, in turn, slapped her.

The newspapers picked up the story, and Merrick was typically overjoyed with the free publicity. He resolutely refused to enter the fray, hoping for more fireworks and more headlines. He got his wish. A reporter from the *New York Herald-Tribune* came to the Boston tryouts and hung around backstage watching the dynamics of the situation. His patience was rewarded when Gray's mother slapped Kidd and was dragged by onlookers into her daughter's dressing room. ✿

SONGS

ACT I "Bottleneck" · "Ladies" · "Hoop-de-Dingle" · "Tomorrow Morning" · "Ballad of the Gun" · "I Know Your Kind" · "I Hate Him" · "(Rose Lovejoy of) Paradise Alley" "Anyone Would Love You" · "Once Knew a Fella" · "Every Once in a While" · "Fair Warning"
ACT II "Are You Ready, Gyp Watson?" · "Only Time Will Tell" · "Respectability" · "That Ring on the Finger" · "I Say Hello"

ABOVE: The one-man Bottleneck vice squad raids the Paradise Alley house of love and pleasure.
RIGHT: The welterweight tag team Golden Gloves champs of 1959, Mama and Dolores Gray.
LEFT: At the party celebrating his tenth anniversary as a Broadway producer, David Merrick proves to Carol Channing that you can have your cake and eat it too.
BOTTOM RIGHT: Two sides of the law: Gray and Griffith.

Backstage
David Merrick often neglected one show in favor of a bigger hit. *Destry* was the poorer cousin to *Gypsy* in the same way that *Foxy* was allowed to wither after *Dolly!* opened.

On opening night the street outside the Imperial Theatre was strewn with sawdust, and horses were tied up outside the theatre.

David Merrick
David Merrick, perhaps the most famous (or infamous) Broadway producer, was known for his cutthroat business tactics, his surly demeanor, and his sometimes outrageous publicity stunts. He scored an incredibly impressive number of hits in the 1950s and '60s: *Fanny* (for which he had a statue of a belly dancer erected in Times Square), *Jamaica*, *Destry Rides Again*, *Gypsy*, *Take Me Along* (feuding with star Jackie Gleason), *Irma La Douce*, *Do Re Mi*, *Carnival!* (feuding with star Anna Maria Alberghetti), *I Can Get It for You Wholesale*, *Oliver!*, *110 in the Shade*, *Hello, Dolly!* (feuding with just about everyone from Gower Champion to the head usher), *I Do, I Do*, and *Promises, Promises*. So particular and predictable were his tastes that advertising agencies referred to a certain color, used over and over again on his posters, as "David Merrick red." His most notorious publicity stunt was for the 1961 flop *Subways Are for Sleeping*: he found seven New Yorkers with the identical names of the major critics and printed their "reviews" of the show, instead of the poor reviews it had actually received. Additionally, he caused a furor when he closed the foundering *Breakfast at Tiffany's* in previews, telling the press that he was sparing the public an incredibly dull evening in the theatre. He was debilitated by a series of strokes in the 1980s, so other than a few last gasps in the 1990s (*Oh, Kay!*, *State Fair*), Merrick's real swan song was *42nd Street*, where, true to fashion, he topped himself once again when he announced the death of director Gower Champion to a stunned theatre at the opening night curtain call.

Dolores Gray

Dolores Gray, thrilling singer and actress who had a belt as solid as Gibraltar, more curves than the Indianapolis raceway, and features that were strangely ugly and beautiful all at once, made her debut wearing little more than a smile in the revue *Seven Lively Arts*. After a triumph in London starring in the British company of *Annie Get Your Gun*, she returned to the States to costar with Bert Lahr in the revue *Two on the Aisle*. Never one to shy away from an offstage battle, her vituperative feud with top banana Bert Lahr made all the papers. Next, opposite John Raitt in *Carnival in Flanders*, she set a still-standing record for the shortest run ever to garner a Tony Award for one of its performers (six performances). Gray then went to Hollywood, lending her inimitable style (perfect for the excesses of the Technicolor musical) to such MGM films as *Kismet* and *It's Always Fair Weather*, where her production number "Thanks a Lot (But No Thanks)" has entered the pantheon of camp heaven. Another famous feud—this time with Michael Kidd, once *Fair Weather* costar, now director and choreographer of *Destry Rides Again*—went as far as fisticuffs. Her last original role in a musical was the short-lived *Sherry!*, in which she considerably brightened the proceedings with her trademark verve. After a run in *42nd Street*, she scored one final musical triumph in England, socking out a clear, strong "I'm Still Here" in the London revival of *Follies*.

ABOVE: Scott Brady and Dolores Gray in "Are You Ready, Gyp Watson?," a prime example of Michael Kidd's knee-sliding, athletic choreography.

LEFT: A beret-clad Gray as a gun moll singing "If" in *Two on the Aisle*.

BELOW: The saloon girls and the outlaws cut loose.

DO RE MI

OPENED DECEMBER 26, 1960; ST. JAMES THEATRE; 400 PERFORMANCES

DO RE MI

Produced by David Merrick

Book by Garson Kanin
Music by Jule Styne
Lyrics by Betty Comden and Adolph Green
Musical Director: Lehman Engel
Music orchestrated by Luther Henderson
Vocal Arrangements and
Vocal Direction by Buster Davis
Dance Arrangements by David Baker

Directed by Garson Kanin
Choreographed by Marc Breaux and Deedee Wood

Scenic Design by Boris Aronson
Costume Design by Irene Sharaff
Lighting Design by Al Alloy

Synopsis

Pursuit of the American dream is the subject of *Do Re Mi*. Hubie Cram is a self-proclaimed dreamer and schemer who is always looking for that lucky break. His long-suffering wife, Kay, loves him but can't help wondering what if. Hubie's latest scheme involves a bright new singer with the name Tilda Mullen. Hubie's surprising success with her leads him into the jukebox business and into trouble with the mob. It's Hubie's fate never to succeed, and he doesn't. But Tilda falls in love with hit record producer John Henry Wheeler, and Kay and Hubie are happily married.

Cast

Kay Cram	*Nancy Walker*
Hubert Cram	*Phil Silvers*
John Henry Wheeler	*John Reardon*
Fatso O'Rear	*George Mathews*
Skin Demopoulos	*George Givot*
Brains Berman	*David Burns*
Tilda Mullen	*Nancy Dussault*

In a tour-de-force number for a pajama-clad Nancy Walker, Kay Cram assures husband Hubie (Phil Silvers) that their marriage has been an "Adventure.

JULE STYNE IS HAILED AS a great tunesmith and a particularly theatrical composer. He also receives kudos for his ability to tailor his music to suit the talents of his stars, but he's not given enough credit for his offbeat songs. While *Do Re Mi* boasts a wonderful standard, "Make Someone Happy," written in the traditional Broadway ballad form, songs such as "Waiting, Waiting," "Adventure," "Take a Job," and "All of My Life" are character-driven monologues, not merely attempts at a chart-topper. The stream-of-consciousness quality that he had explored with "Rose's Turn" in *Gypsy* was utilized here as well, with "C" and "D" sections taking the songs in more and more unexpected directions; even the bridges of these songs have bridges. Of course, these numbers were aided by the wonderful interpretive talents of Nancy Walker and Phil Silvers, not your typical trained voices, with Nancy Dussault and John Reardon handling "Fireworks" and the romantic ballads. It was up to Walker and Silvers to traverse the tricky meter shifts and acting chores of these unusual songs, unlike any other numbers in any other musical.

Do Re Mi is also one of those shows that deal with a particular New York milieu that we'll never see again. Though *The Producers* takes place in and around Broadway, it has none of the feeling of Times Square and its habitués (and sons of habitués – to quote *Finian's Rainbow*). In *Guys and Dolls*, we meet the Broadway gamblers, bookies, and bettors, and the righteous who try to help them. *Wonderful Town* (another Betty Comden and Adolph Green favorite) spends most of its time with the denizens of artsy, offbeat Greenwich Village, and their *On the Town* shows the romantic giddiness of World War II Manhattan, where "twenty-four hours can go so fast." *Do Re Mi* explores the nightclub/record/juke box business.

These days, with Times Square seeming more like a shopping mall food court, no longer do colorful characters such as *Guys and Dolls*'s Harry the Horse, General Matilda B. Cartwright, and Sky Masterson inhabit the area. Or *On the Town*'s Lucy Schmeeler and Maude P. Dilly. Or *Do Re Mi*'s Fatso O'Rear, Skin Demopoulos, and Brains Berman. ❁

Phil Silvers

Inspired clown Phil Silvers was completely at home in the world of musical comedy with his rapid-fire delivery and energetic singing. His persona was most often a variation on the shifty salesman fast-talking his way in and out of trouble, which he developed in his early career in burlesque. After a debut in 1939, playing Punko Parks in *Yokel Boy*, he scored as conman Harrison Floy in his first hit, *High Button Shoes*. Playing the monumental ego Jerry Biffle in *Top Banana*, he exemplified every tyrannical attribute of a TV variety show mega-star (read Milton Berle), driving the show to a frenzied pitch with his breathless double-talk. Although he never let his comedy mask slip too far, he showed a far more dramatic side as lovable loser Hubie Cram in *Do Re Mi*, revealing true vulnerability with a "Rose's Turn"-esque eleven o'clock number, "All of My Life." Turning down the lead in the original *A Funny Thing Happened on the Way to the Forum*, he brilliantly played Pseudolus in *Forum*'s tenth-anniversary production, at the Ahmanson in Los Angeles (costarring his old *Do Re Mi* wife, Nancy Walker). It later transferred to Broadway, where its successful run was cut short by Silvers's stroke.

ABOVE: *Do Re Mi*'s secondary couple, Nancy Dussault and John Reardon, sing the big hit from the show, "Make Someone Happy."

LEFT: The swindlers get swindled: In the Mack Sennett ballet from *High Button Shoes*, Phil Silvers and Joey Faye lose a satchel full of Dough-Re-Mi to little Sondra Lee, youngest of the Charles Addams–inspired crook family and master of the ol' switcheroo.

BELOW: Silvers and company in a scene from *Top Banana*.

"What's New at the Zoo?" was a deliberately cheesy send-up of the mindless pop hits (also spoofed in *Bye, Bye Birdie*) that were soon to push theatre music off the charts entirely.

SONGS

ACT I "Waiting, Waiting" · "All You Need Is a Quarter" "Take a Job" · "It's Legitimate" · "I Know About Love" "Cry Like the Wind" · "Ambition" · "Fireworks" · "What's New at the Zoo" · "Asking for You" · "The Late, Late Show" **ACT II** "Adventure" · "Make Someone Happy" · "Don't Be Afraid of a Teardrop" · "V.I.P." · "All of My Life"

Backstage

President Kennedy wanted to see *Do Re Mi* with only a few hours' notice. There were no seats available anywhere because a synagogue had bought out the theatre. When Jule Styne asked a woman if she would mind giving up her seat for the president elect, she replied that she would if the President asked her personally. Kennedy met her in the lobby, asked for the tickets, and she promptly fainted.

In *Bajour*, Nancy Dussault, as a budding anthropologist, searches for her own tribe through the giant birds... and the boa constrictors... and the jungle cats...and the tse-tse flies (not pictured).

Nancy Dussault

Delightful ingénue Nancy Dussault lent her quirky charm to many musicals of the 1960s. Confidently clowning alongside such pros as Phil Silvers and Nancy Walker in *Do Re Mi*, she never faded into the scenery. Equally comfortable as a pure soprano or a rangy high belter, her versatility was well captured on the *Do Re Mi* cast album: mournful in "Cry Like the Wind," kitschy in "What's New at the Zoo," and pure Jule Styne bliss in "Fireworks," her duet with the sensational baritone John Reardon. After closing the original Broadway run of *The Sound of Music* as Maria, she starred as anthropologist Emily Kirsten in the guilty pleasure *Bajour*, once again demonstrating her curious penchant for making animal noises in her songs. Her Sharon McLonergan in a 1966 City Center revival of *Finian's Rainbow* was exceedingly well received. Well cast as a situation-comedy wife, she spent much of the 1970s and '80s in California, returning to costar with Hermione Gingold, Larry Kert, and Georgia Brown in the second company of *Side by Side by Sondheim*. Her last Broadway appearance to date was as a replacement Witch in *Into the Woods*. Still singing as effortlessly as ever, she waits, along with Donna McKechnie, Anita Gillette, Pamela Myers, Susan Watson, and her great friend Karen Morrow . . . to tackle one more great musical theatre role.

DREAMGIRLS

OPENED DECEMBER 20, 1981; IMPERIAL THEATRE; 1,521 PERFORMANCES

LEFT TO RIGHT: Deena (Sheryl Lee Ralph), Effie (Jennifer Holliday), and Lorell (Loretta Devine).

Effie: "Frontways or backways, wigs ain't natural and this dress doesn't fit."

Lorrell: "You got the same wig I got?"

Effie: "Yeah."

Lorrell: "You got the same dress I got?"

Effie: "Yeah."

Lorrell: "Then shut up!"

DREAMGIRLS

Produced by Michael Bennett, Bob Avian, Geffen Records, and the Shubert Organization

Music by Henry Krieger
Book by Tom Eyen
Lyrics by Tom Eyen
Music orchestrated by Harold Wheeler
Musical Director: Yolanda Segovia
Vocal Arrangements by Cleavant Derricks

Directed by Michael Bennett
Choreographed by Michael Bennett
Co-choreographer: Michael Peters

Scenic Design by Robin Wagner
Costume Design by Theoni V. Aldredge
Lighting Design by Tharon Musser

Synopsis

What happens when a part is greater than the whole—especially in a black vocal group à la the Supremes? The Dreams consist of Deena, Lorrell, and Effie, but it's Effie who creates the conflict. Though her talent is immense, so is she. Curtis Taylor, their agent (and, initially, Effie's lover) finds them a gig as the opening act for a James Brownian soul singer, James Thunder Early, but as they rise up the Motown ladder, Curtis sees dollar signs in the beautiful, marketable Deena, and moves her to the lead role, onstage and in his affections. Soon Effie finds herself not only out of Curtis's bed but out of the group, replaced by the slimmer, prettier Michelle. After a comeback climb from the bottom, Effie finally gets a song on the charts. When Curtis tries to cover the song with the Dreams, Effie, finally believing in herself, fights back and wins. The Dreams break up while Effie's career is just taking off.

Cast

Marty	*Vondie Curtis-Hall*
Curtis Taylor Jr.	*Ben Harney*
Deena Jones	*Sheryl Lee Ralph*
Lorell Robinson	*Loretta Devine*
C. C. White	*Obba Babatundé*
Effie Melody White	*Jennifer Holliday*
James Thunder Early	*Cleavant Derricks*
Michelle Morris	*Deborah Burrell*

Nearly one quarter of the 101 shows in this book feature performers as central characters. From ballets (*On Your Toes*) to strip clubs (*The Full Monty*), from movies (*City of Angels, Kiss of the Spider Woman*) to Wild West shows (*Annie Get Your Gun*), show business has proved a natural setting for exploring the themes of success, failure, and the pursuit of happiness. Nightclubs (*Pal Joey, Guys and Dolls, Cabaret*), saloons (*Destry Rides Again, A Tree Grows in Brooklyn*), and even musicals themselves (*Babes in Arms, Follies*) have provided the backdrops—and some great excuses for musical numbers.

Running neck and neck with *Gypsy*, undoubtedly the greatest musical ever about show business, is *Dreamgirls*, Michael Bennett's masterpiece. Indeed, the musical motif "Show biz. It's just show biz" weaves its way in and out of *Dreamgirls* in the same way that Rose's "I had a dream" theme recurs in *Gypsy*. Telling the story of the rise, fall, and rise of a group of black recording artists in the 1960s and '70s gave Michael Bennett a chance to use the Motown sound he loved growing up in Buffalo and the moves he absorbed working as a young dancer on the television show *Hullabaloo*. With the help of set designer Robin Wagner, he created an abstract, whirling, gliding canvas of a playing area with four revolving towers, where he could transform the action from onstage performance scene to offstage turmoil through a quick shift in the brilliant lighting of Tharon Musser.

The opening of the show, certainly the most stunning sequence in Bennett's career, begins with four women in hot pink, skin-tight dresses. Introduced as the Stepp Sisters, they begin to sing "I'm Lookin' for Something," and the audience thinks, Ah, here are the girls whose story we're going to follow.

> "We did a first workshop and Nell [Carter] was in it. Nell decided she wanted to be a television star and went to Los Angeles."
>
> —*Henry Krieger on delaying the production of Dreamgirls for over a year to wait (in vain) for Carter*

No. The real stars of the show soon enter, scarves on their heads, suitcases in hand, late for the talent contest at New York's Apollo Theatre. (In a wonderful storytelling touch, when our three girls finally get ready to perform, they're wearing exactly the same wigs as the Stepp Sisters.) During the next fifteen minutes, we meet all the main characters of *Dreamgirls*, learn about their ambitions, see the beginning of the relationships that will ravel and unravel over the course of the upcoming two and a half hours, while all the time the show at the Apollo is continuing upstage, the contestants now playing to the back wall as we watch from backstage. After the Dreams (then the Dreamettes) lose the contest (to "Tiny" Joe Dixon, all of six feet four), they prepare to get back on the bus to Chicago. The ambitious Curtis Taylor Jr. ("your Cadillac salesman") approaches them and offers them a job singing backup for headliner James "Thunder" Early (read James Brown), whom Curtis doesn't even manage. All the time the towers are still whirling, the vantage point is constantly shifting—now to the wings, now to the stage. In lesser hands, these shifts of focus would be chaos, but in the hands of Bennett, no doubt strongly abetted by collaborators Bob Avian and Michael Peters, the audience always, always knew where to look.

Winding up this, the most smoothly delivered exposition ever, Lorrell, the lovable "Miss Adelaide" of *Dreamgirls*, declares, "Show business sure has a lot of ups and downs!" And off they go, on tour with Jimmy Early, as we watch their wardrobe improve and their steps become slicker. As the stakes get higher, our leading lady, Effie, gets first shoved to the background and finally unceremoniously dumped from the group altogether. This disintegration forms the basis of another brilliant Bennett sequence, "Heavy, Heavy," where every stage trick possible is employed, from lip-synching as the Dreams sing on television (*Hullabaloo*? No, the fictional *ABC Star Cavalcade*), only to deteriorate into a shouting match among the girls as their prerecorded vocals continue to play over them, to the fastest costume change ever, with the group marching upstage, still arguing as a curtain falls and *Bam!*—they break through the Mylar in entirely new outfits, performing in a different location. One wonders how many hours of technical rehearsals it took Bennett, Theoni Aldredge, the cast, dressers, and stage managers to get that six-second effect just right. The roar of shock from the audience as Jennifer Holliday, Sheryl Lee Ralph, and Loretta Devine burst through, completely transformed and grinning from ear to ear, singing another verse of "Heavy" (a cruel, ironic lyric, considering the girth of Effie's character, about to be ousted from the group) must have been one of those moments creators of theatre live for, when everything goes exactly right. ❋

Theoni V. Aldredge

Theoni V. Aldredge, a costume designer who never met a sequin she didn't like, reached her pinnacle with three shows of the early 1980s: *42nd Street*, in which the ladies of the "Dames" production number spilled onto the stage in a rainbow of 1932 couture; *Dreamgirls*, in which the rise of a pop group could be charted through their ever-deeper plunging necklines; and *La Cage Aux Folles*, in which the pastel pallette of the St. Tropez set was wildly offset by the spangles on her troupe of drag queens. With a career dating back to 1959's *Sweet Bird of Youth*, she designed a myriad of shows set in every era, including *Annie*, *Ballroom*, *I Remember Mama*, *Barnum*, and *The Rink*. Her most iconic work, though, was the everyday dance attire for *A Chorus Line*, where color, fabric, and even size (she deliberately designed Kelly Bishop's leotard to be too small, adding to Sheila's complex combination of confidence and vulnerability) were used to further delineate character.

TOP: Fast-talking manager Curtis (Ben Harney) explains to James "Thunder" Early (Cleavant Derricks) his idea of the American Dream: a "Cadillac Car."

ABOVE: Although "And I Am Telling You" was the most famous moment, Jennifer Holliday's "I Am Changing" featured an effect that best exemplified Michael Bennett's brilliance. With an assist from Theoni Aldredge and lighting genius Tharon Musser, Effie, now on the skids, is reborn through a midsong costume change. (Note the blue sequins on the lining of the sleeves.)

Restaged out of town, the "Party, Party" number was originally a dance centered around Effie.

Backstage

During casting of the original production, a young singer auditioned for the ensemble and, though her singing was extraordinary, her inadequate dancing skills caused Michael Bennett to reject her. Her name? Whitney Houston.

Robin Wagner

Robin Wagner, who revolutionized Broadway with his whirling spinning, gliding scenery, first turned heads with his urban designs for the musical *Promises, Promises*, his first collaboration with Michael Bennett. He was a particular favorite of director/choreographers like Bennett, Gower Champion, and Susan Stroman, helping them to create fluid, seamless transitions in shows such as *Ballroom*, *42nd Street,* and *Crazy for You*. In addition to designing many rock musicals (*Hair*, *Jesus Christ Superstar*, *Inner City*), his two masterpieces were *On the Twentieth Century*, where he literally made an art deco train careen toward the audience, and *Dreamgirls*, in which his spinning towers became a giant game board for the brilliant staging of Bennett. Despite an artistic dry spell after *Crazy for You*, he has contributed fine work of late, with the revival of *Kiss Me, Kate* and the underrated, moody ballroom unit set for *The Wild Party*. His award-winning design for *The Producers* was a cannily constructed Broadway cliché, spoofing himself and totally in tune with that show's winking tone.

TOP: One could immediately tell which rung of the music industry ladder the Dreams (here in their piñata period) were on through Theoni Aldredge's sensational costumes.
ABOVE: In "Hard to Say Goodbye, My Love," the Dreams make their final appearance.

CAST ALBUMS

Cast album giant Goddard Lieberson confers with Julie Andrews during the *Camelot* recording session.

THE INVENTION OF THE PHONOGRAPH coincided with the early development of the musical, and these two would share an intimate history from cylinders to CDs. The first original cast performances captured for posterity were the 1890 recordings (on cylinder) of "You Can Always Explain Things Away" from *Castles in the Air*, sung by DeWolf Hopper, and "The Commodore Song" from *Ship Ahoy*, sung by Edward M. Favor.

As Broadway songs became more and more successful, popular singers and bands recorded hits from the shows, and sometimes, as in the case of Al Jolson, stars would record their numbers in a pop fashion without the Broadway orchestrations. In the 1910s, British casts were regularly recording the major numbers from their shows, and by the 1920s, Victor began issuing a series of studio cast recordings of famous scores under the banner of the Victor Light Opera Company. These long medleys sometimes constitute the only recordings of these early shows.

Victor recorded the Astaires and composer Arthur Schwartz on a series of recordings backed by Leo Resiman and his orch estra. Victor utilized the recently invented 33 1/3 recording speed for this issue but it didn't catch on with the public. By the '30s, 78 rpm albums were regularly issued with members of the original casts. In 1938 a set of songs recorded by original cast members of Marc Blitzstein's *The Cradle Will Rock* was issued on the Musicraft Records label. It was such a success that Blitzstein's next show, *No for an Answer* (1941), was recorded, again with the composer at the piano.

The 1940s saw the emergence of Decca Records as the leader in the cast album field. In 1942 Decca released a set of eight songs from the Irving Berlin

Stephen Douglass, Gwen Verdon, and Ray Walston commit *Damn Yankees* to wax.

revue *This Is the Army*, featuring its all-soldier cast, and following their release of the hugely successful original cast recording of *Oklahoma!*, most important shows received some form of cast recording. Jack Kapp, president of Decca, recorded other notable shows, including *Carousel* and *Porgy and Bess*. Columbia Records didn't jump on the bandwagon until 1946, with their release of the historic revival of *Show Boat*, and newly formed Capitol Records, founded by lyricist Johnny Mercer, issued his and Harold Arlen's score for *St. Louis Woman* that same year. RCA finally caught up in 1947, with the original cast recording of *Brigadoon*. By the 1950s, the cast album was such an important part of a company's bottom line that rights for recordings went for then exorbitant fees; in fact, Under the leadership of the great Goddard Lieberson, Columbia underwrote the entire production cost of *My Fair Lady*, recouping their investment many times over. Lieberson, urbane, witty, and a little snobby, brought the original cast recording to new heights, recording studio cast versions of early shows that did not have cast recordings, and preserving several flops like *Candide*, *Anyone Can Whistle*, and Frank Loesser's entire score for *The Most Happy Fella*.

Show music was so much a part of mainstream music at the time that pop stars regularly covered Broadway scores, as did instrumentalists like Percy Faith and Andre Kostelanetz. During the late 1950s and early '60s, the heyday of the cast recording saw the development of talented producers who specialized in original cast albums: masters of the form, including Andy Wiswell, David Kapp, George Marek, Hugo and Luigi, Dick Jones, Michael Berniker, Thomas Z. Shepherd, and Jay David Saks.

Changes in popular taste marked the end of the heyday of the original cast recording. Once rock was firmly established as the premiere money maker for the labels, expensive Broadway cast recordings were dropped. With the exception of megahits like *Hello, Dolly!*, *The Fantasticks*, or *Rent*, or anything written by Andrew Lloyd Webber or Stephen Sondheim, most cast albums never recoup their investment. The emergence of the compact disc gave a fresh life to original cast recordings, and most were reissued, even as new ones went unrecorded. With the majors disinterested, a number of smaller labels popped up to record shows, including TER Records, Varese Sarabande, Fynsworth Alley, Harbinger Records, and Original Cast Records. As the number and quality of Broadway musicals declined, older shows were given elaborate, complete studio cast recordings to take advantage of the greater playing time of CDs.

Carol Channing, backed up by the other *Hello, Dolly!* principals, belts her boots off.

DU BARRY WAS A LADY

OPENED DECEMBER 6, 1939; 46TH STREET THEATRE; 408 PERFORMANCES

Let them eat cheesecake: Ethel Merman and Bert Lahr find themselves trapped in a French Revolution dream.

DU BARRY WAS A LADY

Produced by B. G. De Sylva

Music by Cole Porter
Lyrics by Cole Porter
Book by Herbert Fields and B. G. De Sylva
Orchestra Arrangements by Hans Spialek
Additional Arrangements by
Russell Bennett and Ted Royal
Choral Arrangments by Hugh Martin
Assistant to Hugh Martin: Ralph Blane

Staged by Edgar McGregor
Choreographed by Robert Alton

Scenic Design by Raoul Pène Du Bois
Costume Design by Raoul Pène Du Bois
Lighting Design by Albert A. Ostrander

Synopsis

A washroom attendant at the Club Petite, Louis Blore is infatuated with the the club's sexy singer, May Daly. Blore is ecstatic when he wins $75,000 in the Irish Sweepstakes, thinking it will help him win the heart of May, but he accidentally drinks the "Mickey Finn" that he had planned to give to May's boyfriend. Louis passes out, dreaming that he is King Louis XV of France and that May is Madame Du Barry.

Cast

Louis Blore .... *Bert Lahr*
May Daly .... *Ethel Merman*
Alice Barton .... *Betty Grable*
Charley .... *Benny Baker*
Alex Barton .... *Ronald Graham*
Harry Norton .... *Charles Walters*

> "Cole Porter was a horrible piano player. Oompah, oompah. He played with a slow, wooden tempo. If you didn't know who it was, you'd have thought he was a learner." —*Bert Lahr*

SONGS

ACT I "Where's Louie?" · "Ev'ry Day's a Holiday" · "It Ain't Etiquette" · "When Love Beckoned" · "Come On In" "Dream Song" · "Mesdames and Messieurs" · "Gavotte" "But in the Morning, No!" · "Do I Love You" · "Du Barry Was a Lady"
ACT II "Give Him the Oo-La-La" · "Well, Did You Evah!" "It Was Written in the Stars" · "L'Après Midi d'un Boêuf" "Katie Went to Haiti" · "Friendship"

"WAIT!" WE HEAR YOU EXCLAIMING. "What in the name of Belle Poitrine is *Du Barry Was a Lady* doing in this damn book?!"—well, we'll tell you. There's nothing wrong with good old-fashioned musical comedy. Man cannot live by *Street Scene* alone. Picture this: You are on a desert island and you can choose one (and only one) Stephen Sondheim show to see every single night, with matinees on Wednesdays and Saturdays. Would you pick *Passion*? Remember, we're talking eight shows a week here. How about *Sweeney Todd*? Nope. *Pacific Overtures*? Nah, too emotionally unsatisfying. *Company*? Want to spend all that time with those angst-filled neurotics? *A Little Night Music*? Beautiful, but maybe a bit too ephemeral. *A Funny Thing Happened on the Way to the Forum*? That's it! You could use a good laugh and a sweet little love story and a great book and score. You'd never get tired of that.

Well, that's our point. One reason the late 1980s and '90s were so dreary was all those dark, self-important, dark, overwrought, dark, well, downers, frankly. You know: *Miss Saigon*, *Thou Shalt Not*, *Marie Christine*, *Jane Eyre*, *Parade*, *Jelly's Last Jam*, *The Civil War*. As a friend of ours says, "Turgid." Add in all the pop junk shows, like *Aida*, *Jekyll and Hyde*, and today's hit—*Wicked*.

Speaking of today, thankfully the tide has turned and musical comedy is coming back to the fore. We've got *The Producers*, *Hairspray*, and *Avenue Q* bringing lighthearted laughter back to the Great White Way. And the revival of *42nd Street* is still giving the rubes their money's worth down on Forty-second Street. So, maybe the future isn't so bleak (and we mean that literally—all those black sets). In times of recession, war, terrorism, and general uncertainty, isn't it great to lose yourself for a few hours in the company of Max Bialystock, Edna Turnblad, or Trekkie Monster… , and … sorry, back to *Du Barry*.

Du Barry Was a Lady was a resolutely risqué, naughty, almost dirty show, and it starred one of the greatest clowns of Broadway, Bert Lahr. Broadway's greatest female star, Ethel Merman, was up there with him, clowning around and belting out such great Cole Porter songs as "Friendship," a funny, silly, tuneful song for a funny, silly, tuneful show. What we'd give for one of them right now. Critic John Mason Brown, in the *New York Post*, exclaimed, "She needs no vitamins; she has plenty to spare. Her throat houses as beguiling a calliope as Broadway knows. The Midas touch is upon her tonsils because she can turn brass into gold. She can do more than that. She can keep it brass. No one can match her in putting a song across, in trumpeting its lyrics, in personifying its rhythms. All the bright lights of Broadway seem to shine behind her face. Hard-boiled she frankly is, but she makes toughness itself an irresistible virtue. She possesses not only great energy, but a kind of shimmering dignity, too; a dignity born of her poise, her skill, her honesty and her magnificent professionalism." Honestly, wouldn't you plunk down your hard-earned bucks to see that today? ❊

Bert Lahr

Bert Lahr, a classic clown who would go to inhuman lengths for the approval of his audience, was a perfect type for the burlesque-flavored musicals and revues of the 1930s and '40s. Like most brilliant comedians, he had a deep vulnerability and a morose quality that offset his buffoonery, along with a vibrato like a flooded automobile engine. His shows are not household names today: *Hold Everything*, *Flying High*, *Hot-Cha!*, and *Life Begins at 8:40*, but in their time, they elevated him to top of the musical comedy field. After laying them in the aisles in *Du Barry Was a Lady*, he next returned to the musical stage in the revues *Seven Lively Arts* (costarring with another utterly brilliant, utterly unique clown, Bea Lillie) and *Two on the Aisle*, costarring (and feuding) with Dolores Gray. Besides a short run in *The Boys Against the Girls* and nonmusical roles in shows ranging from S. J. Perelman's *The Beauty Part* to *Waiting for Godot*, his only other musical was in 1964's *Foxy*, which played its tryout in the most remote of locales: Dawson City, Alaska. Eternally remembered as the Cowardly Lion, Lahr wore many other masks during his illustrious career: always hysterically funny, with acute pain just under the crust.

ABOVE: Lahr's lengths to go for a laugh knew no boundaries; in *Foxy*, he went so far as to climb the proscenium arch to get away from bloomer girl Julienne Marie.

BELOW: All smiles for the camera, archenemies Bert Lahr and Dolores Gray in the revue *Two on the Aisle*.

Backstage

Herbert Fields planned to write a musical featuring Mae West as Madame Du Barry. B. G. De Sylva wanted to write a musical about a washroom attendant in love with a society gal. They got together and merged their two plots—voilà, *Du Barry Was a Lady*.

Bert Lahr examines the million-dollar ankle of Betty Grable.

EVITA

OPENED SEPTEMBER 25, 1979; BROADWAY THEATRE; 1,567 PERFORMANCES

Don't mess with her, fellas: Patti LuPone, as Santa Evita Peron, achieves a "Rainbow High."

EVITA

Produced by Robert Stigwood
Produced in association with David Land

Music by Andrew Lloyd Webber
Book and Lyrics by Tim Rice
Musical Director: Rene Wiegert
Music orchestrated by
Andrew Lloyd Webber and Hershy Kay

Directed by Harold Prince
Choreographed by Larry Fuller

Scenic Design by
Timothy O'Brien and Tazeena Firth
Costume Design by
Timothy O'Brien and Tazeena Firth
Lighting Design by David Hersey

Synopsis

Celebrity takes many forms and can come from the most unlikely sources. The teenage Eva Duarte sees performer Augustin Magaldi as her ticket out of the slums and into the big city of Buenos Aires, only the beginning of her plans for greatness. Unceremoniously dumping the singer, she becomes a second-rate actress. She develops contacts and finds, in the small-time politician Juan Peron, exactly the moldable man who can lead her to her dreams. She makes short work of Peron's sixteen-year-old girlfriend and pushes her lover up the political ladder to the presidency of Argentina. It's still not enough, for Eva doesn't want to be just a faceless first lady. She invents an image of herself in the public's mind, promising good while delivering only evil, nevertheless establishing herself as a saint to the masses. Still hungry for the heroin-like effect of power, she goes even further, naming herself vice president. Faced with suspicion and rising political opposition, she undertakes her greatest sacrifice: She dies, achieving immortal fame. And the Argentineans cry for her.

Cast

Eva	*Patti LuPone*
Che	*Mandy Patinkin*
Peron	*Bob Gunton*
Magaldi	*Mark Syers*
Peron's Mistress	*Jane Ohringer*

Evita GREW OUT OF AN idea that was exploited quite successfully by Andrew Lloyd Webber and Tim Rice—the concept album. The team had previously produced a concept album titled *Jesus Christ Superstar*, which led to a stage mounting, but the idea didn't originate with Lloyd Webber and Rice. In the late 1950s, there was an album titled *Clara* that featured Betty Garrett, adapted for Broadway in 1960 under the title *Beg, Borrow and Steal*. There was also a musical version of *Tom Jones* issued on LP, but it was never produced.

The albums of both *Superstar* and *Evita* were smash hits on their own, and when the shows were produced, audiences entered the theatre humming the scores. "Don't Cry for Me, Argentina" became a pop hit on the British charts, and popular singer Barbara Dickson covered "Another Suitcase in Another Hall" to great success.

Producer Robert Stigwood had the good sense to hire Hal Prince, a master of the concept musical, to direct *Evita*. The show, barely more than a string of songs with hardly a libretto, cried out for Prince's talent for creating dramatic stage pictures and his instinctual recognition of the important beats in the action. It is no accident that fans of *Evita* remember favorite scenes as if they were snapshots in the brain—Eva standing with hands raised on the balcony, the musical rocking chairs of "The Art of the Possible," the dramatic chiaroscuro of "New Argentina," and Che's bitter mockery of the masses mourning Evita's death.

Prince and his designers employed film; harsh, shadow-filled lighting; multilayer scaffolding; and cinematic staging, with the use of the various social strata of Argentina as characters in their own right. *Evita* was a mesmerizing, unforgiving illustration of a human being's increasing hunger for adoration and power, and even though history books excoriate Santa Evita, we, as an audience, are nonetheless drawn to her single-mindedness. Che tries to warn us of her evil, but we can only sense her charisma. Hal Prince's canny use of theatrical magic turns the audience into the masses, who know the evil within but choose to bask in the flair and theatricality of the moment. "Oh What a Circus" indeed. ❋

> "Andrew, the scores which are arriving are totally and utterly unplayable."
>
> —*Musical director Anthony Bowles on Lloyd Webber's early drafts*

Patti LuPone with Topol in *The Baker's Wife* (sometime after LuPone replaced Carole Demas and before Paul Sorvino replaced Topol ... ah, the vagaries of the pre-Broadway tour!).

SONGS

ACT I "A Cinema in Buenos Aires; July 26, 1952" "Requiem for Evita" · "Oh What a Circus" · "On This Night of a Thousand Stars" · "Eva Beware of the City" "Buenos Aires" · "Good Night and Thank You" · "The Art of the Possible" · "Charity Concert" · "I'd Be Surprisingly Good for You" · "Another Suitcase in Another Hall" "Peron's Latest Flame" · "A New Argentina"
ACT II "On the Balcony of the Casa Rosada" · "Don't Cry for Me Argentina" · "High Flying Adored" · "Rainbow High" "Rainbow Tour" · "The Actress Hasn't Learned (the Lines You'd Like to Hear)" · "And the Money Kept Rollin' In (and Out)" · "Santa Evita" · "Waltz for Eva and Che" "She Is a Diamond" · "Dice Are Rolling" · "Eva's Final Broadcast" "Lament"

Patti LuPone

Patti LuPone, who achieved stardom with a singing voice that combined stunning range and strength with sometimes questionable diction, started her career as a dramatic actress, performing with John Houseman's Acting Company. After the out-of-town closing of *The Baker's Wife* and the quick closing *Working*, she rocketed to the top with her performance as Eva Peron in Hal Prince's *Evita*. After a 1984 revival of *Oliver!*, she appeared in London at the Royal Shakespeare Company, as Fantine in the original London production of *Les Misérables*, returning to the States for the Lincoln Center revival of *Anything Goes*. After a hiatus from the stage, during which she starred on television's *Life Goes On*, she was tapped to reunite with Andrew Lloyd Webber and Trevor Nunn for the London production of *Sunset Boulevard*. Contracted to move to Broadway with the show, she was unceremoniously dumped after a mixed review from the *New York Times* critic. She sued for (and won) a large, undisclosed sum for her pain and suffering, coming out unscathed in the eyes of her adoring American fans. Perhaps soured by that experience, she has opted for the hit-and-run approach of late, starring in concert versions of *Sweeney Todd*, *Passion*, *A Little Night Music*, and *Can-Can*, always to through-the-roof raves.

RIGHT: Patti LuPone as Nancy in the 1984 Broadway revival of *Oliver!*

FANNY

OPENED NOVEMBER 4, 1954; MAJESTIC THEATRE; 888 PERFORMANCES

ABOVE: Florence Henderson and William Tabbert as Fanny and Marius, the epitome of tortured young love.

RIGHT: Ezio Pinza (right), basso profundo, and Walter Slezak, comedian profundo, as César and Panisse.

FANNY
Produced by David Merrick and Joshua Logan
Book by S. N. Behrman and Joshua Logan
Music and Lyrics by Harold Rome
Based on the films *Marius*, *Fanny*, and *César*
by Marcel Pagnol
Musical Director: Lehman Engel
Vocal arrangements by Lehman Engel
Music orchestrated by Philip J. Lang
Musical continuity by Trude Rittman

Directed by Joshua Logan
Choreographed by Helen Tamiris

Scenic Design by Jo Mielziner
Lighting Design by Jo Mielziner
Costume Design by Alvin Colt

Synopsis

César, a café owner, and his best friend Panisse, a merchant of maritime goods, watch Fanny, a waitress, and Marius, César's son, grow into adulthood. Fanny is admired by both the seafaring wanderer Marius and his widowed father, Panisse. Marius sleeps with Fanny on the eve of sailing off to sea, and soon Fanny finds herself pregnant. Her virtue is saved by Panisse, who agrees to marry her and call the son his own. When Marius returns from his voyage, he demands Fanny and his son return to him, but César convinces Marius that he has no rights given his past actions. Besides, Panisse has become a doting husband and father. Years later, Panisse dies, and César writes Marius to return to his family.

Cast

Marius	*William Tabbert*
Fanny	*Florence Henderson*
Panisse	*Walter Slezak*
The Admiral	*Gerald Price*
César	*Ezio Pinza*
Honorine	*Edna Preston*
Césario	*Lloyd Reese*
Escartifique	*Alan Carney*

DAVID MERRICK MADE HIS MUSICAL comedy producing debut with *Fanny*, directed and co-authored by Joshua Logan. Because it was a delicate and unique piece, Logan's choice of Harold Rome to musicalize Marcel Pagnol's film trilogy was surprising, for up to this point in his career, Rome had specialized in giving voice to the feelings of the American middle class. Here was an epic story that was decidedly French in both tone and feeling. Luckily, Rome was more than up to the challenge.

As is often the story in the theatre, *Fanny* had to undergo various trials before it would open on Broadway, and it's a great tribute to David Merrick's tenacity that the show ever opened at all. Merrick had only produced three plays up to this point and none were hits; indeed, he was still a relative unknown on Broadway. When Merrick initially sent Marcel Pagnol a series of missives asking him for the rights to his trilogy, they were all ignored. Undeterred, Merrick hopped a plane and knocked on Pagnol's door, and the surprised playwright invited Merrick in and soon agreed to let his works become the basis for an American musical.

With the rights finally sewn up, Merrick had only to find an artistic staff. He first hired playwrights Albert Hackett and Frances Goodrich, who wanted to reset the piece in New England, but after three unproductive years with the Hacketts, Merrick decided on Joshua Logan, who agreed to undertake the writing and direction if he could also have co-producer credit. Logan, in turn, brought in sophisticated playwright S. N. Behrman as a collaborator on the libretto. Having teamed fairly happily with Rodgers and Hammerstein on *South Pacific*, Logan also immediately offered the task of the score to the famous team. They were very interested but, as they insisted with all their shows, they also wanted to produce. Their lawyers drew up an agreement which read: "Rodgers and Hammerstein present *Fanny*," with Merrick's name nowhere to be seen. As this was his first venture into presenting musical comedy, Merrick was more than willing to take second billing to the masters; indeed, he only wanted a line below the title to read, "In association with David Merrick." But Rodgers and Hammerstein, not the most amenable of businessmen, refused, and Merrick decided to go it alone. (Given Merrick's temperament, it's difficult to see him collaborating with anyone, but, as the good lawyer he was, he realized the benefits of such a partnership.) Logan claims in his autobiography that for the rest of his life, Hammerstein regretted not writing *Fanny*.

At the time, Logan was working with Rome on the Catskills musical comedy, *Wish You Were Here*, and the writer/director admired Rome's skill in composing deceivingly simple songs that expressed very deep emotions—exactly what was required for the characters in *Fanny*. Merrick wanted Alan Jay Lerner and Burton Lane, who were then under contract to MGM. Lane worked out a release from the Hollywood contract, so in love was he with *Fanny*, but Logan refused to work with anyone with whom he had not already collaborated, insuring that Rome would be hired.

Rome's score is extremely unusual, difficult to grasp on first hearing, but its richness is all the more surprising given its apparent simplicity. It is probably unsurpassed in the American theatre. To be sure, there is the soaring title song, which became a standard, but the score also contains many unique, almost obtuse songs, like "The Octopus Song," unlike any other written for a Broadway show. Here is a score that is unconcerned with selling itself to the audience, in screaming its importance across the footlights. "Be Kind to Your Parents," "To My Wife," "Never Too Late for Love," and "Love Is a Very Light Thing" are sweet, effortless, yet deeply felt tributes to the basic humanity of the show's characters. By understating its themes, both musically and lyrically, Rome's tender, meaningful score becomes all the more profound. A note must also be made of Philip J. Lang's unobtrusive, supportive orchestrations, for both Rome and Lang eschewed the typical Broadway idea of a French setting. No accordions, no Piaf-like wails, no sexy roués or boulevardiers. The honesty of *Fanny* in writing, performance, and production probably threw some critics in 1954, who gave it only kind reviews. In retrospect, it has turned out to be one of the hallmarks of the American musical theatre, awaiting a major revival. ❦

Florence Henderson

Known to whole generations as Mrs. Brady, Florence Henderson had a whole other career as a successful Broadway star in the 1950s and ´60s. After an early break in the ensemble of *Wish You Were Here* (where she befriended fellow up-and-comer Phyllis Newman—they banded together since the rest of the chorines ignored them, and worse), she went on tour for a year as Laurey in the national company of *Oklahoma!* While out on the road, she auditioned for *Wish You Were Here* director Josh Logan, then casting the ingenue lead of his upcoming musical *Fanny*. Only twenty and sharing the stage with such heavyweights as Ezio Pinza and Walter Slezak, Henderson captivated audiences and critics with her simple, Indiana-bred innocence and a vibrant soprano of near-operatic proportions. Inexhaustible, she spent the remainder of the decade starting a family and was a constant presence on television, appearing on variety shows, often with fellow Rodgers and Hammerstein stalwart Bill Hayes, and as the first female co-host of *The Today Show*. The 1960s brought a reunion with her guardian angel Richard Rodgers (he so respected her that she was one of the few females in his employ that he never made a pass at), playing Maria in the national tour of *The Sound of Music*. Had her next Broadway vehicle, *The Girl Who Came to Supper*, been a hit, perhaps we would have never lost her to an extended stay in La-La Land. Co-starring Jose Ferrer, an actor at the bottom of everyone's list to play a handsome, dashing prince in a musical, its failure wasn't remotely her fault, for Henderson mined everything there was to be had out of Noël Coward's score, and knocked her showstopping, seven-minute encapsulation of an entire Broadway operetta (*The Coconut Girl*), clear out of the park. But after a well-received *South Pacific* at Lincoln Center, Henderson became the mother of "three very lovely girls" and, in spite of rumors that she'd replace Liv Ullman in Rodgers's final musical *I Remember Mama*, Henderson has never returned to the New York stage.

ABOVE: Walter Slezak, thrilled he will have a son to carry on his name, changes the sign outside his sail shop: Now it will be called "Panisse and Son."

RIGHT: Even barefoot and wrapped in a sheet, Florence Henderson had Wessonality singing "Here and Now" in *The Girl Who Came to Supper*.

Backstage

When *Variety* was unable to get grosses from Merrick, he wrote the paper, "Whenever the average high temperature for the preceding week is 63 degrees or less, the gross for *Fanny* is $63,000. Thereafter the gross recedes in inverse ratio to the rise in the average high temperature for the week."

When Florence Henderson left the cast, Merrick cast his current girlfriend in the role.

Harold Rome

Harold Rome's output may not match that of his contemporaries in quantity, but the quality and success of his shows put him near the top of the list of major Broadway songwriters. He contributed both words and music to a variety of shows, spanning a wide range—from the Old West of *Destry Rides Again* to the New York garment district of *I Can Get It for You Wholesale* to the Old South of *Gone with the Wind*. Like many other songwriters, Rome studied law, but the stock market crash forever changed his fortunes (or previous lack thereof). His big break came in 1937, when Rome was hired by the International Ladies' Garment Workers Union to write songs for a topical revue, *Pins and Needles*, to be performed entirely by members of the union. Intended as a limited run of a few weeks, it was so successful that the show was extended and ran over 1,000 performances, a remarkable achievement and a testament to Rome's developing talents. An ardent liberal, Rome continued in a topical, satirical vein with his next shows, *Sing Out the News* (1938), which contained the hit song "Franklin D. Roosevelt Jones," and *Call Me Mister* (1946) with the hit "South America, Take It Away." The high-spirited, loveable *Wish You Were Here* (1952) followed, with its romantic title song and its renowned onstage swimming pool. *Fanny* was a resounding hit, and Rome's good fortune continued with the rare musical oater, *Destry Rides Again*, in 1959. Less successful commercially was *I Can Get It for You Wholesale*, which introduced Barbra Streisand not only to the world at large but to co-star Elliott Gould, who married her. In a career that exemplified diversity of subject matter, Rome's final Broadway production was perhaps his most diverse, 1965's *The Zulu and the Zayda*, and while it only ran 179 performances, the score was Rome at his best. Commissioned to write a musical version of *Gone with the Wind* for a Japanese theatre, the result, *Scarlett*, soon found its way to a spectacular production in London as *Gone with the Wind*, and a pre-Broadway tour that never came into New York. One of the premier collectors of African art, Rome was a true mensch, loved by all who knew and worked with him.

> "My boy, it's a great song. But we open in four weeks."
>
> —*Ezio Pinza to Harold Rome,* explaining why he wouldn't learn a new number

TOP: On his deathbed, Panisse (Walter Slezak) is comforted by César (Ezio Pinza), Honorine (Edna Preston), and the Admiral (Gerald Price).

RIGHT: Little known fact: The delightful singer/dancer Sheila Bond auditioned for director Joshua Logan six times for the role of Fay Fromkin in *Wish You Were Here*. John Perkins, who played the role of "Muscles" Green, only had to take his shirt off to be cast.

OFF BROADWAY, PART I

Way back in the 1950s a phenomenon was born—Off Broadway. A reaction to the perceived commercialism of Broadway and an outlet for a new generation of poets, playwrights, actors, songwriters, and designers, Off Broadway celebrated the small. It was truly a world of la bohème, artists who eschewed fame and money for their art. And this fertile breeding ground, away from the pressures of commercial production and critical brickbats, helped give a leg up to hundreds of future Broadway greats. The first great Off Broadway musical was the 1954 revival of the Brecht/Weill *Threepenny Opera* and from then on producers saw money in Of Broadway. Among the great shows that achieved fame downtown were Jerry Herman's revues, *I Feel Wonderful* and *Parade*; Rick Besoyan's charming spoof, *Little Mary Sunshine*; the all-time greatest Off Broadway musical, *The Fantasticks*; Mary Rodgers and Marshall Barer's *The Mad Show*; and Clark Gesner's *You're a Good Man, Charlie Brown*. The granddaddy of all composer compilation revues, *Jacques Brel Is Alive and Well and Living in Paris*, spawned a rash of imitators, most of which failed. Joseph Papp's Public Theatre presented one of the most radical musicals of all time, *Hair*, while on a much frothier note, Bernadette Peters got her start with the spoof *Curly McDimple*, and followed it up with another spoof, the immensely popular *Dames at Sea*. Another smash hit was *Your Own Thing*, a pop musical retelling of *Twelfth Night*. Many of these shows were great hits but two shows would soon open that would change the tenor of Off-Broadway forever.

TOP: Never to be matched, the original Seymour and Audrey of the long-running *Little Shop of Horrors*, Lee Wilkof and Ellen Greene.

CENTER: Gary Burghoff, Reva Rose, Karen Johnson, Bob Balaban, and brothers Skip and Bill Hinnant are comic strip characters sprung-to-life in Clark Gesner's *You're a Good Man, Charlie Brown*.

RIGHT: Dody Goodman and Charles Nelson Reilly enjoy a "Jolly Theatrical Season" in Jerry Herman's revue *Parade*.

FAR RIGHT: David Campbell and Lauren Ward perform in the belated (by forty-five years) New York premiere of Stephen Sondheim's first musical written for Broadway, *Saturday Night*.

FIDDLER ON THE ROOF

OPENED SEPTEMBER 22, 1964; IMPERIAL THEATRE; 3,242 PERFORMANCES

FIDDLER ON THE ROOF
Produced by Harold Prince
Book by Joseph Stein
Music by Jerry Bock
Lyrics by Sheldon Harnick
Based on Stories by Sholom Aleichem
Music orchestrated by Don Walker
Musical Director: Milton Greene
Vocal arrangements by Milton Greene
Dance arrangements by Betty Walberg

Directed by Jerome Robbins
Choreographed by Jerome Robbins

Scenic Design by Boris Aronson
Costume Design by Patricia Zipprodt
Lighting Design by Jean Rosenthal

Zero Mostel in his greatest role, as Tevye the milkman.

Synopsis

Tevye is the poor dairyman of Anatevka, a shtetl in czarist Russia. He and his wife, Golde, have five daughters, and they live their lives according to their traditions. Those traditions are questioned when the oldest daughter, Tzeitel, wants to marry a poor tailor whom she loves, rather than the elderly butcher, Lazar Wolf, to whom she was promised in marriage by Tevye. Tevye's faith is tested again when his second daughter, Hodel, marries a young revolutionary who is arrested and sent to Siberia. The ultimate challenge comes when Tevye's third daughter, Chava, wants to marry a young, handsome Russian boy who is not Jewish. This Tevye cannot condone. Soon the citizens of Anatevka are commanded to leave their homes. Resigned to their fate, Tevye, Golde, and their two remaining daughters set off with their friends for a new life far from the home they love.

Cast

Tevye	Zero Mostel
Golde	Maria Karnilova
Tzeitel	Joanna Merlin
Hodel	Julia Migenes
Chava	Tanya Everett
Yente	Beatrice Arthur
Motel	Austin Pendleton
Perchik	Bert Convy
Lazar Wolf	Michael Granger
Rabbi	Gluck Sandor

AT THIS WRITING, A NEW production of *Fiddler on the Roof* has opened to decidedly mixed reviews. This revival boasts a "reimagining," what is now known as a "revisal." Now, we're not asking for slavish re-creation of the original production (that would be impossible), and while we can't imagine any staging better than Jerome Robbins's original work, it would be fine with us if another young, talented director/choreographer gave it a shot. Trouble is, there don't seem to be any young director/choreographers who have proven themselves as gifted as Robbins. If you can't improve it, why change it?

The producers of this new *Fiddler* were obviously inspired by the immensely successful revival of *Chicago* and revisal of *Cabaret*. To be sure, these productions caught the public's imaginations. But the old fogies who saw the originals know that something palpable was missing in the remountings. *Chicago* substituted Victoria's Secret titillation and dramaturgic shorthand for the rich, imaginative, vaudeville concept of the original production. Without any sets or costumes to speak of, and with the orchestra on stage level, this revival of *Chicago*, successful though it is, isn't really, truly a Broadway show.

This certainly isn't a new phenomenon, for as the eminent critic George Jean Nathan wrote in the *New York Journal-American* on Sunday, May 25, 1952: "Operating under the delusion, increasingly noticeable among our producers, that if theatergoers loved a show when they first saw it they will not love it any longer unless all sorts of alterations are made in it, the present sponsors

"You don't give awards to the show. You give the awards to *me*!"

—*Zero Mostel, on hearing that* Fiddler *received the Critics Circle Award*

monkeyed the revival out of any public acceptance and right into the can…. In their zeal to bring shows up-to-date the producers succeed not only in diminishing their original values but in making them even more out-of-date…. Thus, the squirting of Stassen gags, Truman sports shirts and the like into *Of Thee I Sing*, far from acceptably modernizing it, only makes an audience doubly conscious of its age, as artificially colored hair and face enamel accentuate a woman's. And thus, when about a half dozen years ago its producer sought to liven up *The Merry Widow* by inserting a banana-eating comedian, not only did he murder the excellent operetta's chances on the spot but caused the people seeing and hearing it for the first time seriously to doubt whether it had ever been what earlier audiences properly appreciated it was."

And it's not only the monkeying with the tone, it's the overhauling of the scripts, muddying the intent of the original book to the point where something that would have seemed nostalgic or slightly creaky is now nonsensical. Would a modern-day producer get away with rewriting *Death of a Salesman* or *The Glass Menagerie*? Why are musicals less sacrosanct? One current writer complained that the original, still-living authors of a classic musical (on most people's ten-best lists) balked at his making too many changes to the book. One would assume that if a theatre company wanted to rework one of his plays, he'd hit the roof. Isn't it hubris to think that a playwright with one or two successful Off-Broadway plays knows better than George Abbott, Joseph Fields, or Jerome Chodorov—all with many successes and decades in the theatre on their résumés? Why is it generally assumed that *Pal Joey*, *Finian's Rainbow*, or *The Boys from Syracuse* need rewrites, and what exactly was wrong with the original books? The 1982 revival of *Little Me*, one of the funniest books ever, reimagined the tour-de-force role originally played by Sid Caesar into a split between two actors, James Coco and Victor Garber (both wonderful actors, by the way). Why?

The problem, it seems to us, is that producers, estates, and writers don't trust the material. If you don't trust it, why produce the show in the first place? The creators of the original *Fiddler*, Joseph Stein, Jerry Bock, and Sheldon Harnick, all under the brilliantly watchful eye of Jerome Robbins, never lost faith or confidence in the raw materials with which they were presented.

During rehearsals, once the theme of the show—"tradition"—was established, Robbins was adamant that every moment exemplify or illuminate that theme. He wanted a show with no extraneous material. Stein, Bock, and Harnick managed to give Robbins what he wanted while keeping a wonderful sense of character and warmth to the proceedings. *Fiddler* is a show that was as much a conceptual show as Sondheim's *Company* or *Follies* but utilized a more traditional structure. And that is why many people feel that *Fiddler* is the greatest musical of all time. ❀

ABOVE: The Sabbath dinner, with guest Bert Convy and the family: Zero Mostel, Maria Karnilova, and daughters Joanna Merlin (later the casting director of the Prince/Sondheim shows), Julia Migenes (later an opera diva), Tanya Everett, Marilyn Rogers, and Linda Ross.
BELOW: Dorothy Johnson and Zero Mostel as the Peachums in *Beggar's Holiday*, a 1946 Duke Ellington musicalization of *The Beggar's Opera*.

Zero Mostel

Zero Mostel began his career as sketch comedian in such revues as *Keep 'Em Laughing* and *Concert Varieties,* and played an early supporting role in the Alfred Drake flop *Beggar's Holiday.* Although he received much acclaim for his dramatic turns in Eugéne Ionesco's *Rhinoceros* and James Joyce's *Ulysses in Nighttown,* Mostel will always be best remembered for creating the role of Max Bialystock in the movie *The Producers,* as well as for his two starring roles in musicals, first as the slave in *A Funny Thing Happened on the Way to the Forum,* then as Tevye in the long-running *Fiddler on the Roof,* creating (when the spirit moved him) five of the most thrilling minutes in Broadway history with his soliloquy "If I Were a Rich Man." After the surprise hit movie *The Producers* failed to bring the swarms of offers he had hoped for, he realized he had had two roles of a lifetime in Pseudolus and Tevye the milkman, and he contined to play both parts in subsequent productions. Unfortunately, his complicated psyche and monumental ego led him to play extremely fast and loose with the text, much to the frustration of his costars and the chagrin of the authors, who were understandably nonplussed by Mostel's liberties. His antics were perhaps more forgivable in Larry Gelbart and Burt Shevelove's burlesque of the works of Plautus, but it was absolutely disgraceful to ad lib about Jimmy Carter from a turn-of-the-century Russian shtetl.

LEFT: Mostel and Michael Granger, as the butcher Lazar Wolf, lift a cold one "To Life."

ABOVE: Bea Arthur dishes the dirt with the gossip hounds of Anatevka in "I Just Heard" (also known as "The Rumor").

BELOW: At Tzeitel and Motel's wedding, the village menfolk celebrate with a klezmer-accompanied bottle dance.

Backstage

Danny Kaye, Tom Bosley, Danny Thomas, Alan King, and Howard Da Silva were all considered for the role of Tevye. Nancy Walker, Kaye Ballard, and Kay Medford were all considered for Golde.

Charles Durning played the village priest in *Fiddler*, but his part was whittled away while the show played Detroit and Washington, and he never opened with the show in New York.

Jerry Bock and Sheldon Harnick

Composer Jerry Bock began his career as coauthor of the Sammy Davis Jr. vehicle *Mr. Wonderful*, while lyricist Sheldon Harnick began writing specialty material for revues, most notably "Boston Beguine" for *New Faces of '52* and "Merry Little Minuet" for *John Murray Anderson's Almanac*. After teaming up and producing an early flop, *The Body Beautiful*, they auditioned and were given a huge break writing a show for director George Abbott. The result, *Fiorello!*, won both the Tony Award and the Pulitzer Prize, a monumental feat for such young, relatively new writers. Its score revealed a great flair for writing specific and unique character songs. After a post-*Fiorello!* flop—*Tenderloin*—they wrote *She Loves Me*, *Fiddler on the Roof*, and *The Apple Tree* in three years, showing an incredible versatility. Highly in demand, twice they doctored scores for troubled shows, adding songs to *Baker Street* (four songs) and *Her First Roman* (three songs). After providing a wonderful score for *The Rothschilds*, they ended their fifteen-year partnership, Harnick to team up with Richard Rodgers on *Rex*, and with Michel Legrand on a musicalization of *A Christmas Carol* and a stage version of *The Umbrellas of Cherbourg*, while Bock kept a very low profile, his attempts at new scores going unproduced. The early end to their collaboration was a great loss, for in songs like "The Very Next Man" from *Fiorello!*, "Tonight at Eight" from *She Loves Me*, and "Oh, to Be a Movie Star" from *The Apple Tree*, they exhibited talent of the highest order.

SONGS

ACT I "Tradition" · "Matchmaker, Matchmaker" · "If I Were a Rich Man" · "Sabbath Prayer" · "To Life" · "Miracle of Miracles" · "The Tailor Motel Kamzoil" · "Sunrise, Sunset" "Wedding Dance"
ACT II "Now I Have Everything" · "Do You Love Me?" "I Just Heard" · "Far from the Home I Love" · "Chavaleh" "Anatevka"

TOP: One of Jerome Robbins's most brilliantly staged sequences, "The Tailor Motel Kamzoil," wherein Tevye concocts a nightmare for Golde, complete with the ghosts of Grandma Tzeitel and Fruma-Sarah, the ten-foot-tall dead wife of Lazar Wolf. RIGHT: Eileen Rodgers and Lee (Becker) Theodore sing "Little Old New York" in Bock and Harnick's *Tenderloin*.

FINIAN'S RAINBOW

OPENED JANUARY 10, 1947; 46TH STREET THEATRE; 725 PERFORMANCES

Sharon (Ella Logan) and Finian (Albert Sharpe) arrive in Rainbow Valley, Missitucky, Finian in search of a place to bury his pot o' gold, Sharon yearning to go home to Glocca Morra.

FINIAN'S RAINBOW

Produced by Lee Sabinson and
William R. Katzell

Book by E. Y. Harburg and Fred Saidy
Music by Burton Lane
Lyrics by E. Y. Harburg
Music orchestrated by Robert Russell Bennett
and Don Walker
Musical Director: Milton Rosenstock
Vocal Arrangements by Lyn Murray
Dance Arrangements by Trude Rittman
Assistant Vocal Arrangements by Ray Charles

Directed by Bretaigne Windust
Choreographed by Michael Kidd

Scenic Design by Jo Mielziner
Costume Design by Eleanore Goldsmith
Lighting Design by Jo Mielziner

Synopsis

Irishman Finian McLonergan has stolen a crock of gold from the leprechaun Og. Finian brings the gold and his daughter Sharon to Rainbow Valley, Missitucky, for Finian believes that if the United States can get rich by burying its gold in Fort Knox, so can he. Og has followed his stolen gold and fallen head over heels for Sharon, but she has eyes only for Woody Mahoney, a union organizer of the local sharecroppers. Woody's sister, Susan the silent, is the only person other than Finian who knows the location of the gold, but she's mute—able to communicate only through dance. A subplot features the racist Senator Billboard Rawkins, who is trying to subvert Woody's plans and buy up Rainbow Valley for himself. When Sharon unwittingly makes a wish while standing over the buried pot of gold, she turns Senator Rawkins into a black man, setting in motion a firestorm of hijinks and ironies.

Cast

Susan Mahoney	*Anita Alvarez*
Finian McLonergan	*Albert Sharpe*
Sharon McLonergan	*Ella Logan*
Woody Mahoney	*Donald Richards*
Og	*David Wayne*
Senator Billboard Rawkins	*Robert Pitkin*

"Dear Yip. I love you. Will you marry me?"

— *Oscar Hammerstein II, in a note to Yip Harburg after opening night*

THE GENERAL RULE ON BROADWAY is that the more changes out of town, the more songs are put in and discarded, the smaller the chance that the show will be a success in New York. *Breakfast at Tiffany's*, *Sail Away*, *Seesaw*, *Big*, *Victor/Victoria*, *La Strada* all underwent drastic changes, with characters axed and new scenes and songs were written. Of course, there are exceptions. Both *Funny Girl* and *Hello, Dolly!* had severe troubles on the road. Many songs were added to and subtracted from *Funny Girl*, and director Garson Kanin was all but replaced by Jerome Robbins. *Hello, Dolly!* endured major recasting between Detroit and New York, and songs and sequences were eliminated.

Still, the biggest hits remained pretty stable during the tryout period. Richard Rodgers and Oscar Hammerstein shows seemed to fare the best. *Oklahoma!* had but one major change: its title. It opened in New Haven as *Away We Go!* (there's very rare sheet music out there with that title); otherwise, only one song, "Boys and Girls Like You and Me," was deleted. *Carousel* suffered hardly any changes, and *South Pacific* had three songs eliminated out of town: "Loneliness of Evening," "Now Is the Time," and "My Girl Back Home."

One of the finest shows of the 1940s was *Finian's Rainbow*, and it, too, underwent very few changes: only one song was dropped. The reason *Finian* didn't change is unusual. On the first day of rehearsal, as composer Burton Lane ran the chorus through their parts, lyricist and co-librettist E. Y. (Yip) Harburg came into the room and told the assembled cast, "Don't listen to him, he's just the piano player." Lane left the room fuming, and didn't speak to Harburg again until long after the show opened on Broadway. Luckily, the team had done their work well and what appeared on the stage of the 46th Street Theatre was, with the exception of one song cut on the road, exactly what went into rehearsal.

The plot of *Finian* is a fantasy involving a leprechaun and a hidden pot of gold, but behind all the fantasy is a strong social statement. In the middle of the show, the bigoted southern senator is turned black. (In one famous story, *Finian* was being performed in a theatre in the round. Each night the actor playing the senator would race up the aisle, where a stagehand would apply blackface on him, to quickly run back down to the stage having been transformed. At one performance, an audience member chose exactly that moment to go up the aisle. Imagine his surprise to find himself slapped with black makeup.) In an ironic twist, *Finian* has gotten the reputation over time (by people who have never actually seen it) of being a racist show. Nothing of course could be further from the truth. Harburg and Lane were died-in-the-wool liberals, with Harburg constantly preaching for the common man and Lane on Nixon's enemies list.

So today, when *Finian's Rainbow* and its exceptional score are most needed, it sadly isn't performed much. A contributing factor is the original cast recording that, because of its poor fidelity, doesn't do the score justice. A recent attempt at a Broadway mounting closed in Cleveland. Whimsy, fantasy, and social consciousness are a delicate balance. The film version, directed by Francis Ford Coppola of all people, wasn't a hit but was extremely faithful to the musical—boasting Fred Astaire in his last musical film role. And in the manner of many film musicals that were lambasted upon their first release (*Hello, Dolly!* and *Star!* come to mind), it isn't bad in retrospect—well, not *so* bad. ✷

Burton Lane

Burton Lane's career wasn't as long or wide ranging as some of his contemporaries, but his work was consistently excellent, possessing an especially good sense of rhythm and depth of melody. Lane wrote the score to a Shubert show at the age of fourteen. It closed out of town but, had it come to New York, Lane would have been the youngest Broadway composer in history. With George Gershwin mentoring the youngster, he finally made it to Broadway, writing in collaboration with Howard Dietz for the revue *Three's a Crowd* (1930). While Lane's career was mainly spent in Hollywood, he made occasional forays to Broadway. He tried again and again to find Broadway projects, but had rocky professional relationships with his main collaborators, E. Y. Harburg (with whom he shared a wonderful nonworking relationship, as well as an unabashed liberalism) and Alan Jay Lerner. His scores for *Finian's Rainbow* and *On a Clear Day You Can See Forever* are among

the finest in Broadway history, thanks to his lush melodies for such songs as "How Are Things in Glocca Morra?," "She Wasn't You," and "It's Time for a Love Song" from his last score, *Carmelina*. Many projects, including an *Upstairs/Downstairs* musical with Sheldon Harnick, never saw production. But the scores that were produced demonstrate an excellence that has seldom been equaled.

TOP: Composer Burton Lane, during rehearsals for *On a Clear Day You Can See Forever*.

ABOVE: *Carmelina*, starring the intense, dramatic Georgia Brown, was Burton Lane's final Broadway score.

LEFT: The charming, whimsical shows of days gone by used trees to create exciting stage pictures and add a hint of realism (e.g., *The Sound of Music*, *Camelot*, and this scene, in which the McLonergans watch the sharecroppers and Woody). The more somber shows of today use trees for the lynching of a southern Jew wrongly accused of raping and strangling a young girl who works in his factory (e.g., *Parade*). All together now: "Everything about it is appealing! Everything the traffic will allow..."

RIGHT: The ebullient Martha Raye in the Burton Lane/Yip Harburg musical *Hold On To Your Hats*.

LEFT: David Wayne as Og the leprechaun near the girl he loves (and nibbles), Anita Alvarez.

Backstage

Finian's Rainbow is the favorite musical of Czechoslovakia (now the Czech Republic). It has been performed there in a series of productions for almost fifty years.

Composer Burton Lane almost became the youngest composer on Broadway. At age fourteen, he was "discovered" by a scout for the Shubert Brothers. J. J. Shubert hired Lane to write songs for a new revue. The show wasn't produced because its star became ill, but later, in Atlantic City, Lane and his father heard his tunes in another Shubert show with credit going to Shubert contract writer Maurie Rubens. Lane's father threatened to sue, and the songs were deleted from the score.

David Wayne

David Wayne, like fellow character actor Eddie Albert, enjoyed a busy career in all media, jumping easily from theatre to film to television, and back again. After beginning his musical career with the flop *Park Avenue*, he really cleaned up in his second show, where his puckish whimsy as Og, the leprechaun in *Finian's Rainbow,* was awarded a Tony and two Donaldson Awards (for Best Supporting Actor and Performance of the Year). After film triumphs (*Adam's Rib* and *The Tender Trap*) and straight play successes (*Teahouse of the August Moon*), he returned to Broadway in the musical satire *Say, Darling*, followed by *The Yearling*, one of those disasters that performed its opening night with the closing notice already posted. He immediately went into the Music Theatre of Lincoln Center revival of *Show Boat*, playing a jaunty Cap'n Andy, followed by his best musical role since *Finian's Rainbow*, the warm and wise Grandpére in *The Happy Time*, charming audiences with "The Life of the Party" and "A Certain Girl."

SONGS

ACT I "This Time of the Year" · "How Are Things in Glocca Morra?" · "Look to the Rainbow" · "Old Devil Moon" "Something Sort of Grandish" · "If This Isn't Love" "Necessity" · "(That) Great Come-and-Get-It Day"
ACT II "When the Idle Poor Become the Idle Rich" Dance of the Golden Crock · "The Begat" · "When I'm Not Near the Girl I Love"

UPPER RIGHT: David Wayne, with the delish Vivian Blaine and Johnny Desmond, in *Say, Darling*.

RIGHT: From the He Shoulda Known Department: David Wayne in a scene from *The Yearling*, breaking the three cardinal rules of show business: never work with children, animals, or Carmen Mathews.

FIORELLO!

OPENED NOVEMBER 23, 1959; BROADHURST THEATRE; 796 PERFORMANCES

FIORELLO!

Produced by Robert E. Griffith
and Harold S. Prince

Book by Jerome Weidman and George Abbott
Music by Jerry Bock
Lyrics by Sheldon Harnick
Musical Director: Hal Hastings
Music orchestrated by Irwin Kostal
Dance Arrangements by Jack Elliott

Directed by George Abbott
Choreographed by Peter Gennaro

Scenic Design by William and Jean Eckart
Costume Design by William and Jean Eckart
Lighting Design by William and Jean Eckart

Synopsis

The story of firebrand Fiorello La Guardia, a hero of World War I, reform congressman from New York, and eventually its mayor. Set against his political life, *Fiorello!* also tells the story of the loves of his life—his first wife, Thea, and his secretary and eventual second wife, Marie.

Cast

Fiorello LaGuardia	*Tom Bosley*
Ben Marino	*Howard Da Silva*
Floyd	*Mark Dawson*
Morris	*Nathaniel Frey*
Thea	*Ellen Hanley*
Dora	*Pat Stanley*
Marie	*Patricia Wilson*
Neil	*Bob Holiday*
4th Player	*Ron Husmann*
Mitzi Travers	*Eileen Rodgers*
Ed Peterson	*Stanley Simmonds*
Fiorello LaGuardia Standby	*Harvey Lembeck*

Ellen Hanley, Howard Da Silva, and Patricia Wilson surround Tom Bosley as he introduces himself to his constituency: "The Name's LaGuardia."

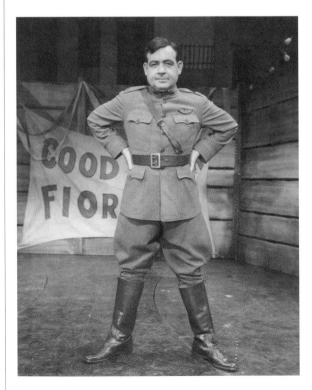

ONE WOULD THINK THAT BIOGRAPHICAL musicals would occupy a larger portion of musical theatre history than they do. After all, biography works in the movies, for the characters and plot are right there in the history books. Why can't musicals do what the movies do and ignore the facts completely? There have been more than a few musical bios, but few have succeeded: There was *Onward Victoria*, the drab, dull life (in its creators' hands, at least) of Victoria Woodhull; *The First*, the story of Jackie Robinson and not the first show to start previews strongly and end up lousy by opening night; *The Firebrand of Florence*, which examined episodes in the life of Benvenuto Cellini to a beguiling Kurt Weill and Ira Gershwin score; *Ben Franklin in Paris*, which wasn't as bad as history recounts; *Sophie*, Steve Allen's attempt at an even more Jewish funny girl; *Ain't Broadway Grand* (one of two musicals with Gypsy Rose Lee as a character); and finally *Kean*, the story of actor Edmund Kean with an underappreciated score. So that leaves us with *Fiorello!*, *The King and I*, *Annie Get Your Gun*, *Gypsy*, *The Sound of Music*, *Evita*, *The Unsinkable Molly Brown*, *Wonderful Town* (yes, the Sherwood sisters were based on real people), and *Funny Girl*; the exceptions to the rule. With the exception of *The First*, which started as a hit and ended as a double play, the flops all deal with people of higher social standing than your average Broadway theatregoer. At this writing. there is *The Boy from Oz.*

Fiorello! succeeded brilliantly due in no small part to the reality-infused acting. director George Abbott's no-nonsense directing. the warm-hearted libretto and score. and the fact that Fiorello LaGuardia was still fondly remembered by the theatregoing public. They loved him in life and they loved him as embodied by Tom Bosley. making his Broadway debut. ❋

SONGS

ACT I · "On the Side of the Angels" · "Politics and Poker" · "Unfair" · "Marie's Law" · "The Name's LaGuardia" · "The Bum Won" · "I Love a Cop" · "Till Tomorrow" · "Home Again"
ACT II · "When Did I Fall in Love?" · "Gentleman Jimmy" · "Little Tin Box" · "The Very Next Man"

"Would Larry Hart have been satisfied with that?"

— *George Abbott, encouraging Sheldon Harnick to write better lyrics*

Pat Stanley

Pat Stanley, a gamine dancer/actress with a charming singing voice who was a quirky potential successor to Carol Haney, made her debut in a small role in the Dolores Gray–John Raitt flop *Carnival in Flanders*. After playing Haney's role in the national tour of *The Pajama Game*, she had an incredibly busy two-year period, playing Carrie Pipperidge in a City Center production of *Carousel* (with Barbara Cook and Howard Keel), followed by a one-two punch in *Goldilocks* (winning a Tony Award for her performance of "Lady in Waiting" and "The Pussyfoot") and *Fiorello!* (where she stopped the show with "I Love a Cop"). After a nonmusical role in the comedy *Sunday in New York*, she disappeared into her marriage, resurfacing twenty years later for a brief, two-week run in the Goodspeed Opera House transfer of *The Five O'Clock Girl*. But, like so many others, she found Broadway had changed and there was no longer a place for her charming, winsome simplicity.

TOP : Pert Pat Stanley, in her showstopping song-and-dance number "I Love a Cop." She later married the brother of *Fiorello!* costar Ellen Hanley, thereby becoming "Pat Stanley Hanley."

RIGHT: Pat Stanley won a Tony Award for her role as Lois Lee (curiously, the same name as the actress who played the ingénue in *High Button Shoes*) in the silent-screen era *Goldilocks.*

Robert E. Griffith

Robert E. Griffith, great gentleman of the theatre who teamed with the younger, super energetic Hal Prince to produce many successful shows of the 1950s and '60s, started as a performer, segueing into assistant director and stage manager on many of George Abbott's musicals of the 1940s, including *Call Me Madam*, *A Tree Grows in Brooklyn*, and *Wonderful Town*. His first show as producer was *The Pajama Game*, followed by other smashes, including *Damn Yankees*, *West Side Story*, and *Fiorello!* His commitment to excellence and creative savvy are sorely lacking in the vast majority of today's producers. He died in 1961 at the age of 54, but his taste and unerring belief in talent lives on through his remarkable protégé Hal Prince.

ABOVE: The beloved Robert E. Griffith visiting his Maria, Carol Lawrence, in her dressing room at the National Theatre during the out-of-town engagement of *West Side Story*.

Backstage

When Tom Bosley performed in a revival of *Fiorello!* in the 1980s, instead of having to whiten his hair for the second act, he had to blacken his hair for the first act.

Though he played the title role, Tom Bosley won the Tony Award for Featured Actor. Just another example of the craziness of the Tony Awards.

TOP: Tom Bosley, seen here with Ellen Hanley, had the requisite talent (and stature) to make an unforgettable Broadway debut as New York City's "Little Flower."

ABOVE: Patricia Wilson as the loyal-to–a-fault secretary Marie, singing the beautiful Bock and Harnick song "Where Do I Go from Here?," unfortunately cut during *Fiorello!*'s tryout

FOLLIES

OPENED APRIL 4, 1971; WINTER GARDEN THEATRE; 522 PERFORMANCES

Florence Klotz's costumes stop the show in the Loveland sequence of *Follies*.

FOLLIES
Produced by Harold Prince
Book by James Goldman
Music and Lyrics by Stephen Sondheim
Musical Director: Harold Hastings
Music orchestrated by Jonathan Tunick
Dance arrangements by John Berkman
Choral arrangements by Harold Hastings
Directed by Harold Prince and Michael Bennett
Choreographed by Michael Bennett
Scenic Design by Boris Aronson
Costume Design by Florence Klotz
Lighting Design by Tharon Musser

Synopsis

A reunion of members of the Weismann Follies brings together many generations of performers who appeared on the stage of the Weismann Theatre. Against the backdrop of their pasts, two couples in particular, Ben and Phyllis—smart, sophisticated intellectuals—and Buddy and Sally—suburbanites—find themselves confronting their feelings as well as their pasts. As the *Follies* performers and their ghosts perform their old numbers, Ben, Phyllis, Buddy, and Sally revisit their past lives, which were filled with hope for the future. But they can't avoid confronting the stark reality of their current lives and relationships. The end of *Follies* finds the principals in a combined nervous breakdown as played out behind the veil of an actual *Follies* performance.

Cast

Sally Durant	Dorothy Collins
Young Sally	Marti Rolph
Christine Crane	Ethel Barrymore Colt
Stella Deems	Mary McCarty
Heidi Schiller	Justine Johnston
Roscoe	Michael Bartlett
Hattie Walker	Ethel Shutta
Solange LaFitte	Fifi D'Orsay
Carlotta Campion	Yvonne De Carlo
Phyllis Rogers Stone	Alexis Smith
Benjamin Stone	John McMartin
Young Phyllis	Virginia Sandifur
Young Ben	Kurt Peterson
Buddy Plummer	Gene Nelson
Young Buddy	Harvey Evans
Dmitri Weisman	Arnold Moss
Young Heidi	Victoria Mallory

"I think I will declare war on this man, and I know there will be a lot of support with me to see that this man is done away with!"

—*Hal Prince on Clive Barnes, critic for* The New York Times

Is *Follies* THE GREATEST MUSICAL comedy of all time? Some would insist that it is. Maybe it was simply the greatest production of all time? For avid theatregoers, one viewing of *Follies* was not enough. It's a sure bet that whatever audiences found their way into the Winter Garden Theatre, a good percentage were repeat visitors. Still, it might also be argued that an equal number walked out, or left the theatre utterly perplexed by the show, and perhaps no other Broadway musical has so divided an audience.

Nary a man is now alive who saw the original *Show Boat* or *Ziegfeld Follies*, or even *Oklahoma!*, so we can't speak firsthand of their greatness. We have to take it on blind faith that Helen Morgan, perched on an upright piano, made people's hearts stand still when she extolled the virtues of "Bill." We have to believe that there was no one funnier than Fanny Brice singing "Becky Is Back at the Ballet" or more touching when she lamented her life with "My Man." People who were around from the 1950s on speak of some of the greatest moments in their theatrical history, highpoints of their years of theatergoing. Moments that caused the heart to leap or break, moments that stayed in their memories forever. They are the reason we return again and again to the theatre: hoping for new revelations of performance, stagecraft, or writing: Elaine

Bennett's choreography for "Who's That Woman?"; and, most impressively, the shocking transition to Loveland, when the emotions swelled to such proportion that time and space seemed to explode into the Follies. Boris Aronson's dark, open setting transformed into the bright, fairytale world of Loveland, with doilied drops plunging to the stage and everything exploding into a visual and aural orgasm of musical theatre bliss.

Follies is a celebration of our past and our present, as well as an admonition. In our time, there can never be another *Follies*, just like there can never be another *Show Boat*,

the regret of "the road you didn't take," it requires attention, an opening of the heart and mind, and a great deal of intelligence and sensitivity. Harold Prince and Michael Bennett's direction and staging were layered in countless ways, and the original cast can never be equaled, for not only was the show beautifully tailored to their specific talents, but fewer and fewer performers today have lived the history of those in *Follies*, a show all about histories.

So, while we can't say definitively that *Follies* is the greatest of all our 101 shows, either in writing or production, we can state unequivocally that its like will never be seen again; and that is the glory and tragedy of theatre—it is at once the most accessible yet most ephemeral of arts. ✻

SONGS

"Beautiful Girls" · "Don't Look at Me" · "Waiting for the Girls Upstairs" · "Rain on the Roof" · "Ah, Paris!" "Broadway Baby" · "The Road You Didn't Take" · "Bolero d'Amour" (dance) · "In Buddy's Eyes" · "Who's That Woman?" · "I'm Still Here" · "Too Many Mornings" · "The Right Girl" · "One More Kiss" · "Could I Leave You?" "Loveland" · "You're Gonna Love Tomorrow" · "Love Will See Us Through" · "The God-Why-Don't-You-Love-Me Blues" · "Losing My Mind" · "The Story of Lucy and Jessie" · "Live, Laugh, Love"

LEFT: Dorothy Collins and Alexis Smith are the girls upstairs.

BELOW: John McMartin and Gene Nelson are the boys who wait for them.

again to the theatre; hoping for new revelations of performance, stagecraft, or writing: Elaine Stritch exhorting, "Everybody rise!" in "The Ladies Who Lunch"; a ragdoll-like Michael Jeter, kicking higher and higher in a Charleston of giddy abandon in *Grand Hotel*; Mary Martin, bursting through the Darlings' nursery window for the first time; Jennifer Holliday's soul-baring intensity in "And I Am Telling You I'm Not Going."

It's the rare show that contains even one such moment, but those who venerate the original *Follies* can name many such breathtaking incidents onstage: Ethel Shutta kicking her imaginary cat while belting out "Broadway Baby;" Yvonne De Carlo, joyfully seen-it-all in "I'm Still Here" (on the rare occasion she didn't blow the lyrics); the harrowing "In Buddy's Eyes" and the poignant simplicity of "Losing My Mind," as sung by Dorothy Collins and staged by Bob Avian; Alexis Smith's exquisite, soignée timing in "Could I Leave You?," only to be topped by her leggy song-and-dance turn in "The Ballad of Lucy and Jessie"; John McMartin's horrific epiphany, "Me ... I've got to love ... me"; Gene Nelson's superhuman swinging around the poles in "The Right Girl" (which Michael Bennett apparently hated; no: it was sheer magic); the ghosts gliding across the stage, existing in both past and present; Jonathan Tunick's ethereal, otherworldly orchestration of the overture; Florence Klotz's astounding Loveland showgirl costumes; the subtextual brilliance of Michael

another *South Pacific*, another *Hair*. All great shows are written in tune with the social, historical, and psychological pulse of their time. *Oklahoma!* was a big hit partly because the world was at war and America needed to be reminded of its noble, yes noble, roots. The sets were mainly painted drops, since lumber was hard to get because of war shortages, and audiences were conditioned to shows opening with a chorus of girls, not a sole cowboy singing from the wings about what a beautiful morning it was. *Oklahoma!* was a product of its time and place in history as much as *The Merry Widow* or *This Is the Army* were, though all great art is defined by its universality and timelessness.

No matter how successful we are in mounting revivals, they can never be as earthshaking as the originals. This isn't to say we shouldn't continue to try, and theatres keep trying to replicate the magic moments of *Follies*, but if ever a show was of its time and place, *Follies* is it. A show about resonance, memory, and

ABOVE: Mary McCarty as Stella Deems, backed up by former chorines Sheila Smith, Alexis Smith, Dorothy Collins, and Yvonne DeCarlo (along with the ghosts of their youth), in arguably the best-staged production number in Broadway musical history, the Michael Bennett masterpiece "Who's That Woman?"

BELOW: Dorothy Collins delivered a killer "Losing My Mind" in a killer gown by Florence Klotz.

LEFT: Harvey Evans and Marti Rolph as Young Buddy and Young Sally declaring in typically bittersweet, Stephen Sondheim fashion, "Love Will See Us Through (Til Something Better Comes Along)."

Harvey Evans

A true legend, although most people outside of Times Square won't be familiar with his name, Harvey Evans is one of the most beloved (and gainfully employed—and did we say beloved?) performers in Broadway history. Appearing in twenty-eight Broadway musicals and national tours over the last fifty years, Evans began his career as Harvey Hohnecker, all of sixteen and a featured dancer with the legendary Gwen Verdon in *New Girl in Town*. His résumé includes the cream of show business of the latter half of the twentieth century: *Gypsy*, *West Side Story* (also appearing in the film), *Hello, Dolly!*, *Anyone Can Whistle* (backing up another legend, Angela Lansbury), *George M!*, *The Boyfriend* (where he Charlestoned to a fare-thee-well with Sandy Duncan), and as Young Buddy in another monumental show, *Follies*. In between, he danced with Judy Garland on her television show, was a chimney sweep in the film *Mary Poppins*, and starred opposite Ann-Margret in the television production of *Dames at Sea*. With later roles as Jim Dale's standby in *Barnum*; a funny, touching Albin in the national tour of *La Cage aux Folles* (opposite longtime friend Larry Kert); and on and on (and on), Harvey Evans was most recently seen in the 2002 revival of *Oklahoma!* as sunny and beloved as the sixteen-year-old Harvey Hohnecker was in 1957.

Alexis Smith

Like Robert Preston and Angela Lansbury, classy, leggy Alexis Smith came to musicals after a long Hollywood career as a film actress. At the time semi-retired, she auditioned unsuccessfully for *Follies*, but after buckling down and working with vocal coach David Craig (husband of Nancy Walker) on every note and gesture of her audition, she campaigned for another shot. This time she nailed it, and received unparalleled love letters from critics and a Tony Award for her performance as Phyllis Rogers Stone, the brittle sophisticate with a wide-eyed chorine still buried somewhere under the icy surface. She returned to Broadway in 1979 in a really lousy show, *Platinum*, albeit with six minutes of sheer brilliance, when Smith's character, in a *Follies*-esque moment, looked back on her Hollywood career in the tour de force "Nothing But," a song so head and shoulders above the rest of the score that wags wondered if John Kander and Fred Ebb had written it on the sly. A national tour in *The Best Little Whorehouse in Texas* followed, and for a while rumors flew that she would return in a full-fledged Broadway revival of *Pal Joey* (she played the hell out of it in stock, opposite a far-too-old Joel Grey), but another great Broadway turn never materialized.

Backstage

Capitol Records wouldn't record a complete original cast recording of *Follies*. Damn them!

Among the unlikely celebrities who have appeared in stock productions of *Follies* are such notables as Maxene Andrews, Yma Sumac, Dorothy Lamour, the incomparable Hildegarde, and in a recent Los Angeles production, the Phyllis and Sally of Patty Duke and Vikki Carr.

ABOVE: A rare look at the last moments of *Follies*: daylight peers down through the skeletal remains of the Weisman Theatre on a sobered Phyllis (Alexis Smith) and a shattered Ben (John McMartin).

TOP LEFT: Alexis Smith in a Sondheim homage to Kurt Weill's "The Saga of Jenny" titled "The Story of Lucy and Jessie."

CENTER LEFT: Lisa Mordente and Alexis Smith in the monumentally disappointing *Platinum*.

LEFT: Ethel Shutta, who made her Broadway debut in *The Passing Show of 1922*, was still laying them in the aisles forty-nine years later, singing "Broadway Baby" in orthopedic shoes.

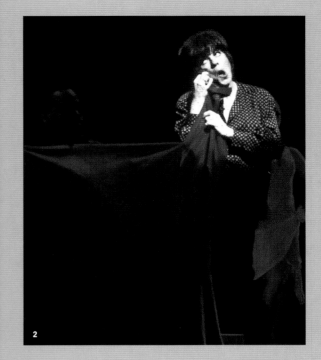

FLOPS, PART I

AND NOW, WE PAUSE FOR a moment to honor those shows that made a wrong turn down a dead-end street; the shows in which talented, experienced people made the mistakes of rank amateurs; the musicals that began with great promise and ended like the Donner party, with every chorus boy for himself. Yes, dear readers, it's time to celebrate the turkeys; the stinkers; the bombs: those immortal classics whose mere mention sends a chill down the spine of the empathetic and quickens the pulse of the Rialto vultures who gleefully attended the first preview of *Legs Diamond*.

1) Nanette Fabray, who evidently doesn't read reviews, jumps for joy as Robert Ryan takes a breather during Irving Berlin's *Mr. President*. **2)** Sock it to her: *Laugh-In*'s JoAnne Worley was a brave soul in the truly lousy *Prince of Central Park*. **3)** Carol Channing gets nasty in her eleven o'clock number from the stinker *The Vamp*, "I'm Everybody's Baby."

Carmen Mathews

I nexplicably drawn to flops like moths to a flame, Carmen Mathews appeared in various straight plays before her first kamikaze musical appearance, in 1951's *Courtin' Time*, which somehow managed to play two different Broadway houses but rack up only 37 performances. Written out of *Candide* during rehearsals, she played Anne Rogers's mother in *Zenda*, which closed pre-Broadway, followed by a musical adaptation of *The Yearling* (1965, 3 performances). Next for Mathews was a role alongside fellow flop maven Karen Morrow in *I'm Solomon* (1968, 7 performances). Then came her biggest smash (comparatively speaking) as one of the madwomen in Jerry Herman's *Dear World* (1969), which managed a 132-performance run. Luckily, Mathews was spared the grueling tedium of a run that long with her next role, in *Ambassador* (1972, 19 performances), before her last flop in 1981, the 13 performances of *Copperfield*. She came dangerously close to appearing in a hit—but she was replaced as George's mother in *Sunday in the Park with George* after the workshop. In reality a talented and versatile character actress, Mathews, along with Morrow, has had perhaps the worst luck of any person to enter a theatre since Abraham Lincoln saw *Our American Cousin* (in which Mathews did not appear).

4) Carmen Mathews and Brian Matthews, in *Copperfield*. At least the costumes were nice. **5)** Have caftan, will travel: Mathews (center) leads David Sabin and Howard Keel down the primrose path toward flopdom in *Ambassador*. **6)** Occidental tourist Carol Lawrence, looking fairly Tibetan considering she's a nice Italian girl from Arlington Heights, Illinois, with Shirley Yamaguchi, Leland Mayforth, and Edwin Kim Ying in the woebegone *Shangri-La*.

7) Alyson Reed should have been awarded the Congressional Medal of Honor for grace under fire for giving a fantastic, should-have-been-a-starmaking performance in *Marilyn: An American Fable*. **8)** A prostheticized and squinty-eyed Don Ameche, as Chun, the Hawaiian father of *13 Daughters*.

THE FULL MONTY

OPENED OCTOBER 26, 2000; EUGENE O'NEILL THEATRE; 770 PERFORMANCES

ABOVE: Marcus Neville, Andre De Shields, John Ellison Conlee, Patrick Wilson, Romain Fruge, and Jason Daniely go *The Full Monty*.

RIGHT: Laura Marie Duncan, Annie Golden, Jannie Jones, and Lisa Datz primp before seeing some prime, Grade-A male talent.

THE FULL MONTY

Produced by Fox Searchlight Pictures, Lindsay Law, and Thomas Hall

Book by Terrence McNally
Music and Lyrics by David Yazbek
Music orchestrated by Harold Wheeler
Dance arrangements by Zane Mark
Musical Director: Ted Sperling
Vocal and incidental music arrangements by Ted Sperling

Directed by Jack O'Brien
Choreographed by Jerry Mitchell

Scenic Design by John Arnone
Costume Design by Robert Morgan
Lighting Design by Howell Binkley

Synopsis

Buffalo, New York: it's the heart of the rust belt, and the economy sucks. Jerry, an unemployed, divorced father, is at the end of his proverbial rope with nowhere to turn. His meets his friend Dave outside a ladies-only strip club. With Dave's wife inside watching the muscles, Jerry and Dave decide to sneak into the club and see what's going on. The two men are transfixed at the spectacle, especially the amount of money tucked into the dancers' G-strings. The day after, things go from bad to worse for Jerry when he's served papers: his ex-wife is seeking sole custody of his son, Nathan. Something has to be done—and now. A neon light bulb goes off over Jerry's head, and he comes up with the idea of getting his friends, a group of "real men," young and old, black and white, fat and buff, gay and straight, to join him in an evening of stripping. They won't stop with G-strings either; the big draw is that the men will go the "full monty." There are many obstacles along the way, but in the end the men pull together, discover their inner he-man, and "let it go."

Cast

Georgie Bukatinsky	*Annie Golden*
Reg Willoughby	*Todd Weeks*
Jerry Lukowsky	*Patrick Wilson*
Dave Bukatinsky	*John Ellison Conlee*
Malcolm MacGregor	*Jason Daniely*
Ethan Girard	*Romain Fruge*
Pam Lukowsky	*Lisa Datz*
Harold Nichols	*Marcus Neville*
Vicki Nichols	*Emily Skinner*
Jeanette Burmeister	*Kathleen Freeman*
Noah "Horse" T. Simmons	*Andre DeShields*

MUSICAL ADAPTATIONS OF FILMS ARE tricky hills to climb, and for every *Sweet Charity, Promises, Promises,* or *The Producers,* there is a *Look to the Lilies, Goodbye Girl,* or (heaven forfend) a *Carrie.* Motion pictures are a decidedly different medium, with close-ups, montages, and the ability to communicate pages of spoken dialogue in a single shot. These visuals are exceedingly difficult to translate to the live theatre, a form all about the conflicting clash of the distancing fourth wall with the intimacy of the shared experience between actor and audience. The 1997 film *The Full Monty,* about a group of Sheffield, England, steel workers forced to become strippers to make ends meet, would not seem to be a natural candidate for musicalization. But Terrence McNally, the brilliant playwright (and book writer of the intensely intimate *The Rink;* another translated film, *The Kiss of the Spider Woman;* and the sprawling and unwieldy *Ragtime*), along with director Jack O'Brien, choreographer Jerry Mitchell, and first-time Broadway composer David Yazbek, saw something that they felt could sing and dance for a New York crowd.

Cannily resetting the action to an Eastern steel town, the Americanization helped transplant the story, and—by always keeping the focus on the father/son relationship—the conflict and motives were delivered straightforwardly, honestly, and accessibly to all audiences. (In fact, at one performance of this most blue-collar musical comedy, the ninety-something Kitty Carlisle Hart, one of the most elegant, urbane women in modern society, was seen leaping to her Pradas during the finale, wildly clapping with the rest of the throng.) The bashful, almost innocent humor emanating from this group of disparate yet average guys thrown together and having to go "the full monty" made for a surprisingly sweet evening in the theatre.

In addition, the subplot in which two of the men find each other in an unexpected fashion provided a gay twist that was utterly refreshing, neither maudlin nor in your face. With a wonderful cast (particularly rising star Patrick Wilson, veteran Andre DeShields, and veteran cum legend Kathleen Freeman as the Thelma Ritterish accompanist), smart, uncluttered direction and choreography by the team of O'Brien and Mitchell on their way to *Hairspray* fame, and the score of Yazbek (with song titles like "Big-Ass Rock," "Big Black Man," and "You Rule My World") providing an ideal musical setting, the show is on its way to becoming a classic working-class musical comedy.

Oh, and regarding the nudity. Rarely has more of a fuss been made over . . . um . . . so little. To be sure, there were the types that went with their night-vision goggles to catch a microsecond peek of the fellas' "monties" (this serves as official notice that Kitty Carlisle Hart most assuredly did NOT whip out her opera glasses during the show's final moments); but all told, *The Full Monty* was about as raunchy as a ladies' auxiliary luncheon, also adding to its wide appeal. ❊

TOP RIGHT: Fruge, Conlee, De Shields, Wilson, Neville, and Daniely in "Michael Jordan's Ball," so cleverly choreographed for character that it signaled Jerry Mitchell's arrival on Broadway as a major force.

ABOVE: When the stooped, hunched Andre De Shields started to slide and glide in his showstopper "Big Black Man," it never failed to elicit roars from the audience.

Jerry Mitchell

Teeming with show-biz smarts, Jerry Mitchell began his career as a dancer in the revival of *Brigadoon* in 1980. Tall, dark, handsome, and reveling in it, Mitchell appeared in the film of *Best Little Whorehouse in Texas* and the workshop of Michael Bennett's last show, *Scandal,* before he, along with fellow choreographic minutiaeist Cynthia Onrubia, assisted Jerome Robbins on the retrospective *Jerome Robbins' Broadway.* Next, Mitchell appeared in *The Will Rogers Follies* while waiting for an opportunity to show his stuff as a choreographer in his own right. He attracted much attention with the all-star, Paper Mill Playhouse production of *Follies*, where he staged a series of period-perfect numbers. One Mitchell touch was to have the ghosts dancing the original numbers in brief, startling flashes of white light behind a scrim, while the oldsters gamely attempted their routines at the footlights. In addition to making a name for himself with the annual *Broadway Bares* benefit, an ultra-sexy, ultra-produced skin show featuring the most beautiful women and men on Broadway, Mitchell made his Broadway debut with the dances for the revivals of *You're a Good Man, Charlie Brown* and *The Rocky Horror Show.* Then came a triumph in *The Full Monty*, with his choreography for the basketball number, "Michael Jordan's Ball," some of the most clever character-driven movement since the heyday of Michael Bennett. Mitchell moved on to *Hairspray* (another show that would have made Bennett proud, with its *Hullabaloo*-like versions of "The Jerk," "The Pony," and "The Mashed Potato") and *Never Gonna Dance*, with period tap numbers on a Stromanesque level. He is the fastest rising star of the Broadway dance world, set to choreograph a revival of *La Cage Aux Folles* and the new *Dirty Rotten Scoundrels* in 2005.

CENTER: Jerry Mitchell as a Wrangler in *The Will Rogers Follies.*
ABOVE: Marissa Jaret Winokur as Tracy Turnblad in *Hairspray*.

SONGS

ACT I "Scrap" · "It's a Woman's World" · "Man" · "Big-Ass Rock" · "Life with Harold" · "Big Black Man" · "You Rule My World" · "Michael Jordan's Ball"
ACT II · "Jeanette's Showbiz Number" (Things Could Be Better) · "Breeze Off the River" · "The Goods" · "You Walk with Me" · "Let It Go"

FUNNY FACE

OPENED NOVEMBER 22, 1927; ALVIN THEATRE; 250 PERFORMANCES

ABOVE: Adele and Fred Astaire at the top of their game.

RIGHT: Victor Moore and William Kent break the law with a glass of hooch.

FUNNY FACE

Produced by
Alex. A. Aarons and Vinton Freedley

Music by George Gershwin
Lyrics by Ira Gershwin
Book by Fred Thompson and Paul Gerard Smith
Musical Director: Alfred Newman

Staged by Edgar MacGregor
Choreographed by Bobby Connolly

Scenic Design by John Wenger
Costume Design by Kiviette

Synopsis

Jimmie Reeve is the caretaker of Frankie, her sister June, and a girl named Dora. Jimmie has taken Frankie's diary and locked it in his safe. Frankie is afraid of what he might find in the diary and arranges for her aviator boyfriend, Peter Thurston, to steal it. He does, but at the same time also manages accidentally to steal a valuable necklace belonging to June. The action hurtles around New York and New Jersey, finally coming to a close at the Two-Million Dollar Pier in Atlantic City.

Cast

Dora .... *Betty Compton*
June .... *Gertrude McDonald*
Frankie .... *Adele Astaire*
Jimmy Reeve .... *Fred Astaire*
Dugsie Gibbs .... *William Kent*
Herbert .... *Victor Moore*
Peter Thurston .... *Allen Kearns*
Duo Pianists .... *Victor Arden, Phil Ohman*

Here's a favorite parlor game of ours called "Hit or Flop?" The moderator takes a random volume of *Best Plays* and reads out a synopsis, and the players guess the fate of the show.

1. Chiquita Hart, a nightclub entertainer; Harry Hart, a carnival pitchman; and Blossom Hart, a war worker, are found by the Court of Missing Heirs and informed that they have inherited a ranch in Texas. Once there, they discover their property abuts Kelly Field and has been taken over by the army for maneuvers, which makes it nice for the boys when they invite their wives and girlfriends down. Then the army interferes.

2. Harvey Casey, big business tycoon, decides to send his rebellious daughter, Consuelo, to Pottawatomie College at Stop Gap, New Mexico. To guarantee her protection, he engages four former All-American football players to go along and, unknown to Consuelo, serve her as bodyguards of sorts. At Pottawatomie, the football players get mixed up with the college eleven, and Consuelo falls in love with one of them. The day of the big game, she discovers that she has been watched and orders the boys back east. Compromise and kisses.

3. A singing-and-dancing romp in which a girl named Frankie induces Peter Thurston to help her steal back the pearls her guardian, Jimmy Reeve, has hidden from her. Dugsie and Herbert, comic burglars, are also after the pearls.

Hits or Flops?
Answers: All were hits. Number 1 is *Something for the Boys*. Number 2 is *Too Many Girls*. Number 3 is, of course, *Funny Face*.

What makes a hit musical? Betty Comden and Adolph Green, librettists/lyricists extraordinaire, felt that the music was more important than the lyrics. They reasoned that people went around humming the tunes, not singing the lyrics. Still, most experts feel that the most important factor in a show's success is the libretto; after all, there are lots of flop shows that feature great songs. Why did they fail? Because of a bad book. What else would explain the relative failure of the original production of *Pal Joey* (not that it actually had a bad script, but the audience at the time certainly thought it was)? Though there were some exceptions, mainly the books written by Oscar Hammerstein II, most early libretti were pretty damn silly.

Since musical theatre grew out of a variety of traditions, it was somewhat of a bastard art form in the early years, with most shows built around established personalities from vaudeville and minstrel shows. From the latter came Al Jolson, arguably the greatest performer of all time, and the libretti for his shows were so inane, Jolson would actually stop the show, go down to the footlights, and ask the audience if they preferred to see the show as written or just have Jolson present a concert of his hits. The hits always won. After a fashion, this tradition exists today, when Hugh Jackman, still in character as Peter Allen, stops the wafer-thin book of *The Boy from Oz* and speaks directly to the audience. Jackman is magnificent, a true Broadway star who can do it all, and audiences eagerly await those times when he breaks the extremely fragile fourth wall.)

Fred and Adele Astaire

More than just the leading dance team of the 1920s, the Astaires entertained audiences with their wit, charm, and sophistication, combined with unparalleled grace and technical virtuosity. The youngsters arrived in New York in 1904, when Fred was just four and Adele was six. Mrs. Austerlitz, their mother, brought her offspring to the Great White Way so that they might becomes stars. They made their professional debut two years later in Keyport, New Jersey, then were booked on the Orpheum Circuit, touring in vaudeville until finally outgrowing their act. They made their Broadway debut in 1911, at a benefit performance at the Broadway Theatre on 42nd Street, but their act, titled "A Rainy Saturday," was such a failure no Broadway producer would touch them. Returning to the world of the two-a-day for the next five years, they got their first true Broadway booking in the 1917 show *Over the Top*, which perfectly described the critical huzzahs that greeted them. After that, there was no stopping them for the next fourteen years, as they marauded through a succession of better and better shows, *For Goodness Sake!*; *Lady, Be Good!*; *Funny Face*; and *Smiles*, culminating in the greatest revue in Broadway history, *The Band Wagon* (1931). Adele, deciding to go out on top, married Lord Charles Cavendish, leaving Fred a single act. The gamble paid off when he opened in the *Gay Divorce* the next year, and once he proved he could go it alone, he, too, left the theatre and made his way to Hollywood, where he became an even greater star, teaming most famously with Ginger Rogers.

Betty Compton gets some dancing lessons from Fred Astaire as the chorus looks on.

For its time. *Funny Face*'s libretto did its job admirably, loading the gentlest of plots with ample opportunities for Fred and Adele Astaire to show their stuff with terrific songs and imaginative choreography. It was all lighthearted fun, never promising more than it could deliver. Still, by 1927, the year *Funny Face* debuted, shows were already striving for a modicum of integration between song and story, and no longer were numbers listed as "Dance Eccentrique" and "The Cabaret," as in the Astaires' 1922 show, *The Bunch and Judy*.

The books of these shows weren't a problem when they were first produced; after all, you got the Astaires in the bargain. But when they are revived, the creakiness of the plots and the low comedy don't hold up without the original stars. So producers find new book writers to "update" the scripts and make them more palatable to today's audiences. Often, all they seem to do is add even more silly puns, then wink at the silliness of musical comedy in general. When new shows are created from old songs, like the recent *Never Gonna Dance*, the shows are neither old nor new, but rather trapped in some strange limbo, uncomfortable in any era.

Perhaps it's best to hear these great scores in concert, with minimal, bridging narration; better still would be a first-class revival, retaining the original book with just a little trimming. It would be fun to hear *Funny Face*, with all those wonderful Gershwin standards, and well worth it to put up with a few creaks of the book—for these shows, like the classic silent films of Charlie Chaplin, Mary Pickford, and Buster Keaton, are part of our cultural heritage. We should have the opportunity every now and again to rediscover our musical-comedy roots. ❋

Alex Aarons and Vinton Freedley

Alex Aarons and Vinton Freedley created a remarkable series of shows at their eponymous Alvin Theatre that changed the history of musical theatre. The son of composer-producer Alfred E. Aarons, Alex Aarons made his Broadway debut in 1919, producing the George Gershwin/B. G. De Sylva show *La, La, Lucille*. His next show, *For Goodness Sake!*, boasted a score by George and Ira Gershwin, and in the cast was young Vinton Freedley, among others. Freedley, giving up his acting career, teamed with Aarons as coproducer and had a hit right out of the gate, *Lady, Be Good!* (1925), thanks to its remarkable Gershwin score and the talent of the Astaires. They continued producing Gershwin shows, including *Tip-Toes*, starring Queenie Smith and Jeanette MacDonald; *Oh, Kay!* (with Gertrude Lawrence); and *Funny Face*. Rodgers and Hart got the Aarons and Freedley treatment with *Spring Is Here* and *Heads Up!*, both in 1929. After the stock market crash, Broadway business went south, but still the team struck gold with *Girl Crazy* in 1930. Their last coproduction prior to Aarons's retirement was the Gershwin's *Pardon My English*. Now producing solo, the dapper Freedley went on to present Cole Porter's *Anything Goes*; *Red, Hot and Blue!*; and *Leave It to Me!*, showing off Freedley's continued penchant for the exclamation point. After the hits *Cabin in the Sky* and *Let's Face It!*, his last three offerings were failures, and Freedley left Broadway for good in 1950. The team of Aarons and Freedley contributed much to Broadway, not the least of which was launching the careers of its two greatest female stars, Ethel Merman and Mary Martin.

SONGS

ACT I "Birthday Party" · "Once" · "Funny Face" · "High Hat" · "S' Wonderful" · "Let's Kiss and Make Up"
ACT II "In the Swim" · "He Loves and She Loves" · "Tell the Doc" · "What Am I Going to Do?" · "Sing a Little Song" · "The Babbitt and the Bromide"

Backstage

The show tried out as *Smarty* with a book by Robert Benchley. It was a disaster.

Mary Ellen Ashley, one of the little girls in the original cast of *Annie Get Your Gun*, reports that producers would top load the cast for opening night (see photo at right). Once the production photos were taken and the show opened, the chorus numbers would be reduced.

TOP: Fred and Adele greet their producers, Aarons and Freedley.
RIGHT: Fred fronts the chorus boys in "High Hat" and establishes his persona.

FUNNY GIRL

OPENED MARCH 26, 1964; WINTER GARDEN THEATRE; 1,348 PERFORMANCES

FUNNY GIRL
Produced by Ray Stark
Music by Jule Styne
Lyrics by Bob Merrill
Book by Isobel Lennart
Musical Director: Milton Rosenstock
Music orchestrated by Ralph Burns
Vocal arrangements by Buster Davis
Dance arrangements by Luther Henderson
Assistant Vocal Arranger: Marvin Hamlisch

Directed by Garson Kanin
Production Supervised by Jerome Robbins
Musical Staging by Carol Haney

Scenic Design by Robert Randolph
Lighting Design by Robert Randolph
Costume Design by Irene Sharaff

Synopsis

Fanny Brice, a bit of a meeskite, yearns for a life on the stage. She finds work at a local Brooklyn theatre. Eddie the stage manager stays up all night teaching her the routines. Before you know it, she's discovered by Ziegfeld and becomes a star of his *Follies*. Along the way she meets the rakish and handsome gambler, Nicky Arnstein. They marry; but while Fanny's fortunes soar, Nick's luck runs out. He's jailed for stock swindling, and Fanny divorces him. But somehow she finds the strength to continue her life.

Cast

Fanny Brice .... *Barbra Streisand*
Mrs. Brice .... *Kay Medford*
Mrs. Strakosh .... *Jean Stapleton*
Tom Keeney .... *Joseph Macaulay*
Eddie Ryan .... *Danny Meehan*
Nick Arnstein .... *Sydney Chaplin*
Florenz Ziegfeld Jr. .... *Roger De Koven*

LEFT: Even though the lyrics are slightly cryptic (Why are people who need people the luckiest people, anyway?), few songs have become so identified with a particular singer as Jule Styne's great ballad has with Striesand.

RIGHT: Barbra "Bloomers" Streisand, singing "Cornet Man."

Funny Girl WAS A TROUBLED production from the beginning, so it's interesting that many consider it one of the best Broadway musicals. Without the star-making performance of Barbra Streisand as Fanny Brice, *Funny Girl* might be best remembered as a great score married to a so-so libretto.

The original idea for the show was that of Hollywood producer Ray Stark, who just happened to be the real Fanny Brice's son-in-law. Stark envisioned the piece as a film musical and hired Ben Hecht to write the screenplay. Fanny Brice, very much alive at the time, thought his draft was "a little fancy" but reasonably accurate by Hollywood standards, and the renewed interest in her career prompted Brice to write her memoirs. When she died in 1951, just as the book was going to press, Stark bought the plates and put the book on hold. He approached several studios about a film version of Brice's life, but was rebuffed by studio execs who recalled a previous, slightly disguised version of Brice and gambler Nick Arnstein's relationship titled *Rose of Washington Square*.

Stark got in touch with Isobel Lennart, a longtime Hollywood screenwriter who had written a screenplay titled *My Man*. He convinced her to redraft the work as a stage play, with the idea of opening the show on Broadway as a precursor to a movie version. It was a good idea, but it turned out that the execution wasn't quite so easy.

Stark, having no experience on Broadway, knew he needed a good producer and turned to David Merrick, who eagerly took on the project. Jule Styne, who had had a recent success with another bio-musical, *Gypsy*, agreed to write the music. Styne went to Stephen Sondheim, who came aboard to write the lyrics until Stark made a presentation to Mary Martin, then a reigning queen of Broadway. Sondheim balked and dropped out of the project. Jerome Robbins was hired to direct and choreograph.

Now all they needed was a lyricist. Fortune intervened when Styne bumped into Bob Merrill, an old friend from his days at Republic Pictures, and asked Merrill if he would write five songs on spec. They played the songs for potential star Anne Bancroft; she was aghast at the vocal range, predicting that no actress would ever be found to sing those songs.

Stark and Merrick discussed the project with Carol Burnett, Shirley MacLaine, and Eydie Gorme (who wanted Steve Lawrence to play Arnstein). Robbins got disgusted and left. Bob Fosse was hired next, but he, too, lost patience and quit. Finally, Garson Kanin was signed as director. Styne then suggested that the team listen to Barbra Streisand, just beginning to make a name for herself, but Stark's wife (Brice's daughter), Fran, was against Streisand, thinking she wasn't classy enough to play the sophisticated (offstage) Brice.

Just as things were looking up, Stark and Merrick had a falling out and a real conflict arose when it was revealed that while Stark owned the property, Merrick owned Streisand's contract.

As rehearsals progressed, the show was extensively reshaped, mostly to show Streisand to better advantage. Other performers had their parts cut down, and actress Allyn Ann McLerie lost her role entirely. Jerome Robbins was brought in to lend an unbiased eye and to help spark the show by tightening the pacing and adding fluid transitions between scenes. When it was suggested that Robbins and Kanin share directing credit, Kanin flatly rejected the idea, since he had been deeply involved in the show for eight months. Ultimately, Robbins's credit read, "Production Supervised by Jerome Robbins" and an ego-bruised Kanin left the show. The constant tinkering resulted in the show's opening being postponed five times, but when it did open, it was a smash hit, due in large part to the score and, of course, Streisand's performance. ✳

SONGS

ACT I "If a Girl Isn't Pretty" · "I'm the Greatest Star" "Cornet Man" · "Who Taught Her Everything" · "His Love Makes Me Beautiful" · "I Want to Be Seen with You Tonight" · "Henry Street" · "People" · "You Are Woman" "Don't Rain on My Parade"
ACT II "Sadie, Sadie" · "Find Yourself a Man" · "Rat-Tat-Tat-Tat" · "Who Are You Now?" · "The Music That Makes Me Dance"

Bob Merrill

Bob Merrill, composer and lyricist, began his career writing novelty songs such as "How Much Is That Doggie in the Window?" before auditioning a score for director George Abbott and producers Robert Griffith and Hal Prince and winning his first Broadway show, *New Girl in Town*. After writing two David Merrick hits, *Take Me Along* and *Carnival!*, he began bouncing back and forth between working as lyricist on such Jule Styne shows as *Funny Girl* and *Sugar*, and writing complete scores (*Henry, Sweet Henry*). Despite the fact that two of his shows, *Prettybelle* and *The Prince of Grand Street*, closed prior to Broadway, and another, the legendary misfire *Breakfast at Tiffany's*, closed in previews, his output over his twenty-year career was impressive. Although cynics accused Merrill of being overly sentimental and musically simplistic (it was often reported that he composed his songs on a toy xylophone), upon closer examination, this simply is not true. While his greatest songs as a composer ("It's Good to Be Alive" from *New Girl in Town*, "Mira" from *Carnival!*, "Here I Am" from the half-great score to *Henry, Sweet Henry*) have an undeniable simplicity, full of joyful innocence, his lyrics to songs like "You Are Woman" from *Funny Girl* and "On the Farm" from *New Girl* reveal the verbal dexterity and bite of an artist in complete control of his craft. His last job, under the pseudonym Paul Stryker, was doctoring the lyrics for old friend Jule Styne's last musical, *The Red Shoes*.

TOP: Frequent collaborators Bob Merrill and Jule Styne.

RIGHT: Eileen Herlie and Jackie Gleason as middle-aged sweethearts in Bob Merrill's *Take Me Along*.

In this cinematic sequence, the action melts from Fanny reminiscing about her youth directly into a flashback of her mother and friends playing poker.

Backstage

Jule Styne named his son Nick after the character Nicky Arnstein.

Robbins, Fosse, and Kanin all wanted "People" cut from the score.

LEFT: The only disappointment of the movie version of *Funny Girl* was the loss of most of the scenes of Fanny Brice performing (a Swan Lake burlesque was filmed but only a few seconds were spared the cutting room floor). Thus, Streisand lost the opportunity to show the clownish side of Brice, here as Private Schwartz from Rockaway in "Rat-a tat-tat."

LOWER LEFT: Kay Medford (here with Jack Carter) replaced Pat Marshall shortly after the opening of *Mr. Wonderful*, also starring future *Bye Bye, Birdie* star Chita Rivera.

BELOW: Streisand as Brice, singing "The Music That Makes Me Dance," the closest thing in Styne and Merrill's score to Brice's real-life trademark song, "My Man."

"You've got to have a Jewish girl, and if she's not Jewish she at least has to have a nose."

—*Stephen Sondheim to Jule Styne, after meeting Mary Martin*

Kay Medford

Kay Medford, a talented character actress whose specialty was Jewish mothers (just to prove how talented an actress she was, her birth name was Maggie O'Regin), made her debut in *Paint Your Wagon*, before appearing in two revues, *John Murray Anderson's Almanac*, and *Almost Crazy*. After replacing Pat Marshall in *Mr. Wonderful*, and a City Center *Carousel*, she struck comic gold as Dick Van Dyke's mother in *Bye, Bye Birdie*. Only five years older than Van Dyke, she was hilarious in her relentless attempts to break up her beloved Albert's relationship. Following a City Center revival of *Pal Joey* in which she sang "Zip" opposite Bob Fosse, Medford landed her best (and best-known) role. As Barbra Streisand's mother in *Funny Girl*, a role she reprised in the film version (albeit without her two big numbers, "Who Taught Her Everything She Knows," prerecorded but never filmed, and "Find Yourself a Man"), she gave a brilliantly nuanced portrayal of Rosie Brice, expressing deep love for her daughter and real concern subtly layered into her deadpan skepticism. Medford was not nearly as lucky with straight plays: with the exception of *A Hole in the Head* in 1957, and Woody Allen's *Don't Drink the Water*, which she left early to film *Funny Girl*, she appeared in six Broadway plays that ran less than a month each.

A FUNNY THING HAPPENED ON THE WAY TO THE FORUM

OPENED MAY 8, 1962; ALVIN THEATRE; 964 PERFORMANCES

Four horny old men with unfortunate hair: John Carradine, Jack Gilford, David Burns, and Zero Mostel proclaim, "Everybody Ought to Have a Maid."

A FUNNY THING HAPPENED ON THE WAY TO THE FORUM

Produced by Harold Prince

Music and Lyrics by Stephen Sondheim
Book by Burt Shevelove and Larry Gelbart
Music orchestrated by
Irwin Kostal and Sid Ramin
Musical Director: Harold Hastings
Dance Arrangements by Hal Schaefer
Additional Dance Music by Betty Walberg

Directed by George Abbott
Choreographed by Jack Cole
Additional Staging and Choreography by
Jerome Robbins

Scenic Design by Tony Walton
Costume Design by Tony Walton
Lighting Design by Jean Rosenthal

Synopsis

This is a farce, so pay particularly close attention: Pseudolus, a slave in the house of Senex, will do practically anything—no, make that absolutely anything—to gain his freedom. Senex's son, Hero (what else?), is just discovering girls and falls in love with Philia, the girl next door. The problem is, the girl next door is a virgin—and a courtesan owned by Marcus Lycus. Hero promises Pseudolus his freedom if he arranges a meeting between Philia and him. Second catch: Roman soldier extraordinaire, Miles Gloriosus, is on his way to retrieve Philia, who he has purchased as a mail-order bride. When Miles Gloriosus arrives to pick up his purchase at the will-call window of the House of Marcus Lycus, Pseudolus tells him that Philia has died from the plague, and show Miles her body—only it's really his friend Hysterium, an extremely nervous slave in a shroud. Miles demands a funeral pyre and.... Well, by the end, Hero and Philia are united; Miles and Philia discover that they are siblings and the lost children of Erronius, who has searched the world for his offspring; and Pseudolus gains his freedom.

Cast

Prologus/Pseudolus	*Zero Mostel*
Senex	*David Burns*
Domina	*Ruth Kobart*
Hero	*Brian Davies*
Hysterium	*Jack Gilford*
Lycus	*John Carradine*
Philia	*Preshy Marker*
Erronius	*Raymond Walburn*
Miles Gloriosus	*Ronald Holgate*

Is there a doctor in the house? It's an oft-asked question, especially for shows experiencing difficulties in tryouts, and the "doctor" most producers and directors turned to was director and choreographer Jerome Robbins. The list of musicals he directed and choreographed is remarkable, and even a partial list of musicals he doctored is impressive: *Funny Girl, Silk Stockings, Wonderful Town, Wish You Were Here, A Tree Grows in Brooklyn,* and *Cabaret,* for starters. And *A Funny Thing Happened on the Way to the Forum.* (He also had a hand in some flops, including *Seventh Heaven, 1600 Pennsylvania Avenue,* and *Ankles Aweigh.*)

A Funny Thing Happened was a smash hit in its gypsy run-through prior to going on the road, but when it opened in New Haven, its reception was lackluster. Not bad, but not especially good either. One problem was that the authors had been convinced to simplify the plot—so they quickly started putting the complications back in. The original ingénue and juvenile were recast. The show moved to D.C., and, as Harold Prince tells it, over half the audience left the theatre before the final curtain rang down.

The original opening was a gentle little song titled "Love Is in the Air," sung by David Burns, one of the supporting leads. Stephen Sondheim had realized that "Love Is in the Air" gave the wrong signal, and he wrote the song "Invocation," but Abbott rejected it as not hummable. Prince knew something was wrong but didn't quite know how to fix the problem, so he called in Jerome Robbins. Robbins had originally agreed to direct *A Funny Thing Happened* but dropped out when he decided that the material wasn't

> "If you don't take this part, I'll stab you in the balls. It's our first chance at security and you're blowing it."
>
> —Kate Mostel, addressing her husband's reluctance to take the role of Pseudolus

ready and that the producer, David Merrick, was too difficult. Once Merrick was out of the picture, Robbins came back, only to withdraw for a second time (Larry Gelbart had sent Robbins a telegram reading in part, "Your cowardly withdrawal is consistent with your well-earned reputation for immorality"). There was some trepidation about whether Robbins would be accepted as director by Jack Gilford and Zero Mostel, for both Gilford and Mostel had been blacklisted by the House Un-American Activities Committee, and Robbins had named names (including Jack Gilford's wife!). But Mostel told Prince that he welcomed Robbins's help because, "we of the left do not blacklist."

Robbins did join the show, tightening some numbers and restaging a few more. He had Sondheim write "I'm Calm" and a couple of reprises of "Everybody Ought to Have a Maid." But most important, Robbins told Sondheim that the opening didn't work and audiences didn't know what the show was about, suggesting that the wild, hilarious farce could work only if the audience was prepared to laugh. Abbott now agreed, so Sondheim went to work on "Comedy Tonight." The song went into the show, and from that moment, *A Funny Thing Happened* was the huge hit everyone expected it to be. ❈

ABOVE RIGHT: Perfectly cast as a cigar-chomping devil, David Burns, along with Tallulah Bankhead (who only occasionally chomped cigars), in a sketch from the out-of-town closer *Ziegfeld Follies of 1956*.

RIGHT: Burns with the only cast member of *70, Girls, 70* to pay full bus fare, Tommy Breslin, during rehearsals for their "Go Visit Your Grandmother" soft shoe.

ABOVE: The fast and loose qualities of farce can lead actors of Zero Mostel's great talent and greater ego to believe that they have been given license to leave the page. Always a mistake, for farce is fragile and intricately constructed chaos. A smart, seasoned director like Hal Prince revisits his shows often, to—as he puts it—"take out the improvements."

David Burns

David Burns, who always looked at home with a cigar and a scowl, had an unbelieveably long career on the Broadway stage, dating back to 1923's *Polly Preferred*. He spent the 1930s on the London stage, then he returned to the United States at the beginning of World War II and was rarely out of work as a second banana in *Billion Dollar Baby*, *Make Mine Manhattan*, *Alive and Kicking*, and *Out of This World*. He costarred with brilliant vocalists Bette Davis (in *Two's Company*) and Tallulah Bankhead (in the *Ziegfeld Follies of 1956*), but luckily, the *Follies* closed in New Haven, freeing Burns to go directly into

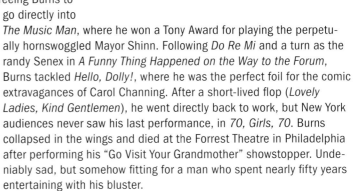

The Music Man, where he won a Tony Award for playing the perpetually hornswoggled Mayor Shinn. Following *Do Re Mi* and a turn as the randy Senex in *A Funny Thing Happened on the Way to the Forum*, Burns tackled *Hello, Dolly!*, where he was the perfect foil for the comic extravagances of Carol Channing. After a short-lived flop (*Lovely Ladies, Kind Gentlemen*), he went directly back to work, but New York audiences never saw his last performance, in *70, Girls, 70*. Burns collapsed in the wings and died at the Forrest Theatre in Philadelphia after performing his "Go Visit Your Grandmother" showstopper. Undeniably sad, but somehow fitting for a man who spent nearly fifty years entertaining with his bluster.

Tony Walton

Tony Walton, set and costume designer, has a flair for vibrant color and larger-than-life scenarios. He made his Boadway debut with *A Funny Thing Happened on the Way to the Forum*. After working on more traditional musicals like *Golden Boy* and *The Apple Tree*, he made Broadway magic with his sets for Bob Fosse's directorial sleight-of-hand in *Pippin*. With the Lincoln Center revival of *Anything Goes* and *Grand Hotel* in the late 1980s, he began long and busy collaborations with directors Jerry Zaks and Tommy Tune, including *The Will Rogers Follies* and his greatest work, the 1992 revival of *Guys and Dolls*. Like Oliver Smith and Jo Mielziner before him, his renderings are true works of art: his atmospheric drawing of five scantily clad women in *Chicago* has become one of the most famous logos ever. Recently, he has tackled directing, adding yet another string to his bow.

SONGS

ACT I "Comedy, Tonight" · "Love, I Hear" · "Free" · "The House of Marcus Lycus" · "Lovely" · "Pretty Little Picture" "Everybody Ought to Have a Maid" · "I'm Calm" · "Impossible" · "Bring Me My Bride"
ACT II "That Dirty Old Man" · "That'll Show Him" "Funeral Sequence" (Dirge)

Backstage

A quirky young actress whose tiny voice couldn't be heard played the role of Philia out of town. The actress's name? Karen Black (of *Nashville* and *Airport 75* fame).

ABOVE: Pseudolus (Zero Mostel) gets up close and personal with the gold medalist in Greco-Roman wrestling, Gymnasia (Gloria Kristy).

RIGHT: Brian Davies and Preshy Marker, hired as out-of-town replacements, singing "Lovely."

GENTLEMEN PREFER BLONDES

OPENED DECEMBER 8, 1949; ZIEGFELD THEATRE; 740 PERFORMANCES

She don't mean rhinestones: Carol Channing sets her sights on stardom as the wide-eyed gold digger Lorelei Lee.

GENTLEMEN PREFER BLONDES
Produced by Herman Levin and Oliver Smith
Book by Joseph Fields and Anita Loos
Music by Jule Styne
Lyrics by Leo Robin
Adapted from the Novel by Anita Loos
Dance Arrangements by Trude Rittman
Vocal Arrangements by Hugh Martin
Musical Director: Milton Rosenstock
Music arranged by Don Walker

Staged by John C. Wilson
Choreographed by Agnes de Mille

Production Design by Oliver Smith
Costume Design by Miles White
Lighting Design by Peggy Clark

Synopsis

It's the 1920s, an era of flappers and gold diggers, and the ultimate good-time girl is Lorelei Lee from Little Rock. Her sugar daddy is the Button King, Gus Esmond. Lorelei's friend Dorothy Shaw acts as a chaperone on a transatlantic cruise, since Gus is too busy with buttons. Lorelei, who espouses the philosophy that diamonds are a girl's best friend (Dorothy comes in second), uses her wiles on Sir Francis Beekman and borrows $5,000 to buy a diamond tiara from his wife. After the ship docks, Lorelei discovers many sights, chiefly Josephus Gage, a physical fitness nut and the Zipper King. Gus arrives in Paris only to find Lorelei in the enemy camp, sporting a zipper on her gown. After giving a spectacular performance in a Parisian nightclub, Lorelei gets Gus, Gus merges his business with Josephus's, and Dorothy hooks up with the millionaire Henry Spofford.

Cast

Dorothy Shaw	*Yvonne Adair*
Henry Spofford	*Eric Brotherson*
Lorelei Lee	*Carol Channing*
Dancer	*Charles "Honi" Coles*
Sir Francis Beekman	*Rex Evans*
Josephus Gage	*George S. Irving*
Gus Esmond	*Jack McCauley*
Mr. Esmond Sr.	*Irving Mitchell*
Louis Lemanteur	*Howard Morris*
Mrs. Ella Spofford	*Alice Pearce*
Lady Phyllis Beekman	*Reta Shaw*

"For Chrissakes, she can't sing and she looks crazy. Those big eyes, that funny voice. She's weird."

—*Milton Rosenstock, musical director, on Carol Channing in* Lend an Ear

DIMINUTIVE (IN HEIGHT ONLY) NOVELIST Anita Loos created flapper Lorelei Lee in her 1925 novel *Gentlemen Prefer Blondes*, first serialized in *Harper's Bazaar*. The book was an immediate sensation, and producer Florenz Ziegfeld approached Loos to adapt her novel into a Broadway musical, but Ziegfeld rival (all other producers were Ziegfeld's rivals) Edgar Selwyn had already signed Loos to write a straight play adaptation.

The play opened in 1926 with June Walker creating the part of Lorelei; Ruth Taylor played the lead in the 1928 silent-film version. After repeated tries, director John C. Wilson convinced Anita Loos to begin work on the musical version of her hit play. Meanwhile, scenic designer and sometime producer

Oliver Smith was sailing across the Atlantic when he ran into music publisher Jack Robbins. Smith mentioned that it would be a good idea to turn *Gentlemen Prefer Blondes* into a musical. While Robbins was in Europe, he let his friend Jule Styne stay at his Essex House apartment while Styne got situated back in New York after a long sojourn in Hollywood. Robbins arrived home and suggested that Styne contact Smith.

The show began to gather momentum once Styne, Smith, Loos, and Wilson signed on. Smith brought in Herman Levin as a coproducer, Loos selected Joseph Fields for help with the libretto, and Styne chose Leo Robin as his lyricist. The songwriters came up with their first song, "Diamonds Are a Girl's Best Friend."

As Styne and Robin worked on the score, Levin began raising the money. It was slow in coming until Billy Rose, owner of the Ziegfeld Theatre, which needed a tenant, invited Leland Hayward, Richard Rodgers, Oscar Hammerstein II, and Joshua Logan over to hear Jule Styne play the score. They were so enthusiastic, they each agreed to pony up $5,000, and once word got out that the masters of the musical had given their approval, the rest of the money was raised the next day.

Still, there was no one signed for the lead role of Lorelei. It was assumed by all involved that a name actress would be cast, and Dolores Gray and Gertrude Niesen were among those who auditioned. Then Jule Styne saw a little Broadway revue, *Lend an Ear*, and first laid eyes on Carol Channing. The following night he returned with Anita Loos in tow. Loos also flipped for Channing, realizing she could give some comic dimension to the dumb blonde Lorelei Lee. Yvonne Adair, also featured in *Lend an Ear*, was cast in the costarring role of Dorothy.

Once rehearsals began, the show quickly fell into shape, quite an achievement considering that both Leo Robin and Joseph Fields made their contributions by telephone and mail from California.

Gentlemen Prefer Blondes has remained an especially vital property. The film musical version was released in 1953, and, in 1974, Carol Channing returned to the part in a revised version titled *Lorelei*. Comden and Green collaborated with Styne on some new, inferior songs, and Kenny Solms and Gail Parent supplied a new libretto, bookending the show as a flashback for the now fifty-something Channing. Still, it managed to run 320 performances on Broadway. Less successful was a revival of the original musical that originated at the Goodspeed Opera House, squeaking out only thirty-two performances in 1995. Still, *Gentlemen Prefer Blondes* enjoys myriad productions around the country as a mainstay of the American musical theatre. ❋

LEFT: Howard Morris, Carol Channing, and Mort Marshall.

BELOW: (left to right) Herman Levin, Channing, Oliver Smith, Anita Loos, and John C. Wilson.

Oliver Smith

Oliver Smith, one of the most gifted and prolific scenic designers in history, began his Broadway career with the operetta *Rosalinda* in 1942. In addition to designing for ballet, opera, and film, his best-known creations were the beautiful, atmospheric drops and sumptuous set pieces for such legendary musicals as *Brigadoon*, *My Fair Lady*, *West Side Story*, *Hello, Dolly!*, and *Camelot*, widely regarded as the most opulent show ever. His career was astonishing, encompassing ten Broadway shows in the 1964–65 season alone (including such scenically demanding ones as *Baker Street*, *Ben Franklin in Paris*, *Bajour*, and flop of flops *Kelly*)! Also carving out a career as producer, he often wore two hats, as both producer and designer of shows such as *On the Town*, *Billion Dollar Baby*, and *Gentlemen Prefer Blondes*. He was involved with the American Ballet Theatre beginning with his co-conception of *On the Town* in 1944. The following year he became co-director of ABT along with Lucia Chase, a position he retained until 1980.

LEFT: Channing and company proclaim "It's Delightful Down in Chile" on Oliver Smith's ocean liner set. Note the trumpet at the lower right that the Brass I player has inadvertently left at the footlights.

Carol Channing

Bizarre yet familiar, gawky yet graceful, outrageously comical yet oddly touching, Carol Channing is one of those performers you have just got to see to understand. And once you've seen her, you may never be the same. Discovered by Marge and Gower Champion, she made her debut in the revue *Lend an Ear*, where her sketch comedy of the 1920s musical spoof *The Gladiola Girl* provided her with such socko material that she continues to use it to this day. Rocketing into the stratosphere with her "comedy comment" as Lorelei Lee in *Gentlemen Prefer Blondes*, she became the toast of New York for her wide-eyed innocence, expert timing, and loony vocals. After she replaced (quite unsuccessfully) Rosalind Russell in *Wonderful Town* and the flopperoo *The Vamp*, skeptics began to wonder if Channing was a one-off, too unique ever to score as any character other than Lorelei. She proved them all wrong; as the original Dolly Gallagher Levi, Channing became the one against whom all subsequent actresses would be judged.

SONGS

ACT I "It's High Time" · "Bye, Bye Baby" · "A Little Girl from Little Rock" · "I Love What I'm Doing" · "Just a Kiss Apart" · "It's Delightful Down in Chile" · "Sunshine" "In the Champs de Mars" · "I'm a'Tingle, I'm a'Glow" "House on Rittenhouse Square" · "You Say You Care" **ACT II** "Mamie Is Mimi" · "Coquette" · "Diamonds Are a Girl's Best Friend" · "Gentlemen Prefer Blondes" "Homesick Blues" · "Keeping Cool with Coolidge" "Button Up with Esmond"

Backstage

Gentlemen Prefer Blondes had one set of orchestrations in the theatre and another for the original cast album.

TOP LEFT: As naive farm girl Flora Weems turned silent screen star Delilah, Channing seemed to have everything going for her in the 1955 vehicle *The Vamp*: a huge cast, ornate sets, Steve Reeves. All that was missing was a show.

CENTER: In *Show Girl*, really an elaborately produced nightclub act, Channing spoofed *West Side Story* in the song "Switchblade Bess."

TOP RIGHT: In *Lorelei*, Channing commandeered the song "Mamie is Mimi" for herself, dancing with Broadway stalwarts John Mineo and Robert Fitch.

LEFT: Both Channing and Yvonne Adair went directly from the ensemble cast of the revue *Lend an Ear* to starring roles in *Gentlemen Prefer Blondes*.

GEORGE WHITE'S SCANDALS OF 1931

OPENED SEPTEMBER 14, 1931; APOLLO THEATRE; 202 PERFORMANCES

ABOVE: *Scandals* staple Helen Wehrle strikes a sophisticated pose.

RIGHT: Stars of the 1931 edition of the *Scandals*, Rudy Vallee and Ethel Merman.

GEORGE WHITE'S SCANDALS OF 1931

Produced by George White

Music by Ray Henderson
Lyrics by Lew Brown
Sketches by George White,
Lew Brown, Harry Conn, and Irving Caesar
Musical director: Al Goodman
Orchestrations by Howard Jackson

Directed by George White

Settings by Joseph Urban
Costumes by Charles LeMaire

Cast

Rudy Vallee, Ethel Merman, Willie and Eugene Howard, Everett Marshall, Ray Bolger, The Gale Quadruplets, and Ethel Barrymore Colt

SONGS

ACT 1 "Life Is Just a Bowl of Cherries" · "Beginning of Love" · "The Thrill Is Gone" · "This Is the Missus" · "Ladies and Gentlemen, That's Love" · "That's Why Darkies Were Born"
ACT 2 "Song of the Foreign Legion" · "Here It Is" · "My Song" · "Back from Hollywood" · "The Good Old Days"

George White's Scandals WAS AN annual series of revues produced, directed, and sometimes written and starring George White. The idea for the show grew out of the premiere Broadway revue series, the *Ziegfeld Follies*. White, at one time a featured performer in Ziegfeld's shows, decided that Ziegfeld was mired in the producing styles of the teens and earlier, and White became convinced he could move the revue format in a more modern direction through his own series. His revues were much faster-paced than Ziegfeld's, reflecting a new trend in jazzy entertainment, and White was the first producer to commission a score especially for a revue; until this time, composers had submitted individual songs to producers, who would pick and choose the best. Because he was a hoofer himself, White's shows had an emphasis on dance, featuring such songs as "The Black Bottom" and such performers as Ann Pennington (famous for the shimmy) and Eleanor Powell.

Ziegfeld felt so threatened by the success of the first edition, in 1919, he offered White and Pennington $3,000 a week to appear in the *Follies*. White countered by offering Ziegfeld and wife Billie Burke $7,000 to come over to the *Scandals*. For the next edition, White hired the young George Gershwin to compose the music, and the first of the great dance crazes to come out of the series premiered in this edition, the Scandal Walk.

Gershwin and lyricist Arthur Jackson repeated their assignments for the 1921 edition and enjoyed a hit with "Drifting Along with the Tide." The next year saw the series officially retitled *George White's Scandals* (prior to this, the show had been called simply the *Scandals*), and for this offering Gershwin teamed with his brother Ira (using the pseudonym Arthur Francis) and B. G. De Sylva on the hit song, "I'll Build a Stairway to Paradise." For one performance only (opening night) in the 1922 edition, Gershwin and De Sylva wrote a 25-minute jazz opera, *Blue Monday Blues* (later titled *135th Street*). White felt it slowed down the proceedings and had it cut, but it served as foreshadowing of Gershwin's ambition and budding genius.

When the Gershwin brothers left revues to concentrate their talents on musical comedy, White hired the team of De Sylva, Brown, and Henderson for the 1925 edition. They hit their stride with the 1926 edition with "The Birth of the Blues," "The Black Bottom," and "Lucky Day." Helen Morgan made her Broadway debut in this edition, but made such a poor impression she was fired. With this edition, considered by many to be the best in the series, White was so confident of its success he charged the then astronomical price of $55 for opening night tickets.

White's most successful offering in the series was the 1931 edition. It boasted a score by Brown and Henderson which included no fewer than five huge hits: "Ladies and Gentlemen, That's Love," "Life Is Just a Bowl of Cherries," "That's Why Darkies Were Born," "This Is the Missus," and "The Thrill Is Gone." The cast, too, was the greatest in *Scandals* history: Ethel Merman, Rudy Vallee, Ray Bolger, Everett Marshall, and Willie and Eugene Howard. In fact, even the lesser players were notable: Ethel Barrymore Colt made her Broadway debut (her final Broadway appearance was forty years later in the musical *Follies*), Alice Faye was a chorus girl, and Eleanor Powell made her Broadway debut in this show. White also wooed away Ziegfeld's designer extraordinaire, Joseph Urban, to create the settings for this magnificent edition.

However fine the material and cast, however, the country was then in the middle of the Depression, so even with all the star power, great music, and dancing, the show didn't run as long as it might have in better times. Indeed, because of the changes in both the country and the theatre itself, there were only two more editions of the *Scandals*, in 1935 and 1939. The latter, featuring Ann Miller, launched the hit song "Are You Havin' Any Fun?" by Sammy Fain and Jack Yellen.

All told, there were a total of eleven editions of the *Scandals*, and three films also used the *Scandals*' name (in 1934, 1935, and 1945). The revue series most in step with the times, its great success was due to the vision of the extraordinary multi-tasker George White, the actor, dancer, producer, director, choreographer, lyricist, and librettist who created them. ❊

George White

George White, a true man of the theatre, was born in Canada and found himself in New York City when his parents moved to the States. He wasted no time in getting theatrical experience, making his first stage appearance at the age of twelve, four years later hitting the vaudeville circuit as half of a dance act with partner Ben Ryan, and finally landing on Broadway at the ripe old age of twenty in *The Echo*. He appeared in a few more forgettable shows, until a moment came that would change his life (and theatrical history) forever, when legendary impresario Florenz Ziegfeld cast White in the 1915 edition of his *Follies*. After observing Ziegfeld at work, White became convinced that he could produce a better revue himself, and in 1919, the first edition of the *Scandals* opened on Broadway. Fast and snappy, with a youthful exuberance and a penchant for slight naughtiness, the *Scandals* were a great success. White also produced a number of hit book musicals, including the black show *Runnin' Wild* in 1923 (which introduced the dance fad the Charleston), *Manhattan Mary*, and *Flying High*. With the failure of *Melody* in 1933, he turned his attention first to movies with three *Scandals* films and then to nightclubs, mainly in Hollywood, where his last show opened in 1963. A presence for nearly six decades, White helped define the 1920s through his shows, launching such revolutionary dance crazes as the Charleston and the Black Bottom. In addition to helping the careers of many artists, he also brought the glamour of Broadway to millions of people through movies and nightclub entertainment. Close friends remember him as a shy, introverted man whose greatest pleasure was sneaking into his box offices and selling tickets.

BELOW: George White surrounded by the *Scandals* girls.

GIRL CRAZY

OPENED OCTOBER 14, 1930; ALVIN THEATRE; 272 PERFORMANCES

Mail (male?) carrier Ginger Rogers and Allan Kearns give in to frontier love in *Girl Crazy*.

GIRL CRAZY

Produced by Alex. A. Aarons and Vinton Freedley

Music by George Gershwin
Lyrics by Ira Gershwin
Book by Guy Bolton and John McGowan

Staged by Alexander Leftwich
Choreographed by George Hale
Music Director: Earl Busby
Orchestrations: Robert Russell Bennett

Settings by Donald Oenslager
Costumes: Kiviette

Synopsis

At the behest of his father, New York bon vivant Danny Churchill goes west (by taxi, natch). Danny doesn't especially want to give up the pulchritudinous pleasures of the big city, but Daddy holds the purse strings. So Danny does what any red-blooded American boy would do, he turns Custerville, Arizona, into Gotham lite. But he ends up finding true love with simple Molly Gray rather than with Kate Fothergill, the daughter of the town's saloon owner and a distaff version of the old Danny.

Cast

Danny Churchill .... *Allen Kearns*
Molly Gray .... *Ginger Rogers*
Gieber Goldfarb .... *Willie Howard*
Flora James .... *Eunice Healy*
Kate Fothergill .... *Ethel Merman*
Slick Fothergill .... *William Kent*
Jake Howell .... *Lew Parker*
"Red" Nichols and His Orchestra
The Foursome

"As soon as I sang 'Sam and Delilah,' I knew I was in."

—*Ethel Merman*

WHEN GEORGE GERSHWIN STEPPED UP to the podium on the opening night of *Girl Crazy*, Broadwayites were expecting just another musical comedy. As librettist Jack McGowan later stated, "We didn't do George justice." The cast was nothing special: Willie Howard was a well-known comedian but hardly a star, and he inhabited a role written for Bert Lahr, who was stuck in the unexpected hit *Flying High* and was unable to escape his contract. Female lead Ginger Rogers had appeared in only one other show, to middling acclaim. The juvenile lead, Allen Kearns, was a good, dependable performer, but not much more. Yes, the Gershwins' score was excellent, especially as conducted on opening night by none other than the composer himself. And onstage, making her Broadway debut, was a stenographer from Queens. This comely lass had auditioned for Guy Bolton, Bert Kalmar, and Harry Ruby for the musical *Top Speed*. But Kalmar was concerned that she was too damn loud! So she took an engagement at the Brooklyn Paramount, where producer Vinton Freedley was taken with her voice. He took her to meet the Gershwins, who liked that she sang too loud, and they wrote songs for her. Oh yes, that neophyte singer was named Ethel Merman.

Bolton and Jack McGowan beefed up her part, but the Gershwins wisely didn't give her anything to sing till almost an hour into the show. As Ira

SONGS

ACT I "Bidin' My Time" · "The Lonesome Cowboy" · "Could You Use Me" · "Bronco Busters" · "Barbary Coast" "Embraceable You" · "Goldfarb!, That's I'm!" · "Sam and Delilah" · "I Got Rhythm"
ACT II "Land of the Gay Caballero" · "But Not for Me" "Treat Me Rough" · "Boy! What Love Has Done to Me" "(When It's) Cactus Time in Arizona"

Gershwin explained it. "Although this young woman was appearing for the first time on any stage, her assurance, timing, and delivery both as a comedienne and singer—with a no-nonsense voice that could reach not only standees but ticket takers in the lobby ... convinced the opening-night audience that it was witnessing the discovery of a new star."

Overnight stardom is one of the most enduring clichés of the theatre. But it does happen very, very rarely. Those who come to mind are Gwen Verdon in *Can-Can*, Edith Adams in *Wonderful Town*, and Eartha Kitt in *New Faces of 1952*. Harry Belafonte's appearance in *John Murray Anderson's Almanac* made him a singing star.

Still, it's our gal Ethel who remains the epitome of an overnight sensation. She had appeared in a couple of nightclubs and, during rehearsals of *Girl Crazy*, took an engagement at the Palace Theatre. But it was her appearance at the Alvin Theatre singing "I Got Rhythm" that launched her fifty-year career. ❁

Backstage

Jazz greats Glenn Miller, Benny Goodman, Red Nichols, Gene Krupa, Jimmy Dorsey, and Jack Teagarden all performed in the pit band of *Girl Crazy*.

Alex Aarons brought in Fred Astaire to beef up the choreography. When they got to "Embraceable You," Fred showed some steps to Ginger Rogers. It was the first time they danced together.

RIGHT: Ginger Rogers, about to go blonde and go Hollywood, would not return to Broadway for thirty-five years.

BELOW: A star is born.

Ethel Merman

Ethel Merman, stenographer from Astoria and the Queen of them all, had more than just a voice like a car alarm, more than just a wisecrack at every turn of the plot, more than just an arm to be flung to the heavens with every note, held till kingdom come. Merman had It, that undefinable quality that is seldom experienced and can't be manufactured. Sure, some her shows were fairly silly (*Red, Hot and Blue*, *Something for the Boys*) and some were merely good instead of legendary (*Stars in Your Eyes*, *Panama Hattie*), but she was in only one true stinker (*Happy Hunting*), and her presence alone kept it running for a year. Her last original role, in the monumental *Gypsy*, provided her with a role that was, for once, not overflowing with the unwavering self-confidence for which she had become famous. Rose experienced moments of terror, anger, sadness, and loss; most of all, she had self-doubt, something that never crossed the mind of Reno Sweeney, Sally Adams, or Nails Duquesne. Knowing she had the role of her career, Merman ran with it, playing the entire Broadway run, even heading the national tour, something she rarely did. After that, there was nothing left to prove. She turned down all offers of new shows, claiming she wasn't interested. Perhaps bored, perhaps worn down by the constant questions, she finally relented and agreed to be the last Dolly Levi of *Hello, Dolly!*'s original Broadway run. Far more complex a personality than many believed, she wavered between a filthy sense of humor and a deeply traditional streak. The subject of the most hilarious (and mostly unprintable) stories in Broadway history, there will truly never, ever be another like her.

STARS WHO TRIED TO CONQUER MUSICALS

A H, THE LURE OF THE Great White Way! You've conquered movies and television, why not the musical theatre? After all, if Rex Harrison could do it, why not you? That's the reasoning, anyway, but it doesn't always work out as planned.

For every Richard Burton there's a Robert Shaw (1). For every Roz Russell there's a Lucille Ball (2). Or, as high school standardized tests would put it: Robert Preston is to Jose Ferrer as Lauren Bacall (3) is to Liv Ullman (4). Some made it look deceptively easy, like Tony Randall, John Lithgow, Tyne Daly, and Angela Lansbury. Then there are those who couldn't sing a lick in the traditional way but managed, through star power and determination, to make audiences think they were every bit as adept as Barbara Cook (we're thinking of Katharine Hepburn (5) as Coco, not Bette Davis (6) as Miss Moffatt). Sid Caesar—yes. Vincent Price —no. Diana Rigg—yes. Shelley Winters—no. Hugh Jackman (7)—a resounding yes. Melanie Griffith—a resounding no (despite what the paper of note thought).

GOOD NEWS

OPENED SEPTEMBER 6, 1927; CHANIN'S 46TH STREET THEATRE; 551 PERFORMANCES

Zelma O'Neal, who introduced "The Varsity Drag."

GOOD NEWS

Produced by Laurence Schwab
and Frank Mandel

Music by Ray Henderson
Lyrics by B. G. De Sylva and Lew Brown
Book by Laurence Schwab and B. G. De Sylva

Directed by Edgar MacGregor
Musical Numbers staged by Bobby Connolly

Settings designed by Donald Oenslager
Frocks designed by Kiviette
Conducted by Alfred Goodman
Advice in Football Technique by Knute Rockne

Synopsis

Will star football player Tom Marlowe play in the big game despite flunking astronomy? Constance Lane tutors him so he'll pass the test, win the game, and get the girl (Constance). And that's exactly what happens.

Cast

Tom Marlowe .... *John Price Jones*
Bobby Randall .... *Gus Shy*
"Pooch" Kearney .... *John Sheehan*
Patricia Bingham .... *Shirley Vernon*
Constance Lane .... *Mary Lawlor*
Babe O'Day......................... *Inez Courtney*
Sylvester .... *Don Tomkins*
Millie................................. *Ruth Mayon*
Flo .... *Zelma O'Neal*
The Glee Club Trio .... *Bob Rice, Fran Frey,*
                                              Bob Borger
Orchestra Leader .... *George Olsen*

THEATRE IS EPHEMERAL, LIKE *BRIGADOON*. It returns out of the mist eight times a week and then disappears forever, and productions and performers live on, a few bootleg videos aside, solely in the memories of their audiences. No man alive can tell us firsthand of the particular magic of the *Ziegfeld Follies*, Willie Howard, Julia Sanderson, or Fay Templeton. The shows are gone, too, existing only in photographs, posters, and maybe an early recording, with newer generations of audiences increasingly embracing their own time only, with little regard for the past. B. G. De Sylva, Lew Brown, and Ray Henderson, composers of *Good News*, were among the most successful writers in the 1920s and '30s. But today, apart from a handful of songs, they are forgotten. And the stars of *Good News*—Gus Shy, John Price Jones, Zelma O'Neal, and Inez Courtney—have left a legacy of lists. Lists of their credits appear in *Theatre World* and *Best Plays*, and on www.imdb.com. But we don't know anything about their acting or singing. In fact, we don't know anything about them at all.

Mary Lawlor was a pretty big star in her time. The titles of the shows in which she appeared give a sense of her talents: *No, No, Nanette; Queen High; Cross My Heart; Hello, Daddy; You Said It*—and *Good News*, of course. None of these had cast albums, and Lawlor, a minor figure in musical theatre history, isn't mentioned in autobiographies. But we do know she wanted to grow up to be a nun or an actress, actually attending a convent, where she couldn't help dancing. Upon being told she was going directly to hell, she quit the nunnery and entered show business. What went around came around, for after the smash opening of *Good News*, she was asked by those very same nuns to perform at their graduation ceremony.

Gus Shy and Inez Courtney, the comic couple of *Good News*.

But go to Google, and there's only one reference to her—for the film version of *Good News*. She's luckier than most performers of the 1930s in that she appeared in a film version of her stage hit, but still she's unknown today. Today's stars, Bernadette Peters, Patti LuPone, and Donna Murphy, will be remembered through video tapes, films , and recordings. Meanwhile, let's take a moment to remember Mary Lawlor.

She was just one of the reasons *Good News* was a success. The stock market was booming (for a while, anyway) and American cities were growing at a previously unknown pace. The energy of the cities was reflected in every aspect of the jazz age. For the first time, a sizable number of children had the opportunity to enter college, and all things collegiate became faddish. Youth was everything and *Good News* reflected the enthusiasm of flaming youth. Critic Burns Mantle wrote of the cast, "They sway from the hips. They wear their trousers baggy and their panties short. They sing with raucous abandon and dance like all get out. They rah-rah with gusto. They are very collegiate. Oh, very!"

Though *Good News* espoused modernity, the popularity of the show was based on the age-old values of the hit songs "The Best Things in Life are Free" and "Just Imagine." It might have been "Flaming Youth" and "The Varsity Drag" that propelled *Good News*, but at heart it was a simple story of boy meets girl. It's telling that when the first film version was made by MGM, Zelma O'Neal, the irrepressible energy that fueled "The Varsity Drag," wasn't cast. Rather, shy, demure good girl Mary Lawlor was picked to reprise her role. *Good News* had one foot in the future and another firmly planted in homespun homilies. ✻

B. G. De Sylva, Lew Brown, and Ray Henderson

The songwriters B. G. "Buddy" De Sylva, Lew Brown, and Ray Henderson are the most underappreciated of all major Broadway tune-smiths. Their shows were so rooted in their flapper era, they have failed to transcend time. In fact, the three, together and separately, wrote some of Broadway's most enduring standards, including "It All Depends on You," "Lucky Day," "The Birth of the Blues," "The Best Things in Life Are Free," "Lucky in Love," "You're the Cream in My Coffee," and "Button Up Your Overcoat." When De Sylva left the team, his partners continued with "Life Is Just a Bowl of Cherries," and "The Thrill Is Gone." Aside from his work with Brown and Henderson, De Sylva collaborated on such Jolson standards as "Avalon," "April Showers," and "California, Here I Come." With Victor Herbert, De Sylva produced "A Kiss in the Dark" and with Jerome Kern the enduring "Look for the Silver Lining." George Gershwin provided the music for De Sylva's lyrics to "I'll Build a Stairway to Paradise" and the plaintive "Somebody Loves Me." Among his other standards are "If You Knew Susie," "Eadie Was a Lady," and "You're an Old Smoothie." He went on to become an executive at Paramount Pictures and produced four hit musicals. Brown produced, cowrote the libretti, and directed three Broadway shows.

Backstage

Ushers wearing letter sweaters led audiences to their seats. Even before the overture, George Olsen marched his band down the aisles of the 46th Street Theatre bedecked in letter sweaters and cheering for Tait College.

SONGS

ACT I "A Ladies' Man" · "Flaming Youth" · "Just Imagine"
"The Best Things in Life Are Free" · "On the Campus"
"The Varsity Drag" · "Baby! What?" · "Lucky in Love"
ACT II "Girls of the Pi Beta Phi" · "In the Meantime"
"Good News"

TOP: Songwriters Brown, De Sylva, Henderson, and Robert Crawford (seated).

ABOVE: The lovely Mary Lawlor.

LEFT: Alice Faye, Marti Rolph, and kids of Tait College in the title song of the short-lived 1974 revival.

GRAND HOTEL

OPENED NOVEMBER 12, 1989; MARTIN BECK THEATRE; 1,017 PERFORMANCES

GRAND HOTEL

Produced by Martin Richards, Mary Lea
Johnson, Sam Crothers, Sander Jacobs,
Kenneth D. Greenblatt, Paramount Pictures
Corporation, and Jujamcyn Theaters

Book by Luther Davis
Music and Lyrics by
Robert Wright and George Forrest
Additional music by
Maury Yeston and Wally Harper
Additional lyrics by Maury Yeston
Based on "Grand Hotel" by Vicki Baum
Music orchestrated by Peter Matz
Musical and Vocal Direction: Jack Lee

Directed and Choreographed by Tommy Tune

Scenic Design by Tony Walton
Costume Design by Santo Loquasto
Lighting Design by Jules Fisher

Synopsis

The scene is Berlin in 1928. Through the revolving doors
of the Grand Hotel enters a varied cast of characters.
Colonel Doctor Otterschlag has seen it all from his perch
in the lobby of the Grand Hotel. Checking in are Elizaveta
Grushinskaya, a ballerina afraid of her advancing years;
Felix von Gaigern, her dashing lover who is also a jewel
thief; Otto Kringelein, a sweet, nebbishy man who visits
the hotel for one last fling before his imminent death; and
General Director Preysing with his secretary, Flaemmchen,
who dreams of fame in Hollywood. Fate has brought them
together at the hotel, and they will find themselves inter-
acting in surprising ways.

Cast

Colonel Dr. Otterschlag .... *John Wylie*
Rohna .... *Rex D. Hays*
Front Desk .... *Bob Stillman*
Zinnowitz .... *Hal Robinson*
General Director Preysing ..... *Timothy Jerome*
Flaemmchen .... *Jane Krakowski*
Otto Kringelein .... *Michael Jeter*
Raffaela .... *Karen Akers*
Elizaveta Grushinskaya .... *Liliane Montevecchi*
Felix von Gaigern .... *David Carroll*

ABOVE: "People come, people go..." *Grand Hotel* doorman Charles Mandracchia welcomes Michael Jeter, in his Tony Award-winning role as a mousy accountant on a final spree.

RIGHT: Cabaret singer Karen Akers made her second appearance in a Tommy Tune musical in *Grand Hotel*, as Rafaella, the (completely) devoted companion to Liliane Montevecchi's ballerina.

ALONG WITH *Dreamgirls, Kiss of the Spider Woman*, and Tommy Tune's other visual extravaganza, *Nine, Grand Hotel* was one of the truly towering directorial achievements of the last twenty-five years, with music and dialogue flowing seamlessly and, above all, visual elements coordinated so perfectly that, had an *auteur* of Tune's talent not been in control of the audience's focus, one might not have known where to look, so rich was the storytelling. Based more on Vicki Baum's original book than the MGM Garbo/Barrymores/Crawford opus, it had the longest gestation period of any Broadway musical, over thirty years from an out-of-town closing to a triumphant resurrection on Broadway. Originally titled *At the Grand*, it opened (and closed) on the West Coast in 1958, directed by Albert Marre and starring legendary actor Paul Muni; Marre's wife, the ample Joan Diener; and film star Cesare Danova. Songwriters Robert Wright and George Forrest believed the piece had never received its due, and Tune took

the project on, restoring the action from *At the Grand*'s Rome setting to the original Berlin location. The diva leading lady in the first version, an opera star à la Callas, reverted to a fading ballerina in *Grand Hotel* (allowing former Roland Petit dancer Liliane Montevecchi to dance *en pointe* after a thirty-year hiatus). After a workshop in the old Diplomat Hotel with Tune incorporating the mirrored pillars of the dilapidated ballroom into the floor plan of the set, plans were made for a full production. During the Boston run, as the tapestry of song, dialogue, and dance began to take shape, Tune called in friend (and *Nine* composer) Maury Yeston to supplement Wright and Forrest's score, much to the disappointment of the original authors. Originally only asked to contribute a few songs (most importantly a ballad for the golden-voiced David Carroll), Yeston agreed to join the project only if he were allowed to write at least one number for each of the six principals. All told, he wrote eleven new songs, sometimes retaining Wright and Forrest's verse, sometimes just a snatch of the original.

Word from out of town was that Tune had a disaster on his hands, as the cast never played the same show twice, even through a long preview period at the Martin Beck, but those in the show knew they had something special, and *Grand Hotel* opened to mostly positive reviews, with raves for Tune's tour de force direction and choreography. The original cast of *Grand Hotel* contributed to its great appeal, with lovable Michael Jeter, as the dying accountant Otto Kringelein, giving a transcendent performance, resuscitating his career, and delivering one of the most powerful Tony acceptance speeches ever. In addition, David Carroll struck a dashing, romantic figure as the Baron, finally appearing in a hit show before his death. Jane Krakowski, in the role played by Joan Crawford, achieved much acclaim and validation as a major musical theatre presence after a career as a

teen actress, with other principals Timothy Jerome, and former *Nine* stars Montevecchi and Karen Akers all giving elegant, shaded performances. It was a show with many unique touches: seating the orchestra (the orchestrations, on a par with the master Jonathan Tunick's, were by Hollywood conductor Peter Matz, in one of his rare forays to Broadway) on catwalks above the action; the sensational ballroom dance team of Yvonne Marceau and Pierre Dulaine; and the joyful showstopping Charleston by Jeter, Carroll, and company that had some audience members swearing that the lighter-than-air Jeter was dancing with the aid of unseen wires.

To be sure, some sniped that the book was subpar and the score was a patchwork, some

thought the use of the morphine-addicted doctor/narrator a bit heavy-handed, some found the scullery workers slamming their crates of cutlery noisy and unnecessary—but when the good things in a show are as good as *Grand Hotel*'s, it becomes easy to overlook its shortcomings. Above all, it was Tune's show, with every possible location created using only chairs and a pole, held horizontally to represent locales as varied as a coffee bar and a ladies' room. With the ring of a bell we were transported to the front desk, and the march downstage of three women carrying chairs signified the hotel switchboard. Its spartan use of scenery was a triumph of Tune's imagination, flying in the face of the lumbering spectacles of such shows as *Starlight Express*, *Legs Diamond*, and *Meet Me in St.*

Louis, which opened the week before *Grand Hotel.* Finally recorded three years after its opening (with the equally golden-voiced Brent Barrett filling in for David Carroll), its reputation as a directorial masterpiece has grown in the intervening years. In addition, it was a show that, like *Dreamgirls,* improved greatly during its run, for shows that are woven so intricately need time to find their heart and rhythm. ❊

SONGS

"The Grand Parade" · "As It Should Be" · "Some Have; Some Have Not" · "At the Grand Hotel" · "Table with a View" · "Maybe My Baby Loves Me" · "Fire and Ice" "Twenty-two Years" · "Villa on a Hill" · "I Want to Go to Hollywood" "Everybody's Doing It" · "The Crooked Path" · "Who Couldn't Dance with You" · "The Boston Merger" · "No Encore" · "Love Can't Happen" · "What She Needs" "Bonjour Amour" · "Happy" · "We'll Take a Glass Together" · " I Waltz Alone" · "Roses at the Station" "How Can I Tell Her" · "The Grand Waltz"

Backstage

1989's *Grand Hotel* was the first American musical since 1983's *La Cage Aux Folles* to run over 1,000 performances.

MGM musical star Cyd Charisse made her belated Broadway debut at the age of 71 as a replacement for Liliane Montevecchi.

ABOVE: The tremendous Brent Barrett, who replaced David Carroll as the Baron, and Liliane Montevecchi strike an appropriately dramatic pose

RIGHT: Jane Krakowski, as Flaemmchen, proclaims "I Want to Go to Hollywood."

BELOW LEFT: Kate Draper, David Garrison, Peggy Hewett, Stephen James, and a Tony Award-winning Priscilla Lopez—with Frank Lazarus at the eighty-eights—in Tommy Tune's clever *A Day in Hollywood/A Night in the Ukraine.* BELOW RIGHT: Darcie Roberts and Tommy Tune in a show that was variously titled during its pre-Broadway tour *Buskers, Stage Door Charley,* and *Busker Alley,* before finally running out of names and cancelling its Broadway stand entirely.

Tommy Tune

Tommy Tune, six feet six inches of show-business acumen, made his way through the Broadway gauntlet with jobs in the shows *Baker Street* and *A Joyful Noise.* After a stint in Hollywood on *The Dean Martin Show* and the film of *Hello, Dolly!,* Tune went to Detroit as part of Michael Bennett's *Seesaw* doctoring team, replacing the supporting lead and choreographing his own showstopping number, "It's Not Where You Start." Finally achieving recognition as codirector/choreographer of *The Best Little Whorehouse in Texas,* which transferred to Broadway for a three-year run, he had subsequent successes with *A Day in Hollywood/A Night in the Ukraine,* the stunning *Nine,* and a ninth-inning save taking over as director of *My One and Only.* After another out-of-town turnaround with *Grand Hotel,* where nearly every song

was either replaced or entirely restaged during its Boston run, and the hit *The Will Rogers Follies,* Tune had a run of exceedingly bad luck, helming *The Best Little Whorehouse Goes Public; Busker Alley,* which closed after a long out-of-town tour, finally derailed by Tune's broken foot; and a stage version of *Easter Parade,* with a workshop (starring Tune and Sandy Duncan, in a reportedly career-transforming performance) that failed to reach fruition. Perhaps understandably soured by numerous disappointments, Tune spent two years making a king's ransom in the Las Vegas revue *EFX.* Now in his sixties and still intensely creative, he is eagerly awaited by the Broadway theatregoers he has enriched and invigorated.

AL JOLSON

J OLSON IS CONSIDERED THE GREATEST performer of all time
by those who were lucky enough to see him in action.
His immense energy was fueled by his unstinting belief
in himself. Jolson was the ultimate egotist, a trait that
didn't endear him to friends but gave him the confidence to convince
audiences of his monumental talents. Jolson's greatest challenge was in breaking down any resistance to his charms and abilities. A little of his dynamic
personality comes through in his movie performances, which offer a hint of
his prodigious energy and humor. But although Jolson enjoyed early success
in talking pictures—*The Jazz Singer* and 1928's *The Singing Fool* (the biggest
money-maker in Hollywood history until *Gone with the Wind*), Jolson was
ultimately too big for the screen. Audiences need distance, and that accounts
for some of his fame, for even in the farthest reaches of the balcony, his clarion
voice and attenuated personality rang through. George Jean Nathan wrote of
Jolson, "The power of Jolson over an audience I have seldom seen equaled....
Possessed of an immensely electric personality, a rare sense of comedy, considerable histrionic ability, a most unusual music show versatility in the way of
song and dance, and, above all, a gift for delivering lines for the full of their
effect, he so far outdistances his rivals that they seem like the wrong ends of
so many opera glasses."

Theatre, to paraphrase Marshall McLuhan, is a "warm" medium, relying
on the interaction between audience and performer. Al Jolson was the ultimate
performer in such an environment. A corollary today would be the rock musician able to whip up a crowd, elevate emotions, and appear to be speaking to
the individual while addressing the masses. A persona is everything with a
rock musician, and so it was with Jolson.

LEFT: Al Jolson as Gus Jackson, a recurring blackface character he played in a series of Winter
Garden shows produced by the Shuberts.

ABOVE: Al makes his final Broadway appearance in *Hold on to Your Hats*.

Think of rockers like Mick Jagger when you read the following description
of Jolson's performance as related by Robert Benchley, writing in the first *Life*
magazine, "The word 'personality' isn't quite strong enough for the thing that
Jolson has. Unimpressive as the comparison may be to Mr. Jolson, we should
say that John the Baptist was the last man to have such a power. There is
something supernatural at the back of it, or we miss our guess. When Jolson
enters, it is as if an electric current has been run along the wires under the
seats where the hats are stuck. The house comes to a tumultuous attention. He
speaks, rolls his eyes, compresses his lips, and it is all over. You are a member
of the Al Jolson Association. He trembles his underlip, and your heart breaks
with a loud snap. He sings a banal song and you totter out to send a night letter
to your mother. Such a giving-off of vitality, personality, charm, and whatever
all those words are, results from a Jolson performance."

Jolson introduced more hit songs than any other performer, with the possible exception of Bing Crosby. He even received credit for writing many of his
hits, though it's doubtful that he ever wrote any music or lyrics. Jolson's shows
were full of interpolations—lucky was the music publisher who could boast on
his sheet music, "as sung by Al Jolson at the Winter Garden Theatre."

GUYS AND DOLLS

OPENED NOVEMBER 24, 1950; 46TH STREET THEATRE; 1,200 PERFORMANCES

Vivian Blaine and the Hot Box Girls, against the eye-poppingly colorful set design of master Jo Mielziner.

GUYS AND DOLLS
Produced by Feuer & Martin
Music and Lyrics by Frank Loesser
Book by Abe Burrows and Jo Swerling
Based on a Story and Characters
by Damon Runyon
Musical Director: Irving Actman
Music arranged by
George Bassman and Ted Royal
Vocal Arrangements by Herbert Greene
Vocal Direction by Herbert Greene

Staged by George S. Kaufman
Dances and Musical Numbers
staged by Michael Kidd

Scenic and Lighting Design by Jo Mielziner
Costume Design by Alvin Colt

Synopsis

Against the colorful backdrop of Times Square, a bunch of gamblers have a run-in with the Salvation Army, and Sky Masterson, an inveterate man-about-town, bets that he can woo the uptight Salvation Army lass Sarah Brown. Sky makes the wager with Nathan Detroit, a nogoodnik sharpie who has been engaged for fourteen years to showgirl Miss Adelaide, who has developed psychosomatic symptoms due to her perpetually unmarried status. Sky manages to get Sarah to go to Havana with him by promising her that he'll fill up her Save-a-Soul Mission with sinners, and once in Cuba, Sarah gets stone-cold drunk while resolutely refusing to fall in love with Sky. In the meantime, Nathan capitalizes on Sarah's absence by holding his "permanent floating crap game" right in the mission headquarters. By curtain's fall, everything is straightened up, and the two couples find themselves wed.

Cast

Sky Masterson	Robert Alda
Miss Adelaide	Vivian Blaine
Nathan Detroit	Sam Levene
Miss Sarah Brown	Isabel Bigley
Arvide Abernathy	Pat Rooney, Sr.
Big Jule	B. S. Pully
Nicely-Nicely Johnson	Stubby Kaye
Harry the Horse	Tom Pedi
Benny Southstreet	Johnny Silver

"I remember one time when I had a funny joke that I repeated two more times in my script. Kaufman looked at it and said, 'Abe, you've done that same joke three times.' I answered in a rather patronizing tone, 'George, we often do that on radio. We call it a running gag.' Kaufman said, 'Abe, radio is free. The people coming to see your show have to buy tickets. Give them a new joke.'"

—Abe Burrows

IT MAKES SENSE THAT SINCE Broadway represents the heart and soul of New York that the city itself, with all its accompanying glamour and sleaze, has served as an inspiration and setting for many musical comedies. *Guys and Dolls* is a valentine to the Times Square of Damon Runyon, with its host of colorful characters and exotic locations (exotic, at least, to the tourists who flocked to see the show), and the denizens of *Guys and Dolls* couldn't be confused with people from anywhere else in the world: their manners, slang, dress, and actions all spoke to the land of nightclubs, floating crap games, and blintzes. Although hundreds of other shows have been set in Manhattan, few have been so creatively inspired by the Big Apple.

The world of *Guys and Dolls* was the world of Damon Runyon, creator of the original short stories upon which the show was based. Like the Sholom Aleichem stories that formed the basis of *Fiddler on the Roof*, Runyon's world was based in reality but featured characters and situations bigger than life, often incorporating subtle twists and offering a moral in the bargain. Both writers reveled in the humanity of their subjects, for Runyon and Aleichem believed in the essential goodness of people, and although they skirted stereotypes, neither ever denigrated his characters.

Like Aleichem, Runyon knew of what he spoke and wrote about his own world. Runyon was a fixture at Lindy's Restaurant, immortalized as Mindy's in his stories and newspaper columns. He recorded and celebrated the patois of the streets, and *Guys and Dolls*'s lyrics make use of the unique phraseology of characters like Harry the Horse, Big Jule, Nicely-Nicely Johnson, and Joey Biltmore. In this world, "guys" are men and "dolls" are women, and other gender labels include "bum," "broad," "John," and "Jane." "Can do" meant that a horse could win a race, and the "morning line" was found in the well-known newspaper the *Racing Form*. "Shooters" were men who played craps with their "bundle"—the amount they had to bet with—and free tickets to shows were "Chinee" because the tickets had holes punched in them, making them resemble Chinese coins. Money was "potatoes," and a guy "tore a herring" at his favorite deli.

The slang certainly didn't make the songs or dialogue difficult to understand and added much in terms of ambiance and characterization. Runyon made up some of the slang, but even those words felt true to the period and personalities, for his stories are based on such real denizens of the Square as Titanic Thompson, the model for Sky Masterson. This honesty and exactness make *Guys and Dolls* one of the few shows that creates a complete and realistic world. The world of the Biltmore Garage and the Save-a-Soul Mission is in some ways just as foreign and exotic as the Siam of *The King and I* or the Morocco of *The Desert Song*, but those shows have modern dialogue and characters who behave much as contemporary audience members do. Perhaps the only shows that approach *Guys and Dolls* in creating a unique and specific universe are *Oklahoma!* and *West Side Story*, two other shows that make exquisite use of colloquial speech.

The brilliance of the score and book are deservedly revered elements in the success of *Guys and Dolls*, one of the most performed musicals in Broadway history, but above all else, Runyon's language is the mortar that binds all the elements together into a magical, musical comedy world. ✷

ABOVE: The saviors flank the sinner: Pat Rooney, Sr., Robert Alda, and Isabel Bigley, as Arvide Abernathy, Sky Masterson, and Miss Sarah Brown.

BELOW: Stubby Kaye raises the roof of the 46th Street Theatre as he leads the cast of *Guys and Dolls* through encore after encore of "Sit Down, You're Rockin' the Boat."

Backstage

Billy Rose invested $10,000 in *Guys and Dolls*, but when he found out Abe Burrows was going to replace Jo Swerling's libretto, he demanded his money back.

Feuer and Martin went through eleven writers before settling on Jo Swerling. When Swerling's script was deemed inappropriate, Abe Burrows replaced him. But Swerling's contract demanded credit whether or not any of his work was retained.

SONGS

ACT I "Runyonland" · "Fugue for Tinhorns" · "Follow the Fold" · "The Oldest Established" · "Travelling Light" · "I'll Know" · "A Bushel and a Peck" · "Adelaide's Lament" "Guys and Dolls" · "Havana" · "If I Were a Bell" · "My Time of Day" · "I've Never Been in Love Before"
ACT II "Take Back Your Mink" · "More I Cannot Wish You" · "The Crapshooters' Dance" · "Luck Be a Lady" "Sue Me" · "Sit Down, You're Rockin' the Boat" · "Marry the Man Today"

ABOVE: Walter Bobbie leads the revival meeting at the Save-a-Soul Mission in the 1992 Broadway revival of *Guys and Dolls*.

FAR LEFT: Vivian Blaine urges Isabel Bigley to "Marry the Man Today."

LEFT: Anthony Perkins and Ellen McCown declare, "Gideon Briggs, I Love You," in a rare Frank Loesser failure, *Greenwillow*.

RIGHT: Unchaperoned young love: Doretta Morrow, Ray Bolger, Byron Palmer, and Allyn Ann McLerie sing "Better Get Out of Here" in *Where's Charley*.

Frank Loesser

One of the most chameleon-like of all songwriters, Frank Loesser hit Broadway after a long career as a Hollywood lyricist, where he wrote lyrics for such greats as Hoagy Carmichael, Jule Styne, and Burton Lane. After an early revue, he wrote his first book show, *Where's Charley*, and scored a standard with "Once in Love with Amy." His second show was the smash hit and instant classic *Guys and Dolls*, still as fresh today as it was in 1950, and perhaps the most admired show ever by fellow musical-comedy writers. Every song is a perfectly musicalized character moment. His most ambitious undertaking was *The Most Happy Fella*, a three-act piece of near-operatic proportions, followed by his only flop to reach Broadway, *Greenwillow*. Loesser's final Broadway show, *How to Succeed in Business Without Really Trying*, won the Pulitzer, the Tony, and practically every other award short of the Medal of Freedom. *Pleasures and Palaces*, another ambitious project with a mostly wonderful score, seemed cursed from the start (after all, it was Bob Fosse's only out-of-town closer as well). He was working on *Señor Discretion* at the time of his death in 1969, and it was finally produced at the Arena Stage in Washington in early 2004. Although he wrote many standards, Loesser's greatest legacy is songs such as "Make a Miracle" from *Where's Charley*, "Marry the Man Today" from *Guys and Dolls*, and "Cinderella Darling" from *How to Succeed*. With their highly unusual song structures, they reveal an artist eager to stretch himself with every new project.

Nathan Lane

Nathan Lane is that rarest of things in today's world—a truly bankable Broadway star. After a musical debut as Chita Rivera's son in *Merlin* starring musical comedy genius Doug Henning (as Lane remarked, Henning's greatest magic trick was making the audience disappear), he appeared as Toad in *Wind in the Willows*, another flop. Building a name for himself in Off-Broadway plays such as *The Common Pursuit* and *The Lisbon Traviata*, Lane finally found himself in a hit musical. Directed by Jerry Zaks, whose sense of pace and business was well suited to both Lane and "Miss Adelaide"

Faith Prince, the 1992 revival of *Guys and Dolls* found Lane and Prince, cast as the traditional secondary couple, garnering most of the attention with their comic trapeze act. Next up for Lane was the slave Pseudolus in the revival of *A Funny Thing Happened on the Way to the Forum* (also directed by Zaks), a role that lent itself to his self-deprecating wisecracks and facility for the ad-lib. He appeared with Victor Garber in several workshops of the most recent Sondheim project, at that point titled *Wise Guys*, before winning a second Tony for *The Producers*, a show whose runaway success (at least with Lane and Matthew Broderick on the marquee) was among the most unstoppable in recent times. Like most great clowns, he has an admitted dark side, oceans of self-doubt underpinning his great comic gifts. His latest venture finds Lane wearing multiple hats, as both star and adaptor of Burt Shevelove's original book of *The Frogs*, reuniting him with *Producers* director Susan Stroman and *Forum* composer Stephen Sondheim.

TOP LEFT: Max Bialystock (Nathan Lane) pushes the very classily named "Lick-me Bite-me" (the hilarious Jennifer Smith) in a scene from the unstoppable hit, *The Producers*.

ABOVE: David Carroll, Nathan Lane, and Vicki Lewis in the unsuccessful 1985 musical, *Wind in the Willows*.

TOP RIGHT: Lane was both star and co-author of the Lincoln Center production of Stephen Sondheim's musical, *The Frogs*.

LEFT: Finding there was already a "Joe Lane" in Actors Equity, a young actor from New Jersey chose his favorite character from *Guys and Dolls* and became Broadway star Nathan Lane.

RIGHT: The perpetually engaged Nathan and Adelaide (Sam Levene and Vivian Blaine) get off at Saratoga for the fourteenth time.

GYPSY

OPENED MAY 21, 1959; BROADWAY THEATRE, 702 PERFORMANCES

Rose (Ethel Merman) gets ready to hit the road with her girls, just as soon as her father leaves the room so she can steal the gold plaque on the wall behind her.

GYPSY

Produced by David Merrick and Leland Hayward

Book by Arthur Laurents
Music by Jule Styne
Lyrics by Stephen Sondheim
Based on the Memoirs of Gypsy Rose Lee
Musical Director: Milton Rosenstock
Music orchestrated by
Sid Ramin and Robert Ginzler
Dance Arrangements by
John Kander and Betty Walberg
Additional Dance Music by Betty Walberg

Directed and Choreographed by
Jerome Robbins

Scenic Design by Jo Mielziner
Lighting Design by Jo Mielziner
Costume Design by Raoul Pène Du Bois

Synopsis

Ruthless stage mother Rose Hovick propels her two children, June and Louise, through the dying years of vaudeville. Along the way, Rose connives and wheedles to keep the act alive, but when June finally abandons both mother and act, Rose is left with the musically untalented Louise. Rose and Louise, now on a downward spiral, eventually land in the tawdry world of burlesque, where Louise unexpectedly finds her niche and becomes star stripper Gypsy Rose Lee. In the end, having achieved at least half her goals, Rose is left alone, having alienated everyone.

Cast

Rose	Ethel Merman
Louise	Sandra Church
Herbie	Jack Klugman
June	Lane Bradbury
Tulsa	Paul Wallace
Mazeppa	Faith Dane
Electra	Chotzi Foley
Tessie Tura	Maria Karnilova
Baby June	Jacqueline Mayro
Baby Louise	Karen Moore
Pop	Erving Harmon
Agnes	Marilyn Cooper
Uncle Jocko, Mr. Goldstone	Mort Marshall
Weber	Joe Silver
Kringelein, Cigar	Loney Lewis
Miss Cratchitt	Peg Murray

CONSIDERED BY MANY TO BE the ultimate Broadway musical, *Gypsy* is an ultrashrewd, deeply felt spectacle of life and show business. Subtitled "A Musical Fable," it romanticizes life up and down the ladders of vaudeville and burlesque. Every character in *Gypsy* desperately wants something, and it's that clash of needs that gives the show its dramatic drive. Its, loosely based on the memoirs of stripper/actress/author Gypsy Rose Lee, follows the good and bad fortunes of Rose and her two daughters, June and Louise, as they live out Rose's dreams of stardom in the theatre. *Gypsy*, a rare tragicomic musical, doesn't remotely turn out neatly packaged at the final curtain. The eleven o'clock number, "Rose's Turn," is as dramatic as anything in grand opera, a true aria for Broadway.

While the entire production team, including producers David Merrick and Leland Hayward, composer Jule Styne, lyricist Stephen Sondheim, librettist

SONGS

ACT I "May We Entertain You?" · "Some People" · "Small World" · "Baby June and Her Newsboys" · "Mr. Goldstone, I Love You" · "Little Lamb" · "You'll Never Get Away from Me" · "Dainty June and Her Farmboys" · "If Momma Was Married" · "All I Need Is the Girl" · "Everything's Coming Up Roses"
ACT II "Madame Rose's Toreadorables" · "Together, Wherever We Go" · "You Gotta Have a Gimmick" · "Let Me Entertain You" · "Rose's Turn"

Arthur Laurents, director/choreographer Jerome Robbins, designers Raoul Pène du Bois and Jo Mielziner, and orchestrators Sid Ramin and Robert Ginzler were at the top of their game, above all else, it was Ethel Merman's performance of Rose that provided the backbone of *Gypsy*. Constantly driving the show forward, Merman's powerhouse presence propelled the musical toward its conclusion, worthy of a Greek tragedy. Merman dispelled all criticism that she was simply a "belter," a woman whose lungs were disproportionately large in comparison to her heart or brain. As Rose, Merman's persona was perfectly captured by music and lyrics, allowing her to show off her expected brass as well as her all-too-seldom-utilized sensitivity. In addition, Laurents's libretto allowed Merman a rare opportunity to *really* act, enthralling audiences with the emotional tightrope walk of a decidedly unsympathetic character. Unfortunately, Merman would never again originate a musical character on Broadway.

One other ingredient of *Gypsy*'s success is worth noting: its legendary, thrilling overture. Jule Styne strongly believed in the power of the first notes heard by an audience, going so far as to handpick the pit musicians. Beginning with its trumpet fanfare of the "I Had a Dream" motif, *Gypsy*'s overture is one of the most recognizable elements in a production chock-full of perfect theatrical moments.

Gypsy provides a juicy star opportunity in Rose, making it the Promised Land for many actresses. After Merman (who played the entire Broadway run) came Angela Lansbury, first in London's West End in 1973, then on Broadway in 1974. Whereas Merman's Rose hurtled through life without reflection until her explosive moment of self-awareness at the end, Lansbury mined the psychological complexity under the surface of her vicarious pleasure, electrifying theatregoers with a particularly harrowing "Turn." Her sorrow and disillusionment in the last moments of the final scene with Louise, magnified by the theatrical magic of the revival's director, Arthur Laurents, added yet another haunted layer to the character. Tyne Daly was the next Broadway Rose, giving the part a willful, single-minded core. In Daly's portrayal, the "dream" became obsession, as she pointed to the same spot in the balcony of the St. James every time her goal came into view. Daly had scant need for the subtle wiles of Lansbury's Rose, becoming a truly unstoppable force of nature, sometimes physically knocking down those who stood in her way. Most recently, Bernadette Peters undertook this dream role. Peters, without the imposing physicality of her predecessors, explored the coy, manipulativeness of the character, creating a sensuous minx of a Rose. That this, the most famous of female characters in the Broadway musical, who could hold her own with Shakespeare's fatally flawed creations, can be interpreted by such a disparate group of women without growing stale as the years pass is a final, lasting testament to the brilliance and universality of *Gypsy*. ❈

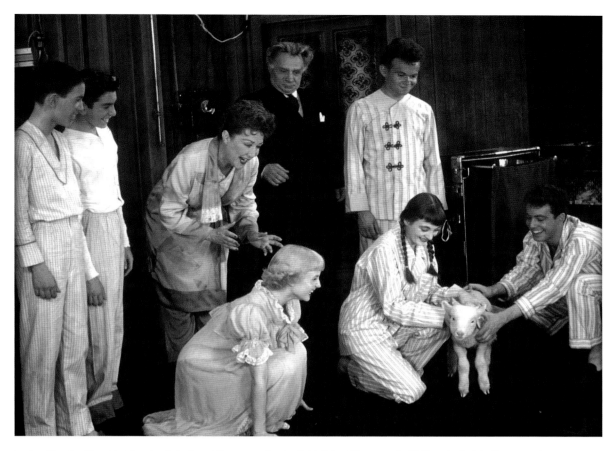

Louise (Sandra Church) gets a lamb for her sixth consecutive tenth birthday. Of course, it will fit perfectly into the new act her mother has devised.

Jule Styne

Composer Jule Styne had a prodigious output unequaled by his contemporaries and a staggering versatility and melodic fecundity. After early days as a Hollywood tunesmith, Styne and lyricist Sammy Cahn attempted to write for Broadway, and their second show (their first, *Glad to See Ya*, had closed out of town), *High Button Shoes*, starring Phil Silvers and Nanette Fabray, scored a hit. Styne again hit pay dirt with *Gentlemen Prefer Blondes*, working with Leo Robin as lyricist. Though it was only his third score for the theatre, we see in the song "Little Girl from Little Rock" Styne's uncanny knack for perfectly tailoring songs to match the unique charms of star Carol Channing. Through the 1950s and '60s, his stock rose, as he teamed often with longtime collaborators Betty Comden and Adolph Green. Their scores for *Peter Pan*, *Bells Are Ringing*, and *Do Re Mi* were in perfect step with the personas of Mary Martin, Judy Holliday, and Phil Silvers, respectively. In 1964, the smash *Funny Girl* became Styne's longest-running hit. With lyrics by Bob Merrill, the powerhouse songs "People" and "Don't Rain on My Parade" are so brilliantly tailored to Barbra Streisand's range and intensity that the show remains one of the few major musicals without a major revival. With the rise of the rock musical in the 1970s, Broadway seemed to let Jule Styne down. He dismissed the success of the British invaders of the 1980s and '90s and proclaimed himself the greatest living American composer—and he was right. At the 1993 opening of *Miss Saigon*, during the show's ballad "Why God Why," he turned to his date and proclaimed, "You gotta be kidding me ... they stole that melody from 'There's a Small Hotel'!" Even at that late date, you couldn't put one over on him.

ABOVE: Premier Broadway composer Jule Styne at the keyboard during a rehearsal for his 1962 show *Subways Are for Sleeping*.

LEFT: One of the highlights of *Fade Out, Fade In* was the song "You Mustn't Be Discouraged," with Carol Burnett as Shirley Temple and Tiger Haynes as Bill (Bojangles) Robinson.

LEFT: Maria Karnilova, as former ballerina, current ecdysiast "dressy" Tessie Tura, is mortally offended when asked by Cigar (Loney Lewis) to "feed lines to a bum comic."

BELOW: Jule Styne plays, Stephen Sondheim sings at a January 1959 backer's audition for *Gypsy*.

BELOW LEFT: Ethel Merman, Jack Klugman, and Sandra Church make an unholy pact to remain "Together."

BELOW: With the tug of a zipper, Rose Louise (Sandra Church) becomes Gypsy Rose Lee.

> "I thought he might hit me over the head, knowing that he wanted to do the whole show. He was young, ambitious, and a huge talent. But he was also very gentle, and we got along fine."

> — *Jule Styne on Stephen Sondheim and* Gypsy

Arthur Laurents

In 1957, playwright Arthur Laurents, along with Leonard Bernstein, Stephen Sondheim, and Jerome Robbins, sent shock waves through the musical theatre with his daring work on *West Side Story*. After reteaming with Sondheim and Robbins on *Gypsy*, a one-two punch of amazing artistic scope for the three collaborators, Laurents directed a musical for the first time, *I Can Get It for You Wholesale*. By hiring the largely unknown Elliott Gould to carry the show and a young cabaret singer named Streisand with an odd yet undeniable charisma, Laurents showed bravery in his casting choices. This continued in his next Sondheim collaboration, the fascinating *Anyone Can Whistle*, starring musical theatre neophytes Lee Remick, Angela Lansbury, and Harry Guardino. *Do I Hear A Waltz?*, a musicalization of his play *Time of the Cuckoo*, was, despite some lovely songs, by most accounts a miserable experience for those involved. In 1973, he reunited with Angela Lansbury, directing her in the West End premiere of *Gypsy*, which later came to Broadway and proved a great triumph for both director and star. In 1983, he directed the smash musical version of the French farce *La Cage Aux Folles*, musicalized by Jerry Herman and Harvey Fierstein. Another revival of *Gypsy* starring the gifted Tyne Daly made it a hit all over again, cementing the title of one of the finest books ever written for a musical. Laurents's fierce intellect, strong societal beliefs, and great craftsmanship have made him one of the mammoth talents of the American theatre.

BELOW: *Hallelujah, Baby!*, another Laurents/Styne collaboration, starred the magnetic Leslie Uggams. In the finale, "Now's the Time," Uggams's character Georgina has emerged from years of oppression and racism as a modern, confident African American woman.

Backstage

In the out-of-town tryout, the song "Mama's Talkin' Soft" was sung in counterpoint to "Small World," as Baby June and Baby Louise, perched high in the flies of the theatre, watched their mother trap an agent in one fell swoop. When one of the young actresses became so afraid of the height, she became hysterical, and the song, along with a wonderful moment illustrating the girls' awareness, was cut.

When the creators approached the real-life June, June Havoc, to sign a release allowing them to depict her by name, she initially refused, and the character was temporarily renamed Baby Claire. Havoc soon realized that everyone would recognize her as the character anyway, and she relented. During rehearsals the name change so confused the cast, they often referred to her as Baby Clune.

HAIR

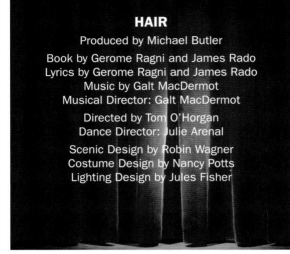

HAIR

Produced by Michael Butler

Book by Gerome Ragni and James Rado
Lyrics by Gerome Ragni and James Rado
Music by Galt MacDermot
Musical Director: Galt MacDermot

Directed by Tom O'Horgan
Dance Director: Julie Arenal

Scenic Design by Robin Wagner
Costume Design by Nancy Potts
Lighting Design by Jules Fisher

Synopsis

The American Tribal Love-Rock Musical concerns Claude, a young, free spirit (hippie) who is about to be drafted and presumably sent to Vietnam. He enjoys a last tryst with his friend Berger and Berger's girlfriend, Sheila. Jeanie, pregnant by a friend of hers, is upset that Claude is going into the army, as is everyone else in the tribe. But he does.

Cast

Claude	*James Rado*
Ron	*Ronald Dyson*
Berger	*Gerome Ragni*
Woof	*Steve Curry*
Hud	*Lamont Washington*
Sheila	*Lynn Kellogg*
Jeanie	*Sally Eaton*
Dionne	*Melba Moore*
Crissy	*Shelley Plimpton*
General Grant	*Paul Jabara*

ABOVE: Oatis Stephens, a replacement for James Rado, and "the tribe."

RIGHT: Jeanie (Sally Eaton) sings "Air."

THE SMASH HIT *My Fair Lady* introduced a new concept: the musical star who couldn't sing. You could say that this led in some ways to the demise of the big Broadway voice, and paved the way to musical stardom for actors whose main forte was not singing. Once the bar was lowered, it became acceptable to bring other talents to the musical theatre table that might compensate for a lack of vocal prowess: the likes of Richard Burton (who had a musical speaking voice, even if he couldn't exactly sing) in *Camelot*, Maurice Evans in *Tenderloin*, Vivien Leigh in *Tovarich*, and nightingales Katharine Hepburn, Lauren Bacall, and Liv Ullmann in *Coco*, *Applause*, and *I Remember Mama*, respectively. More important, this development drove writers to find new ways to evoke emotions that ordinarily would have been expressed musically.

And that, believe it or not, leads us to *Hair*. Once singers didn't have to have "round tones," the operetta form truly became passé, and new kinds of musicals developed. Coincidently, *My Fair Lady* had come to Broadway just as the first stirrings of rock and roll were being felt in the Deep South. *Hair* was the first true rock musical, not only because of the driving rhythms of the music, but because the singers had true rock voices. Later rock shows like *Your Own Thing* suffered the consequences of employing Broadway singers who didn't have the rock edge. For proof of this just take a listen to *Two Gentlemen of Verona*, like *Hair* with music by Galt MacDermot. It has a rock score but doesn't sound authentic, despite the talents of the cast. Lloyd Webber and Rice

were smart: when they cast *Jesus Christ Superstar* they employed performers with true rock voices (save Ben Vereen).

The other great Broadway musical that made *Hair* possible was *Annie Get Your Gun*, starring the potent combination of Ethel Merman and Ray Middleton, both enormously powerful singers. Given the then current vogue of the big band, the orchestrations were hot and loud, but these two performers could easily sing over them. For subsequent voices less clarion than a Merman or Middleton, microphones were introduced into musical theatre, never to leave. Soon, even performers with a pure, well-focused sound (like Barbara Cook) and belters (like Dolores Gray) used microphones because audiences had become accustomed to the sound. Furthermore, the existence of a sound board freed up orchestrators to work with a greater tonal palette, and without regard for bringing the level down for the singer. Hans Spialek's original orchestrations for *On Your Toes*, for example, were carefully calibrated to allow even the smallest of voices to cut through the orchestra, whereas today, the balance of sound is controlled electronically from the back of the theatre.

The rock performers of *Hair*, freely using the microphone in their performances, could be heard clearly throughout the Biltmore Theatre over the wailing of the guitars. Today, rock inflections have stormed Broadway: the pop-rock sound of *Les Misérables* and *Jekyll & Hyde* is delivered by singers who scoop notes, add syllables to single-syllable words in a mock gospel fashion, and depend on an increase in volume to indicate extreme emotion. All too often, the range of modern Broadway emotion can be summed up as *American Idol* meets *Aida*.

In *Hair*, the actors onstage really did feel what they were singing because they were expressing the spirit of the times. The events and ideas of *Hair* mirrored what was happening outside the theatre: people were antiestablishment and protested the war; belief in free love and equal rights for those of all races and sexual proclivities were new, hot-button issues, and they were being squarely faced at the Biltmore. Yes, there was earnestness in *Hair*, and much disorder and dissent backstage, but there was also happiness, fear, horniness, passion, and silliness. The cast members of *Hair* didn't just act their parts, they felt them, giving it an abject sincerity and raw truthfulness previously unseen on Broadway. Oh, and it also had the famous nude scene. What more could one ask for in a musical? ❋

Backstage

On April 26, 1970, more than 10,000 people were treated to an open-air performance of *Hair* in Central Park.

Late in the run, the cast of *Hair* was paid an extra $1.50 if they took part in the nude scene. Paul Jabara once mooned the audience and was paid only 75 cents.

The show grossed around $73 million in all its companies throughout the world, with the Broadway production earning over $6 million profit on a $150,000 capitalization.

"In a show like *Hair* you were professional if you showed up."

—*Lorrie Davis*, original cast member

Galt MacDermot

Galt MacDermot, a noted classical composer, made a name for himself as composer of the electric, eclectic rock score for *Hair*, written with Gerome Ragni and James Rado. His subsequent show, written with John Guare, was *Two Gentlemen of Verona*, a rock version of Shakespeare that transferred from the Delacorte Theatre in Central Park to a successful run on Broadway, beating out Stephen Sondheim's *Follies* for the Tony Award in 1972, an event that causes fisticuffs among fanatics to this day. His follow-ups to *Two Gentlemen* were not remotely as successful. *Dude*, cowritten with Ragni, and the legendary flop *Via Galactica*, written with Christopher Gore, had a combined run of twenty-three performances. Not particularly prolific, MacDermot's most recent work was 1984's *The Human Comedy*, featuring a highly interesting score and bearing many similarities to a folk opera. It transferred from the Public Theatre for a brief run on Broadway.

SONGS

ACT I "Aquarius" · "Donna" · "Hashish" · "Sodomy" · "Colored Spade" "Manchester (England)" · "Ain't Got No" · "I Believe in Love" · "Air" "Initials" · "I Got Life" · "Going Down" · "Hair" · "My Conviction" · "Easy to Be Hard" · "Hung" · "Don't Put It Down" · "Frank Mills" · "Hare Krishna" ("Be-In") · "Where Do I Go?"
ACT II "Electric Blues" · "Black Boys" · "White Boys" · "Walking in Space" "Abie Baby" · "Prisoners in Niggertown" ("3-5-0-0") · "What a Piece of Work Is Man" · "Good Morning Starshine" · "The Bed" · "The Flesh Failures" ("Let the Sunshine In")

TOP: Melba Moore, lyricist Gerome Ragni, and the cast of The American Tribal Love-Rock Musical exhort us all to "Let the Sunshine In."

ABOVE: Raul Julia and Virgina Vestoff in the Galt McDermot flop *Via Galactica*.

HELLO, DOLLY!

OPENED JANUARY 16, 1964; ST. JAMES THEATRE; 2,844 PERFORMANCES

"Wa, wa, wow, fellas ..." Many have followed her in the role, from Betty Grable to Nell Carter, but no one has put her inimitable stamp on the character of Dolly Levi (born Gallagher) like the irrepressible, irreplaceable Carol Channing.

HELLO, DOLLY! WAS, ALBEIT BRIEFLY, the longest-running musical of all time. Fiddler surpassed its astounding run a short time later and subsequently, in an era of never-closing shows, many lesser shows ran longer. When the waiters of the Harmonia Gardens sang, "Dolly'll never go away again," they weren't kidding. Dolly! has been a frequent presence on Broadway ever since its original run. The show closed on December 27, 1970, with Ethel Merman in the lead. Only five years later, on November 6, Pearl Bailey brought her touring company to the Minskoff Theatre for the Christmas season. Channing returned to Broadway less than three years after that, on March 5, 1978, this time with the Lunt-Fontanne Theatre as home to the theatrical favorite. After staying away from Broadway in the 1980s (while embarking on yet another tour), Carol brought Dolly! back for one last (we assume) spin, also at the Lunt-Fontanne.

Dolly! succeeded despite enormous problems out of town. The title was originally Dolly, a Damned Exasperating Woman, and an ad even appeared in the New York Times with that title. By the time it came to its out-of-town opening in Detroit, the name was changed to Hello, Dolly! But nomenclature was the least of the show's problems.

David Merrick believed that stress and tension among the creative staff made them work harder, so he terrorized the young Jerry Herman, who, admittedly, was scared to death. Merrick brought in songwriter Bob Merrill to mentor Herman and even contribute a few lines to the songs "Elegance" and "Motherhood March."

HELLO, DOLLY!

Produced by David Merrick and Champion-Five Inc.

Book by Michael Stewart
Music and Lyrics by Jerry Herman
Suggested by *The Matchmaker* by Thornton Wilder
Musical Director: Shepard Coleman
Vocal Arrangements by Shepard Coleman
Music orchestrated by Philip J. Lang
Dance and Incidental Music arranged by Peter Howard

Directed and Choreographed by Gower Champion

Scenic Design by Oliver Smith
Costume Design by Freddy Wittop
Lighting Design by Jean Rosenthal

Synopsis

Widow Dolly Gallagher Levi plies an innumerable variety of trades to make ends meet after the death of her beloved husband, Ephraim. Her chief occupation is as a matchmaker, and in that capacity she is hired by the chauvinistic, blowhard Horace Vandergelder, a very, very rich owner of a feed and grain store in Yonkers, New York. Dolly sets up Horace with the much younger milliner, Irene Molloy. Meanwhile, with the boss out of town, Vandergelder's two shop assistants, Cornelius and Barnaby, take the day off to see the city, determined to kiss a girl. The two miscreants run into Irene and her friend Minnie Fay, and the two pairs quickly fall in love. After a farcical meeting at the Harmonia Gardens (a fancy restaurant featuring a huge, red staircase), all are matched up correctly, with Dolly landing Vandergelder, much to his bewilderment.

Cast

Mrs. Dolly Gallagher Levi	*Carol Channing*
Ernestina	*Mary Jo Catlett*
Ambrose Kemper	*Igors Gavon*
Horace Vandergelder	*David Burns*
Ermengarde	*Alice Playten*
Cornelius Hackl	*Charles Nelson Reilly*
Barnaby Tucker	*Jerry Dodge*
Irene Molloy	*Eileen Brennan*
Minnie Fay	*Sondra Lee*
Rudolph	*David Hartman*
Judge	*Gordon Connell*

Backstage

The original cast album of *Hello, Dolly!* features a photo of "Come and Be My Butterfly," cut from the show just after it opened.

Harold Prince was offered the direction of *Dolly!* He agreed, provided Stewart and Herman would cut the title song.

Herman had composed a song titled "When I Lead the Parade"—close to being a good song but not close enough for Merrick, who brought in Charles Strouse and Lee Adams to lend a hand. They supplied a song titled "Before the Parade Passes By." Once Herman heard the Strouse and Adams song, he figured he could write one just as good—and did—retaining only the title of the first-act closer. During its gestation, David Burns's show-stopping number "Penny in My Pocket" was cut, as were several reprises. Gower Champion felt, and rightly so, that the show needed to move along as quickly as possible. Cast members James Dybas and Gloria LeRoy were replaced, and a performer had a tempestuous affair with (and got pregnant by) a member of the production staff. And to top it all off, the reviews in Detroit were kind but raised concerns.

Today, creative staffs of Broadway musicals are often so self-satisfied they ignore the out-of-town critics—or, even worse, believe them—and never make any changes. Most producers earned their stripes on Wall Street or through the time-honored tradition of inheritance and have no theatrical sense at all, while many songwriters steadfastly refuse to cut any of their songs. Our current wave of choreographers-turned-directors may know how to stage wonderful, boffo numbers, but when there's trouble with the book or performances, they have absolutely no idea how to fix it. You've got to hand it to the crew of Hello, Dolly!: they knew what had to be done and buckled down to fix the show. Herman, Champion, and Michael Stewart, under the watchful eye of showman/madman Merrick, addressed Dolly's problems and solved them to the tune of 2,844 performances on Broadway, with countless productions around the world. ✤

RIGHT: Carol Channing exudes generosity.

This full stage shot of "Put on Your Sunday Clothes" shows the vibrant, near flourescence of Freddy Wittop's costumes, perfectly supported by the neutrals of Oliver Smith's line-drawing-like scenery. Not pictured is the passarelle (borrowed from burlesque and later used by Tommy Tune in *Nine* and *The Will Rogers' Follies*) which director/choreographer Gower Champion exploited to the hilt, breaking the fourth wall, bringing the action as close to the audience as possible.

"It was like being tossed into a pool of show-business sharks."

—Jerry Herman on his first meeting with Champion, Stewart, and Merrick

SONGS

ACT I "I Put My Hand In" · "It Takes a Woman" · "Put on Your Sunday Clothes" · "Ribbons Down My Back" "Motherhood" · "Dancing" · "Before the Parade Passes By"
ACT II "Elegance" · "The Waiter's Gallop" · "Hello, Dolly!" "Come and Be My Butterfly" · "It Only Takes a Moment" "So Long Dearie"

ABOVE: Ethel Merman (here with her Vandergelder, Jack Goode) made her final Broadway appearance in the role she had turned down six years earlier. TOP LEFT: The wonderful Betty Grable elicited roars from the audience when she flashed her million-dollar legs. BOTTOM LEFT: Martha Raye delivered perhaps the most touching "Before the Parade Passes By" of any Broadway Dolly.

Michael Stewart

Michael Stewart, one of the most successful book writers ever, made his musical libretto debut with *Bye Bye Birdie*. Always the first to be blamed for a show's failure and last to be hailed for its success, the book writer is musical theatre's unsung hero, too often the glue that holds a show together. It's difficult enough to adapt a preexisting property, and to write an original musical for Broadway has given even experienced writers fits, but perhaps ignorance truly was bliss for Stewart. His book for *Birdie* is astonishingly confident in its breezy, generation-gap humor. He reteamed with *Birdie* director Gower Champion four more times, on the hits *Carnival!*, *Hello, Dolly!*, and *42nd Street*, as well as the cult flop *Mack and Mabel* and another flop, *The Grand Tour*. Stewart took much of the blame for that show's failure, but, as time goes on, one begins to realize just how difficult the story of Mack Sennett and Mabel Normand is to musicalize. He had hits with two Cy Coleman shows of the late 1970s: the wife-swapping *I Love My Wife,* and *Barnum*, a triumph for all, particularly star Jim Dale and director Joe Layton. Before his death, Stewart completed one more musical for Broadway: *Harrigan 'n' Hart* (another failed bio-musical, with a story just as tricky to tell as *Mack and Mabel*'s).

LEFT: David Burns's tour-de-force number "Penny in My Pocket" was one of the unfortunate out-of-town casualties of *Hello, Dolly!* BELOW: Pearl Bailey (with her register) registering suspicion. BELOW LEFT: Pearl Bailey (as escaped slave Connecticut) and Nanette Fabray in a comedy scene from *Arms and the Girl*, the Underground Railroad musical.

Pearl Bailey

Pearl Bailey, a comedienne and singer who combined folksiness with super-sophisticated musicality, made her Broadway debut in 1946, after carving out a major career in nightclubs. Often referring to herself in the third person ("Pearlie Mae has to take a load off, children"), her faux-lazy delivery became her trademark, lulling her audiences into blissful complacency, while she played fast and loose with both lyric and melody, suddenly kicking the tempo into high gear, jolting everyone in a twelve-block radius into the stratosphere with a burst of near-nuclear energy. In *St. Louis Woman*, *Arms and the Girl*, and *House of Flowers*, she stopped the shows cold with her renditions of "Legalize My Name," "There Must Be Something Better Than Love," and "One Man Ain't Quite Enough," all pitch-perfect songs for her persona. After appearing in clubs, television, and film (where she played Maria in the movie version of *Porgy and Bess*), she made Broadway history leading the all-black company of *Hello, Dolly!*, costarring Cab Calloway, to rapturous reviews and frequent revivals.

HOW TO SUCCEED IN BUSINESS WITHOUT REALLY TRYING

OPENED OCTOBER 14, 1961; 46TH STREET THEATRE; 1,417 PERFORMANCES

ABOVE: Buttoned up for the last two and a half hours, Ruth Kobart finally lets it rip with an unlikely combination of Valkyrie and Mahalia Jackson, while Sammy Smith, Robert Morse, and the rest of the executives declare a "Brotherhood of Man."

RIGHT: Charles Nelson Reilly as the obsequious Bud Frump.

HOW TO SUCCEED IN BUSINESS WITHOUT REALLY TRYING

Produced by Feuer & Martin Produced in association with Frank Productions, Inc.

Book by Abe Burrows, Jack Weinstock, and Willie Gilbert
Music by Frank Loesser
Lyrics by Frank Loesser
Musical Director: Elliot Lawrence
Music orchestrated by Robert Ginzler
Additional Scoring by Elliot Lawrence

Directed by Abe Burrows
Musical Staging by Bob Fosse
Choreographed by Hugh Lambert

Scenic Design by Robert Randolph
Lighting Design by Robert Randolph
Costume Design by Robert Fletcher

Synopsis

J. Pierrepont Finch, a window cleaner, finds a book, *How to Succeed in Business Without Really Trying*. By following the often underhanded advice in the book, he soon rises through the ranks of the World Wide Wickets Company. Through connivance, wheedling, and taking the main chance, he eventually ends up in the boardroom and gets the girl.

Cast

J. Pierrepont Finch	*Robert Morse*
J. B. Biggley	*Rudy Vallee*
Hedy La Rue	*Virginia Martin*
Bud Frump	*Charles Nelson Reilly*
Rosemary Pilkington	*Bonnie Scott*
Miss Jones	*Ruth Kobart*
Milt Gatch	*Ray Mason*
Bert Bratt	*Paul Reed*
Peterson	*Casper Roos*
Twimble, Wally Womper	*Sammy Smith*
Smitty	*Claudette Sutherland*

CAN ONE THINK OF ANOTHER musical that was so embraced by the public and critics (not to mention the Pulitzer Prize committee) that is so unabashedly mean-spirited? Our hero connives his way to the top in a single-minded leapfrog over the other poor wretches who would gladly do the same to him. Whereas *What Makes Sammy Run?* was a serious exposé of nasty doings in Hollywood, *How to Succeed* chose to go the satirical route. And since all the characters (well, all the male ones) were either morally despicable or completely incompetent, the audience, who never trusted those buttoned-down executives anyway, felt eminently superior. On second glance, the women were really no loftier in their motives, but instead of angling for a promotion they were conspiring to land a husband to take them away to the suburbs. Remember, this is the era of *The Man in the Grey Flannel Suit* and *The Organization Man*, two books that reached the best-seller list, while over at the Plaza Hotel, Julius Monk was satirizing Madison Avenue-speak.

Composer Frank Loesser and author/director Abe Burrows were two tough customers—indeed, they could have stepped off the stage of their own *Guys and Dolls*. But they were humorists, too, and their reteaming (along with Jack Weinstock and Willie Gilbert) sardonically and brilliantly captured the manners and mores of contemporary life. Rudy Vallee could be known as a cheap son of a bitch in real life, so he didn't stretch too far for motivation in playing J. B. Biggley. The J. Pierrepont Finch of Robert Morse used the mischievous glint in his eye, his cockeyed smile, and his kinetic energy with nary a wink to the audience—devious he was, yes; but like Rosemary, we loved him all the more for it. We'd have given anything to be swept off our feet to New Rochelle and a life of wedded bliss complete with a two-car garage.

Could such a show succeed now? The 1995 revival certainly didn't, artistically anyway, misconceived and miscast with Matthew Broderick in the lead. Nor did a recent, more serious look at the underbelly of the climb to the top, *Sweet Smell of Success*, with audiences staying away despite its many excellent qualities. As George S. Kaufman famously proclaimed, "Satire is what closes on Saturday night." Still, *How to Succeed* managed to stay open through many, many Saturdays by being the right show at the right time. ❋

Abe Burrows

Abe Burrows, one of the more intelligent writer/directors, contributed his slightly askew comic sense to some of musical theatre's greatest hits. He hit a home run his first time at bat in the Broadway league with his book for *Guys and Dolls*. He jumped back and forth easily among directing (*Two on the Aisle*, *Happy Hunting*, *What Makes Sammy Run?*), writing (an uncredited rewrite of Preston Sturges's *Make a Wish*, *Silk Stockings*), and undertaking both jobs simultaneously (*Three Wishes for Jamie*; *Can-Can*; *Say, Darling*; *First Impressions*). After winning a Pulitzer Prize for wearing two hats on *How to Succeed*, he wrote and directed the disastrous *Breakfast at Tiffany's*, where he was replaced during a nightmarish out-of-town tryout. He had much greater success as director of the hit play *Forty Carats* and his own comedy, *Cactus Flower*, both of which were adapted from French stage hits. He directed the unsuccessful 1974 revival of *Good News*, indicating that Broadway had gone to the nostalgia well one too many times after the hits *No, No, Nanette* and *Irene*.

TOP RIGHT: Smitty (Claudette Sutherland) and the girls in the typing pool dub Rosemary (Bonnie Scott) their "Cinderella Darling."

RIGHT: Rudy Vallee as Boss Biggley and Virginia Martin, who put the "va" in "va-va-va-voom."

Backstage
Bob Fosse came in and redid the original chore-ography by Hugh Lambert, save for Lambert's work on "Pirate Dance." Fosse insisted that Lambert retain his credit as chore-ographer, taking credit for Musical Staging.

How to Succeed was the second show for which Abe Burrows was asked by Cy Feuer and Ernest Martin to come in and rewrite an existing script. The first was *Guys and Dolls*.

ABOVE: Tony Roberts and Robert Morse on the lam from the mob in *Sugar*, extolling their new look, "The Beauty That Drives the Men Mad."

RIGHT: A typical Robert Morse shot: tousled hair, furrowed brow, twinkling eye. He's plotting something.

SONGS

ACT I · "How to (Succeed)" · "Happy to Keep His Dinner Warm" · "Coffee Break" · "The Company Way" "A Secretary Is Not a Toy" · "Been a Long Day" · "Grand Old Ivy" · "Paris Original" · "Rosemary"
ACT II · "Cinderella Darling" · "Love from a Heart of Gold" · "I Believe in You" · "Brotherhood of Man"

Robert Morse

With a goofy, gap-toothed grin hiding a slyly subversive side, Robert Morse made a splashy debut as budding producer Ted Snow (a thinly veiled Hal Prince) in *Say, Darling*. He supported fellow ham Jackie Gleason in *Take Me Along*, particularly standing out in a scene where Richard Miller, drunk for the first time, envi-sions a world full of women of low morals and lower necklines. Aside from his star-making turn in *How to Succeed,* his greatest perfor-mance came in a less-than-great show, *Sugar* (1972), based on the classic film *Some Like It Hot*. After a stunning comeback, winning raves and every award possible for *Tru*, his one-man re-creation of Truman Capote, he's twice been announced for Broadway musi-cals in the last decade, first in the Hal Prince revival of *Show Boat* and again in *Wicked* (2003). Though neither opportunity panned out for Morse, one suspects he's still got one great trick up his sleeve.

I CAN GET IT FOR YOU WHOLESALE

OPENED MARCH 22, 1962; SHUBERT THEATRE; 300 PERFORMANCES

"Momma, Momma": Lillian Roth and Elliott Gould as doting mother and ambitious son in *I Can Get It For You Wholesale*.

I CAN GET IT FOR YOU WHOLESALE

Produced by David Merrick
Book by Jerome Weidman
Music and Lyrics by Harold Rome
Based on the Novel by Jerome Weidman
Musical Director: Lehman Engel
Vocal arrangements by Lehman Engel
Music orchestrated by Sid Ramin
Dance and Incidental
Music arranged by Peter Howard

Directed by Arthur Laurents
Musical Staging by Herbert Ross

Scenic Design by Will Steven Armstrong
Costume Design by Theoni V. Aldredge
Lighting Design by Will Steven Armstrong

Synopsis

Harry Bogen begins his climb up the garment center ladder by hiring scabs to take over the jobs of his boss's striking employees. Furthering his career by underhanded schemes, Harry swindles his friend Tootsie by selling him half interest in a failing company. Meanwhile, he steals his ex-employer's head designer, salesman, and secretary for his own firm. He has an affair with a Broadway showgirl while bleeding the company dry, all the time making sure someone else is framed. By the end, Harry is back at his old job, under his old boss—and ready to make another rise to the top.

Cast

Mrs. Bogen	*Lillian Roth*
Ruthie Rivkin	*Marilyn Cooper*
Harry Bogen	*Elliott Gould*
Teddy Asch	*Harold Lang*
Martha Mills	*Sheree North*
Miss Marmelstein	*Barbra Streisand*
Tootsie Maltz	*James Hickman*
Meyer Bushkin	*Ken Le Roy*
Blanche Bushkin	*Bambi Linn*

"Her Miss Marmelstein came from the fingernails, not from the outside. She was simply incapable of just standing and listening.... Luckily, it was a musical: she had that incredible voice. But also the fingernails."

—Arthur Laurents on Barbra Streisand

THE AMERICAN DREAM IS A potent subject for the modern musical. Some musicals feature ruthless protagonists who will do anything for fame, money, and power, and who don't hesitate to step on anyone in their way. In this category are Sammy Glick of *What Makes Sammy Run?*, Joey Evans of *Pal Joey*, Eva Peron of *Evita*, and Harry Bogen of *I Can Get It for You Wholesale*. Those are dramatic musicals. For good ol' musical comedy schemes, you've got characters like J. Pierrepont Finch in *How to Succeed in Business Without Really Trying*, using the same ruthless tactics to climb the ladder at World Wide Wickets, this time to comedic effect. Straddling the line between comedy and tragedy is Hubie Cram in *Do Re Mi*.

It's hard for American audiences to warm up to these self-absorbed souls. Americans want to see a bit of themselves onstage, hoping for a happy ending with their song and dance. If they do get drama, they want to be uplifted at the end, as in *Carousel* or *Porgy and Bess*. Somehow, English audiences, coming from an outwardly more stratified and conservative society, will embrace questionable morals, along with salty language, nudity, and sex onstage, without feeling personally affronted. They can somehow differentiate between life on the stage and their own lives, and can much more readily accept the dark side of the human condition. They don't need happy endings or neatly resolved morals. Schmucks can be schmucks but interesting nonetheless.

But Americans are different. That's why none of the above shows, save *How to Succeed* and *Evita*, were successes. *I Can Get It for You Wholesale* certainly spoke to the Jewish audiences that were a mainstay of Broadway, but they didn't cozy up to the characters, mainly because Jerome Weidman didn't pull any punches in his adaptation of his original novel. *Wholesale*'s director, Arthur Laurents, believed in a more mature musical theatre, exemplified by *Gypsy*; but that show balanced unsympathetic lead characters with the satire of their vaudeville act and the broad burlesque comedy of the three strippers. *Wholesale*, fine though it was, turned off audiences who wanted at least the faintest glimmer of hope in their musicals. *Wholesale* has integrity and artistry to spare; what it doesn't have is hope. It's a closed room without any chance of light slipping in through the cracks—just like the room without windows in *What Makes Sammy Run?* ❋

Herbert Ross

Herbert Ross, talented choreographer/director, made his debut in 1951 with *A Tree Grows in Brooklyn*, followed by fine work in *House of Flowers*, *Tovarich* (where his delicate Charleston for Vivien Leigh garnered most of the reviews), *The Gay Life*, and *I Can Get It for You Wholesale*, where he staged the rolling-office-chair showstopper "Miss Marmelstein." His greatest choreography was seen by scant few: the "Cookie Ballet" and Angela Lansbury's Kay Thompsonesque numbers in *Anyone Can Whistle*. His directorial debut of a Broadway musical was also his swan song: the legendary one-performance fiasco *Kelly*. After that, it was back to the barre, with dances for *Do I Hear a Waltz?* and *On a Clear Day You Can See Forever*. After *The Apple Tree*, his second consecutive Barbara Harris musical, he moved to the film world, adding his theatrical sensibilities to such films as *The Turning Point*, *Pennies from Heaven,* and *Footloose*. He staged the *Follies* concert at Lincoln Center in 1985, reuniting with former leading ladies Barbara Cook and Lee Remick.

FAR LEFT: Two amazingly talented dancer/actors who should have been major stars: Sheree North and Harold Lang, both looking for a leg up, wonder "What's in it for Me?"

LEFT: Although she now claims the casters were her idea, Barbra Streisand's rolling-office-chair "Miss Marmelstein" number was actually envisioned and executed by choreographer Herbert Ross.

Backstage

Barbra Streisand's understudy was Louise Lasser.

Twenty-five years later, Barbra Streisand recorded *Wholesale*'s "A Funny Thing Happened" but the album was never released.

The entire *Wholesale* company at the unveiling of Harry Bogen's new dress line. (Little known fact: shortly after opening, the name of the company was changed from Apex Modes, Inc. to Acme Modes, Inc.)

Marilyn Cooper

Marilyn Cooper—comedienne, singer, and the original "Puerto Rico" girl of *West Side Story*—possesses unerring comic timing and a huge singing voice so at odds with her tiny frame that it has become both her trademark and her curse. She created the role of Hollywood Blonde Agnes in *Gypsy*, continuing her association with Arthur Laurents with her only leading role, in *I Can Get It for You Wholesale*. After a supporting role in *Hallelujah, Baby!*, understudying Eydie Gorme in *Golden Rainbow*, and a memorable Lucy Schmeeler in the 1971 revival of *On the Town* (where her piercingly nasal speaking voice was put to good use), she was richly rewarded for her years of trouping with a plum role in Kander and Ebb's *Woman of the Year*. Not appearing until halfway through the second act, she won a Tony Award for her single scene, one of the shortest stage times ever to yield a Tony. Bedecked in curlers, slippers, and nightgown, sitting next to the chic, put-together Lauren Bacall, "Coopie" (as she is known to her intimates) stopped the show stone cold every night with her deadpan delivery of zinger upon zinger in "The Grass Is Always Greener."

LEFT: In the 1971 revival of *On the Town*, Marilyn Cooper (here flanked by Jess Richards and Bernadette Peters) scored as "Lucy Schmeeler, girl of mystery."

BOTTOM LEFT: Proving that all you need for a showstopper is two stools and pinpoint comedy timing, Bacall and "Coopie" compare their lives in the ultimate Kander and Ebb good news/bad news duet, "The Grass Is Always Greener" from *Woman of the Year*.

SONGS

ACT 1 "I'm Not a Well Man" · "The Way Things Are" "When Gemini Meets Capricorn" · "Momma, Momma" "The Sound of Money" · "Family Way" · "Too Soon" · "Who Knows?" · "Have I Told You Lately?" · "Ballad of the Garment Trade"
ACT 2 "A Gift Today" · "Miss Marmelstein" · "A Funny Thing Happened" · "What's in It for Me?" · "What Are They Doing to Us Now? " · "Eat a Little Something"

GUILTY PLEASURES

In *Bajour*, the eternal guilty pleasure, each character was goofier than the next, from Chita Rivera's gypsy to Mae Questel's Rego Park Jewish mother. Still, it had a highly enjoyable score by Walter Marks with often clever lyrics (the animal noises of "Where Is the Tribe for Me?" aside).

ALL RIGHT, YOU CAN COME out from behind that veil of shame, stand up, chest out, and proclaim, "My name is _____ and I like *Bajour!*" Listen, you're not alone. What is it that we're livin' for (to quote Lee Adams in the guilty pleasure *Applause*)? Not *The Cradle Will Rock* or *Assassins*; and, face it, the really greatest of the greats, *Fiddler on the Roof* or *My Fair Lady*, aren't suitable for standing in your living room in your BVDs, waving your arms like a madman as you conduct the original cast album. You'll get a much bigger grin on your face hopping around, making faces, and singing at the top of your lungs to "Nobody Throw Those Bull" (from *Whoop-Up*), "Everyone Who's 'Who's Who'" (from *Happy Hunting*), "Five Growing Boys" (from *Minnie's Boys*), "Addie's at It Again" (from *I Had a Ball*), "Desert Moon" (from *Golden Rainbow*), or "Where Is the Tribe for Me?" (from *Bajour*). We just love that all-American, 100 percent pasteurized processed cheese, and the cheesier the better. Don't get us wrong, these are perfectly good songs, but they don't have any, shall we say, "depth." And they have to be either really catchy ("There Goes the Neighborhood" from *I Had a Ball*) or really maudlin ("The Game of Love" from *Happy Hunting*). Can you believe Frank Gorshin, Anita Gillette, and Julie Wilson all jockeyed to sing "I Only Wanna Laugh" from *Jimmy*? We've even heard tell of an actress whose audition piece was the overture to *Jimmy* (adding the lyrics as the songs flew by). Somehow, she didn't get cast.

Listen, the people who wrote these songs had talent. Moose Charlap might have written the guilty pleasure *Whoop-Up* but he also composed wonderful music for *Peter Pan*. Sammy Fain is a distinguished composer of many standards, including "I'll Be Seeing You," but he also gave us *Ankles Aweigh!* And please understand, though many guilty pleasures were flops, they weren't all bad shows. Bad shows include such dogs as *Seventh Heaven*, *Her First Roman*, *Christine*, and *Victor/Victoria* ("Paris Makes Me Horny." Need we say more?).

So, crank up the stereo and let 'er rip with "Walk Like a Sailor" from *Ankles Aweigh!* And play the album over and over again until the needle (CDs don't have that nice crackly, well-worn sound) digs through the vinyl and your mother (or your wife, or your boyfriend, or your neighbor) screams at the top of his/her lungs, "What are you doing up there!?" Then you know you're really celebrating a guilty pleasure.

1) In *Subways Are for Sleeping*, Orson Bean is enthralled by a towel-clad (and Tony-winning) Phyllis Newman as Miss America–loser "Martha Vail, in a musical dramatic playlet written and directed by herself." **2)** Homoerotic even by the standards of a Joshua Logan show, dancers in the 1962 Guilty Pleasure *All American* combine physics with the mating ritual of the woolly caterpillar, while Ray Bolger (far right), looking on, realizes he isn't in Kansas anymore. **3)** One of the cheesiest musicals ever, *Let it Ride!* starred "Lonesome George" Gobel, Sam Levene, and the bodacious Barbara Nichols, who got all the reviews singing the preposterous "I Wouldn't Have Had To." **4)** Shelley Winters as Minnie Marx, mother to "Five Growing Boys" in the Guilty Pleasure *Minnie's Boys*, with an often enjoyable score by the flop-prone team of Larry Grossman and Hal Hackady. **5)** In the Guilty Pleasure *I Had a Ball*, starring Buddy Hackett (in window at upper left) as a Coney Island fortune-teller, any profits were gobbled up by the millions spent in body makeup for the chorus kids' need for a perpetual tan. **6)** Ethel Merman only had one flop but it was a lulu, the silly *Happy Hunting*. Here, a candid shot of "The Merm's" dresser dragging Ethel to the stage to perform a matinee.

THE KING AND I

OPENED MARCH 29, 1951; ST. JAMES THEATRE; 1,246 PERFORMANCES

ABOVE: The King (Yul Brynner) and I (Gertrude Lawrence).

RIGHT: Anna Leonowens exclaims, "Hello, Young Lovers!"

THE KING AND I

Produced by Rodgers & Hammerstein
Music by Richard Rodgers
Book and Lyrics by Oscar Hammerstein II
Based on the novel
"Anna and the King of Siam" by Margaret Landon
Musical Director: Frederick Dvonch
Ballet Arrangements by: Trude Rittman
Music orchestrated by Robert Russell Bennett
Directed by John Van Druten
Choreographed by Jerome Robbins
Scenic Design by Jo Mielziner
Costume Design by Irene Sharaff
Lighting Design by Jo Mielziner

Synopsis

Anna Leonowens sails to Bangkok to teach the children of the despotic King of Siam. The two irritate and constantly challenge each other, but as the months pass they come to a grudging admiration, as close to love as two such vastly different people can ever come. The king makes the first steps toward civility, while Anna learns to appreciate the difficult job that being a king is. With the death of the king at the end of the play, each of these two headstrong individuals has undeniably influenced the other.

Cast

Anna Leonowens	*Gertrude Lawrence*
The King	*Yul Brynner*
Lady Thiang	*Dorothy Sarnoff*
Tuptim	*Doretta Morrow*
Lun Tha	*Larry Douglas*
Prince Chulalongkorn	*Johnny Stewart*
The Kralahome	*John Juliano*

"Shave it!"

—Irene Sharaff to Yul Brynner on the matter of his hair

THE STORY OF ANNA LEONOWENS's adventures in Siam was brought to Rodgers and Hammerstein by star Gertrude Lawrence. At that point riding high from their third smash, *South Pacific*, they hardly needed someone suggesting properties to musicalize, but they jumped at the chance, renaming the piece *The King and I*. A dizzying hit for all involved, the triumph of *The King and I* was all the more remarkable since the dramatic action of the piece is rather slight. Also, the stars, Lawrence and Yul Brynner, were not trained singers, so Rodgers and Hammerstein could not supply them with the usual soaring melodies routinely created for their shows, reserving those songs for Doretta Morrow's Tuptim and her beautiful soprano voice. Instead, for Lawrence, the songwriters composed simple, gentle songs that were filled with character, perfect for a great star of Lawrence's caliber to tackle. The verse to "Hello, Young Lovers,"

for instance, adroitly fills the audience in on Anna's past, explaining why a proper English gentlewoman would travel thousands of miles with her child. For the king, the songwriters created staccato, introspective numbers, and for a sense of orientalism, Rodgers approximated (but did not reproduce) a sort of Asian tonality in the numbers. In addition, Hammerstein removed all articles in the king's spoken words, reflecting the lack of "a," "the," and other articles in Asian languages. This is certainly not to say that the leads didn't have emotionally heightened moments in their numbers, but they took the form of frustrated soliloquies: Anna with "Shall I Tell You What I Think of You" and the king with "A Puzzlement." Each of these highly controlling individuals is frustrated by lack of control over the other. The subtext is that their upbringing and prevailing mores won't let them communicate, or even acknowledge, their deep feelings for each other.

Rodgers, Hammerstein, and director John Van Druten were greatly helped in creating three-dimensional characters by their performers. Lawrence was a multi-faceted personality, on stage and off, steely when necessary and yet incredibly vulnerable. Brynner exhibited a remarkable strength, both emotionally and physically, and a fierce intelligence married to a surprising sensitivity. The King was like a lit fuse, ready to blow at any time, a ruler who could easily either kill, kiss, or rape Mrs. Anna and get away with it—after all, he was the king. The tension between the strong personalities of these two stars gave the show its life, and the moment when the two finally came together in a magnificent polka (the only instance in the show when they actually touch), the electricity was akin to two power lines coming into contact.

Their frustrated and confusing relationship is paralleled by the secondary characters Lun Tha, a Burmese envoy, and Tuptim, one of the king's concubines. Unlike many supporting characters, they are not a humorous couple in the style of Ado Annie and Will Parker or Carrie Pipperidge and Enoch Snow. Lun Tha and Tuptim are permitted to express their love to each other, but they cannot show the world their love, for it would mean certain death under the king's laws. Anna sees in them her own lost love and, overestimating the king, encourages the two. When the king sentences Lun Tha to death, Anna is appalled at the king's barbarism and vows to leave. Soon thereafter, she hears that the king is dying and her heart is overcome, as is her reason. With the king on his deathbed and Anna at his side, Oscar Hammerstein provides his leads with a magnificent final scene, one that rivals the famous Bench Scene from *Carousel*. The hopefulness that must come at the end of all Rodgers and Hammerstein shows is not expressed in the rip-roaring declarations of *Oklahoma!* or the stirring anthem of *Carousel*. Rather, the emotion comes out of character when the king's son, now the king himself, changes the rules of the court in concordance with the teachings of Mrs. Anna.

While *Carousel* is considered to be the team's masterpiece, *The King and I* is the most deeply emotional of their works, and even though the show will forever be identified with Brynner, it is much, much more than a star vehicle. The true strength of *The King and I* is in the exquisite writing, the dramatic fight of wills between the two lead characters, the beautiful songs, and the way the piece continues to speak to succeeding generations. *The King and I* is a classic musical and like great operas, is timeless. ❈

TOP: Anna and her son Louis (Sandy Kennedy) whistle a happy tune.

RIGHT: Anna meets Prince Chulalongkorn (Johnny Stewart) under the watchful eye of the king.

LEFT: Doretta Morrow and Larry Douglas as the doomed lovers Tuptim and Lun Tha.

Jerome Robbins

One of the greatest director/choreographers of the Golden Age of Broadway musicals, Jerome Robbins began as a ballet dancer, also appearing in the choruses of a few musicals. Rising to the top of the ballet world with *Fancy Free* (1944), he was pivotal in turning the piece about three gobs on a twenty-four hour leave into the first rate musical comedy *On the Town*. Major hits followed, including 1947's *High Button Shoes* (where his Mack Sennett-inspired bathing beauty ballet became an instant classic), *The King and I* (ditto for his "Small House of Uncle Thomas" ballet), and *Peter Pan* (1954). Even in mediocre shows like *Billion Dollar Baby* (1945), *Look Ma, I'm Dancin'* (1948), and *Miss Liberty* (1949), Robbins created dances that were unlike anything Broadway had ever seen, using ultra-specific, stylized character movement to historic effect. His greatest triumphs, *West Side Story* (1957), *Gypsy* (1959), and *Fiddler on the Roof* (1964), were the pinnacle of a brilliant career carving out a new path in staging musicals, influencing all who followed.

After *Fiddler*, Robbins stayed away from the theatre (other than an aborted worshop of a Sondheim/Bernstein collaboration of Bertolt Brecht's *The Exception and the Rule*) for nearly twenty-five years, working in the world of the dance. Returning in 1989 with a retrospective of his life's work, he put the cream of the crop of Broadway dancers through a grueling series of workshops that resulted in *Jerome Robbins Broadway*, winning him a whole new generation of admirers. That said, for a director and choreographer who used shy humor and delicate tenderness in his fancy free work, he was an exceedingly unpopular individual, positively hateful to many of his dancers and reviled by many who collaborated with him. He lost many friends when he named names before HUAC (the House Un-American Activities Committee) during the McCarthy era, spending much of his later life in the unenviable role of despised genius.

ABOVE LEFT: Jerome Robbins testifies before HUAC, in a moment that forever changed his life (and the lives of the people against whom he testified). LEFT: In the Mack Sennett-inspired "Sunday by the Sea" ballet from *High Button Shoes*, remounted for *Jerome Robbins Broadway*, the bathing beauties spot the audience and say "Helllllllooooooooo!" RIGHT: Jerry Robbins, working with dancers Kelly Patterson and Steve Ochoa, demonstrates the proper way to express the abject terror of working for a tyrannical director/choreographer.

Backstage

The original billing of *The King and I* had Gertrude Lawrence above the title, with Yul Brynner below. By the time Brynner returned to the role in the 1977 Broadway revival, the order was reversed, "King" billed above and "I" below. Brynner was paired with Constance Towers in the revival and when they took a vacation, the producers brought in Angela Lansbury and Michael Kermoyan, thus returning the star balance (and billing) to its original hierarchy.

When the show was trying out, it was Gertrude Lawrence's idea to have a song with the children. Mary Martin, who had invested in the show, suggested that Rodgers and Hammerstein go into their trunk and pull out "Suddenly Lucky," cut from *South Pacific*. With new lyrics, it became the charming "Getting to Know You."

LEFT: Wicked Simon of Legree, et al., in Jerome Robbins' brilliant ballet, ""The Small House of Uncle Thomas."

ABOVE: Three of the many productions of *The King and I*. Left, Barbara Cook was a young but well-received Anna opposite Farley Granger in the 1960 City Center revival. Center, believe it or not, Elaine Stritch actually played Anna in stock (opposite Renato Cibelli as the King). Right, Angela Lansbury (here with an exceedingly ruddy Michael Kermoyan), the biggest female star to play the role in New York since Gertrude Lawrence, restored the star wattage ratio of Anna and the King to its original 1951 configuration.

RIGHT: Catherine Lee Smith and Brynner in a scene from *Odyssey* during its tortuous, yearlong pre-Broadway tour, wherein it lost its title (which ultimately became *Home, Sweet Homer*), its bookwriter and lyricist (Erich Segal), its choreographer (Billy Wilson), and Catherine Lee Smith herself, who played the nymph Kalypso.

Yul Brynner

Yul Brynner, born in Vladivostok, reared in China and then in Paris, used his geographically untraceable accent to the hilt, thriving on an air of exotic mystery. He came to the States and worked as an instrumentalist before making his debut in 1946, supporting Mary Martin in *Lute Song*. When Alfred Drake turned down the lead in Rodgers and Hammerstein's new musical, Martin recommended Brynner for the job, which he got. The musical, of course, was *The King and I*, and the role would become the one he would be forever identified with, one that he ended up playing over 4,000 times. Powerful, angular, and fiercely charismatic in the role of the king, he was the perfect foil for superstar Gertrude Lawrence, winning a Tony Award (for featured actor, the last time that role would be thought as such) and repeating his role in the film. Becoming a movie star in such films as *The Ten Commandments*, *The Magnificent Seven,* and *Westworld*, Brynner stayed away from a new musical project for nearly twenty-five years. His choice for a return was ill-advised: starring with Joan Diener in a lengthy pre-Broadway tour of *Odyssey* (later titled *Home Sweet Homer* for its one-night run in New York), the show did nothing for Brynner's reputation, save making him seem impossible to please. To offset the show's failure, he almost immediately returned to his most famous role, starring in a first-class revival opposite Constance Towers. In 1985, suffering from terminal lung cancer, he died not long after costarring with Mary Beth Piel in his final return to Broadway, once and forever "The King."

KISMET

OPENED DECEMBER 3, 1953; ZIEGFELD THEATRE; 583 PERFORMANCES

ABOVE: The opulent scenery and costumes for *Kismet* by the design genius Lemuel Ayers.

RIGHT: Alfred Drake and Doretta Morrow as the father/daughter team of Hajj and Marsinah.

KISMET

Produced by Charles Lederer
A Production by Edwin Lester

Music from Alexander Borodin
Musical Adaptation and Lyrics by
Robert Wright and George Forrest
Book by
Charles Lederer and Luther Davis
From the Play by Edward Knoblock
Music orchestrated by Arthur Kay
Choral arrangements by Arthur Kay
Musical Director: Louis Adrian

Directed by Albert Marre
Dances and Musical Numbers by
Jack Cole

Scenic Design by Lemuel Ayers
Costume Design by Lemuel Ayers
Lighting Design by Peggy Clark

Synopsis

Remarkably, all of the events of *Kismet* take place in a twenty-four-hour period. A public poet assumes the identity of Hajj, a beggar, when it becomes expedient, and the pretender (we might as well just call him Hajj) is accompanied to Baghdad with his daughter, Marsinah, who is admired by the young Caliph. The captain of police, the Wazir, has his own plans to wed the Caliph to a bevy of foreign princesses, but the ever-resourceful Hajj tricks the Wazir into drowning, winning the Wazir's wife Lalume for himself while ensuring the two lovers a perfect future. Whew.

Cast

First Beggar	*Earle MacVeigh*
Omar	*Philip Coolidge*
Public Poet (Hajj)	*Alfred Drake*
Marsinah	*Doretta Morrow*
Hassan-Ben	*Hal Hackett*
Jawan	*Truman Gaige*
Chief Policeman	*Tom Charlesworth*
The Wazir of Police	*Henry Calvin*
Lalume	*Joan Diener*
The Caliph	*Richard Kiley*
Princess Zubbediya	*Florence Lessing*
Princess Samaris	*Beatrice Kraft*

*K*ismet WAS THE LUCKY SHOW to open during a newspaper strike. While strikes have hurt many shows, they've also helped a few. Producer David Merrick knew he was in trouble with his transfer of the London hit *Oliver!* He had the smarts to keep the show in an extended West Coast tryout (which put the production in the black!) and to record the original cast album prior to New York and plant the songs on the airwaves. When *Oliver!* opened in New York, the reviews didn't matter, the songs were already ingrained in the public's mind, and the show was a hit.

Kismet opened during a newspaper strike and featured a score that far surpassed a deficient libretto. Alfred Drake's bravura performance had a lot to do with the show's success, as did the opulent production. But it's the Robert Wright and George Forrest score that accounts for its success. "Stranger in Paradise" and "Baubles, Bangles and Beads" were huge hits on radio, television, and records. Although both Walter Kerr and Brooks Atkinson derided the score (especially the lyrics), their colleagues recognized the excellent work of Wright and Forrest in adapting Alexander Borodin's themes.

The idea of adapting a classical composer's works for the Broadway stage was not a new one. *Blossom Time* (1921), produced by the Shubert brothers, had music by Franz Schubert (no relation), as reinterpreted by Sigmund Romberg and with lyrics by Dorothy Donnelly. Then it was Jacques Offenbach's turn in 1925's *The Love Song*. Pyotr Tchaikovsky was first heard on Broadway with *Nadja* in 1925. He would return in 1947 with *Music in My Heart*. Frédéric Chopin's melodies were the basis for *White Lilacs* in 1928. Johann Strauss' père and fils had an immense success with the favorite *The Great Waltz* in 1934. Their success was so great that they returned to Broadway, along with Oscar Straus (no relation) in the 1937 musical *Three Waltzes*. The songs of Offenbach, who had actually written operettas, provided the music for *The Happiest Girl in the World*, which boasted new, original English lyrics by E. Y. Harburg.

Fritz Kreisler's romantic tunes were the basis of *Rhapsody*, produced in the same year as *The Song of Norway*: 1944. Kreisler had actually written a show, 1919's *Apple Blossoms*, a big hit running over 200 performances, starring Fred and Adele Astaire. He also had songs interpolated into two shows, *Continental Varieties* and *Reunion in New York*. Kreisler made history as the first living composer to have his works adapted for a Broadway musical. The others had the bad luck (or wisdom) to have passed away.

Of all the songwriters who adapted the works of their classical brethren, Robert Wright and George Forrest enjoyed the most success and turned out the best-loved shows. They were the only ones to enjoy Hit Parade success and the only ones with works that are still in the international repertoire. ❋

Joan Diener

Joan Diener, of the eye-popping silhouette and the eardrum-popping vocals, made her Broadway debut at the age of seventeen (if one believes her biographical data) in the revue *Small Wonder*. She first gained widespread acclaim in 1953 for her performance as the lusty, busty Lalume in *Kismet*, her style perfectly suited to the exotic songs "Not Since Nineveh" and "Rahadlakum." After the out-of-town closing of the 1956 version of the *Ziegfeld Follies* with Tallulah Bankhead, she worked exclusively with her husband, director Albert Marre, on two out-of-town folders (*La Belle,* and *At the Grand*, which was miraculously revised and revived thirty years later as *Grand Hotel*), two fast flops (*Cry for Us All* and *Home Sweet Homer*, both with scores by composer Mitch Leigh), and one super smash, *Man of La Mancha* (also with music by Leigh), in which Diener created and re-created, in London, Paris, and on Broadway as late as 1992 (well into her sixties, she became a kind of Slattern Emeritus), the role of the lusty, busty Aldonza. Instantly identifiable from the sound of her dizzying soprano range colliding with her chest voice, Diener had two of the most extraordinary voices ever heard on Broadway.

ABOVE: Joan Diener, as Lalume, in her opener "Not Since Nineveh."

LEFT: Diener and George Segal in a scene from the flop *La Belle*. Maybe it was the disappointment of an out-of-town closing; maybe it was a phobia he developed from his frighteningly close proximity to Diener's imposing decolletage; but Segal never appeared in another musical.

BELOW: Steve Arlen and Diener in *Cry for Us All*, a Mitch Leigh musicalization of William Alfred's *Hogan's Goat*.

Backstage

While the show was still out of town, Alfred Drake noticed that his costar, Richard Kiley, was also a baritone. Drake didn't want the vocal competition, so by the time the show opened on Broadway, Kiley was singing in the tenor range, a range that he never attempted again.

Borodin was the first of several long-dead people to win Tony Awards. T. S. Eliot of *Cats* "book" fame is another.

"Rahadlakum" is the only song without origins in Borodin. Wright and Forrest had originally used the melody for the nightclub song "I'm Going Moroccan for Johnny."

Robert Wright and George Forrest

The indisputable kings of classical theme adaptations are Robert Wright and George "Chet" Forrest. A long-running team both on and off the Broadway boards, Wright and Forrest succeeded with a series of shows featuring music derived from the works of classical composers. The songs had more weight and depth than the typical Tin Pan Alley Broadway tune, and the lyrics were equally dense, exhibiting a particular propensity for internal rhyme and sophisticated wordsmithery. Wright and Forrest began their career writing for nightclub revues and then found their way to Hollywood and three Oscar nominations. Their first two shows, *Thank You Columbus* (1940) and *Fun for the Money* (1941) were produced there. Their biggest hits, *Song of Norway* (1944—based on the works of Edvard Grieg) and *Kismet,* also began life on the West Coast and contained the standards "Strange Music," "Freddie and His Fiddle," "Stranger in Paradise," and "Baubles, Bangles and Beads." Their other Broadway shows, *Gypsy Lady* (1946—based on Victor Herbert's melodies) and *Anya* (1965—Sergey Rachmaninoff), were unsuccessful. They actually collaborated with a famous composer, Hector Villa-Lobos, on 1948's *Magdalena,* and the result was sadly unappreciated. Along the way they wrote two scores without the help of dead white composers—*The Love Doctor* (1959) and *Kean.* The latter contains some of their most felicitous music and would have been a major success but for Alfred Drake's health problems at the time. The album on Columbia Records has become a kind of cult hit. Their final musical, *Grand Hotel* (1989), was a success, capping a remarkable career.

SONGS

ACT I "Sands of Time" · "Rhymes Have I" · "Fate" · "Bazaar of the Caravans" · "Not Since Nineveh" · "Baubles, Bangles and Beads" · "Stranger in Paradise" · "He's in Love" · "Gesticulate"

ACT II "Night of My Night" · "Was I Wazir?" · "Rahadlakum" · "And This Is My Beloved" · "The Olive Tree" · "Presentation of Princesses"

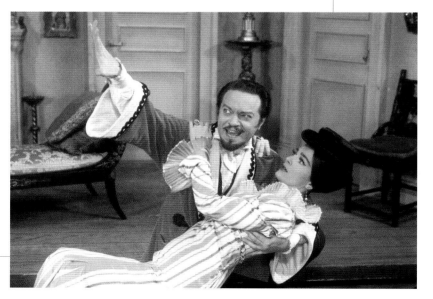

ABOVE LEFT: Alfred Drake and Joan Diener covered in baubles, bangles, and beads.

TOP RIGHT: Romantic leads Richard Kiley and Doretta Morrow sing the beautiful "Stranger in Paradise."

LEFT: In the Wright and Forrest show *Kean,* Joan Weldon gets "Swept Away" by Alfred Drake, as legendary actor Edmund Kean.

KISS ME, KATE

OPENED DECEMBER 30, 1948; NEW CENTURY THEATRE; 1,077 PERFORMANCES

ABOVE: Mistaking her cleavage for a meat locker, Kate (Patricia Morison) gets busted for carrying concealed weenies by the Petruchio of Alfred Drake.

RIGHT: Harry Clark and Jack Diamond, listed in the playbill simply as First Man and Second Man, kick 'em right in the Coriolanus in the eleven o'clocker "Brush Up Your Shakespeare."

KISS ME, KATE

Produced by Saint Subber and Lemuel Ayers

Music and Lyrics by Cole Porter
Book by Bella Spewack and Samuel Spewack
Based on *The Taming of the Shrew*
by William Shakespeare
Musical Director: Pembroke Davenport
Music Orchestrated by Robert Russell Bennett
Incidental Ballet Music Arranged by
Genevieve Pitot

Choreographed by Hanya Holm
Staged and Directed by John C. Wilson

Scenic Design by Lemuel Ayers
Costume Design by Lemuel Ayers
Lighting Design by Al Alloy

Synopsis

A tryout of a musical version of *The Taming of the Shrew* is playing Ford's Theatre in Baltimore, starring the tempestuous Lilli Vanessi and her former husband, the hammy Fred Graham. It's clear from the beginning that, despite their constantly bickering, Fred and Lilli are still in love and meant for each other. The secondary couple are both actors in the show, the chronic (and unlucky) gambler Bill Calhoun; and his girlfriend, the flirtatious Lois Lane. With scenes presented both on stage and off, by the end of the show, everyone is happily fated to be mated again.

Cast

Fred Graham/Petruchio........ *Alfred Drake*
Harry Trevor .... *Thomas Hoier*
Lois Lane/Bianca .... *Lisa Kirk*
Lilli Vanessi/Kate .... *Patricia Morison*
Hattie.................................. *Annabelle Hill*
Paul .... *Lorenzo Fuller*
Bill Calhoun/Lucentio .... *Harold Lang*
First Man............................ *Harry Clark*
Second Man .... *Jack Diamond*

THE SCORE TO *Kiss Me, Kate* is widely considered Cole Porter's masterpiece, not to slight the many many classics he wrote before *Kiss Me, Kate*, or the great songs he would write after it. What set *Kate* apart from his other works was the brilliance of the libretto in setting up the numbers, always keeping the evening on its toes. Porter didn't often have libretti that equaled his songs; nor did he often have performers who devoted themselves wholeheartedly to their characters in the way Alfred Drake and Patricia Morison did in inhabiting the roles of Fred Graham and Lilli Vanessi.

Porter shocked Broadway when *Kiss Me, Kate* opened to rapturous reviews and stellar business at the box office. Wags along the Rialto declared Porter's prospects dim, not only because of his recent record, but had taking into account the tragic riding accident he suffered in 1937, which left him in excruciating pain for the rest of his life.

Those in the theatre and on its periphery are all too quick to revel in a celebrity's fall. The "whatever happened to" game can be lots of fun, especially when "the bigger they are the harder they fall" cliché is really true. For those of a more humane nature, it's especially gratifying when a somebody who's become a nobody all of a sudden is a somebody again. It certainly happened with Porter, who was down for the count after a series of mediocre shows: *Mexican Hayride* (1944), *The Seven Lively Arts* (1944), and the out-and-out debacle *Around the World* (1946). While these shows contained the occasional good song. (*Mexican Hayride* had "I Love You" and *Seven Lively Arts* boasted one of Porter's best, "Ev'ry Time We Say Goodbye"), in general, they were sodden affairs.

Let's take a moment to remember some other comebacks—like that of Oscar Hammerstein II—for it's easy to overlook the fact that the greatest musical theatre artist of all time had his ups and downs. Never one to overlook the fickle nature of show business, after *Oklahoma!* was hailed as the second coming of musical theatre, Hammerstein took out the following advertisement in *Variety*:

Holiday Greetings
from Oscar Hammerstein 2nd
Author of

SUNNY RIVER (6 weeks at the St. James)
VERY WARM FOR MAY (7 weeks at the Alvin)
THREE SISTERS (7 weeks at the Drury Lane)
FREE FOR ALL (3 weeks at the Manhattan)

"I've Done It Before and I Can Do It Again!"

In addition, modern music-makers have seen their careers sink only to rise again. Jerry Herman had three big hits in a row at the beginning of his Broadway career, with *Milk and Honey*, *Hello, Dolly!*, and *Mame*. Then came the fall—*Dear World*, *Mack and Mabel*, and *The Grand Tour*, beautiful scores all, but flops. Really, really big flops. Then came *La Cage Aux Folles*, and Herman's star ascended again. Stephen Sondheim, the master of the last thirty years, had two classics under his belt with his exceptional lyrics to *West Side Story* and *Gypsy*. When he tried his hand at creating both words and music, he wrote *A Funny Thing Happened on the Way to the Forum*, certainly a success. But after *Anyone Can Whistle*, a fast flop lambasted by the critics, and an unwilling return to just lyric writing on *Do I Hear a Waltz?*, Sondheim went fallow for almost five years, and many wondered if he was too esoteric ever to succeed as composer and lyricist. Then in came *Company*, and he was back on top, having changed the history of the musical theatre. Stephen Schwartz made a welcome return to the theatre with *Wicked*, his first hit Broadway show since 1974's *The Magic Show*, and Charles Strouse hasn't had a hit since *Annie* in 1977. Don't count him out, however; he's as talented as ever and has five new shows in the wings.

So let Cole Porter and *Kiss Me, Kate* be your inspiration no matter what your goal. Keep Porter and Hammerstein and Sondheim and Herman and Schwartz in mind—keep trying, don't give up, and understand that you may never be on top again but as long as you do your best you can't really lose. And for those of you who are quick to proclaim someone's career dead, remember: you might find yourself in the same position someday. ❉

TOP RIGHT: Fred Graham (Alfred Drake) gives Lili Vanessi (Patricia Morison) a spanking for being a big old shrew.
CENTER: Harold Lang defies the laws of gravity.
RIGHT: Lang and Helen Wood dance to "If You Got Music" in the *Ziegfeld Follies of 1957*.

Harold Lang

The handsome, charismatic dancer Harold Lang attracted attention in the Jerome Robbins ballet *Fancy Free* before making his Broadway debut dancing in the chorus of *Mr. Strauss Goes to Boston*. Hired three years later for the lead in *Look Ma, I'm Dancin'* opposite Nancy Walker, Lang revealed a fine singing voice and an ability to speak as well as dance. Later that year, as Bill Calhoun in *Kiss Me, Kate*, he finally had a hit, and after playing Ricky in the short lived *Make a Wish* (1951), he took the title role in a long running revival of *Pal Joey*, costarring with original Vera Simpson Vivienne Segal and *Make a Wish* costar Helen Gallagher. Dogged by personal and alcohol problems, he wasn't able to sustain the fame that *Pal Joey* brought him, and the flops, including *Shangri-La* and the *Ziegfeld Follies* with Beatrice Lillie, didn't help. Considered a has-been by 1962, Lang was hired by old friend Arthur Laurents for *I Can Get It for You Wholesale*, winning excellent reviews. Also appearing in the well-received Off-Broadway revue *The Decline and Fall of the Entire World as Seen Through the Eyes of Cole Porter*, he retired to Chico, California, in the 1970s to teach dance, where he died in 1985.

Lisa Kirk

Shapely Lisa Kirk, with a husky alto and impeccable comic timing, became an overnight sensation in 1947 as Emily, the reliable, lovelorn nurse in Rodgers and Hammerstein's *Allegro*, stopping the show with her lament "The Gentleman Is a Dope." The following season she hit the jackpot again, as Lois Lane in *Kiss Me, Kate*, introducing the Cole Porter standards "Why Can't You Behave," and "Always True to You in My Fashion." Spending the 1950s recording, on television, and playing the Las Vegas and nightclub circuit, Kirk was the worst kept secret in Hollywood when she acted as ghost singer for Rosalind Russell in the movie version of *Gypsy*. Replacing Janis Paige in *Here's Love*, she didn't return in a new show until 1974, in Jerry Herman's *Mack and Mabel*, belting out throaty renditions of "Big Time" and "Tap Your Troubles Away." Kirk's last musical before her death from lung cancer was one that she wisely bailed out of during the out-of town tryout: Cy Coleman's *Home Again, Home Again*, which closed before reaching Broadway in 1979.

Backstage

Bella Spewack and Sam Spewack were separated at the time of the writing of *Kiss Me, Kate* and barely speaking. Bella wrote the libretto, but the characters of the gangsters were Sam's idea.

At the dress rehearsal for *Kate*, before it went on its pre-Broadway tour, Moss Hart and Agnes de Mille proclaimed it a flop.

Patricia Morison's Broadway debut was in the short-lived *The Two Bouquets*, in which she performed opposite Alfred Drake.

SONGS

ACT I "Another Op'nin', Another Show" · "Why Can't You Behave" · "Wunderbar" · "So In Love" · "We Open in Venice" · "Tom, Dick or Harry" · "I've Come to Wive Wealthily in Padua" · "I Hate Men" · "Were Thine That Special Face" · "I Sing of Love" · "Kiss Me, Kate"
ACT II "Too Darn Hot" · "Where Is the Life That Late I Led?" · "Always True to You (in My Fashion)" · "Bianca" "Brush Up Your Shakespeare" · "I Am Ashamed That Women Are So Simple"

TOP LEFT: Alfred Drake as the hammy Fred Graham, with Lisa Kirk as the full-of-moxie Lois Lane (no, not the one who works at the *Daily Planet*).

CENTER: Lisa Kirk taps her troubles away in her last Broadway musical, *Mack and Mabel*.

TOP RIGHT: Whereas many modern revivals disappoint, in the hands of a smart director like Michael Blakemore and a talented choreographer like Kathleen Marshall, Marin Mazzie and Brian Stokes Mitchell were truly smashing in the 2000 revival of *Kate*.

RIGHT: Charles Wood, Edward Clay, and Harold Lang serenade Lisa Kirk, as Bianca, with "Tom, Dick or Harry."

"Cole is a naughty boy."

—*Kate Porter, Cole's beloved mother, on hearing his lyrics on opening night*

KISS OF THE SPIDER WOMAN

OPENED MAY 1, 1993; BROADHURST THEATRE, 906 PERFORMANCE

In the song "Where You Are," Aurora (Chita Rivera) reveals the benefits of escapism, telling the cellmates to use their imagination to "build a palace where you're the Czar."

KISS OF THE SPIDER WOMAN

Produced by Livent (U.S.) Inc.
Book by Terrence McNally
Music by John Kander
Lyrics by Fred Ebb
Based on the Novel by Manuel Puig
Music orchestrated by Michael Gibson
Dance music by David Krane

Directed by Harold Prince
Choreographed by Vincent Paterson
Additional choreography by Rob Marshall

Scenic Design by Jerome Sirlin
Costume Design by Florence Klotz
Lighting Design by Howell Binkley

Synopsis

Based on *El Beso de la Mujer Arana*, a novel by Manuel Puig, *Kiss of the Spider Woman* explores the complex relationship between two men caged together in a Latin American prison. One of them, a gay window dresser, has been imprisoned for allegedly making sexual advances to a young boy. In order to escape the brutality of prison life, he spends his days dreaming of Aurora, a B-movie actress from the '40s who once played the role of the sinister Spider Woman. His dreams, however, become more complicated when the warden asks him to spy on his cellmate, a political activist jailed for his involvement in the Argentinian revolution.

Cast

Brent Carver .... *Molina*
Anthony Crivello .... *Valentin*
Chita Rivera .... *Aurora*
Herndon Lackey .... *Warden*
Merle Louise...................... *Molina's mother*
Kirsti Carnahan .... *Marta*
Jerry Christakos .... *Gabriel*

THAT RARE THING, A SUCCESSFUL musical tragedy, *Kiss of the Spider Woman* is a piece of integrity and seriousness, of purpose and idea. The mysterious title character, B-movie star Aurora, is remembered, recounted, and fabulously reenacted by Molina, an imprisoned gay window dresser, forced to share his cell with the handsome young revolutionary, Valentin. As their relationship grows in intensity and intimacy and the window dresser is manipulated into betraying his cellmate, Molina's fantasy woman reveals her true designs, and he tragically learns that no one can escape his fate. Despite the flash and style of the movie fantasies, the heart of the show is the spirit and optimism of Molina, reflected in the history of the musical itself.

The show premiered in 1990 at the State University of New York's Purchase campus, the inaugural production of New Musicals, created as a breeding ground for the development of new works. *Spider Woman* was promoted as a work in progress (in a season also including future Broadway musicals *The Secret Garden* and *My Favorite Year*), and the press was asked not to review it. Led by the *New York Times*, critics attended performances anyway, explaining that since it was a full production created by Broadway heavyweights and presented to a paying audience, it was open to criticism. The reviews were universally devastating and the entire New Musicals project died a quick and unfortunate death.

However, composer John Kander and lyricist Fred Ebb continued to see *Spider Woman* as the perfect marriage of their two favorite themes: innocents caught up in historical events beyond their control and an unbeatably optimistic view of life. So, along with librettist Terrence McNally and director

Hal Prince, the creators decided to keep working on the show and solve its problems.

Practically a wholesale rewriting of the piece was undertaken and the revised and remounted *Spider Woman* opened far from Broadway at Toronto's St. Lawrence Centre. Out of the largely rewritten score, the most important addition was the song "Where You Are," staged by then-rising director/choreographer Rob Marshall and socked over by Chita Rivera in a commanding star turn that firmly centered the show. The showstopper, with Aurora in a white suit and fedora and the prisoners as her backup dancers, brought the story into sharp focus: the fantasy numbers, previously unmotivated, now contrasted with the bleakness of the prison scenes and commented on the downward spiral of the doomed cellmates. Good reviews in Canada prompted another move, not to New York as expected, but still farther from the Great White Way, London. The production won the London Evening Standard Award for Best Musical, and, with its reputation established, was finally presented on Broadway, where it became an immediate success, winning Tony Awards for Rivera, Kander & Ebb, McNally, and Brent Carver and Anthony Crivello as Molina and Valentin. As the final number proclaims, *Kiss of the Spider Woman*, once declared dead by Broadway wags, had a triumphant rebirth in the final reel that one sees "Only in the Movies." ❋

Brent Carver and Anthony Crivello as Molina and Valentin, striking an unusual bond as cellmates.

John Kander and Fred Ebb

John Kander and Fred Ebb comprise Broadway's longest lasting songwriting teams. Their first effort, *Flora, the Red Menace*, began a professional and personal friendship with its star, Liza Minnelli, that has lasted for 40 years. The next year, they shot to the front of the pack with the brilliant score for *Cabaret*. Their next three musicals, *The Happy Time*; *Zorba*; and *70, Girls, 70*, were all underappreciated, and *Chicago*, while successful, was not fully appreciated at the time. *Woman of the Year*, in 1980, featured a brassy, highly enjoyable Kander and Ebb score and a bona fide star turn from Lauren Bacall. The loyalty of longtime friend Chita Rivera, dating back to the national tour of *Zorba*, was rewarded with their intimate songs for *The Rink*.

The recent, wildly successful Broadway revivals of *Cabaret* and *Chicago*, now deemed ahead of its time in 1975, are testament to the lasting appeal and relevancy of their work. John Kander, composer of the most infectious vamps in Broadway history, has a chameleon-like quality of disappearing into a show's milieu, as evidenced by the romance and regret of *The Happy Time* and the world-weary bouzouki flavor of *Zorba*. Fred Ebb's ruefully optimistic lyrics ("Sing Happy" from *Flora* and "Yes" from *70 Girls, 70*) are rivaled only by Stephen Sondheim for their adult, ironic views. Their shows *The Visit*, starring the indefatigable Chita Rivera, and a musicalization of *Skin of Our Teeth*, have both had regional theatre productions and are awaiting the next step.

ABOVE LEFT: John Kander (left) and Fred Ebb rehearse with their *70, Girls, 70* leading lady, the delightful Mildred Natwick.

LEFT: Two of Kander and Ebb's favorite inspirations, Chita Rivera and Liza Minnelli, playing an estranged mother and daughter, in rehearsal for their deeply fe◀musical, *The Rink*.

LEFT: Lauren Mitchell and John Rubinstein as Aurora and Molina in the ill-fated Purchase production of *Kiss of the Spider Woman* in 1990.

FAR LEFT: Chita Rivera as Aurora, the woman of every man's dreams, doesn't mind being a caged bird—all she wants is someone to "Gimme Love."

BELOW: As the duplicitous Anyanka in *Bajour*, Chita delights in telling the gypsy women of her tribe just how "Mean" she can be.

BOTTOM LEFT: Chita Rivera and Alfred Drake are entangled, both romantically and literally, in a number from the out-of-town casualty, *Zenda*.

Backstage

When Chita Rivera left the Broadway company of *Spider Woman* to launch the national tour, she was replaced by actress, pop artist, and deposed Miss America Vanessa Williams, then by Cuban film actress Maria Conchita Alonso. Rivera was also spelled on the tour by Carol Lawrence, her longtime friend and *West Side Story* costar.

Chita Rivera

Chita Rivera, one of a handful of true triple-threat performers, worked her way up through the ranks from chorus to featured dancer, to supporting roles in *Seventh Heaven* and *Mr. Wonderful*. She was catapulted to stardom with *West Side Story*, finally achieving leading lady status in 1960's *Bye Bye Birdie*. In addition to the guilty pleasure *Bajour* were two West coast closings: *Zenda* with Alfred Drake, and *1491*, the Christopher Columbus "musical speculation," with John Cullum. After a seven-year hiatus in California, she made a smashing return to Broadway in Kander and Ebb's *Chicago* and in 1984, won a long-deserved Tony Award for *The Rink*, written specifically for her by longtime friends Kander and Ebb and costarring Liza Minnelli. Despite a traffic accident in 1986 which shattered her left leg and threatened to permanently end her dance career, she was back onstage in six months, kicking higher and surer than ever. After a second Tony for *Spider Woman*, as she enters her sixth decade on Broadway, she continues to work her magic, most recently in the revival of *Nine*, tangoing with Antonio Banderas. To many, her performances as Anita, Rose Grant, and Velma Kelly will never be equaled—at once edgy and ultra-confident, yet with a warmth and humor that many successors have failed to find. Whether playing to a star-studded crowd on opening night or 300 matinee ladies on a Wednesday afternoon in St. Louis, Chita Rivera never, ever fails to give it her considerable all.

LA CAGE
AUX FOLLES

OPENED AUGUST 21, 1983; PALACE THEATRE; 1,761 PERFORMANCES

LA CAGE AUX FOLLES

Produced by Allan Carr, Kenneth D. Greenblatt,
Stewart F. Lane, James M. Nederlander,
Martin Richards and Marvin A. Krauss

Music and Lyrics by Jerry Herman
Book by Harvey Fierstein
Based on the play
La Cage Aux Folles by Jean Poiret
Musical Director: Don Pippin
Vocal Arrangements by Don Pippin
Music Orchestrated by Jim Tyler
Dance Music Arranged by: G. Harrell

Directed by Arthur Laurents
Choreographed by Scott Salmon

Scenic Design by David Mitchell
Costume Design by Theoni V. Aldredge
Lighting Design by Jules Fisher

Synopsis

Albin and Georges live a happy life, days spent with their son Jean-Michel and evenings at La Cage Aux Folles, where Georges is the emcee and Albin transforms himself into the flamboyant drag queen "Zaza." All is well until Jean-Michel (Georges's biological progeny) announces he is getting married. How do you present your two fathers to your fiancée's rabidly conservative parents? Lying seems to be the way to go and Albin appears at the meeting of the in-laws dressed as "maman," in sensible shoes and pearls. Farcical proceedings abound, until everything turns out well, all maintaining their pride.

Cast

Georges .... *Gene Barry*
Albin .... *George Hearn*
Jean-Michel......................... *John Weiner*
Anne .... *Leslie Stevens*
Jacqueline .... *Elizabeth Parrish*
Edouard Dindon .... *Jay Garner*
Marie Dindon .... *Merle Louise*

ABOVE: George Hearn applies "A Little More Mascara" to tranform himself from the humdrum, everyday Albin...

RIGHT: ...into the fabulous "Zaza"!

AFTER THE SMASH HITS *Hello, Dolly!* and *Mame*, Jerry Herman had a series of disappointments with *Dear World*, *Mack and Mabel*, and *The Grand Tour*. The first two, particularly, deserved a far greater success, but all three shows were of a darker nature than the ever-sunny Dolly Levi and Mame Dennis, and audiences evidently expected the usual Broadway razz-ma-tazz from Herman. Of course, there was much more than just glitz to the those long-running smashes; still, audiences wanted Herman to give them more and more of the same, while he yearned to expand his artistry. Luckily, along came *La Cage Aux Folles* and Herman was able to have it both ways. With equal doses of Broadway splash and political astuteness, *La Cage Aux Folles* achieved the miracle of succeeding on both fronts.

After an early false start, titled *The Queen of Basin Street*, resetting the action to New Orleans and with a score by *Nine* composer Maury Yeston, Herman joined the project and the show reverted to its original title as well as its St. Tropez setting. With a book by *Torch Song Trilogy* author and gay activist Harvey Fierstein, and direction by the outspoken and highly politicized Arthur Laurents, *La Cage* might have easily become a polemic diatribe on gay rights. Herman's presence undoubtedly helped offset the other creators, balancing the scales between "issue" and "entertainment" and telling a universal story of individuality and freedom of self-expression. Still, with a highly human story at its core, it wasn't easy making a gay-themed show palatable to the bridge-and-tunnel crowd without turning the characters into caricatures. One thing the audience didn't want was a message shoved in their faces; they

just wanted a big Jerry Herman musical with lots of hummable songs, a few tears, and lots of big song and dance. The powers that be followed the rule of Herman's lyric, "I don't want praise; I don't want pity," and by delivering their sentiments in a sweetly entertaining manner, the creative team made more of an impact than they ever could have with mere rhetoric. The first act closer "I Am What I Am" (recorded by singers as varied as Gloria Gaynor, Tony Bennett, and Pia Zadora), is a powerhouse tune, strongly sung by George Hearn, but the reason the song truly brought the house down was the fully realized character behind all the bravado, a person driven to take a stand for himself—a notion that all people could relate to.

It was a triumph for all involved, mainly its composer, for, contrary to the then popular opinion, Jerry Herman was far from washed up, proving that despite the well-deserved reign of the Stephen Sondheim/Hal Prince collaborations, Herman's style of well-crafted, emotionally rich, snazzy Broadway was still necessary. In fact, with the dearth of new shows being produced, audiences were hungrier than ever for "the best of times" in the theatre, and Herman's innate optimism and unthreatening melodies were a breath of fresh air amidst all the thinking-man's shows. For a certain element of the population, that's what Broadway's all about.

With its long run, you might think that the tale of *La Cage Aux Folles* had a typical happy ending. It doesn't, for after all the rough treatment he had received through all the dark years, enduring constant comparisons to the more cerebral Sondheim, Jerry Herman was fed up. When the curtain rang down on opening night of *La Cage*, Herman walked out onto Broadway, the street to which he had devoted his entire life, vowing to himself never to write another Broadway show. He had nothing more to prove and, sadly, it's a vow he's kept for more than twenty years. No matter how many times Carol Channing promises that "Dolly will never go away again," all of us, his fans and supporters alike, are the poorer that we will never again have the special thrill of a brand new Broadway score by a master of the musical, Jerry Herman. ❋

SONGS

ACT 1 "We Are What We Are" · "A Little More Mascara" · "With Anne on My Arm" · "The Promenade" · "Song on the Sand" · "La Cage Aux Folles" · "I Am What I Am"
ACT 2 "Masculinity" · "Look Over There" · "Cocktail Counterpoint" · "The Best of Times"

Jerry Herman

As upbeat and unflaggingly optimistic as his songs, Jerry Herman is, in some ways, a walking Broadway show tune. After several Off-Broadway revues, Herman made his Broadway debut composing the score to *Milk and Honey*, perfectly geared to the Jewish theatre party crowd. Next came "The Show," the one with "The Song": *Hello Dolly!* Given its legendary status, many are surprised to know that all was not smooth sailing for Herman out of town, and Bob Merrill came to Detroit to offer his advice on some of the stickier moments. Herman classily gave credit to Merrill for the lyric ideas for "Motherhood March" and "Elegance," just as generously returning the favor and writing two songs for *Ben Franklin in Paris* and three songs for Tommy Tune's *A Day in Hollywood/A Night in the Ukraine*. A second smash, *Mame*, followed, and during the late 1960s it seemed as if Herman was the only game in town. In his next project, Herman and Angela Lansbury reteamed on *Dear World*, a major disappointment considering the receptions of his prior shows. With another heartbreaking failure, *Mack and Mabel*, the unsuccessful movies of *Mame* and *Dolly* (made during the last gasp of the Hollywood musical), and his one true misstep, *The Grand Tour*, many wondered if Herman was washed up. This is, however, the man who wrote the song "I Promise You a Happy Ending," and in 1983, Herman had a career rebirth with *La Cage Aux Folles*. Everyone hoped he would dive right into another Broadway show, but after flirting with musicalizing Kaufman and Ferber's *The Royal Family*, decided better, preferring to leave the Broadway party on top. Then, in 1998, invigorated by an upturn in his health, Herman wrote the first major television musical in decades, with Angela Lansbury singing several new jaunty tunes in the title role of *Mrs. Santa Claus*. Keeping his promise to stay away from Broadway, he wrote the concept album for *Miss Spectacular*, and is still eyeing a run in Las Vegas. Whatever he sets his sights on, the best of times for Jerry Herman, to paraphrase Herman himself, is always now.

TOP: The dangerous Cagelles, sans wigs.
ABOVE: The eternally sunny Jerry Herman, in a rare pensive mood during rehearsals for *Mack and Mabel*.
RIGHT: Robert Weede, Mimi Benzell, Molly Picon, and an unidentified goat in a scene from Herman's *Milk and Honey*.

George Hearn

The wonderful actor/singer George Hearn has had three distinctively different careers. Starting out as a budding opera singer, he segued into acting jobs, both in straight plays like *The Changing Room* as well as the occasional musical (a supporting role in *A Time For Singing*, a replacement John Dickinson in *1776*). His Broadway musical career began in earnest when he was cast as the leading man of the "I never miss a Liv Ullmann musical" epic, *I Remember Mama*. Despite its quick failure, he segued into the title role of *Sweeney Todd*, replacing Len Cariou, later touring with original star Angela Lansbury, and committing his powerfully sung Sweeney to video for cable television. Reteaming with director Hal Prince, as well as *Sweeney* costars Betsy Joslyn and Edmund Lyndeck in the interesting but unfortunate *A Doll's Life*, he bounced back and won a Tony Award for his star-making portrayal of Albin in *La Cage Aux Folles*. In a complete 180 from a St. Tropez drag queen, Hearn next appeared as Long John Silver in *Pieces of Eight*, the Jule Styne musical version of *Treasure Island* that closed in Canada prior to Broadway. In a job that was more about a paycheck than a career move, he played the father in the gargantuan *Meet Me in St. Louis*. He finally found another juicy musical role as Max, the all-too-dutiful manservant of Glenn Close's Norma Desmond in *Sunset Boulevard*, winning a second Tony in the process. In addition to continued dramatic work (portraying Mr. Frank in the 1999 revival of *The Diary of Anne Frank*), Hearn's most recent singing appearance on Broadway was in the Sondheim revue *Putting it Together*, playing husband to Carol Burnett (and Kathie Lee Gifford, at the Tuesday evening performance).

TOP LEFT: George Hearn, one of the straightest arrows on Broadway, had an absolute ball playing against type as the flamboyant Zaza, here in an eye-popping Theoni Aldredge creation.

TOP RIGHT: Hearn and Liv Ullmann in *I Remember Mama*, singing the beautiful "You Could Not Please Me More."

RIGHT: As the long-suffering Max in *Sunset Boulevard*, Hearn's quiet magnetism made for a perfect mix of stolidity and creepiness.

LEFT: George Hearn and Gene Barry made an extremely touching couple in *La Cage*. They both just happened to be men.

Backstage

The television commercial for *La Cage*, written by gravel voiced Harvey Fierstein, featured the gravel voice of Elaine Stritch.

For all of the producers' open-mindedness, the ten-story high billboard above the Palace ironically featured a high-kicking, beautiful chorus girl, one of only two women in the twelve-member cross-dressing team of Cagelles.

George Hearn auditioned for the show singing, "My Heart Belongs to Daddy," in full drag.

LADY, BE GOOD!

OPENED DECEMBER 1, 1924; LIBERTY THEATRE; 184 PERFORMANCES

Adele and Fred Astaire.

LADY, BE GOOD!

Produced by
Alex. A. Aarons and Vinton Freedley
Book staged by Felix Edwardes

Music by George Gershwin
Lyrics by Ira Gershwin
Book by Guy Bolton and Fred Thompson
Orchestra under the Direction of Paul Lannin
Orchestrations by Robert Russell Bennett,
Charles N. Grant, Paul Lannin, Stephen Jones,
and Max Steiner

Dances and Ensembles staged by Sammy Lee
Settings designed by Norman Bel Geddes
Costumes by Kiviette, Jenkins, P. Leone

Synopsis

Dick Trevor is in love with sweet, simple Shirley. His sister, Susie, is in love with Jack Robinson, a down-on-his-luck Lothario. Jack: "I'm just a poor hobo." Susie: "Then I must be in Hoboken." But the road to love is rocky, especially before the intermission. Dick, you see, is pursued by the rich and wanton Josephine Vanderwater. And Susie is cajoled into impersonating a rich Mexican widow whose husband was killed in an "accident" before leaving her his fortune. Unbeknownst to Susie, the widow, or the scheming lawyer who represents said widow, Jack is really the husband and is very much alive, having escaped the plot on his life. Jack is also really a millionaire. The audience is not surprised when Dick gets Shirley and Susie weds Jack.

Cast

Dick Trevor.......................... *Fred Astaire*
Susie Trevor........................ *Adele Astaire*
Jack Robinson..................... *Alan Edwards*
Josephine Vanderwater .... *Jayne Auburn*
J. Watterson Watkins .... *Walter Catlett*
Shirley Vernon.................... *Kathlene Martyn*
Jeff..................................... *Cliff Edwards*
Pianos............................... *Victor Arden*
and Phil Ohman

"For God's sake, George, what kind of lyric do you write to a rhythm like that? It's a fascinating rhythm...."

—Ira Gershwin, on hearing the music for "Fascinating Rhythm" for the first time

Lady, Be Good! WAS GEORGE Gershwin's first great musical comedy. Perhaps the show's success was due to George's brother, Ira, collaborating with his brother on a full score for the first time. Ira seemed to inspire George to give freer reign to his melodies and forgo completely any operetta influences that remained in his compositions. *Lady Be Good!* might not have been as faddish and manic as *Good News*, which debuted a few years later, but it was certainly a musical of its time. The plot was breezy and verged on the silly, the voices of the cast, from Fred Astaire to Cliff Edwards, were opposite to the trained opera-like voices that warbled Romberg, Friml, and Herbert. Astaire and Edwards had a nonchalance and free-wheeling quality to their singing and those qualities lent themselves perfectly to George and Ira's jaunty score.

"Fascinating Rhythm" seems to have been George's breakthrough number with its bold unconventionality. "Little Jazz Bird" and "Hang on to Me" saw George in a playful mood, keeping the tone light, a perfect match with Ira's witty, literate lyrics.

By the time *Lady, Be Good!* went on at the Liberty Theatre, thirty-nine musicals had opened that year (there was to be one more, *Princess April*, making an uneven forty-one). *Lady, Be Good!* was the Gershwin's fourth show of 1924. With so many shows opening, not to mention holdovers from past seasons, Broadway's theatres were fully booked. *Lady, Be Good*'s producers, Alex A. Aarons and Vinton Freedley, were lucky enough to get the Liberty Theatre on Forty-second Street.

Forty-second Street was the premiere theatre venue in New York, anchored by the New Amsterdam at the head of the block. The Liberty was owned and designed by the same men who built the New Amsterdam. But for the Liberty, architects Henry B. Herts and Hugh Tallant were commanded by producers Marcus Klaw and Abe Erlanger to make simplicity their byword.

Since the property values on Forty-second Street were so high, the theatres had long, narrow lobbies fronting the street with the theatre house proper on either Forty-first or Forty-third Streets, where the real estate costs were much lower. When the *Evening Post* covered the opening, along with all the major New York dailies, their reporter opined, "Every seat on the three floors has a direct view of the stage, and one feels—no matter where one is sitting—that there is no great distance between himself and the people back of the footlights." Impressive for a theatre that seated 1,054 patrons. Most of the theatres of the time had an orchestra section, a mezzanine/first balcony, and a second balcony. Before the advent of movies and television, audiences were not used to seeing actors close up, and they were content to sit far from the stage—especially for ten cents.

Another of the shows in this book, *Little Johnny Jones*, played the Liberty. But for the most part, although quite successful in attracting bookings, the theatre had few notable tenants—in 1907 no fewer than seven shows opened at the Liberty. Among the more successful were Cohan's *Little Nellie Kelly*, and a series of shows by Jerome Kern, including *Have a Heart*, *The Night Boat*, and *The City Chap*. An early Cole Porter Broadway show, *Hitchy-Koo of 1919*, played the Liberty. Gershwin saw two other shows premiere at the Liberty in addition to *Lady, Be Good!*—George White's *Scandals of 1920* and *Tip Toes*. Among the biggest successes at the Liberty was Lew Leslie's production of *Blackbirds of 1928*, the show starred Elisabeth Welch, Bill Robinson, Adelaide Hall, and Mantan Moreland and introduced the song, "I Can't Give You Anything but Love" by Dorothy Fields and Jimmy McHugh.

Like most of the Forty-second Street theatres, the Liberty fell on hard times when the Depression hit. Because of its popularity, it managed to stay open until 1933 when the poor economy won out and the Liberty became a grind movie house. Today, the theatre sits behind a makeshift wall at the exit of the AMC Empire movie theatre—the lobby was demolished when the Empire theatre was rolled down Forty-second Street to its present position. The Times Square Redevelopment Plan called for the theatre to be used for nonprofit theatre productions from around the country, but currently plans are afoot to turn the orchestra level into a restaurant.

In its heyday, the Liberty was one of Broadway's most intimate theatres. It would seem, in this era of big, barnlike auditoria with bad sightlines and worse acoustics, that a treasure like the Liberty would be cherished. But we don't have many small, intimate musicals like *Lady, Be Good!* nor intimate performers like the Astaires, and Broadway isn't the same as it was in the heyday of the 1920s. ❈

Adele Astaire, Cliff Edwards, Kathlene Martyn, and Fred Astaire.

SONGS

ACT I "Hang on to Me" · "A Wonderful Party" · "End of a String" · "We're Here Because" · "Fascinating Rhythm" "So Am I" · "Oh, Lady, Be Good"

ACT II "Weatherman"/"Rainy Afternoon Girls" · "The Half of It Dearie Blues" · "Juanita" · "Leave It to Love" "Little Jazz Bird" · "Insuffcent Sweetie" (music and lyrics by Cliff Edwards) · "Carnival Time" · "Swiss Miss" (lyrics by Arthur Jackson and Ira Gershwin)

LEFT: George Gershwin on stage for opening night of the original production of *Porgy and Bess*.

BELOW LEFT: This rare shot of George Gershwin, one of only two color photos of the composer that exist, was taken when George went to Mexico to meet artist Diego Rivera.

BELOW RIGHT: Ira Gershwin in retirement at his house in Beverly Hills.

Backstage

Financier Otto Kahn decided to invest $10,000 in *Lady, Be Good!* after hearing "The Man I Love." Unfortunately, it was dropped before the premiere, although it was published (under the name "The Man I Loved"). Kahn didn't complain—he more than doubled his investment.

Lady, Be Good! was the first Broadway show to have a complete score by the Gershwins. Their *Primrose* had opened in London just prior to *Lady, Be Good!*

The show was originally titled *Black-Eyed Susan*, with Adele Astaire in the title role. She was considered the more talented of the dance team.

George and Ira Gershwin

George Gershwin's aggressive rhythms and blues-inspired melodies were a perfect match for his brother Ira's ingenious rhyming and impudent humor. They constantly sought to expand the scope of the musical while eschewing artiness and pretension. Their range included sophisticated revues (*George White's Scandals*), smart and bubbly musical comedies (*Oh, Kay!; Lady, Be Good!; Funny Face*), lightly satirical comic operettas (*Let 'Em Eat Cake* and *Strike Up the Band*), and a heartfelt, emotional folk opera (*Porgy and Bess*). Gershwin began his career with a variety of lyricists including Arthur Jackson (*George White's Scandals*), B. G. DeSylva (*Sweet Little Devil*), Otto Harbach and Oscar Hammerstein II (*Song of the Flame*), and Brian Hooker (*Our Nell*) before teaming with his brother Ira, who originally used the pseudonym Arthur Francis, a name he created from the first names of two of his siblings. George and Ira's perfectly attuned talents resulted in a remarkable body of work for both the stage and screen, with George's composing talents extending to classical music. Ira also contributed lyrics to the music of Vernon Duke (*Ziegfeld Follies*) and Harold Arlen (*Life Begins at 8:40*). After George's death, Ira contributed to three more scores, *Lady in the Dark* and *The Firebrand of Florence* (both with Kurt Weill), and *Park Avenue* (with Arthur Schwartz). Among the better known Gershwin brothers songs are: "Looking for a Boy," "I Got Rhythm," "Strike Up the Band," "Bidin' My Time," "But Not for Me," "There's a Boat That's Leavin' Soon for New York," "I've Got a Crush on You," "My One and Only," and "Do Do Do."

LADY IN THE DARK

OPENED JANUARY 23, 1941; ALVIN THEATRE; 467 PERFORMANCES

"Girl of the Moment" Gertrude Lawrence is Liza, a *Lady in the Dark*.

LADY IN THE DARK

Produced by Sam H. Harris
Book by Moss Hart
Music by Kurt Weill
Lyrics by Ira Gershwin
Musical Director: Maurice Abravanel
Music orchestrated by Kurt Weill
Vocal arrangements by Kurt Weill

Play staged by Moss Hart
Musical sequences staged by Hassard Short
Choreographed by Albertina Rasch

Production Design by Hassard Short
Lighting Design by Hassard Short
Scenic Design by Harry Horner
Costume Design by Irene Sharaff
Gowns by Hattie Carnegie

Synopsis

Magazine editor Liza Elliott finds it increasingly difficult to make up her mind, whether on the job or in her personal life. She does decide to see a psychiatrist in order to get to the root of her problem. Among her predicaments is the choice between marrying her lover, publisher Kendall Nesbitt, or her magazine's sarcastic advertising manager, Randy Curtis. As the musical progresses, her dreams are illustrated and, little by little, Elliott finds the key to her problem—and makes the right choices.

Cast

Liza Elliott	*Gertrude Lawrence*
Miss Foster	*Evelyn Wyckoff*
Alison Du Bois	*Natalie Schafer*
Russell Paxton	*Danny Kaye*
Charley Johnson	*MacDonald Carey*
Randy Curtis	*Victor Mature*
Kendall Nesbitt	*Bert Lytell*

Backstage

Transparent Lucite panels were used on Broadway for the first time in *Lady in the Dark*. The brilliant scenic designer Harry Horner used the panels to make the transitions between Liza's dreams and reality.

Decca Records released an album of songs from *Lady in the Dark* sung by the incomparable Hildegarde before the original cast album was even recorded. Gertrude Lawrence was incensed and threatened not to record her songs at all.

The cast of *Lady in the Dark* included fifty-six performers; fifty-one stagehands were needed to move the elaborate settings.

MOSS HART, IRA GERSHWIN, AND Kurt Weill had a unique idea: make a musical in which all of the musical numbers take place in the lead character's subconscious. Out went the formula established by *Show Boat*; now, instead of just expressing emotion or advancing the plot, the songs gave insight into a character's psyche.

Lady in the Dark borrowed an idea from an older show, the operetta *Naughty Marietta*. Liza Elliott cannot complete the song "My Ship." She remembers snatches of the melody and lyrics but can't quite put it all together. The cynical Charley Johnson completes the song, and Liza recognizes him as her soul mate. In *Naughty Marietta*, the title character chooses between the dashing pirate leader and the rangers' Captain Dick when the latter completes

"Ah. Sweet Mystery of Life." a song Marietta dimly recalls from her youth. *Lady in the Dark* also resembles Richard Rodgers and Lorenz Hart's *Peggy Ann*. Both treat dreams. sometimes surrealistically. as insights into their title character's psyche.

We're sure that Moss Hart. Ira Gershwin. and Kurt Weill didn't think of *Peggy Ann* when they set out to write *Lady in the Dark*. In fact. Hart began writing the musical in 1937 along with his frequent collaborator. George S. Kaufman. The intended star was Marlene Dietrich. When Dietrich dropped out and Kaufman became busy with *My Sister Eileen*. Hart turned the idea into a straight vehicle for Katherine Cornell. The play. titled "I Am Listening." was similar in form to *Lady in the Dark*. but before it could move to the next level. there would be a chance meeting between Hart and composer Kurt Weill at a birthday party for Walter Huston. star of Weill's *Knickerbocker Holiday*.

Weill and Hart discussed the state of the musical. and both agreed that the insipid libretto of the typical musical was beneath their interest. They wanted to write an innovative show like Rodgers and Hart's *Pal Joey*. in which the plot was advanced through song. not a typically lame story with non-character-specific songs dropped into the action haphazardly.

Moss Hart brought up "I Am Listening." and he and Weill came up with the idea that the patient's monologues to her therapist could be treated as musical numbers. Hart believed they had found "a new technique and a new musical form." and he dubbed it a musical play. Weill. Gershwin. and Hart's experiment paid off.

Theatre is an evolving art form. By being bold enough to try out new ideas. the trio advanced the musical theatre another small step. ❈

Moss Hart

Moss Hart, author and director, began his association with musicals by writing *Jonica* in 1930 and *Face the Music* in 1932. After contributing sketches to *As Thousands Cheer*, he collaborated with George S. Kaufman on many successful plays (including *You Can't Take It With You* and *The Man Who Came to Dinner*) and musicals (*Jubilee* and *I'd Rather Be Right*). Hart's lifelong fascination with psychoanalysis made him the perfect book writer for the struggles of Liza Elliott in *Lady in the Dark*. As director of the smash *My Fair Lady*, he saved the job (and possibly the career) of Julie Andrews, shepherding her through the challenging role of Eliza Doolittle during legendary closed rehearsals where he built her performance line by line and inflection by inflection. His last musical, *Camelot*, was a trial for all involved, sending most of the creative team to the hospital at one time or another during its genesis; indeed, there are some who say its tortured birth process killed him.

"This is not a song for me. This is Ethel Merman, and it's not very funny anyway."

— *Gertrude Lawrence on first hearing "The Saga of Jenny "*

TOP: In the spectacular circus dream sequence, Liza relates "The Saga of Jenny."

ABOVE: The dapper Moss Hart, surrounded by the ladies of *Lady in the Dark*.

RIGHT: Moss Hart's final show, *Camelot*, like the earlier *My Fair Lady*, starred a serious actor turned musical-comedy star. This time it was Richard Burton.

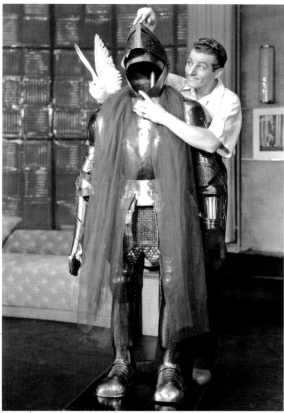

LEFT: One of the first musicals to delve into the subconscious minds of its characters, *Lady in the Dark* featured flashbacks of Liza's unhappy childhood.

RIGHT: In addition to its other groundbreaking aspects, *Lady in the Dark* was one of the first musicals to feature an openly gay character, the flamboyant Russell Paxton, played by Danny Kaye in his star-making role.

BELOW: Kaye checks the weather outside the ark in *Two By Two*. Apparently, there were as many storm clouds backstage as onstage.

Danny Kaye

Danny Kaye, a brilliant but decidedly complicated movie star, also had a spotty but long-spanning career in musicals. He became a star with his turn as a mincing photographer in *Lady in the Dark*, in which he stopped the show with the tongue twister "Tchaikovsky." His first starring role, alongside other rising stars Vivian Vance, Nanette Fabray, and Eve Arden in *Let's Face It*, catapulted him to a thirty-year stay in Hollywood. Turning down the roles of Harold Hill in *The Music Man* and Tevye in *Fiddler on the Roof*, Kaye didn't choose wisely when he finally returned to Broadway, as Noah (of ark fame) in *Two by Two*, with a score by Richard Rodgers. Kaye found Broadway to have changed greatly since 1943. The collaborative aspect of musical theatre was at odds with the more rigid hierarchy of motion pictures and the casual, improvisational qualities of television, where he had complete control over the four-year run of his CBS variety show. He was thoroughly unpopular with both cast and crew of *Two by Two*, even screaming at fellow actors onstage during a performance. After breaking his leg, he returned to the show and performed first in a wheelchair, then on crutches, his behavior going from bad to worse. This tarnished his reputation as the warm and funny Hans Christian Andersen.

SONGS

ACT I "Oh Fabulous One in Your Ivory Tower" "The World's Inamorata" · "One Life to Live" "Girl of the Moment" · "It Looks Like Liza" "This Is New" · "The Princess of Pure Delight" "This Woman at the Altar"
ACT II "The Greatest Show on Earth" "The Best Years of His Life" · "Tchaikowsky" "The Saga of Jenny" · "My Ship"

(L to R) Vivian Vance, Edith Meiser, Nanette Fabray, Eve Arden, Joseph Macaulay, Danny Kaye (with tuba), Benny Baker, and Jack Williams in a scene from the Cole Porter wartime romp, *Let's Face It!*

LES MISERABLES

OPENED MARCH 12, 1987; BROADWAY THEATRE; 6,680 PERFORMANCES

LES MISERABLES

Produced by Cameron Mackintosh
Book by Claude-Michel Schönberg
and Alain Boublil
Music by Claude-Michel Schönberg
Lyrics by Herbert Kretzmer
Based on the novel by Victor Hugo
Original French text by
Alain Boublil and Jean-Marc Natel
Additional text by James Fenton
Music orchestrated by John Cameron
Musical Director: Robert Billig

Directed and Adapted by
Trevor Nunn and John Caird

Scenic Design by John Napier
Associate Scenic Design: Keith Gonzales
Lighting Design by David Hersey

Synopsis

Jean Valjean, released from jail for stealing bread, assumes another identity and begins a new life, working his way up to the post of mayor of a country town. By disappearing, he neglects the terms of his ticket of leave, and the obsessed policeman Javert vows to track him to the ends of the earth. Meanwhile, the tragic Fantine, driven to prostitution, dies, and Valjean adopts her daughter, Cosette, by stealing her away from her foster parents, the evil innkeepers the Thenardiers. As the play jumps forward in time, the handsome student Marius falls in love with the now grown Cosette. When revolution breaks out, Javert and Valjean find themselves confronting each other. When Valjean spares the policeman's life, Javert goes mad, unable to comprehend this man who he has hunted for years. He commits suicide, and Valjean, now an old man, finally finds peace.

Cast

Jean Valjean	*Colm Wilkinson*
Javert	*Terrence Mann*
Fantine	*Randy Graff*
Madame Thenadier	*Jennifer Butt*
Thenardier	*Leo Burmeister*
Eponine	*Frances Ruffelle*
Enjolras	*Michael McGuire*
Marius	*David Bryant*
Young Cosette	*Donna Vivino*
Gavroche	*Braden Danner*
Cosette	*Judy Kuhn*

SONGS

ACT I "Soliloquy" · "At the End of the Day" · "I Dreamed a Dream" · "Lovely Ladies" · "Who Am I?" · "Come to Me" "Castle on a Cloud" · "Master of the House" · "Thenardier's Waltz (of Treachery)" · "Look Down" · "Stars" · "Red and Black" · "Do You Hear the People Sing?" · "In My Life" · "A Heart Full of Love" · "On Day More"
ACT II "On My Own" · "A Little Fall of Rain" · "Drink With Me to Days Gone By" · "Bring Him Home" · "Dog Eats Dog" · "Javert's Suicide" · "Turning" · "Empty Chairs at Empty Tables" · "Wedding Chorale" · "Beggars at the Feast"

The entire *Les Misérables* company in the Act I finale, "Do You Hear the People Sing?"

Other than *Irma La Douce*, no musicals originating in France have successfully transferred to Broadway—except, of course, *Les Misérables*. The show, which started as a concept recording, went on to a fully-staged production in Paris's Palais des Sports arena. From Paris, the show went to London's Royal Shakespeare Company, where it received mixed reviews, but producer Cameron Mackintosh so believed in the show, he transferred it to the Palace Theatre on Cambridge Circus, where it ran. And ran. And ran. Then on to New York's Broadway Theatre, where it ran. And ran. And ran.

And therein lies a problem of sorts. Back in the 1920s, a good, long run was around 100 performances. Certainly, some shows ran 500 performances and longer, but they were the vast exceptions, and after a few months or even weeks in New York, a show could go on the road, advertising "direct from Broadway" on their poster. The Broadway engagement was seen as a stepping stone to the far more lucrative road. As the country's population and economy grew, travel became easier and more tourists flocked to New York, with increases in a hit show's run as a result. Most shows in the years before air conditioning closed for good when the summer months hit but more and more were either weathering the summer's heat or closing for a vacation to reopen in the fall. By the 1950s, a run of 500 performances was still considered a hit; by the late 1960s, that long a run didn't spell success (the shows *Sugar, Irene*, and *Follies* being prime examples of that phenomenon). The road began to dry up in the early 1970s, as downtowns, home to the large touring houses, were deserted by an exodus to the suburbs, with many historic theatres demolished in the name of urban renewal. Yes, there were long runs like *Grease* and *A Chorus Line*, that began their runs of more than a decade in the 1970s, spinning off numerous tours, but those shows were also very inexpensive to tour, with minimal production values and no stars.

By the 1980s, the birth of the mega-show meant shows were running for decades, not years. Herein lies a potential downside. With these shows occupying the most desirable musical houses for years on end, and the producers of those super hits making money hand over fist, there's less incentive to develop new shows and risk their hard earned squillions on new, untried authors and composers.

So, we have the *Phantoms* and *Lion Kings* and *Mamma Mias* and *Rents* rolling along. Now, we're not suggesting that these shows close before they run out of steam; that would be idiotic, business-wise. If the junkyard of *Cats* had vacated years before, would there be brilliant new shows to take their place? Perhaps not, but it just seems strange that some avid theatregoers can go nearly twenty years between visits to the *Winter Garden*, one of the most beloved and unique musical houses.

Meanwhile, while we question these long running smasheroos, we can't deny that *Les Misérables* has entertained millions of people, on Broadway and around the world (in fact, ironically, everywhere but France). Countless audiences have thrilled to its stagecraft, courtesy of Trevor Nunn and John Caird, its pop-opera score, written by Claude-Michel Shoenberg and Alain Boublil, and its epic story, penned by some dude named Hugo. We've got to admit that's a very, very good thing. ❋

RIGHT: Randy Graff as the tragic Fantine, about to sell her body and her hair to make a quick buck.

Trevor Nunn

Director Trevor Nunn, who guided the majority of the British super hits of the eighties, began his career in the classical realm. While serving as artistic director of The Royal Shakespeare Company, he made a splash on Broadway with his two-part, eight-hour *Nicholas Nickleby*. He teamed with Andrew Lloyd Webber on four shows, including the unstoppable *Cats*, as well as the more gargantuan but less successful *Starlight Express*. In between he helmed *Les Misérables*, imported from Paris to the RSC, to the West End. From there, it went on to Broadway, then conquering the world, with innumerable productions spanning the globe. In addition, there was the American transfer of his successful West End *Chess*, rethought for New York and one of the biggest flops of his Broadway career. After that, it was back to collaborations with Lloyd Webber, on the small-sized *Aspects of Love* and the most traditional musical of the British imports, *Sunset Boulevard*. By then acting as director of the Royal National Theatre, Nunn directed a revival of *Oklahoma!* in 1999, which came to Broadway in 2002 but failed to ignite America the way it had Great Britain. In addition, he staged National Theatre productions of *My Fair Lady*, *South Pacific*, and *Anything Goes*. Having relinquished the reins at the National to the brilliant Nicholas Hytner, Nunn is slated to direct another American musical, a 2005 Broadway revival of *A Little Night Music* starring Glenn Close.

RIGHT: Alan Campbell and Glenn Close, in a highly dsyfunctional relationship in the Trevor Nunn-directed *Sunset Boulevard*.

ABOVE: Colm Wilkinson, the original Jean Valjean, with a voice so high that dogs would come running.

BROADWAY HOUSES

The Winter Garden Theatre featuring the *Passing Show of 1916*.

THE HISTORY OF THEATRES devoted to musical theatre is also the story of Times Square, for as the musical comedy was in its infancy so too was the area where Seventh Avenue crossed Broadway. The area was originally named Long Acre Square and its main industry was carriage production. Where the Winter Garden Theatre now stands was Tattersall's American Horse Exchange. In fact, during the early years of the Winter Garden, when a show flopped the critics claimed they could still smell the horses. By 1893, New Yorkers were spending six million dollars a year on entertainment and producers saw dollar signs in theatre development. In 1895, Oscar Hammerstein I built his Olympia theatre complex just as electric lights made their way up to the Square. In 1904, the *New York Times* built its headquarters exactly on the Square, which was renamed for the paper. Early owners of theatres were the dreaded Theatrical Trust of Klaw and Erlanger and their main rivals, the Shubert brothers, with noted developers The Chanins also building an impressive number of houses around the Square; by the 1927–1928 season, the busiest in Broadway history, 257 shows opened in the area's 71 theatres. With the invention of motion pictures, additional theatres were built on Broadway as the flagships of major studios.

During the 1930s, the Depression hit Broadway hard. The Shuberts lost many of their theatres to foreclosure, and promptly bought them back at reduced prices at the bank auctions. Many theatres were converted to radio (and later television) studios, or became burlesque houses, and when Mayor LaGuardia outlawed burlesque, many of the theatres on 42nd Street became grind movie houses. The 1950s and '60s were relatively calm periods in the history of the Broadway theatres but the 1970s and 1980s saw crime escalate and the theatre district became a haven for drugs and prostitutes. Many of Times Square's landmarks were demolished, further adding to the woes of the neighborhood, with the skyscrapers that replaced them destroying the low-rise ambiance of the area. During this period, zoning changes made it more profitable to build in the area and, despite the best efforts of preservationists, the Helen Hayes, Bijou, Morosco, Astor, and Victoria Theatres were demolished. Mayor Koch, the man most responsible for selling out to developers, promised a renewed Times Square, but a stock market crash in October 1987 put the plans on hold.

It was the Walt Disney Corporation's refurbishment of the New Amsterdam Theatre that proved to be the most important catalyst in the renovation of 42nd Street. The resurgent economy, especially during the Clinton

Oscar Hammerstein's Olympia theatre complex.

Joseph Urban's magnificent Ziegfeld Theatre on Sixth Avenue.

presidency, as well as the emergence of popular musicals (usually British and produced by Cameron Mackintosh) provided momentum. More theatres were lost despite the improved economy, although a few new theatres were built, including the Uris (now Gershwin) in 1972, the Minskoff in 1973, and the Marquis in 1986. These theatres are badly designed, however, with poor sight lines, huge barn-like auditoria, and severe acoustic problems—not to mention the fact that they are architectural eyesores. The Ford Center, on the lot once shared by the beautiful Lyric and Apollo theatres, opened in 1998 and proved to be just as ill-suited to theatrical purposes as its modern predecessors. Meanwhile, the Liberty and Times Square theatres on 42nd Street remain empty, and the intimate Empire (Eltinge) Theatre serves as the lobby for a movie complex. The great musical theatre houses of the past, the Majestic, the Imperial, the St. James, the Richard Rodgers, the Shubert, the Palace, and the Broadway, help to keep the great history of Times Square alive for future generations.

LI'L ABNER

OPENED NOVEMBER 15, 1956; ST. JAMES THEATRE; 693 PERFORMANCES

After Abner (Peter Palmer) and Marryin' Sam (Stubby Kaye) return from their trip to Washington, D.C., they declare "The Country's in the Very Best of Hands."

RIGHT: The stunning Edith Adams, whose dishiness would make anyone wonder why Li'l Abner would run away.

LI'L ABNER

Produced by Norman Panama, Melvin Frank, and Michael Kidd
Music by Gene de Paul
Lyrics by Johnny Mercer
Book by Norman Panama and Melvin Frank
Based on Cartoon Characters by Al Capp
Musical Direction and Continuity: Lehman Engel
Vocal Arrangements by Lehman Engel
Music orchestrated by Philip J. Lang
Ballet Music arranged by Genevieve Pitot
Directed and Choreographed by Michael Kidd

Scenic and Lighting Design by
William and Jean Eckart
Costume Design by Alvin Colt

Synopsis

The denizens of Dogpatch lead their quiet hillbilly lives until they discover that the government plans to wipe them out due to their very unnecessariness. But Mammy Yokum's Yokumberry Tonic proves to be a medical miracle, transforming scrawny men into muscle-bound hunks (but with the unfortunate side effect of eliminating their libido—just like steroids do today). With the discovery of a proclamation by none other than Abraham Lincoln, the day is saved for Abner, Daisy Mae, Moonbeam McSwine, Romeo Scragg, and the other Dogpatchians.

Cast

Daisy Mae	Edith Adams
L'il Abner	Peter Palmer
Marryin' Sam	Stubby Kaye
Mammy Yokum	Charlotte Rae
Gen. Bullmoose	Howard St. John
Pappy Yokum	Joe E. Marks
Stupefyin' Jones	Julie Newmar
Earthquake McGoon	Bern Hoffman
Moonbeam McSwine	Carmen Alvarez
Appassionata Von Climax	Tina Louise
Evil Eye Fleagle	Al Nesor

Li'l Abner is SIMPLY ONE of the funniest, cleverest shows ever. Sharply drawn characters, sprightly music by Gene de Paul, hilarious and satirical lyrics by Johnny Mercer, a ridiculous and all-too-timely (or timeless) book by farce masters Norman Panama and Melvin Frank, inventive, witty choreography by the deeply underrated Michael Kidd, pointed, precise, and perfect orchestrations by Phil Lang, and wonderfully broad, unwinking performances. Its like will never be seen again.

New York's City Center Encores series recently tried a concert version of *Li'l Abner*, with rather dire results. And who got the blame? The show, of course, with many in the audience at City Center accusing *Li'l Abner* of being a not-very-good or funny show. No matter that the performers and production team couldn't master the tone or begin to understand the sweet, wry, non-ironic style necessary to the piece. "Dated" is the all-purpose word used for shows that the audience just doesn't understand, never pausing to consider that they, in fact, are the ones who might be "dated," unable to take on the mind-set of an older, different tradition of theatre. It's like when modern audiences laugh at the emotive excesses of silent movies. Opera audiences are sophisticated enough to view operas for what they are and accept them on their own terms; otherwise, every single one would be dubbed "dated."

Musical comedies, especially the truly funny kind, sometimes get short shrift on Broadway, while "message" musicals win the critics' approval. Of course, it wasn't always this way. There was a time when shows could do anything to get laughs, with no restraints on their endeavor to please. Think of some of the funniest musical comedies: *Hellzapoppin'*, *Little Me*, *Whoopee*, *Cocoanuts*, *A Funny Thing Happened on the Way to the Forum*,

Two on the Aisle. Sugar Babies. Off-Broadway's *The Mad Show.* With the exception of *Forum,* they are seldom revived. Admittedly, most were star vehicles, tailored to the talents of such veterans as Olsen and Johnson, Sid Caesar, Eddie Cantor, or the Marx Brothers, but they made audiences positively rock with laughter. Perhaps the triumph of *The Producers* will help put the "comedy" back in "musical comedy." And if it happens, will we be able to pull it off? Doubtful, since the kind of clowns Broadway once employed to such success no longer exist. Whereas comics of the past captured the energy and vitality of the city (even when they were born in the sticks), performers today are weaned on television and film—both "cool" media. The days of working week in and week out in front of vaudeville and burlesque audiences, honing one's skills, are gone. Too, with the advent of microphones, a high level of physical energy is no longer required, and, as a result, most modern comics are more passive than their predecessors. Broadway has slowly slid, for the most part, into a non-threatening blandness. There's a reason many of the great comics of the past were first-generation Americans (and often Jewish). They needed to be accepted, and acceptance was gauged by applause and laughter. And, as the replacement casts of *The Producers* have shown, there just ain't a lot of really funny, really dynamic performers who naturally have that kind of attack. That's why Nathan Lane is wooed back to reprise his role of Max Bialystock at sums unheard of in the annals of Actors' Equity. Luckily for us, we have the film version of *Li'l Abner,* faithfully re-creating the raucous hilarity of one of the musical theatre's great, silly achievements, to remind us of a time when that kind of exuberance was as typical as a typical day in Dogpatch U.S.A. ✾

Michael Kidd

Michael Kidd, choreographer and director whose high-energy dances brightened many Broadway musicals from the 1940s through the 1970s, made his debut in 1947 with *Finian's Rainbow* and two Nanette Fabray shows, *Love Life* and *Arms and the Girl.* In numbers such as "The Crapshooter's Dance," "Quadrille," and "Every Once in a While" from the hits *Guys and Dolls, Can-Can,* and *Destry Rides Again,* respectively, Kidd created a new dance vocabulary with his gymnastic, sometimes treacherous routines. He was not above controversy, getting in much-publicized fisticuffs with both *Destry* star Dolores Gray and her mother. After *Destry,* he had disappointments with projects like *Wildcat, Subways Are for Sleeping, Here's Love, Breakfast at Tiffany's,* and *Skyscraper,* none of which exploited his exuberant character- and situation-driven choreography. His most startling work was his subtle, elegant staging of *The Rothschilds,* completely unlike his previous work and evidence of the growth and maturation of a deeply talented man whose unfortunate choice of properties in the 1960s kept him from the elite club of Jerome Robbins, Bob Fosse, Gower Champion, and Michael Bennett.

TOP: Charlotte Rae and Joe E. Marks as the Yokums, doing their hoedown dance specialty in Michael Kidd's rambunctious "Rag Offen the Bush."

ABOVE: Michael Kidd with a soon-to-be-disillusioned Mary Tyler Moore during dance rehearsals for the catastrophic *Breakfast at Tiffany's.*

LEFT: Abner, under the thrall of a whammy, nearly makes it down the aisle with the aptly named Appassionata Von Climax (Tina Louise). That's the Machiavellian General Bullmoose (Howard St. John) in the center.

Stubby Kaye

Stubby Kaye made his presence known with his clarion tenor voice and his portly frame. After raising the roof nightly with "Sit Down, You're Rocking the Boat" as Nicely-Nicely Johnson in *Guys and Dolls*, he became a star with his showstopper "Jubilation T. Cornpone" in *Li'l Abner*. After a sojourn in Hollywood, playing, among other roles, a banjo-playing, singing narrator alongside Nat "King" Cole in the film *Cat Ballou*, and a mini-career in London starring in musicals and television, he returned to Broadway for two short runs, sounding much the same as he did in 1950, first in the Abe Burrows revival of *Good News* (singing "Keep Your Sunny Side Up"), then in Hal Prince's *Grind*, as a burlesque performer whom time has passed by.

Backstage

Originally to be written by Alan Jay Lerner and Arthur Schwartz, *Li'l Abner* was then planned for Lerner and Burton Lane.

After Charlotte Rae was cast as Mammy Yokum, Billie Hayes was a sensation in *New Faces of 1956*. The producers wanted to replace Rae with Hayes, but Rae had a contract and wouldn't budge. They even went so far as to cut her song. When the tour and movie came up, Hayes got the part.

TOP LEFT: In *Grind*, Stubby Kaye touchingly played a burlesque comic in the twilight of his career.

LEFT: Four of Al Capp's beloved characters: Daisy Mae Scragg (Edith Adams), Pansy Yokum (Charlotte Rae), Earthquake McGoon (Bern Hoffman), and Marryin' Sam (Stubby Kaye).

"He liked to pinch the girls and be obscene... exposed himself and did all kinds of charming things."

— *Edie Adams on Al Capp*

LITTLE JOHNNY JONES

OPENED NOVEMBER 7, 1904; LIBERTY THEATRE; 52 PERFORMANCES

LITTLE JOHNNY JONES
Produced by Sam H. Harris
Music, Book, and Lyrics by
George M. Cohan
Orchestra under the Direction of
Charles J. Gebest
Orchestrations by Charles J. Gebest
Directed by George M. Cohan
Scenic Design by W. Franklin Hamilton
Costumes by Mme. Freisinger, Lord & Taylor

Ethel Levey and the girls.

Synopsis

Johnny Jones, an American jockey, arrives in England set to ride the horse Yankee Doodle in the Derby. He is charged with throwing the big race by the stereotypical upper-class Englishman Anthony Anstey, who resents the upstart American. Meanwhile, Jones's love interest, Goldie Gates, is forced by her mother, Mrs. Kenworthy, to become engaged to a dud of a rich Englishman. Unsurprisingly, the bad guys get their due and the true-blue American is found innocent by the fall of the final curtain.

Cast

Anthony Anstey	*Jerry J. Cohan*
Sing Sing	*J. Bernard Dyllyn*
Timothy D. McGee	*Sam J. Ryan*
Henry Hapgood	*Donald Brian*
The Unknown	*Tom Lewis*
Johnny Jones	*George M. Cohan*
Mrs. Andrews Kenworthy	*Helen F. Cohan*
Florabelle Fly	*Truly Shattuck*
Edith Tyler/Rosario Fauchette/ Earl of Bloomsbury	*Ethel Levey*

ALONG WITH JEROME KERN, GEORGE M. COHAN contributed a distinctly American flavor to the embryonic musical theatre form—a welcome break from operettas, whose plots often revolved around class issues and were finding themselves increasingly passé. By breaking with the European traditions of William Gilbert and Sir Arthur Sullivan, Jacques Offenbach, and the Strausses, both Cohan and Kern introduced Tin Pan Alley melodies and American stories to the theatregoing public, with farcical elements that were precursors to today's situation comedies. Lyrics containing current slang also helped to lower the often high-pitched emotional levels of the somewhat staid operetta form.

Cohan had written two other musicals, *The Governor's Son* (1901) and *Running for Office* (1903), but neither was a success, and Broadway took little notice. With *Little Johnny Jones*, Cohan reached his stride. He wrote the book, composed the score, directed, and coproduced with Sam H. Harris. The show further refined his formula, mixing a healthy dose of patriotism with a strong dash of farce and a liberal sprinkling of good old American corn.

After Cohan read a newspaper story about the American jockey Tod Sloan, he joined up with producer Sam H. Harris, beginning a long and fruitful collaboration. Cohan wrote the entire score without the customary interpolations or the heretofore expected vaudeville turns, which usually intruded. A less original plot of the period would have found Johnny returning to London in the last act to win the Derby once and for all. In *Little Johnny Jones*, the hero loses the race fair and square.

Today's audiences are familiar with *Little Johnny Jones* via the Cohan movie biography *Yankee Doodle Dandy*, starring James Cagney. Although

> "George is not the best actor or author or composer or dancer or playwright. But he can dance better than any author, write better than any actor, compose better than any manager, and manage better than any playwright."
>
> —*Actor William Collier*

much of the screenplay is simply Hollywood fiction (Cohan didn't want either of his wives depicted in the film), the last scene of the second act of *Little Johnny Jones* is quite faithfully represented. After a signal flare from his detective friend (named The Unknown) indicates Anstey's guilt in framing Johnny, our hero lets loose with a rousing reprise of "Give My Regards to Broadway."

Once the show established itself as a Broadway hit, Cohan—for the first time billed above the title and not as one of The Four Cohans—took *Little Johnny Jones* on tour. That's where he enjoyed performing most, before audiences who were thrilled to see a talent they had watched grow up before their eyes, season after season. The money on the road wasn't so bad, either; and when he got the urge, he could always bring the show back to Broadway (which he did three more times). All told, *Little Johnny Jones* played more than 240 performances on Broadway, a long run for the time.

The show featured the first hit standards to come from an American musical: "Life's a Funny Proposition After All" and "Give My Regards to Broadway." The musical theatre was on the road to becoming a true native art form. ❋

George M. Cohan

In the first three decades of the century, George M. Cohan was the symbol of American ingenuity, can-do attitude, and patriotic fervor. Cohan did it all: producer, writer, director, actor, dancer, singer, and songwriter. And he did all of his jobs brilliantly. The Cohan persona—brash, energetic, sentimental, and naïve, was the same onstage and off. Cohan fought for his ideals, even when he was on the wrong side of the issue. During the actors' strike of 1919, he naively took the side of management and later received special dispensation from Actors' Equity. Cohan grew up in a theatrical family, The Four Cohans, along with his parents, Nellie and Jerry, and sister Josie accompanied him from vaudeville to Broadway. His first wife, Ethel Levey, also became part of the Cohan troupe. Cohan's shows were an important transition from European operetta to the American vernacular. Among his most important songs are "Over There," "Give My Regards to Broadway," "The Yankee Doodle Boy," "You're a Grand Old Flag," and "Mary's a Grand Old Name." Early in his career he wrote, produced, and acted in his own shows, but he and his producing partner, Sam H. Harris, presented others' works as well. He acted in two historic productions—the only two that he did not write—Eugene O'Neill's *Ah, Wilderness!* and Richard Rodgers and Lorenz Hart's musical *I'd Rather Be Right*. He is immortalized in the James Cagney film *Yankee Doodle Dandy* and the musical *George M!*

Backstage

A. L. Erlanger asked George M. Cohan sarcastically, "Think you could write a play without a flag?" Cohan responded, "I could write a play without anything but a pencil."

The show was revived on Broadway in 1982 with Donny Osmond in the lead, in a production that had originated at the Goodspeed Opera House. Unfortunately, it lasted but one performance.

RIGHT: An elderly Cohan stars as Franklin Roosevelt in *I'd Rather Be Right*.
TOP: Donny Osmond in the flop revival of *Little Johnny Jones*.

LITTLE ME

NOVEMBER 17, 1962; LUNT-FONTANNE THEATRE; 257 PERFORMANCES

Sid Caesar, as a Chevalier-like Val du Val, sings "Boom-Boom."

LITTLE ME

Produced by Feuer & Martin

Music by Cy Coleman
Lyrics by Carolyn Leigh
Book by Neil Simon
Based on a novel by Patrick Dennis
Music orchestrated by Ralph Burns
Dance arrangements by Fred Werner
Vocal arrangements by Clay Warnick
Musical Director: Charles Sanford

Directed by Cy Feuer and Bob Fosse
Choreographed by Bob Fosse

Scenic Design by Robert Randolph
Costume Design by Robert Fletcher
Lighting Design by Robert Randolph

Synopsis

The top-heavy Belle Schlumpfert has a mighty urge to get ahead in life; she loves Noble Eggleston, but he was born on the right side of the tracks (the far right) and she on the wrong. She marries Fred Poitrine, who dies in World War I (by getting his fingers caught in the keys of a typewriter). Next, she marries French *chanteur* Val du Val, who perishes when the liner *Gigantic* sinks. Then she meets Prince Cherney of Rosenzweig, finally garnering a title. At last ready for Noble, she is about to toast her impending nuptials when Noble becomes an instant alcoholic and a bum. There's nothing left for Belle but to marry George Musgrove, who's had her number since the first act. Noble's son and Belle's daughter end up having the romantic finish their parents could never achieve.

Cast

Patrick Dennis...........................*Peter Turgeon*
Belle, today...............................*Nancy Andrews*
Momma.....................................*Adnia Rice*
Belle, Baby ....*Virginia Martin*
Noble Eggleston, Mr. Pinchley,
Val du Val, Fred Potrine,
Otto Schnitzler, Prince Cherney,
Noble Junior ....*Sid Caesar*
Mrs. Eggleston..........................*Nancy Cushman*
Pinchley Junior, Defense Lawyer,
German Officer, Production
Assistant, Yulnick ....*Mickey Deems*
Bernie Buchsbaum ....*Joey Faye*

Little Me WAS A BRIGHT spot in the 1962–63 Broadway season, and is considered by many to be the funniest musical ever written. It's not easy to write a truly funny musical, for the libretto is by necessity an outline linking the songs together, leaving little room for funny business. (In fact, the librettist's credit for the book of *42nd Street* (1980) reads "Lead Ins and Cross Overs by Michael Stewart and Mark Bramble," acknowledging the low spot on the totem pole that the book writer can occupy.) Lyrics, too, are extremely difficult to make funny—especially *smart* and funny.

There aren't a lot of truly hilarious book shows. *A Funny Thing Happened on the Way to the Forum* (1962) comes to mind. It works so well because the show follows the rules of farce so the exposition, by definition, is funny; the

> "The people aren't coming to see me. They're coming to see Swenson."
>
> —*Sid Caesar,* alarmed when Swen Swenson got applause for "I've Got Your Number"

characters and their needs are over the top; and the story accelerates at an increasingly manic pace. Book writer Burt Shevelove and Larry Gelbart are masters of verbal humor and so is composer/lyricist Stephen Sondheim. And between them, they still left lots of room for the performers to make the parts of *Forum* their own.

Of Thee I Sing (1931) and *How to Succeed in Business Without Really Trying* (1961) are funny because they're satires, not because their characters actually say funny things. *Guys and Dolls* (1950) is funny because it's incredibly stylized yet also incredibly real. Some shows, like *Sugar* (1972), an adaptation of a brilliantly funny film, weren't particularly well written, but the authors left enough leeway so that when the clowns were sent in, they landed the comedy successfully. If you read the scripts of *As the Girls Go* (1948), *Whoopee* (1928), *Du Barry Was a Lady* (1939), and *Foxy* (1964), you might chuckle once or twice, but in reality they were funny for the same reason that *Sugar* was—they were excellent vehicles for Bobby Clark, Eddie Cantor, and Bert Lahr, brilliant clowns all. *The Producers* (2001) is a damn funny show, but somehow a little less so than the movie. *City of Angels* (1989) was extremely clever—but as a rule, cleverness is more admired than laughed at.

Mirth-inducing lyrics are even harder to produce than laugh-out-loud libretti, given the restrictions of music, rhyme scheme, and scansion. The funniest lyricists, in no particular order, are Leo Robin, who is in that rare camp of lyricists that could actually make a joke within a song, with some of his lyrics for *The Girl in Pink Tights* actually making one laugh out loud; Stephen Sondheim, a brilliant wit whose humor relies on wordplay and a mostly benign ridicule of human foibles; Marshall Barer, who could write an extremely funny song (listen to *The Mad Show* [1966] or *Once Upon a Mattress* [1959] for proof); David Zippel, an extremely clever lyricist (some might say too clever), who wrote the funny and smart lyrics to *City of Angels* (1989); and Carolyn Leigh, the lyricist of *Little Me*, who rose to the challenge of Neil Simon's book to pen some of the funniest (and sweetest) lyrics ever heard on Broadway.

Little Me starred the comically gifted Sid Caesar along with an excellent supporting cast of clowns, including Nancy Andrews, Virginia Martin, Joey Faye, Mickey Deems, and Mort Marshall. It employs all manner of humor: exaggeration, incongruity, surprise, slapstick, situational humor, ridicule, satire, and wordplay. The show also gave free rein to Caesar, who brought his special talents for improvisation and slapstick. And there's one more ingredient in the mirthful mix—the breather. Swen Swenson's character isn't funny, just showstoppingly sexy, providing the audience with a much-needed break from all the laughs. Finally, *Little Me* isn't as pushy as *The Producers*, which is positively hell-bent on reducing the audience to hysterics—*or else*! It's a gentler show, one that earns its laughs in an utterly honest manner. Unlike many of its counterparts, it truly merits the title of "musical comedy." ❉

ABOVE: Caesar as Mr. Pinchley, just married to the scrumptious Belle Poitrine (Virginia Martin). Yes, he'll die on his wedding night, but he'll go with a smile on his face. LEFT: Nancy Andrews, lyricist Carolyn Leigh, and composer Cy Coleman during *Little Me* rehearsals. BELOW: Keith Andes plays "Pin the Sombrero on the Donkey" with Lucille Ball in a scene from Leigh and Coleman's first Broadway musical, *Wildcat*.

Carolyn Leigh

Wildly talented yet with a reputation for being poisonously difficult, the witty lyricist Carolyn Leigh collaborated on pop songs like "Young at Heart" before segueing to Broadway with *Peter Pan* in 1954. Although much of her and Moose Charlap's score was supplemented by Styne, Comden, and Green, she contributed greatly to the proceedings with her infectious words to "I Gotta Crow," "I Won't Grow Up," and "I'm Flying." After contributing to several revues and writing more pop songs, often with Cy Coleman, she and Coleman hit Broadway, first writing some rejected spec songs for *Gypsy* (including the Tony Bennett hit, "Firefly") before contributing the songs for the Lucille Ball vehicle *Wildcat* in 1960. With such catchy, jaunty songs as "Hey, Look Me Over" and "Give a Little Whistle," the team seemed a natural for the verve of musical theatre. With *Little Me* two years

later, Leigh revealed a wickedly comic side, matching Neil Simon's hysterical book zinger for zinger. The songs "On the Other Side of the Tracks," "To Be a Performer" (reworked from their rejected *Gypsy* score), "Real Live Girl," and "I've Got Your Number" were perfect for the smart ass, comically loose style of Sid Caesar and company. Teaming with Elmer Bernstein on the thoroughly mediocre *How Now Dow Jones* (1967), Leigh's words and Bernstein's music clearly outshone the rest of the show. After writing two new songs for the 1982 revival of *Little Me*, she teamed with Marvin Hamlisch in 1985 to write *Smile* (1986). The score nearly complete, her death prompted Hamlisch to write a completely new score with Howard Ashman.

SONGS

ACT I · "The Truth" · "The Other Side of the Tracks" · "The Rich Kids' Rag" · "I Love You" · "Deep Down Inside" · "Be a Performer!" · "(Oh! Dem Doggone) Dimples" · "Boom-Boom" · "I've Got Your Number" · "Real Live Girl"
ACT II · "Poor Little Hollywood Star" · "Little Me" · "The Prince's Farewell" (Goodbye) · "Here's To Us"

ABOVE: Nancy Andrews, as the older Belle Poitrine, gets rubbed the right way as she dictates her memoirs.

FAR RIGHT: The sublime Swen Swenson has got Virginia Martin's number in his showstopping song and dance, a kind of male version of Fosse's own "Whatever Lola Wants" striptease number.

RIGHT: Sada Thompson, Nancy Andrews, Jean Stapleton, and Beulah Garrick are four widows singing "You Poor Thing" in *Juno*.

BOTTOM: Poor Nancy Andrews... a veritable shrinking violet... just can't relax for the camera as she sings her showstopping "Miss Platt Selects Mate" in the revue *Touch and Go*.

Nancy Andrews

The wonderful comedienne Nancy Andrews made her Broadway debut in the quick flop *Hilarities* in 1948. With a much better showcase for her talents the next season in *Touch and Go* (1949), Andrews won all the reviews for her showstopper "Miss Platt Selects Mate." Replacing in *Gentlemen Prefer Blondes* and *Hazel Flagg* (when Benay Venuta vacated during its summer hiatus), she next appeared on Broadway in *Plain and Fancy* (1955), winning laughs with the song "City Mouse, Country Mouse." She replaced a miscast Helen Traubel in *Pipe Dream* (1955), and many said her presence in the role of Flora made the whole show fall into place. Two flops followed: the serious *Juno* (1959), and the seriously bad *Christine* (1960). Also appearing Off-Broadway in the title role of the early Jerry Herman musical *Madame Aphrodite* (1961), Andrews was a campy hoot as the older Belle Poitrine in *Little Me*, singing a rousing title duet with her younger self. Her last Broadway job was as understudy to Mildred Natwick and Lillian Roth in the short-lived *70, Girls, 70* (1971).

A LITTLE NIGHT MUSIC

OPENED FEBRUARY 25, 1973; MAJESTIC THEATRE; 601 PERFORMANCES

The bewitching Glynis Johns (center, with Judy Kahan and Despo), living "The Glamorous Life."

ONCE UPON A TIME, BROADWAY musicals were the primary suppliers of American popular song, with any Broadway show worth its salt containing at least one future standard. Among the earliest were 1891's *Robin Hood*, which gave us "O, Promise Me"; *The Merry Widow* (1907) offered "Waltz at Maxim's"; and *The Girl from Utah* (1914), provided the hit "They Didn't Believe Me." These songs and many, many more from early Broadway musicals entered the Hit Parade and remained favorites until the rise of rock and roll and the singer/songwriters forever changed the face of popular music in the early 1960s (though the Beatles did record "Till There Was You" from *The Music Man*). By the 1970s, the record companies had largely abandoned their classical, jazz, and show catalogues, the variety show was banished from television, and radio stations had switched over to rock and news formats. The last popular song to come from a Broadway show just might be "One Night in Bangkok" from *Chess*, which opened in 1988, and while some producers hold out hope that scores by immensely popular singer/songwriters like Paul Simon and Elton John might contribute to the Billboard charts, it hasn't come to pass.

Stephen Sondheim, by general consensus the greatest Broadway songwriter of our time (and maybe of all time), has had only one pop song come out of a show for which he created both words and music, "Send in the Clowns" from *A Little Night Music*. Recorded by Judy Collins after the show had left the boards, it won a Grammy Award for Song of the Year in 1975, a year after the show had closed.

Collins's benign, folk-like rendition of "Send in the Clowns," although responsible for the song's immense popularity, is in many ways the antithesis of its meaning in the show. Sondheim himself was surprised by its hit status, for it was originally written late in rehearsals as a bitter musing for the character of Desirée, and a small song, musically speaking, tailored to the wispy, honey-

A LITTLE NIGHT MUSIC
Produced by Harold Prince
Produced in association with Ruth Mitchell
Music and Lyrics by Stephen Sondheim
Book by Hugh Wheeler
Suggested by the film
Smiles of a Summer Night by Ingmar Bergman
Music orchestrated by Jonathan Tunick
Musical Director: Harold Hastings
Directed by Harold Prince
Choreographed by Patricia Birch
Scenic Design by Boris Aronson
Costume Design by Florence Klotz
Lighting Design by Tharon Musser

Synopsis

Months after his marriage to Anne, lawyer Fredrik Egerman finds himself increasingly frustrated. It seems that Anne is still protecting her virginity. It's a May–December romance, and Anne is actually closer in age to Fredrik's also-frustrated son, Henrik. As Fredrik's patience slowly crumbles, a theatre company comes to town starring none other than Desirée Armfeldt, an old lover of Fredrik's. Desirée is having an affair with the hussar, Carl Magnus Malcolm, an unrepentant chauvinist who is married to Charlotte. Desirée's illegitimate daughter, Fredrika (please note the similarity to Desirée's ex-lover's name) is ensconced with her grandmother, Madame Armfeldt, while Desirée tours the hinterlands. They all wind up spending a weekend in the country at Madame Armfeldt's and the complex couplings soon sort themselves out—Anne running away with Henrik, Carl Magnus back with his wife, and Fredrik with Desirée.

Cast

Frederika Armfeldt	*Judy Kahan*
Madame Armfeldt	*Hermione Gingold*
Henrik Egerman	*Mark Lambert*
Anne Egerman	*Victoria Mallory*
Fredrik Egerman	*Len Cariou*
Petra	*D. Jamin-Bartlett*
Desirée Armfeldt	*Glynis Johns*
Count Carl-Magnus Malcolm	*Laurence Guittard*
Countess Charlotte Malcolm	*Patricia Elliott*
Frid	*George Lee Andrews*

"I'd played for royalty but Steve Sondheim and Hal Prince were too much for me. The only one who frightened me more was Noël Coward."

— Hermione Gingold on her audition

dipped vocals of actress Glynis Johns. Completely at odds with the straight haired, crunchy-granola, macramé world of the Collins recording, the original Broadway production of *Night Music* was witty, romantic, and one of the most elegant musicals to ever be seen on Broadway. The show was perfectly cast, from the three leads of Johns, Len Cariou, and Hermione Gingold, through the crystal-voiced ingénue of Victoria Mallory and shiny tenor of juvenile Mark Lambert (who, like their onstage counterparts, ended up together in real life as well), the Count of Laurence Gittard, with a perfect pomposity and a baritone of operatic proportion; and the Countess of Patricia Elliott, who, not taking anything away from her marvelous performance, was provided with dialogue by Hugh Wheeler that is among the most surefire in the history of theatre (in actor terms, the role is known as a "gimme"). Add into the mix a delightful quintet of *lieder* singers, a precocious daughter, a lusty maid, and one of the most beautiful physical productions ever, with Boris Aronson's gliding panels of birch trees, Flossie Klotz's sumptuous costumes, and the legendary Tharon Musser's evocation of the eternal Swedish summer night, and you've got a commercial and critical hit. It even converted longtime Sondheim sorehead Clive Barnes of the *New York Times*, who finally opened his eyes and ears and recognized the importance of the Prince/Sondheim collaboration, exclaiming in his rave review, "Good God, finally an adult musical!"

Long announced for a Broadway revival, first starring Lee Remick and later Glenn Close, we still await a first-class, open-ended production. Imagine the show starring Meryl Streep, Kevin Kline, and Angela Lansbury. ✳

"Now" vs. "Soon": Len Cariou, in amorous mood as lovesick lawyer Fredrik Egerman, once again gets the brush-off from his virgin wife, Anne (Victoria Mallory).

Hermione Gingold

Hermione Gingold, who made hauteur hilarious, made her Broadway debut in the revue *John Murray Anderson's Almanac* in 1953, where her number "Which Witch?," her coronation as Miss Rheingold, and "Dinner for One," her sketch with fellow ham Billy DeWolfe, made Gingold the toast of the town. Difficult to cast due to her unique looks and delivery, her next musical was not until 1959, when she played Mrs. Bennett, the mother of "Five Daughters" in *First Impressions*, followed quickly by a brief run in the flop revue *From A to Z*. She replaced Molly Picon in *Milk and Honey*, and had a non-musical success in *Oh, Dad, Poor Dad...* A frequent guest on talk shows through the 1960s, she regaled audiences with her skills as a raconteur and her persona of a dotty, sometimes smutty aunt that one alternately adores and is embarrassed by. She won the creators of *A Little Night Music* over in her audition, for they had an entirely different type in mind for the role of Madame Armfeldt. It gave her career a jolt, proving she had could rein in her comic bravura and be truly touching.

ABOVE: Gingold as Madame Armfeldt, who "acquired some position, plus a tiny Titian." FAR RIGHT: There she is, Miss Rheingold: Hermione Gingold, in the Richard Adler and Jerry Ross song "Queen for a Day," from the 1953 revue *John Murray Anderson's Almanac*. RIGHT: Polly Bergen (whose smoky singing was most definitely un-Austenlike) and Gingold sing "Let's Fetch the Carriage" in *First Impressions*.

SONGS

ACT I "Night Waltz" · "Now" · "Soon" · "Later" "The Glamorous Life" · "Remember?" · "You Must Meet My Wife" · "Liaisons" · "In Praise of Women" · "Every Day a Little Death" · "A Weekend in the Country"
ACT II "The Sun Won't Set" · "It Would Have Been Wonderful" · "Perpetual Anticipation" "Send in the Clowns" · "The Miller's Son"

ABOVE: During a weekend in the country, partners waltz romantically with different partners; here, Fredrik (Len Cariou) and Charlotte (Patricia Elliott) commiserate over their plights. RIGHT: Glynis Johns in The Dress, a crimson stunner by designer Florence Klotz. BELOW: Rebecca Luker wearing another trademark red Klotz, as Magnolia in the 1993 Prince revival of *Show Boat*.

Backstage

On the national tour, Madame Armfeldt was played by Wicked Witch of the West Margaret Hamilton. When she was cast, Stephen Sondheim quipped, "She's never had a liaison in her life."

The 1991 LA production featured the original Desiree, Glynis Johns, now graduated to the role of Madame Armfeldt.

Florence Klotz

Florence Klotz, costume designer of many of the historic Hal Prince shows, started out as a costume supervisor at City Center, making her debut as a Broadway musical designer with Prince's *It's A Bird . . . It's A Plane . . . It's Superman* in 1966. For her staggering, Ziegfeldian inspirations for *Follies*, undisputedly the most beautifully designed Broadway musical ever, Klotz's place in history would be guaranteed had she never designed another show. In addition to her sumptuous work for *Follies*, her red dresses for leading ladies became her signature: for Alexis Smith in *Follies*, the ladies of *Jerry's Girls*, Teresa Stratas in *Rags*, Chita Rivera in *Kiss of the Spider Woman*, Georgia Brown in *Roza*, and Rebecca Luker in Prince's 1994 revival of *Show Boat*. One of the most famous costumes in modern musical theatre history, the red sequined dress in which Glynis Johns delivered "Send in the Clowns" in *A Little Night Music*, never failed to elicit gasps from the audience.

LOST IN THE STARS

OPENED OCTOBER 30, 1949; MUSIC BOX THEATRE; 273 PERFORMANCES

Stephen Kumalo (Todd Duncan) beseeches the Lord to help him find his son.

LOST IN THE STARS

Produced by The Playwrights' Company
Book and Lyrics by Maxwell Anderson
Music by Kurt Weill
Based on the novel *Cry, the Beloved Country*
by Alan Paton
Music orchestrated and arranged by Kurt Weill
Conducted by Maurice Levine
Choral group trained by Maurice Levine
Directed by Rouben Mamoulian
Choreographed by La Verne French
Scenic Design by George Jenkins
Costume Design by Anna Hill Johnstone
Johannesburg backdrop by Horace Armistead

Synopsis

Black minister Stephen Kumalo has lost touch with his son, Absalom, who left his home for Johannesburg to earn money for school and hasn't been heard from since. He leaves for the capital to search for his son and at the train station, Kumalo runs into James Jarvis, a white, liberal lawyer and his two sons, Arthur and Edward. Soon, in a burglary gone wrong, Absalom murders Arthur Jarvis. Absalom is captured, and Kumalo finds his son in jail, awaiting execution. Eventually, Kumalo and James Jarvis must come to terms with their lives as they attempt to understand the polarization of whites and blacks in apartheid South Africa.

Cast

Leader	*Frank Roane*
Stephen Kumalo	*Todd Duncan*
James Jarvis	*Leslie Banks*
John Kumalo	*Warren Coleman*
Alex	*Herbert Coleman*
Linda	*Sheila Guyse*
Matthew Kumalo	*William Greaves*
Absalom Kumalo	*Julian Mayfield*
Irina	*Inez Matthews*

SONGS

ACT I "The Hills of Ixtapo" · "Thousands of Miles" · "Train to Johannesburg" · "The Search" · "The Little Gray House" "Who'll Buy?" · "Trouble Man" · "Murder in Parkwold" "Fear" · "Lost in the Stars"

ACT II "The Wild Justice" · "O Tixo, Tixo, Help Me" · "Stay Well" · "Cry, the Beloved Country" · "Big Mole" · "A Bird of Passage"

THE LATE 1930s AND THE 1940s were a time of experimentation in the theatre, when Broadway was still a force in American culture, generally attracting highly educated people with a genuine interest in ideas who were drawn to serious themes in their art. With the events in Europe preceding and surrounding World War II, the more evolved realized that in order for humanity to survive, we must not only stand up for our beliefs but must take responsibility for our actions.

Musical theatre concerned itself less with lofty goals than did straight plays, but there were definitely brave new voices to be heard. Two of the boldest examples of "issue" musicals were *Porgy and Bess* and *Lost in the Stars,* which shared many elements: Rouben Mamoulian directed both productions; Todd Duncan, the original Porgy, starred as Stephen Kumalo in the new show; and Warren Coleman, who had played Crown in *Porgy,* played Stephen Kumalo's brother in *Stars.*

Lost in the Stars was the first and last show to be dubbed a "musical tragedy" by its creators, composer Kurt Weill and lyricist/librettist Maxwell Anderson, who used the term to distinguish it from musical comedy. Certainly, it does deal with tragedy, but despite its examination of the horrors of apartheid, by the end of the evening the white and black protagonists have come to a tentative understanding.

Weill began his career in the political, or *agitprop,* theatre of Germany, partnering with playwright Bertolt Brecht, and continued to explore serious themes in his American works. Anderson, one of the finest playwrights of his generation, also deeply believed in the goodness of the common man, despite the obstacles he must overcome. Together and separately, they wrote shows espousing their deeply felt political and societal ideas, reaching a broad audience. While they certainly craved commercial success, they were equally interested in delivering a message.

Weill and his collaborators, Anderson, Paul Green, Ira Gershwin, Alan Jay Lerner, and Ogden Nash, believed in, if not a serious musical theatre, at least one that spoke to its audience in a mature, intelligent way and was unafraid to deal with serious ideas in an entertaining manner. Fifty-five years later, Weill and Anderson's *Lost in the Stars* continues to challenge and thrill, with its soaring melodies and deeply felt story. ✻

Backstage

Many of the songs in *Lost in the Stars* came from an unfinished score by Weill and Anderson titled *Ulysses Africanus,* which was meant to star Paul Robeson.

Todd Duncan

A serious singer with a fervent sense of right and wrong, confidence in his fellow blacks, and an unswerving faith in the possibilities of mankind, Todd Duncan graced the Broadway stage with his strong presence and commanding voice. He made an auspicious Broadway debut in the title role in *Porgy and Bess.* After a run at London's Drury Lane Theatre in *The Sun Never Sets* (1938), he returned to Broadway in the Vernon Duke/John Latouche musical, *Cabin in the Sky* (1940), starring as the Lawd's General opposite Ethel Waters and Dooley Wilson. He returned to *Porgy and Bess* on Broadway in the historic 1943 revival, and in subsequent productions worldwide, acting as an unofficial ambassador of culture. Also assaying many opera roles and appearing in a few films, he played his last Broadway role in the powerful *Lost in the Stars.* Occasional concertizing alternated with teaching at the prestigious Howard University in Washington, D.C.

ABOVE: Todd Duncan and Kurt Weill during rehearsals.

BELOW: Minister Stephen Kumalo (Todd Duncan) leads his congregation in prayer. Note James Jarvis (Leslie Banks) at the far right of the photo.

MAME

OPENED MAY 24, 1966; WINTER GARDEN THEATRE; 1,508 PERFORMANCES

Angela Lansbury as the irrepressibly zany Mame Dennis.

MAME

Produced by Fryer, Carr & Harris, Inc.
Book by Jerome Lawrence and Robert E. Lee,
based on their play and the novel
by Patrick Dennis
Music and Lyrics by Jerry Herman
Musical Director: Donald Pippin
Vocal arrangements by Donald Pippin
Music orchestrated by Philip J. Lang
Dance arrangements by Roger Adams
Directed by Gene Saks
Choreographed by Onna White
Scenic Design by William and Jean Eckart
Costume Design by Robert Mackintosh
Lighting Design by Tharon Musser

Synopsis

Mame Dennis finds herself with a ward, her ten-year-old nephew Patrick. She raises him in the only manner she knows, living life to its utmost. But when the Great Depression hits, Mame struggles to find work to keep her household together. After she meets, marries, and loses a wealthy Southern gentleman, Mame must learn to let go of the only other man in her life, the now-grown Patrick. After a close call with a Connecticut snob, Patrick finds true love. They soon have their own son, whom Mame will mold in the same way she did Patrick, her boy with the bugle.

Cast

Mame Dennis .... *Angela Lansbury*
Vera Charles .... *Beatrice Arthur*
Agnes Gooch .... *Jane Connell*
Ito .... *Sab Shimono*
Patrick Dennis, age 10 .... *Frankie Michaels*
Dwight Babcock .... *Willard Waterman*
Mr. Upson .... *John C. Becher*
Beauregard Burnside .... *Charles Braswell*
Pegeen Ryan .... *Diane Coupé*
Mrs. Upson .... *Johanna Douglas*
Sally Cato .... *Margaret Hall*
Mother Burnside .... *Charlotte Jones*
Patrick Dennis, age 19–29 ... *Jerry Lanning*
Peter Dennis .... *Michael Maitland*
Gloria Upson .... *Diana Walker*

SONGS

ACT I "St. Bridget" · "It's Today" · "Open a New Window" "The Man in the Moon" · "My Best Girl" · "We Need a Little Christmas" · "The Fox Hunt" · "Mame"
ACT II "The Letter" · "Bosom Buddies" · "Gooch's Song" "That's How Young I Feel" · "If He Walked into My Life"

You CAN LOOK AT THE career of Jerry Herman in two ways. Either he had the misfortune of being born too late, at the tail end of the golden years of the American musical, or he had the luck to come on the scene just before the American musical began its long slide into irrelevance.

In the 1920s, composers might have as many as five shows produced on Broadway in one season; even in the 1960s, composers like Herman, Charles Strouse, and Cy Coleman premiered new shows every other season. But by the 1970s and '80s, productions of new musicals had practically ground to a halt and the emergence of rock-style musicals and British imports further lessened the number of original musicals by the great masters of the form.

Mame came right at the last gasp of a century-long tradition. There was still a solid, professional pool of talent upon which to draw. And, due to the immense success of *Hello, Dolly!* and the reputation of producers Robert Fryer, Allan Carr, and Joseph Harris, *Mame* had its pick of the best musical theatre talents. The actresses available for the title role included such veterans as Kaye Ballard, Nanette Fabray, Dolores Gray, and Lisa Kirk, but the role, as everyone knows, ended up going to the magical Angela Lansbury, who had previously appeared in only one musical, the nine-performance Sondheim flop *Anyone Can Whistle*.

Once Lansbury relinquished the role, there were still plenty of fine actresses to play it on Broadway and the road, including (in no particular order) Celeste Holm, Ann Miller, Janis Paige, Janet Blair, Ginger Rogers, Jane Morgan, and even Susan Hayward (in the Las Vegas production). If a first-class production were to be cast now, one would be hard-pressed to think of an actress with the stage smarts, glamour, and star quality of any of the above-named performers.

The success of *Mame* was due only in part to the magic of the lead actress, for it was a smart, sophisticated, and energetic production in which all the elements jelled into a unified whole. However, as brilliant as the players and production staff were, the success of *Mame* was primarily due to three men: Jerome Lawrence and Robert E. Lee, both of whom authored the libretto and the original play; and Jerry Herman, the composer and lyricist.

In *Hello, Dolly!* the "Waiters Gallop" and the title song certainly thrill, but it is "Ribbons Down My Back" and "It Only Takes a Moment" that give the show its heart. Likewise, while *Mame* may be best remembered as a splashy, glitzy, Broadway extravaganza with its jubilant title song, effervescent "It's Today" and joyful "We Need a Little Christmas," the small, intimate moments are what anchor its standing as one of the greatest Broadway musicals. "My Best Girl" and "If He Walked into My Life" are what really matter to an audience. And once you've won the audience's heart, you're home free.

Looking at our list of the 101 greatest musicals, the one element they all share is heart. And of them, *Mame* is one of the most touching of all. ✻

Left to right, Charles Braswell, Angela Lansbury, Sab Shimono, Jane Connell, and Frankie Michaels in the reprise of "We Need a Little Christmas."

Angela Lansbury

Angela Lansbury, a brilliant motion-picture character actress, surprised most New York critics when she revealed a theretofore untapped flair for musical comedy, clowning as the zany yet evil mayoress Cora Hoover Hooper in Stephen Sondheim and Arthur Laurents's *Anyone Can Whistle*. Despite its quick failure, she was composer Jerry Herman's first choice to play Mame Dennis, and *Mame*'s smash success and her uncanny mix of fine dramatic acting and knockout singing and dancing catapulted her into the highest stratosphere of Broadway stardom (winning her first Tony). Her follow-up show, reuniting many of the *Mame* team, was *Dear World*, which, a second Tony Award notwithstanding, was a distinct letdown to audiences expecting more of the same Mame. Her next show, *Prettybelle*, was an out-and-out disaster, closing in Boston. After a self-imposed hiatus, she returned, first to the West End, then to Broadway, in the riveting revival of *Gypsy* in 1974, with a most harrowing "Rose's Turn." Her least-known musical performance was as a three-week replacement Anna in the 1977 revival of *The King and I*. Her dizzyingly mad/comic/poignant turn as Mrs. Lovett in Sondheim's *Sweeney Todd* assured her place as one of the greatest actresses in musical theatre history.

LEFT: Stephen Sondheim's songs for Cora Hooper Hoover (Angela Lansbury, here with Harvey Evans) in *Anyone Can Whistle* were deliberately modeled on the nightclub act of Kay Thompson, who, like Cora, Sondheim considered "brilliant and heartless."

RIGHT: As Countess Aurelia in *Dear World*, Lansbury won a second Tony Award.

Onna White

Onna White got her choreographic start re-creating Michael Kidd's dances for the City Center revivals of *Finian's Rainbow* and *Guys and Dolls*. Her greatest success came from staging dances for period shows, including the turn-of-the-century cakewalks and polkas of *The Music Man*, *Take Me Along*, and *Half a Sixpence;* her tangos, Lindy hops, and jitterbugs of *Mame;* and her stately stage pictures and gavottes of *1776*. Her track record in shows set in the present day was less than stellar: *Whoop-Up*, *Let It Ride!*, *I Had a Ball*, and *Illya Darling* were all failures, despite White's always classy work. In addition, she had unfortunate luck in the 1970s (aside from her witty, low-key musical staging in the hit *I Love My Wife*) with such credits as *70, Girls, 70; Goodtime Charley;*

and *Working*. One of the most underrated of the great chore-ographers, Onna White's work always reflected character, advanced the plot, and displayed abundant invention. Comparisons of her work on the original productions with that of recent revivals show exactly how brilliant Onna White could be.

Backstage

Judy Garland begged to be considered to replace Angela Lansbury as Mame on Broadway, but the producers were unwilling to risk their investment on an erratic genius.

Mame is one of the rare examples of a show that opened with one song in Philadelphia, "That's How Young I Feel," then replaced it in Boston with "Do You Call That Living," but went back to the original song in New York.

TOP: Bea Arthur, as Great Lady of the American Theatre Vera Charles, reminds us once and for all that she was *never* in the chorus.

ABOVE RIGHT: Elegant choreographer Onna White adding her customary class to the Tommy Steele starrer *Half a Sixpence*.

RIGHT: In another Jerry Herman title song lovefest, the boys at the foxhunt also prove to have had extensive ballet training.

MAN OF LA MANCHA

OPENED NOVEMBER 22, 1965; ANTA WASHINGTON SQUARE THEATRE; 2,328 PERFORMANCES

ABOVE: Richard Kiley dreams "The Impossible Dream."

RIGHT: She was born in a ditch: Joan Diener as Aldonza the wench.

MAN OF LA MANCHA

Produced by Albert W. Selden and Hal James

Book by Dale Wasserman
Music by Mitch Leigh
Lyrics by Joe Darion
Musical Directors:
R. Bennett Benetsky and Neil Warner
Dance Arrangements by Neil Warner
Music arranged by Music Makers, Inc.

Musical Staging by Albert Marre
Directed by Albert Marre
Choreographed by Jack Cole

Scenic Design by Howard Bay
Lighting Design by Howard Bay
Costume Design by
Howard Bay and Patton Campbell

Synopsis

Novelist Miguel de Cervantes and his servant have been arrested by the Spanish Inquisition. Thrown into a communal cell surrounded by whores and thieves, Cervantes tells his fellow inmates the story of Don Quixote de la Mancha, a dreamer who may be mad—at least in the view of his relatives. Cervantes takes the part of Quixote, who meets the downtrodden wench Aldonza. She was born in a ditch, but the idealist Quixote sees her as a beautiful lady, his "Dulcinea." Along his journey, the knight faces many obstacles, not the least of which is The Enchanter. When this foe holds up a mirror to Quixote, forcing him to see the reality of his life, it sends the woeful knight into a breakdown and to his eventual death. As Cervantes completes the story, he is called to appear before the inquisitors. Climbing the long staircase out of the cell, he remains optimistic, just like his creation Don Quixote, always dreaming the impossible dream.

Cast

Don Quixote (Cervantes) ...... *Richard Kiley*
Sancho Panza .... *Irving Jacobson*
Aldonza .... *Joan Diener*
The Innkeeper .... *Ray Middleton*
Dr. Carrasco .... *Jon Cypher*
The Padre .... *Robert Rounseville*

Man of La Mancha SHARPLY divided audiences and critics alike, for while some hearts soared upon hearing "The Impossible Dream," others of a more cynical nature cringed. The romantics certainly won out, for the show became an international hit that has continued to uplift audiences for almost forty years.

A lot of the credit, of course, goes to Richard Kiley's magnificent performance and Howard Bay's impressive unit set, with a central staircase worthy of *Hello, Dolly!* or *Follies*. And, of course, there's that anthem. For better or worse, "The Impossible Dream" spawned a slew of sappy imitations whose orchestrations went up, up, up the scale, indicating lofty goals. We might not have had an "I Dreamed a Dream" (ah, that dream thing) or "Music of the Night" or "Wheels of a Dream" (there's that dream again) if it weren't for Mitch Leigh and Joe Darion's original. Richard Rodgers and Oscar Hammerstein had been the kings of uplift with *Carousel*'s "You'll Never Walk Alone" and *The Sound of Music*'s "Climb Every Mountain," but those lung busters didn't spawn musical offspring in the same fashion, perhaps because of their religious undertones.

The long-lasting appeal of *Man of La Mancha* is even more surprising given that Mitch Leigh (whose best known composing credit up to that point had been "Nobody Doesn't Like Sara Lee"), director Albert Marre, and his wife, original Aldonza Joan Diener (both of *Kismet* fame) would never enjoy another success. Leigh and Marre were responsible for the only "Zen-Buddist-Hebrew musical comedy" (as it was billed), *Chu-Chem*. Their next musical, *Cry for Us All*, had an anthem of a title song and an often terrific score, but Leigh, Marre, and Diener couldn't make it work. And the threesome's *Home Sweet Homer*, a musical retelling of Homer's *Odyssey*, was such an embarrassment that it drove Yul Brynner back to revivals of *The King and I* for the rest of his career. Two other Leigh/Marre musicals—*Halloween* and *April Song*—never got past the summer-stock circuit. All in all, one out of six ain't a bad track record when the one is *Man of La Mancha*.

Oddly, *La Mancha*'s librettist and lyricist didn't fare any better. Book writer Dale Wasserman was best known for his play *One Flew Over the Cuckoo's Nest*, a failure on Broadway but a hit Off-Broadway that came into its own as a movie. Lyricist Joe Darion had done good work on *Shinbone Alley*, a musical based on Don Marquis's *archy and mehitibel*. Darion cowrote that libretto with some young upstart named Mel Brooks, but the show wasn't a popular hit (though it does have a marvelous score by Darion and George Kleinsinger). Darion went on to musicalize the film *Never on Sunday*, retitled *Illya Darling*—again good work but no cigar.

Ultimately, no one remembers their flops (and wasn't it nice of us to remind you): they just remember their one, gigantic, mega-hit. That's the way it should be, of course, and somewhere in the world, as you read this right now, some seventeen-year-old kid with shoe white in his hair, a middle-aged star of Belgian television, and an elderly former matinee idol now working South Florida's "condo circuit" are all walking up that central staircase into the light, trying to reach the unreachable star. ❋

SONGS

"Man of La Mancha" (I, Don Quixote) · "It's All the Same" · "Dulcinea" · "I'm Only Thinking of Him" · "I Really Like Him" · "What Does He Want of Me?" · "Little Bird, (Little Bird)" · "Barber's Song" · "Golden Helmet of Mambrino" · "To Each His Dulcinea (To Every Man His Dream)" · "The Quest" (The Impossible Dream) · "The Combat" · "The Dubbing" (Knight of the Woeful Countenance) · "The Abduction" · "Aldonza" · "The Knight of the Mirrors" · "A Little Gossip" · "The Psalm"

TOP: Joan Diener, of the wide-ranging vocals, sings "What Does He Want of Me?"

RIGHT: Chita Rivera and Jack Cole rehearse for *Zenda*, their 1963 flop.

Jack Cole

Simultaneously reviled and worshipped by his dancers, choreographer Jack Cole was a notorious taskmaster. He began in the world of modern dance, performing with the Denishawn Company before graduating to the nightclub scene, where he began to develop his unique choreographic style. His most traditional Broadway show was his first, the Ethel Merman vehicle *Something for the Boys*. Bringing African, Indian, and Latin styles into his work, he was most successful in musicals with an emphasis on ethnic dance, from the South American rhythms of *Magdalena* and the "Calypso Celebration" in *Alive and Kicking* to the Middle Eastern ceremonies of *Kismet*, the native island dances of *Jamaica*, and the exotic courtesans in *A Funny Thing Happened on the Way to the Forum*. *Zenda* and *Mata Hari* closed prior to New York. He tried to move into directing with *Kelly* and *Donnybrook!* An early mentor (and tor-mentor) of Gwen Verdon, Cole was responsible for originating what we now call Broadway jazz dance, greatly influencing the work of later choreographers Bob Fosse, Peter Gennaro, and Michael Bennett. His most recognizable work is the "Diamond's Are a Girl's Best Friend" number for Marilyn Monroe in the film *Gentlemen Prefer Blondes*. Ironically, Cole's contribution to *La Mancha*, his best-known stage work, was minimal—just the Aldonza rape ballet.

Richard Kiley

Actor Richard Kiley, who, in addition to a long career in dramatic roles, used his rich baritone voice to great advantage in Broadway musicals. He made his musical debut as the juvenile lead in *Kismet*, singing "Stranger in Paradise" and "And This Is My Beloved." He won his first Tony Award opposite Gwen Verdon in *Redhead*, and was almost continually employed through the 1960s, as the romantic lead of *No Strings* and in the Buddy Hackett vehicle *I Had a Ball*. Kiley's career took an unexpected turn and he became a character actor of the highest order with his performance as Don Quixote in *Man of La Mancha*, inspiring lounge singers on seven continents with "The Impossible Dream." His biggest flop was his first post–*La Mancha* outing, the short-lived musical version of *Caesar and Cleopatra* titled *Her First Roman*, costarring Leslie Uggams. Like Zero Mostel, Carol Channing, and Yul Brynner, the lack of worthy new projects in the 1970s led Kiley to reprise *La Mancha* twice, first at Lincoln Center, then back on Broadway at the Palace. Twice slated for a return to Broadway in the 1980s, first as Scrooge in the Michel Legrand and Sheldon Harnick's *A Christmas Carol* then in a revival of *South Pacific,* neither came in.

TOP LEFT: Gwen Verdon and Richard Kiley sing "Look Who's In Love" in *Redhead*.

ABOVE: Kiley and a bevy of beauties in his opening number from *No Strings*, "How Sad."

LEFT: Irving Jacobson as the faithful Sancho.

Backstage

Michael Redgrave was the original choice to play Don Quixote. Poets, librettists, and partners W. H. Auden and Chester Kallman were set to write the lyrics.

THE MERRY WIDOW

OPENED OCTOBER 21, 1907; NEW AMSTERDAM THEATRE; 416 PERFORMANCES

ABOVE: Widow Ethel Jackson doesn't look too merry at Maxim's.

RIGHT: In the 1955 television version of *The Merry Widow* (cowritten by Neil Simon!), Ann Jeffreys (here with Brian Sullivan) made for an especially glamorous Sonia.

THE MERRY WIDOW

Produced by Henry W. Savage

Music by Franz Lehár
Book by Basil Hood
Original Book (*Die Lustige Witwe*) by Victor Leon and Leo Stein after *L'Attache d'Ambassade* by Henri Meilhac
English Lyrics by Adrian Ross
Musical Director: Louis F. Gottschalk
Orchestra under the Direction of Louis F. Gottschalk

Staged by George Marion

Settings by Walter Burridge
Costumes by Percy Anderson, Mme. Hermann, Mme. Zimmerman

Synopsis

The Ambassador of Marsovia is on a mission to raise money for his country's depleted treasury. He decides that a marriage between Prince Danilo and "the merry widow," Sonia Sadoya, would enrich his country's coffers. Indeed, Danilo was once in love with the wealthy widow but is now concerned that he would be viewed as a fortune-hunter, marrying her for his country's greater good rather than for love. Of course, that is exactly the plan set forth by Baron Popoff, the ambassador. The widow throws a ball in her Paris home and convinces Danilo that she is broke, in addition to using her womanly wiles to make him jealous of another suitor. He falls for the bait and proposes.

Cast

Popoff .... *R. E. Graham*
Natalie .... *Lois Ewell*
Prince Danilo .... *Donald Brian*
Sonia .... *Ethel Jackson*
Camille de Jolidan .... *William C. Weedon*

ie Lustige Witwe was FIRST presented in Vienna in 1905, and its staggering success led to an English adaptation by Basil Hood, which premiered at Daly's Theatre in London in June 1907, with composer Franz Lehar himself conducting the opening night. When *The Merry Widow* premiered on Broadway, it caused a similar sensation, influencing European operetta as well as fashion on both sides of the Atlantic. Women all over the world were soon seen sporting Merry Widow hats and gowns (along with their unseen Merry Widow corsets).

Hit shows of the time were burlesqued, and *The Merry Widow* proved no exception. Lulu Glaser starred in *The Merry Widow Burlesque* (1908) under the auspices of Joe Weber of Weber and Fields fame. Germany had its own burlesque, *Der Lustiger Witwer* (with music by future Hollywood film scorer Max Steiner), while Vienna had a fake sequel titled *Die Lustige Witwe in Zweite Ehe*, and Philadelphia saw *The Merry Widow Remarried*. There were also parodies in Hungary (*A Vigado Ozvegy*) and more than a dozen in Paris. *His Honor the Mayor* featured the song "I Wish I Could Find the Man Who Wrote the Merry Widow Waltz." These parodies spoke to the worldwide success of a show that has continued to entertain audiences for almost 100 years. ❄

SONGS

ACT I Opening Chorus · Ball-Music · "A Dutiful Wife" · "In Marsovia" · "Maxim's" (Girls, Girls, Girls) · Finale
ACT II Opening Chorus · "Villa" · "The Cavalier" "Women" · Duet · "Oh, Say No More" · "Love in My Heart"
ACT III Opening Scene · "The Girls at Maxim's" "Butterflies" (Dance) · "I Love You So" (The Merry Widow Waltz) · Finale

Franz Lehár

One of the traditions from which the American musical descended was the European operetta. Franz Lehár was the preeminent Viennese composer, with a string of successful shows beginning in 1902 with *Wiener Frauen* and continuing through the 1934 production of *Giudetta* (he concluded his career writing film scores). Lehár made an auspicious Broadway debut with the famed production of *The Merry Widow*. Lehár's music was a constant presence on Broadway with such shows as *The Count of Luxembourg* (1912), *Eva* (1912), *The Man with Three Wives* (1913), *Maids of Athens* (1914), *Alone at Last* (1915), and *The Star Gazer* (1917). After operetta went out of vogue following World War I, Broadway continued to amuse itself with revivals of *The Merry Widow* (four in all) and one of *The Count of Luxembourg* (1930). Lehár's Broadway career concluded with *Frederika* (1937) and *Yours Is My Heart* (1946), two failures. Naturally, Lehár's work continued in opera houses throughout the country and through three film versions of *The Merry Widow*.

Backstage

The score for the 100-year-old *Merry Widow* has been recorded in English, Russian, Italian, Swedish, Hungarian, Spanish, Romanian, and French.

ABOVE: Ethel Jackson surrounded by the "girls, girls, girls" of Maxim's.

ABOVE LEFT: Franz Lehar and renowned opera singer Richard Tucker in 1946.

RIGHT: Early musical theater superstar Donald Brian as Prince Danilo.

STAR TURNS, PART II

Tammy Grimes

With an immediately identifiable voice halfway between the purr of a minx and the gurgle of a drain, Tammy Grimes suffered from arrested career development. Tapped in 1955 to play the lead in *The Amazing Adele*, which featured a book by Anita Loos, the show proved not so amazing and folded in Boston. Grimes would have to wait another five years to become a Broadway musical star, playing the title role in Meredith

Willson's *The Unsinkable Molly Brown*. Because of the Tony Awards' strange rules that determine an actor's eligibility based on her billing, Grimes won a Tony Award for Best Featured Actress, though she was clearly the lead of the show. Following that with *High Spirits*, a musicalization of Noël Coward's *Blithe Spirit*, Grimes's touched, otherworldly delivery was perfect for the ghostly Elvira. Rumored to be waiting in the wings twice—to replace Mary Tyler Moore in *Breakfast at Tiffany's* and an ailing Glynis Johns in *A Little Night Music*—she spent much time in straight plays, winning another Tony for a revival of *Private Lives* with Brian Bedford. She returned to the musical stage in *42nd Street*, playing the temperamental Dorothy Brock, still perfectly wonderful and quite odd. Her last singing appearances have been Off Broadway, in the reworking of the 1978 flop *Platinum*, retitled *Sunset*, and the chamber piece *Mademoiselle Colombe*.

William Gaxton & Victor Moore

Singer and actor William Gaxton possessed an odd combination of conflicting talents. A leading man without matinee-idol looks, his comic gifts set him apart, and he was fortunate to work with the giants of the musical theatre, introducing standards by Berlin, Porter, Gershwin, and Rodgers and Hart. He had a star-making lead in *A Connecticut Yankee*, and more success in Cole Porter's *Fifty Million Frenchmen*. As President John P. Wintergreen in the Gershwins' *Of Thee I Sing*, his career changed forever when Gaxton found an unlikely foil in character actor Victor Moore. Moore, who had achieved Broadway stardom way back in 1906 in George M. Cohan's *Forty-Five Minutes from Broadway*, had been a musical comedy stalwart for twenty-five years, as a stammering clown in such hits as *Oh, Kay!*, *Funny Face*, and *Hold Everything*. They were wildly different in age and type, and something about the oil-and-water of Gaxton's slickness and Moore's buffoonery clicked in a magical way. They became partners in comic crime through a total of seven Broadway musicals, including the *Of Thee I Sing!* sequel, *Let 'Em Eat Cake*; *Anything Goes*; *Leave It to Me* (aided and abetted by Sophie Tucker); and *Louisiana Purchase*. After two flops (both with Moore), *Hollywood Pinafore* and *Nellie Bly*, Gaxton retired, realizing that with the rise of the Rodgers and Hammerstein form of musical play, his presence was

viewed as distinctly "old school." Moore made only one more appearance, ironically, in an R&H show, as the Star-keeper in the Howard Keel/ Barbara Cook *Carousel* at City Center, fifty-one years after becoming a star.

TOP: Tammy Grimes as *The Unsinkable Molly Brown*, with brothers Sterling Clark, Bill Starr, and Bob Daley, who've evidently been dipping into the henna. TOP RIGHT: Joy Hodges, with William Gaxton and Victor Moore, in their final show as a musical comedy team, *Nellie Bly* (1946). RIGHT: Gaxton, Shirley Booth, and Moore in the 1945 flop *Hollywood Pinafore*. ABOVE: Madame Arcati (Beatrice Lillie) performs an exorcism on Green Goddess Grimes, as the "passed over" Elvira, in *High Spirits*.

Donna Murphy

One of the few true leading ladies of the contemporary musical theatre, Donna Murphy has shown an astounding versatility. After a Broadway debut fresh out of college as one the Alter Egos in *They're Playing Our Song*, Murphy took an ensemble part in *The Mystery of Edwin Drood*, eventually replacing Betty Buckley in the title role and paralyzing audiences with her comic expertise. After Off-Broadway jobs in such shows as *Birds of Paradise, Song of Singapore,* and *Privates on Parade*, she got her star-making opportunity as the tragic Fosca in Stephen Sondheim's *Passion*. Following that triumph with a second Tony Award for her re-evaluation of Anna Leonowens in the 1996 revival of *The King and I*, costarring Lou Diamond Phillips, she spent time in California before returning to Broadway in the revival of *Wonderful Town*, recreating the role she received accolades for in the 2002 City Center Encores version. Though she remains determined to make a name for herself in film and television, New York audiences await her return in a new musical written especially for her unique talents.

TOP: In the 1996 revival of *The King and I*, Donna Murphy was one of the most intense, complicated Annas ever. ABOVE: Murphy, cutting loose comically on Broadway for the first time since *Drood*, climbs a chain link fence to escape the "Conga!"-crazed cadets in the 2003 revival of *Wonderful Town*. BELOW: Larry Blyden tries to determine whether Bert Lahr has a heart, in a scene from the farcical *Foxy*.

Leslie Uggams

After a childhood spent singing on television with Mitch Miller, the powerhouse singer Leslie Uggams took the lead in Styne/Comden & Green/Laurents multi-generational tale *Hallelujah, Baby!* Though the role was originally written for Lena Horne, Uggams made it her own, winning a Tony Award and electrifying audiences with her vibrant combination of rangy vocals, poignant vulnerability, and comic flair. Her next role was a mistake, as Cleopatra opposite Richard Kiley's Caesar in the stinker *Her First Roman*, which opened the same season as the Angela Lansbury flop *Dear World* and proved to all three stars just how fleeting the high of a Broadway smash can be. Like so many of her theatre contemporaries (including Bernadette Peters and Sandy Duncan), she decamped to Hollywood for much of the 1970s, starring in her own variety show and winning raves for the landmark miniseries *Roots*. Returning to New York in 1986 in *Jerry's Girls,* with Chita Rivera and Dorothy Loudon (she had toured with Carol Channing and Andrea McArdle in an earlier version), she next replaced Patti LuPone in the revival of *Anything Goes*, belting the bejesus out of "Blow, Gabriel, Blow." After numerous stock performances (playing the Witch in *Into the Woods*, Sally Adams in *Call Me Madam*, and Sally Bowles in *Cabaret*), she spent 2003-2004 as Muzzy van Hossmere in *Thoroughly Modern Millie*, utterly ageless.

TOP RIGHT: Alan Weeks, Leslie Uggams, and Winston DeWitt Hemsley shout *Hallelujah, Baby!* ABOVE: With a wig that looks not unlike the valance over the proscenium at the Winter Garden, Cleopatra Uggams smiles through clenched teeth in *Her First Roman*. RIGHT: Miyoshi Umeki (who would later achieve TV fame as the housekeeper to Mr. Eddie's father) and Larry Blyden in *Flower Drum Song*.

Larry Blyden

The character actor and singer Larry Blyden first hit Broadway joining the cast of *Wish You Wish Here*. His original cast debut came when he replaced Larry Storch during the out-of-town tryout of *Flower Drum Song*, playing the slick Sammy Fong. Blyden was married to the show's choreographer, the brilliant dancer/comedienne Carol Haney, and they had a highly tempestuous relationship, divorcing before her death in 1964. He made further appearances in *Foxy* (sharing the stage with the over-the-top antics of Bert Lahr) and *The Apple Tree*, playing various incarnations of the Devil opposite rising stars Barbara Harris and Alan Alda. Bouncing between television, film (*On a Clear Day You Can See Forever*), and straight plays, Blyden returned to musicals as Hysterium in the Phil Silvers revival of *A Funny Thing...*, producing the Broadway transfer after a successful run in Los Angeles. Belting a memorable "Buddy's Blues" at the Sondheim "Scrabble" benefit in 1973, he was the host of the television show *What's My Line?* when he was killed in an automobile accident while vacationing in Morocco in 1975.

THE MOST HAPPY FELLA

OPENED MAY 3, 1956; IMPERIAL THEATRE; 676 PERFORMANCES

Robert Weede and Jo Sullivan (the future Mrs. Loesser), sing the soaring "My Heart is So Full of You."

THE MOST HAPPY FELLA

Produced by Kermit Bloomgarden
and Lynn Loesser

Book, Music, and Lyrics by Frank Loesser
Based on *They Knew What They Wanted*
by Sidney Howard
Music orchestrated by Don Walker
Orchestra and Choral Direction by
Herbert Greene

Staged by Joseph Anthony
Choreographed by Dania Krupska

Scenic Design by Jo Mielziner
Lighting Design by Jo Mielziner
Costume Design by Motley
Assistant Designer to Mr. Mielziner:
John Harvey
2nd Assistant Designer to Mr. Mielziner:
Ming Cho Lee

Synopsis

Tony, an elderly grape grower in the Napa Valley, proposes in a letter to a waitress, Amy, whom he saw once in a greasy spoon in San Francisco. In his embarrassment over his age and looks, he sends a photo of his handsome foreman, Joe. Tony goes speeding off to pick up "Rosabella," (his name for Amy), and crashes his truck. Rosabella arrives at Tony's farm and is shocked by his appearance, and in her despair, she falls into the arms of Joe. She nurses Tony back to health and learns to love him. She is pregnant by Joe—but Tony agrees to call the baby his own.

Cast

Rosabella .... *Jo Sullivan*
Tony .... *Robert Weede*
Cleo .... *Susan Johnson*
Herman .... *Shorty Long*
Marie .... *Mona Paulee*
Tessie .... *Zina Bethune*
The Cashier, The Postman.... *Lee Cass*
Pasquale .... *Rico Froehlich*
Clem .... *Alan Gilbert*
The Doctor.......................... *Keith Kaldenberg*
Joe.................................... *Art Lund*

"I was chattering away for Frank [Loesser] about the marvelously funny stuff in his show *The Most Happy Fella*. He cut me off angrily. 'Abe, the hell with that! We both know I can do that kinda stuff. Tell me where I made you cry.'"

– Abe Burrows

I N WRITING *Porgy and Bess*, George Gershwin had one foot in the classical world and one squarely in Tin Pan Alley. Frank Loesser, the most courageous of composers, put both feet squarely in Times Square for his operatic excursion, *The Most Happy Fella*. Yes, he included soliloquies, trios, and quartets as in all operas, but the speech and rhythms were definitely of the common man. And not only did he create an immense score, he also undertook the libretto, based on Sidney Howard's *They Knew What They Wanted*. Loesser had the smarts to blow the 1920s cobwebs off of the original play and give it a lighter, more lyrical flavor, downplaying the tragic in favor of the heart. The story is still full of anguish, and where Howard viewed his characters as a little desperate and pathetic, Loesser brought out their humanity and inspired us to forgive their failings. As Loesser tells it, any one of us might be in the same position one day; in fact, most of us have been.

This is among the richest, lushest scores in Broadway history. The show was gently criticized as too rich and too inventive, but Loesser's music mimics the grapes hanging heavy on the vines, ready to be picked and savored and squeezed. These grapes are the lifeblood of the Napa community in *The Most Happy Fella*, and most of its characters are in need of a bit of squeezing themselves. They are all just on this side of being over-ripe; still, it's invigorating to experience a score and performances just this close to bursting.

Too many musicals today put stock in the sere, minimalist lives of the cynical, sucking the air out of the theatre with their all-wise, all-knowing nihilism. This is the lesson many composers and librettists feel they have learned from Sondheim. But they don't see the heart behind the farce of *A Little Night Music*, the wry, self-deprecation of "Send in the Clowns." Where they see fools with a critical, jaundiced eye, Sondheim (and Loesser) see people as people, albeit theatrically. Sondheim makes us care about his characters by allowing them rare insight that comes with self-examination. Likewise, Loesser makes us care about the characters in *The Most Happy Fella:* their sadness, their mistakes, and even their deceptions. It is a show that provides an all-too-rare opportunity to revel in real feelings. Loesser gives us the permission we need to relax, let the music envelop us and bring us into the spirit of joy and heartbreak. *The Most Happy Fella* is truly a great opera for Americans, brought to life through the language of the musical theatre. ✳

Herman (Shorty Long) declares to Cleo (Susan Johnson) "I Like Everybody" ... but mostly her.

Susan Johnson

Susan Johnson, whose creamy alto voice was described as melting honey by numerous critics, had her biggest hit as the chiropodist's dream Cleo in *The Most Happy Fella*. Always an utterly reliable standout no matter what the quality of her vehicle, she made her career as the soubrette in such middling shows as *Oh Captain!, Whoop-Up,* and *Donnybrook!*, often riding motorcycles and always working in a restaurant, saloon, or nightclub. After an offstage motorcycle accident in the early 1960s, she developed health problems that took her away from the New York stage. She was not yet forty and sorely missed. She resurfaced again in the 1980s for the occasional benefit, movie role, or California civic light opera production, her luscious tones and moxie still intact. With her arms akimbo she could belt with the best of them or cradle a song with warmth and sensitivity.

LEFT: In *Oh Captain!*, Susan Johnson, of the big voice and the lavender rinse, sang two of the show's best songs, "Give It All You Got" and "The Morning Music of Montmartre."

ABOVE RIGHT: *Whoop-Up* provided Johnson yet another opportunity to prove her mettle as musical comedy maven/biker chick. (Note that since her elevation from soubrette to leading lady, Susan now primly sits on her cycle sidesaddle.)

SONGS

ACT I · "Ooh! My Feet!" · "I Know How It Is" · "Seven Million Crumbs" · I Don't Know" · "Maybe He's Kind of Crazy" · "Somebody, Somewhere" · "The Most Happy Fella" · "A Long Time Ago" · "Standing on the Corner" "Joey, Joey, Joey" · "Soon You Gonna Leave Me, Joe" "Rosabella" · "Abbondanza" · "Plenty Bambini" "Sposalizio" · "Special Delivery" · "Benvenuta" · "Aren't You Glad" · "No Home, No Job" · "Don't Cry"
ACT II · "Fresno Beauties" · "Love and Kindness" "Happy to Make Your Acquaintance" · "I Don't Like This Dame" · "Big D" · "How Beautiful the Days" · "Young People" · "Warm All Over" · "Old People Gotta" · "I Like Everybody" · "I Love Him" · "I Know How It Is" · "Like a Woman Likes a Man" · "My Heart Is So Full of You" "Hoedown" · "Mamma, Mamma"
ACT III · "Goodbye Darlin'" · "Song of a Summer Night" "Please Let Me Tell You" · "Tell Tony and Rosabella Goodbye for Me" · "She Gonna Come Home wit' Me" "Nobody's Ever Gonna Love You" · "I Made a Fist"

Backstage

Composer Frank Loesser embarked upon *The Most Happy Fella* with one wife, Lynn Loesser, and landed with another, Jo Sullivan. The former, who had stuck by Frank from his earliest struggles to establish himself, was sometimes dubbed "the evil of two Loessers."

Robert Weede

Robert Weede, the Metropolitan Opera star who lent his rich baritone to three Broadway shows, initially made his name performing the works of Puccini and Verdi, singing *Tosca* (with Maria Callas) and *Aida* in opera houses around the world. He seemed, then, a perfect choice for ranch owner Tony in *The Most Happy Fella*, the closest thing to Italian opera in the world of the Broadway musical. After *The Most Happy Fella*, he returned to the legit world, next appearing on Broadway with fellow Met star Mimi Benzell as an Israeli émigré, wrapping his golden voice around Jerry Herman's "There's No Reason in the World" and "Let's Not Waste a Moment" in *Milk and Honey*. His final musical was 1970's unfortunate *Cry for Us All*, singing the songs "The Mayor's Chair" and "Aggie, Oh Aggie," while losing much of his stage time to the ever-expanding role of Broadway's version of Maria Callas, the lusty/busty diva Joan Diener.

ABOVE: *Cry for Us All*'s Helen Gallagher, Tommy Rall, and Robert Weede, all considering firing their agents for getting them into this one.
BELOW: All ends happily for Tony and Rosabella, now Mr. and Mrs. *Most Happy Fella.*

THE MUSIC MAN

OPENED DECEMBER 19, 1957; MAJESTIC THEATRE; 1,375 PERFORMANCES

ABOVE: The irreplaceable Robert Preston alerts the parents of River City to "Trouble" in their midst.

RIGHT: Barbara Cook sings the beautiful, freeform "My White Knight."

THE MUSIC MAN

Produced by Kermit Bloomgarden

Book, Lyrics, and Music by Meredith Willson
Story by Meredith Willson and Franklin Lacey

Music orchestrated by Don Walker
Additional Orchestrations by Sidney Fine, Irwin Kostal, Seymour Ginzler, and Walter Eiger
Dance Arrangements by Laurence Rosenthal
Musical Director: Herbert Greene
Vocal Arrangements by Herbert Greene

Staged by Morton Da Costa
Choreographed by Onna White

Scenic Design by Howard Bay
Lighting Design by Howard Bay
Costume Design by Raoul Pène Du Bois

Synopsis

Traveling salesman Harold Hill comes to River City, Iowa, selling band uniforms and instruments under the pretext of teaching the local children to play said instruments. Hill knows nothing about music but touts the "think system," and plans to blow town as soon as the uniforms and instruments are paid for. But he meets up with the town librarian, Marian, and sees a challenge in her uptight demeanor. Although he does win over Marian, it is she who has changed Hill—domesticated him, as it were. And by the final curtain, just as the torch-bearing towns-people track down Hill for a dose of tar and feathers, the River City youngsters march down Main Street in their uniforms playing, in the minds of their proud parents, just as if they were led by the great John Philip Sousa himself.

Cast

Charlie Cowell .... *Paul Reed*
Harold Hill .... *Robert Preston*
Mayor Shinn .... *David Burns*
The Buffalo Bills .... *Al Shea, Wayne Ward, Vern Reed, Bill Spangenberg*
Marcellus Washburn .... *Iggie Wolfington*
Tommy Djilas .... *Danny Carroll*
Marian Paroo .... *Barbara Cook*
Mrs. Paroo .... *Pert Kelton*
Amaryllis .... *Marilyn Siegel*
Winthrop Paroo .... *Eddie Hodges*
Eulalie Mackencknie Shinn .. *Helen Raymond*
Zaneeta Shinn .... *Dusty Worrall*

THE ROAD TO BROADWAY IS often rough, and one hopes that those shows that take a long time gestating are worth the effort. That was certainly the case of *The Music Man*. Composer/author Meredith Willson became interested in celebrating the Iowa of his youth in an all-American musical comedy, and after writing, writing, and rewriting, he finally showed a rough draft and a few songs to Cy Feuer and Ernest Martin, reigning producers of their day. They were enthusiastic about the project and went to CBS, who was interested in presenting the musical as a two-hour television special, but when the network wanted input in the casting process, Feuer and Martin backed out. Jesse Lasky, Hollywood producer at MGM, wanted to buy the material for a movie musical, pairing it with a documentary titled *The Big Brass Band*. As you may have guessed, that project never materialized, either. Daunted, Feuer and Martin dropped their option on the project. Then, movie producer Sol Siegel, still seeing potential in the star role of the swindler Harold Hill, offered the role to Bing Crosby. No dice, replied Der Bingle. Subsequently, Ray Bolger heard it and loved it but was tied up with television for the following year.

Frustrated, Willson enjoined Franklin Lacey to come on board and help trim, simplify, and focus the piece. During this cut-and-paste period, Willson was ready to excise a long piece of dialogue concerning the problems facing River City parents. When he reread it, he discovered it sounded almost like a lyric, even though there were no rhymes, and he composed music to accompany the dialogue, turning an almost-cut sequence into the showstopping song "Ya Got Trouble." Somehow, the exciting birth of that number gave Willson and Lacey the hope they needed to continue.

After the thirty-second draft was completed, Ernie Martin showed up with an offer, not to produce *The Music Man*, but for Willson to musicalize a book titled *Indian Joe*. Disappointed, Willson turned him down (the show eventually opened and quickly closed as the guilty pleasure *Whoop-Up*, with a score by Moose Charlap and Norman Gimbel). Willson finally contacted Kermit Bloomgarden, producer of his mentor Frank Loesser's *The Most Happy Fella*. Once Bloomgarden came aboard, the momentum quickly picked up, and, in a remarkably short time, the show was cast and opened, a smash hit. Of course, between Willson's first jottings and the out-of-town opening in Philadelphia, around forty songs were written, and twenty-two were cut for one reason or another. Looking to stretch the boundaries of musical theatre, he also devised fifty-three different rhythmic numbers, written as experiments for the opening of the show, the salesmen's spoken "Rock Island." "My White Knight," which is very nearly an aria, and the aforementioned "Ya Got Trouble," have few, if any rhymes.

This "overnight success" took a long, long time to come to fruition, a rich embodiment of the memories and history that Meredith Willson carried in his mind and heart. That's an important lesson for all musical-comedy writers: Don't try to write the sure thing, write what you feel passionate about. Having a little talent couldn't hurt either. ✻

"If ya don't mind me sayin' so": Pert Kelton, as the Widder Paroo, meddles her way into little Amaryllis's piano lesson. She sure didn't get her money's worth that day.

Meredith Willson

Meredith Willson, a relative novice who hit the jackpot with his first venture, wrote book music and lyrics, a rarely attempted feat, for the surprise smash *The Music Man*. With the spoken opening number "Rock Island," the barbershop harmonies of "Lida Rose," and the songs "Goodnight, My Someone" and "Seventy-six Trombones," which shared the same melody but with wildly different tempi, Willson flew in the face of the Broadway music tradition of the 1950s. Inspired by his mentor Frank Loesser, another renegade as far as song form, he gambled and won big, overshadowing competition as fierce as *West Side Story* in the 1957–1958 season and spawning countless other productions, as well as a movie version that faithfully captures the seminal Harold Hill of Robert Preston. Not unlike *Oliver!* composer Lionel Bart, Willson never remotely approached *Music Man*'s success. Each of his successive shows yielded diminishing returns, with his scores for *The Unsinkable Molly Brown* (half buoyant, half just barely afloat), *Here's Love* (treading water), and *1491* (going down for the third time) on a decided downward trajectory of quality. Still and all, through the pure melody of songs such as "Till There Was You," "I Ain't Down Yet," or "I'll Never Say No" (hands down the two best songs in *Molly Brown*), Willson carved out a niche for himself as a major Broadway success story.

ABOVE: Preston, Cook, and Willson.

RIGHT: Janis Paige, as an executive so successful she color coordinates her skirt with the floor pillows in her penthouse, sings "Arm in Arm" to daughter Valerie Lee in the not-so-miraculous *Here's Love*.

LEFT: Iggie Wolfington as Marcellus, the huckster who came in from the cold, with the beloved "Pres."

Robert Preston

I t's an odd thing when an actor, in his first foray into a genre, puts such an unmistakable stamp on a role that everyone who attempts to follow in his strutting footsteps can't quite keep up the pace. Indeed, Robert Preston, the one and only Music Man, made it look deceptively easy. Like Rosalind Russell and Angela Lansbury, he came to the Broadway musical after a long career in motion pictures, and, interestingly, all three performers were utterly liberated by the experience, seeming more alive, more human, and more, well, fun than they'd ever been allowed to be in the less immediate world of film. Considering his resounding success as Harold Hill, Preston's remaining five Broadway musicals had spotty track records at best. His follow-up to *The Music Man*, *We Take the Town*, closed on the road, and while *Ben Franklin in Paris* was a personal triumph, it was only a modest success. His last true hit won him a second Tony Award, playing opposite Mary Martin in *I Do, I Do*. Despite many wonderful qualities, *Mack and Mabel* proved a deeply crushing failure, and *Prince of Grand Street*, Preston's last musical, closed in Boston. Sadly, he never got to re-create his wise and warm movie portrayal of the aging "queen with a head cold," Toddy, in *Victor/Victoria*'s Broadway incarnation. Never remotely a "method" actor who disappeared into his characters, his Ben Franklin basically behaved and sounded like his Mack Sennett, his Harold Hill like his Pancho Villa. They were all first and foremost Robert Preston, and, considering his limitless energy and invigorating appeal, that was just fine with audiences.

In a scene that demonstrates the artistic liberties of the Yiddish Theatre, a sixtyish "Huckleberry Preston" in *The Prince of Grand Street*, a 1978 out-of-town closer.

Backstage

Danny Kaye, Gene Kelly, Jason Robards, Dan Dailey, Milton Berle, Jackie Gleason, Ray Bolger, Art Carney, and Bert Parks were the first names bandied about to lead the company. The second go-round, once it was decided that an actor, not a song-and-dance man, would do the trick, included Lloyd Bridges, Phil Harris, Van Heflin, Laurence Olivier, Alec Guinness, James Whitmore, James Cagney, Andy Griffith, and a movie actor by the name of Robert Preston.

SONGS

ACT I "Rock Island" · "Iowa Stubborn" · "(Ya Got) Trouble" "Goodnight, My Someone" · "Seventy-six Trombones" · "Sincere" "The Sadder-but-Wiser Girl" · "Pickalittle (Talkalittle)" "Goodnight Ladies" · "Marian the Librarian" · "My White Night" "Wells Fargo Wagon"
ACT II "It's You" · "Shipoopi" · "Lida Rose" · "Will I Ever Tell You" "Gary, Indiana" · "Till There Was You"

TOP: I Did, I Did: Preston and Mary Martin as newlyweds Michael and Agnes, about to get nervous on their wedding night.

ABOVE: Barbara Cook and the terrific child actor Eddie Hodges.

RIGHT: "Marbles. Six steelies, eight aggies, a dozen peewees, and one big glassie with an American flag in the middle. I think I'll drop 'em."

MY FAIR LADY

OPENED MARCH 15, 1956; MARK HELLINGER THEATRE; 2,717 PERFORMANCES

MY FAIR LADY

Produced by Herman Levin
Book and Lyrics by Alan Jay Lerner
Music by Frederick Loewe
Adapted from *Pygmalion* by
George Bernard Shaw
Music arranged by
Robert Russell Bennett and Phil Lang
Dance arrangements by Trude Rittman
Musical Director: Franz Allers
Choral arrangements by Gino Smart
Assistant to Mr. Allers: Peter Howard

Staged by Moss Hart
Choreographed by Hanya Holm

Production Design by Oliver Smith
Costume Design by Cecil Beaton
Lighting Design by Feder

Synopsis

Eliza Doolittle, a poor cockney flower girl plying her wares in Covent Garden, London, is chosen by Professor Henry Higgins for an experiment in linguistics. Higgins bets his friend Colonel Pickering that he can turn Eliza into a proper lady and, in fact, pass her off as a princess. Eliza moves in with Higgins and undergoes a rigorous and impersonal training. After a false start at the Ascot Races, Eliza passes the test at the Embassy Ball with flying colors, and Higgins, a confirmed bachelor, finds that he's grown strangely accustomed to Eliza's being around the house.

Cast

Eliza Doolittle	*Julie Andrews*
Henry Higgins	*Rex Harrison*
Colonel Pickering	*Robert Coote*
Alfred P. Doolittle	*Stanley Holloway*
Mrs. Higgins	*Cathleen Nesbitt*
Mrs. Pearce	*Philippa Bevans*
Zoltan Karparthy	*Christopher Hewett*
Freddy Eynsford-Hill	*John Michael King*

ABOVE AND RIGHT: In a series of short comedy scenes punctuated by blackouts and accompanied by a chorus of servants perpetually singing "Quit! Professor Higgins!," Harrison and Andrews brilliantly demonstrate the progress of Eliza's English instruction. The scenes build in tension until, utterly exhausted, Andrews quietly enunciates the famous "Rain in Spain" line, sending them (along with Robert Coote as Colonel Pickering) into an eruption of tango madness, complete with a mock bullfight.

ASK A MUSICAL THEATRE AFICIONADO what the best musical of all time is, and four shows surface again and again: *Follies*, *Gypsy*, *Fiddler on the Roof*, and *My Fair Lady*. All are undoubtedly great, and each has its particular strengths. *Follies* is a multileveled tribute to show business past as well as an examination of its characters' psyches. *Gypsy* is a seamless blend of song and story building up to the psychological explosion of "Rose's Turn." *Fiddler* is an unabashedly emotional work celebrating the indomitable human spirit and the delicate balance between honoring one's traditions and growing with society.

My Fair Lady is a traditional musical done in the greatest of taste and with the utmost technique. The musical captures the sophistication, wit, and intellect of George Bernard Shaw's *Pygmalion*. That an Austrian and an American could capture the brittle, wry English upper class as well as the lower-class mores of the cockney is extraordinary.

But the road to production of *My Fair Lady* wasn't an easy one. Producer Gabriel Pascal had, remarkably, obtained the motion picture rights to Shaw's plays. He contacted several composers and lyricists about turning *Pygmalion* into a musical, but every one found himself stymied by the play itself. Many felt the source material was so strong to begin with that it didn't need music to help embellish or extend the story. It was a drawing room comedy and didn't fit into the Richard Rodgers and Oscar Hammerstein formula: a central couple in love and a secondary, usually comic couple. Not only wasn't there a secondary love story, there wasn't a primary love story, for Professor Higgins and Eliza Doolittle are neither profoundly nor overtly in love.

Rodgers and Hammerstein themselves worked on the project for over a year before declaring the play impossible for musicalization. Pascal approached countless others, even Sam Coslow, the composer of "Cocktails for Two," before Alan Jay Lerner and Frederick Loewe accepted the assignment. After working together on the piece, they reached the same conclusion as Rodgers and Hammerstein and went their separate ways, Loewe to collaborate with Harold Rome and Lerner to team with Burton Lane on *Li'l Abner*. But neither of those collaborations worked out, so Loewe and Lerner made a second attempt to tackle *Pygmalion*. Slowly, it dawned on the team that the play's strengths had nothing to do with formula musical comedy, so they mustn't try to squeeze it into that box. Instead, they decided simply to musicalize the play on its own terms.

Having unlocked the play's inner heart, they encountered another obstacle. In the intervening years, Gabriel Pascal had had the unfortunate luck of dying, and his estate was in litigation, being challenged by both his wife and mistress. So Lerner and Loewe, along with their producer Herman Levin, broke the most basic rule of writing for Broadway: never, under any circumstances, work on a show for which you have not obtained the rights. Luckily, the team ignored this inconvenience and set about writing the songs and libretto, even casting the leads.

When it did come time to acquire the rights, it emerged that Chase Bank, the executor of Pascal's estate, had deemed itself incapable of making an artistic decision (a miracle that has never been repeated—everyone today seems

Backstage

Mary Martin expressed interest in *My Fair Lady* as a possible vehicle. Lerner and Loewe obliged and auditioned the score for her. Later Martin's husband, Richard Halliday, told them that Martin had exclaimed, "Those dear boys have lost their talent."

In the 1981 Broadway revival, the then septuagenarian Rex Harrison reprised his role as Henry Higgins. Cathleen Nesbitt—well into her nineties—again played his mother. She was the only actress old enough to do so.

ABOVE: The men in Eliza's life: Professor Henry Higgins (Rex Harrison) and her father, Alfred P. Doolittle (Stanley Holloway).

LEFT: Julie Andrews as the violet selling guttersnipe Eliza Doolittle.

Eliza and Higgins enter the Embassy Ball. Will she pull it off? The hairy hound from Budapest, Proessor Zoltan Karpathy, approaches Eliza for the ultimate test ... and ... and ... Intermission.

to see themselves as arbiters of taste, from lawyers to steamfitters, and, most egregiously, distant relatives of deceased artists). After Chase hired the agent Harold Freedman to make the decision, Lerner and Loewe set up a meeting with him and accomplished two things: they hired Freedman as their own agent; then they asked for the rights to the play. The rights were granted.

On to London, to obtain the legal blessings of the Shaw estate: only there was no real Shaw estate and the great writer's will was impossibly oblique. Undeterred, the two merry partners soldiered on and left London having achieved three coups: Rex Harrison as star, Cecil Beaton committed to designing the costumes, and the rights to the play.

Because of oddities in Shaw's will, the authors decided to approach the NBC and CBS television networks to back the production. NBC showed no interest, but Goddard Lieberson, a vice president of Columbia Records (with Herman Levin's aid) convinced William Paley, the president of Columbia, to bankroll the entire project.

And so it only remained for Lerner and Loewe to finish writing the work, which they most famously did. ✻

Stanley Holloway (center, with Gordon Dilworth and Rod McLennan) sings "With a Little Bit of Luck."

Al Hirschfeld

Al Hirschfeld, artist extraordinaire, captured nearly seventy years of Broadway history with his witty caricatures. His drawing of George Bernard Shaw, Rex Harrison, and Julie Andrews became inextricably linked with the smash hit *My Fair Lady*—which was adapted from an earlier caricature for *Arms and the Man*—and his uncanny ability to capture the larger-than-life personalities of stars such as Carol Channing, Zero Mostel, and Ethel Merman made him the premiere caricaturist of the twentieth century. Finding the "Nina's" (in honor of his beloved daughter) hidden in his drawings became an obsession for readers of the Sunday *New York Times*, (they were so deftly concealed that the U.S. Army used his artwork to train bombing pilots to recognize targets and aid in the study of camouflage techniques). The flair of his drawings went so perfectly hand-in-hand with the energy, movement, and emotions of musical theatre that an overview of its important contributors would be incomplete without a debt of gratitude to one of its keenest observers. In 2003, the Martin Beck Theatre was renamed the Al Hirschfeld Theatre.

Julie Andrews

Julie Andrews, a great star of the musical theatre whose temporary vacation from the rigors of eight shows a week lasted over thirty years, made her debut in the Broadway version of an English hit. Described by Andrews herself as a "piece of lace," *The Boy Friend* provided her with a prime opportunity for stardom. Absolutely nailing the innocence of "perfect young lady" Polly Browne, she never, ever winked at the audience, realizing that the humor of her character lay in her unalloyed naïveté, along with the audience's familiarity with the formulaic musicals of the 1920s. After her triumph in *My Fair Lady* (it now seems unfathomable that she came *this* close to being fired in rehearsal), she reteamed with Lerner, Loewe, and Moss Hart for *Camelot.* The show's delivery was decidedly not an easy one, but the lighter vocal demands of the role of Guenevere made it Andrews's favorite of her Broadway roles. Offered the role of Amalia Balash in the original *She Loves Me*, she instead segued into a film career, not returning to Broadway until 1995, when she appeared in the stage version of her wonderful film *Victor/Victoria.* Her voice had lost some of its luster, but the dignity, presence, and no-nonsense style that had endeared her to a whole generation as Mary Poppins and Maria von Trapp were still there in abundance.

SONGS

ACT I "Why Can't the English?" · "Wouldn't It Be Loverly" "With a Little Bit of Luck" · "I'm an Ordinary Man" · "Just You Wait" · "The Rain in Spain" · "I Could Have Danced All Night" · "Ascot Gavotte" · "On the Street Where You Live" · "The Embassy Waltz"
ACT II "You Did It" · "Show Me" · "Get Me to the Church on Time" · "A Hymn to Him" · "Without You" · "I've Grown Accustomed to Her Face"

TOP RIGHT: "Move yer bloomin' arse!" In a trial run for the new, improved Eliza Doolittle, the thrill of the Ascot Races makes for an-ever-so-slight faux pas.

TOP LEFT: Andrews as "Poor Little Pierette" Polly Browne in *The Boy Friend.*

CENTER: Über-cheesy, the second-act opener of *Victor/ Victoria* sported Andrews as Marie Antoinette in the punny "Louis Sez."

LEFT: Trying to get that old nag Mrs. Pearce off her case, Julie Andrews is just pretending to go to sleep. After all, she's got one more chorus of "I Could Have Danced All Night" to go.

THE NEW MOON

OPENED SEPTEMBER 19, 1928; IMPERIAL THEATRE; 509 PERFORMANCES

Robert Halliday, Evelyn Herbert, and William O'Neal strike a fetching pose.

THE NEW MOON

Produced by
Laurence Schwab and Frank Mandel

Music by Sigmund Romberg
Lyrics by Oscar Hammerstein II
Libretto by Oscar Hammerstein II, Frank Mandel
and Laurence Schwab
Orchestrations by
Emil Gerstenberger and Alfred Goodman
Orchestra under the direction of
Alfred Goodman

Musical numbers staged by Bobby Connolly
Settings by Donald Oenslager
Costumes Designed by Charles LeMaire

Synopsis

It's the late 18th century and our hero, Robert Mission, works in the French colony of New Orleans as a bondservant. In reality he is a French aristocrat in hiding from the authorities, who are seeking him on a charge of murder. Robert is in love with Marianne Bewaunoir. Both she and Robert are captured and put on a ship bound for France. In a daring act of piracy, Robert and his followers take over *The New Moon* and sail to the Isle of Pines, where they establish a free colony. The French invade the island but in the meantime things have changed in France. The monarchy has been deposed and the Republic has emerged. The French take over the colony but with Robert as Governor and Marianne as his wife.

Cast

Julie .... *Marie Callahan*
Monsieur Beaunoir .... *Pacie Ripple*
Captain Paul Duval .... *Edward Nell Jr.*
Vicomte Ribaud .... *Max Figman*
Robert .... *Robert Halliday*
Alexander .... *Gus Shy*
Besac .... *Lyle Evans*
Marianne .... *Evelyn Herbert*
Philippe .... *William O'Neal*
Clotilde Lombaste .... *Esther Howard*

SONGS

ACT 1 "Dainty Wisp of Thistledown" · "Marianne" · "The Girl on the Prow" · "Gorgeous Alexander" · "An Interrupted Love Song" · "Tavern Song" · "Softly, as in a Morning Sunrise" · "Stouthearted Men" · "Fair Rosita" · "One Kiss" "Ladies of the Jury" · "Wanting You"
ACT 2 "A Chanty" · "Funny Little Sailor Man" · "Lover, Come Back to Me" · "Love Is Quite a Simple Thing" · "Try Her Out at Dancing" · "Never"

THE GIANTS OF THE WORLD of musical theatre in the 1920s were busy men indeed. Jerome Kern opened seventeen shows in the decade, including his masterwork, *Show Boat*. That show's lyricist/librettist, Oscar Hammerstein II, beat Kern's record by one, and Hammerstein's collaborator on *The New Moon*, Sigmund Romberg, beat them all with a whopping twenty-four musicals and revues opening in that historic decade. It's an even more remarkable achievement for Hammerstein and Romberg in that they wrote two largely different scores for *The New Moon*, one of their biggest successes.

The New Moon was first produced by Schwab and Mandel in Philadelphia (one week after the opening of Hammerstein's *Show Boat* on Broadway) with much the same team as their smash hit, *The Desert Song*: the same producers (of course), composer, lyricist, librettists, choreographer, and male lead. But lightning refused to strike twice in Philadelphia, where the show suffered insurmountable problems from the start. Apart from the usual rewrites, the show suffered from cast replacements, technical snafus, and a complete turnover of the stage crew due to union problems. Schwab and Mandel wisely decided to shut down the show for major revisions.

The new version, which opened in Cleveland barely eight months later, had only a few songs from the original score, only two of the original leads, and a new libretto. It was a smash hit, bigger even than the team's previous smash, *The Desert Song*. *The New Moon's* magnificent score launched six standards, more than any other operetta. It proved to be a hit throughout the world and continues to entrance audiences who find it amazingly easy to get lost in the romantic, swashbuckling story and songs. ❃

Oscar Hammerstein II

The greatest theatrical figure of the 20th century is undoubtedly Oscar Hammerstein II, author, lyricist, producer, and humanist. Hammerstein was at the forefront of the movement to create a musical theatre form where song and story are fully integrated. His triumphs *Show Boat* and *Oklahoma!* changed the direction of musical theatre as he attempted to illustrate serious themes through popular entertainment. Oscar came from one of the most prestigious theatrical families: he was the son of William Hammerstein, the manager of the Victoria Theatre; grandson of the great theatre builder and impresario (and unofficial founder of Times Square) Oscar Hammerstein I; and the nephew of noted producer Arthur Hammerstein. Hammerstein's career was equaled in length and breadth only by that of author, director, and producer George Abbott and by Hammerstein's partner, Richard Rodgers. He had his failures but also remarkable successes. His lyrics and libretti were warm and humane and touched on themes of tolerance and understanding.

Backstage

In 1792, New Orleans was actually under Spanish rule, not French—but no matter. The historic mistake also found its way into the operetta *Naughty Marietta*.

During the tumultuous gestation of *The New Moon*, Hammerstein was in the midst of divorcing his wife and courting his future wife who was then married.

TOP: Oscar "Ockie" Hammerstein II celebrates his fiftieth birthday with (clockwise from lower left) Jan Clayton, Rosemarie Schaeffer, Fay Smith, Katharine Sergava, and Nona Feid.

ABOVE: Richard Rodgers, Julie Andrews, and Oscar Hammerstein on the set of their 1957 television musical, *Cinderella*.

LEFT: Annamary Dickey and William Ching in *Allegro*, one of Hammerstein's most frustrating failures.

NO, NO, NANETTE

OPENED SEPTEMBER 16, 1925; GLOBE THEATRE; 321 PERFORMANCES

ABOVE: Helen Gallagher (here singing "Too Many Rings Around Rosie"), weathered locusts, pestilence, and *Portofino* to become the ultimate show-biz survivor with her Tony-winning turn as Lucille in *No, No Nanette*.

RIGHT: Patsy Kelly, also a Tony winner, played the dry-as-bone maid, Pauline, in the 1971 revival.

NO, NO, NANETTE

Produced by H. H. Frazee
Book by Otto Harbach and Frank Mandel
Music by Vincent Youmans
Lyrics by Irving Caesar and Otto Harbach
Based on the Comedy *My Lady Friends* by
Frank Mandel and Emil Nyitray
Musical Director: Nicholas Kempner
Directed by H. H. Frazee
Musical Staging by Sammy Lee
Scenic Design by P. Dodd Ackerman
Costume Supervisor: Corinne Barker
Costumes provided by Milgrims,
Schneider-Anderson, and Frances

Synopsis

Bible publisher Jimmy Smith wants to live it up, but his wife, Sue, doesn't approve. So Jimmy becomes a close personal friend of Flora (from Frisco), Betty (from Boston), and Winnie (from Washington). When his involvement with the trio becomes too much to handle, Jimmy's lawyer, Billy, takes the girls down to Atlantic City to arrange the breakup. Unbeknownst to the lawyer, Jimmy has also decided to retreat to the shore along with his young ward, Nanette. And unbeknownst to them both (this is a 1920s musical, after all), Sue and Billy's jealous wife, Lucille, also decide to take in the sea breezes. You can guess what happens, but we should tell you that Billy's assistant, Tom, who is in love with Nanette (and vice versa), adds to the door-slamming confusion.

Original Cast

Pauline .... *Georgia O'Ramey*
Sue Smith .... *Eleanor Dawn*
Billy Early........................... *Wellington Cross*
Lucille .... *Josephine Whittell*
Nanette .... *Louise Groody*
Tom Trainor .... *Jack Barker*
Jimmy Smith .... *Charles Winninger*

Today musicals belong to one of two camps—those that try out on the road and then come to Broadway, and those that open cold with just a few previews. Touring has become prohibitively expensive, so many shows prefer to forgo the benefits of time spent away from the prying eyes of Broadway and the usefulness of audience response. Shows that have opened cold include *City of Angels*. Others open cold on Broadway but with many workshops under their belts. Today, many regional theatre companies present musicals with "enhancement money" provided by producers who want to test the waters without having to raise all the money necessary for a full Broadway production with Broadway costs for actors, sets, and so forth. *The Full Monty* (Old Globe Theatre), *A Year with Frog and Toad* (Children's Theatre Company of Minneapolis), *High Society* (ACT), *Jane Eyre* (La Jolla), *Urban Cowboy* (Cocoanut Grove Playhouse), *Bounce* (Goodman Theatre Company), *Aida* (Alliance Theatre), and *Over and Over* (Signature Theatre) are just a few examples. Given the lackluster success of the aforementioned, perhaps the regional theatre route is not the way to proceed. Less-than-sophisticated but enthusiastic homegrown audiences sometimes aren't the most reliable gauges of reception on Broadway.

But for some producers, a long out-of-town engagement with Broadway as an ultimate goal seems the best way to proceed. *Sunset Boulevard* played in Los Angeles for a year before moving to Broadway. *Kiss of the Spider Woman* played a long engagement in Toronto before opening in London and finally New York. *Mamma Mia* did it backward, opening first in London then setting down in Toronto before a new company opened in Chicago on the way to New York.

The idea of a long engagement prior to Broadway isn't a new one. *No, No, Nanette* played for a year in Chicago before opening in New York. In fact, Chicago had its own homegrown musical theatre tradition. Mort H. Singer produced a series of shows at the La Salle Theatre with music by Joseph E. Howard, Frank R. Adams, and Will M. Hough. Many of these shows never came to New York. *Nanette*, in fact, opened in London, Philadelphia, Los Angeles, and even Melbourne, Australia, for long runs prior to opening on Broadway.

Nanette was the first true international hit Broadway musical. In addition to the dozen companies playing the United States, there were engagements in Paris (and four revivals over the years), Germany, Vienna, and Budapest. The show has been revived continuously and filmed on two occasions. Just about the time that *Nanette* fell out of favor, replaced by more current fare, producer Harry Rigby came along and presented the legendary 1971 Broadway revival starring Ruby Keeler, Patsy Kelly, Jack Gilford, Bobby Van, and Helen Gallagher. There were the requisite national tours, London mounting, an Australian revival, and, later, a production in Berlin.

Nanette's great success inspired Harry Rigby to resurrect *Irene* on Broadway. It, too, was a success, but his revival of *Good News* didn't ignite, and Broadway's reexamination of early musicals ended.

Nanette proved that a show could succeed before opening on Broadway, that Broadway had international appeal, and that, fifty years on, an entertaining Broadway musical could succeed again throughout the world. ❊

RIGHT: While the 1971 revival of *Nanette* was a nostalgic (but not campy) look at the quaint naughtiness of 1925, the original production was thoroughly modern in its frisky morality.

The stunningly colorful costumes and scenery of Raoul Pène DuBois made the "Peach on the Beach" number (with Susan Watson, at center) in the 1971 revival a visual feast.

Backstage

Louise Groody, playing the title role, cut her trademarked curls for an up-to-date bob, thereby changing women's hairstyles.

In 1971, they had difficulty finding enough gypsies who could tap-dance as tap hadn't been in vogue on Broadway for years.

LEFT: As if time has stood still, sixty-one-year-old Ruby Keeler urges chorus kids forty years her junior to "Take a Little One-Step."

Donald Saddler

Donald Saddler started as a hoofer, getting a huge break choreographing a smash his first time up, with his "Conga!" and "Swing!" production numbers centering each act of *Wonderful Town*. Saddler was saddled with more than his share of stinkers (*Shangri-La*, *Sophie*, *Tricks*, *Teddy and Alice*), and his greatest work was in the revivals of *No, No, Nanette* and *On Your Toes*. In *Nanette*, he devised a ballroom dance showstopper for the ages with the "You Can Dance With Any Girl At All" stunner for old friend Helen Gallagher and Bobby Van, incorporating the polka, waltz, Castle Walk and two step, and in *On Your Toes*, his challenge dance between the ballet troupe and the hoofers was thoroughly exhilarating. He danced his way back to Broadway as a performer at the age of 81, as half of the dancing Whitmans (here, opposite Marge Champion) in the revival of *Follies*.

Still graceful and elegant with more than 150 years of performing experience between them, Donald Saddler and Marge Champion step out in the 2001 revival of *Follies*.

Otto Harbach

Otto Harbach was one of the most prolific librettist/lyricists of the American musical theatre—in 1926 alone he had five shows premiere on Broadway. His career spanned the most important decades of the young art form's formative years. Harbach's words graced shows from 1908's *The Three Twins* to 1936's *Forbidden Melody*. Along the way he worked with some of the greatest composers of operetta and musical comedy including, Rudolf Friml, Jerome Kern, Sigmund Romberg, Vincent Youmans, and Harry Tierney. His first show, *The Three Twins*, written with composer Karl Hoschna, yielded his first hit, "Cuddle Up a Little Closer." He struck Tin Pan Alley gold again with *Madame Sherry*'s "Every Little Movement," in 1910. His other hit songs include, "Indian Love Call," "Who," "One Alone," "I Won't Dance" (all in collaboration with Oscar Hammerstein II), "She Didn't Say 'Yes'," "The Night Was Made for Love," "Try to Forget," "You're Devastating," "Smoke Gets in Your Eyes," and "Yesterdays."

SONGS

ACT 1 "Flappers Are We" · "The Call of the Sea" · "Too Many Rings Around Rosie" · "I'm Waiting for You" · "I Want to Be Happy" · "No, No, Nanette"
ACT 2 "The Deep Blue Sea" · "My Doctor" · "Fight Over Me" · "Tea for Two" · "You Can Dance with Any Girl at All"
ACT 3 "Hello, Hello, Telephone Girlie" · "Who's the Who?" · "Pay Day Pauline"

REVUES, PART II

THE AMERICAN REVUE CAN TRACE its lineage to the first edition of the *Ziegfeld Follies* in 1907. That era of great revues included several long-running series in addition to the *Ziegfeld Follies*, including *The Passing Shows*, *George White's Scandals*, the *Greenwich Village Follies*, the *Music Box Revues*, and *The Earl Carroll Vanities*. Though many songwriters contributed material to revues, the masters were Howard Dietz and Arthur Schwartz, who wrote the score to the greatest of all revues, *The Band Wagon* (1931), along with a host of others including *Flying Colors* (1932), *At Home Abroad* (1935), *Between the Devil* (1937), and *Inside U.S.A.* (1948). Important revue producers included Lew Leslie (*Blackbirds of 1928*), Max Gordon (*The Band Wagon*), Billy Rose (*Sweet and Low* and *Seven Lively Arts*), Michael Todd (*Star and Garter, Seven Lively Arts, Michael Todd's Peep Show*) and Leonard Sillman (*New Faces of 1952*). The British contributed *Charlot's Revue of 1924*, *This Year of Grace* (1928), *Wake Up and Dream* (1929), and *Set to Music* (1939)—most with the participation of Noël Coward. Harold Rome's *Pins and Needles* (1937) was the most successful revue of the 1930s, closely followed by Olsen and Johnson's *Hell-zapoppin'* (1938) and *The Show Is On* (1936), starring Bea Lillie (a revue stalwart on both sides of the Atlantic) and directed by Vincente Minnelli. The war years saw several themed revues including *This Is the Army* (1942), *Winged Victory* (1943), and *Call Me Mister* (1946), which had its successful run in the postwar years. The last great decade of original revues, the 1950s, contributed *Two on the Aisle* (1951), *John Murray Anderson's Almanac* (1953), and *La Plume de Ma Tante* (1958). More recently, Broadway has been treated to two great revues, the burlesque-themed *Sugar Babies* (1979), starring Mickey Rooney and Ann Miller, and *Black and Blue* (1989), featuring Ruth Brown, Linda Hopkins, and Carrie Smith.

TOP: "Tops in Taps" Ann Miller shows off her legendary legs and her truly mammoth hair in the patriotic finale of the 1979 burlesque revue *Sugar Babies*, "You Can't Blame Your Uncle Sammy."

TOP RIGHT: The dotty Bea Lillie (here with Bruce Laffey) in the "Milady Dines Alone" sketch from the *Ziegfeld Follies of 1957*.

RIGHT: She's an Indian, Too: Lillie and company in "Frahngee-Pahnee" from 1944's *Seven Lively Arts*.

ABOVE: Eartha Kitt making a splash in *New Faces of 1952*, growling out "Monotonous."

Beatrice Lillie

Although many thought she was British, the zany, irrepressible Beatrice Lillie was actually Canadian by birth. She had a truly subversive side lurking just under a surface demeanor of a veddy proper lady, and audiences (and indeed, many of her costars) never knew what Lillie would do next. Having spent her youth in the London music halls, she became a star in the revues produced by André Charlot. Coming to the States in the 1920s (along with great friends Noël Coward and Gertrude Lawrence), Lillie's comic genius made her the toast of New York for over thirty years, in revues such as *At Home Abroad* (1935), *The Show Is On* (1936), *Inside U.S.A.* (1948), and the *Ziegfeld Follies of 1957*, where she had audiences on the floor with her sketch comedy, clowning as a geisha girl, an airline hostess, and a housewife shopping in a modern supermarket. Her last Broadway appearance was as the dotty, bike-riding, bunny-slipper-clad Madame Arcati in the Broadway musical *High Spirits* (1964), only her second book show—the other was *She's My Baby* in 1928. By the time she did the movie *Thoroughly Modern Millie* in 1967, she was exhibiting the early signs of Alzheimer's Disease, which she would battle for the next twenty-five years. Forever known for her rendition of "There Are Fairies at the Bottom of Our Garden," Lillie was one of the most insanely hysterical, hysterically insane performers ever.

OF THEE I SING

OPENED DECEMBER 26, 1931; MUSIC BOX THEATRE; 441 PERFORMANCES

OF THEE I SING

Produced by Sam H. Harris
Music by George Gershwin
Lyrics by Ira Gershwin
Book by
George S. Kaufman and Morrie Ryskind
Music director: Charles Previn
Orchestrations by
Robert Russell Bennett and William Daly

Staged by George S. Kaufman
Choreographed by Chester Hale
Settings by Jo Mielziner
Costumes by Charles LeMaire

Synopsis

John P. Wintergreen and his running mate Alexander Throttlebottom campaign for the White House on the LOVE platform. Wintergreen is in love with simple Mary Turner, and he handily wins the election. Then scandal hits. A beauty contest winner accuses him of alienation of affection and the scandal rocks the White House, but by the end of the evening, all is well, after Mary Turner reveals she's about to give birth to twins. The impeachment is called off and the country is restored to glory.

Cast

Louis Lippmann .... *Sid Mann*
Francis X. Gilhooley .... *Harold Moffet*
Arnold Fulton .... *Dudley Clements*
Senator Robert E. Lyons ...... *George E. Mack*
Senator Carver Jones .... *Edward H. Robbins*
Alexander Throttlebottom ..... *Victor Moore*
John P. Wintergreen .... *William Gaxton*
Sam Jenkins .... *George Murphy*
Diana Deveraux................... *Grace Brinkley*
Mary Turner .... *Lois Moran*
Miss Benson .... *June O'Dea*
The Chief Justice .... *Ralph Riggs*
The French Ambassador....... *Florenz Ames*

Vice President Alexander Throttlebottom (Victor Moore) can't quite believe in President John P. Wintergreen's (William Gaxton) "love platform."

HERE ARE SOME LEGENDARY MUSICAL comedy quotes—classic quips that have entered into the realm of legend. We can't vouch that all of them are true, nor would we swear that the words are exactly right, but they are truly witty, and any musical comedy aficionado knows most of them. Interestingly, many have to do with Rodgers and Hammerstein, together and apart:

"No legs, no jokes, no chance," is ascribed to Mike Todd, who left after the first act of *Away We Go!* in New Haven (the show became *Oklahoma!*).

"Can you draw sweet water from a foul well?" wondered Brooks Atkinson in the *New York Times* after the opening of *Pal Joey*.

"The world of woozy song" was how critic Kenneth Tynan summed up Rodgers and Hammerstein's *Flower Drum Song*.

When asked about how he liked Rodgers and Hammerstein, Cole Porter replied that they were fine, dryly adding, "if you can imagine it taking two men to write one song."

When a woman gushed to Mrs. Jerome Kern how much she admired "Ol' Man River," Mrs. Hammerstein, standing nearby, commented, "My husband wrote 'Ol' Man River.' *her* husband wrote, Dum, dum, dum, dum."

Not all famous quotes revolve around Rodgers and Hammerstein, of course. "Throw it away and keep the store open nights" suggested wag Cy Howard to producer Alfred Bloomingdale after seeing *Allah Be Praised*. During tryouts of *Guys and Dolls*, Frank Loesser wanted to reprise songs from the first act in the second. George S. Kaufman, the director, responded, "I'll let you reprise the songs if I can reprise the jokes."

SONGS

ACT 1 "Wintergreen for President" · "Who Is the Lucky Girl to Be?" · "The Dimple on My Knee" · "Because, Because" · "As the Chairman of the Committee" · "How Beautiful" · "Never Was There a Girl So Fair" · "Some Girls Can Bake a Pie" · "Love Is Sweeping the Country" · "Of Thee I Sing" · "Here's a Kiss for Cinderella" · "I Was the Most Beautiful Blossom"
ACT 2 "Hello, Good Morning" · "Who Cares?" · "Garcon, S'il Vous Plait" · "Entrance of French Ambassador" · "The Illegitimate Daughter" · "We'll Impeach Him" · "The Roll Call" · "Impeachment Proceeding" · "Jilted" · "Who Could Ask for Anything More" · "Posterity Is Just Around the Corner" · "Trumpeter, Blow Your Horn" · "On That Matter No One Budges"

Kaufman also quipped, "Satire is what closes on Saturday night." The show to which he was referring was the Gershwins's *Of Thee I Sing* and, for once, the genius Kaufman was wrong. So wrong, in fact, that *Of Thee I Sing* enjoyed the longest run of any book musical that opened in the 1930s. Kaufman can't quite be blamed, as history seemed to support his view, but *Of Thee I Sing* wasn't your usual satire. The book, by Morrie Ryskind and Kaufman himself, was the first to lampoon the Congress, Supreme Court, the Presidency, and that most sacrosanct of American institutions, motherhood.

The show was unique in other ways, too, owing much to the Gilbert and Sullivan school of writing, with many recitative passages and choral commentary. As Ira himself explained, "In the show there are no verse-and-chorus songs; there is a sort of recitative running along, and lots of finales and finalettos." That structure was so innately theatrical, it made the satire easy for audiences to swallow. The characterizations were broad and the plot ridiculous, yet the barbs and shafts of the writers still hit their marks. A true comic opera, *Of Thee I Sing* owed as much to Brecht and Weill (though a good deal sillier and more affectionate than their works) as to Gilbert and Sullivan.

Initially, there was nervousness on the parts of the creators and the cast. Thinking back to the era in which *Of Thee I Sing* flourished, patriotism and a belief in the American way of life was high. The country was in a Depression and needed to believe that their government would pull them through, and while there had been some precedents to political satire (Mark Twain, and in more recent times, Will Rogers laconically pointing up idiocies in the democratic society), the Presidency, not to mention the Vice Presidency, was held in high regard, almost above satire. The show's stars, William Gaxton and Victor Moore, seriously worried whether they would get in trouble with the government for their somewhat disrespectful characterizations of the country's leaders, but they needn't have worried. *Of Thee I Sing* was a smash hit, and forever more the office of the Vice President would be seen as somewhat of a joke; in fact, the show became one of the few musicals to inspire a sequel, *Let 'Em Eat Cake*. That show didn't achieve the success of its predecessor—perhaps the public was tired of the joke, or maybe the writers became overly confident—but the relative failure of *Let 'Em Eat Cake* certainly does nothing to diminish the great accomplishment of *Of Thee I Sing*. ❊

George S. Kaufman

Known as one of the greatest playwrights of the twentieth century, George S. Kaufman was responsible for some the most important comedies of the 1930s and '40s, collaborating with other legendary wits Moss Hart and Edna Ferber on such plays as *The Royal Family* (1927), *Once in a Lifetime* (1930), *Merrily We Roll Along* (1934), and *The Man Who Came to Dinner* (1939)—(all of which have been musicalized)—as well as *Dinner at Eight* (1932), *Stage Door* (1936), and *The Solid Gold Cadillac* (1953)—all of which will undoubtedly be musicalized, someday. Kaufman also wrote or co-wrote the books for many musicals, including *Animal Crackers* (1928), *The Band Wagon* (1931), *Of Thee I Sing*, *I'd Rather Be Right* (1937), the flops *Hollywood Pinafore* (1945) and *Park Avenue* (1945), and his last, *Silk Stockings* in 1955. A successful director of many of his owns plays, Kaufman also staged the original productions of other playwrights' work, with such varied credits as *The Front Page* (1928), *Of Mice and Men* (1937), *My Sister Eileen* (1945), and the musical *Guys and Dolls* (1950).

Backstage

The national company starred Gershwin favorite Oscar Shaw and Harriette Lake. She became better known when she changed her name to Ann Sothern.

Victor Moore was set to reprise his role in the 1952 revival, starring Jack Carson, but he withdrew before the opening.

The librettists and lyricists of *Of Thee I Sing* were awarded the Pulitzer Prize, the first ever given to a musical. Poor George Gershwin was never so honored during his lifetime, to everyone's dismay. (He received it posthumously on the occasion of his centenary.)

Love is sweeping the country, according to Presidential hopeful John P. Wintergreen and his loving wife, Mary Turner.

OH, BOY!

OPENED FEBRUARY 20, 1917; PRINCESS THEATRE; 463 PERFORMANCES

Ouch! Tom Powers, Anna Wheaton, and Hal Forde sing "Flubby Dub, the Caveman" —or maybe, "The First Day of May."

THE TEAM OF JEROME KERN, P. G. Wodehouse, and Guy Bolton created a new form of American theatre with the Princess Theatre shows, aptly named after the intimate venue in which they were presented. The third Princess Theatre musical and the third-longest-running book musical of the teens was *Oh, Boy!* The show followed Bolton and Kern's *Nobody Home* and *Very Good Eddie* with Wodehouse joining the team for the first time. Like other Princess musicals, simple and unpretentious with one setting for the first act and another for the second, *Oh, Boy!* eschewed exotic, foreign locales, and used modern American settings and themes. These early shows were musicalized comedies of manners featuring romantic and marital mix-ups and misunderstandings. The Princess shows were another step forward in true integration of song and story. While there were no interpolated specialty numbers or wildly off-base songs, there was room for the occasional piece of special material somewhat subtly jammed into the plot. And if the characters were sometimes more like caricatures, all were essentially good people dutifully playing the roles society demanded. Above all, the tone and style of the show was unwavering, eschewing overly energetic farce and overworked emotions.

OH, BOY!

Produced by
William Elliott and F. Ray Comstock
Staged by Edward Royce

Music by Jerome Kern
Book by Guy Bolton and P. G. Wodehouse
Lyrics by Guy Bolton and P. G. Wodehouse
Orchestra under the direction of
Max Hirschfeld
Orchestrations by Frank Saddler

Scenery designed by D. M. Aiken
Costumes designed by Faibsey

Synopsis

George and his new wife, Lou Ellen, return to George's house on Long Island after their honeymoon only to find a party going on. Because they eloped, Lou Ellen's parents don't yet know they were married and, to ease telling them, the couple decides to separate till the parents can be informed. Once Lou Ellen has left George's bedroom, in through the window comes zany actress (is there any other kind?) Jackie Sampson, escaping from a lecherous judge down below. Much madcap farce follows, as Jackie is forced to disguise herself as George's Quaker aunt and then his wife.

Cast

Jane Packard	Marion Davies
Polly Andrus	Justine Johnstone
Jim Marvin	Hal Forde
George Budd	Tom Powers
Lou Ellen Carter	Marie Carroll
Jackie Sampson	Anna Wheaton
Judge Daniel Carter	Frank McGinn
Miss Penelope Budd	Edna May Oliver

SONGS

ACT 1 "Let's Make a Night of It" · "You Never Knew About Me" · "A Package of Seeds" (Lyrics by Herbert Reynolds and P.G. Wodehouse) · "An Old-Fashioned Wife" "A Pal Like You" · "Till the Clouds Roll By" (Lyrics by P.G. Wodehouse and Jerome Kern) · "A Little Bit of Ribbon" "The First Day of May"

ACT 2 "Koo-La-Loo" · "Rolled Into One" · "Oh, Daddy, Please!" · "Nesting Time in Flatbush" (Lyrics by P.G. Wodehouse and Jerome Kern) · "Words Are Not Needed" "Flubby Dub, the Cave-Man"

Oh, Boy! represented the transition from the haphazard musicals of the past to the newer, more methodical modern musical comedy. Though tertiary characters' names illustrate the old-time penchant for puns—Sheila Rive, Inna Ford, Annie Olde-Knight, B. Ava Little, Phil Ossify, and Hugo Chaseit—the libretto is remarkably pun-free and the plot is natural and unforced. Charm was uppermost in the creators' minds so they designed an evening in which the audience could relax, have a few laughs, feel slightly superior to the silly undertakings on stage, and smile along with the simple, melodic, lyrically witty but undemanding songs. The hit song of the show proved to be one of Kern's most beautiful and enduring works, "Till the Clouds Roll By." The heartfelt, romantic sentiment of the lyrics is perfectly matched to the lilting, rolling melody.

Simplicity, a good sense of clean fun, and tender emotions seem a world away from today's musical theatre. While its plot might seem a bit silly to today's audiences, we would be wise to take a tip from Bolton, Wodehouse, and Kern and their adherence to honest, non-ironic, hardworking theatre. ❀

ABOVE RIGHT: Hal Forde and Anna Wheaton.
BELOW: Dramatic doings on stage at the intimate Princess Theatre. We don't really care what's going on—that wonderful set has us longing for Old Broadway.

Princess Theatre

While the New Amsterdam Theatre is closely associated with the *Ziegfeld Follies*, only one theatre is noted for its importance in a theatrical movement. That theatre is the tiny, intimate Princess Theatre, which was located at 104 West 39th Street. Its long-term failure to attract worthy tenants was resolved through a series of productions that became known as the Princess Theatre Shows, thus insuring the Princess Theatre an important role in the history of the American musical. The 299-seat house was built nearby the immense Metropolitan Opera House. The Princess presented a simple interior design, with fourteen rows of seats in the orchestra section and four boxes. After it hosted a series of failures, agent Elisabeth Marbury was asked to help book the space. She represented many of the best-known playwrights, and her business sense was legendary. (She was the first agent to get her playwrights a percentage of the gross receipts.) Marbury suggested small, intimate musicals for the Princess's stage, but it was generally assumed that established writers wouldn't work for such minuscule monetary returns. So, Marbury approached the young Jerome Kern, who suggested teaming with Guy Bolton. Their series of historic and popular shows, later in collaboration with P. G. Wodehouse, changed the course of the American musical. Following their presentations, the theatre again slipped into hard times, changing names several times, even being transformed into a movie house. Fame came again to the Princess in 1937, renamed the Labor Stage, with the opening of *Pins and Needles*, a topical revue from the ILGWU (International Ladies' Garment Workers Union). The show played almost 1,000 performances at the theatre before moving. In June of 1955, the historic theatre was razed to make room for an office building.

OH, KAY!

OPENED NOVEMBER 8, 1926; IMPERIAL THEATRE; 256 PERFORMANCES

Gertrude Lawrence, with her little rag doll, sings "Someone to Watch Over Me."

OH, KAY!

Produced by Alex. A. Aarons
and Vinton Freedley
Book by Guy Bolton and P. G. Wodehouse
Music by George Gershwin
Lyrics by Ira Gershwin
Based on the play *La Presidente*
by Maurice Henniquin and Pierre Veber
Orchestra under the direction of William Daly

Staged by John Harwood
Musical Staging by Sammy Lee

Scenic Design by John Wenger
Costumes designed by Hattie Carnegie
Brooks Costume Company

Synopsis

It's the Roaring Twenties and Prohibition is rampant throughout the land. So, by the way, is bootlegging, and unbeknownst to him, Jimmy Walker's Long Island estate is being used to stash illegal liquor. The ringleaders of this operation are the Duke of Durham and his sister, Lady Kay, aided and abetted by the rather dim bulbs Story McKee and Larry Potter. Jimmy returns home from his honeymoon with his new wife, Constance (the daughter of a judge... naturally), but unfortunately for the newlyweds, there's a slight problem with the legality of the marriage: Jimmy has neglected to divorce his first wife. Now wed to a bigamist, Constance flees to a hotel for the night. Kay accidentally enters Jimmy's bedroom in search of the hooch. Much confusion of identities occurs (Kay appears in disguise, both as a maid and Jimmy's Cockney wife), but true to form, Jimmy ends up with Kay.

Cast

Molly Morse	*Betty Compton*
The Duke	*Gerald Oliver Smith*
Larry Potter	*Harland Dixon*
Phil Ruxton	*Marion Fairbanks*
Dolly Ruxton	*Madeleine Fairbanks*
'Shorty' McGee	*Victor Moore*
Jimmy Winter	*Oscar Shaw*
Kay	*Gertrude Lawrence*
Mae	*Constance Carpenter*

"It was the opposite of plagiarism; we'll call it donorism."

—*Howard Dietz on Ira Gershwin,* who gave him credit for the lyrics of the title song for which Dietz wrote a rejected lyric

THE MUSICAL COMEDY *Oh, Kay!* is utterly conventional yet thoroughly enchanting. In the tradition of a bygone era, the songwriters wrote the entire score before the librettists ever put pen to paper. In fact, going into the project, all the Gershwins knew was that rising star Gertrude Lawrence would headline. It's no surprise, then, that no fewer than eight songs were dropped before the show made it to New York; after all, once the Gershwins were confronted with what could loosely be called a plot, some of the pre-libretto songs just couldn't be shoehorned into P.G. Wodehouse and Guy Bolton's libretto, set among the world of bootleggers and

rum-runners, plucked directly from the headlines. The characters, in addition to Lawrence's title character, included her British fop of a brother; a pompous, blustering judge; and a ne'er-do-well playboy. In the role of the bumbling comic, a staple in most twenties and thirties musical comedies, beloved character man Victor Moore, famous for his stuttering, slow-motion simplicity, was hired. Co-producer Vinton Freedley was so unsure of Moore's slow delivery, however, he had two comics standing by in Philadelphia should Moore hold up the farcical proceedings; of course, it wasn't necessary, for Moore was a delight. Aarons and Freedley saw *Oh, Kay!* as a Princess Theatre-type show (single setting, farcical goings on and only the slightest attempt to integrate song and story), although they provided Broadway-sized trappings, including a female chorus and a troupe of dancers.

The main draws of most twenties musicals were the stars and the songs. In this case, anyway, expectations were overwhelmingly surpassed for although Gertrude Lawrence had made quite a splash in the *André Charlot Revues* of 1924 and 1925, she became the toast of New York as the zany Kay. (Note: Guy Bolton always claimed he discovered Lawrence performing in a London revue, improbably titled *Rats*. Bolton immediately spotted her star appeal and sent her a note, promising to write a show especially around her talents.) As for the score, it contained marvelous, jaunty tunes in the typical Gershwin manner, but the big hit of the show, "Someone to Watch over Me," was exemplary in its perfectly simple staging, with Lawrence plaintively singing the jazzy yet tender plea to a rag doll that George Gershwin had found in a Philadelphia toy store window. It stopped the show cold, becoming one of the Gershwins' best-loved standards.

Oh, Kay! might have been one of the finest of twenties musicals, but it was also to be one of the last of its kind, for just over the theatrical horizon a miracle was about to occur on the stage of the Ziegfeld Theatre. After *Show Boat*, musical theatre would never quite be the same, and shows like *Oh, Kay!* would become quaint reminders of musical comedy with nothing more on its pretty little mind than bumbling comics, stuttering English asses, and the occasional beautiful, lovelorn ballad. ✽

Bolton & Wodehouse

Guy Bolton, P.G. Wodehouse, and Jerome Kern comprised the most celebrated musical theatre trio in the early years. While Kern's many accomplishments in musical theatre are fondly recalled, many people have no idea of the importance of Bolton and Wodehouse. The former enjoyed a long life in the theatre from his first show, *The Rule of Three* in 1914, to his last, *Anya*, in 1965. Along the way, he wrote many other musicals and plays, many of which have been recently revived or adapted (including *Very Good Eddie*, *The Five O'Clock Girl*, *Anything Goes*, and *Oh, Kay!*) and the hit *Crazy for You* was based on his original work. P.G. Wodehouse's musical career is forgotten, largely because of the great number of other writings he produced; he was, however, responsible for the libretti of almost forty musical comedies, the most successful of which were written in collaboration with Bolton and Kern for the tiny Princess Theatre. Wodehouse's lyrics were the first to use popular slang and speech patterns rather than poetic musings, and made inroads to integrating songs into plots that were less idiotic than usual. Wodehouse was the most influential of all the early lyricists, with many later greats citing him as their inspiration.

TOP: Harland Dixon, Gertrude Lawrence, Oscar Shaw, Victor Moore, and Constance Carpenter—good help is so hard to find.

CENTER: (left to right) George Gershwin, Guy Bolton, and Ira Gershwin.

LEFT: Morris Gest, P.G. Wodehouse, Guy Bolton, F. Ray Comstock, and Jerome Kern were in Detroit on April 8, 1924, for the opening of *Sitting Pretty*, the seventh Princess Theatre show.

SONGS

ACT I · "The Woman's Touch" · "Don't Ask" · "Dear Little Girl" · "Maybe" · "Clap Yo' Hands" · "Do-Do-Do"
ACT II · "Bride and Groom" · "Someone to Watch Over Me" · "Fidgety Feet" · "Heaven on Earth" · "Oh, Kay!"

Gertrude Lawrence

Gertrude Lawrence had "It," that indefinable, unteachable, ineffable quality that separates a superstar from a competent, solid performer. An unlikely person to make her fame in musicals, she was an average dancer and highly "pitchy" as a singer, but like Marilyn Miller, Gertie could stand center stage, beam, and any vocal deficiencies were immaterial. Coming to the States with Beatrice Lillie in *André Charlot's Revue of 1924*, Lawrence walked off with the show and became an overnight sensation to American audiences with her songs "Parisian Pierrot" and "Limehouse Blues." Subsequently, the Gershwins tapped her to play the lead in *Oh, Kay!*, introducing "Do, Do, Do" and "Someone to Watch Over Me." A wonderful stage comedienne, she became a beloved star, forever associated with Noël Coward after their sensational pairings in *Private Lives* and *Tonight at 8:30*. Actually leading the kind of dramatic personal life one imagines most actresses lead, she was considered flighty, self-centered, and undependable by those who worked her, but none of that mattered to audiences. After playing the searching Liza Elliott in *Lady in the Dark*, Rodgers and Hammerstein wrote the role of Anna Leonowens in *The King and I* at her request. It should have been her greatest triumph, a role she could have played for years. Not long into the run, however, it became apparent that Lawrence was seriously ill, and when she finally left the show, her decline was rapid—she died from cancer within a few weeks.

Backstage

When Ira Gershwin was laid up in the hospital for an emergency appendectomy during production, lyricist Howard Dietz came to the rescue and contributed lyrics to the title song and three others in the score, plus the title to "Someone to Watch over Me."

Gertrude Lawrence, appearing in the States in her first book musical, was the first Englishwoman to originate a role in an American musical prior to its traveling to the West End.

Lawrence didn't make her entrance in *Oh, Kay!* until forty minutes into the first act.

TOP LEFT: "Has Anybody Seen Our Ship?" Noël Coward and Gertrude Lawrence in *Tonight at 8:30*.

TOP RIGHT: Oscar Shaw protects Gertrude Lawrence from a gangster.

ABOVE: Gertrude Lawrence looks positively divine in a Hattie Carnegie design.

Oscar Shaw surrounded by a bevy of beauties.

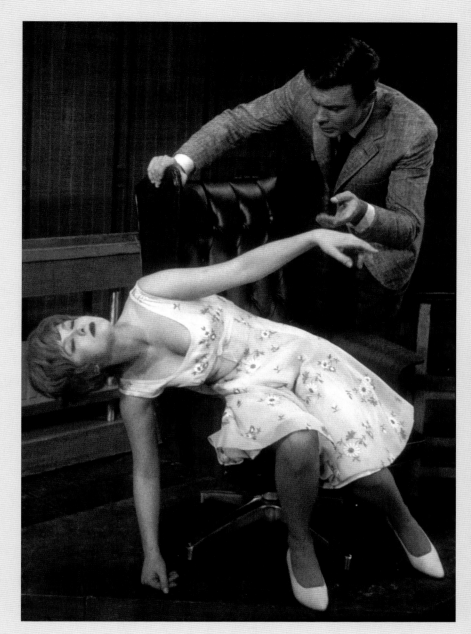

PINK SLIPS

AUDITIONING ACTORS IS A TRICKY thing. Once in a while, the powers that be in a Broadway musical look at each other after the first rehearsal and whisper, "Kids, we've made a big mistake." There are certain performers who are known as professional auditioners: brilliant with their uptempo and ballad, but unable to deliver the goods in the show itself. When it doesn't work out, it's not always the actor's fault, however; for producers and directors, summoning up a sense of false bravado, can convince themselves that they will be able to extract a stellar performance from an iffy prospect. Not measuring up is not the only reason their are those unexpected inserts in the programs of previewing shows reading "The role of Boris Lermontov is now being played by Steve Barton" (as in the case of *The Red Shoes*) Sometimes, a star wisely bails out when they he or she sees the writing on the wall, as in the case of Eddie Foy, Jr. in *Drat! the Cat!*, Ella Logan in *Kelly*, and Barbara Cook, who left the cast of *Carrie* during its Stratford tryout after almost being decapitated by an errant set. Chaotic out–of–town rewrites can lead to an actor losing her gig, as in the case of Anita Gillette in *The Gay Life*, Allyn Ann McLerie in *Funny Girl*, or Madeline Kahn in *How Now, Dow Jones*. In

the case of *Legs Diamond*, a famous recent episode of a Broadway bloodbath, the talented Christine Andreas and Bob Stillman both saw their major roles excised when the creators went into panic mode. Most painfully, an injury can lead to dismissal, as when Ron Orbach hurt his knee during the Chicago tryout of *The Producers*. The creative team fell in love with his understudy, Brad Oscar, and Orbach never returned, losing out on a chance for a Tony nomination. Orbach's consolation prize? A role in *Dance of the Vampires*.

TOP LEFT: Fired in Boston, Louis Jourdan was so ill-equipped for his role in *On A Clear Day You Can See Forever* he often put costar Barbara Harris to sleep during performances. LEFT: Lainie Kazan was a victim of the Detroit bloodbath of *Seesaw*. TOP RIGHT: Christine Andreas was written out of *Legs Diamond* during previews. We hope she now views this as a gift from the theatrical gods. CENTER RIGHT: Much more believable piloting a crippled 747 than singing in a Broadway musical, Karen Black didn't make it into town as Philia in *Forum*. CENTER LEFT: Elaine Stritch shows Jean Fenn the door during the pre-Broadway shakedown of *Sail Away*. BOTTOM RIGHT: Garn Stephens, not up to the vocal demands of "The Miller's Son," saw her big break evaporate when she was let go out-ot-town in *A Little Night Music*.

OKLAHOMA!

OPENED MARCH 31, 1943; ST. JAMES THEATRE; 2,212 PERFORMANCES

ABOVE: Hoedown at the Skidmore Ranch: A bright-golden Agnes de Mille moment from "The Farmer and the Cowman."

RIGHT: Alfred Drake and Joan Roberts, the original Curley and Laurey of *Oklahoma!*

OKLAHOMA!
Produced by the Theatre Guild
Music by Richard Rodgers
Book and Lyrics by Oscar Hammerstein II
Based on the play
Green Grow The Lilacs by Lynn Riggs
Musical Director: Jay Blackton
Music orchestrated by Russell Bennett
Directed by Rouben Mamoulian
Choreographed by Agnes de Mille
Scenic Design by Lemuel Ayers
Costume Design by Miles White

Synopsis

Aunt Eller Murphy has two ranch hands, Curly and Jud Fry, both of whom have taken a liking to Eller's niece, Laurey. Curly is handsome and virile; Jud is a lonely, angry misfit. Laurey uses Jud in order to make Curly jealous, giving Jud reasons to believe that he has a chance with the young farm girl. With the assist of a surrey with fringe on top, Curly wins over Laurey and they are married. Jud picks a fight with Curly, during which Jud falls on his knife and is killed. After a trial lasting a few sentences, Curly is exonerated and ranchers and cowmen join together to celebrate the new state of Oklahoma.

Cast

Curly .... Alfred Drake
Laurey .... Joan Roberts
Ali Hakim .... Joseph Buloff
Jud Fry .... Howard Da Silva
Will Parker .... Lee Dixon
Aunt Eller........................... Betty Garde
Ado Annie Carnes .... Celeste Holm
Jess, Dream Jud .... George Church
Aggie, Dream Child .... Bambi Linn
Chalmers, Dream Curley ...... Marc Platt
Dream Laurey .... Katharine Sergava
Andrew Carnes .... Ralph Riggs

CHANGES IN THE MUSICAL THEATRE form came fast and furious in the 1940s. This was mainly due to the successful run of Rodgers and Hammerstein's shows, beginning in 1943 with the groundbreaking *Oklahoma!* In actuality, however, *Oklahoma!* wasn't as revolutionary a triumph as Hammerstein and Kern's *Show Boat* (1927). Structurally speaking, *Oklahoma!*—and most of Rodgers and Hammerstein's shows—were essentially operettas, though more mature and sophisticated, better integrated, and with more complex characterizations than the usual lighthearted operetta fare. People are often killed or die in R & H shows: Jud is killed in *Oklahoma!*, Billy commits suicide in *Carousel*, Lieutenant Cable is killed in *South Pacific*, and the king dies in *The King and I*. All of their shows share a strong sense of community and characters must strive for happiness and overcome obstacles in order to reach their goals. Sometimes, as in the cases of Jud Fry, Cable, and Tuptim, that happiness remains elusive.

The greater integration of book, music, and dance had been explored by both writers prior to joining forces. Many of their shows (*Oklahoma!*, *Carousel*, *Allegro*, *The King and I*, even *Flower Drum Song*) included a lengthy ballet, usually psychological in nature and always heavily metaphoric. In addition, the shows tend to be heavily weighted toward the first act with a lighter, shorter second act. The Rodgers and Hammerstein formula further demanded a main romantic couple, with a secondary subplot built around a humorous couple; there was often an earth mother figure, such as Aunt Eller in *Oklahoma!*, Nettie Fowler in *Carousel*, the Grandmother in *Allegro*, Fauna in *Pipe Dream*, and the Mother Superior in *The Sound of Music*. In fact, a repertory company could easily produce a season of Rodgers and Hammerstein shows utilizing one group of actors who could fit all of the roles.

Some of the shows by others that successfully followed the Rodgers and Hammerstein formula were *Brigadoon* (1947, with three couples), *Bloomer Girl* (1944), *Finian's Rainbow* (1947), and *Kiss Me, Kate* (1948), but these were works by up-and-coming heavyweights (in the case of Lerner and Loewe) or Rodgers and Hammerstein's contemporaries reinventing themselves (in the case of Cole Porter). Just following the formula didn't guarantee a success, and there were plenty of derivative flops.

Unlike many other writers, Rodgers and Hammerstein believed in the essential humanity of all their characters. They never wrote a part purely for comedy's sake, or treated their characters lightly or with disdain. They respected the villains and the romantic leads alike, loving them for their mistakes as well as their triumphs, allowing their characters an unusual depth and three-dimensionality. The King is at once a barbarian (by our standards), and an intelligent ruler who cares about his country and people. Billy Bigelow goes down the wrong road because he cares so much for his wife and unborn child. The audience can even empathize with poor Jud, isolated in his lonely room with his girlie pictures.

Sixty years after its premiere. *Oklahoma!*'s groundbreaking nature can still be appreciated, and the Rodgers and Hammerstein structure lives on in such shows as *Side Show* (1997), *Ragtime* (1998), and *Parade* (1998). In an unsure time, *Oklahoma!* hit a nerve with an America in the midst of war. It celebrated our country's homespun values, determination, and triumph over obstacles. It wasn't just a flag-waver, however; it told the story of honest, three-dimensional characters who had dreams as well as disappointments. The Rodgers and Hammerstein formula worked then and it works today, because, while time and circumstances change, basic human values and dreams are eternal. ❈

LEFT: Howard Da Silva and Alfred Drake eulogize "Poor Jud."

BELOW: Joseph Buloff, Celeste Holm, and Ralph Riggs are gettin' ready for a good ol' shotgun weddin'.

BOTTOM LEFT: Laurence Guittard and Christine Andreas in the wonderful 1979 revival. Note how much moodier, almost seductive, "The Surrey with the Fringe on Top" seems here, compared to the Drake and Roberts version across the page, staged thirty-five years earlier.

ABOVE: The epitome of Broadway sophistication, circa 1962: Diahann Carroll and Richard Kiley, adult, romantic, and glamorous in Richard Rodgers's first post-Hammerstein musical, *No Strings*.

TOP RIGHT: Richard Rodgers congratulates leading lady Elizabeth Allen on the opening night of *Do I Hear a Waltz?* His wife Dorothy dutifully looks the other way.

Richard Rodgers

Richard Rodgers, who along with George Abbott had the richest, longest lasting career in Broadway history, made his debut as a composer in 1925, teaming with Lorenz Hart on *The Garrick Gaieties* which introduced the standard "Manhattan." For the next twenty years, Rodgers and Hart had a hand in one classic musical comedy after another, and with their witty, romantic, and tuneful scores for *A Connecticut Yankee, Babes in Arms, Too Many Girls, On Your Toes, The Boys From Syracuse*, and *Pal Joey,* among many others, they were the musical engine that drove both Broadway and popular music. When Hart's personal problems interfered, Rodgers began a collaboration with Oscar Hammerstein II, becoming a pioneering force in the development of story and character through song. With *Oklahoma!*, they started forging a path that has become so ingrained in the history of the musical that all writers, whether they know it or not, are mimicking their structure on some unconscious level. Wonderful show after wonderful show followed; some were not smash hits, but they were all intelligent, worthy pieces: *Carousel, South Pacific, The King and I, Flower Drum Song*, and *The Sound of Music* remain among the bravest, best and most frequently performed of musicals. After Hammerstein's death, Rodgers wrote his first show with his own fine lyrics, the highly enjoyable *No Strings*. After proving there were sweet sounds still inside his head, he teamed with a series of lyricists, to diminishing results, with *Do I Hear a Waltz?* (lyrics by Stephen Sondheim), *Two by Two* (Martin Charnin), *Rex* (Sheldon Harnick), and *I Remember Mama* (Charnin and Raymond Jessel), containing passing glimmers of melodic beauty. A complicated man with as many demons as Lorenz Hart, but much more functional, he could at times be stubborn, condescending, prejudiced, suspicious, and vindictive, but like Jerome Robbins and Zero Mostel, was often afforded a pass for behavior that would otherwise be considered unacceptable. He died in 1979, having made the sound of music on Broadway for over half a century.

ABOVE RIGHT: The magnificent Penny Fuller was every inch Elizabeth I of England in Rodgers's penultimate musical, *Rex*.

LEFT: Great kissers Elizabeth Allen and Sergio Franchi in a scene from the Rodgers/Sondheim collaboration *Do I Hear A Waltz?*

Alfred Drake

With the bravura of a great Shakesperean and a singing voice of operatic proportions, Alfred Drake was perhaps the most successful and in demand leading man of the 1940s and '50s in plays as well as musicals. After an early featured role alongside other talented youngsters in *Babes in Arms*, he won acclaim and became a first-class star in 1943 as Curly in the revolutionary *Oklahoma!*, opening the show with "Oh, What a Beautiful Morning" and flying in the face of the then-traditional opening chorus. After roles in *Sing Out Sweet Land* and Duke Ellington's *Beggars Holiday*, Drake tackled two roles that cemented his place in Broadway history. Perfectly suited to his oversized persona and his lush baritone, the hammy Fred Graham in *Kiss Me, Kate* provided Drake with a prime opportunity to chew the scenery with fellow diva Patricia Morison and stop the show with "Where Is the Life That Late I Led?" One of his biggest regrets was turning down the role of the king in *The King and I*; nevertheless, he replaced Yul Brynner while on vacation and received excellent reviews, and he soon delivered another star turn as Hajj in *Kismet*, winning a Tony Award. In 1961, he played the title role in *Kean*, which, despite a wonderful score and a heroic effort on his part, suffered from a weak book and Drake's lengthy illness, leading to vocal problems and many missed performances, a true anomaly for such a solid, committed performer. After two out of town closings, both playing dual roles, in *Zenda* (costarring Chita Rivera and Anne Rogers) and *After You, Mr. Hyde* (costarring Nancy Dussault), he went into retirement from musical theatre, coming out only to give a wonderful, understated turn as Honore in the stage version of the musical film *Gigi*, utterly unlike Maurice Chevalier and completely valid.

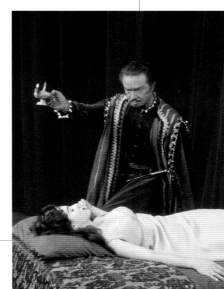

SONGS

ACT I "Oh, What a Beautiful Mornin'" · "The Surrey With the Fringe on Top" · "Kansas City" · "I Can't Say No" "Many a New Day" · "It's a Scandal! It's an Outrage!" "People Will Say We're in Love" · "Poor Jud" · "Lonely Room" · "Out of My Dreams" · "Laurey Makes Up Her Mind" Ballet
ACT II "The Farmer and the Cowman" · "All er Nothin'" "Oklahoma"

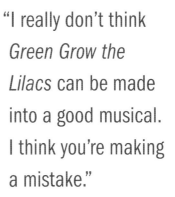

"I really don't think *Green Grow the Lilacs* can be made into a good musical. I think you're making a mistake."

—*Lorenz Hart to Richard Rodgers*

TOP LEFT: Anne Rogers and Alfred Drake in *Zenda*, which closed out of town despite an often lovely Vernon Duke score.

TOP RIGHT: Alfred Drake and Lee Venora enact a scene from *Othello* in the musical *Kean*.

ABOVE: Katharine Sergava, as "Dream Laurey," is tormented by the girlie-pictures-come-to-life from Jud's shack, in the landmark "Laurey Makes Up Her Mind."

LEFT: Celeste Holm in her star-making role as Ado Annie Carnes.

ON THE TOWN

OPENED DECEMBER 28, 1944; ADELPHI THEATRE, 462 PERFORMANCES

Miss Turnstiles (Sono Osato) appears as a subway car vision to sailor Gabey (John Battles) at the beginning of the "Playground of the Rich" ballet.

ON THE TOWN

Produced by Oliver Smith and Paul Feigay

Music by Leonard Bernstein

Book and Lyrics by
Betty Comden and Adolph Green
Based on an idea by Jerome Robbins
Additional Lyrics by Leonard Bernstein
Orchestrations by Leonard Bernstein,
Hershy Kay, Don Walker, Elliott Jacoby,
and Ted Royal
Musical Director: Max Goberman

Directed by George Abbott
Choreographed by Jerome Robbins

Production Design by Oliver Smith
Costume Design by Alvin Colt
Lighting Design by Sam Amdurs

Synopsis

Three sailors, Gabey, Chip, and Ozzie, on twenty-four-hour leave, hit the Big Apple. Along the way they get involved with three women who are equally interested in companionship. Hildy is a taxi driver, Claire is a prominent anthropologist, and Ivy is a struggling dancer who has recently been crowned Miss Turnstiles. The boys and girls travel from the Bronx to Battery Park to Coney Island in Brooklyn, singing, dancing, and smooching all the way.

Cast

Hildy Esterhazy	Nancy Walker
Claire DeLoone	Betty Comden
Ozzie	Adolph Green
Chip	Cris Alexander
Gabey	John Battles
Ivy Smith	Sono Osato
Lucy Schmeeler	Alice Pearce
Pitkin W. Bridgework	Robert Chisholm
Madame Maude P. Dilly	Susan Steell

THE 1940S WERE A MOMENTOUSLY rich decade in the development of the musical theatre. While *Oklahoma!* is credited as the show that united all creative elements, resulting in the perfect formula for the modern musical, *On the Town*, opening a year later, introduced a new wave of musical comedy geniuses, ones who would expand on the legacy of the previous generation of talents.

The project began at Ballet Theatre as the piece *Fancy Free*, when dancer Jerome Robbins was commissioned to make his choreographic debut with the company. Leonard Bernstein, following his remarkable conducting debut with the New York Philharmonic, was hired to write his first ballet score, and designer Oliver Smith also made his Ballet Theatre debut. Amazingly, Robbins, Bernstein, and Smith's collaboration took place almost exclusively by telephone and mail, since both Robbins and Bernstein were touring and Smith was working in Mexico.

The slim plot of *Fancy Free* dealt with the adventures of three sailors on a one-day leave in New York City and their misadventures in trying to pick up women. The ballet was so successful it was used as the basis for a Broadway musical. Bernstein, Robbins, and Smith would reprise their roles, with Smith also acting as co-producer. Needing words to accompany the dancing, Bernstein suggested friends Betty Comden and Adolph Green, then successful cabaret performers, as librettists/lyricists. All five would be making their Broadway debuts.

They've "got one day here and not another minute": The six principals of *On the Town* (clockwise from lower right: Sono Osato, Adolph Green, Nancy Walker, Cris Alexander, Betty Comden, and John Battles).

Raising money for the show proved difficult until George Abbott, the legendary producer/director/writer, agreed to direct. Work began, a cast was assembled (including authors Comden and Green, also making their Broadway debuts as performers; dancer Sono Osato; and comic forces Nancy Walker and Alice Pearce), and, only eight months and ten days after the opening of *Fancy Free*, Broadway audiences were *On the Town* at the Adelphi Theatre in New York—by today's standards, an absolutely remarkable achievement. The speed with which the show was written, rehearsed, and opened mirrored the speed and youthful enthusiasm of the entire proceedings. Besides the authors, there were other notable Broadway debuts associated with *On the Town*: Hershy Kay's first orchestrations, Alvin Colt's first costumes, along with the Broadway debuts of Cris Alexander and John Battles.

Comden and Green's first libretto shows their off-kilter conceits and bittersweet romanticism—two qualities of all their best work. Even the names of *On the Town*'s characters reveal Comden and Green's playful imagination. What other writers, save S. J. Perelman (or Guy Bolton), would name characters Pitkin W. Bridgework, Lucy Schmeeler, or Claire DeLoone? And Bernstein brought a brash, modern sensibility to the Broadway musical, mixing hip jazz, modern classicism, and languorous blues motifs.

Broadway revivals of *On the Town* in 1971 and 1999 were failures, but the piece remains a favorite with its complicated balance of classical dance, jazz, farce, and heart—a delicate mixture of tones that is extremely difficult to reproduce. ❋

Backstage

Miss Turnstiles was based on the real-life Miss Subways. (This is not to be confused with Miss Rheingold.)

When *On the Town* was filmed in 1949, MGM deemed Leonard Bernstein's music too atonal, keeping the ballet music but tossing out almost all of his songs. The only Bernstein songs remaining were "I Feel Like I'm Not Out of Bed (Yet)," "New York, New York," and "Come Up to My Place." Roger Edens composed the balance of the songs, with lyrics by Betty Comden and Adolph Green.

TOP RIGHT: The sailors and their girls see Miss Turnstiles (Sono Osato) and future star Allyn Ann McLerie (far left) dancing the hootchy-kootch at Coney Island.

CENTER: Nancy Walker (right), crazy for the Boogie Woogie; June Allyson (left), an aficionado of the Barrelhouse; and Victoria Schools, lover of the Blues, extol "The Three B's" in *Best Foot Forward*.

FAR RIGHT: In *Copper and Brass*, Nancy Walker had a rare opportunity to play a romantic lead.

Nancy Walker

Nancy Walker, an eternal comic sourpuss, made her Broadway debut in 1941 at the age of nineteen in *Best Foot Forward*, where her unique combination of brass and hangdog expression made her an instant smash. After *On the Town*, she had a great triumph costarring with Harold Lang in the Hugh Martin musical *Look Ma, I'm Dancin'*. As the unlikely owner of a ballet troupe, her number "I'm the First Girl (in the Second Row)" perfectly captured her ability to simultaneously charm and kvetch. Despite her inability to find a perfect property, she never failed to make an impression, whether singing of

her love "Irving" in *Along Fifth Avenue* or wrestling a nightstick as policewoman Katey O'Shea in *Copper and Brass* (cowritten by husband David Craig). She finally got another hit as Phil Silvers's long-suffering wife in the 1960 show *Do Re Mi*. To see her priceless stage business as she sat in a nightclub, stood up on her anniversary, was to see a master of the slow burn, an actress not afraid to use her anger as a comic weapon. Despite appearing in the L.A. run of the 1972 revival of *A Funny Thing Happened on the Way to the Forum,* and performing a touchingly understated "I'm Still Here" at the 1973 Sondheim tribute, she unfortunately never returned to Broadway in a musical, gaining her greatest fame on the TV series *Rhoda* and as Rosie, the Bounty Paper Towel lady.

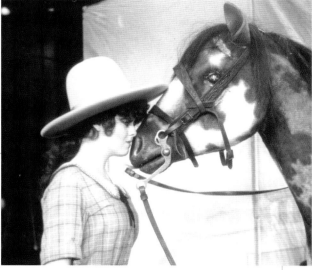

Bernadette Peters

Bernadette Peters, an ageless adorable whose sex appeal belies her versatility as an actress, made her debut at the age of thirteen in a tour of *Gypsy* starring Mary McCarty. She made her Broadway musical debut in the bio-musical *George M!*, starring Joel Grey, and, after costarring in the mega-flop *La Strada* and an *On the Town* revival, she portrayed tragic silent-screen star Mabel Normand opposite the wonderful Robert Preston in *Mack and Mabel*. After that show's lamentable failure, she spent the next nine years working in television, film, and nightclubs. When she resurfaced to theatergoers in 1983 in Sondheim's *Sunday in the Park with George*, Broadway welcomed her with open arms and she became the most beloved musical star of her generation, her performance in *Song and Dance* winning her a well-deserved Tony Award. A rare misstep was costarring with Martin Short in 1994's *The Goodbye Girl*, which proved just how elusive the magic of onstage chemistry can be. She won a second Tony Award for the revival of *Annie Get Your Gun*, reasserting her popularity by drawing huge audiences to a less-than-inspired production. Her career came full circle in 2003, as she returned to *Gypsy* forty-two years later, this time playing Rose. Her commitment to excellence in the theatre was no more clearly exemplified than when, in 1987, as Broadway's reigning queen, she accepted a supporting lead in *Into the Woods*, unwilling to pass up an opportunity to create another role in a Sondheim show. Long may she reign.

TOP: Bernadette Peters (as taxi driver Hildy) picks up the fare of her dreams (Jess Richards) in the 1971 Broadway revival.

ABOVE RIGHT: As tragic silent-screen star Mabel Normand, Bernadette Peters shares a winsome moment during the filming of a Western in *Mack and Mabel*.

ABOVE: Momentarily freed from the confines of her bustle, Dot frolics on the Island of the Grand Jatte in *Sunday in the Park with George*.

RIGHT: In *The Goodbye Girl*, Peters played a dancer coming out of retirement. Here she realizes she is "A Beat Behind."

ON THE TWENTIETH CENTURY

OPENED FEBRUARY 19, 1978; ST. JAMES THEATRE; 460 PERFORMANCES

ABOVE: Musical comedy simile: The four porters (Keith Davis, Quitman Fludd III, Ray Stephens, and Joseph Wise) in the Entr'acte of *On the Twentieth Century*, "Life Is Like a Train."

RIGHT: George Coe, Madeline Kahn, and Dean Dittman at odds.

ON THE TWENTIETH CENTURY
Produced by The Producers Circle 2, Inc.
Robert Fryer, Mary Lea Johnson, James
Cresson and Martin Richards
Book and Lyrics by
Betty Comden and Adolph Green
Music by Cy Coleman
Based on the Play by Ben Hecht,
Charles MacArthur, and Bruce Milholland
Musical Director: Paul Gemignani
Music orchestrated by Hershy Kay
Directed by Harold Prince
Musical Staging by Larry Fuller
Scenic Design by Robin Wagner
Costume Design by Florence Klotz
Lighting Design by Ken Billington

Synopsis

Producer on the skids Oscar Jaffee escapes town after the failure of his latest fiasco, the story of Joan of Arc. He books himself in a compartment on the Twentieth Century Limited, a train traveling from Chicago to New York. The roomette is next to that of Lily Garland, a Hollywood actress, who is traveling with her boyfriend, the very, very handsome and very, very stupid Bruce Granit. Jaffee is desperate to sign Garland for his next religious spectacle, the story of Mary Magdalene. To add to his headache, also traveling on the train is a rival producer also seeking to sign Garland, and a certifiable lunatic, Letitia Primrose—very religious, very rich, and very addled. By curtain's end, Garland and Jaffee have reconciled, celebrating their mercurial onstage/offstage relationship.

Cast

Letitia Primrose	*Imogene Coca*
Owen O'Malley	*George Coe*
Oliver Webb	*Dean Dittman*
Oscar Jaffee	*John Cullum*
Max Jacobs	*George Lee Andrews*
Mildred Plotka/Lily Garland	*Madeline Kahn*
Bruce Granit	*Kevin Kline*
Agnes	*Judy Kaye*

HAROLD PRINCE HAS ENJOYED MANY successes (both artistically and financially) in his long, unsurpassed career in the musical theatre—some shows got good reviews but never did good business, while some went on to enjoy long runs despite so-so reviews. Many received raves and did good business, too, but whatever kind of success his shows have enjoyed, one thing has marked all of Prince's productions: the unparalleled producing (even when he wasn't actually the producer).

Fans of *On the Twentieth Century* consider it the last good, traditional Broadway musical. To be sure, there have been satisfying shows since, but this one had it all: great material, terrific performances (from John Cullum, Imogene Coca, and a truly madcap Kevin Kline in a role that Jack Cassidy would have played fifteen years earlier), and a magnificent design by Robin Wagner, not to mention Prince's excellent and precise pacing and staging.

Betty Comden and Adolph Green expanded the original play with their inimitable spoofery, their lyrics and book equal to the best of their comedy work, while Cy Coleman's endlessly inventive music kept the show hurtling along. Some critics complained that Coleman's music didn't sound vaguely Depression-era, but they were missing the point, for the purpose of a Broadway score is to characterize a setting or period while retaining its own unique sound. The music must at once seem contemporary (as opposed to old-fashioned) yet timeless, all the while supporting the characters and becoming a chief dramatic component.

Madeline Kahn, as audition-pianist-Mildred-Plotka-turned-movie-star-Lily-Garland, turned in a performance of wacky unconventionality and near operatic scope. The energy and concentration of an eight-show-a-week run proved too much, however, and Kahn unceremoniously left the show shortly after its opening. The wonderful Judy Kaye, Kahn's understudy, "pulled a Shirley MacLaine," truly becoming an overnight sensation when she assumed the role. Unfortunately, despite a fine career, the changing state of the musical theatre did not provide Kaye with more roles tailored to her talents. She starred in *Oh, Brother* (a sadly underappreciated show that closed after only three performances) and *The Mooney Shapiro Songbook* (closed on opening night), and she soon became typecast as a character actress. She handled these roles superbly, but one always got the feeling that she was constrained by the small size of the roles she was given. Prince, however, never forgot Kaye's importance to the artistic success of *On the Twentieth Century* and later cast her in another spectacle, *Phantom of the Opera*.

Twentieth Century was one of the last pure musical theatre entertainments on Broadway to date. Apart from the occasional lighthearted revival (*Forum, Guys and Dolls*), Broadway became a pretty serious place, mounting self-important epics with epic themes. And it was the hugely successful *Evita*, which Prince directed, that laid the groundwork for serious, power-ballad musical theatre.

Strangely enough, in some ways *On the Twentieth Century* was a precursor to Prince's work on *Phantom of the Opera*. Both are operettas and both contain shows within the show which are parodies. They lampoon life in the theatre as well as celebrate that life. Both *Twentieth Century* and *Phantom* are performed in an over-the-top style, one for comic effect and the other for dramatic intensity. The physical productions of both shows, thanks to the talents of Robin Wagner and Maria Bjornson, respectively, help reinforce their exaggerated styles.

Twentieth Century succeeded on all levels and was one of the last Broadway shows to spotlight Comden and Green's off-kilter view of the world. It stands among their very best works, featuring their trademark wit, energy, and zest for living. It may have been the last great Broadway musical comedy. ❀

Cy Coleman

Cy Coleman, one of a handful of Broadway composers who is a brilliant pianist in his own right, and perhaps second only to Harold Arlen in his ability to translate the jazz idiom to the musical stage, made his debut as Broadway composer with the Lucille Ball vehicle *Wildcat*. Working with the gifted yet troubled lyricist Carolyn Leigh, he next tackled *Little Me*, this time writing a delightfully funny score for Sid Caesar. Coleman wrote his next two shows with another female lyricist, the brilliant Dorothy Fields, and in *Sweet Charity* and *Seesaw*, he became a master of capturing, through his music, the rhythmic grit and sexual drive of contemporary urban life, further developed in his later shows *I Love My Wife* and *The Life*. Just as easily, however, Coleman could drop the down-and-dirty sound and switch gears to write the operetta-flavored *On the Twentieth Century* and the jaunty calliope sounds of *Barnum*. In *City of Angels*, he joyfully returned to his jazz roots, with the hottest band in a Broadway pit since the original production of *Gypsy*. Reteaming with his *Twentieth Century* lyric team Betty Comden and Adolph Green, he struck Tony gold again with *The Will Rogers' Follies*. After forty years, and with a tunestack including such finger-snappers as "I've Got Your Number," "Big Spender," "Hey, Look Me Over," and "Nobody Does It Like Me," Cy Coleman is still the embodiment of Broadway brass.

TOP RIGHT: The unrepentant Messrs. Dittman, Coe, and Cullum, bamboozling their angel of an angel, Letitia Primrose (played by the comically inspired Imogene Coca).

ABOVE RIGHT: Coleman, Dorothy Fields, and Bob Fosse confer during *Sweet Charity* rehearsals.

RIGHT: Ken Howard and the ladies of the morning, afternoon, or evening of *Seesaw*: Michon Peacock, Baayork Lee, Judy Gibson, the brilliant Anita Morris, and Loida Iglesias. Twenty-five years later, still haunted by their unspoiled beauty, Cy Coleman would musicalize these same five hookers in *The Life*.

Two of the greatest hams in the modern theatre duke it out: John Cullum and Kevin Kline, vying over Lily Garland, vow to make her "Mine."

Backstage

The role of Letitia Primrose was originally offered to Mildred Natwick, who turned it down because she thought the song "Repent" was too vulgar.

Co-librettest/lyricist Betty Comden replaced a vacationing Imogene Coca as Letitia Primrose—constantly forgetting her own lyrics. Her one previous Broadway musical comedy appearance was in the original company of *On the Town*, thirty years earlier.

SONGS

ACT I "On the Twentieth Century" · "I Rise Again" "Indian Maiden's Lament" · "Veronique" · "I Have Written a Play" · "Together" · "Never" · "Our Private World" "Repent" · "Mine" · "I've Got It All"
ACT II "Life Is Like a Train" · "Five Zeros" · "Sextet" "She's a Nut" · "Max Jacobs" · "Babette" · "The Legacy" "Lily, Oscar"

ABOVE: In "Veronique," Madeline Kahn (here with Sal Mistretta) revels in one of Comden and Green's wittiest musical scenes ever, showing the transformation of audition pianist Mildred Plotka into silver screen goddess Lily Garland.

LEFT: John Cullum replaced a vocally overtaxed Louis Jourdan in *On A Clear Day ...* , becoming a musical theatre star forever. And ever. And e-ver more.

LEFT: Robin Wagner's set for *Twentieth Century*, a marvel of elegance and modern stage wizardry, showed the speeding train from every possible angle, from caboose to cowcatcher.

John Cullum

John Cullum, with the acting chops of a Shakespearean and a superb, rich baritone, has lent his strong voice and presence to many Broadway musicals. From Civil War–era patriarch to hammy Svengali to modern-day psychiatrist, his range is amazing, equaling that of Richard Kiley in its ability to span eras and styles. After understudying both Richard Burton and Roddy McDowell in *Camelot*, he made his leading-man debut replacing Louis Jourdan in *On a Clear Day You Can See Forever*. He followed that up with a true flopperoo, the Christopher Columbus musical *1491*, which folded in California, then replacement stints in *Man of La Mancha* and *1776*. He won his first Tony Award for his robustly sung soliloquies as Charley Anderson in *Shenandoah*, and another three years later for his Barrymore-inspired Oscar Jaffee in *On the Twentieth Century*. After turning down the title role in *Sweeney Todd*, he branched out into television, starring in *Northern Exposure*. He returned, still in fine form and voice, as the venal Caldwell B. Cladwell in *Urinetown* in 2001.

ON YOUR TOES

OPENED APRIL 11, 1936; IMPERIAL THEATRE; 315 PERFORMANCES

Tamara Geva and Demetrios Vilan in George Balanchine's "Princess Zenobia" ballet.

ON YOUR TOES

Produced by Dwight Deere Wiman

Music by Richard Rodgers
Lyrics by Lorenz Hart
Book by
Richard Rodgers, George Abbott, and Lorenz Hart
Music orchestrated by Hans Spialek
Music Director: Gene Salzer

Staged by
C. Worthington Miner and George Abbott
Choreographed by George Balanchine

Scenic Design by Jo Mielziner
Costume Design by Irene Sharaff

Synopsis

Junior Dolan, youngest member of the Dolan family vaudeville act, grows up to teach music in New York City. Among his pupils are Sidney Cohn, an up-and-coming composer, and Frankie Frayne, a pretty songwriter. Frankie introduces Junior to Peggy Porterfield, wealthy patron of the arts with a passion for the ballet. Junior convinces Peggy to produce Sidney's jazz ballet, even though the ballet's Russian artistic director is completely against the idea. Vera Barnova, the company's tempestuous prima ballerina, having split yet again with her costar and lover Morrosine, meets Junior and convinces him to dance the lead role in what is now titled "Slaughter on Tenth Avenue." Junior obliges, but Morrosine, jealous of Junior, hires a gangster to kill him at the end of the ballet. On opening night, Junior (tipped off to the hit) dances and dances (and dances), until the police can save him.

Cast

Phil Dolan III	*Ray Bolger*
Frankie Frayne	*Doris Carson*
Vera Barnova	*Tamara Geva*
Peggy Porterfield	*Luella Gear*
Vassilli	*Robert Sidney*
Serge Alexandrovitch	*Monty Woolley*
Konstantine Morrosine	*Demetrios Vilan*
A Singer	*Earle MacVeigh*
Featured Dancer	*George Church*
Sidney Cohn	*David Morris*
Pianists	*Edgar Fairchild*
	Adam Carroll

"I met with Balanchine one afternoon. . . . I didn't know a thing about choreography and told him I was unsure how we should go about it. Balanchine smiled and said simply, 'You write. I put on.'"

—*Richard Rodgers*

HISTORY WAS MADE WHEN LORENZ Hart appeared in the Columbia University Varsity Show of 1915, but not for his memorable appearance as Mary Pickford. Also onstage that day was Oscar Hammerstein II, while in the audience sat the thirteen-year-old Richard Rodgers with his brother Mortimer. Morty took his brother backstage and introduced him to Hammerstein.

The team of Rodgers and Hart wrote a remarkable number of shows over the next eleven years—seventeen musicals produced either on Broadway or in London, as well as three filmed versions of their stage shows. In 1926 alone, Rodgers and Hart premiered four shows in New York and one in London, while from 1931 to 1935, the duo sojourned in Hollywood and turned out six film scores. Then it was back to Broadway, where, before 1942, they wrote ten more shows and three more films, enjoying (save 1941) a hit show every season.

Today's musical theatre writers are lucky to have one show on Broadway. Since the 1996 premiere Off-Broadway of his first musical, *Floyd Collins*, Rodgers's own grandson, Adam Guettel, has had only one show in concert and one tryout out of town. Stephen Flaherty and Lynn Ahrens, writers of *Ragtime*, a score some consider the best of recent times, have had only five shows produced in ten years. These are talented people, but the simple economics of the modern theatre doesn't afford them the opportunities to hone and develop their craft. There's too much money on the line: too few creative, artistic producers with smarts to go along with their checkbooks; cutbacks in the budgets of regional theatres…. The excuses are legion. But it's the art and audiences that suffer.

Rodgers and Hart were lucky enough to get their start in college—and what schools today produce original shows? Afterward, Lew Fields took a chance and gave them their Broadway debuts. And Broadway supported them.

Although they were by now Broadway veterans, they retained their youthful spirit. Though their words and music were often smart and sophisticated, they could still entertain a few somewhat sophomoric ideas. This playful quality was matched by Rodgers and Hart's interests in exploring the new. Their songs leavened their sophistication and dexterous craft with charm and humor.

On Your Toes is a particularly felicitous merging of book and song, perhaps due to the fact that Rodgers and Hart (along with George Abbott) also contributed the libretto. Both songwriters were concerned about the problems inherent in musical comedies where song and plot often coexist on seemingly different planes. They wanted to write integrated scores. It would have been too easy and too boring to write the typical silly mish-mash that defined most musical comedies, so to keep themselves from getting bored, they tried to improve their craft with each show. These shows reflect the joy they felt in the writing process. While Rodgers was often exasperated by Hart's inconsistencies of character, he never questioned his partner's abilities. In fact, it bothered him that Hart didn't have to work as hard to achieve great effects.

Rodgers and Hart's constant striving toward perfection was a double-edged sword, though. At first hearing, their shows were cheered for the artistry of the songs, story, and staging. But as they moved on, trying to outdo themselves with each project, the older shows seemed dated and old-fashioned. And why? Because Rodgers and Hart themselves had educated audiences to accept better and better theatrical offerings. In only one case did they slip up, *Pal Joey*. Here was a show that was a great leap ahead of its predecessors, with its cynical sophistication and the ingenuous antihero at its core. But by the time *Pal Joey* was revived, audiences had caught up and the revival was a great success. The show hadn't changed but the audiences had.

On Your Toes was a precursor to *Pal Joey*, even if not in spirit. It was another step in the remarkable evolution of two great artists of the American theatre who had started their careers at college and had found people who believed in their talents and supported their dreams. ✽

RIGHT: In the 1983 revival, George S. Irving suggests possible cosmetic surgery to Dina Merrill.

FAR RIGHT: Musical comedy used to be populated with truly unique characters; one wonders if such quirkies as Ed Wynn, Carol Channing, or Barbara Harris could ever make a mark today. Here, three one-of-a-kinds: Luella Gear, Ray Bolger, and Monty Woolley.

Ray Bolger

Ray Bolger, eccentric dancer extraordinaire, trained his rubber legs on the vaudeville stage. With the exception of *Heads Up!*, a 1929 Rodgers and Hart show, his career prior to *On Your Toes* was solely in revues, including *Life Begins at 8:40*, where he starred alongside future *Wizard of Oz* cohort Bert Lahr. With *On Your Toes* and his third Rodgers and Hart show, *By Jupiter* in 1942, he rose from sidekick roles to become a first-rank, quirky leading man. His delivery of the soft shoe "Once in Love with Amy" in *Where's Charley* was the stuff Broadway legends are made of, every evening leading the audience in a sing-along, through encore after encore. After turning down the role of Harold Hill in *The Music Man*, his choice for a return, *All American*, was a miscalculation. He also found that during his absence from Broadway in the 1950s, audiences had become more sophisticated with the rise of the Rodgers and Hammerstein style of musical play, and his style of performing, down front and playing out, even breaking the fourth wall, had been replaced by a more naturalistic approach. The reception of his final show, *Come Summer*, so soured him on the theatre that he never returned.

LEFT: *Wizard of Oz* reunion? No, it's a scene from Bolger's last musical—the ill-fated *Come Summer*—in which he costarred with Margaret Hamilton.

BELOW: Bolger in a pose from Rodgers and Hart's last musical, *By Jupiter*.

SONGS

ACT I "Two a Day for Keith" · "The Three B's" · "It's Got to Be Love" · "Too Good for the Average Man" · "There's a Small Hotel" · "The Heart Is Quicker Than the Eye" "La Princesse Zenobia" Ballet
ACT II "Quiet Night" · "Glad to Be Unhappy" · "On Your Toes" · "Slaughter on Tenth Avenue" Ballet

George Balanchine

Choreographic genius George Balanchine brought a new, higher level of dance artistry to the musical theatre. His "Princess Zenobia" and "Slaughter on Tenth Avenue" ballets for *On Your Toes* raised the bar (and the barre) of dance on Broadway from the usual kick line of chorus girls, paving the way for subsequent legends Jerome Robbins and Agnes de Mille. His brilliant work graced such productions as *Babes in Arms*, *I Married an Angel*, *The Boys from Syracuse*, *Song of Norway*, and *Where's Charley*. After the flop *Courtin' Time* in 1951, and being replaced by Herbert Ross on *House of Flowers* (1954), he left the Broadway scene to focus solely on ballet. He built the New York City Ballet into the world-class company it remains today, returning only to oversee the re-creation of his ballets for the two Broadway revivals of *On Your Toes*.

ABOVE LEFT: Balanchine, muse (and sometimes wife) Vera Zorina, and Lorenz Hart in 1937.
ABOVE: Tamara Geva and Ray Bolger in George Balanchine's "Slaughter on Tenth Avenue."
LEFT: Prima ballerina Natalia Makarova (with Lara Teeter) was surprisingly hilarious in the 1983 revival, and "Slaughter" proved still fresh and inventive forty-seven years after the original production.
BELOW: Phillip Arthur Ross, Betty Ann Grove, and Eugene J. Anthony as the dancing Dolan family hoofing "Two a Day for Keith."

Backstage

This was the first musical comedy credit for choreographer George Balanchine. The show also marked the acting debut of Monty Woolley. Rodgers and Hart originally wrote the show for Fred Astaire to perform in the movies, but Astaire turned them down.

ONE TOUCH OF VENUS

OPENED OCTOBER 7, 1943; IMPERIAL THEATRE; 567 PERFORMANCES

In the "Forty Minutes for Lunch" ballet, Venus (Mary Martin) hits the streets of the Big Apple and meets Sono Osato (in purple). Miss Martin's gown is by Mainbocher.

ONE TOUCH OF VENUS

Produced by Cheryl Crawford
Associate Producer: John Wildberg

Music by Kurt Weill
Book by S. J. Perelman and Ogden Nash
Lyrics by Ogden Nash
Suggested by *The Tinted Venus* by F. Anstey
Music orchestrated by Kurt Weill
Music arranged by Kurt Weill
Musical Director: Maurice Abravanel

Staged by Elia Kazan
Musical Staging by Agnes de Mille

Scenic Design by Howard Bay
Costume Design by
Paul Du Pont and Kermit Love
Miss Martin's gowns by Mainbocher

Synopsis

Barber Rodney Hatch is about to be engaged to Gloria when he visits the Whitelaw Savory Foundation of Modern Art and finds himself drawn to a marble statue of Venus. On an unexplainable whim, Rodney slips Gloria's engagement ring onto the statue's finger and, to his bewilderment, the statue comes to life. Rodney retreats to his apartment, but Venus, in love with Rodney for giving her life (and wanting to explore her carnal desires), follows him. Gloria asks Rodney for the ring and is surprised to hear that a statue is wearing it and won't return it. Venus wants Gloria out of the picture and sends her to the North Pole. The police arrive, arresting Rodney for stealing the statue, also charging him and Venus with killing Gloria. Venus arranges for their escape to a nearby hotel. Rodney dreams about life with his beloved goddess in the suburbs of Long Island. He awakens to find Venus gone, summoned by a messenger of the gods and returned to her marble form. The spell on Gloria is broken, and she returns from her frigid trip north understandably angry with Rodney. Alone, Rodney returns to the museum and looks at the statue with a new admiration. His reverie is interrupted by a young girl who looks amazingly like Venus. She asks Rodney for directions, and they go off together.

Cast

Whitelaw Savory	*John Boles*
Molly Grant	*Paula Laurence*
Taxi Black	*Teddy Hart*
Rodney Hatch	*Kenny Baker*
Venus	*Mary Martin*
Gloria Kramer	*Ruth Bond*
Premier Danseuse	*Sono Osato*

"To hell with posterity. I want to hear my music now, while I'm alive."

— *Kurt Weill*

I N 1943, PRODUCER CHERYL CRAWFORD had just enjoyed a success with the transfer of her production of *Porgy and Bess* to Broadway from her Maplewood, New Jersey, summer-stock theatre. She followed it up with *One Touch of Venus*, but the road to *Venus* wasn't nearly as smooth.

Costumer Irene Sharaff brought Kurt Weill the novel *The Tinted Venus* by F. Anstey (Thomas Anstey Guthrie). She suggested that the novel would make a fine musical, with Weill in turn bringing Crawford aboard. As Crawford wrote in her autobiography, "It could involve the world as we see it and as the goddess sees it and allow us to compare the two views, which would of course be quite different. I thought it could have social bearing and also be amusing." And that is as apt a description of Weill's choice of material throughout his career as has ever been stated.

Crawford obtained the rights to the novel and, after turndowns by both Ira Gershwin for the lyrics and Arthur Kober for the libretto, hired poet Ogden Nash to provide the lyrics and Bella Spewack to provide the libretto. Crawford and Weill had Marlene Dietrich in mind to play the title role. Weill and Crawford traveled to Hollywood, where he played a few songs for the star and they explained the concept of the script. As Crawford described their meeting with Dietrich, "We would talk about the show for a while, then Marlene would take up the musical saw and begin to play. That, we soon found out, was the cue that talk was finished for the evening."

On a trip to New York, Dietrich visited the Metropolitan Museum of Art and draped herself in yards of gray chiffon approximating various poses for Venus. She even sang an audition at the 46th Street Theatre, but wavered when it came to formally committing to the project. An incredibly shrewd businesswoman, Crawford took advantage of Dietrich's migraine headache one day and got her to sign a contract. Now, armed with a star, all that remained was to actually write and produce the piece.

When Spewack appeared stuck on the script, Crawford replaced her with humorist S. J. Perelman. His revision was a lot racier, and, when their star read it, Dietrich bowed out, explaining to Weill, "I have a daughter who is nineteen years old, and for me to get up on the stage and exhibit my legs is now impossible."

After turndowns by several Europeans, the writers and producer turned to all-American Mary Martin. After hearing some of the score, especially the tune "That's Him," Martin visited the Museum of Modern Art to see how artists had interpreted the character of Venus. Martin's husband, Richard Halliday, contacted the renowned designer Mainbocher and asked him to supply Martin's costumes, but the couturier was undecided and asked to hear some of the songs. Halliday, Martin, Mainbocher, and Crawford all assembled in Weill's apartment, where he again played "That's Him." While he was playing the song, Martin drew a chair over to the designer and sang along with the composer. When the song was finished, Mainbocher agreed to design the show, and provided a charming bit of blocking in the process. He told Martin, "Promise me you'll always sing this song that way: take a chair down to the footlights, sing across the orchestra to the audience as if it were just one person." And that's exactly how the song was staged.

Martin accepted the role, balking at only one of Perelman's typically risqué lines, "Love is not the moaning of distant violins—it's the triumphant twang of a bedspring," but after reciting it onstage and receiving a huge laugh, she acquiesced without further complaint. In Boston, the show concluded with the "Venus in Ozone Heights" ballet, climaxing with Venus's return to her original form: a statue. When both audiences and the creative team voiced their unhappiness with this ending, choreographer Agnes de Mille suggested that another scene be written, in which Rodney returns to the museum to look once more at the statue, wondering why she has returned to stone. Just then, a young girl enters looking for an art class. She is the image of Venus, only "her clothes are simple and she has an attractive awkward grace; she might be Venus's country cousin." She tells Rodney that she is from Ozone Heights and can't think of living anywhere else. And the two exit to the strains of "Speak Low."

Oscar Hammerstein was quite taken with that image of Mary Martin. As she wrote in her autobiography, "He wanted to write a part for the innocent, eager little girl in the white-pique blouse, pink polka-dot skirt, and matching rolled-brim hat. He wrote it, too—Nellie Forbush in *South Pacific* was a descendant of Venus." ✺

Some claim that Broadway musicals either deify or demonize women. In this number from *One Touch of Venus*, the local membership of the Misogynist He-Man Woman-Haters club (Kenny Baker, John Boles, Harry Clark, and Teddy Hart), enumerate "The Trouble with Women."

Kurt Weill

The first half of Kurt Weill's career took place in Germany, in an especially fruitful collaboration with Bertolt Brecht on a series of agitprop entertainments satirizing and lambasting German politics and society. With the rise of the Third Reich, Weill fled, first to France and then to Britain, finally ending up in America. Weill continued to explore intellectual themes in his musical theatre work, mainly with playwrights and poets as his lyricists. Critics called him chameleon-like in his ability to reflect the styles of his adopted homelands in his work, but they failed to recognize that even in his Weimar Republic days, he had flirted with Tin Pan Alley–inspired themes. True, the sardonic qualities of his early work were toned down and his music became more lyrical, but at the core they were every bit as cutting as in his German works. *The Threepenny Opera*, his best-known work, was a failure in its first American incarnation, only to find wide acceptance with Marc Blitzstein's English words in a 1954 historic revival Off Broadway. His first Broadway show, *Johnny Johnson*, found his dissonance and attacking rhythms intact. He voiced his interest in society and its injustices in the musical/opera *Street Scene* and in his last work, *Lost in the Stars*, while he tackled political issues in *The Firebrand of Florence* and *Knickerbocker Holiday*, which boasted his first American hit song, "September Song." Although Kurt Weill was a gentleman in the true sense of the word, he was quick to use his talents to voice his political and social ideas.

The "Punch and Judy Get a Divorce" scene from the Kurt Weill concept musical *Love Life*.

RIGHT: When Venus's doppelganger (guess who?) walks into the art museum at the end of the show, she starts to tell Kenny Baker her name. "You don't have to tell me. I know," he replies, and the curtain comes down. Miss Martin's simple, country-bumpkin frock by Mainbocher.

BELOW RIGHT: In *Lute Song*, Occidental tourist Mary Martin shared the stage with that musical comedy genius Nancy Davis (Reagan). Miss Martin's gown by Valentina.

BELOW: *I Do, I Do* featured a cast small in number but enormous in star wattage. Miss Martin's nightgown by Sears-Roebuck.

Mary Martin

Mary Martin, a truly beloved Broadway star, basked in the glow of her audiences' adoration for almost forty years. She was never as socko a singer nor as powerhouse a clown as Ethel Merman, her contemporary and only true rival for the title of Broadway musical demi-goddess; nevertheless, she had it all over Merman in versatility, easily jumping among roles—here a nun, there an ageless boy, now a Roman goddess, later an Army nurse. No matter what she played, she always, always imbued her performances with her own, ineffable brand of charm and coy, Texas-bred humility, as if each audience of twelve hundred people had sprung a surprise birthday party on her eight times a week and she just happened to have a show to perform for them. Although she's best remembered for her family-friendly roles and her all-American, fresh-scrubbed goodness, she began her career as a sly sexpot. After her overnight, star-making performance of "My Heart Belongs to Daddy" in the 1938 Cole Porter show *Leave It to Me*, she took on her first leading-lady role in *One Touch of Venus*. Martin turned down her share of plum roles (in *Oklahoma!*, *Kiss Me, Kate*, *My Fair Lady*, *Funny Girl*, and *Mame*) and had her share of flops (*Dancing in the Streets*, Noel Coward's *Pacific 1860* in London, and *Jennie*); but oh, the winners she chose: Nellie Forbush, Peter Pan, and Maria von Trapp, any one of them enough to assure her place as an all-time great.

Backstage
After Dietrich balked, Crawford approached Ilona Massey, ballerina Vera Zorina, Gertrude Lawrence, and Lenora Corbett to play Venus. All turned the part down.

SONGS

ACT I "New Art Is True Art" · "One Touch of Venus" · "How Much I Love You" · "I'm a Stranger Here Myself" · "Forty Minutes for Lunch" Ballet · "West Wind" · "Way Out West in Jersey" · "Foolish Heart" · "The Trouble with Women" "Speak Low" · "Dr. Crippen"
ACT II "Very, Very, Very" · "Catch Hatch" · "That's Him" "Wooden Wedding" · "Venus in Ozone Heights" Ballet

POSTERS

The theatre is an ephemeral art form, which is its blessing and its curse. Once a show passes into memory, little that is tangible remains, excepting programs, photos, cast recordings, an occasional video, and posters. Of these, the poster is the most decorative, but for years the poster was looked at simply as a utilitarian object without collectible value, and thousands were printed, distributed, and discarded. Only a few individuals had the forethought to collect them when their value was considered infinitesimal.

Since theatre needs an audience, broadsides were an inevitable part of the strategy to put people into seats, with early playbills also serving as posters. With the advent of the lithograph in the early 19th century, posters and playbills enjoyed greater variety, genuine fine artists began illustrating them, and printing techniques became more sophisticated. Probably the best American printing house was the Strobridge Lithographing Company of Cincinnati, which printed thousands of posters for theatrical shows and circuses in addition to its other graphic products.

Strobridge's dominance of poster art was waning by the early 1920s, and the Artcraft Lithograph and Printing Company, founded in 1922, became the premier theatre poster printer in America. Until then, posters were printed on whatever size of paper stock the artist and producer requested, but Artcraft began standardizing the poster's size to fourteen by twenty-two inches, the size of a Broadway window card to this day. Sizes of larger posters were also regularized, and the Shubert Alley–sized poster became known as a "three-sheet" because it was three times as tall as the "one-sheet" lobby card.

Among the recent poster designers whose work is highly prized by collectors are Berta (*Mame, La Cage aux Folles, How Now, Dow Jones*), Byrd (*Follies, Godspell, The Grand Tour*), Eula (*The Act, Timbuktu*), Fay Gage (*Dear World, 1776, All American*), Gilbert Lesser (*Rex, Equus, The Elephant Man*), Oscar Liebman (*Canterbury Tales, What Makes Sammy Run?*), Frederick Marvin (*70, Girls, 70, Look to the Lilies*), James McMullen (All the shows at the Lincoln Center Theatre Company, *I Remember Mama*), Morrow (*Fiddler on the Roof, Candide, Wildcat*), Mozelle (*The Gay Life*), Nicholas (*On the Twentieth Century*), Clyde Smith (*Applause*), Gil Spear (*Caesar and Cleopatra*), and Stubbs (*Flower Drum Song*).

Sometimes, the set designers of a show also come up with the poster, as did Raoul Pène Du Bois for *Doctor Jazz* (1975), Lee Simonson for *Porgy* (1927) and *Strange Interlude* (1928), Vertés for *Seventh Heaven* (1955), and Tony Walton for *Pippin* (1972) and *Chicago* (1975). Famous illustrators include Peter Arno (*The Pajama Game*), Saul Bass (*Golden Boy*), Whitney Darrow, Jr. (*Something More*), Mort Drucker (*Bob and Ray: The Two and Only*), Don Freeman (*A Streetcar Named Desire, The Skin of Our Teeth*), Al Hirschfeld (*My Fair Lady, Man of La Mancha, Fade Out—Fade In*), Hoff (*Borscht Capades*), Hilary Knight (*Half a Sixpence, Come Summer, Meet Me in St. Louis, Irene, No, No, Nanette*), and Leroy Nieman (*Busker Alley*).

No matter the artist, theatre posters all share basic elements: the name of the producer, title of the show, and name of the theatre. But as the decades have passed, more and more names have been added, to the detriment of the artwork; in fact, many modern posters have no logo, consisting only of type. The exception to this rule is the British show poster, especially those designed by DeWynters: *Cats, Miss Saigon, Phantom of the Opera*. Of course, no poster can convince anyone to run out and see a show, but they are secondary forms of advertising, acting as a reminder to the theatergoer that the show is still playing. Older posters, apart from their beauty as art, remind us of great nights in the theatre, favorite stars and shows, and the romance of it all.

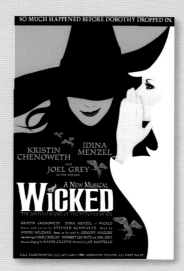

THE PAJAMA GAME

OPENED MAY 13, 1954; ST. JAMES THEATRE; 1,063 PERFORMANCES

Janis Paige, John Raitt, and the rest of the gang have a "Once a Year Day" at the Union picnic.

THE PAJAMA GAME

Produced by Frederick Brisson,
Robert E. Griffith and Harold S. Prince

Music and Lyrics by
Richard Adler and Jerry Ross
Book by George Abbott and Richard Bissell
Based on the novel *7½ Cents*
by Richard Bissell
Musical Director: Hal Hastings
Music orchestrated by Don Walker
Dance arrangements by Roger Adams

Directed by George Abbott and Jerome Robbins
Choreographed by Bob Fosse

Scenic Design by Lemuel Ayers
Costume Design by Lemuel Ayers

Synopsis

Babe Williams is a member of the Grievance Committee of the Local Union at the Sleep Tite pajama factory. The union wants a 7½-cent raise but Mr. Hassler, the owner of the factory, won't budge. Sid Sorokin, the new foreman, and Babe quickly fall in love. Can management and labor work and love together despite their differences? That is the question answered by curtain's fall.

Cast

Hines	*Eddie Foy*
Prez	*Stanley Prager*
Hasler	*Ralph Dunn*
Gladys	*Carol Haney*
Sid Sorokin	*John Raitt*
Mabel	*Reta Shaw*
Second Helper	*Buzz Miller*
Babe Williams	*Janis Paige*
Mae	*Thelma Pelish*
Brenda	*Marion Colby*
Salesman	*Jack Waldron*
Worker	*Peter Gennaro*

"Isn't it a wonder? Isn't it a limitless wonder?"

– Harold Prince the day after the opening of The Pajama Game, *seeing a long line at the box office when only a day before they had sold just enough tickets to run one week*

*T*he Pajama Game IS ONE of the most influential and innovative musicals ever. That might seem like an odd statement, but changes in the arts are often undertaken in small steps. The shows that introduce the bravest new ideas are often those that mask them with entertainment, never letting on that another barrier has fallen. In *The Pajama Game*, one of these revolutions happened in a small, simple moment. After the song "Small Talk," when the heroine, Babe, cooks a midnight snack for the hero, Sid, she takes off her dress so as not to spatter it with grease. She's left wearing only a slip. In that moment, audiences saw for the first time in a musical that two unmarried characters were going to spend the night together. No big deal was made of it, and audiences didn't make an uproar, even though this was the chaste America of 1954. (Interesting to note: when the show was filmed, with great allegiance to its stage origins, Babe did not disrobe. But then, the movies have always been behind the times, at least when it came to intimations of sex and drugs and other Production Code breakers.)

Even the lyrics of such an innocent show as *The Pajama Game* came under scrutiny. When Mabel tests Heinsie's jealousy quotient in the song "I'll Never Be Jealous Again," she asks him would he be jealous if he unexpectedly dropped in on his girlfriend, Gladys, and found her looking guilty with the window open and there in front of him, "a shirt and a tie and a pair of pants in a nice, neat little pile." That's what Broadway audiences heard, anyway, for Hollywood insisted on the sanitized lyric, "a hat and a tie and a pair of socks in a nice, neat little pile," as if movie audiences didn't get the point anyway.

Perhaps the relative boldness came from the fact that most of the creators of *The Pajama Game* had limited or no Broadway experience, and not much was expected of their efforts. Producers Robert E. Griffith, Harold Prince, and Frederick Brisson had never before produced a Broadway show; the script was co-librettist Richard Bissell's first, based on his novel, *7 ½ Cents*. The songwriting team of Richard Adler and Jerry Ross provided their first ever score for a book show, and Bob Fosse made his choreographic debut with *The Pajama Game*. This is reminiscent of another sleeper almost a decade later.

Bye Bye Birdie, where the producer, librettist, and songwriting team had never been involved with a Broadway musical. Twenty years after that, *Urinetown*'s creators were also Broadway neophytes, as were the writers of the recent Tony Award-winner *Avenue Q*.

The only true veteran on *The Pajama Game* was Broadway legend George Abbott, who co-produced, co-wrote, and co-directed. Much of the credit must also go to the wonderful cast, including the beautiful, intelligent, and sometimes pitch-challenged Janis Paige, and the handsome, manly, John Raitt, he of the greatest male voice in modern Broadway history. With the superb dancer Carol Haney making her Broadway debut, and Broadway veterans Eddie Foy, Jr. and Reta Shaw, the show was teeming with talent.

In typical Abbott fashion, the piece moved fast and contained a lot of sweet and gentle moments, juxtaposed with awfully adult feelings. Sex ran rampant through the entire show, as frisky couples pursued each other around the factory, at the company picnic, and in Hernando's Hideaway, with the union plot simply a front for the multi-couple examination of love in all its incarnations. While early operettas went to pains to be set in exotic lands, *The Pajama Game* took place in the most prosaic of settings, the Sleep Tite pajama factory. (Actually, the location was probably just as foreign to most Broadwayites as the operetta locale Ruritania.)

The Pajama Game is notable for a few other reasons. First, a mere six months after the show closed, it was revived by New York's City Center, already having achieved classic status. Second, while *The Pajama Game* didn't have a sequel, it had something unique: a play with music written about its creation. The show was *Say, Darling*, and Richard Bissell, who wrote the roman a clef novel of the same name, also co-authored the libretto. In that show, David Wayne played Bissell, Robert Morse gained stardom as a lightly disguised Harold Prince, and Jerome Cowan stood in for the real-life George

Buzz Miller, Carol Haney, and Peter Gennaro in the number that defined the Fosse style, "Steam Heat."

Carol Haney

The quirky comic dancer Carol Haney began her career in California, first as a pupil of Jack Cole, then assisting Gene Kelly on MGM musicals such as *On the Town* and *Singin' in the Rain* (where she dubbed Kelly's taps in the legendary title song). Also partnering Bob Fosse in the movie of *Kiss Me, Kate*, dancing the first steps that Fosse choreographed on film, she was chosen by Fosse for the star-making role of Gladys in *The Pajama Game*, stopping the show with "Her Is," "Hernando's Hideaway," and "Steam Heat," one of the seminal Fosse dances. She saw her chance for Hollywood stardom go down the drain when, while she was injured and out of the show, producer Hal Wallis spotted her understudy, a chorus girl named Shirley MacLaine, and gave her the movie contract that well may have gone to Haney. After the out-of-town closing of *The Ziegfeld Follies* starring Talulah Bankhead, Haney never again appeared on Broadway, segueing into a career as a choreographer, creating the charming dances for *Flower Drum Song* (directed by Hollywood friend Gene Kelly and costarring husband Larry Blyden), *Bravo Giovanni*, the wittily staged romantic atmosphere of *She Loves Me*, and *Funny Girl*, where her big set piece, the "Cornet Man" dance, was cut when Jerome Robbins took over the directorial reins. She suffered from paralyzing stage fright, ruining several chances to play leads in Broadway shows by sabotaging herself in auditions. Her personal demons, magnified by severe diabetes and other health problems, cut her life tragically short at the age of thirty-nine.

ABOVE: Carol Haney and Stanley Prager in "Her Is."
LEFT: Reta Shaw promises a nervous Eddie Foy, Jr., "I'll Never Be Jealous Again."
RIGHT: Haney in the out-of-town closer *Ziegfeld Follies of 1956* (starring Talulah Bankhead).

Abbott. Johnny Desmond had a harder role, as songwriters Adler and Ross all rolled into one. Third, George Abbott announced a racially integrated Broadway revival in 1969 that would star Nipsy Russell, Gerri Granger, and Paula Kelley, but that production would have to wait until 1973, with Hal Linden, Barbara McNair, and Cab Calloway heading the cast. A funny, witty, adult musical comedy with one of the theatre's most unprepossessing, tuneful scores, *The Pajama Game* is a warmhearted, smart show that deserves a first-class revival on Broadway. ❋

Richard Adler and Jerry Ross

With only two hit shows, the songwriting team of Richard Adler and Jerry Ross was one of the most successful yet shortest-lived in Broadway history. A rarity in that both men wrote words and music, they contributed several songs for *John Murray Anderson's Almanac*, after which they were given a golden opportunity, considering their unproven track record. With turndowns from other songwriters, Adler and Ross were tapped to write the score for the smash *The Pajama Game*, reteaming with many of the creators the following season on another hit, *Damn Yankees*. After Ross's death from leukemia in 1955, Adler was never able to approach his previous success. He wrote a television musical version of *Little Women*, followed by the quick flop (with a sometimes fine score) *Kwamina*, starring then-wife Sally Ann Howes. Next was a true disaster: *A Mother's Kisses*, starring Bea Arthur, which closed out of town in 1968. The unfortunate *Music Is*, Adler's last show for Broadway and one of many musicalizations of Shakespeare's *Twelfth Night* (along with *Your Own, Thing, Love for Love*, and *Play On!*, among others), was smacked down by New York critics, despite a highly enjoyable score and a bright, energetic young cast featuring such rising talents as Catherine Cox and Joel Higgins.

SONGS

ACT I "The Pajama Game" · "Racing With the Clock" · "A New Town Is a Blue Town" · "I'm Not at All in Love" · "I'll Never Be Jealous Again" · "Hey There" · "Her Is" · "Sleep-Tite" · "Once a Year Day" · "Small Talk" · "There Once Was a Man"

ACT II · · "Steam Heat" · "Think of the Time I Save" · "Hernando's Hideaway" · "Jealousy Ballet" · "7½ Cents"

Backstage

Rodgers and Hammerstein, Jule Styne, Frank Loesser, Burton Lane, Harold Rome, and Cole Porter all turned down the chance to write the songs for *The Pajama Game*.

Janis Paige refused to wear the costumes Lemuel Ayres designed for her. So, Rosalind Russell, wife of producer Frederick Brisson, piled everyone into a limo and they went shopping for Paige's outfits.

Sleep Tite was modeled after the H.B. Glover Co. of Dubuque, Iowa, where Richard Bissell's father had worked.

PAL JOEY

OPENED DECEMBER 25, 1940; ETHEL BARRYMORE THEATRE; 374 PERFORMANCES

ABOVE: June Havoc and Nelson Rae (center) tend "The Flower Garden of My Heart."

RIGHT: Original *Pal Joey* stars Vivienne Segal and Gene Kelly, in their little den of iniquity.

PAL JOEY

Produced by George Abbott

Music by Richard Rodgers
Lyrics by Lorenz Hart
Book by John O'Hara
based on his novel of the same name
Orchestra conductor: Harry Levant
Orchestrations by Hans Spialek

Directed by George Abbott
Dance direction by Robert Alton

Settings and lighting by Jo Mielziner
Costumes by John Koenig

Synopsis

Joey Evans is not too bright, but that's all right because he has self-assurance and sex appeal to spare. Joey works in a nightclub and there meets the wealthy, married Vera Simpson. She's interested in his animal magnetism and he's drawn to her pocket book. Vera sets Joey up in a classy apartment and even buys him his own dream nightclub, Chez Joey. Still, Joey mistreats her, which only makes her fall more deeply in love with him. When Vera learns of a plan to blackmail her she calls the police on the hoods and realizes that slumming in Joey's world isn't quite the aphrodisiac it once seemed. She leaves Joey back where he began, down and out and looking for the main chance.

Cast

Joey Evans........................... *Gene Kelly*
Gladys................................. *June Havoc*
Linda English .... *Leila Ernst*
Albert Doane....................... *Stanley Donen*
Vera Simpson .... *Vivienne Segal*
Melba Snyder...................... *Jean Castro*
Ludlow Lowell .... *Jack Durant*

THE ORIGINAL PRODUCTION OF *Pal Joey* met with, shall we generously say, mixed reviews. Many were shocked at such a charming, charismatic, sexy antihero as lead of a musical. The usual song and dance show for the tired businessman it certainly wasn't. It was only with the revival that *Pal Joey* achieved its great fame and success. That revival was spurred by the success of a studio cast recording of the score by Columbia Records under the leadership of Goddard Lieberson, with Harold Lang playing Joey and Vivienne Segal reprising her original role of Vera. When Jule Styne decided to produce a revival based on the great reception of the recording, he cast Lang and Segal.

Revivals have always been a staple of the American theatre, though never as much as in recent times. The most revived show in Broadway history is the Shubert Brothers's production of *Blossom Time*, playing Broadway a minimum of six times. The exact number is unknown since the Shuberts would put the show on for one or two performances then yank it out and put it on the road advertised as "direct from Broadway."

It wasn't always so on Broadway. In fact, once upon a time when the musical was alive and kicking, revivals were the rarity rather than the mainstay of the theatrical season.

The first successful revival was Victor Herbert's *The Red Mill* in 1945. There were a few revivals in the early '50s—*Pal Joey* in 1952 and 1954's *On Your Toes*, but, aside from a brief Broadway transfer of the Lincoln Center production of *Annie Get Your Gun*, there were no more Broadway revivals of note until *The Boy Friend* in 1970. (One reason was a spate of Off-Broadway revivals including *Leave It to Jane*, *Anything Goes*, and *Best Foot Forward*).

There was, however, producer Jean Dalrymple's fabulously successful series of musicals at City Center. When a show closed on Broadway, Ms. Dalrymple would take possession of the scenery and kept it in storage until the time was right for a revival at the former Masonic Temple. In the 1960s, Richard Rodgers headed up the Music Theatre of Lincoln Center which performed at the astoundingly unsatisfactory New York State Theatre.

With the unexpected success of producer Harry Rigby's nostalgic production of *No, No, Nanette* in 1971, Broadway went revival crazy. Rigby tapped the market again with Debbie Reynolds in *Irene*, opening the cavernous Minskoff Theatre in 1973. Rigby's tribute to the olden age of American musicals came to a crashing halt with the revival of *Good News* starring Alice Faye.

As the flow of original musicals slowed to a crawl, the revival offered pre-tested product. Just recast, slap it up with road-show-quality sets, a star of television, and on with the show! Only it wasn't that easy. A spate of terrible musical revivals hit Broadway in the '70s. An all-Black *Guys and Dolls* starring Robert Guillaume wasn't a bad idea, but it didn't equal the success of the similarly cast *Hello, Dolly! Kismet* made its way back to Broadway renamed *Timbuktu!* Other revivals of note were *Oklahoma!* and *Peter Pan*, the latter with Sandy Duncan.

The '80s found a terrific revival of *On Your Toes* directed by George Abbott but few others of interest.

In the '90s the Dodgers produced a series of revivals that included *Guys and Dolls, A Funny Thing Happened on the Way to the Forum, Once Upon a Mattress* (1997), starring a vocally undercast Sarah Jessica Parker, and *How to Succeed* starring her husband, Matthew Broderick. Other revivals of the '90s included *Fiddler on the Roof, Man of La Mancha, Damn Yankees, My Fair Lady, Carousel, Grease, Show Boat, The King and I, Candide, 1776, The Sound of Music, On the Town, You're a Good Man Charlie Brown, Annie Get Your Gun, She Loves Me*, and *Kiss Me, Kate*.

The most successful revivals of all time took place in the '90s (and into the next century). They were *Cabaret*, based on a British staging at the Donmar Warehouse, and *Chicago*, a transfer of the City Center Encores concert staging, both of which ran longer than the original productions.

So far this century we've seen *Follies, 42nd Street, The Music Man, Bells Are Ringing, Gypsy, Man of La Mancha, Jesus Christ Superstar, Little Shop of Horrors, Flower Drum Song, Fiddler on the Roof*, and *Oklahoma!* With the exception of *42nd Street*, which equaled the original at least in terms of its physical production and its energy, they were all pale imitations or unfortunate rethinkings of the originals.

Strangely, there has only been one other revival of *Pal Joey*, at Circle in the Square in 1976, starring Christopher Chadman and Joan Copeland. Perhaps the failure of that revival has made producers shy away from further attempts to bring the show into New York. The Rodgers and Hammerstein Organization has commissioned several new libretti but none has equaled the original. In this era when revivals explore the darker elements of musicals like *Chicago* and *Cabaret*, it seems odd that *Pal Joey* isn't tops on any producer's list. ❁

SONGS

ACT 1 "You Mustn't Kick It Around" · "I Could Write a Book" · "Chicago" · "That Terrific Rainbow" · "What Is a Man?" · "Happy Hunting Horn" · "Bewitched, Bothered and Bewildered" · "Joey Looks into the Future" (Ballet)
ACT II · "The Flower Garden of My Heart" · "Zip" · "Plant You Now, Dig You Later" · "In Our Little Den (of Iniquity)" "Do It the Hard Way" · "Take Him"

Backstage

Gene Kelly left Broadway for Hollywood after *Pal Joey*. He only returned to direct Rodgers and Hammerstein's *Flower Drum Song*.

The original *Pal Joey's* songs didn't achieve standard status because of a ban on their radio play by ASCAP. Once the ban was lifted, in the late 1940s, the songs came into their own.

TOP: Triple threats Helen Gallagher (on her way to her first Tony Award) and Harold Lang, in the 1952 revival of *Pal Joey*.

ABOVE: Gene Kelly, on his way to Hollywood stardom.

Jo Mielziner

Jo Mielziner, the most successful set designer of the Golden era of Broadway, worked equally on musicals and straight plays. With his beautiful, atmospheric drops, mammoth set pieces and use of imagination, color, and startling shifts of perspective, Mielziner boasted a resume that reads like a history of the Broadway musical: *Gay Divorce*, *Jubilee*, *On Your Toes*, *I Married an Angel*, *Knickerbocker Holiday*, *Boys From Syracuse*, *Stars in Your Eyes*, *Too Many Girls*, *Pal Joey*, *Best Foot Forward*, *By Jupiter*, *Carousel*, *Annie Get Your Gun*, *Street Scene*, *Finian's Rainbow*, *Allegro*, *South Pacific*, *Guys and Dolls*, *The King and I*, *A Tree Grows in Brooklyn*, *Top Banana*, *Can-Can*, *Wish You Were Here* (for which he designed Broadway's first functional swimming pool), *Me and Juliet*, *By the Beautiful Sea*, *Fanny*, *Silk Stockings*, *Most Happy Fella*, *Happy Hunting*, *Oh, Captain*, *Gypsy*, *Mr. President*, and *1776*.

TOP: Gene Kelly and company, in a shot that shows the scope of Jo Mielziner's stunning scenic design.

RIGHT: Quintessentially elegant, Vivienne Segal reprised the role of Vera Simpson in the 1952 revival, making the age difference between her and Joey even more marked.

June Havoc

June Havoc, one of only two people profiled in this book who is also represented as a character in one of the 101 Greatest Shows (the other being Florenz Ziegfeld, Jr.), began her career as a precocious moppet in vaudeville as "Baby" June Hovick, later portrayed (perhaps more than a little mythically) in the musical *Gypsy*. As she matured, Havoc became one of the rare and lucky child performers that segued into an equally successful adult career. With a career that spanned over six decades, she made a debut in the 1936 Sigmund Romberg flop *Forbidden Melody*. Finally gaining stardom after a quarter century in the business, she played Gladys Bumps, singing "That Terrific Rainbow" and "The Flower Garden of My Heart" in the original production of *Pal Joey*, followed by leading lady roles in *Mexican Hayride* and *Sadie Thompson*. A great beauty and an extremely versatile performer, perhaps her graduation from the school of hard knocks left her without the vulnerability of a Mary Martin, but she had great wit and fierce intelligence, which led to a wide-ranging and productive journey. She became a playwright, author, director, and producer, returning to Broadway as a replacement Miss Hannigan in *Annie*, and Mrs. Lovett in the bus and truck tour of *Sweeney Todd*.

ABOVE: June Havoc played the title role in *Sadie Thompson*, the show that Ethel Merman quit during rehearsals.
RIGHT: "Hello, everybody! My name's June! What's...yours?"
BELOW: Harold Lang and Vivienne Segal (center) in the 1952 version of the "Joey Looks into the Future" ballet.

PETER PAN

OPENED OCTOBER 20, 1954; WINTER GARDEN THEATRE; 152 PERFORMANCES

ABOVE: Mary Martin flies the friendly skies with Kathy Nolan, Joseph Stafford, and Robert Harrington, the darling Darling children.

RIGHT: Sondra Lee and the rest of the tribe (note the sneakers) get ready to dine on an "Ugg-a Wugg-a-meatball."

PETER PAN

Produced by Richard Halliday
A production by Edwin Lester
Lyrics by Carolyn Leigh
Music by Moose Charlap
Based on the play by James M. Barrie
Additional music by Jule Styne
Additional lyrics by
Betty Comden and Adolph Green
Incidental music by
Elmer Bernstein and Trude Rittman
Music orchestrated by Albert Sendrey
Directed and Choreographed by
Jerome Robbins
Scenic Design by Peter Larkin
Costume Design by Motley
Lighting Design by Peggy Clark

Synopsis

The Darlings, a middle-class family in England, have three children, John, Wendy, and Michael, along with their nanny Nana (a dog). One evening, Peter Pan, the boy who wouldn't grow up, flies in the nursery window looking for his shadow and is discovered by the children. Along with his fairy friend Tinkerbell, he teaches them to fly and takes them to Neverland, where they meet up with a group of lost boys, a band of Indians, and Peter Pan's archenemy, Captain Hook and his gang of cutthroat pirates. Many exciting adventures ensue, and the children return home to their parents' loving arms (lost boys in tow).

Cast

Wendy/Jane	*Kathy Nolan*
John	*Robert Harrington*
Liza	*Heller Halliday*
Michael	*Joseph Stafford*
Nana/Crocodile	*Norman Shelley*
Mrs. Darling	*Margalo Gillmore*
Mr. Darling/Captain Hook	*Cyril Ritchard*
Peter Pan	*Mary Martin*
Smee	*Joe E. Marks*
Tiger Lily	*Sondra Lee*

A CURIOUS SUB-GENRE OF THE BROADWAY theatre is the children's musical. From the beginnings of the musical, fairy tales and legends were used as the basis for plots, and as early as 1881, New Yorkers were treated to "family entertainment" with *Cinderella at School*. The classic *Robin Hood*, with its standard "O Promise Me," entertained audiences for decades following its 1891 opening, and other shows based on fairy tale origins include *Aladdin, Jr.* (1895), *Jack and the Beanstalk, Mother Goose, Little Red Riding Hood, and Sleeping Beauty* and *the Beast*, all produced on Broadway around the turn of the century. One of the greatest of all fairy tale shows (although the plot was an original) is Victor Herbert and Glen MacDonough's classic, *Babes in Toyland*. The great success of that show led to a spate of fairy tale-based shows over the next decade.

All these shows share one thing in common: they were all written with adults in mind and the children who tagged along were an added bonus. In more modern times, shows like *Annie* and Doug Henning's *Merlin* were geared for the children's market. The recent *A Year with Frog and Toad*, from the Children's Theatre of Minneapolis, was especially conceived for children, although the adults who accompanied them were equally enchanted. The quality of the show didn't guarantee its success, however; with a top ticket

price nearly 100 dollars, families were understandably loath to drop nearly half a thousand dollars on an evening in the theatre for a family of four.

Today we're lucky to have the Disney musicals *The Lion King* and *Beauty and the Beast* bringing in thousands of new theatregoers. Exposing children to theatre at a young age and making it a habit is of the utmost importance if we are to cultivate new audiences. Everyone who enjoys the theatre remembers how enchanted they were at their first live performance, be it a puppet show, a school play, or even a Broadway musical. Of all modern art forms, theatre requires the most suspension of disbelief, and therefore, children, with boundless sense of wonder and imagination can be the most responsive to the magic of the theatre.

That, in a roundabout way, leads us to *Peter Pan*. J.M. Barrie's 1904 play has always been a staple of the English and American theatre. The first actress to play Peter (it was always played by actresses until a 1952 German production) was Nina Boucicault, sister of the great playwright Dion Boucicault (who served as director), while the most famous American Peter was Maude Adams. For many of us, though, there will only be one Peter Pan, and that is Mary Martin. Presented live on NBC for the first time in 1955, it soon became an annual event, with seven additional showing over the next decades. Surprisingly, the Mary Martin Peter Pan we all know came about because of an entirely different version.

An earlier adaptation was begun by Leonard Bernstein, starring Jean Arthur and Boris Karloff, with Jerome Robbins set to direct. When Bernstein left the project after supplying only five songs (writing lyrics as well as music), Robbins saw the piece becoming more play than musical and quit. After the Jean Arthur "play with songs" version closed, Robbins felt the time was right for the full-fledged musical he had envisioned all along. The songwriting team of Moose Charlap and Carolyn Leigh were hired to write the songs, with songwriters Nancy Hamilton and Morgan Lewis, and Tom Adair also contributing numbers (all of which were eventually cut).

When the show was beset by problems during its Los Angeles tryout, Robbins brought in Jule Styne, Betty Comden, and Adolph Green to supplement the Charlap/Leigh score. That seemed to do the trick, and *Peter Pan* came to the Winter Garden Theatre in excellent shape, with Martin and Cyril Ritchard, as a soignée, foppish Captain Hook, thoroughly enchanting all audiences. While the Broadway production only played 152 performances, it was never intended for an open-ended run, actually mounted as a launching pad for the television broadcast. The Jean Arthur version had been a huge hit only a few years earlier.

Subsequently, the piece has become a staple of the American theatre, with successful Broadway revivals featuring the remarkable Sandy Duncan, and later, Cathy Rigby (acquitting herself well as a singer, and an absolutely first-rank flier).

The story of *Peter Pan* is still a perennial favorite, 100 years after its first presentation. It lives on through countless theatrical productions around the world of both the straight play and musical version, bringing joy and happiness to children of all ages and making many lifelong devotees to the theatre. ❊

Cyril Ritchard

The witty, epicene comedian Cyril Ritchard will forever be known to an entire generation as the Captain Hook of their youth. Originally from Australia, he came to the States in 1925, appearing in several revues, before he moved to London to become a musical star, often alongside his wife Madge Elliott. He came back to the States after almost thirty years to direct the revue *John Murray Anderson's Almanac* in 1953, and was cast shortly thereafter in *Peter Pan* by Mary Martin herself, winning a Tony for his flamboyant yet sniveling portrayal. With many appearances on the early days of television (including a musical version of *Aladdin*, with Cole Porter's last score), he wore two hats in 1961 in the short-lived *The Happiest Girl in the World*, both directing and starring in a number of roles. Next co-starring with Anthony Newley in *The Roar of the Greasepaint, The Smell of the Crowd*, Ritchard had his final role in a book show as dirty old man Osgood Fielding in *Sugar*, falling head over heels for a lipsticked Robert Morse. He died in Chicago at the age of eighty, while appearing as the Narrator in the national tour of the revue *Side By Side By Sondheim*.

TOP: Lu Leonard finds Cyril Ritchard a real drag in *The Happiest Girl in the World*.
ABOVE: Ritchard made a most satisfyingly foppish Captain Hook.
LEFT: Peace prevails in Neverland with the new Captain.

Backstage

Tony Awards were given to Mary Martin, Cyril Ritchard, and Richard Rodda, the last for Best Stage Technician.

J.M. Barrie refused to allow musical adaptations of *Peter Pan*. After his death, his estate continued to refuse requests until the 1953 Disney animated version.

"You've got two big stars and they never sing together. That's appalling."

—*Jule Styne*, when called in to write additional songs

SONGS

ACT I "Tender Shepherd" · "I've Got to Crow" · "Neverland" · "I'm Flying"
ACT II "Pirate Song" · "A Princely Scheme" · "Indians!" · "Wendy" "Neverland Waltz" · "I Won't Grow Up" · "Mysterious Lady" · "Ugg-a-Wugg" "Distant Melody"
ACT III "To the Ship" · "Captain Hook's Waltz"

Sandy Duncan

The vivacious Sandy Duncan first appeared on a New York stage in City Center revivals, playing Louise in *Carousel*, Susan the silent in *Finian's Rainbow*, and Liesl in *The Sound of Music* in the 1967 season. She made her Broadway debut playing the ingenue in the flop musical *Canterbury Tales*, and as the Charleston crazy Maisie, she stole the revival of *The Boy Friend* from star Judy Carne, getting two Tony nominations in two years. After a rollercoaster seven years in California, losing sight in one eye due to a tumor on her ocular nerve, she returned to New York playing the high flying Peter Pan, costarring former *Canterbury Tales* castmate George Rose. The joy she communicated in the role was truly magical, and Duncan became the longest-flying Peter Pan ever on Broadway. In 1984, she and husband Don Correia replaced Twiggy and old Texas chum Tommy Tune in *My One and Only*, later costarring in an international tour with Tune. Back to California with a four year stint on television, nightclub work, and an L.A. production of *South Pacific* (tackling another Mary Martin signature role and making it her own), she moved her family back to New York a decade ago, anxious to return to Broadway. Reportedly brilliant to the lucky few who saw her in several workshops of an aborted stage version of *Easter Parade*, she finally made it back to the boards in 1999 as a magnetic, hysterical replacement Roxie in the *Chicago* revival. In a City Center Center concert in 2003, a fifty-seven-year-old Duncan sang "A Wonderful Guy" from *South Pacific*, ending with a cartwheel into the splits, to a thunderous ovation. Perhaps more than any other performer, this woman deserves a new musical written just for her.

PHANTOM OF THE OPERA

OPENED JANUARY 26, 1988; MAJESTIC THEATRE; 6,845 AND STILL RUNNING

ABOVE: This sure doesn't look like Venice: The creepiest gondolier you've ever seen, the Phantom kidnaps Christine and takes her to his lair.

RIGHT: Leila Martin is the mysterious Madame Giry.

PHANTOM OF THE OPERA

Produced by Cameron Mackintosh and
The Really Useful Theatre Company Ltd.
Music by Andrew Lloyd Webber
Lyrics by Charles Hart
Book by
Richard Stilgoe and Andrew Lloyd Webber
From the novel *Le Fantôme de L'Opéra* by
Gaston Leroux
Additional lyrics by Richard Stilgoe
Musical Director: David Caddick
Music orchestrated by
David Cullen and Andrew Lloyd Webber

Directed by Harold Prince
Musical Staging and Choreography by
Gillian Lynne
Scenic and Costume Design by Maria Björnson
Lighting Design by Andrew Bridge

Synopsis

Christine Daaé, a dancer in the corps of the Paris Opera, is also a budding singer, coached by a secret admirer whom she has never seen but only hears when alone in her dressing room. The voice belongs to the seductive and shadowy Phantom, a frustrated composer. He plans to have his beloved protégée Christine sing his opera, and to meet this end blackmails the producers into giving her bigger and bigger roles. Christine is terrified by the disfigured genius, but is mesmerized by his power and talent. The Phantom, tortured by his love for Christine (who only has eyes for the handsome Raoul), captures her and takes her to his secret lair in the catacombs beneath the Opera House, where they are pursued by the police, Raoul, and anyone who can carry a torch. Trapped, he vanishes into the music of the night.

Cast

The Phantom of the Opera ...	*Michael Crawford*
Christine Daaé	*Sarah Brightman*
Raoul, Vicomte de Chagny	*Steve Barton*
Carlotta Guidicelli	*Judy Kuhn*
Monsieur André	*Cris Groenendaal*
Madame Giry	*Leila Martin*

WHICH NOVEL HAS BEEN MUSICALIZED more than any other? If you guessed Gaston Leroux's 1911 masterpiece, *The Phantom of the Opera*, you'd be wrong. The correct answer is Charles Dickens' novella *A Christmas Carol*, with countless musical versions trudged out each holiday season to line the coffers of regional theatres. A production starring Richard Kiley with a score by Michel Legrand and Sheldon Harnick toured but never made it to New York, so it's had only two musical versions play Broadway, the Alan Menken and Lynn Ahrens rendition at Madison Square Garden (not technically a Broadway house, but close enough), which ran every Christmas from 1994 through 2003; and *Comin' Uptown*, an all-black version starring Gregory Hines and written by the team that gave us *Purlie* (1970) and *Shenandoah* (1975). Unfortunately, that one played only forty-five performances back in 1979.

Phantom must certainly come in second place, with many different musicalizations performed worldwide, to varying degrees of success. The first was written by Ken Hill and played London's Theatre Royal, Stratford East in 1984 (ironically, Sarah Brightman was offered the part of Christine in that production but turned it down, and Andrew Lloyd Webber attended a performance). In 1986, the Capital Repertory Company of Albany, New York, presented its own version with music by David Bishop and lyrics and libretto by Kathleen Masterson, later remounted in Germany to great acclaim. That same year, Andrew Lloyd Webber, Charles Hart, and Richard Stilgoe's production opened at Her Majesty's Theatre in London, becoming the greatest sensation of the decade (and it still hasn't closed), and then a smash of equal proportions when mounted on Broadway in 1988. *Nine* composer Maury Yeston wrote his own version of the oft-told tale prior to Lloyd Webber's, but that show wasn't mounted until 1989. Still another *Phantom* appeared at the Al Hirschfeld Theatre (not the one on Broadway) in Miami Beach, and, to complete the fad,

there was *The Phantom of the Country Palace*, which premiered in 1994 at Marriott's Lincolnshire Theatre outside Chicago.

It's the Andrew Lloyd Webber version, however, that has outlasted them all. Now in its sixteenth year on Broadway, an upcoming film version may give its box office the same kind of jolt that *Chicago* got from its film incarnation. *Phantom* shows no signs of closing soon. Its assets include a soaring score (and a tip of the hat to Mr. Puccini), a sumptuous production directed by Hal Prince at the top of his game, and above all, a passionate and mysterious love story at its core that has resonated with millions of theatregoers worldwide. ❋

SONGS

ACT I "Think of Me" · "Angel of Music" · "Little Lotte"/ "The Mirror" · "The Phantom of the Opera" · "The Music of the Night" · "I Remember"/"Stranger Than You Dreamt It" · "Magical Lasso" · "Prima Donna" · "Poor Fool, He Makes Me Laugh" · "Why Have You Brought Me Here"/ "Raoul, I've Been There" · "All I Ask of You"
ACT II Masquerade"/"Why So Silent" · "Twisted Every Way" · "Wishing You Were Somehow Here Again" · "Wandering Child"/"Bravo Bravo" · "The Point of No Return" "Down Once More"/"Track Down This Murderer"

The Phantom (Michael Crawford) beguiles Christine (Sarah Brightman) with "The Music of the Night."

Andrew Lloyd Webber

Andrew Lloyd Webber, the most successful British composer in the modern musical theatre, teamed with fellow Oxford student Tim Rice in 1967 to write *Joseph and the Amazing Technicolor Dreamcoat*, a children's cantata that was later brought to the London and Broadway stages. When he and Rice wrote a conceptual rock opera album called *Jesus Christ Superstar*, it became a sensation and triggered stage versions, first in London, then on Broadway (in 1971), where it was a smash. Trying the same approach with a pop opera biography of Argentinean icon Eva Peron, Lloyd Webber and Rice struck gold once more with *Evita* in 1978, teaming with director Hal Prince for the first time. Lloyd Webber and director Trevor Nunn collaborated on *Cats*, turning T. S. Eliot's *Book of Practical Cats* poems into *Cats*, which opened in London in 1981 and hit Broadway like a tidal wave in 1982, thus beginning a decade-long domination of the Broadway musical by British imports. After Broadway transfers of *Song and Dance*, his evening of two one-act musicals in 1986; and *Starlight Express*, with its speeding trains and overwhelming physical production in 1987, Lloyd Webber reunited with Prince on *Phantom of the Opera*, another megasmash on the level of *Cats*. Since then, however, Lloyd Webber's track record has been less than stellar. *Aspects of Love*, despite a run of almost a season and a lengthy tour, along with his most traditional book show, *Sunset Boulevard*, failed to repay their investors. Another collaboration with Hal Prince, Lloyd Webber's *Whistle Down the Wind*, closed prior to Broadway in 1996; and the first New York production of his intimate 1974 musical *By Jeeves* failed to captivate audiences. With his latest show, *The Beautiful Game*, still without a production in the States, Lloyd Webber is preparing the film of *Phantom* and the stage production of *The Woman in White*, which opens in London in the fall of 2004 with lyrics by David Zippel and starring Michael Crawford. While many have accused him of borrowing many themes from other composers, Lloyd Webber has an undeniable gift for writing sweeping, accessible melodies that he knows will win the hearts of theatergoers everywhere.

LEFT: The former Mrs. Lloyd Webber, Sarah Brightman, as the original Christine Daaé. RIGHT: As an engine named Greaseball, Robert Torti is "Pumping Iron" in *Starlight Express*, the Andrew Lloyd Webber musical that did for trains what *Cats* did for the animal kingdom.

Cameron Mackintosh

The most successful producer at the end of the last century, Cameron Mackintosh has an ongoing love affair with the Broadway musical. Intensely loyal and fully supportive of his projects, both emotionally and financially, Mackintosh got his start as a producer in England when only twenty years old, making a mark on the West End with his 1976 production of *Side by Side by Sondheim*. After another hit with a revival of *Oliver!* (a show Mackintosh had appeared in as a child), he struck box office gold with *Cats*, later continuing his association with Andrew Lloyd Webber with *Starlight Express* and the remarkable *Phantom of the Opera*. When *Les Miserables*, produced in association with the Royal Shakespeare Company, opened to mostly negative reviews, Mackintosh so believed in the piece, he moved it to London's Palace Theatre, where he proved his unerring taste when it, too, became a sensation. All four shows came to Broadway between 1982 and 1988 and, with the exception of *Starlight*, repeated their amazing smash success in the States and subsequently around the world. A 1984 Broadway revival of *Oliver!* (starring movie Fagin Ron Moody and Patti LuPone) and a softened, retooled 1987 revival of *Follies* in the West End were rare missteps. In 1989, he produced his fourth smash hit, *Miss Saigon*, spanning the globe with the Vietnam-era "popera." While his next megaproduction, *Martin Guerre,* failed in London and has yet to reach Broadway, and *The Witches of Eastwick* also failed on the West End, he has been concentrating on revivals of late, including the well-received National Theatre productions of *Carousel, Oklahoma!,* and *Anything Goes.*

Backstage

Phantom includes several moments prerecorded on tape. During the transition into the sewers in the title song, the Phantom's singing and Christine's high notes are taped. *Bye Bye, Birdie* was the first show to use prerecorded voices. Other shows that have relied on the technique include *Follies* (Mary McCarty's last lines in "Who's That Woman?"), *The Act* ("Hot Enough for You" and "Turning"), and *Victor/Victoria* (Julie Andrews's high notes).

LEFT: Lea Salonga and Brian Baldomero, caught up in the Viet Nam conflict in Cameron Mackintosh's worldwide triumph *Miss Saigon*.

BELOW: Wielding textbook-perfect control over all elements—music, story and design—Hal Prince was at the height of his directorial powers in this scene depicting the finale of the opera *Hannibal*.

FLOPS, PART II

AFTER PAGES AND PAGES CELEBRATING wonderful examples of dramaturgical and musical genius, it's once again time to take a moment to honor those shows that, despite the blood, sweat, and tears of their creators and cast, resolutely stunk up the theatre district (if they were lucky enough to make it into town). Or better yet, as a friend said after seeing *Carrie*, "The King is dead. Long live the Queen."

TOP LEFT: Horton hears a boo: Kevin Chamberlin in *Seussical*. TOP RIGHT: The ever-valiant Julie Wilson asks the audience if they like her knockers in *Legs Diamond*, the show that converted the Mark Hellinger into a church. ABOVE: Betsy Joslyn pleads to be released for good behavior from the prison that is *A Doll's Life*. LEFT: Michael Crawford, feeling like Tom Jones but wearing more makeup than Jennifer Jones, headlines the most recent entry in the Broadway Hall of Shame, *Dance of the Vampires*.

Karen Morrow

Karen Morrow, who could (and should) have been the Merman of the 1960s and 1970s, had what can only be called rotten luck. After a splash in the Off-Broadway *Sing Muse!* and the revival of *The Boys from Syracuse*, she made her Broadway debut as the leading lady of the Buddy Hackett vehicle *I Had a Ball* (1964), socking the title number out with such abandon and joy that her belt (akin to the most beautiful, glorious air raid siren you've ever heard) is still reverberating somewhere up in the rafters of the Al Hirschfeld. Some of her longest runs were in two-week stands at New York's City Center, playing the soubrette in revivals of *Carnival*, *Brigadoon*, and *The Most Happy Fella*. After *A Joyful Noise* (1966) and *I'm Solomon* (1968, costarring with fellow jinxed one Carmen Mathews), she spent time in California, supporting Jim Nabors on his short-lived variety show. Returning to New York only to star in two more bombs, *The Grass Harp* (1971), where she stopped the show with her tour-de-force "Babylove Miracle Show"; and *The Selling of the President* (in 1972, with 5 performances, in which Morrow didn't even sing—what were they thinking?), she decamped permanently to Hollywood, occasionally appearing on television and in Los Angeles theatre (as a terrific Carlotta in *Follies*, Dolly Levi, and most recently, a rock solid Sally Adams in the Reprise! version of *Call Me Madam*), only returning to New York in 1985 to replace Cleo Laine in *The Mystery of Edwin Drood*. She still sings like a dream: Where oh where is her show?

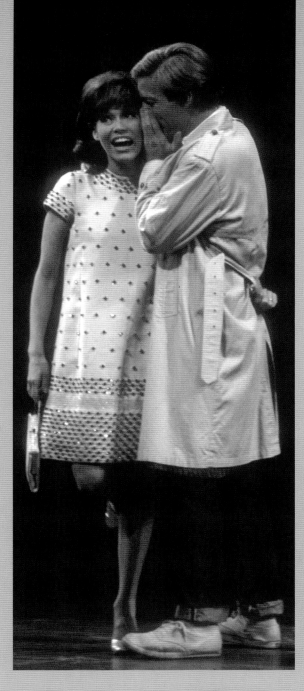

TOP LEFT: The amazingly talented Karen Morrow, drawn to flops as a dowser is drawn to water, plays Babylove in *The Grass Harp*. TOP RIGHT: Richard Chamberlain to Mary Tyler Moore during *Breakfast at Tiffany's*: "We're breakin' outta this dump... pass it on." BOTTOM RIGHT: Barbara Perry and Eddie Foy, Jr., singing "In Times Like These" from the 1958 bomb, *Rumple*. LEFT: Dick Shawn, Salome Jens, and, vying for the title of "Miss Flop 1968," Carmen Mathews and Karen Morrow in a rehearsal shot from *I'm Solomon* (then titled *In Someone Else's Sandals*). BOTTOM LEFT: Andrea Marcovicci is the titular Egyptian Queen in *Nefertiti*. (The show closed in Chicago in 1977.) Clearly, the chorus members think they're performing the "Magic to Do" number in a road company of *Pippin*.

PORGY AND BESS

OPENED OCTOBER 10, 1935; ALVIN THEATRE; 124 PERFORMANCES

Porgy (Todd Duncan) reassures Bess (Anne Brown) as the hurricane approaches.

PORGY AND BESS
Produced by The Theatre Guild
Music by George Gershwin
Libretto by DuBose Heyward
Lyrics by DuBose Heyward and Ira Gershwin
Based on the play
Porgy by DuBose Heyward and Dorothy Heyward
Conducted by Alexander Smallens
Orchestrations by George Gershwin
Staged by Rouben Mamoulian
Scenic Design by Sergei Soudeikine

Synopsis

Porgy, a crippled beggar on Catfish Row in Charleston, South Carolina, falls in love with Bess, the girlfriend of Crown, a particularly hot-tempered and violent man. When Crown kills a man during a crap game and goes into hiding, the flashy Sportin' Life, also with his eye on Bess, urges her to accompany him to New York. Bess declines and settles down with Porgy, who treats her well. A picnic on Kittiwah Island is a happy occasion until Crown materializes and forces Bess to leave with him. A few days later she returns to Porgy, tired and sick of Crown's abuse. As they reiterate their love, the hurricane bell sounds, and Crown appears, attempting to win Bess back. Porgy fights with Crown and kills him. With Porgy in jail for questioning, Bess is again alone when the seductive Sportin' Life reappears and, with the help of drugs, convinces Bess to come to New York with him. Porgy, finally freed from prison, finds Bess gone and begins a journey to get his woman back.

Cast

Mingo	*Ford L. Buck*
Clara	*Abbie Mitchell*
Sportin' Life	*John W. Bubbles*
Jake	*Edward Matthews*
Maria	*Georgette Harvey*
Lily	*Helen Dowdy*
Serena	*Ruby Elzy*
Porgy	*Todd Duncan*
Crown	*Warren Coleman*
Bess	*Anne Brown*
Frazier	*J. Rosamond Johnson*

"My people are American, my time is today. Music must repeat the thought and aspirations of the times."

—George Gershwin

Porgy and Bess, a MASTERPIECE of the American theatre, had an unusually rocky start. Before Ira Gershwin even paired up with DuBose Heyward, Al Jolson was interested in Heyward's play, *Porgy*. It's one of history's near misses on a par with Shirley Temple as Dorothy in *The Wizard of Oz* and Ronald Reagan in *Casablanca*. It wasn't even the first all-black opera: that distinction went to Virgil Thomson's *Four Saints in Three Acts*. The original production's reviews were less than splendid, and there wasn't even an original cast recording. By the time of the show's revival in 1942, some of the score was familiar to the public, and critics and audiences hailed the piece.

Shows that are lucky enough to be successful on Broadway have lives for decades to come. There are Broadway revivals, national tours, community theatre productions, high school and college mountings, summer stock and regional theatre presentations, international productions, sometimes a film version, and, for some, production by opera houses.

Musical theatre is one of America's most influential exports. *Finian's Rainbow*, as positive a message about America that you could hope for, has played in the Czech Republic on and off for more than thirty years. *Grease* has toured Italy for a decade. *I Do! I Do!* was recently presented in Paris. Disney has even premiered new musicals like the *Hunchback of Notre Dame* in Germany—a long way to go for an out-of-town tryout. Cy Coleman wrote a musical about Princess Grace (titled *Grace*, natch) for production in Holland. And Japan regularly presents American musicals with all-female casts.

Here are a couple of stories about the wildly successful afterlife of *Porgy and Bess*, as told by the original Porgy, Todd Duncan, in an interview with Berthe Schuchat; and by the original Bess, Anne Brown, in a later interview with Jeff Lunden, Amy Asch, and Ken Bloom.

Anne Brown: When we were supposed to sing at the National Theatre in Washington, we realized it was a segregated theatre. And I think I was the very first one [who] protested vehemently that I would not sing if the theatre was segregated. And Todd Duncan very soon joined me, and we had made such a protest, of course with the help of Gershwin and the Theatre Guild, that they changed their policy for that one week we were there. But the next week they went back to their old policy, which continued for twenty years.

Todd Duncan: We closed the 1935 tour here in Washington at the National Theatre. The 1938 tour went to California. It was all the same cast. It ended in disaster because of the floods in Los Angeles and San Francisco. I came back home to Washington until 1942. I taught at Howard University. The 1942 revival was done by Cheryl Crawford, who had been a Theatre Guild assistant. I did it in Copenhagen in Danish in the late 1940s at the Royal Opera. I'd been doing concerts in Europe and heard about the production of *Porgy and Bess* during the war. The Gestapo closed a lot of theatres, but they wanted more music and allocated money for that. The Danish staged four new operas. They chose *Porgy and Bess* to show how they hated the Nazis. After all it was performed by Negroes and written by a Jew. They thought the Nazis would veto it. Money was poured into *Porgy and Bess*; people were sent to America to get real Negro wigs. At the premiere, 200 Nazis were in the audience. They enjoyed the first act, but during intermission they got up and walked out. They allowed the Danish to do the next two performances because they were sold out.

But the Danes gave forty more performances underground during the war. The Germans would always find out that it was done the night before, but they never knew when it was going to be done. The Royal Opera was dark on the outside. And that was the Danish performers' fight. They performed it at the cost of not knowing if they'd be blown up or killed by the Nazis. The Danes used "It Ain't Necessarily So" to jam Gestapo radio lines. That became a symbol of resistance.

I was proud to relearn the role and do it for them. I was learning it in Danish while they rehearsed it in Danish. For most of the rehearsals, though, I'd sing in English while they all sang in Danish. They gave me one dress rehearsal with all these blondes in the cast. And that night, for the performance, when I went out onstage and saw all these Negroes, I couldn't believe my eyes. They'd done something to make their noses broader, they were lovely dark shades from light brown to black. Up to high yellow Negroes, mulattos. All kinds of hair textures. Not only that but they had the Negro flavor. They were just so wonderful. I cried.

On the night of the opening, when we sang the duet "Bess, You Is My Woman Now," I sang to Bess in Danish, and she sang to me in English. I thought I would die. It took my breath away when I heard her say, "Porgy, I'se your woman now."

I stopped the show with "Plenty o' Nuttin'." They wouldn't let me go on. I had to encore the song. That opera house was 300 years old, and that was only the third time that had happened. The first time was with Caruso, the second time was with Chaliapin, the basso from Russia. Caruso had to sing "I Pagliacci" twice, and Boris Godunov had to die twice. They said it would go down in history.

Anne Brown: I stage-directed *Porgy and Bess* in eight different cities in France and also in Oslo. The French people, the chorus, and the people who lived in Catfish Row—when the makeup was right, you almost believed they were in South Carolina.

It appeals because Porgy is a cripple; he is disadvantaged in more ways than one. And he wins over this. He wins a beautiful woman, he wins the respect of the other people in Catfish Row, and he, in the end, is going to go off with his goat and his little wagon to New York to find Bess. Of course we don't know if he ever reaches there. But the idea is that one can surmount one's difficulties, and what difficulties they had! ❋

Porgy (Todd Duncan), Bess (Anne Brown), and company hunker down and sing "Oh, Doctor Jesus" as a hurricane hits Catfish Row.

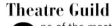
Theatre Guild

One of the most important producing companies in Broadway history, the Theatre Guild was founded in 1919 by Lawrence Langner; his wife, Armina Marshall; and Theresa Helburn. The guild was most famous for its plays, including eighteen by George Bernard Shaw, seven by Eugene O'Neill, and others by Robert E. Sherwood, Maxwell Anderson, William Saroyan, Philip Barry, and Sidney Howard. Also among the Guild's 228 Broadway productions were some of the most important Broadway musicals. The Guild was responsible for Richard Rodgers and Lorenz Hart's first Broadway success, *The Garrick Gaieties*; Richard Rodgers and Oscar Hammerstein's first collaboration, the groundbreaking *Oklahoma!*; as well as *Porgy and Bess*, *Carousel*, *Bells Are Ringing*, and *The Unsinkable Molly Brown*. Among the Guild's other musical offerings were several quite respectable efforts, including *Sing Out Sweet Land*, *Arms and the Girl*, *Allegro*, and *Darling of the Day*. Naturally, not all of the Guild's musical offerings were successful; in fact, their finances were among the most mercurial of all production companies.

TOP: Robert Breen's 1952 revival of *Porgy and Bess* featured William Warfield and Leontyne Price.

ABOVE: Todd Duncan, Ella Waters, and famed actor/composer Rosamond Johnson.

RIGHT: Rouben Mamoulian directs the original cast of *Porgy and Bess*.

PROMISES, PROMISES

OPENED DECEMBER 1, 1968; SHUBERT THEATRE; 1,281 PERFORMANCES

As the hapless, affable Chuck Baxter, Jerry Orbach (here with Adrienne Angel and Paul Reed) had an actor's dream of a role, able to talk directly to the audience and land the wonderful jokes of Neil Simon's book.

PROMISES, PROMISES

Produced by David Merrick
Book by Neil Simon
Music by Burt Bacharach
Lyrics by Hal David
Based on the Film
The Apartment by Billy Wilder and I. A. L. Diamond
Musical Director: Harold Wheeler
Dance Arrangements by Harold Wheeler
Music orchestrated by Jonathan Tunick

Directed by Robert Moore
Choreographed by Michael Bennett

Scenic Design by Robin Wagner
Costume Design by Donald Brooks
Lighting Design by Martin Aronstein

Synopsis

The executives at Consolidated Life spend their extracurricular time at lowly Chuck Baxter's apartment, where they make whoopee with various distaff members of the firm. Baxter's boss, Mr. Sheldrake, is involved with Fran Kubelik, a sensitive girl who soon falls for Baxter. Chuck slowly finds the confidence to stand up to Sheldrake just as Fran despairs of her position as "the other woman" and attempts suicide. In the end, Fran and Chuck end up together.

Cast

Fran Kubelik	*Jill O'Hara*
Chuck Baxter	*Jerry Orbach*
Dr. Dreyfuss	*A. Larry Haines*
J. D. Sheldrake	*Edward Winter*
Sylvia Gilhooley	*Adrienne Angel*
Karl Kubelik	*Ken Howard*
Miss Wong	*Baayork Lee*
Vivien Della Hoya	*Donna McKechnie*
Marge MacDougall	*Marian Mercer*
Mr. Eichelberger	*Vince O'Brien*
Jesse Vanderhof	*Dick O'Neill*
Mr. Dobitch	*Paul Reed*
Miss Polansky	*Margo Sappington*
Mr. Kirkeby	*Norman Shelly*
Peggy Olson	*Millie Slavin*

"I kind of went through the whole thing like I didn't know what I was doing, you know?"

— *Burt Bacharach*

THE ELECTION OF JOHN F. Kennedy created a dividing line between the stolid, postwar Eisenhower era and a glorious, optimistic future, and while they certainly didn't live up to their promise politically, the "Camelot" years were assuredly a time of amazing change. It was a period of assassination, war, and civil rights disturbances, and also a time of freedom of speech, free love, experimentation with drugs, and a vast sea change in the arts. Theatre became looser, and current events were tackled dramatically, with a vigor not seen since the height of the Depression. Art became Pop and then Op, popular music embraced the new rhythms of Brazil and free jazz, and the tide in the musical theatre promised to turn with the advent of *Hair*. But successive rock musicals were flops, with writers like Charles Strouse, Jerry Herman, and Jerry Bock still writing in the traditional style, with others like Cy Coleman providing scores that synthesized traditional sounds and structures with more up-to-date elements.

There were two new masters of the American popular song in the 1960s, both working extensively in the movies. The first was Henry Mancini—who wouldn't show up on Broadway until the 1990s with the egregiously mediocre (and posthumous) *Victor/Victoria*. The other was Burt Bacharach. After the team of Bacharach and Hal David enjoyed enormous success with a series of pop songs introduced by Dionne Warwick, it seemed inevitable for them to take a stab at Broadway. But it took the genius of David Merrick to bring the team to Broadway success.

Merrick provided Bacharach and David with top-drawer support. *Promises, Promises* boasted a libretto by the most financially successful playwright in the history of American theatre—Neil Simon—then at the height of his abilities. The young Michael Bennett provided the upbeat, high-energy dances for such greats as Donna McKechnie (making her first big splash on Broadway) and Baayork Lee. The slick, fluid direction was by the sadly underrated Robert Moore (making his Broadway debut). Leads Jerry Orbach and Jill O'Hara were perfectly teamed, and Marian Mercer almost walked off with the show in the pocket of her owl coat. Credit for the successful pop sound of the show went to dance arranger Harold Wheeler and orchestrator Jonathan Tunick (making their Broadway debuts). In fact, a quartet of women sat in the orchestra pit and provided pop vocal accompaniment along with the instruments. While David's lyrics, for the most part, were barely passable by Broadway standards, Bacharach's melodies and rhythms were highly inventive and theatrically satisfying. Sadly, Bacharach loathed the experience and for thirty-five years has refused entreaties to work on another score. David returned but once, teaming with Michel Legrand on the flop *Brainchild*, which closed out of town. ❋

In *Promises, Promises*, Jerry Orbach and Jill O'Hara got to sing Bacharach and David's "I'll Never Fall in Love Again," one of the last popular music standards to come out of a Broadway musical.

Jerry Orbach

Jerry Orbach's easygoing charm, versatility, and fine singing voice made him one of the most gainfully employed actors on Broadway in the 1960s and '70s, rarely out of work or in a flop. After creating the role of El Gallo in the original Off-Broadway production of *The Fantasticks*, he played the crippled puppeteer Paul in the Bob Merrill/Gower Champion hit *Carnival!*, providing baritone auditioners with a template for forty years to come with his powerful rendition of the ballad "Her Face." After a terrifically received *Guys and Dolls* at City Center, opposite former *Carnival!* understudy Anita Gillette, he became a full-fledged Broadway star as Chuck Baxter in *Promises, Promises*, shooting to the top of everyone's list for every new musical. He chose his projects exceedingly well, and his roles as Billy Flynn in *Chicago* and Julian Marsh in *42nd Street* provided him with long runs and rave reviews. Also known as the voice of Lumiere the candelabra in the animated classic *Beauty and the Beast*, he has, since 1992, been best known as Detective Lennie Briscoe in the long-running crime drama *Law & Order*. Yet again, Orbach has chosen exceedingly well.

ABOVE: As Julian Marsh in *42nd Street*, Orbach made his last appearance in a musical to date.
ABOVE RIGHT: Rita Gardner, Orbach, and Richard Stauffer in the unstoppable Off-Broadway legend, *The Fantasticks*.

SONGS

ACT I · "Half as Big as Life" · "Grapes of Roth" · "Upstairs" · "You'll Think of Someone" · "Our Little Secret" · "She Likes Basketball" · "Knowing When to Leave" · "Where Can You Take a Girl?" "Wanting Things" · "Turkey Lurkey Time"
ACT II · "A Fact Can Be a Beautiful Thing" · "Whoever You Are" · "A Young Pretty Girl Like You" · "I'll Never Fall in Love Again" · "Promises, Promises"

Michael Bennett

Director/choreographer Michael Bennett proved his brilliance again and again in his ability to emotionally build a showstopping number. In shows such as *Promises, Promises; Coco; Company;* and *Follies,* Bennett surprised his older, more educated collaborators with his innate understanding of an audience's visceral reaction to song and dance. After taking the reins of *Seesaw* during its chaotic out-of-town-tryout, he next set out to create a new musical celebrating the individuality of the anonymous Broadway dancer. *A Chorus Line* (much like *My Fair Lady* and *The Producers* did in their times) turned New York on its ear with its runaway success. Bennett's staging of the last measures of "At the Ballet," when three dancers step back into "the line" as it advances from the darkness upstage, returning with a sigh of Jonathan Tunick's wonderful orchestration to the show's now famous tableau, is poetic in its simplicity and beauty. Everyone, including Bennett, knew that whatever his next venture might be, it would pale in comparison. That show, *Ballroom*, contained some classic Bennett touches, but it was ultimately let down by a weak score and lack of conflict. The flow and character detail in the stunning, cinematic opening sequence of his directorial masterpiece, *Dreamgirls*, shows a genius at the absolute top of his sometimes tortured powers, and his death while still at his peak is one of the great losses in the history of Broadway.

LEFT: State of the art is the best way to describe Bennett's direction of *Dreamgirls*. Here he is in rehearsal with Loretta Devine (hidden), Sheryl Lee Ralph, and Jennifer Holliday.

Backstage

"I'll Never Fall in Love Again," the big hit from the show, was a last-minute addition to the score.

In the film *The Apartment,* upon which *Promises, Promises* was based, Chuck Baxter has tickets to the Broadway musical *The Music Man.* In the musical, he's stood up at a basketball game.

ABOVE: Dorothy Loudon and Victor Griffin trip the light fantastic in Michael Bennett's *Ballroom*.

LEFT: In the lyrically insipid yet fabulously choreographed "Turkey Lurkey Time," (left to right) Baayork Lee, longtime Bennett muse Donna McKechnie, and Margo Sappington kick it up, Michael Bennett-style, at the office Christmas party.

RAGTIME

OPENED JANUARY 18, 1998; FORD CENTER FOR THE PERFORMING ARTS; 834 PERFORMANCES

Peter Friedman and Lea Michele, at center, with the other tired, poor, and hungry at Ellis Island.

RAGTIME
Produced by Livent (U.S.) Inc.

Book by Terrence McNally
Music by Stephen Flaherty
Lyrics by Lynn Ahrens
Based on the novel by E. L. Doctorow
Music orchestrated by William David Brohn
Musical Director: David Loud
Dance music arranged by David Krane
Vocal arrangements by Stephen Flaherty

Directed by Frank Galati
Musical Staging by Graciela Daniele

Production Design by Eugene Lee
Costume Design by Santo Loquasto
Lighting Design by Jules Fisher
and Peggy Eisenhauer

Synopsis

1902: Mother, Father, and Mother's Younger Brother live in New Rochelle; Coalhouse Walker and his love, Sarah, are blacks confronting racism; and the immigrant Tateh and his Little Girl have escaped from Eastern Europe. When Sarah abandons her new baby in Mother's garden, she is brought into the family, setting the wheels in motion for a remarkable tale of human courage and growth in America at the beginning of the twentieth century. Mother becomes a modern woman, Coalhouse evolves into a radical and then a terrorist, and Tateh rises from the factories to become a movie pioneer. All the characters' paths intertwine more than once and each is changed forever, just as their country is.

Cast

Father .... *Mark Jacoby*
Mother .... *Marin Mazzie*
Mother's Younger Brother..... *Steven Sutcliffe*
Coalhouse Walker .... *Brian Stokes Mitchell*
Sarah .... *Audra McDonald*
Tateh .... *Peter Friedman*
Emma Goldman .... *Judy Kaye*
Evelyn Nesbit .... *Lynnette Perry*

SONGS

ACT I · "Ragtime" · "Goodbye, My Love" · "Journey On" "The Crime of the Century" · "What Kind of Woman" "A Shtetl Iz Amereke" · "Success" · "Gettin' Ready Rag" "Henry Ford" · "Nothing Like the City" · "Your Daddy's Son" "New Music" · "Wheels of a Dream" · "The Night That Goldman Spoke at Union Square" · "Lawrence, Massachusetts" · "Gliding" · "Justice" · "President" · "Till We Reach That Day"
ACT II · "Harry Houdini, Master Escapist" · "Coalhouse's Soliloquy" · "Coalhouse Demands" · "What a Game" "Atlantic City" · "Buffalo Nickel Photoplay, Inc." · "Our Children" · "Sarah Brown Eyes" · "He Wanted to Say" "Back to Before" · "Look What You've Done" · "Make Them Hear You"

THE ERA IN WHICH THE musical *Ragtime* is set was an unbeatably rich period in American history: with new-fangled inventions seemingly changing people's lives overnight; the emergence of cities; class struggles and racial conflicts; throngs of huddled masses flowing in from Europe, looking for a better life and finding near slavery in factories of a newly industrialized land; ruthless robber barons juxtaposed with the honest, rags-to-riches optimism of the self-made man; and above all, the wonderful, syncopated new music that seemed to encompass all the hopes, dreams, and bittersweet regret of a country.

The moving and expansive novel *Ragtime*, by E. L. Doctorow, encompassed all of these themes, throwing in many real-life historical names in the bargain. Though it seemed a wonderful choice for musicalization, Doctorow wasn't enthusiastic about an adaptation of his novel for Broadway, since the film version had not met his liking. Producer Garth Drabinsky, the P. T. Barnum of his day, finally convinced the author that his work would be presented in a first-class production by top-drawer talent. Harold Prince, then intimately involved in Drabinsky's company, Livent, through his productions of *Show Boat* and *Kiss of the Spider Woman*, suggested that ten songwriting teams write four songs each on spec. Eight teams agreed, among them composer Stephen Flaherty and lyricist Lynn Ahrens. Hardly household names, Ahrens and Flaherty showed an impressive versatility as the writers of the Off-Broadway charmer *Lucky Stiff*, the Caribbean-flavored hit *Once on This Island*, and *My Favorite Year*, adapted from the film of the same name. Buckling down and submitting their audition score, they got the assignment.

Meanwhile, Drabinsky, never a producer to do anything halfway, gained control of the Lyric and Apollo Theatres on 42nd and 43rd Streets in order to demolish them and build a new theatre that would open with *Ragtime*. As the theatre took shape, brick by brick, the production set off on its road to Broadway, with productions in Toronto and Los Angeles before the Broadway opening. When it arrived in New York, the paint on the brand-new Ford Center was barely dry. Along the way, Ahrens and Flaherty, along with book writer Terrence McNally, director Frank Galati, and choreographer Graciela Daniele, had had two years to hone the material, writing and rewriting, always under the micromanaging eye of Drabinsky. Perhaps Drabinsky saw himself as David O. Selznick marshalling the resources for his epic *Gone with the Wind*, for *Ragtime* was truly a theatrical epic—a musical of great scope, historically, socially, and emotionally.

The finished product couldn't possibly please everyone and was not quite as faithful to the novel as Doctorow might have wished—but after all, it was an extraordinarily vast, unwieldy source to distill into three hours. In addition, the necessarily episodic nature of the script made some of the score seem more narrative that experiential; still, in the stunning opening sequence, with the three storylines of Tateh, Coalhouse, and Mother swirling about the stage in a foreshadowing of the dramatic interweaving to come, *Ragtime* was a joy to behold. The score, criticized by some as consisting of one anthem after another, beautifully captured the emotional landscape of its characters: "Our Children," "Back to Before," "Your Daddy's Son," and "Wheels of a Dream" are all stunningly modern theatre songs. There were those who thought the proceedings appropriately grand and moving but also those who decried the sentimentality and epic proportions, preferring *The Lion King*, which opened the same season. Audiences, however, loved the show, and *Ragtime* appeared to have settled in for an extended run, perhaps even rivaling the English mega-hits. With incredibly high running costs, however, compounded with the implosion of Livent, Inc., amid lawsuits, charges of bookkeeping irregularities, and fraud, the show closed prematurely, denying the authors a super-hit. Maybe McNally, Ahrens, and Flaherty should write their next show about the rise and fall of Garth Drabinsky, a character as complex and colorful as any of those in *Ragtime*. ✻

The phenomenal actress and singer Audra McDonald gets ready to meet her doom in the song "President."

Brian Stokes Mitchell

The charismatic singer and actor Brian Stokes Mitchell made an early name for himself on television (starring with other Broadway musical actors Mary McCarty, Gregory Harrison, and Pernell Roberts, who had the bad luck to star in two shows that closed out of town: *Mata Hari* and *Gone with the Wind*), as "Jackpot" Jackson on *Trapper John, MD*. Coming East with the Michael Rupert musical *Mail*, which began at the Pasadena Playhouse, he starred in David Merrick's ill-fated revival of *Oh, Kay!* After ably acquitting himself as Gregory Hines's replacement in *Jelly's Last Jam*, and starring opposite Howard McGillin and Vanessa Williams in the strongly sung second cast of *Kiss of the Spider Woman*, Mitchell took on the role of Coalhouse Walker in *Ragtime*, singing, acting, and dancing with star-making power. Exploring his comic, hammy side opposite *Ragtime* costar Marin Mazzie in the very fine revival of *Kiss Me, Kate*, he won a Tony Award for his performance as Fred Graham, and after a dramatic performance in August Wilson's *King Hedley II*, Mitchell returned to the Martin Beck Theatre as Don Quixote in the 2002 revival of *Man of La Mancha*. Becoming a star in revivals, Mitchell, along with other talented performers like Donna Murphy, Brent Barrett, and Christine Ebersole, desperately deserves a brand-new Broadway show tailored to his gifts.

LEFT: The *Ragtime* company makes the most of the classy character movement supplied them by the talented Graciela Daniele.

THE RED MILL

OPENED SEPTEMBER 24, 1906; KNICKERBOCKER THEATRE; 274 PERFORMANCES

Bertha (Alline Crater), Kid Connor (Dave Montgomery), Con Kidder (Fred Stone), and Tina (Ethel Johnson).

THE RED MILL

Produced by Charles Dillingham

Book and lyrics by Henry Blossom
Music by Victor Herbert
Orchestra under the direction of
Max Hirschfeld
Orchestrations by Victor Herbert
Directed by Fred G. Latham
Scenic Design by Frank E. Gates,
E. A. Morange, Homer Emens, Joseph Wickes,
and Edward G. Unitt
Costume Design by Wilhelm

Synopsis

Kid Connor and Con Kidder, two American nincompoops abroad, are stranded and broke in Katwyk-aan-Zee, Holland. The two innocents undergo a series of farcical adventures with the comely Gretchen, who loves Captain Karl Van Damm, while her father wishes her to wed the governor of Zeeland. Connor and Kidder contrive to bring Gretchen together with her intended, despite making an enemy of the governor. A daring rescue in the titular red mill and a hilarious series of impersonations by the stars follows. At the end, it is revealed that Van Damm is set to inherit a vast fortune, at which point Gretchen's father removes all objections to their union.

Cast

Con Kidder	*Fred A. Stone*
Kid Conner	*David Montgomery*
Jan Van Borkem	*Edward Begley*
David I. Don	*Joseph M. Ratliff*
The Governor of Zeeland	*Neal McCay*
Gretchen	*Augusta Greenleaf*
Bertha	*Allene Crater*
Tina	*Ethel Johnson*

THE CREATIVE TEAM IS A phenomenon that has seemingly gone the way of the TV Western. Once, all American entertainment—stage, film, radio, and television—was lousy with teams, usually comic in nature. Film had Stan Laurel and Oliver Hardy, Lou Abbott and Bud Costello, Ma and Pa Kettle, and Dean Martin and Jerry Lewis. Radio featured Edgar Bergen and Charlie McCarthy, Fibber McGee and Molly, and George Burns and Gracie Allen. The stage boasted Joe Weber and Lew Fields, Bobby Clark and Paul McCullough, and Ed Gallagher and Al Shean. Today all but forgotten, one of the most famous and successful stage teams consisted of David Montgomery and Fred Stone, who achieved great success in the Victor Herbert musical *The Wizard of Oz*. Always one to know a good thing when he saw it, Herbert called upon librettist Henry Blossom to write a show especially for the comic duo.

The result, *The Red Mill*, transcended its purpose as a showcase for the two comics. An exceptional hit in its time, the show was revived in 1945 and ran twice as long as the original. By necessity, the libretto, fashioned around the particular talents of Montgomery and Stone, has dated, but the score is still one of the masterpieces of the American musical theatre. "Every Day Is Ladies' Day" and "The Streets of New York" are two of Herbert's most beloved melodies, still performed today. Certainly a musical of its time and a vehicle for Montgomery and Stone, *The Red Mill* is occasionally revived with a somewhat updated libretto, and it never fails to amuse and entertain, making the heart soar with its beautiful melodies. ✳

SONGS

ACT 1 "By the Side of the Mill" · "Mignonette" · "You Can Never Tell About a Woman" · "Whistle It" · "A Widow Has Her Ways" · "The Isle of Our Dreams" · "Always Go While the Goin' Is Good" · "An Accident" · "Moonbeams"
ACT 2 "Gossip Song" · "Legend of the Mill" · "Good-a-Bye John" · "I Want You To Marry Me" · "Every Day Is Ladies' Day with Me" · "Because You're You!" · "The Streets of New York" · "Entrance of Wedding Guests"

Montgomery and Stone

Two of America's most beloved performers, David Montgomery and Fred Stone were acrobatic talents who could sing, dance, act, and mime, gaining their fame with the historic 1903 musical version of *The Wizard of Oz*, Montgomery playing the Tin Man and Stone the Scarecrow. They had met in their early twenties, and in 1894 created a blackface song and dance act which they toured in vaudeville for nearly ten years. They reached the top of the prestigious Keith circuit before making their Broadway debut in *The Girl from Up There* in 1901, also co-starring in *The Red Mill*, *The Old Town* (1910), *The Lady of the Slipper* (1912), and *Chin-Chin* (1914), among other shows. In between Broadway assignments, they headed vaudeville bills throughout the nation, until Montgomery died in 1917, leaving Stone for the first time in his career without a partner. He continued to star in Broadway musicals, including *Jack O' Lantern* (1917) and *Tip Top* (1920), and tried to make a name in silent movies, but theatre was clearly his forte. In a sense, he made his family a partner when his daughters, Dorothy and Paula, and wife, Allene, joined his act, known as the Stepping Stones, also the title of one of their musicals. He worked steadily through the next decade, before retiring following the 1945 revival of *You Can't Take It With You*.

Backstage

The 1945 revival of *The Red Mill* starring Eddie Foy was coproduced by Fred Stone's daughter Paula, and featured his other daughter, Dorothy, in a major role.

LEFT: Fred Stone and Dave Montgomery in the roles that made them the most beloved performers of the early part of the twentieth century.

BELOW: Franz the Sheriff (Charles Dox) is not fooled by Connor and Kidder.

ROSE-MARIE

OPENED SEPTEMBER 2, 1924; IMPERIAL THEATRE; 311 PERFORMANCES

ABOVE: Sergeant Malone (Arthur Deagon, far left) and his Royal Canadian Mounted Police.

RIGHTt: The girls of "Totem Tom Tom."

ROSE-MARIE

Produced by Arthur Hammerstein
Book staged by Paul Dickey
Music by Rudolf Friml and Herbert P. Stothart
Book and Lyrics by
Otto Harbach and Oscar Hammerstein II
Orchestra under the direction of
Herbert Stothart
Orchestrations by Robert Russell Bennett

Dances arranged by Dave Bennett
Gowns and costumes designed by
Charles LeMaire
Settings by Gates and Morange

Synopsis

Rose-Marie, a singer in a hotel deep in the Canadian Rockies, is at the center of a love triangle. Trader Ed Hawley is in love with Rose-Marie, who in turn loves Jim Kenyon. When the Indian Black Eagle is murdered, Ed tries to frame Jim and get him out of the way. Rose-Marie, knowing the plots of operettas only too well, tells Ed that if he exonerates Jim, she will marry him to save the man she loves. Before the wedding can take place, Sergeant Malone of the Canadian Rockies saves the day, clearing Jim of the charges and discrediting Ed.

Cast

Sergeant Malone .... *Arthur Deagon*
Lady Jane .... *Dorothy MacKaye*
Black Eagle .... *Arthur Ludwig*
Edward Hawley .... *Frank Greene*
Emile La Flemme .... *Edward Chianelli*
Wanda .... *Pearl Regay*
Hard-Boiled Herman .... *William Kent*
Jim Kenyon .... *Dennis King*
Rose-Marie La Flamme .... *Mary Ellis*
Ethel Brander .... *Lela Bliss*

THERE ARE MANY REASONS WHY shows are written. Some for money, some for fame, and some for other reasons that have nothing to do with art. The Shubert brothers, Lee and J.J., were known to have songs written for their shows simply because they had a warehouse full of, say, bird costumes or wooden shoes. Similarly, producer Arthur Hammerstein wanted to produce a new operetta but couldn't figure out how shake up what had become a formulaic style. Instead of changing the way the shows were written, he focused his energies on constantly finding new, exotic settings for his operettas to give them variety. Thus, *The Three Musketeers* took place in France, *Naughty Marietta* had dibs on New Orleans, The *Merry Widow* waltzed in Paris, and *The Fortune Teller* used the Czardas sounds of Hungary as its background. Hammerstein was at a loss for an untapped locale for his new show until he heard of a winter carnival in Quebec, at the conclusion of which snowshoed revelers took lit torches to the extravagant ice sculptures. Arthur sent his nephew, Oscar, and Otto Harbach to Quebec to see this magnificent ceremony. While the idea for the winter fest operetta was left out in the cold, the two librettists, now in a Canadian state of mind, looked further west to the Rockies, and voila, *Rose-Marie* was born.

The idea was so stupendous that two composers would be necessary to write the score. Both Rudolf Friml and Herbert Stothart were hired (Stothart would later achieve great fame at MGM as the incidental musical composer for *The Wizard of Oz*), and the splendor of the Rockies demanded no less a talent than Mary Ellis, then a star of the Metropolitan Opera, to play the title role.

SONGS

ACT I "Vive la Canadienne" · "Hard-Boiled Herman" "Rose-Marie" · "The Mounties" · "Lak Jeem" · "Indian Love Call" · "Pretty Things" · "Why Shouldn't We?" · "Totem Tom-Tom"

ACT II "Only a Kiss" · "I Love Him" · "The Minuet of the Minute" · "One Man Woman" · "The Door of My Dreams"

Already Oscar Hammerstein II was working hard to break from convention and create a new kind of musical, and the show marked the first time a murder was the center of an operetta plot. The curtain fell on the two lovers alone on stage, not on a typical full-company chorale. Hammerstein was even making early strides to integrate song and story, for a note in the program read: "The musical numbers of this play are such an integral part of the action that we do not think we should list them as separate episodes."

Rose-Marie became the longest running musical of its time, surpassed only later by Hammerstein and Jerome Kern's *Show Boat*, which ran two weeks longer. There were no fewer than five national tours and a first-class revival on Broadway in 1927, and MGM filmed the story twice, in 1936 and again in 1954. Since its debut, *Rose-Marie* has become one of the most produced operettas in musical history. ❊

Rudolf Friml

Czechoslovakian Rudolf Friml was the ultimate operetta composer. When he tried to write for musical comedy, his romantic themes and broad melodies didn't quite suit the more up-to-the-minute style of jazz-influenced musicals. Friml came to America from Prague as a pianist whose flashy technique served him rather more than the music. When the Metropolitan Opera diva Emma Trentini was cast in *The Firefly* (1912), Victor Herbert refused to write for her. Friml gladly took the job and made a smash immediately with both the public and Trentini, with whom he began a passionate affair. Friml's next show, *High Jinks* (1913), was also a smash hit, and the young composer was on his way. He hit his stride in 1924 with the magnificent *Rose-Marie* and followed that with another classic, *The Vagabond King* (1925) and, a few years later, another huge hit, *The Three Musketeers* (1928). By the 1930s, the Depression took its toll on Broadway's finances as well as on the public's taste for operettas. Friml wrote two more shows, *Luana* (1930) and *Annina* (1934), but both were failures. He spent the rest of his life in California, mainly working on film adaptations of his hits.

ABOVE: Even the secondary couples find love in the Canadian Rockies.
BELOW: Eileen Brennan in the affectionate *Rose-Marie* spoof, *Little Mary Sunshine*.

Dennis King

Dennis King was a strong-voiced, dashing leading man of operetta and early musical comedy. In his Broadway musical debut, in 1924's *Rose-Marie*, King warbled the duet "Indian Love Call" with costar Mary Ellis, giving those heretics who roll their eyes at the earnest, heart on the sleeve emotions of musicals a perfect target to spoof. He followed up with other Rudolf Friml operettas, *The Vagabond King*, *The Three Musketeers*, and the Franz Lehar flop *Frederika*. Also carving out a career as a wonderful dramatic actor, he returned to singing in 1938, introducing "Spring Is Here" and the beautiful title song of Rodgers and Hart's *I Married an Angel*. In a real-life changing-of-the-guard moment, King's last Broadway musical, the bomb *Shangri-La*, opened three months after the runanway smash *My Fair Lady*, featuring his son, John Michael King. As Freddy Eynsford-Hill, King Junior sang "On the Street Where You Live," a song that, thirty years earlier, would have been introduced by his father.

Backstage

Oscar Hammerstein II asked theatre critics not to review the tour of *Rose-Marie* since he felt they "do not recognize what a good libretto is, and do not realize that a good musical comedy must not necessarily be a good play."

TOP LEFT: Jim and Rose-Marie (Dennis King and Mary Ellis). TOP CENTER: Dennis King in *The Vagabond King*. TOP RIGHT: Dennis King in the Harry Warren/Lawrence and Lee bomb, *Shangri-La*. ABOVE: Mary Ellis and company in the "Bridal Finale"—the perfect ending to any operetta.

T & A, PART II

SINCE NEW YORK THEATRE IN part existed as entertainment for the tired businessman (the 1913 edition of *The Passing Show* actually had a character named The Tired Businessman, played by Herbert Gilfoil), there was a direct correlation between the demise of burlesque and the rise of its eye-popping elements in the Broadway musical. Through shows like *As the Girls Go, Ankles Aweigh*, and the Mike Todd revues of the 1940s and '50s (*Star and Garter*), beauty changed from the idolized, pedestal-placed lovelies to the brazen bustiness and naughty sexuality of the Cy Feuer/Ernie Martin shows *Can-Can* and *Whoop-Up*, which started a trend (with the exotically named Asia) of having a single monikered bombshell enliven the proceedings with her mere presence. Virginia Martin was another dumb blonde bimbo (although usually she was a redhead) in shows like *Little Me, New Faces of 1956, How to Succeed*, and others.

Then too, the tired businesswoman (or the tired businessman with alternative tastes) was not ignored, for the shows of Joshua Logan always provided acres of male pulchritude, the sweaty Seabees of *South Pacific*, the swimsuit-clad campers of *Wish You Were Here*, and the locker room action of *All American* raising the temperature of many a Broadway theatregoer.

Unfortunately, not all of the reforms to morality were for the better, for we can point to *The Best Little Whorehouse in Texas Goes Public*, one of the most unabashedly trashy shows ever (playing in a house named for theatre royalty Alfred Lunt and Lynn Fontanne, no less), where the girls, encased in Plexiglas cubes, had phone sex with middle-aged businessmen, clad in boxer shorts and black socks and sitting atop the cubes. Classy.

Surely the pendulum of what is acceptable and what is not will swing again, as it always does—but after full frontal nudity and whores in Plexiglas, what barrier is left to break?

ABOVE: Rachel York, wearing little more than a smile, sings "Lost and Found" in *City of Angels*.

RIGHT: Anita Morris, who kidded sexuality better than any musical actress since Gwen Verdon, gives Guido "A Call from the Vatican," one of the many tour de force numbers in *Nine*.

TOP RIGHT: *The Will Rogers Follies* sported the most stunning chorines in recent memory, seen here in "The Powder Puff Ballet."

Anita Morris

Anita Morris, perhaps the most overtly sexual actress to ever appear in a Broadway musical, offset her remarkable physical attributes with a near-coloratura range, the flexibility of a contortionist, and razor-sharp comic gifts. After a debut in the original cast of *Jesus Christ Superstar*, she gained attention as the gymnastic leader of a pack of hookers in the "My City" number in *Seesaw* (where she met future husband, director and choreographer Grover Dale). After more exposure (in every way) in *Rachel Lily Rosenbloom . . . and Don't You Ever Forget It, The Magic Show*, and a missed opportunity for stardom with a showstopping song and dance in the out-of-town disaster *Home Again, Home Again*, she replaced as Miss Mona in *The Best Little Whorehouse in Texas*, further solidifying her friendship with her *Seesaw* costar, by now the rising director/choreographer Tommy Tune. In Tune's state of the art *Nine*, unfortunately Morris's last Broadway musical before her death from cancer, her tour de force "A Call from the Vatican" was something that no one, and we mean no one, could ever approach in its combination of musical comedy expertise and bewildered yet naughty sensuality.

SALLY

OPENED DECEMBER 21, 1920; NEW AMSTERDAM THEATRE; 561 PERFORMANCES

ABOVE: The ethereal Marilyn Miller as Sally.

RIGHT: Rubber-legged comedian, Leon Errol.

SALLY

Music by Jerome Kern and Victor Herbert
Book by Guy Bolton
Lyrics by Clifford Grey
"Butterfly Ballet" Music by Victor Herbert
Orchestra under the direction of Gus Salzer

Produced by Florenz Ziegfeld Jr.
Staged by Edward Royce

Settings designed by Joseph Urban
Costumes designed by Alice O'Neil

Synopsis

Poor orphan Sally Rhinelander is brought by the rich society lady Mrs. Ten Broek to the Alley Inn, a theatrical boardinghouse, to work as a dishwasher. Sally's dream, however, is to be a dancer in the *Ziegfeld Follies*, and she is encouraged in her fantasies by the often drunk waiter, Connie. Blair Farquar, son of one of the richest men on Long Island, bumps into Sally, who immediately falls in love with the handsome man. Connie is invited to a ball on the Farquar estate, and meets theatrical agent Otis Hooper who is looking for a Russian ballerina to entertain at the ball. Sally pretends to be Russian but when her real identity is revealed she is banished to the kitchen. Hooper, still believing in the girl, casts her in the *Follies*. And like all *Follies* girls, Sally weds a millionaire—Blair!

Cast

Pops	*Alfred P. James*
Rosalind Rafferty	*Mary Hay*
Otis Hooper	*Walter Catlett*
Mrs. Ten Broek	*Dolores*
Sally of the Alley	*Marilyn Miller*
Blair Farquar	*Irving Fisher*
Jimmy Spelvin	*Stanley Ridges*
Connie	*Leon Errol*

STAR POWER CAN BE AN engine to propel a musical into the stratosphere. A star can make an otherwise lackluster show into a hit— Lauren Bacall in *Applause* and Hugh Jackman in *The Boy from Oz*, are good examples. Sometimes, as in *Funny Girl*, *The King and I*, or *The Music Man*, a star is so identified with a role that all subsequent productions pale in comparison. In the case of a *Hello, Dolly!* or a *Fiddler on the Roof*, a show can open with a big star who defines a role, but other performers are capable of keeping the show running. Sometimes, as in *The Producers*, when the star (or stars) leaves, the box office plummets. Sometimes stars turn out to be actors who aren't billed as stars, as in the case of Gwen Verdon, who became an overnight sensation in *Can-Can*, much to the chagrin of Lilo, the show's nominal star. And Judy Carne was the billed star of the revival of *The Boy Friend*, but it was a featured Sandy Duncan who got all the reviews.

"Hello, you lousy son of a bitch."

Marilyn Miller, greeting Ziegfeld when he took his daughter Patricia backstage after Sally, *her first musical*

What is it about stars that makes them so special? Talent alone isn't enough; in fact, many of Broadway's biggest stars weren't the best singers, dancers, or actors, but what they all shared was a wonderful rapport with the audience and an indefinable quality that projected their personality up to the highest balcony. We don't mean to disregard talent, of course. A great performer has to work on honing his or her natural gifts.

Marilyn Miller, whose biggest success was *Sally*, knew that she hadn't built upon the talent she was born with. And she had the good sense to realize that unless she improved, her career and fame could not blossom. Once she was hired by Florenz Ziegfeld for *Sally*, Miller got serious about her craft, spending up to eighteen hours a day on singing, acting, and dancing lessons, and exercise classes. Her singing and acting markedly improved, and the critics said as much in reviewing the show. Since the show featured a score by the team of P. G. Wodehouse, Guy Bolton, and Jerome Kern and additional lyrics by Clifford Gray, Miller had to rise to meet her material—and excellent material it was, too.

The two biggest hits of the score, "Whip-poor-will" and "Look for the Silver Lining," came from the Kern and B. G. DeSylva show, *Zip Goes a Million*, which closed out of town. Another hit song, "Wild Rose," perfectly showcased Miller's delightful charm. All her hard work had paid off, and Miller became a bigger star than ever (at one performance, the applause became so deafening, Miller ran out to Forty-second Street with members of the audience following her, bringing her back to the theatre for an encore).

She became the toast of Broadway, and thanks to the generosity of Ziegfeld, she was the first female musical star to receive a percentage of the box office gross. In order to ensure that she didn't decamp to Hollywood (which in fact she had no intention of doing), Ziegfeld gave Miller a chauffeur-driven limousine, jewels, and furs. Marilyn Miller's success in the role resulted in a long run on Broadway, an extensive national tour, and, most important to us, a filmed version of the show with Miller, providing today's audiences with a brief taste of the lighter-than-air persona of the radiant Marilyn Miller, a star, it turns out, for all ages. ❋

Marilyn Miller

Marilyn Miller, the personification of the term "charm star," achieved an unparalleled popularity during her brief reign in the late 1920s. After appearing in vaudeville, she became a sensation dancing en pointe and adding her teeny-tiny singing voice and delicate beauty to editions of *The Passing Shows* and *The Ziegfeld Follies*. Catapulted to superstardom in the title role in *Sally* in 1925, her follow-up vehicles were all in a similar vein, primarily variations on a scrappy, rags-to-riches heroine. In *Sunny*, *Rosalie*, and *Smiles*, she introduced the standards "Look for the Silver Lining" and "Who?," among others. In her final Broadway show, the revusical *As Thousands Cheer*, Miller revealed an untapped flair for sophisticated comedy, playing Barbara Hutton and Joan Crawford in sketches with the soigné Clifton Webb. Leading a much more complicated life than her ever-optimistic characters (she was married four times, had a long-running affair with Ziegfeld, and had a reputation for being impossible to work with), Miller died at the age of thirty-seven, from health issues magnified by alcoholism.

ABOVE: Marilyn as spritely Sally.
RIGHT: Here she is as the title character in *Sunny*.
BELOW: Our star runs through her songs with musical director Gus Salzer.

SONGS

ACT I "Way Down East" · "On with the Dance" · "This Little Girl" · "Joan of Arc" "Look for the Silver Lining" (lyrics by B. G. DeSylva) · "Sally"
ACT II "The Social Game" · "The Wild Rose" "(On the Banks of) the Schnitza-Komisski" "Whip-poor-Will" (lyrics by B. G. DeSylva) "The Lorelei" (lyrics by Anne Caldwell) · "Little Church Around the Corner" (lyrics by P.G. Wodehouse)

Backstage

Marilyn Miller was the first person named Marilyn. Her given name was Marilynn, an amalgam of the names of her maternal grandparents, Mary and Lynn. It was soon shortened to Marilyn and every other Marilyn owes her a debt of gratitude.

As John Adams, William Daniels sang in roughly the same sonorous tone in which he spoke, proving that acting ability is far more important than perfectly placed high notes when you're handed a musical as superbly written as *1776*.

1776

OPENED MARCH 16, 1969; 46TH STREET THEATRE; 1,217 PERFORMANCES

1776

Produced by Stuart Ostrow
Book by Peter Stone
Music and Lyrics by Sherman Edwards
Musical Director: Peter Howard
Music orchestrated by Eddie Sauter
Dance Arrangements by Peter Howard
Vocal Arrangements by Elise Bretton

Directed by Peter Hunt
Musical Staging by Onna White

Scenic Design by Jo Mielziner
Lighting Design by Jo Mielziner
Costume Design by Patricia Zipprodt

Synopsis

John Adams is frustrated that the Continental Congress refuses to recognize the importance of the Colonies' independence from Great Britain. A thoroughly abrasive personality, Adams teams up with Benjamin Franklin, a more level-headed statesman, to convince the members to break from the mother country. Richard Henry Lee, a delegate from Virginia, convinces his fellow Southerners to entertain the idea. It's finally decided that a declaration of independence is in order, and Thomas Jefferson is elected to draft the paper. Arguments as to its contents ensue. The Northerners want slavery abolished, the Southerners call the brethren hypocrites. Jefferson's writing progresses slowly until Adams and Franklin arrange for Martha Jefferson to pay her husband a conjugal visit and restore his concentration. Finally, the Declaration of Independence is ratified—just in time for the Fourth of July holiday.

Cast

John Adams	*William Daniels*
Stephen Hopkins	*Roy Poole*
Benjamin Franklin	*Howard Da Silva*
John Dickinson	*Paul Hecht*
Richard Henry Lee	*Ronald Holgate*
Thomas Jefferson	*Ken Howard*
Edward Rutledge	*Clifford David*
Abigail Adams	*Virginia Vestoff*
Martha Jefferson	*Betty Buckley*

THE MUSICAL *1776* BELONGS TO that rare breed of show in which the libretto is stronger than the score. This isn't to say that *1776* has a bad score, but the libretto could conceivably stand alone, without Sherman Edwards's contributions. There are a few other shows, very few, in which the librettos stand out as the premiere element. *City of Angels* comes to mind (though we like the score, too), as does the more recent *Sweet Smell of Success*. And today's *Wicked* and *The Producers* have serviceable scores married to excellent books.

Peter Stone, a librettist with a track record unequal to his reputation, certainly struck dramatic gold with his libretto for *1776*. The libretto does follow actual historical events, and it's a remarkable story in its own right. But Stone accomplishes a miracle. Although the audience certainly knows the outcome of the story (unless they slept through seventh-grade civics class), Stone instills a real sense of suspense. There's an actual moment of doubt as to whether the damned declaration will be signed or not.

In his second historic libretto, for *Titanic* (the first letterboxed musical), Stone had much more difficulty grasping on to a narrative line. The action bounces around the decks, zeroing in on one or another passenger or crew member and connecting emotionally with only the few characters who had clear-cut motivations (the stoker, the telegraph operator, and a second-class woman desperate to mingle with society). With a story fully equal to the signing of the Declaration of Independence in dramatic impact, Stone was reduced

> "If you were Thomas Jefferson and hadn't seen your wife for six months, wouldn't you finish writing the Declaration of Independence the minute that Betty Buckley walked in the door?"
>
> —*Stuart Ostrow to Peter Stone and Sherman Edwards, following Buckley's audition*

to pointing up the ironies of history in his libretto, assigning many of the characters banalities about the frigid weather and the lack of lifeboat drills.

But in *1776*, Stone gave the many characters distinct personalities, using the historical data to develop the characters. He had the added foresight (after cutting an unnecessary scene at a tavern) to set the play almost entirely within the confines of what would become Independence Hall.

Sherman Edwards, who had written a few minor teenage-oriented pop songs, surprised everyone with the quality of his score—his first and only for the Broadway stage. Like Meredith Willson of *Music Man* fame, he seemed to have only one really good show in him. But, as fine as Edwards's score is (and a lot of the praise has to go to orchestrator Eddie Sauter and the cast), Peter Stone's book is a revelation. He created a realistic milieu and three-dimensional characters, and imbued the proceedings—somewhat stolid and archaic political discussions—with a real sense of urgency and drama. ✻

Peter Stone

Book writer Peter Stone began his career with two shows that didn't quite set the world ablaze: *Kean*, starring Alfred Drake, and *Skyscraper*, Julie Harris's only foray into musicals. Undeterred, Stone finally achieved success in 1969 with his greatest work, the highly literate book for *1776* (really a play with songs, as one thirty-five-minute stretch is completely without music). After that, the 1970s found Stone scripting the unhappy Danny Kaye vehicle *Two by Two* and adapting the screenplay of Some *Like It Hot*, (musicalized as *Sugar*). Stone racked up two hits in the 1980s: *Woman of the Year*, and *My One and Only*, salvaged during a particularly hellish Boston tryout. *My One and Only*'s director, Tommy Tune, called upon Stone to write another historical piece, the vaudeville biomusical *The Will Rogers' Follies*. Tune then hooked Stone up with another frequent collaborator, the composer Maury Yeston, and together they wrote the Tony-winning *Titanic*. His last work was his most unnecessary. In order to make the 2000 Bernadette Peters revival of *Annie Get Your Gun* palatable for modern audiences, the book was rewritten in the name of every untutored producer's catchphrase, "political correctness." Unfortunately, in Stone's revisal, instead of an increased relevancy, the book somehow became much more inane and creaky than Herbert and Dorothy Fields's excellent original.

ABOVE: This photo from the tavern scene, which was cut out of town, is a real rarity. Franklin (Howard Da Silva) fraternizes with assorted strumpets and wenches.

TOP RIGHT: As Abigail and John Adams, Virgina Vestoff and William Daniels made American history not only interesting but tuneful.

RIGHT: Two of the most talented and nicest people working on Broadway today, Brian d'Arcy James and Martin Moran, played the stoker and the wireless operator in the Maury Yeston/Peter Stone *Titanic*.

Backstage

Sherman Edwards worked on *1776* for ten years before the show opened in New York.

The musical played the Nixon White House on Washington's birthday, just about one year after it opened on Broadway. It was the first show performed in its entirety at the White House.

TOP: Clifford David (center) and his fellow conservatives espouse the views of "Cool, Cool Considerate Men."

ABOVE: John Zacherle, Howard Da Silva, and Thayer David in the out of town flop *La Belle*.

RIGHT: Daniels and Da Silva bemusedly watch reunited newlyweds Thomas and Martha Jefferson, played by Ken Howard and a twenty-year-old Betty Buckley who was right off the bus from Texas.

Howard Da Silva

Howard Da Silva, a brilliant character actor whose presence in a few landmark shows made him an important figure, first sang in the historic *The Cradle Will Rock* in 1938. Never a natural for musicals (his singing voice could best be described as highly audible), his excellent acting made him the choice of Richard Rodgers and Oscar Hammerstein to create the role of Jud Fry in the original production of *Oklahoma!* After being blacklisted for refusing to testify before HUAC during the 1950s communist witch hunt, Da Silva maintained a low profile until he was cast as Ben Marino in *Fiorello!*, stopping the show with his two numbers—"Little Tin Box" and "Politics and Poker." After writing the book to the undeniably strange *The Zulu and the Zayda* in 1965, he next appeared as Benjamin Franklin in *1776*, and even with his tour-de-force scene cut from the show out of town, Da Silva was a resounding success, repeating his performance in the film version. Health problems forced him to leave the *1776* cast immediately after the opening, so he was replaced on the cast album by Rex Everhart. His stage appearances in the 1970s and '80s were limited, but Da Silva continued to work as producer and director.

SHE LOVES ME

OPENED APRIL 23, 1963; EUGENE O'NEILL THEATRE; 302 PERFORMANCES

Amalia Balash (Barbara Cook), waiting for the man of her dreams, meets the man of her nightmares (Daniel Massey). Violinist Gino Conforti provides the "romantic atmosphere."

SHE LOVES ME

Produced by Harold Prince
Music by Jerry Bock
Lyrics by Sheldon Harnick
Book by Joe Masteroff
Based on a Play by Miklos Laszlo
Musical Director: Harold Hastings
Music orchestrated by Don Walker
Incidental Music arranged by Jack Elliott

Directed by Harold Prince
Musical Staging by Carol Haney

Scenic and Lighting Design by
William and Jean Eckart
Costume Design by Patricia Zipprodt

Synopsis

Georg Nowack, a salesman at Maraczek's Parfumerie, is carrying on a romantic pen pal relationship with "Dear Friend," a woman he believes he has never met. In fact, the woman in question is Amalia Balash, who works alongside Georg. In real life, they hate each other. What will happen when they discover it's a thin line between love and hate?

Cast

Amalia Balash	Barbara Cook
Georg Nowack	Daniel Massey
Ilona Ritter	Barbara Baxley
Steven Kodaly	Jack Cassidy
Mr. Maraczek	Ludwig Donath
Ladislav Sipos	Nathaniel Frey
Arpad Laszlo	Ralph Williams
Headwaiter	Wood Romoff
Violinist	Gino Conforti
Busboy	Al De Sio

FEAR OF INTIMACY IS A common problem among humans. And so it is with musicals. Many a wonderful, intimate show has been injected, stretched, inflated, embellished, and enlarged beyond its tender means. The process ruined the otherwise wonderful *Dear World*. It overwhelmed the tender memory musical *The Happy Time*. It kitsched up the simplicity of *Here's Love*. And it buried the soft gentility of *Sugar Babies*. All right, maybe not *Sugar Babies*. Okay, definitely not *Sugar Babies*.

Some shows just scream to be big—*Show Boat*, *42nd Street*, *Phantom of the Opera*, *Jumbo* (well, the name says it). But others would benefit from the adage "less is more." Director/producer Harold Prince had the wisdom to keep *She Loves Me* small. The trials and tribulations of the employees of a perfume shop don't demand big production numbers, dazzling settings, or huge, blasting orchestrations.

Barbara Cook, who could raise the roof as she amply exhibited in *Candide*, pulled back and drew the audience into her character, allowing her acting to come to the forefront. This is only fair since she was paired with Daniel Massey, who was a marvelous actor but only a middling singer.

Though it's been called a "jewel box of a musical," a "candy box," and a "bonbon," *She Loves Me* isn't quite as small and intimate as it seems. It did, after all, fill the stage of the Eugene O'Neill Theatre. But the orchestrations, reliance on stage movement rather than choreography, restrained use of the chorus, and general lightness of touch make it an intimate, romantic musical of the first rank. Not surprisingly, it is especially difficult to revive successfully. The urge is always there to expand the moments, enlarge the performances, and insert a few sight gags. That was one of the problems of the 1993 Roundabout Theatre revival; if you are going to present a cream puff, don't give the audience a ten-tiered wedding cake with rose columns and too much schlag. ✻

Ilona (Barbara Baxley) and Amalia (Barbara Cook) bond while wrapping Christmas presents at Maraczek's Parfumerie.

The basis for of the story for *She Loves Me* has inspired movies for over sixty years, from Ernst Lubitsch's *The Shop Around the Corner* through the MGM musical *In the Good Old Summertime,* to the Tom Hanks/Meg Ryan vehicle *You've Got Mail.*

At the opening-night party for the New Haven tryout of *She Loves Me*, director Harold Prince surprised the company by playing singer Lena Horne's soon to be released pop recording of the show's title song. When star Daniel Massey (son of actor Raymond Massey, best known for playing Abraham Lincoln in films) commented on how nice it was that Lena Horne wanted to sing his big number, Jack Cassidy, without missing a beat, replied, "Why wouldn't she—after all, your father freed her people."

LEFT: Amalia (Barbara Cook) makes a sale in "No More Candy."

BELOW LEFT: Barbara Cook, as Amish girl Hilda Miller, sizes up a modern contraption she's never seen in *Plain and Fancy*. Shirl Conway looks (and laughs) on.

BELOW: Cook during her Viennese period, at her most glorious and gorgeous in 1962's *The Gay Life*.

Barbara Cook

Barbara Cook, an exceptional singing actress and owner of one of the most distinctive and ageless soprano voices ever, has had as varied a career in the musical theatre as is possible. Playing every imaginable female type, she has traveled the entire range of musical theatre territory: as ingénue (*Flahooley*), soubrette (*Plain and Fancy*), comic ingénue (*Candide*), leading lady (*The Music Man*), above-the-title star (*The Gay Life*), diva (*She Loves Me*) and bikini-clad temptress (*Something More!*). After *The Grass Harp* (another flop with another treasurable "magic moment," the thrilling "Chain of Love"), she entered the concert world with a Carnegie Hall evening and, finally, became a full-fledged legend. Since 1985, apart from the *Follies* concert at Lincoln Center, the closest Cook has come to starring in a book musical on Broadway was in the pre-Broadway Stratford production of the legendary misfire *Carrie*, where she was nearly decapitated one evening by an errant piece of scenery. She wisely took it as an omen and bailed out. Today she's regarded as our greatest interpreter of American Popular Song.

Jack Cassidy

Jack Cassidy, the epitome of the debonair matinee idol with a deeply vain streak, started his career with almost ten years in the chorus. He first garnered attention as a young leading man in the shows *Wish You Were Here* and *Shangri-La*, hitting his stride in the 1960s in *She Loves Me; Fade Out, Fade In;* and *It's a Bird ... It's a Plane ... It's Superman*. His tour de force turns in those three shows, (titled, respectively, "Grand Knowing You," "My Fortune Is My Face" and "The Woman for the Man") helped him create his own type, cornering the market of the slightly smarmy, self-possessed lady killer. After an out-of-town closing (replacing Alfred Marks in Frank Loesser's last musical *Pleasures and Palaces*) and the disappointing *Maggie Flynn* opposite wife Shirley Jones, he fought the changing tide of Broadway and personal demons while touring nightclubs and working in television. His death in a 1976 fire robbed us of the third act of Cassidy's Broadway musical career.

ABOVE: As movie star Byron Prong in *Fade Out, Fade In*, Cassidy points to the dimple that says it all: "My Fortune Is My Face."

LEFT: Smooth operator Steven Kodaly (Jack Cassidy) spins his web for the gullible Ilona (Barbara Baxley).

"The chances are, if you work often enough, some of your best work will be underestimated, some of your poorer work will get by. If you work consistently enough, it balances out."

— *Harold Prince*

SONGS

ACT I · "Good Morning, Good Day" · "Thank You, Madam" "Days Gone By" · "No More Candy" · "Three Letters" "Tonight at Eight" · "I Don't Know His Name" · "Perspective" · "Will He Like Me?" · "Ilona" · "I Resolve" · "A Romantic Atmosphere" · "Tango Tragique" · "Dear Friend" **ACT II** · "Try Me" · "Where's My Shoe" · "(Vanilla) Ice Cream" · "She Loves Me" · "A Trip to the Library" · "Grand Knowing You" · "Twelve Days to Christmas"

SHOW BOAT

OPENED DECEMBER 27, 1927; ZIEGFELD THEATRE; 572 PERFORMANCES

Cap'n Andy (Charles Winninger) on the stage of the *Cotton Blossom*, acts out the melodrama *The Parson's Wife*, to the astonishment of the audience.

SHOW BOAT

Produced by Florenz Ziegfeld
Music by Jerome Kern
Lyrics by Oscar Hammerstein II
Book by Oscar Hammerstein II
Based on "Show Boat" by Edna Ferber
Music orchestrated by Robert Russell Bennett
Musical director: Victor Baravalle
Choral director William Vodery

Directed by
Zeke Colvan and Oscar Hammerstein II
Choreography by Sammy Lee

Settings by Joseph Urban
Costumes by John Harkrider

Synopsis

Cap'n Andy and Aunt Parthy run a showboat on the Mississippi river. When their daughter, Magnolia, sees riverboat gambler Gaylord Ravenal, it's love at first site for both of them. Also on the boat is the sultry singer/actress Julie, who takes Magnolia under her wing. Julie is exposed as partially black and is forced to leave the showboat, and Gaylord and Magnolia marry and have a daughter, Kim. Although they are still in love, Gaylord's gambling destroys the marriage and Magnolia is forced to seek work in nightclubs. Cap'n Andy catches up with Magnolia at the Chicago World's Fair and convinces her to come back to the showboat. She returns with Kim and many years later Gaylord returns to complete the family.

Cast

Queenie	Aunt Jemima (Tess Gardella)
Parthy Ann Hawkes	Edna May Oliver
Cap'n Andy	Charles Winninger
Ellie	Eva Puck
Frank	Sammy White
Julie	Helen Morgan
Gaylord Ravenal	Howard Marsh
Magnolia	Norma Terris
Joe	Jules Bledsoe

"Hammerstein's book in present shape has not got a chance except with critics. By the public, no, and I have stopped producing for critics and empty houses."

—*Florenz Ziegfeld*

W HAT *Gone with the Wind* is to movies, *Show Boat* is to the musical theatre. The staggering achievement of this epic musical play is all the more remarkable given its place in musical theatre history, for when *Show Boat* opened in 1927, the art form was still in its adolescence. Operettas were the rage, as were light musical comedies with an emphasis on their burlesque and vaudeville roots. Social commentary of any kind was unheard of, as were three-dimensional characterizations. In addition, musicals of its era shied away from tragic elements, and white audiences (the vast majority of Broadway theatregoers) were quite unused to seeing blacks portrayed on stage in anything but the most stereotypical ways. Going against the grain in every way, *Show Boat* had a unique setting—not the cutout cardboard mountains of the Rockies or the cabarets of Paris but the environs of the mighty Mississippi River. Only the scenes set at the Chicago World's Fair can be construed as typical operetta locale.

While the show had its roots in operetta, the plot was something totally new, uncompromising in its seriousness. Few of the characters in *Show Boat* are without flaws, and although most are sympathetic, happy endings aren't in the cards for many of them. The struggles of the all-too-human Ravenal, Magnolia, and Julie for better, happier futures give the show its drive. *Show Boat* is also unique in that there is no villain, and the ensemble (comprised of 36 white chorus girls, 16 white chorus boys, 16 black male singers, 16 black female singers, and 12 black female dancers) was used in a new way—as characters on the Mississippi, audiences on the showboat, and visitors to the World's Fair, rather than the prancing-pony chorus lines previously used to pump up production volume. *Show Boat* was also different in a way that was noted by Florenz Ziegfeld in a historic letter to Jerome Kern: "After marriage remember your love interest is eliminated." The show's epic qualities give it weight and importance and the mature and serious nature of its sympathetic characters make it a classic.

The score by Kern and Hammerstein was, of course, a huge part of the show's success. In addition to the important leap forward in the integration of song and story that had long been pursued by Kern, Hammerstein, and a few of their contemporaries, the scope of the composition is frankly stunning. Reflecting the epic nature of the story with its own breadth, it offers soaring ballads, spirituals, cakewalks, jazz, and torch songs. Hammerstein's use of vernacular and poetic language in both the lyrics and dialogue was unlike that of any other musical. In the songs, especially, Hammerstein expressed his compassion with the characters; where the story might lead them to heartache and strife, the music bared their souls. The score to *Show Boat* spawned no fewer than six standards, a record for musical theatre.

Producer Florenz Ziegfeld doesn't seem the obvious choice of a producer of a seriously artistic and uncompromising musical, but perhaps he didn't realize how groundbreaking it would be. Kern and Hammerstein, however, believed in the possibilities of the musical theatre and were determined to treat Edna Ferber's sprawling novel with the respect it deserved. Ziegfeld built his new theatre on Sixth Avenue expressly for *Show Boat*, but the time needed to write such a daunting work caused the show to be postponed, and Ziegfeld had to open his new house with a good but typical operetta, *Rio Rita*. Its success meant that *Show Boat*'s opening would have to wait till *Rio Rita* closed. Although Ziegfeld had major doubts about the commercial viability of *Show Boat*, he was keenly aware of his reputation of never, ever scrimping on a show's physical production, so despite his misgivings, he spent money lavishly, ensuring that its opulent look equaled the excellence of the writing.

When it finally opened after sellout engagements in Washington, D.C., Pittsburgh, Cleveland, and Philadelphia, *Show Boat* proved to be the biggest success yet in the American theatre and an influential show for decades to come. It played for almost two years in New York to sold-out houses, grossing nearly $50,000 a week. It has been revived many times on Broadway and throughout the world, and has been filmed three times. ❅

Backstage

Show Boat ran longer than any other Jerome Kern show.

Dorothy Blanchard, cast in *Charlot's Revue of 1924*, told her future husband, Oscar Hammerstein II, that being in show business "wasn't nearly as wicked as I thought it would be." A song lyric was born.

The main melodic theme of the song "Ol' Man River" is the same as that of "Cotton Blossom," but inverted and slowed down in tempo.

TOP: Magnolia Ravenal (Norma Terris) and Gaylord Ravenal (Howard Marsh) in happier times.
BOTTOM: Rebecca Luker, Lonette McKee, and Tony Award-winner Gretha Boston in the Hal Prince revival of *Show Boat* in 1994.

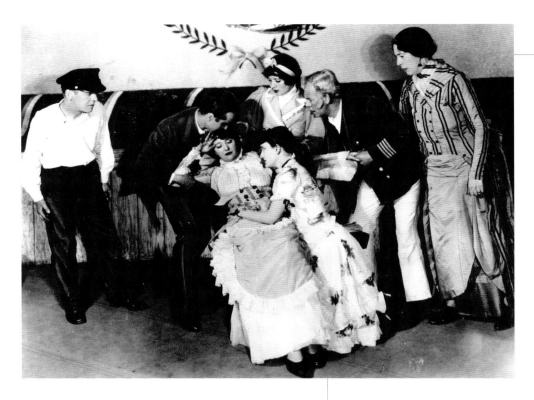

Helen Morgan

With an early career in Chicago saloons and honky-tonks, Helen Morgan, the most famous torch singer of all time, made her theatrical debut in a touring company of *Sally*. Hitting New York, she became a sensation in the speakeasies of the Prohibition era, singing her "my man done me wrong" songs sitting atop an upright piano so as to be seen above the crowd at the underground clubs. Perfectly suited to the musical revue format of Broadway in the 1920s, she attracted notice from a more legitimate audience in *George White's Scandals of 1925* and *Americana* (1926), before producer Florenz Ziegfeld, composer Jerome Kern, and lyricist Oscar Hammerstein II cast Morgan as the tragic octaroon Julie LaVerne in *Show Boat* in 1927. She gave a performance that is still considered legendary more than seventy-five years later, full of helpless joy as she stopped the show with "Can't Help Lovin' Dat Man," later dissolving the Ziegfeld Theatre to tears with her forlorn, fragile rendition of "Bill" (perched atop her trademark piano). Morgan starred in *Sweet Adeline* two years later, once again with a score

by Kern and Hammerstein, introducing the weepy standards "Why Was I Born?" and "Don't Ever Leave Me." She made a few film appearances, but she was beginning to lose her long battle with alcohol. With a personal life as tragic as any of her songs, Morgan retired due to poor health and years of drinking, soon after filming the magnificent 1936 movie version of *Show Boat*. At the age of 41, she succumbed to cirrhosis of the liver in 1941.

ABOVE: Rubber Faced (Francis X. Mahoney), Steve (Charles Ellis), Ellie (Eva Puck), Magnolia (Norma Terris), Cap'n Andy (Charles Winninger), and Parthy (Edna Mae Oliver) console Julie (Helen Morgan).

RIGHT: Helen Morgan in *Sweet Adeline*.
BELOW: Cap'n Andy and the belles of Chicago.

SONGS

ACT 1 "Cotton Blossom" · "Ballyhoo" · "Where's the Mate for Me?" · "Make Believe" · "Ol' Man River" · "Can't Help Lovin' Dat Man" · "Life Upon the Wicked Stage" "Till Good Luck Comes My Way" · "Misery" · "I Might Fall Back on You" · "C'mon Folks" · "You Are Love"
ACT 2 "At the Fair" · "Dandies on Parade" · "Why Do I Love You?" · "In Dahomey" · "Bill" (Lyrics by P.G. Wodehouse and Oscar Hammerstein II) · "Can't Help Lovin' Dat Man" · "Goodbye, My Lady Love" · "After the Ball" (Music and lyrics by Charles K. Harris) · "Hey, Feller"

Jerome Kern

Jerome Kern, one of the greatest composers of the early days of the musical theatre, became a success when his lovely song "They Didn't Believe Me" was interpolated into *The Girl from Utah* in 1914. Teaming with Guy Bolton and P. G. Wodehouse to write a series of musicals for Broadway's intimate Princess Theatre, their hits *Very Good Eddie* (1915), *Oh, Boy!* (1917), and *Leave It to Jane* (1917) made strides toward the integration of plot and songs and, with their accessible settings and regular-Joe characters, were a refreshing change from the exotic, foreign locales of the operetta. He continued with hit after hit, including the Marilyn Miller vehicles *Sally* (1920), with its standard "Look for the Silver Lining" and *Sunny* (1925). With lyricist-librettist Oscar Hammerstein II, he changed the course of musical theatre history with his versatile, sophisticated, and deeply felt score for *Show Boat, which* includes such classic songs as "Make Believe," "You Are Love," "Ol' Man River," and "Can't Help Lovin' Dat Man." Kern also teamed with Hammerstein on *Sweet Adeline* (1929) and *Music in the Air* (1932) and worked with Otto Harbach on *The Cat and the Fiddle* (1931) and *Roberta* (1933). After a sojourn in Hollywood, he and Hammerstein wrote their most beautiful and admired song, "All the Things You Are" for the 1939 *Very Warm for May.* After more movie musicals, he returned to New York to begin composing *Annie Get Your Gun*, with lyrics by Dorothy Fields, but he suffered a stroke while walking the streets of Manhattan, dying at the age of 60.

TOP LEFT: Lonette McKee played Julie LaVerne in two Broadway revivals of *Show Boat*. Here, she is singing "Bill" in the 1983 revival, starring Donald O'Connor as Cap'n Andy.

TOP RIGHT: Paul Robeson was unable to play Joe in the original, but he did act the part in the original London cast and the 1943 Broadway revival.

LEFT: Irene Dunne plays "Smoke Gets in Your Eyes" in *Roberta*.

SHUFFLE ALONG

OPENED MAY 23, 1921; 63RD STREET MUSIC HALL; 504 PERFORMANCES

Flournoy Miller (left) and Aubrey Lyles (right), authors and performers, redundantly black up in *Shuffle Along*.

SHUFFLE ALONG

Produced by Nikko Producing Company

Music by Eubie Blake
Lyrics by Noble Sissle
Book by Flournoy Miller and Aubrey Lyles

Directed by Walter Brooks
Dances arranged by
Charles Davis and Lawrence Deas
Orchestra under the direction of Eubie Blake
Musical arrangements by Will Vodery

Synopsis

Jimtown is holding an election and there are three candidates—Steve Jenkins, Sam Peck, and Harry Walton. Peck and Jenkins, co-owners of a grocery, promise that whoever is elected, they will name the other chief of police. Of course, neither can be trusted, for both are skimming money from the store's till to finance their campaigns. Unbeknownst to each other, they hire the same private eye to spy on their partner. Jenkins wins the election and promptly gets into a fight with his chief of police, but by the curtain's fall, Harry Walton (the guy everyone's wild about) leads a reform movement and unseats the crooks.

Cast

Piano .... *Eubie Blake*
Jessie Williams .... *Lottie Gee*
Ruth Little .... *Gertrude Saunders*
Harry Walton .... *Roger Matthews*
Tom Sharper .... *Noble Sissle*
Steve Jenkins .... *Flournoy E. Miller*
Sam Peck .... *Aubrey Lyles*

"[The orchestra played without music on their stands] because it was expected of us. People didn't believe that black people could read music— they wanted to think that our ability was just natural talent."

—*Eubie Blake*

THE PROBLEMS FACING BLACKS ON Broadway in many ways mirrored societal issues. The minstrel shows that led up to the emergence of musical comedy employed white performers in blackface, indulging in the most outrageous stereotypes. Black minstrel companies began to tour the country, further cementing the stereotypes of the white shows, with black performers themselves forced to don blackface. Soon after the end of the Civil War, a new, middle class emerged in the black population and began to strive for equality, both in society and in the theatre. Many of these blacks were educated in the new African American universities, and those with music majors yearned for equality both socially and professionally.

Legendary black performers Bert Williams and George Walker starred in *The Gold Bug* (1896) at the Casino Theatre, but the first all-black Broadway musical, written by and starring African Americans, was *A Trip to Coontown* (1898), with songs by Bob Cole. Cole wanted to emulate traditional (white) musical theatre. The second black show on Broadway was *Clorindy*, also in 1898, with music by Will Marion Cook and starring Ernest Hogan. When it arrived, Cook exclaimed, "Negroes are at last on Broadway, and here to stay!" Cook believed that the African American should make his own style of theatre and not emulate what "the white artist could always do as well, generally better." Cook also wrote the first black musical to play London's West End, *In Dahomey*

(1903), and the first interracial musical to play Broadway, *The Southerners* (1904).

Black Broadway shows continued to emerge sporadically, including *Mr. Lode of Coal* and *The Red Moon*, both produced in 1909. The last all-black Broadway show of this period was 1911's *His Honor, the Barber* with music by J. T. Brymn. By 1909, the number of black shows had diminished due to the deaths of Ernest Hogan, Bob Cole, and George Walker, for in addition to their skills as performers or songwriters, these men also managed their companies—companies that were on constantly shaky financial ground. Still, companies like Williams and Walker (without Walker), the Black Patti Troubadours, the Smart Set, and the Negro Players all produced shows throughout the United States until the 1920s.

Following the limited integration of World War I and a newfound interest by society folk in black artists, the time was ripe for a new generation of black songwriters to try their hand on Broadway. Whereas their black predecessors leaned toward operetta forms for their musicals, Noble Sissle and Eubie Blake straddled the line between ragtime and Tin Pan Alley. Performers and producers Flournoy Miller and Aubrey Lyles, along with Sissle and Blake, chose Miller and Lyles's popular vaudeville sketch "The Mayor of Dixie" as their basis for conquering the Great White Way. To get there, they realized they needed the help of a white producer, so Al Miller, a white booker for the Keith circuit and friend of Miller and Lyles, took his friend Harry Cort to lunch. Harry, the son of theatre owner and producer John Cort (after whom the Cort Theatre is named) liked the idea, and an

audition was set up with his father. The audition went well, and John Cort agreed to give the company a lecture hall a half mile from the northernmost point of Times Square, the 63rd Street Music Hall. Al Mayer became the show's manager.

Opening-night audiences were enthusiastic, but reviewers from the major papers were slow in attending. When they finally appeared, the reviews were mostly excellent, and business started picking up. The company added a Wednesday midnight performance, which was heavily attended by theatrical folk. *Shuffle Along* soon grew into the most successful show on Broadway. Adding to the fame of the show was the popularity of the song "(I'm Just) Wild About Harry," which earned as many as ten encores a show for singer Lottie Gee and dancer Bob Lee and was recorded hundreds of times, eventually serving as Harry Truman's campaign song. Another song from the show, the beautiful ballad "Love Will Find a Way," also became a hit, despite trepidation that white audiences would not accept blacks singing a romantic love song.

Among the famous performers who got their start in various companies of *Shuffle Along* were Paul Robeson, Josephine Baker, and the legendary Florence Mills. William Grant Still, the famed classical composer, and Hall Johnson, founder of the Hall Johnson Choir, played in its original pit orchestra. Still, the most important legacy of *Shuffle Along* is not its excellent score or its star-studded alumni: it brought a new respect and regard for black performers, opening the door for shows like Lew Leslie's *Blackbirds* series and *Porgy and Bess*, among many others. ❋

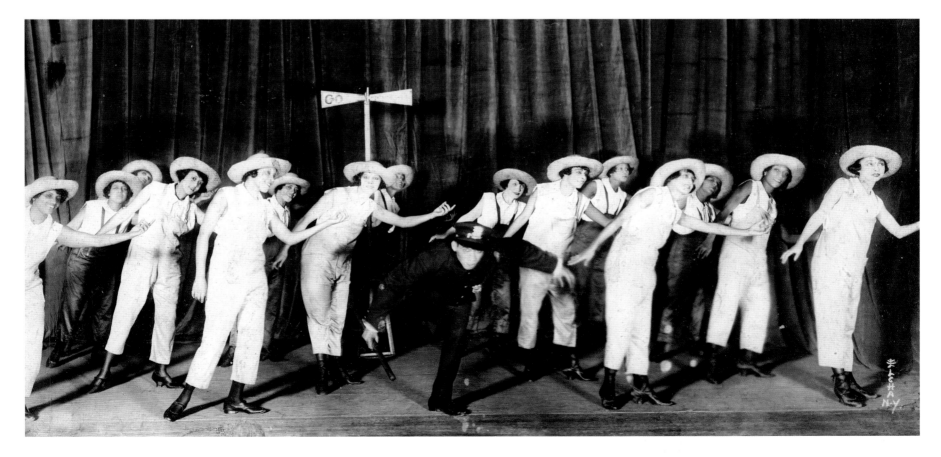

TOP: "I'm Just Wild About Harry," sung by Lottie Gee and danced by Bob Lee. ABOVE: Charlie Davis and the chorus hoof it up in the title song, "Shuffle Along."

Backstage

Shuffle Along was such a success that 63rd Street was made a one-way street to handle the increased traffic.

Shuffle Along's costumes were recycled from the shows *Roly-Boly* and Frank Fay's *Fables*.

SONGS

ACT I "(I'm) Simply Full of Jazz" · "Love Will Find a Way" "Bandana Days" · "Sing Me to Sleep, Dear Mammy" "(In) Honeysuckle Time" · "Gypsy Blues"

ACT II "Shuffle Along" · "(I'm Just) Wild About Harry" "Syncopation Stenos" · "If You Haven't Been Vamped by a Brownskin, You Haven't Been Vamped at All" · "Uncle Tom and Old Black Joe" · "Everything Reminds Me of You" · "Oriental Blues" · "I Am Craving That Kind of Love" (Kiss Me)/"Daddy (Won't You Please Come Home)" "Baltimore Buzz" · "African Dip"

Noble Sissle and Eubie Blake

The team of Noble Sissle and Eubie Blake met on May 15, 1915, in Baltimore, Maryland, at a rehearsal for Joe Porter's Serenaders. They teamed up the same day and began a lifelong friendship and collaboration. Sissle was an accomplished vocalist, and Blake was one of the finest ragtime players and composers. After their theatrical debuts with *Shuffle Along*, Sissle and Blake contributed to a number of Broadway shows, the last being *Shuffle Along of 1952*. Among their songs were such standards as "I'm Just Wild About Harry," "You Were Meant for Me" (in *André Charlot's Revue of 1924*) and the Blake/Andy Razaf standard "Memories of You" from *Blackbirds*. That men of their talents (also including Razaf and his sometime partner Thomas "Fats" Waller) never achieved more fame on Broadway or were summoned to Hollywood was simply due to racism. Both Sissle and Blake achieved a new appreciation and renaissance with the publication in 1972 of Robert Kimball and William Bolcom's *Reminiscing with Sissle and Blake*.

THE SOUND OF MUSIC

OPENED NOVEMBER 16, 1959; LUNT-FONTANNE THEATRE; 1,443 PERFORMANCES

ABOVE: "That will bring us back to Do-oh-oh-oh...."

RIGHT: Martin, as Maria Rainer, who, perched on a branch in her habit, was once mistaken by a group of Tyrolean birdwatchers for a lark who was learning to pray.

THE SOUND OF MUSIC

Produced by Leland Hayward, Richard Halliday, Richard Rodgers, and Oscar Hammerstein II

Music by Richard Rodgers
Lyrics by Oscar Hammerstein II
Book by Howard Lindsay and Russel Crouse
Based on "The Trapp Family Singers"
by Maria Augusta Trapp
Musical Director: Frederick Dvonch
Music orchestrated by Robert Russell Bennett
Choral arrangements by Trude Rittman

Directed by Vincent J. Donehue
Musical staging by Joe Layton

Scenic Design by Oliver Smith
Costume Design by Lucinda Ballard
Lighting Design by Jean Rosenthal
Mary Martin's clothes by Mainbocher

Synopsis

A postulant at Nonnberg Abbey in Austria isn't quite suited for the nunnery. Instead, Maria is encouraged by her Mother Superior to take a job as governess of the seven unruly children of the widowed Captain Von Trapp. Maria's free-wheeling ways rub the Captain the wrong way, but while he is away on business, she teaches the children to express their emotions through song. The Captain returns with his fiancée, but is gradually won over by the innocent charms of Maria. With the rise of the Third Reich, the family escapes across the Alps, filled with the sound of music.

Cast

Maria Rainer	*Mary Martin*
The Mother Abbess	*Patricia Neway*
Captain Georg von Trapp	*Theodore Bikel*
Liesl	*Lauri Peters*
Rolf Gruber	*Brian Davies*
Elsa Schraeder	*Marion Marlowe*
Max Detweiler	*Kurt Kasznar*
Postulant	*Bessie Mae Sue Ella Yaeger*

TRULY, *The Sound of Music* was a show better suited to the movies than the stage. As the curtain rose in the stage version, Maria was seen in a tree with a backdrop of the Alps behind her. No matter what they did to make it look real, it was still a chicken wire and papier-mâché tree in the Lunt-Fontanne Theatre. In the movie version, Julie Andrews twirled in a meadow, amid the real Alps, as captured by a magnificent helicopter shot. A song like "Do Re Mi" that came across as slightly insipid on stage became a rouser on the screen, what with the quick cutting of travelogue shots of Salzburg. The final chase and escape over the mountains was more vivid in the film, and *The Sound of Music*, a show that on Broadway was a hit, took on mammoth proportions after the film version was embraced by the public.

Of course, had the show been written a century earlier, it would have been gladly accepted by the local gentry, for most operettas took place in faraway kingdoms, usually Austria or some other Eastern European setting. Fake drops and less-than-accurate accents didn't matter, since most theatregoers had only seen black-and-white pictures of foreign lands and probably had never met an actual person from Eastern Europe, unless of course they had mistakenly ventured into the poorer sections of Manhattan.

Not all locales and genres are suited to the stage. That's one reason Westerns have never enjoyed much caché as a musical form. How do you get all those horses on stage? And where would you ride them? *Destry Rides Again* solved the problem by taking place mainly in a saloon. Baseball musicals were always considered impossible to stage until *Damn Yankees* came along, but it proved an exception to the rule, while *Sweeney Todd* is an exception to the generally held belief that horror themes aren't suitable for musicalization.

In truth, there's probably no subject that can't be made into a successful musical if the right approach can be found. Everyone thought that Shaw's *Pygmalion* was impossible to transform as a song-and-dance show. No less than the great Rodgers and Hammerstein took a crack at it and Lerner and Loewe's first attempts evoked nothing but despair. And if anyone had told you that a musical would be made from a group of T. S. Eliot's poems about cats or the signing of the Declaration of Independence or the opening of trade with feudal Japan or.... well, the list goes on and on.

The Sound of Music begins as a sweet (some say saccharine) story of a governess winning over a bunch of recalcitrant children and their strait-laced father, when all of a sudden the Nazis enter the picture and the show transforms into *The Great Escape*. That the two halves peacefully coexist is thanks to the skills of Rodgers, Hammerstein, Lindsay, and Crouse. In its best moments, *The Sound of Music* is a superbly well-constructed audience pleaser in the best tradition of the old-fashioned book musical. ❋

Lucinda Ballard

Costume designer Lucinda Ballard had a career on Broadway dating back to 1938. Her greatest work was the stunningly opulent costumes for the Viennese-flavored *The Gay Life*, written by her husband, Howard Dietz. She created the clothes for many plays (including the original *A Streetcar Named Desire*—that historic T-shirt) and such musicals as *Annie Get Your Gun*, *Street Scene*, the fascinating experiments of *Allegro* and *Love Life*, *Silk Stockings* and the stylish lederhosen and wimples of *The Sound of Music*. Ballard retired after *The Gay Life* (although she received many, many offers) to take care of Dietz, who suffered from Parkinson's disease. Until the 1970s, Ballard had received more Tony Awards than anyone else.

ABOVE: Theodore Bikel and Mary Martin, still in the combative stage of their relationship as the captain and the postulant.

BELOW: When the two songs for the Baroness and Max were cut for the film version, *The Sound of Music* lost much of its edge. Here, Bikel, Marion Marlowe, and Kurt Kaszner sing "No Way to Stop It."

SONGS

ACT I "The Sound of Music" · "Maria" · "My Favorite Things" · "Do-Re-Mi" · "You Are Sixteen" (Sixteen Going on Seventeen" · "The Lonely Goatherd" · "How Can Love Survive?" · "So Long, Farewell" · "Climb Every Mountain" **ACT II** "No Way to Stop It" · "(An) Ordinary Couple" "Edelweiss"

"Much has been written of the success of *The Sound of Music* play and motion picture. Is it immodest of me to point out, because no one else *ever* does, that Russel Crouse and I had a hand in it?"

—*Howard Lindsay, in a letter to* The New York Times Magazine

Joe Layton

Joe Layton, as director and choreographer, had a career wildly varied in quality, with every smash hit tailed by at least two dismal failures. After two early successes, *Once Upon a Mattress* and *The Sound of Music*, he had a flop in *Tenderloin*. After his stylish, groundbreaking work on *No Strings*, he directed the misguided *The Girl Who Came to Supper* and *Sherry*, and his sharp, nonstop staging of *George M!* was followed by the relative tedium of *Dear World* and *Two By Two*. A failure truly undeserving of its fate was *Drat! The Cat!*, which like *Love Life*, *Anyone Can Whistle*, and a handful of other shows, was too special, too quirky to ever succeed in a commercial environment. Starring Elliott Gould and the delightful Lesley Ann Warren, *Drat! The Cat!* featured stunning Layton set pieces, including a kabuki burlesque and a choreographed overture showing a jewel thief on a spree, that are still talked about today. Spending much of the 1970s directing concerts and nightclub acts, including Bette Midler's *Clams on the Half Shell* and *An Evening with Diana Ross*, Layton returned with a vehicle for newly crowned Broadway star Alexis Smith. Rebounding from that show, the flop *Platinum*, he surprised everyone with his wonderful, confident direction of the circus concept of *Barnum*. Thereafter, it it was all downhill for Layton, with the quick failure of *Bring Back Birdie*, a show that seemed like a mistake to everyone in New York save the producers, *Rock and Roll: the First 5,000 Years* (a show ahead of its time), *The Three Musketeers*, and *Harrigan and Hart*.

RIGHT: Grover Dale and Patricia Harty (aloft) execute the Joe Layton choreography for "Beatnik Love Affair" in *Sail Away*.

Backstage

Howard Lindsay and Russel Crouse referred to the operatic ladies who portrayed the nuns as "the bull-nuns."

Mary Martin commemorated a childhood friend, Bessie Mae Sue Ella Yaeger, by putting her name into each of her movies as Martin's character name or another character. It soon became a good luck charm and Martin began putting the name into her shows. It didn't work for *One Touch of Venus* or *Lute Song* but in *South Pacific* Martin introduced the girl doing barrel rolls in the Seabees's show as Bessie Mae. Oscar Hammerstein caught on to the superstition and vowed to find a place for Bessie Mae's name. It wasn't exactly an Austrian name, but Martin's understudy, Renee Guerin, also played a postulant in a crossover. So it was decided to bill her in the credits as: Postulant ... Bessie Mae Sue Ella Yaeger. Two years later the government sued the real Bessie Mae for not declaring her income from her appearance in *The Sound of Music*.

TOP LEFT: In the stage version of *The Sound of Music*, Maria sang "The Lonely Goatherd" during the thunderstorm, not as part of a puppet show, as in the film. Rodgers and Hammerstein had hoped to procure the talents of the Bil Baird Marionettes for the original Broadway production, but the puppets were still in deep analysis, scarred by their poisonous *Flahooley* reviews.

ABOVE: This shot of Martin and Bikel in the Wedding Processional offers but a glimpse of the stunning Oliver Smith scenery, which played ingeniously with perspective.

SOUTH PACIFIC

OPENED APRIL 7, 1949; MAJESTIC THEATRE; 1,925 PERFORMANCES

ABOVE: Absolutely true bit of Broadway history: Using a fake bar of soap, Mary Martin concealed a dollop of Prell in her palm to work up the lather needed to "wash that man right outta her hair."

RIGHT: Martin and Pinza at the top of their game.

Synopsis

Emile de Becque, a middle-aged French planter, falls in love with the nurse Ensign Nellie Forbush. One of the islanders, the crafty Bloody Mary, has her eyes on the handsome Lieutenant Cable for her beautiful daughter, Liat. They fall in love, but Cable finds it difficult to reconcile the differences of their races. Nellie, meanwhile, meets de Becque's children and is shocked that they are of mixed-race descent. De Becque and Cable are recruited to spy on Japanese troop movements in a very dangerous mission. While they are away, Nellie bonds with the children and grows to love them. Cable and de Becque's mission is successful, but Cable is killed by the Japanese. De Becque returns home to find Nellie and his children waiting with open arms.

Cast

Nellie Forbush...................... *Mary Martin*
Emile de Becque .... *Ezio Pinza*
Lt. Joe Cable .... *William Tabbert*
Bloody Mary........................ *Juanita Hall*
Liat .... *Betta St. John*
Luther Billis .... *Myron McCormick*

JUST PURCHASING THE RIGHTS TO a novel or film or play with the idea of musicalizing said property is not enough to ensure that the resulting show is a hit; nor is the fame or excellence of the source an indication of how well the adaptation will run. In fact, there's a theory that a moderately successful source makes for the best musical, since there's more room for expansion and tinkering.

When choosing a property to adapt, Rodgers and Hammerstein never went after the A-list commodities. *Green Grow the Lilacs* (the basis of *Oklahoma!*) was a failure on Broadway and generally unknown to the general public. The reminiscences of Anna Leonowens were only known because of the film *Anna and the King*. *Cannery Row* wasn't one of Steinbeck's best selling novels, nor was C.Y Lee's novel *Flower Drum Song* well known. So it was, too, with the stories that comprised *Tales of the South Pacific* by James Michener, though the collection did win the Pulitzer Prize. Josh Logan was the first to read the story "Fo' Dolla'," and grew so excited he immediately called producer Leland Heyward with the idea of Rodgers and Hammerstein musicalizing the tale.

Richard Rodgers, flat on his back due to recurring back pains, had nothing much better to do than read the story; he loved it and recommended it to Oscar Hammerstein II. Rodgers had the foresight to suggest that he and his partner buy the rights to the entire book, not just the one story (cutting out Josh Logan in the bargain). They did so, and scoured the book for a second story to merge with the first, finding it in "Our Heroine," the story of Emile de Becque and Nellie Forbush.

With two plots intertwined (breaking their own rule of one serious plot, and a secondary, comic one), they looked for a third story to leaven the seriousness of the first two. To help the team, Michener penned a third story especially for them, creating the character of Luther Billis. Once they had their basic characters in place and a plot to link them, they received a lucky phone call from Edwin Lester, the producer of the Los Angeles Civic Light Opera. Lester had signed Ezio Pinza for a musical to be decided upon later, but couldn't find an appropriate property and was about to lose the great singer.

With Pinza signed, the rest of the package fell quickly into place. Mary Martin was playing Annie Oakley in the Rodgers and Hammerstein-produced *Annie Get Your Gun* on the West Coast. She agreed to play the part, provided that she not have a duet with Pinza, fearing that the great singer would blow her off the stage. Rodgers and Hammerstein brilliantly solved the problem by writing the "Twin Soliloquys."

Though *South Pacific* has its lighter moments, at heart it is a serious piece with the theme of racial prejudice running through the two main plots. Everyone is familiar with Cable's song "You've Got to Be Carefully Taught," which he sings when confronting his own difficulties in imagining marriage to a Polynesian girl, Liat. Nellie also confronts her insensitivities when, ready to marry Emile de Becque, she has second thoughts on meeting his children of mixed ancestry. Nellie overcomes her prejudice, but Cable is killed before he can completely come to terms with what he knows is wrong.

The writing came extremely slowly to Hammerstein, and Logan was called to the librettist's farm in Pennsylvania for a few days of consultation. Logan was such a help that he stayed until the script was essentially complete, collaborating on every aspect with Hammerstein. A few weeks later Logan, spurred on by his wife Nedda Harrigan, confronted Hammerstein with the request that they share credit. Hammerstein immediately agreed, later refusing to share royalties with Logan; after all, Rodgers and Hammerstein had the rights to the underlying material, even if it was at the behest of Logan. Because he had worked so hard on the project and deeply believed in it, Logan agreed, but it caused a rift between him and his former friends.

Some people have observed that Rodgers was the tough businessman and Hammerstein had the heart. While Rodgers was indeed intractable and impossible (he cheated the Hart family out of royalties after Lorenz Hart died), Hammerstein went along with all of Rodgers' wishes and never stood up to his partner. Now, when Rodgers' personality has been permanently scarred by recent comments of his friends and family, Hammerstein is still portrayed as the great humanitarian.

No matter what the failings of each of these giants, their work lives on, thrilling audiences of every generation with their sense of humor, wisdom, and drama. ✳

ABOVE: Barbara Luna, Michael DeLeon, and Mary Martin sing "Dites-Moi."

LEFT: Juanita Hall, Betta St. John, and William Tabbert perform the charming "Happy Talk" number.

"Of course, it goes without saying that you won't get anything whatsoever of the author's royalties."

—*Oscar Hammerstein II to Josh Logan,* after agreeing to give him credit for co-authorship of the libretto but no money

Backstage

At the last performance of *South Pacific* on Broadway, Myron McCormick, who played Billis for the entire run, led the cast and audience in a rendition of "Auld Lang Syne." The audience stayed in their seats, for another half hour unwilling to leave the magic behind in the theatre.

Before going on stage for the first time each evening, Mary Martin would sit on the toilet until her maid called her entrance. It was her way of overcoming stage fright.

Scalpers sold tickets to *South Pacific* for as much as $100 each.

Juanita Hall

African-American singer/actress Juanita Hall, who made a career out of crossing racial boundaries, made her musical debut in the ensembles of *Sing Out Sweet Land* in 1944 and the 1946 revival of *Show Boat*. After supporting roles in *St. Louis Woman* and *Street Scene*, she broke through as the unflaggingly businesslike Bloody Mary in *South Pacific*, winning a Tony Award and becoming a star introducing the songs "Bali Hai" and "Happy Talk." She played the wise yet unflaggingly businesslike Madam Tango in *House of Flowers* before she recreated her role of Bloody Mary in the movie version of *South Pacific* (where, inexplicably, she was dubbed). After another switch of races, as the thoroughly sensible Chinese woman Madame Liang in *Flower Drum Song* (which she also played in the film, this time singing for herself), she retired due to health problems, having created three major Broadway roles in ten years.

ABOVE RIGHT: William Tabbert sings one of Oscar Hammerstein II's darkest and most pointed lyrics, "You've Got to Be Carefully Taught."

ABOVE: Juanita Hall spans the globe: (top) as Bloody Mary in the South Pacific; (center) as Madame Tango in the British West Indies of *House of Flowers*; and (right) as the Chinese Madame Liang in *Flower Drum Song* (here singing "The Other Generation" with Keye Luke, an actual, real-life Asian).

SONGS

ACT I "Dites-Moi" · "A Cockeyed Optimist" · "Twin Soliloquies" · "Some Enchanted Evening" · "Bloody Mary (Is the Girl I Love)" · "There Is Nothin' Like a Dame" · "Bali Ha'i" · "I'm Gonna Wash That Man Right Outa My Hair" · "(I'm in Love With) A Wonderful Guy" · "Younger Than Springtime"
ACT II "Happy Talk" · "Honey Bun" · "You've Got to Be Carefully Taught" · "This Nearly Was Mine"

Joshua Logan

As writer and director, Joshua Logan was a major force in the Broadway theatre for over thirty years. Beginning his musical career directing the hits *Knickerbocker Holiday*, *By Jupiter*, and *This Is the Army*, Logan became a hot commodity when he directed the wonderful *Annie Get Your Gun* in 1946. With another smash in *South Pacific* (which he co-authored), he turned around the problematic *Wish You Were Here* in 1952, finding another long running hit in *Fanny* two years later. All of his efforts displayed an inordinate amount of male pulchritude, an apparent obsession that raised many an eyebrow along the Great White Way. After *Fanny* (and such straight drama hits as *Mister Roberts*), Logan's golden touch seemed to disappear, and he turned out flop after flop, including *All American* (where his staging of the "Physical Fitness" number seemed

LEFT: Joshua Logan doing what he loves best: directing scantily-clad, well-built men (here in a rehearsal for *Wish You Were Here*).

gratuitously fleshy, even for him), *Mr. President*, *Hot September* (a musicalization of play *Picnic*, which he also directed), *Look to the Lilies*, and the out of town disaster *Miss Moffat*. Also a film director, his versions of *South Pacific*, *Camelot*, and *Paint Your Wagon* are among the most disappointing of all Broadway musical transfers. When he died at the age of 79, he was working on a musical version of *Huckleberry Finn*, even though the musical *Big River* had opened and won the Tony Award.

TOP RIGHT: The unbeatable combination of Rodgers & Hammerstein, golden girl Mary Martin, and opera star Ezio Pinza made *South Pacific* into a super-smash hit, turning New York on its ear as few shows in Broadway history have done (with the possible exceptions of *My Fair Lady*, *A Chorus Line*, and *The Producers*).

THE STUDENT PRINCE IN HEIDELBERG

OPENED DECEMBER 2, 1924; JOLSON'S 59TH STREET THEATRE; 608 PERFORMANCES

THE STUDENT PRINCE IN HEIDELBERG

Produced by Messrs. Shubert
Book and all ensembles staged by J. C. Huffman
Dances by Max Scheck

Music by Sigmund Romberg
Lyrics and Libretto by Dorothy Donnelly
Based the play *Old Heidelberg*
by Rudolf Bleichmann
Adapted from *Alt Heidelberg* by
Wilhelm Meyer-Foerster
Orchestra under the direction of Oscar Bradley
Orchestrations by Emil Gerstenberg

Settings by Watson Barratt
Costumes by Weldy of Paris
and Vanity Fair Costume Company

ABOVE: The Student Prince (Howard Marsh) in all his finery.

RIGHT: Dagmar Oakland as Countess Leyden.

Synopsis

Prince Karl Franz of Karlsberg and his tutor, Doctor Engel, arrive in Heidelberg incognito. Karl Franz enrolls in the university and soon falls in love with a local waitress, Kathy. Suddenly the king, Karl's father, dies and Karl must return home to assume the throne. He must leave Kathy, a commoner, and assume his royal duties, but he cannot stop thinking about her. He returns to Heidelberg and Kathy's arms. While they are still in love, the reality of the situation overwhelms their ability to remain together and Karl Franz leaves forever.

Cast

Prime Minister von Mark ...... *Fuller Mellish*
Dr. Engel .... *Greek Evans*
Prince Karl Franz .... *Howard Marsh*
Gretchen .... *Violet Carlson*
Detlef .... *Raymond Marlowe*
Kathie .... *Ilse Marvenga*
Lutz .... *George Hassell*
Grand Duchess Anastasia .... *Florence Morrison*
Princess Margaret .... *Roberta Beatty*
Captain Tarnitz .... *John Coast*
Countess Leyden .... *Dagmar Oakland*

A MOST UNUSUAL (SOME MIGHT SAY daring) show, *The Student Prince* is a rarity, particularly for its time: a musical with an unhappy ending. Boy gets girl, boy loses girl, and . . . that's it. Still, audiences were entranced by the lush, romantic melodies of Sigmund Romberg and the bravura lyrics of Dorothy Donnelly, one of the musical theatre's unsung heroines. *The Student Prince* didn't contain any of the usual operetta shenanigans—comic-relief turns by low clowns or secondary romantic couples. The emphasis was squarely on Prince Karl and Kathy and their doomed love, and to make up for the lack of comedy and lightness. Donnelly and Romberg substituted rousing student songs to enliven the proceedings and give the show depth. Set at Heidelberg University, there was ample time to spend in the beer halls where Kathy worked as a waitress. Ironically, the score is surprisingly muscular and virile given the rather feminine subject. It was startling to all involved, including its producers. The Shubert brothers expected the usual lackluster Romberg operetta. Jake Shubert, who oversaw the musicals, was astonished by the lack of a female chorus and the unusual ending, and, despairing of what he thought was a sure failure, began tinkering with the show. Romberg (a salaried employee, after all) objected strongly, and Jake took Romberg's name off the billing. Romberg sued and, just prior to the Broadway opening, received his due. The show, to Jake's surprise (and grudging pleasure), was a smash hit, making millions for the Shuberts in successive engagements on Broadway and around the country. One of the most widely performed musicals throughout the world, *The Student Prince* has succeeded beyond expectations due to its uncompromising but wholly entertaining libretto and the magnificent score by Romberg and Donnelly. ✴

"Forty men singing that crap? Who needs it?"

—Lee Shubert, on learning there would be no female chorus

Backstage

Arthur W. Tams Music Library, the music publisher of *The Student Prince in Heidelberg,* was on the brink of bankruptcy when sales of the operetta's sheet music saved the day.

The underlying play, the 1901 *Alt Heidelberg,* had been adapted into two straight plays in New York: *Old Heidelberg* (1902) and *Prince Karl* (1904); an Austrian sequel operetta, *Jung Heidelberg* (also in 1904); a Romanian operetta (later in 1904); an Italian operetta (1908); and a D. W. Griffith silent film in 1915. Two film versions of the Romberg operetta were made, one in 1927 (directed by Ernst Lubitsch and one of the last silent classics) and another in 1954.

SONGS

ACT I "By Our Bearing So Sedate" · "Golden Days" · "Garlands Bright" · "Drinking Song" · "To the Inn We're Marching" · "You're in Heidelberg" · "Welcome to Prince" "Deep in My Heart Dear" · "Serenade"
ACT II "Farmer Jacob" · "Student's Life" · "Farewell, Dear"
ACT III "Waltz Ensemble" · "Just We Two" · "Gavotte" "What Memories" ·
ACT IV "Sing a Little Song" · "To the Inn We're Marching" "Come Boys"

ABOVE: Howard Marsh and Ilse Marvenga, the Prince and the girl who loves him, in happier times—before the Finale.
BELOW: Pretty as a picture, or should we say lithograph, the enchanting "Currier and Ives" from Romberg's surprise hit, *Up in Central Park.*

Sigmund Romberg

Sigmund Romberg composed more than sixty musicals in his forty-year career—making him the most prolific of all Broadway composers. Although Romberg was proficient in most musical theatre styles, he achieved lasting fame as a composer of operettas, and his most enduring shows are still performed, with *Blossom Time, The New Moon, The Desert Song,* and *The Student Prince* still favorites of light opera companies and summer theatres. Romberg's most famous songs are still sung today, including "Deep in My Heart," "Lover Come Back," "Stouthearted Men," "The Desert Song," "Close as Pages in a Book," "Softly, as in a Morning Sunrise," "Serenade," and "Will You Remember?" Romberg came to the United States from Vienna in 1909, almost immediately finding work with the Shubert brothers, desperate for shows to fill their theatres, especially the Winter Garden, home of the revues called the Passing Shows. When Romberg became a Shubert employee, his job was to write numbers that allowed the showgirls to show off their assets in rhythm. He briefly left the Shubert fold in 1919, but after three flops, Romberg returned to the safety of a regular paycheck, to compose a remarkable series of successful operettas. *The New Moon,* produced in 1928, was Romberg's last successful operetta, for musical tastes were changing, and Romberg's lush, romantic style fell out of vogue. More shows and Hollywood followed, with little acclaim; however, in 1945 Romberg returned with a vengeance with the smash hit, *Up in Central Park,* written in collaboration with Dorothy Fields. His last show, *The Girl in Pink Tights,* was completed in 1954, more than two years after his death.

OFF BROADWAY, PART II

WHAT BEGAN AS AN ANTI-BROADWAY phenomenon, the Off-Broadway theatre still clung to its more bohemian roots. However, two shows were about to open that would revolutionize Off Broadway and make it, in essence, an adjunct to Broadway. The first of these two historic musicals was *Grease* which opened at the Eden Theatre, previously a home for the Yiddish Theatre. It soon moved to Broadway's Broadhurst Theatre for a remarkable 3,338-performance run. The Public Theatre had its second long-running musical with 1975's *A Chorus Line*, whose runaway success is covered elsewhere in this book. But suffice it to say, the one-two punch of smash hits *Grease* and *A Chorus Line* moving to Broadway opened the floodgates of uptown producers looking to move Off-Broadway hit musicals to the Main Stem. Some shows wisely chose not to make the move uptown. William Finn's *March of the Falsettos* stayed put at Playwrights' Horizons and the creators of 1982's *Little Shop of Horrors* chose to stay put at the Orpheum Theatre.

Gerard Alessandrini's annual ribbing of Broadway musicals, *Forbidden Broadway*, opened at a small club on 72nd Street. It has played continuously in varying editions and various venues ever since. *Nunsense*, opened in 1985 and spawned several sequels and many productions around the country. More recently, *Forever Plaid* opened in the same space where *Forbidden Broadway* premiered, and Playwrights Horizons had another hit with Stephen Sondheim and James Weidman's *Assassins*. The Kander and Ebb songbook revue, *And the World Goes Round*, and the Sondheim mishmash, *Putting It Together*, showed the inconsistencies in quality of composer revues. The late '90s had one mega-hit that was below the radar of most Manhattanites but pure theatrical bliss for out-of-towners. In 1996, a little show called *I Love You, You're Perfect, Now Change*, by composer Jimmy Roberts and lyricist/librettist Joe DiPietro, opened at the Westside Arts theatre. The show has thrilled people with big hair for over 3,000 performances in New York and has enjoyed over 150 productions worldwide.

The new millennium saw fewer and fewer new musicals opening Off Broadway. An exception was 2001's *Bat Boy*. With costs rises as well as ticket prices, Off Broadway doesn't seem much like an experimental alternative to Broadway anymore.

Harvey Schmidt and Tom Jones

Composer Harvey Schmidt and lyricist Tom Jones are authors of the longest-running professional musical production ever in the United States, the indestructible Off-Broadway perennial *The Fantasticks*, which ran for a staggering forty consecutive years. Schmidt and Jones's music and lyrics have made their works at once accessible and utterly singular in their innocence and pure melody, with unwavering, unmistakable spirit. Their first show for Broadway, *110 in the Shade*, a musicalization of the play *The Rainmaker*, had a wonderful, aching score, on par with the best of Richard Rodgers and Oscar Hammerstein, and featured a true star performance for the ages in the Lizzie of Inga Swenson. After *I Do, I Do*, memorable more for the performances of stars Mary Martin and Robert Preston than for the score, they never again had a success, despite fine, heartfelt work on such shows as Off Broadway's *Philemon*, the fascinating yet ultimately perplexing *Celebration*, the out-of-town casualty *Collette* (featuring a heroic turn by star Diana Rigg),

and the as-yet-unproduced-in–New York musical version of *Our Town* titled *Grover's Corners*. With Harvey Schmidt's recent retirement, Tom Jones has teamed with Joseph Thalken to write the musical *Harold and Maude*.

TOP: Those who only know Eileen Brennan from her dry, deadpan performances in such films as *The Sting* and *Private Benjamin* may be surprised that she started out as as an ingenue, lending her quirky soprano and comic genius to such shows as Off Broadway's *Little Mary Sunshine*. ABOVE: Mandy Patinkin is a transsexual father who has clearly hit the sale rack at Casual Corner, and Devon Michaels is his thoroughly befuddled son in the preposterous 1987 musical, *The Knife*. CENTER RIGHT: In 1960, could Rita Gardner and Jerry Orbach ever have predicted that the simple, low-budget Off-Broadway musical they were hired for would end up running for more than forty years? BOTTOM RIGHT: Schmidt and Jones wrote a lovely score for *Colette*, starring Martin Vidnovic and the delicious Diana Rigg. Unfortunately, it closed in Denver prior to Broadway.

SWEENEY TODD

OPENED MARCH 1, 1979; URIS THEATRE; 557 PERFORMANCES

SWEENEY TODD

Produced by Richard Barr, Charles Woodward,
Robert Fryer, Mary Lea Johnson, and
Martin Richards

Music and Lyrics by Stephen Sondheim
Book by Hugh Wheeler
Based on a version of "Sweeney Todd" by
Christopher Bond
Music orchestrated by Jonathan Tunick
Musical Director: Paul Gemignani

Directed by Harold Prince
Dance and movement by Larry Fuller

Production Design by Eugene Lee
Costume Design by Franne Lee
Lighting Design by Ken Billington

"Those up above will serve those down below": Angela Lansbury and Len Cariou in the morbidly hilarious first-act closer of *Sweeney Todd*, "A Little Priest."

Synopsis

Benjamin Barker, a barber, arrives in a London consumed by the Industrial Revolution and its myriad of vices, having escaped from an unjust imprisonment. He returns to Fleet Street, unrecognizable and having assumed the name Sweeney Todd, to once again take up his craft. Todd finds a room above the pie shop of Mrs. Lovett, a woman of questionable sanitary values. Todd sets up shop and waits for his chance to give the venal Judge Turpin a very, very close shave, for it was Turpin who commanded Todd to jail, ravished his wife, and is now on the verge of doing the same to his ward, Todd's daughter, Johanna. While waiting for his intended victim, Todd practices on the throats of his customers, sending their bodies into the ovens of Mrs. Lovett, to be used in her meat pies (and just in time, as the local cat population has mysteriously dwindled). Achieving vengeance, Todd (along with Mrs. Lovett) tragically learns what the Judge has learned: that one must accept the consequences of his actions.

Cast

Anthony Hope	*Victor Garber*
Sweeney Todd	*Len Cariou*
Beggar Woman	*Merle Louise*
Mrs. Lovett	*Angela Lansbury*
Judge Turpin	*Edmund Lyndeck*
The Beadle	*Jack Eric Williams*
Johanna	*Sarah Rice*
Tobias Ragg	*Ken Jennings*
Pirelli	*Joaquin Romaguera*

> "I have forgotten how this f....ing thing ends."
>
> —*Len Cariou at the end of a marathon technical rehearsal*

Sweeney Todd IS A UNIQUE, almost unclassifiable musical. We can all agree that it isn't a musical comedy, though it has moments as hilarious as any in musical comedy. It isn't really an opera, although it doesn't have much dialogue and is performed by opera companies around the world. The best way to describe it might be as a Grand Guignol musical. The most amazing thing about *Sweeney Todd* is that it makes audiences sympathetic to a mass murderer and a woman who cooks people into meat pies!

What saves *Sweeney Todd* from being a musicalized horror movie is the intelligence and integrity of the writing (by Stephen Sondheim and Hugh Wheeler) and production (by a top-of-his-game Hal Prince); nevertheless, it's the horror aspect at its core that has made its story a perennial. Playwright George Dibdin Pitt's play, *A String of Pearls, or the Fiend of Fleet Street*, was first presented in London in 1847, and the story of the demon barber of Fleet Street has continued to entertain audiences for a century and a half on stage, in film, and in print. The self-proclaimed arbiters of modern morality might look at the history of this show and realize that audiences have always been interested in the grisly and gruesome. Sex and sexuality are the backdrop to most stories, and escapism and fantasy are an undeniably necessary part of human psychology. *Sweeney Todd* has it all: violence, sex, deviance, romance, suspense, and humor. Given the richness and theatricality of the material, it's surprising that Hollywood, or better yet, England, hasn't seen fit to film the musical *Sweeney Todd*.

Since the majority of the action in the original staging took place on a small, raised platform containing Mrs. Lovett's pie shop, Sweeney Todd's rooms upstairs, and the belowground kitchen, the only drawback was its huge set, a recreation of an iron foundry. Although technically impressive, it distracted many from concentrating on the brilliance of the score and book. Of course, the barnlike size of the Uris Theatre (now the Gershwin) didn't help matters, for here was a show that was meant to be seen up close. After all, when one sees a horror movie in the cinema, the murders are usually committed in a Technicolor close-up. Then again, the distance from the stage might have worked in *Sweeney Todd*'s favor; after all, reality, particularly a violent one, is certainly heightened when the action is taking place by real people right before your eyes.

Sweeney Todd is a musical that can be enjoyed by all audiences equally. It is entirely accessible to both intellectuals and the masses, who are equally startled by the flashes of steel and the spurting of blood. It accomplishes what the best drama strives for, bringing audiences together in a common experience. Hundreds of viewers share laughs, thrills and, in the case of *Sweeney Todd*, chills at the same time—it's the most important reason to go to the theatre. ❁

Sweeney Todd (Len Cariou) and Mrs. Lovett (Angela Lansbury), about to hear the pitch for "Pirelli's Miracle Elixir."

Len Cariou

The very fine actor/singer Len Cariou had been employed for years as a Shakespearean stage actor in his native Canada. Supporting Lauren Bacall in *Applause*, his solid baritone and masculine presence made him a sought-after leading man. In his next musical, as the frustrated lawyer Frederik Egerman in *A Little Night Music*, Cariou became a first-rank star on Broadway, and his scenes with Glynis Johns were funny, bittersweet, and deeply touching, flying in the face of those who accused Sondheim's collaborations with Hal Prince of being too cerebral and emotionally distancing. Cariou's greatest role was as the vengeful barber Benjamin Barker, now reinvented and hellbent (and Hellbound) on revenge as Sweeney Todd. Perhaps that show's near-operatic score was too demanding for singers without vocal chords of steel, for although the role has never been as chillingly acted, Cariou's singing voice never sounded quite the same after *Sweeney*, and indeed, in his next show, the flop *Dance a Little Closer*, he seemed to have lost it entirely. In better voice in 1987's *Teddy and Alice*, Cariou gave a thoroughly committed performance in a show not worthy of his talent. Also successful in film (*The Four Seasons*) and straight plays (*The Dinner Party*), Cariou is still a frequent face on the New York stage, waiting for another musical on a level with his early triumphs.

SONGS

ACT I "The Ballad of Sweeney Todd" · "No Place Like London" · "The Barber and His Wife" "The Worst Pies in London" · "Poor Thing" "My Friend" · "Green Finch and Linnet Bird" "Ah, Miss" · "Johanna" · "Pirelli's Miracle Elixir" "The Contest" · "Wait" · "Kiss Me" · "Ladies in Their Sensitivities" · "Pretty Women" · "Epiphany" "A Little Priest"
ACT II "God, That's Good!" · "By the Sea" "Not While I'm Around" · "Parlor Songs" "City on Fire!"

LEFT: Cariou, backed up by Diane Pennington, Cheryl Howard, and Alyson Reed in the one-performance *Dance a Little Closer*.

BELOW: Edmund Lyndeck, in the Judge's version of "Johanna" (cut during previews), where the Judge flagellates himself as he watches his ward Johanna through a keyhole.

Jonathan Tunick

Jonathan Tunick, successor to Robert Russell Bennett as the premiere orchestrator of his time, began by revolutionizing the Broadway sound with the pit voices and synthesizer-laden charts for *Promises, Promises*. In orchestrating the six Sondheim/Prince collaborations of the 1970s and '80s, he showed a versatility and complexity that perfectly complemented Sondheim's. In the metallic urban sounds of *Company*, the pastiches of *Follies*, the lush, string-heavy *A Little Night Music*, the Japanese influences of *Pacific Overtures*, the operatic scope of *Sweeney Todd*, and, at his most brassy and Broadway, for *Merrily We Roll Along*, he helped create the sound of some of the most important works of the last forty years. One of the many orchestrators credited on *A Chorus Line*, Tunick is so gifted that he has the ability to make a good score sound great (*Goodtime Charley*, *Nine*, *Nick and Nora*, *Titanic*). To truly understand his genius, go to your CD player and listen to the various layers and countermelodies of "Another Hundred People" from *Company*, perhaps the greatest orchestration ever written.

Backstage

It took 271 investors to bring *Sweeney Todd* to the stage—possibly a theatrical record.

Pirelli's wagon was made of old wood designer Eugene Lee scavenged from a junkyard. There were huge wood lice in it and they soon infiltrated the set and costumes.

ABOVE: In "By the Sea," Mrs. Lovett (Angela Lansbury) plans for a future that will never come.

FAR LEFT: Sweeney (Len Cariou) and his "friend" Pirelli (Joaquin Romageura) finish off the competition.

LEFT: Sarah Rice, as the Dresden doll Johanna, receives a gift of a caged bird (not unlike herself) from a mutton-chopped Victor Garber, as the sailor Anthony Hope.

SWEET CHARITY

OPENED JANUARY 29, 1966; PALACE THEATRE; 608 PERFORMANCES

Even facing upstage, audiences roared with applause at the first image of *Sweet Charity*, for there was no mistaking Broadway's most beloved dancing star since Marilyn Miller: the cocked head, curved spine, and flexed foot could only belong to Gwen Verdon.

SWEET CHARITY

Produced by Fryer, Carr & Harris Inc.

Music by Cy Coleman
Lyrics by Dorothy Fields
Book by Neil Simon
Based on the Screenplay *Nights of Cabiria*
by Federico Fellini
Musical Director: Fred Werner
Dance Arrangements by Fred Werner
Music orchestrated by Ralph Burns

Conceived, Directed, and Choreographed by
Bob Fosse

Scenic Design by Robert Randolph
Lighting Design by Robert Randolph
Costume Design by Irene Sharaff

Synopsis

Charity Hope Valentine is a dance hall hostess, the 1960s version of Ruth Etting's character in *Simple Simon*, who sang "Ten Cents a Dance." Charity does indeed have a heart of gold and is determined to break out of the Fan-Dango Ballroom. She accidentally finds herself in the bedroom of Italian film star Vittorio Vidal and dating the neurotic, shy, somewhat nerdy Oscar. When the strait-laced and high-strung Oscar proposes, he insists that he doesn't care about Charity's profession. But in the end he cares very much, and Charity is soon back to having her toes and her heart stepped on.

Cast

Charity .... *Gwen Verdon*
Helene .... *Thelma Oliver*
Nickie................................ *Helen Gallagher*
Vittorio Vidal .... *James Luisi*
Oscar .... *John McMartin*
Good Fairy .... *Ruth Buzzi*
Herman .... *John Wheeler*
Ursula .... *Sharon Ritchie*
Rosie .... *Barbara Sharma*

BASED ON THE ITALIAN FILM *Nights of Cabiria*, *Sweet Charity* was a perfect property for the married team of musical comedy legend Gwen Verdon—the closest thing to a singing, dancing Giulietta Masina—and genius director/choreographer Bob Fosse—an auteur much like Federico Fellini, with boundless imagination and an instantly recognizable style. Even though it sported a truly funny book by Neil Simon—the undisputed champ of modern-day New York comedy—and a fresh, pop-influenced score by Cy Coleman and legendary lyricist Dorothy Fields, *Sweet Charity* was undoubtedly Fosse's triumph. The show was all about dance, from Verdon's solo dance to "Charity's Theme" as the curtain rose to "I'm a Brass Band," the joyful strut for Charity and a battalion of drumstick-toting drum majors. In between those was the star turn for Verdon, "If My Friends Could See Me Now," where all Fosse needed was a top hat, a cane, and Verdon's incandescent charm to wrap the entire Palace Theatre around her crooked, choreographed little finger; "There's Gotta Be Something Better Than This," a foot-stamping, flamenco trio for Verdon, Helen Gallagher, and Thelma Oliver; and "The Rich Man's Frug," a three-part ensemble dance for the Eurotrash patrons of the Club Pompeii. Also, there were the beatniks of the jazzy "Rhythm of Life," and, perhaps most memorably, the showstopper "Big Spender," with its lineup of deadpan taxi dancers sizing up fresh meat, each with her own come-on as she slinked down to the footlights: "Hey, mister, can

> "I want her in a plain black dress, and she'll wear it the entire time."
>
> —*Bob Fosse to Irene Sharaff*

SONGS

ACT I "Charity's Theme" · "You Should See Yourself" "Big Spender" · "Charity's Soliloquy" · "Rich Man's Frug" "If My Friends Could See Me Now" · "Too Many Tomorrows" · "There's Gotta Be Something Better Than This" "I'm the Bravest Individual"
ACT II "Rhythm of Life" · "Baby Dream Your Dream" "Sweet Charity" · "Where Am I Going?" · "I'm a Brass Band" · "I Love to Cry at Weddings"

I talk to you for a minute ..." "Hey Monsieur, you speak French?" "Ooh, yer so tall...." Actually, "Big Spender" is a unique dance number whose great power comes from the utter *lack* of movement: the tense poses the girls freeze into as they lean over the railing of the Fan-Dango Ballroom corral elicit applause every time a new one is struck.

In his use of cinematic staging, Fosse streamlined the action. After she gets robbed and pushed into Central Park lake, Charity begins to tell her story to the police. Then, with only a blast from the orchestra as the locker room set glides in, Verdon still midsentence, she finishes her tale to her taxi dancer coworkers. And since Verdon possessed the comic pathos of a Charlie Chaplin, it was entirely fitting that Fosse created a scene for her, trapped in movie star Vittorio Vidal's closet while he made love to his latest conquest, that was the closest thing to the giddiness of silent movie comedy since Jerome Robbins's "Keystone Cop Ballet" in *High Button Shoes*. Verdon, watching through the keyhole, executed a series of comedy bits (drinking a beer, smoking a cigarette, then, when she realizes her mistake, blowing the smoke into a zippered suit bag hanging in the closet) that not only cemented the character of the lovable, sad clown Charity Hope Valentine, but preserved Verdon's always fragile singing voice (Fosse took a similar tack in *Chicago*, where he had Verdon front and center in one of the biggest production numbers, "We Both Reached for the Gun," but since she was a ventriloquist dummy sitting on Jerry Orbach's lap, she never had to sing a note). With one foot solidly in old-school craft but with an eye toward the refreshingly new and innovative, Fosse made *Sweet Charity* into a kind of "bridge" show of the 1960s, linking the musical comedies of the George Abbott era and the state-of-the-art stagings of Hal Prince, Michael Bennett, and Tommy Tune to come. ❃

RIGHT: "Hi girls, it's me—Charity!" In the apartment of Italian movie star Vittorio Vidal, Charity wishes her friends could see her now.

BELOW RIGHT: "Doc" Simon and Mike Nichols outside the Biltmore Theatre the morning after the triumphant opening of their smash *Barefoot in the Park*.

BELOW: Verdon, a claustrophobic John McMartin, and a stalled elevator provided Neil Simon with a prime opportunity to hark back to his sketch comedy roots.

Neil Simon

Neil Simon, the most successful American playwright ever, has had a long association with Broadway musicals. After contributions to the revues *Catch a Star* and *New Faces of '56*, he earned his stripes as a sketch writer on early television. After a smash with his first play, *Come Blow Your Horn*, he started his book-writing career with one of the funniest musicals ever, *Little Me*, which boasted more laughs per page than most others have per show. In between his remarkable string of hit comedies, his hit musicals included *Sweet Charity*; *Promises, Promises;* and *They're Playing Our Song*. His only flop came with the musicalization of his movie *The Goodbye Girl* in 1993. The premiere joke man of all time, "Doc" has also made uncredited contributions to many other shows, from *Seesaw* to *A Chorus Line*.

Helen Gallagher

Helen Gallagher, the ultimate survivor, began as a hoofer in the chorus, graduating to a tango specialty in *High Button Shoes,* and gaining real attention with a splashy revue feature in *Touch and Go.* After the failure of her next show, the Nanette Fabray vehicle *Make a Wish,* she and costar Harold Lang segued directly into the 1952 revival of *Pal Joey,* with Gallagher winning her first Tony Award for playing the delightfully named Gladys Bumps. She had found a fan in *Pal Joey*'s producer, Jule Styne, and he cast her as the star of his next show, *Hazel Flagg.* A marathon role with singing and dancing enough for three shows, it foundered, and its failure tarnished Gallagher's stock as a star. She slipped back into replacement jobs (in *Pajama Game* and *Mame*) and supporting roles (in *Sweet Charity* and *Cry for Us All*), even standing by for Kaye Ballard in the out-of-town closer *Royal Flush.* With the revival of *No, No, Nanette* in 1971, she became a hit all over again, with her "Where-Has-My-Hubby-Gone Blues?" giving her the star spot she hadn't had in twenty years. She shrewdly parlayed her new acclaim into a steady gig on the long-running soap opera *Ryan's Hope.*

Backstage

Bob Fosse spent hours in Times Square dance halls doing research, and Gwen Verdon went undercover and worked as a dance hall hostess.

When she got tired, Gwen Verdon would cut the number "Where Am I Going?" from the show. When she received an angry letter from a theatergoer, Gwen calculated the time the number took in the show, the length of the show, and the price of a ticket; then she sent the audience member a pro-rated refund.

Alison Williams and Bebe Neuwirth vie for a dance partner in the showstopper "Big Spender."

TOP LEFT: The girls of the Fan-Dango (Verdon, Helen Gallagher, and Thelma Oliver) bond in "There's Gotta Be Something Better Than This." Giddy and electrifying, it is one of Fosse's most jubilant dances, without the hooded eyes that accompanied much of his later work.

ABOVE: John Brascia and Helen Gallagher cutting a rug in *Hazel Flagg,* a musicalization of the screwball comedy *Nothing Sacred.* Hazel's got a helluva lotta energy for a girl with radium poisoning.

FAR LEFT: With great tunes, great dresses, and a simply smashing hairdo, Gallagher stopped each of the three acts of the 1971 revival of *No, No, Nanette.*

A TREE GROWS IN BROOKLYN

OPENED APRIL 19, 1951; ALVIN THEATRE; 267 PERFORMANCES

ABOVE: Shirley Booth, as Cissy in *A Tree Grows in Brooklyn*.

RIGHT: Nomi Mitty and Marcia Van Dyke as Francie and Katie Nolan.

A TREE GROWS IN BROOKLYN

Produced by George Abbott
Produced in Association with Robert Fryer

Book by Betty Smith and George Abbott
Music by Arthur Schwartz
Lyrics by Dorothy Fields
Based on the Novel by Betty Smith
Music arranged by Joe Glover
and Robert Russell Bennett
Musical Director: Max Goberman
Ballet Music arranged by Oscar Kosarin

Directed by George Abbott
Choreographed by Herbert Ross

Scenic Design by Jo Mielziner
Lighting Design by Jo Mielziner
Costume Design by Irene Sharaff

Synopsis

On the way to meet his girlfriend Hildy, Johnny runs into Katie and falls instantly in love. He woos her and wins her and soon they are married with a baby daughter. Johnny understands his responsibilities but is unable to hold a job. The vicious circle of drinking to ease the pain and going from job to job only escalates. Working as a sandhog one day, Johnny is killed by a collapsing tunnel, leaving only enough money for some flowers for his daughter on her graduation. Katie, left to raise Francie with her sister Cissy, is left with the knowledge that Johnny tried his best and loved her and their daughter with all his heart.

Cast

Johnny Nolan	*Johnny Johnston*
Hildy O'Dair	*Dody Heath*
Katie	*Marcia Van Dyke*
Cissy	*Shirley Booth*
Francie	*Nomi Mitty*
Petey	*Lou Wills Jr.*
Harry	*Nathaniel Frey*

WHAT HAPPENS WHEN YOU CAST two relative unknowns in the lead roles of a musical and then are lucky enough to snag a big star for a supporting role? For the answer, take a look at *A Tree Grows in Brooklyn*. The leads were Johnny Johnston and Marcia Van Dyke. Once the producers had Shirley Booth for comic relief, the writers expanded her role—after all, why waste the talents of the great Shirley Booth? Marcia Van Dyke comes on strong with two big songs, the exquisite "Make the Man Love Me" in Scene 3 and "Look Who's Dancin'" in Scene 5. After a brief reprise of "Make the Man Love Me" in Scene 7, she doesn't sing another note. Is it a surprise that this was Ms. Van Dyke's only Broadway show?

A couple of other off-balance shows leap to mind. In *Minnie's Boys*, it's the Marx brothers you care about, but the lead went to Shelley Winters, playing their mother, Minnie—a sort of poor man's Madame Rose. *House of Flowers* was ostensibly the story of Ottile, but Pearl Bailey as the madam stole the show, as well as some of the songs from others in the cast.

A Tree Grows in Brooklyn had some other hurdles to overcome, for it was a decidedly downbeat show. The lead character, Johnny Nolan, is an alcoholic who is killed while working as a sandhog. A close cousin to Billy Bigelow in *Carousel*, he's a strong man who lives more for his dreams than for reality. Yet, where Billy turns to crime to give his wife and daughter security, Johnny is simply overwhelmed. His dreams, modest though they are, can never be fulfilled, and while he has oceans of heart, he can't quite make his life work and he turns to drink as his escape. Ultimately, it's a heartwarming story, but still a downer.

The show was up against some pretty big musical theatre guns that season: 1950–51 began with *Michael Todd's Peep Show*, a glorified burlesque revue. That highbrow theme continued with Ole Olsen and Chic Johnson's *Pardon Our French*. The *Hellzapoppin'* stars gave way to Irving Berlin's *Call Me Madam*, the story of socialite ambassadress Sally Adams and her adventures, political and personal, in the fictional Lichtenburg. The atmosphere began looking way up when *Guys and Dolls* opened at the 46th Street Theatre, and Harold Rome's revue *Bless You All* was followed by Cole Porter's *Out of This World*. After the eight-performance run of the revue *Razzle Dazzle*, Michael Stewart's Broadway debut as a writer/lyricist, came Richard Rodgers and Oscar Hammerstein's monster smash *The King and I*. The lighthearted *Make a Wish*, with a sprightly score by Hugh Martin, was up next, opening one night before *A Tree Grows in Brooklyn*. The Yip Harburg/Sammy Fain show *Flahooley*, Barbara Cook's first Broadway outing, rounded out the theatrical year.

What a season—and by the way, nobody thought it was an especially notable year—more like business as usual on Broadway in the 1950s. Despite the comic highjinks of Shirley Booth and Nat Frey, *A Tree Grows in Brooklyn* was the most sober of the pack that year. (Even though the lead character in *The King and I* dies, it's right at curtain's fall.) Most of the other shows that year were decidedly brighter fare: *Call Me Madam*, a typical Merman romp, or *Guys and Dolls*, where one of the leads has a very bad cold, or *Michael Todd's Peep Show*, where the entire female element of the cast were in imminent danger of pneumonia. Yep, *A Tree Grows in Brooklyn* had an uphill battle. Still, its heartfelt sentiment, its excellent score, and the central performance of the wonderfully warm Shirley Booth made it the fifth-longest-running musical of the season. ✤

Dorothy Fields

Dorothy Fields, lyricist/bookwriter whose work never seemed out of step with the quickly changing times, made her debut as part of the Fields theatrical dynasty. Working with brother Herbert, she wrote the books for such musicals as *Let's Face It*, *Something for the Boys*, *Up in Central Park*, and their biggest hit, *Annie Get Your Gun*. As lyricist and book writer, she created *Stars in Your Eyes*, *Arms and the Girl*, *A Tree Grows in Brooklyn*, *By the Beautiful Sea*, and *Redhead*. The lyrics for her last shows, *Sweet Charity* and *Seesaw*, are so in touch with contemporary language that they completely belie her age, making her sound like the hippest sixty-something chick in the biz. Listen to "You Should See Yourself" from *Charity* (1966) or "Nobody Does It Like Me" from *Seesaw* (1973), and consider that this woman first wrote songs for *Blackbirds of 1928*. Like fellow female lyricist Carolyn Leigh, she was a highly complicated person, and personal troubles kept her away from the theatre for much of the 1950s and '60s.

ABOVE: She won't dance, don't ask her: Two of the greatest lyricists of the twentieth century, Dorothy Fields and Oscar Hammerstein II, trip the light fantastic.

RIGHT: In *By the Beautiful Sea*, also set in Brooklyn during the same time period as *A Tree Grows*, Dorothy Fields, Arthur Schwartz, and producer Robert Fryer reunite with Shirley Booth (here with Wilbur Evans and an exceedingly disapproving Mae Barnes).

BELOW: In an out-of-town casualty, "Tuscaloosa," sung by Johnny in the beer garden and Dorothy Fields's favorite tune in the score, was lost.

In her only Broadway appearance, former concert violinist Marcia Van Dyke listens to Johnny Johnston sing "I'll Buy You a Star."

SONGS

ACT I "Payday" · "Mine 'Til Monday" · "Make the Man Love Me" · "I'm Like a New Broom" · "Look Who's Dancin'" · "Love Is the Reason" · "If You Haven't Got a Sweetheart" · "I'll Buy You a Star"

ACT II "That's How It Goes" "He Had Refinement" "Growing Pains" · "Is That My Prince?" · "Halloween" Ballet "Don't Be Afraid"

Shirley Booth

Along with Elaine Stritch and Glenn Close, Shirley Booth was one of the few great dramatic actresses who has also made a mark in musical theatre. She made her musical debut in 1945 in the short-lived *Hollywood Pinafore*. She had a phenomenal career, with roles in plays as varied as *My Sister Eileen*, *Time of the Cuckoo*, *Come Back, Little Sheba*, and *Desk Set*. After her performance as the fun-loving Cissy in *A Tree Grows in Brooklyn*, she returned to the musical stage three years later, reuniting with Arthur Schwartz and Dorothy Fields in *By the Beautiful Sea*. Her biggest failure, *Juno* (1959), had a powerful score by Marc Blitzstein that has attracted a great cult following. She spent the 1960s on television as the lovable maid Hazel (a role that many of her grander theatre associates looked upon as true slumming), achieving the kind of fame and security she had never had as a theatre actress. Her final Broadway musical was the short-lived *Look to the Lilies*, a Jule Styne musicalization of the hit film *Lilies of the Field*, in which, despite her shortcomings in some departments, she gave a customarily heartfelt and touching performance, particularly in her exceedingly well-played scenes with Al Freeman Jr. A few more brief, nonmusical roles followed, then a long and happy retirement in Massachusetts.

FAR LEFT: Shirley Booth, equally at home in comedy or drama, in the "Song of the Ma" in *Juno*.

ABOVE: In her last Broadway musical, *Look to the Lilies*, Shirley Booth and Al Freeman Jr. forged an unlikely partnership.

WEST SIDE STORY

OPENED SEPTEMBER 26, 1957; WINTER GARDEN THEATRE; 732 PERFORMANCES

ABOVE: Riff (Mickey Calin) finds himself on the wrong end of Bernardo's (Ken LeRoy) switchblade in "The Rumble."

RIGHT: On opposite sides of a gang war, Carol Lawrence and Larry Kert fall in love at "The Dance at the Gym."

WEST SIDE STORY

Produced by
Robert E. Griffith and Harold S. Prince
Produced by arrangement with
Roger L. Stevens

Book by Arthur Laurents
Music by Leonard Bernstein
Lyrics by Stephen Sondheim
Musical Director: Max Goberman
Music orchestrated by Leonard Bernstein
Co-Orchestrator: Sid Ramin and Irwin Kostal

Conceive, Directed, and Choreographed by
Jerome Robbins
Co-Choreographer: Peter Gennaro

Scenic Design by Oliver Smith
Costume Design by Irene Sharaff
Lighting Design by Jean Rosenthal

Synopsis

The Sharks and the Jets rule their turf on the West Side of Manhattan. Tony, a former Jet, is trying to grow up, holding down a job at Doc's drugstore. Riff, the current leader, pleads with Tony to come to a dance at the school gym where the Jets will challenge the Sharks to a rumble. Bernardo, the head of the Sharks, has a younger sister, Maria, and when she and Tony meet it's love at first sight. At the rumble, a knife is pulled and Riff is killed by Bernardo. Tony, who has come to stop the fighting, kills Bernardo in a moment of blind rage. Bernardo's girlfriend, Anita, runs to tell Tony that Maria wants to meet him and run away, but the gang mocks her and she, in a fit of pique, lies and tells them that Maria has been killed by Chino. Tony goes to find Chino to avenge Maria's death, only to find her alive. Chino shoots Tony dead. The Jets and Sharks begin to understand the tragedies their actions have caused.

Cast

Riff	Mickey Calin
Tony	Larry Kert
Baby John	David Winters
Snowboy	Grover Dale
Anybodys	Lee Becker
Bernardo	Ken LeRoy
Maria	Carol Lawrence
Anita	Chita Rivera
Doc	Art Smith
Krupke	William Bramley

SINCE THE IMPETUS FOR THE show came from legendary choreographer Jerome Robbins, dance played an integral part in the development of *West Side Story*. Until this point, dance in most Broadway musicals was used as a break between choruses of songs, or as full-blown dream ballets in the Agnes de Mille tradition. In *West Side Story*, Robbins integrated dance into the show in the same way an opera integrates song, hardly a moment going by without some movement expressing the emotions of the characters: be it rage, bluster, love, or fear. At times, notably when Maria and Tony meet for the first time at the gym, the naturalism of the show gives way to a dreamlike lyricism, expressed purely through dance and music.

Robbins was not content simply to cast the finest dancers on Broadway. He wanted each dancer to embody a different character, knowing the motivation behind every step. Because these dancers could truly act, they exhibited the kinetic energy necessary to keep hurtling the momentum of the show to its inevitable conclusion. To help his cause, Robbins kept the actors playing the Sharks and Jets separate during rehearsals, naturally forming cliques in their own groups, with a real animosity developing between the onstage gangs (which the ruthless Robbins exploited to the hilt). The director also had each dancer write his or her character's autobiography, giving each role a singular personality with a specific dance vocabulary that could be identified by the audience, whether consciously or not. By understanding their roles in the drama, the dancers were made to feel that their presence was much more than simply to meaninglessly prance about the stage; instead, they had a deep purpose in the dramatic action, and this sense of identity helped *West Side Story* maintain a consistent tone.

The tone set by the dance is further heightened by the show's aural language: the libretto, and the music and lyrics. Far from being raw and direct, the entire proceedings are steeped in poetry that takes the story out of naturalism and toward the heightened world of musical theatre. Sondheim and Laurents invented a new type of slang for the gangs, the lyricist even ending "Officer Krupke" with the nonsensical expletive, "Krup you!" In addition, the juxtaposition of the beauty and ugliness in the poetry give the piece an unreal quality, where the tragic events seem to have the inevitability of a nightmare, and the music of Bernstein, near operatic in sweep and melody, but at once restless, angular and tragic, adds to the dreamlike quality.

The one element that *West Side Story* has that saves the evening from unmitigated tragedy—an element that Shakespeare's Romeo and Juliet does not have—is its sense of forgiveness. Tony, maturing and trying to escape the cycle of violence, dies while trying to stop his peers from their self-imposed code of honor. When, in their immaturity, the Jets and the Sharks allow their emotions to escalate the violence, it is their own who are hurt, and only then do the gangs begin to understand what all their posturing, taunting and insecurities have wrought. The show may make fun of Officer Krupke and all the bleeding hearts that try to excuse the actions of the delinquents on sociological grounds, but the show itself, while in no way condoning the actions or shying away from their consequences, still has a moment of togetherness and hope at the end. It's that hope that makes the intensity of the evening bearable, and makes *West Side Story* eternal. ❋

"Jerry's artistic ruthlessness was combined with real sadism... The only two men who were never afraid of him were Arthur [Laurents] and Jule Styne."

—Stephen Sondheim

"Mambo!"

Leonard Bernstein

With one foot firmly in the classical world and one forever connected with Broadway, composer Leonard Bernstein wrote his first score for a musical in 1944, where his use of jazz and blues in *On the Town* signaled the arrival of the most individual musical voice to be heard since George Gershwin burst onto the scene. After five songs for a slightly musicalized *Peter Pan*, Bernstein reteamed with George Abbott and lyricist Comden and Green on *Wonderful Town*, providing another quirky, delightful set of songs. His great experiment *Candide* was underappreciated in its original, problematic staging, but has become a widely accepted classic through Hal Prince's 1974 rethinking, and countless opera productions worldwide. His masterpiece *West Side Story* still sounds fresh and electrifying, nearly fifty years later. After *West Side*, Bernstein took up the baton as conductor of the New York Philharmonic until 1969, creating a sensation with his vigorous, vital conducting and his popular young people's concerts. Away from the theatre for nearly twenty years, he returned to Broadway with the troubled production *1600 Pennsylvania Avenue*, with a incredibly sophisticated score that was overhauled countless times during its development, and still hasn't had a proper representation of its worth. The last two songs he wrote for the theatre were for longtime friend Phyllis Newman for her one-woman show *The Madwoman of Central Park West*.

ABOVE: Bernstein (top) and Sondheim share a laugh during the Washington, D.C., tryout of *West Side Story*.

TOP RIGHT: Barbara Cook and Irra Petina model the latest in everyday mantilla-wear in *Candide*.

FAR RIGHT: Ken Howard and Patricia Routledge play George and Martha Washington in Bernstein's fascinating failure, *1600 Pennsylvania Avenue*.

RIGHT: Chita Rivera and the Shark Girls explode into an "America" dance break.

SONGS

ACT I "Jet Song" · "Something's Coming" · "The Dance at the Gym") · "Maria" · "Tonight" · "America" "COOL" · "One Hand, One Heart" · "The Rumble"
ACT II "I Feel Pretty" · "Somewhere" · "Gee, Officer Krupke" · "A Boy Like That" · "I Have a Love" · "The Taunting"

Backstage

Leonard Bernstein and Stephen Sondheim collaborated on the lyrics to *West Side Story*. When Sondheim went uncredited in the Washington, D.C. reviews, Bernstein graciously removed his credit for the lyrics.

The role of Anita was written for Arthur Laurents's good friend and Larry Kert's sister, Anita Ellis but she couldn't dance.

Larry Kert

Singer/actor Larry Kert made his Broadway debut in the chorus of the revue *Tickets Please!* in 1950. Easily spottable (along with George Chakiris) backing up Marilyn Monroe in the "Diamond's Are a Girl's Best Friend" number in the movie version of *Gentlemen Prefer Blondes*, he returned to Broadway in the revue *John Murray Anderson's Almanac* before landing the role that would change his life. Originally auditioning to play Shark leader Bernardo, he jumped to the other side of the gang war and was cast as Tony in *West Side Story*, being the first person to sing the standards "Something's Coming," "Maria," and "Tonight" to an audience. Kert introduced the lovely "There's a Room in My House" in *A Family Affair* and (briefly) joined the cast of *Breakfast at Tiffany's* after Edward Albee overhauled the show. Bouncing back from another disaster in *La Strada*, he replaced Dean Jones in *Company* shortly after opening, becoming the only actor in history to be deemed eligible for a Tony Award nomination though not a member of the original cast. Repeating his triumph as the bachelor Bobby in London, he spent much of the 1970s on the nightclub circuit, returning to Broadway with Nancy Dussault and Georgia Brown as the replacement cast of *Side By Side By Sondheim*. He played Teresa Stratas's assimilated husband in the heartbreaking *Rags*, and his last Broadway job before his death from AIDS in 1990 was as standby for Peter Allen in the fiasco *Legs Diamond*. One of Johnny Carson's favorite guests in the 1970s, Kert was one of the funniest people in show business, with a caustic irreverence hidden behind a shining tenor voice.

TOP: A buff Larry Kert joins Mary Tyler Moore for a short stay in the cast of *Breakfast at Tiffany's*.

ABOVE: Kert and Bernadette Peters in a rare photo from the flop *La Strada*.

TOP RIGHT: In a scene closely following its Shakespearean source, Kert and Carol Lawrence perform the balcony scene that leads into "Tonight."

RIGHT: Grover Dale, Eddie Roll, and the Jets perform "Gee, Officer Krupke," providing some much-needed comic relief.

GREAT SCORES FROM SO-SO SHOWS, PART II

LEFT: Josh Blake and Teresa Stratas were unforgettable in *Rags* (1986).

RIGHT: Sammy Davis, Jr. putting over Strouse and Adams' powerful score in 1964's *Golden Boy*.

CENTER: Ivor Emmanuel and Shani Wallis in a show perfect for a City Center Encores! production, *A Time for Singing* (1966).

BOTTOM RIGHT: She's got the world on a string: Barbara Cook and the Bil Baird Marionettes in *Flahooley* (1951).

H ERE ARE A FEW MORE of our favorite scores from shows that didn't make the grade as all-around entertainment.

Charles Strouse and Lee Adams's *Golden Boy* was a hit because of the incandescent presence of Sammy Davis Jr. The reviews were decidedly mixed, but oh, that score! *It's a Bird . . . It's a Plane . . . It's Superman* needed a little more edge; still, the score has many wonderful surprises. Strouse collaborated with Stephen Schwartz on *Rags*, a show that has its vociferous partisans and detractors, too, but all agree that the score is heavenly. Anthony Newley and Leslie Bricusse produced two remarkable scores for Broadway. *Stop the World—I Want to Get Off* boasted two mega-ballads, "Once in a Lifetime" and "What Kind of Fool Am I?" *The Roar of the Greasepaint—The Smell of the Crowd* contained "The Joker" and "Who Can I Turn To," songs that are the precursors to modern, dreaded power ballads like "This Is the Moment" (among others). Howard Dietz and Arthur Schwartz's *The Gay Life* contains "Magic Moment," a beautiful ballad, especially as sung sincerely by Barbara Cook, who also brightened the Sammy Fain/E. Y. Harburg mishmash *Flahooley* (please ignore the Moises Vivanco numbers for Yma Sumac). Orchestrator Don Walker completed Sigmund Romberg's last score, *The Girl in Pink Tights*, after the great composer's death, with Romberg's lush melodies wedded to the romantic and witty words of a very underrated lyricist, Leo Robin. Vernon Duke gets our vote as the best composer of unsuccessful shows, case in point *Cabin in the Sky*, with lyricist John Latouche's brilliant wordplay. Johnny Burke and Jimmy Van Heusen's *Swingin' the Dream* is another neglected score that deserves to be rediscovered, while Marc Blitzstein's searing *Juno* is Broadway drama at its best, and the John Morris/Gerald Freedman flop, *A Time for Singing*, has a stunning score and magnificent vocal arrangements. In more recent times, Boy George's score for *Taboo* thrilled audiences.

WONDERFUL TOWN

OPENED FEBRUARY 25, 1953; WINTER GARDEN THEATRE; 559 PERFORMANCES

Echoing the sentiments of most transplanted Midwesterners on their first night in New York, Rosalind Russell and Edie Adams as the Sherwood sisters wonder why they ever left "Ohio."

Synopsis

Ruth Sherwood and her sister, Eileen, have traveled from Ohio to New York to make their fortunes: Ruth as a writer and Eileen as an actress. In their basement apartment in Greenwich Village, they meet a motley group of Village denizens. Ruth has problems with men—she always says the wrong thing. Pretty Eileen has the opposite problem—she can't quite hold 'em off. When Ruth tries her hand at newspaper work, she gets herself arrested, along with half of the Brazilian navy. By the end of the evening, Ruth is hooked up with the editor of the *Manhatter* magazine and Eileen has a bevy of men circling her like moths to a flame.

Cast

Tour Guide .... *Warren Galjour*
Appopolous .... *Henry Lascoe*
Officer Lonigan .... *Walter Kelvin*
Helen .... *Michele Burke*
Wreck................................ *Jordan Bentley*
Violet .... *Dody Goodman*
Eileen Sherwood .... *Edith Adams*
Ruth Sherwood .... *Rosalind Russell*
Robert Baker .... *George Gaynes*
Frank Lippincott .... *Cris Alexander*
Chick Clark .... *Dort Clark*

> "Roz was so insecure about the opening note of 'Ohio' that I had to hum it quietly for her every night of the run."
>
> —Edie Adams

THE ROAD TO SUCCESS ON Broadway is often strewn with the bodies of its creators. A case in point is *Wonderful Town*, regarding the gestation of which, director George Abbott proclaimed, "There was more hysterical debate, more acrimony, more tension, and more screaming connected with this play than with any other show I was ever involved with."

In 1950, George Abbott read a treatment of *Wonderful Town* written by Joseph Fields (brother of Dorothy and Herbert) and Jerome Chodorov. Abbott was interested and suggested changes, which the writers were abjectly unwilling to accept. Rosalind Russell was hired as the star, and Leroy Anderson and Arnold Horwitt signed on to write the score. But as rehearsals loomed on the horizon, the score was not nearly ready for production, and it was decided to replace the writers with a trio known for their fast writing of *On the Town*, Leonard Bernstein (music), Betty Comden, and Adolph Green.

Trouble. Whereas book writers Fields and Chodorov had a more old-fashioned musical in mind, gently warm and sentimental, Comden, Green, and Bernstein saw many opportunities for their trademark satire and edginess, leading to an atmosphere in rehearsals rife with conflict, suspicion, and mixed signals. Ingénue Edie Adams, who made a splashy Broadway debut as Eileen, recalled getting direction from Mr. Abbott and then another, different set of notes from Chodorov and Fields, who wanted Adams to re-create the blocking of the play *My Sister Eileen*. Adams's confusion was compounded exponentially when Comden and Green offered their suggestions, and choreographer Donald Saddler sent her down yet another path. When Adams, a stage neophyte, began to hear rumors that others were auditioning to replace her, she had a meeting with Abbott, refusing to become the "fall gal" for the creators' lack of singular vision.

Emotions continued to build, and everything erupted just prior to the out-of-town opening. Fields and Chodorov declared the show a disaster and demanded drastic changes. In addition, the stress of the situation and vocal demands upon an untrained singer caused star Rosalind Russell to lose her voice the day after the New Haven opening and miss some performances. Slowly, the show began to find its footing, and Jerome Robbins helped things along when he was called in to polish the flow. By the time it hit Broadway, *Wonderful Town* was a smash hit, but the rift between the writers and the rest of the creative staff was never healed. ✼

ABOVE: Forty years into their partnership, Comden and Green greatly added to the nostalgia quotient of the 1985 *Follies* concert with their spry rendition of "Rain on the Roof."

BELOW: The most delightful thing about Rosalind Russell's star turn in *Wonderful Town* was that she seemed to be having the absolute time of her life, even when (or especially when) all hell broke loose in the jazzy "Swing!"or here, taking over the 'hood with her Brazilian cadets, in "Conga!"

Betty Comden and Adolph Green

Betty Comden and Adolph Green, as book writers, lyricists, performers, and general all-around bon vivants, started downtown at the Village Vanguard in a group called the Revuers, alongside great good friend Judy Holliday and others. Given the break of a lifetime by George Abbott when he tapped them to write the book and lyrics for *On the Town*, they became a sensation with their youthful brio. In addition to reteaming with *On the Town* composer Leonard Bernstein for *Wonderful Town*, and their classic screenplays for MGM musicals, they brightened the scene with a series of seven musicals written with Jule Styne, their sole collaborator from 1954 to 1967. With the invigorating presence they projected, their good-natured wit, and endless optimism, they became the toast of New York with their two-person show *A Party with Comden and Green*, transferring the ineffable atmosphere of a swank Central Park West cocktail hour to a Broadway house. After writing the book for the musical *Applause* in 1970, they began a successful relationship with Cy Coleman, penning *On the Twentieth Century* and *The Will Rogers Follies*. When they reprised their *A Party with ...* act at a New York cabaret spot in 1999, they teetered onto the stage, the audience holding their collective breaths. All for naught, for as soon as their longtime accompanist Paul Trueblood began the vamp to "I Said Good Morning" from their film *It's Always Fair Weather*, the years melted away and they were bounding about the stage like the energetic gob and man-hungry anthropologist they had created in *On the Town* fifty-five years earlier.

Backstage

Wonderful Town was originally to be written by Leroy Anderson and Arnold Horwitt. George Abbott asked Leonard Bernstein to interpolate a few numbers, but Bernstein suggested he write a completely new score, which he, Comden, and Green did in only five weeks.

Deeply buried in the credits for *Wonderful Town* were future directors Joe Layton (in the chorus) and Hal Prince (as assistant stage manager and understudy for Frank Lippincott).

RIGHT: Edie Adams charms the boys of the Christopher Street station house in "My Darlin' Eileen."

BELOW: In Rodgers and Hammerstein's television musical of the fairy tale, Edie Adams found something wonderful and unexpected opposite Julie Andrews's Cinderella. Instead of a Fairy Godmother in the befuddled, Marion Lorne mold, she played her as Andrews's contemporary, more like a sorority sister showing a new pledge the ropes.

Edith Adams

Unfortunately, delectable Edie Adams added her beauty and lovely soprano voice to only two Broadway musicals. Untrained as a stage actress (she had extensive television experience opposite her husband, Ernie Kovacs), her performance as Eileen in *Wonderful Town* came into focus when, after floundering in the police station scene wherein she wraps an entire Greenwich Village precinct around her perfectly appointed little finger, she was thrown a life preserver by director George Abbott. He instructed her to treat the policemen as the mistress in an English manor would her servants, the scene began to click and Adams became a star. A few years later, she was offered two roles in new musicals at once, and once again turned to her guardian angel Mr. Abbott for advice. Should she take the lead in *Candide* or *Li'l Abner*? Abbott instructed her to accept the sexier role of Daisy Mae (allowing Barbara Cook to tackle "Glitter and Be Gay"), which took Adams in a new career direction in television and film. She became best known as the Tiparillo "spokes-pot."

SONGS

ACT I "Christopher Street" · "Ohio" · "Conquering New York" (Dance) · "One Hundred Easy Ways" · "What a Waste" · "Story Vignettes" · "Never Felt This Way Before (A Little Bit in Love)" · "Pass the Football" · "Conversation Piece (Nice People, Nice Talk)" · "A Quiet Girl" · "Conga!"
ACT II "My Darlin' Eileen" · "Swing!" · "It's Love" · "The Village Vortex Blues" (Dance) · "Wrong Note Rag"

ABOVE: Rosalind Russell loses a man in "One Hundred Easy Ways."

ZIEGFELD FOLLIES OF 1919

OPENED JUNE 16, 1919; NEW AMSTERDAM THEATRE; 171 PERFORMANCES

ZIEGFELD FOLLIES OF 1919

Music and lyrics by Irving Berlin
Additional music and lyrics by Gene Buck,
Rennold Wolf, Dave Stamper,
Harry Tierney and Joseph McCarthy
Ballet composed by Victor Herbert
Sketches by
Dave Stamper, Gene Buck, and Rennold Wolf
Musical Director: Frank Darling
Orchestrations for Buck and Stamper Songs by
Stephen Jones

Produced by Florenz Ziegfeld
Staged by Ned Wayburn

Scenery designed by Joseph Urban
Costumes designed by
Lady Duff-Gordon and Mme. Francis

Cast

Marilyn Miller, Eddie Cantor, Johnny Dooley, Ray Dooley, Van and Schenck, Bert Williams, John Steel, Delyle Alda, Eddie Dowling, The Fairbanks Twins, Jessie Reed, Phil Dwyer, George LeMaire

"Half the great comedians I've had in my shows and that I paid a lot of money to and who made my customers shriek were not only not funny to me, but I couldn't understand why they were funny to anybody."

—*Florenz Ziegfeld*

ABOVE: A typical Ben Ali Haggen tableau from the *Follies of 1919*—sexy, no?

RIGHT: Showgirl Hilda Ferguson strikes a typically sultry pose—head tilted back, heavy-lidded eyes, parted beehive lips. Va va voom!

THE *Ziegfeld Follies* WAS AMERICA'S first musical revue, opening on July 8, 1907. That first edition was an immediate hit, and, following a move to the Liberty Theatre on 42nd Street, became the first Broadway show to run through the hot summer months.

It was such a success that it led to several other series of revues, including *The Passing Show*s (1912), *George White's Scandals* (1919), the *Greenwich Village Follies* (1919), the *Music Box Revue*s (1921), *The Earl Carroll Vanities* (1923), and *Artists and Models* (1923), but it was Florenz Ziegfeld's *Follies* that enjoyed the longest life and the greatest reputation. Will Page, Ziegfeld's brilliant publicist, explained that the Follies were "musical entertainment for tired business men which should represent almost the possible limit of what could decently be done upon the stage." The same thing might have been said for other shows, from *The Black Crook* (1866) through *Oh! Calcutta!* (1969).

The 1919 edition of the *Follies* was among the best of the series and introduced the song that would become its theme, "A Pretty Girl Is Like a Melody." This thirteenth edition of the revue boasted a first-act finale minstrel show featuring Eddie Cantor and Bert Williams as Tambo and Bones, and Marilyn Miller as George Primrose, an early minstrel leader. The show's finale was a tribute to the Salvation Army and its contributions to World War I.

Imaginative, sometimes surreal costumes were the rage in early revues. In this edition, the showgirls were dressed as salad ingredients, as classical music, and as popular beverages such as Bevo, lemonade, grape juice, sarsaparilla, and Coca-Cola. Lavish costumes and settings, not to mention the talent costs, made the budget soar, costing Ziegfeld and his investors over $100,000.

(Remember, this was 1919, and the top ticket price was $3.) Among the many hit songs that came out of this edition were "You'd Be Surprised," "You Cannot Make Your Shimmy Shake on Tea," "Tulip Time," and "My Baby's Arms." With many interpolations over the run, this edition of the *Follies* ultimately included more than thirty songs. Marred by the Actors' Strike of 1919, the show was forced to close on August 12, but reopened on September 10, after the strike was settled and Actors' Equity had been established as the legal bargaining agent for stage performers.

The 1919 *Follies* was so well regarded and financially successful, Broadway was soon inundated with revues from the likes of George White, Earl Carroll, and even composer Irving Berlin. Ziegfeld would produce another ten editions before his death in 1932. ✸

SONGS

ACT I "The Follies · Salad" · "My Baby's Arms" · "Sweet Sixteen" · "The Popular Pests" · "Tulip Time" · "Shimmy Town" · "You'd Be Surprised" · "How Ya' Gonna Keep 'Em Down on the Farm (After They've Seen Paree)?" "You Don't Need the Wine to Have a Wonderful Time" "I've Got My Captain Working for Me Now" · "When They're Old Enough to Know Better" · "(Oh! She's the) Last Rose of Summer" · "I Love a Minstrel Show" · "The Follies Minstrels" · "Mandy"
ACT II "Harem Life" · "I'm the Guy Who Guards the Harem (and My Heart's in My Work)" · "When the Moon Shines on the Moonshine" · "Bring Back Those Wonderful Days" · "It's Nobody's Business But My Own" "Somebody (Else, Not Me)" · "The Circus Ballet" · "A Pretty Girl Is Like a Melody" · "Prohibition" · "You Cannot Make Your Shimmy Shake on Tea" · "The Near Future" "A Syncopated Cocktail" · "Sweet Kisses (That Came in the Night)" · "They're All Sweeties" · "Oh, How She Can Sing" · "My Tambourine Girl" · "We Made the Doughnuts Over There"

Florenz Ziegfeld

Florenz Ziegfeld was the greatest, or at least the most flamboyant, of all early producers. He was a man of superlatives for whom the show was everything. Lousy at business but excellent at raising money, he was often broke, and preferred to plow the fortunes he made into the highly speculative world of theatrical producing. Ziegfeld's organization and methods (although not his financial practices) were the precursors to the famous Hollywood studio star system, and his great monument, the *Ziegfeld Follies*, has become a legend, while his competitors' shows are practically forgotten. Even without the *Follies*, Ziegfeld would have made his mark on Broadway history with his productions of the musicals *Sally* (1920), *Kid Boots* (1923), *Rio Rita* (1927), his masterwork, *Show Boat* (1927), *The Three Musketeers* (1928), *Whoopee* (1928). Surprisingly, he coproduced Noel Coward's *Bitter Sweet* (1929). Ziegfeld provided all of these musicals and others the sumptuous physical production that was his hallmark.

TOP: Florenz Ziegfeld's all-girl orchestra.

ABOVE: Collette Ryan wears her street clothes to a *Ziegfeld Midnight Frolic*.

RIGHT: Ziegfeld surrounded by the girls he glorified.

Fanny Brice

One of the most versatile and popular entertainers on the Broadway stage, Fanny Brice's range of characterizations was incredible. Equally adept at slapstick, self-deprecating humor and intensely emotional ballads, Brice got her start at Keeney's Theatre in Brooklyn, where she entered an amateur contest singing "When You Know You're Not Forgotten by the Girl You Can't Forget." George M. Cohan cast her in one of his early shows, but soon fired her when she couldn't dance. Dancing lessons then brought her to the Traveling Burlesque Company, and when the leading lady dropped out of an evening performance, Brice took over but was unable to play it straight. She was cast in the musical *College Girls*, having the smarts to get Irving Berlin to write a song for her, "Sadie Salome," which made her a star. That led to nine editions of the *Ziegfeld Follies*, seven produced by Ziegfeld and two produced by the Shubert Brothers. Her other musicals were unexceptional, though she introduced many fine songs, including "My Man," "Rose of Washington Square," "Second Hand Rose," and "I Found a Million Dollar Baby in a Five and Ten Cent Store." After leaving the theatre, she made a few movies and starred on radio, usually portraying her most famous creation Baby Snooks. Her life provided the material for the Broadway hit *Funny Girl* and its screen sequel, *Funny Lady*.

FAR LEFT: Bobby Clark and Fanny Brice, er, we mean Adam and Eve, in the *Ziegfeld Follies of 1924*.

LEFT: Bob Hope and Fanny Brice (as Baby Snooks) in the *Ziegfeld Follies of 1936*.

Backstage

Actress Anna Held, then Ziegfeld's wife, suggested that the showman could produce an American version of the French Folies Bergere.

The Ziegfeld Follies were the first American revues.

By the time *The Ziegfeld Follies of 1919* had closed, there were so many interpolations in the score that no less than forty-one songs had been sung on the stage sometime during the run.

Librettist-lyricist Harry B. Smith suggested that Ziegfeld name the revue series after an old newspaper column of Smith's, "Follies of the Day." But Ziegfeld, who was superstitious, wanted the name of the show to contain 13 letters. He settled on *Follies of 1907*.

Ziegfeld added his name to the *Follies* for the first time in the 1911 edition.

Some of the *Follies* girls who went on to greater fame include Irene Dunne, Peggy Hopkins Joyce, Mae Murray, Marion Davies, Justine Johnstone, Paulette Goddard, and Barbara Stanwyck.

Ziegfeld's favorite words were "glorification," "femininity," and "pulchritude."

Gene Buck was the uncredited director of many of the *Follies*.

Julian Mitchell, the famed director of many of the *Follies* was the inspiration for the character Julian Marsh in the film (and musical) *42nd Street*—only the real Julian Mitchell was deaf!

ABOVE: Here's Martha Graham, er, Fanny, in the *Ziegfeld Follies of 1934*.

LEFT: Fanny Brice does a number on Aimee Semple McPherson in "Soul Saving Sadie," in the 1934 edition of the *Follies*.

Eddie Cantor

Possessing energy, a pop-eyed impish glee, and a desire to please at almost any cost, Eddie Cantor achieved stardom portraying weak men made strong by women, adversity, and intelligence. Growing up on the Lower East Side and dancing for money on the street, his professional career started in blackface, playing variations on an enthusiastic, bouncy, sometime effeminate rascal. His professional musical

theatre debut was in the Philadelphia company of *Smiling Island* in 1905, also appearing in a West Coast tour of *Canary Cottage*. From there, it was on to the *Ziegfeld Follies*, where he became one of Florenz Ziegfeld's favorites, though the producer admitted that Cantor's humor escaped him (as did that of most of the comedians he booked). Still, audiences warmed to Cantor, and that was good enough for Ziegfeld to feature him in four *Follies* and innumerable *Midnight Frolics*. Cantor also appeared in *Make It Snappy* (1922), *Kid Boots* (1923, also under Ziegfeld's auspices), and his most famous show, *Whoopee* (1928). Ziegfeld brought his production of the latter to Hollywood, where it was filmed in early Technicolor with much of the original cast. Cantor stayed on the West Coast and made a number of very popular movies, then moved into radio and television. His last Broadway performance was in Vernon Duke and John Latouche's *Banjo Eyes* in 1941. Among the many great songs he introduced are "Dinah," "Alabamy Bound," "If You Knew Susie," "Makin' Whoopee," and "We're Havin' a Baby."

Joseph Urban

Joseph Urban was one of the most talented scenarists and architects at the early part of the twentieth century, and his magnificent scenery for the *Ziegfeld Follies* was a model of the Art Nouveau style. Born in Vienna, Urban's influences were artists such as Gustav Klimt, Josef Hoffman, and Josef Olbrich, known as the Secession for their modern ideas. Coming to the United States in 1912, he worked as art director of the Boston Opera, two years later heading to New York to work for Ziegfeld and the Metropolitan Opera, among other notable clients. Urban's designs stripped away the rococo excesses of the period, utilizing painterly and lighting effects with a simplicity of suggestion that was seldom seen in the theatre up to that time. Where the usual settings of the period were naturalistic, Urban gave his imagination flight and came up with fanciful motifs that utilized color in a new and exciting way. His architecture was equally famous and includes such landmarks as the New School for Social Research, the Palm Beach estate Mar-a-Lago, and the Ziegfeld Theatre. Urban designed film settings for William Randolph Hearst's Cosmopolitan Pictures, book illustrations (notably a series on the fairy tales of Hans Christian Andersen), costume designs, and even the color scheme for the 1933 Chicago World's Fair. Urban designed over 500 stage sets for more than 168 productions, some of which he also directed.

LEFT: The famed New Amsterdam Theatre in 1925. TOP RIGHT: Julie Newmar strikes a comely pose in the *Ziegfeld Follies of 1956*. CENTER LEFT: Eddie and his faithful steed (no relation despite the similarity) in the Vernon Duke/John Latouche *Banjo Eyes*. CENTER RIGHT: Will Rogers perches atop a pyramid of pulchritudinous beauty in the *Ziegfeld Follies of 1924*. ABOVE: "Any Old Place with You" as performed by W.C. Fields, Will Rogers, Lillian Lorraine, Eddie Cantor, and Harry Kelly in the *Ziegfeld Follies of 1918*.

ZORBA

OPENED NOVEMBER 17, 1968; IMPERIAL THEATRE; 305 PERFORMANCES

Hortense (Maria Karnilova) is overjoyed when Zorba (Herschel Bernardi) returns and proposes. They celebrate their engagement in the song "Y'assou."

ZORBA

Produced by Harold Prince
Produced in association with Ruth Mitchell

Music by John Kander
Lyrics by Fred Ebb
Book by Joseph Stein
Adapted from *Zorba the Greek* by
Nikos Kazantzakis
Musical Director: Harold Hastings
Music orchestrated by Don Walker
Dance Arrangements by Dorothea Freitag

Directed by Harold Prince
Choreographed by Ronald Field

Scenic Design by Boris Aronson
Costume Design by Patricia Zipprodt
Lighting Design by Richard Pilbrow

Synopsis

Nikos arrives in Piraeus to supervise the reopening of a mine and meets the force of life named Zorba. Nikos falls in love with the village widow, and Madame Hortense yearns for Zorba. Despite the tragedy of the women's deaths and the collapse of the village mine, Nikos learns from Zorba how to value life and embrace it.

Cast

Zorba .... Herschel Bernardi
Madame Hortense .... Maria Karnilova
The Widow .... Carmen Alvarez
Niko .... John Cunningham
Leader .... Lorraine Serabian
Konstandi .... Joseph Alfasa
Mimiko .... Al De Sio

Herschel Bernardi aloft in the "Mine Dance," staged by Ron Field.

O F THE HUNDREDS OF WRITERS, directors, designers, and performers in this compendium, it is Harold Prince who is associated with the most shows. His remarkable career as producer and director spans the second half of the twentieth century. After a time as a stage manager, he graduated to producer, then producer/director. In his first period he produced a series of excellent entertainments, including *Damn Yankees*, *The Pajama Game*. With *West Side Story*, he began his second phase, the exploration of the concept musical.

Although *Cabaret* is considered the best of these shows, many feel (and as many disagree) that *Zorba* is the show that really put it all together—exploring a theme, life in this case, in all its permutations. The show opens with the cast seated in a half circle facing the audience. The Leader, played brilliantly by Lorraine Serabian, informs us that "Life is what you do while you're waiting to die." (In later productions the lyric was changed to, "Life is what you do till the moment you die.") Zorba speaks of an old man planting an almond tree. "He said, 'I live every minute as if I would never die.' Think of that, boss? He lived as if he would never die. I live as if I would die any minute."

Zorba celebrates life in its entirety: the sound of a bouzouki, the sight of a flower, the smell of a woman, lost love, heartbreak, and death, too. This is a rich, uncompromising musical. People live and die, and not always nicely. But through it all is the spirit of Zorba—the spirit of life.

Just as in *Cabaret*, the central theme is expressed in song by the protagonist. *Cabaret*'s Cliff asks, "Why Should I Wake Up?" In *Zorba*, Nikos asks, "Why Can't I Speak?" *Zorba* teaches us not to wait, because "later" might be too late: to speak now, to embrace life and live it to the fullest. ✤

SONGS

ACT I · "Life Is" · "The First Time" · "The Top of the Hill" "No Boom Boom" · "Viva La Difference" · "The Butterfly" "Goodbye, Canavaro" · "Grandpapa" · "Only Love" · "The Bend of the Road"
ACT II · "Y'assou" · "Why Can't I Speak" · "Mine Dance" "The Crow" · "Happy Birthday" · "I Am Free"

TOP: With the entire cast sitting in a bouzouki circle, the story of *Zorba* is narrated by The Leader (Lorraine Serabian), who espouses her particular viewpoint: "Life Is."

RIGHT: Hal Prince with his Eva Peron (Patti LuPone) during rehearsals for *Evita*.

FAR RIGHT: One of Prince's unsuccessful shows of the 1980s was *A Doll's Life*, a musical sequel to Henrik Ibsen's *A Doll's House*. While it proved problematic, it contained many expectedly stunning stage pictures, an often beautiful score by Larry Grossman, and a valiant performance by the inexhaustible Betsy Joslyn (here with George Hearn), in a role rivaling Eva Peron in terms of total stage time.

Harold Prince

The most important figure in the musical theatre in the second half of the twentieth century, Harold Prince's work as producer and director is unequaled. Having begun his career as a brash young upstart, he was fascinated with every aspect of theatre and yearned to somehow become involved in his great passion. He learned much from his mentors, director George Abbott and producing partner Robert E. Griffith, not only about what makes the theatre work, but more importantly, how to get the best results from your fellow artists by always treating them with honor

and respect. A master at casting and a superb editor of texts, Prince also excels in creating thrilling stage pictures and environments. A pioneer in the development of the concept musical, his instinct for theatre is unsurpassed, with his shows often set against a larger canvas of societal and political conflict. He has worked with many of the seminal figures of the modern musical, including John Kander and Fred Ebb (three shows), Jerry Bock and Sheldon Harnick (four shows), and Richard Adler and Jerry Ross (two shows). His most important collaboration, however, has been with Stephen Sondheim, on a series of truly historic, revolutionary productions including *Company*, *A Little Night Music*, *Pacific Overtures*, *Sweeney Todd*, and the brilliant *Follies*. Following his collaborations with Sondheim and the worldwide success of *Evita*, Prince had a streak wherein he seemed unable to produce a hit, only to roar back with one of the most successful shows in Broadway history, *The Phantom of the Opera*, continuing a collaboration with Andrew Lloyd Webber. *Bounce*, his recent reteaming with Sondheim after a twenty-year hiatus, remains a question mark for Broadway, but his fierce intelligence and talent are undisputed.

Maria Karnilova

Maria Karnilova started out as a ballerina in the American Ballet Theatre, and, after befriending fellow dancer Jerome Robbins, segued into musical theatre with a featured dance role in the postwar revue *Call Me Mister* (where she met husband of over fifty years, the delightful character actor George S. Irving). After discovering that she could talk as well as dance, she began to play speaking roles, breaking through as "dressy" Tessie Tura in *Gypsy*. Her comic timing, range, and European look led to a globetrotter's delight of roles: as an Italian signora leading the novelty dance "The Kangaroo" in *Bravo, Giovanni*; as the Russian Jew Golde in *Fiddler on the Roof*; and, in her most touching performance, as the French former prostitute Hortense in *Zorba*. She went into semiretirement after the stage version of *Gigi* and *God's Favorite*, coming out only to play the Kay Medford role in the ill-fated sequel *Bring Back Birdie,* and the Queen (opposite her beloved husband) in the New York City Opera production of Richard Rodgers and Oscar Hammerstein's *Cinderella*.

Backstage

Lorraine Serabian was originally the understudy for The Leader. During previews, the original Leader missed the first act, returning late from a wedding, and Serabian went on. She did so well that the original actress never played the part again.

Lila Kedrova played Fraulein Schneider in the Harold Prince production of *Cabaret* in London. But when it came to casting Madame Hortense, Prince didn't choose to cast Kedrova, who had played the part in the movie and would eventually win a Tony, finally playing the role on stage in the Anthony Quinn revival.

TOP: Carmen Alvarez (here with Al De Sio and John Cunningham) had previously only played heavy dance roles. As the doomed widow in *Zorba*, she proved herself as a fine dramatic actress.

ABOVE LEFT: Karnilova, a unique combination of superb dancer and character actress, lifts the just-this-short-of-good *Bravo, Giovanni* with the exhausting dance "The Kangaroo."

LEFT: Karnilova as Hortense, recounting to Herschel Bernardi and John Cunningham her unparalleled ability to control the course of war through her womanly wiles, in the showstopping number "No Boom Boom."

INDEX
(photos indicated in **bold**)

Ann Reinking, one of the premier dance stars of the 1970s, in *Goodtime Charley* (top), and *Dancin'* (above).

331

The singular Barbara Harris doubles her assets in *The Apple Tree* (above), one of only two Broadway musicals she appeared in. The other was *On a Clear Day You Can See Forever* (top).

In addition to his long career in Hollywood, Don Ameche appeared in four Broadway musicals including *Silk Stockings* (top, with Hildegarde Neff), and *Henry, Sweet Henry* (above, with Louise Lasser).

Howard McGillin's Ivy-League looks and pure, shining tenor add class to any show in which he appears. He performs alongside another pro, George Rose, in *The Mystery of Edwin Drood* (top) and with Michael McCormick and Brian Stokes Mitchell in *Kiss of the Spider Woman.*

British import Georgia Brown has lent her impassioned vocals to many Broadway musicals, including *Oliver!* (top), and *Roza* (above, with Max Loving).

Fosse favorite Ben Vereen, dancer extraordinaire, provides sinuous grace and star quality to *Pippin* (top) and *Grind* (above).

CHRONOLOGY OF THE 101 GREATEST BROADWAY MUSICALS

PHOTO CREDITS

We are grateful to the following individuals and institutions for permission to publish the photographs in this book:

MICHAEL FEINSTEIN: 182–Top. RICHARD GIAMMANCO: Copyright page. GOODSPEED OPERA HOUSE LIBRARY: 16: 17: 18–Top: 20–Left: 21–Top and Bottom Right: 22: 25–Bottom: 51–Top Right: 79–Left: 81–Top Left and Top Right: 103–Center: 116 (2 photos): 117–Top and Bottom Left: 120–Top: 132: 133 (two photos): 180: 181: 201–Top Right: 203 (two photos): 274: 275 (three photos). COURTESY OF THE IRA AND LENORE GERSHWIN TRUST, USED BY PERMISSION: 182–Center and Bottom. PAUL KOLNIK: 50–Bottom Right: 65–Left: 117–Bottom Right: 145–Top Left and Right: 206–Bottom Right. NEW YORK PUBLIC LIBRARY, BILLY ROSE THEATRE COLLECTION AT LINCOLN CENTER: Opposite Title Page: 8–Top: 9: 12 Top Right: 14–Top: 18–Bottom: 19–Top Right: 20–Right: 21–Left: 23–Top: 24: 27–Left and Right: 28–Top: 29–Top: 31–Top Left and Bottom: 31–Top: 35–Bottom: 36: 37–Top and Bottom: 38–Bottom Right: 40: 42: 43–Top and Bottom Right: 44 (three pictures): 45 (two pictures): 49–Right: 49–Top: 50–Top Right: 51–Top Left, Bottom Left, Bottom Right: 52 (Two photos): 53–Top Right: 54–Top Left and Top Right: 61–Bottom Right: 63–Top Right: 67–Bottom Right: 73–Center and Bottom Right: 74: 75–Bottom and Top: 78–Center and Right: 79–Right: 80: 81–Bottom Right: 83–Center Right: 87–Nancy Dussault photos (three): 97–Bottom: 99–Center: 101–Bottom: 106–Center: 108–Bottom: 109–Bottom Left: 114–Left: 115–Bottom Left:118–Right: 119–Bottom: 120–Bottom: 122–Center: 125–Center: 128–Center: 129–Center: 130 (two photos): 131–Bottom: 136–Left:134–Bottom Left: 135–Bottom Left and Top and Bottom Center:137–Top and Center: 141–Left: 144–Center Right: 146: 147–Top and Bottom: 148–Top Left and Bottom Left and Right: 149–Bottom: 155–Bottom Left and Right: 156 (two photos): 157–Top and Bottom Right: 158–Bottom: 162–Top Left and Bottom: 163–Top Left and Right and Bottom Right: 167–Top Left and Right and Bottom Right: 169–Center and Bottom: 170–Bottom: 172–Bottom: 176–Bottom Right: 183: 184–Top and Bottom: 185–Top Center and Left and Right: 189 (two photos): 196 (three photos): 191–Bottom: 192: 195–Right: 196–Center Left: 198–Bottom Right: 200: 203–Bottom Left and Right: 204–Center: 207–Right: 208–Left: 209–Center: 210–Top Left and Right: 211–Top Right: 213–Bottom Left and Right: 214–Top: 215 (two photos): 216–Top, Bottom Left and Right: 217–Center and Bottom Left and Right: 219–Top Right: 222–Center, Bottom Left and Right: 224–Left: 225–Bottom: 226–Top: 228: 229–Right: 230: 231 (two photos): 232: 233–Top: 234–Bottom Left: 235–Top Left and Center Left: 237–Bottom Right: 238–Top Left and Right and Bottom Right: 239–Top Left and Right: 240–Center Bottom Right: 241–Top: 244–Bottom: 246: 247–Top: 256–Bottom: 251–Bottom: 255–Top Right: 257–Bottom: 258–Bottom Left: 259–Top Left: 261–Top: 267–Left Center: 271–Center: 272–Top and Bottom Right: 273–Bottom: 277–Top: 278 (two photos): 279–Bottom: 280–Top Center and Bottom: 282–Left: 283 (three photos): 286–Center: 287 (two photos): 288–Top and Bottom Right: 289–Top: 297–Left: 298 (three photos): 299–Top Left and Right: 304 (two photos): 305–Top:315–Center and Bottom: 318–Top Right: 319–Bottom: 320–Center and Bottom Right: Left: 324–Left: 325–Bottom Left: 326–Bottom Left and Right: 327–Top Right: 328 (two photos): 329–Top: 330 (three photosJOAN MARCUS: 15–Bottom: 49–Bottom Right: 50–Bottom Right: 66–Top Left: 99–Bottom: 135–Top Left: 173–Top Right: 179–Bottom Right: 186: 187 Bottom Left: 211–Top Right: 221–Center: 226–Bottom: 266–Top Left: 285–Bottom Right. MARTHA SWOPE: Table of Contents: 10: 11 (2 photos) 12–Bottom Left: 20–Top Right: 58 (two photos): 59–Top Right: 64: 65–Top Right and

Bottom Right: 66–Bottom Left and Top Right: 145–Bottom Left: 156 (two photos): 151–Top Right: 177 (two photos): 178–Top: 179–Top and Bottom Left: 187–Center Left: 204–Center and Bottom Right.

ABOUT THE AUTHORS

KEN BLOOM is the author of three seminal works on American popular song: *American Song, Hollywood Song,* and *Tin Pan Alley*. His *Broadway: An Encyclopedic Guide to the History, People and Place of Times Square* was named one of the top reference books of the year by the New York Public Library and was recently reissued in a new edition. In 2003 he published *Jerry Herman: The Lyrics: A Celebration* and a two-volume history of Twentieth Century-Fox music. Bloom is also a playwright, a theatre director, a radio host, an arts consultant, and the president of Harbinger Records. He dedicates this book to his sister Barbara and the memory of two musical theatre chroniclers, Stanley Green and Edward Jablonski.

FRANK VLASTNIK is an actor who appeared in the original casts of the Broadway musicals *Big, Sweet Smell of Success,* and *A Year with Frog and Toad,* as well as the New York premiere of Stephen Sondheim's *Saturday Night.* This is his first first foray into writing, having previously done the photo research and editing for Ken Bloom's *Jerry Herman* and Richard Norton's *A Chronology of American Musical Theatre.* He dedicates this book to his mother, who started buying him *Theatre World* annuals when he was thirteen: his Aunts Mary and Joan: and his brother John and sister Mary (even though she once buried his album collection in a snow drift). Vlastnik is a proud graduate of Illinois Wesleyan University.

Both authors live in New York City.